Insurgent Empire

Insurgent Empire

*Anticolonial Resistance
and British Dissent*

Priyamvada Gopal

VERSO
London • New York

First published in paperback by Verso 2020
First published by Verso 2019
© Priyamvada Gopal 2019

Every effort has been made to ascertain the copyright status of images appearing herein and, where necessary, to secure permission. In the event of being notified of any omission, Verso will seek to rectify the mistake in the next edition. The images reproduced here are in the public domain, with the following exceptions: 'Shapurji Saklatvala speaking to crowds at Speakers' Corner, Hyde Park, September 1933' © Keystone / Getty Images; 'The League against Imperialism canvassing at, Trafalgar Square in London in August 1931' © Fox Photos / Getty Images; 'Nancy Cunard in her print studio in France' © Keystone-France / Gamma-Rapho via Getty Images; 'C. L. R. James giving a speech at a rally for Ethiopia in London' © Keystone-France / Gamma-Keystone via Getty Images.

3 5 7 9 10 8 6 4 2

Verso
UK: 6 Meard Street, London W1F 0EG
US: 20 Jay Street, Suite 1010, Brooklyn, NY 11201
versobooks.com

Verso is the imprint of New Left Books

ISBN-13: 978-1-78478-413-3
ISBN-13: 978-1-78478-415-7 (US EBK)
ISBN-13: 978-1-78478-414-0 (UK EBK)

British Library Cataloguing in Publication Data
A catalogue record for this book is available from the British Library

The Hardback Edition Has Been Cataloged by the Library of Congress as Follows:

Names: Gopal, Priyamvada, 1968– author.
Title: Insurgent empire : anticolonial resistance and British dissent /
  Priyamvada Gopal.
Description: London ; New York : Verso, 2019. | Includes bibliographical
  references and index.
Identifiers: LCCN 2019005764| ISBN 9781784784126 (hardback : alk. paper) |
  ISBN 9781784784157 (US ebk.) | ISBN 9781784784140 (UK ebk.)
Subjects: LCSH: Anti-imperialist movements – Great Britain – History. | Great
  Britain – Colonies – History.
Classification: LCC JV1011 .G66 2019 | DDC 325/.341 – dc23
LC record available at https://lccn.loc.gov/2019005764

Typeset in Sabon by MJ & N Gavan, Truro, Cornwall
Printed in the UK by CPI Group (UK) Ltd, Croydon CR0 4YY

Contents

Acknowledgements

In the early summer of 2006, I took part in an episode of *Start the Week*, the BBC radio show hosted by prominent journalist Andrew Marr. The topic was the British Empire and my fellow guests were the theologian Robert Beckford, the historians Linda Colley and Eric Hobsbawm, and, most significantly in this context, the media face of the case for British imperialism, Niall Ferguson. Although I was familiar with the unquestioned celebration of imperial figures such as Winston Churchill and the silence around the more questionable legacies of the empire which Churchill famously didn't wish to liquidate, this programme was my first close encounter, after moving to Britain in 2001, with bullish assertions about the greatness of Britain's imperial project and the benevolence of its legacies. In this mythology, a version of which is peddled in Ferguson's book on the British Empire and accompanying television series, massacres, violence, slavery and famine were acknowledged as passing unfortunate occurrences rather than as constitutive dimensions of imperialism. While both Colley and Hobsbawm demurred from the matey complacency which marked Marr's and Ferguson's dialogue on the topic, it was largely left to Beckford and me, the two people of colour on the panel, to raise doubts about the benevolence and munificence which was being attributed to the British Empire. We made rather more of the land grabs, dispossession, racism, enslavement, expropriation, ethnic cleansing and resource theft that had taken place over centuries and continued to have lethal afterlives in those countries which had felt the heavy hand of colonial rule on their backs. That in itself was perhaps unremarkable but more striking was the palpable shock and outrage that Ferguson felt at being denied a free pass on a string of questionable assertions. A vituperative opinion piece from him would follow, and he would reference the episode almost obsessively elsewhere.

That evening the BBC took the unprecedented step of replacing the usual repeat of the morning's episode with a phone-in programme to discuss the morning's 'barny', the term Marr used to refer to the exchange. Sitting alongside him in what can only be described as an embarrassingly proto-colonial gesture was a young American woman of Indian descent whose main purpose, it would seem, was to reassure the BBC's listeners that I by no means represented young Indians who, she suggested, were either indifferent to or very positively disposed to the Empire. In a particularly bizarre piece of apparently clinching evidence, she noted that her grandfather, who had grown up in British India, routinely saluted her white husband when they visited him. This incident and the significant amounts of both angry and appreciative mail I received after writing a related piece for the *Guardian* newspaper heralded what would become for me a somewhat unexpected dozen years of engagement with Britain's relationship to its imperial past and the manifold silences and lacunae in the British public understanding of that past. My own students at Cambridge, studying what was then coyly referred to as 'Commonwealth Literature', came to class with very little knowledge of what the Empire was or how it lived on in the present and were, to their credit, keen to know more. It became clear to me that some form of reparative history was desperately needed in the British public sphere which is still subject to a familiar ritual where politicians of various stripes will periodically announce that Britain has 'nothing to apologize for' or call for active 'pride' in the legacies of the Empire. These calls often sit alongside the somewhat contradictory claim that to criticize imperial misdeeds, supposedly by 'the values of our time', is an anachronistic gesture.

But is it anachronistic to subject the Empire to searching criticism? This book is in part a response to that question and in part a very different take on the history of the British Empire to what is generally available in the British public sphere. In academia, a retrograde strain of making the so-called case for colonialism is now resurgent. As a scholar whose prior work had been on dissident writing in the Indian subcontinent as it transitioned to independence, I was aware that all societies and cultures have radical and liberationist currents woven into their social fabric as well as people who spoke up against what was being done in their name: why would Britain in the centuries of imperial rule be an exception? At the same time, I also wanted to probe the tenacious mythology that ideas of 'freedom' are uniquely British in conception and that independence itself was a British 'gift' to the colonies along with the railways and the English language. The result is a study which looks at the relationship between British critics of empire and the great movements of resistance to British rule which emerged across colonial contexts. The case against colonialism, it will be seen, was made repeatedly over the last couple of centuries and it emerged through an understanding of resistance to empire.

My first thanks are to those historians whose vital scholarly texts on British critics of empire I have drawn on extensively: Stephen Howe, Gregory Claeys, Nicholas Owen, Mira Matikkala and Bernard Porter. Writing this book through their work in an age where higher education and research are being privatized and monetized, I have been repeatedly reminded of how fundamentally collaborative the production of knowledge is. I have also learned a great deal from the work of pioneering scholars of anticolonialism, such as Hakim Adi, Marika Sherwood, Mimi Sheller, Brent Hayes Edwards, Anthony Bogues, Ken Post, Gelien Matthews and Minkah Makalani. My mistakes, of course, are not theirs. I am grateful to the Leverhulme Trust for taking a chance on this project and granting to me a two-year research fellowship that enabled substantial amounts of work towards this book. The Faculty of English at the University of Cambridge and Churchill College have also generously provided additional research monies. It would be unseemly not to acknowledge both the BBC and Niall Ferguson for setting me off on a road to discovering a trajectory of British thought and political practice so different from the mythologies they routinely and damagingly peddle. I hope Ferguson will forgive the temerity of 'an obscure Cambridge lecturer', as he has dubbed me, in daring to venture into terrain where only the mighty may expound.

Many people have encouraged this study and rallied my spirits when I've faltered. My thanks to Neil Lazarus, Timothy Brennan and

Benita Parry for the support they gave this project at the outset. My intellectual debts to them are numerous, as also to the many great teachers I had in my formative years as a graduate student at Cornell: the late Martin Bernal, Susan Buck-Morss (whose work on Hegel in Haiti has been foundational), Biodun Jeyifo, Hortense Spillers and Satya P. Mohanty. The late Edward Said's work continues to nourish my mind and the impact of his thought will, hopefully, be evident throughout this book. A number of people have read either all or portions of the manuscript: huge thanks to Sue J. Kim, Shamira Meghani and Joel Fredell for reading an early draft and suggesting revisions, and to Neil Lazarus for going over the near-finished article. Two anonymous readers provided just the kind of challenging and sceptical feedback a project of this scope requires. Christian Høgsbjerg has been the most generous of readers and interlocutors, and I'm very grateful to him and to two other historians, Kim A. Wagner and Kama Maclean, for reading several individual chapters between them. Others who have been generous with suggestions, assistance and materials include John Drew, Paul T. Simpson, Owen Holland, Alaric Hall, Paul Flewers, Joe Shaughnessy and Alf Gunvald Nilsen. Heba Youssef's translations of Arabic texts are integral to Chapter 3 which is on Wilfrid Blunt's travels in Egypt.

I've been extremely fortunate to have had the support and interest of numerous excellent colleagues at Cambridge. First among them is Christopher Warnes, truly the best of friends and most supportive of colleagues. David Trotter has been a kind and skilful mentor, and his exemplary support in that capacity has meant more than he realizes. Tim Cribb has been the most generous friend and advocate from my rookie days as an 'assistant lecturer'. My thanks also to Chana Morgenstern, Drew Milne, Deborah Bowman and Andrew Taylor. I also want to thank a wider community of critical scholars at Cambridge, in particular those who are precariously positioned – their commitment to the public university as a space for transformative thought has been inspirational. In the face of the political onslaughts of the last several years, many of my colleagues in the Faculty of English have repeatedly stood up for a democratic ideal of what a university ought to be and it has been an honour to have had their comradeship, particularly that of Jason Scott-Warren. Thanks also to those many colleagues and students across the institution engaging with the complicated question of 'decolonizing' the curriculum. Two Cambridge historians, David Washbrook and John Lonsdale, very kindly shared their enormous knowledge in talking through some ideas with me, and Christopher Clark gave me his thoughts on an early project plan. I am particularly grateful to the English Faculty Research Seminar and the South Asia Seminar series for inviting me to present my work and for the enriching discussions both occasions generated. Graduate students for whom I've served as supervisor or advisor over the years have also been a great source of intellectual engagement and, since those days, they've forged their own brilliant paths: my particular thanks to Anna Bernard, Rachel Bower, Ben Etherington, Mike Perfect, Anouk Lang, Graham Riach, Desha Osborne, Mukti Mangharam and Megan Jones. I'm indebted to the support and good cheer that Sam Dean, Jen Pollard, Anna Fox, Vicky Aldred, Lauren Lalej, Marica Lopez Diaz and Marina Ballard have provided over the years. To the generations of immensely engaged and bright undergraduates, too numerous to name individually, who have kept me on my toes: this book is for you.

Over the years, I have profited from conversations with audiences at various institutions where I was invited to present work in progress. Many thanks to them and to those who hosted me at the University of Lancaster (Deborah Sutton), the University of Glasgow (Gerard McKeever), the Open University–Institute of English Studies (Alex Tickell), the University of Kent (Ole Birk Laursen, Maria Ridda and Enrique Galvan-Alvarez), the University of Brighton (Bob Brecher, Cathy Bergin and Anita Rupprecht), the University of East Anglia (James Wood), Kings College London (Anna Bernard), Cornell University (Satya Mohanty), the University of Toronto (Kanishka Goonewardena and Ajay Rao), the City University of Dublin (Hari Krishnan, Arpita Chakrabarty, Shruti Neelakantan and Eileen Connolly), Jawaharlal Nehru University, New Delhi (Ayesha Kidwai, G. J. V. Prasad and Udaya Kumar), the University of New South Wales (Laetitia Nanquette), and the University of Western Sydney (Ben Etherington). My thanks also to Becky Gardiner and Joseph Harker for giving me space to try out some related ideas in pieces I've written for the *Guardian*.

A project of this scope would have foundered without the uncomplaining assistance of librarians and archivists at the following institutions: the University Library, in particular Rare Books and Manuscripts, Cambridge; the Fitzwilliam Museum (Blunt Papers) and the Churchill Archives Centre (Brockway Papers); the British Library (Saklatvala Papers); the Modern Records Centre at the University of Warwick; the School of Oriental and African Studies (the Movement for Colonial Freedom Archives), the Bodleian Library and Rhodes House at the University of Oxford (Eyre Defence Fund Papers), Olin Library at Cornell University, the Schomburg Center for Research in Black Culture (Padmore Papers); the Hull History Centre (Bridgeman Papers); and the Harry Ransom Center at the University of Texas–Austin (Cunard Papers). I would also like to acknowledge research and editorial assistance provided by Duncan Thomas, Max Compton, Anna Nickerson and Roberta Klimt. At Verso, my thanks to Leo Hollis, Maya Osborne, Sebastian Budgen, Cian McCourt, Dan O'Connor (who truly went the extra mile), Charles Peyton and Mark Martin for their assistance.

So many people have kept me intellectually, emotionally, politically and literally nourished over the years of writing. My love and lasting gratitude to my parents, Gopal and Kausalya, who have so generously allowed this book to rudely intrude into so many home visits and steal time that was meant to be spent with them. My brother, Anant, has been a huge source of support, insight and good times. My other brother and dearest friend, Jay D'Ercola, has kept my spirits up at the worst of times and leavened numerous missteps with his wisdom, compassion and unique humour. Sue J. Kim has kept cats, dogs and crime drama in my life over nearly twenty years. Kanishka Goonewardena has kept the faith in all the ways that matter. M. Indrani has cooked me very many sustaining meals and shared life wisdom in conversation. To my Ithaca family, I owe the joys of so many working summers: thanks to Roberta Crawford (and Manny, Alma and Kimchi), Franklin Crawford, Tuulikki Tammi, Paul Wilson and Ilmari. Bindia Thapar and Dwijen Rangnekar, both of whom left us far too soon, are sorely missed. Everyone in KPTI (you know who you are) – thanks for the vital doses of bracing silliness. Miss Luna Woodruff has made life in Cambridge that much more fun. Gautam Premnath, Jacqueline Stuhmiller, Shamira Meghani, Antara Dutta, Tanika Sarkar, Gurminder Bhambra, John Meed, Lisa Tilley, Juan Jose Cruz, Gavan Titley, Gyunghee (April) Park, Nadine el-Enany, Vahni

Capildeo, Dave Wearing, Kate Tunstall, Dibyesh Anand, Sandeep Parmar, Rashmi Singh, David Shulman, Isobel Urquhart, Asiya Islam and many other comrades across networks real and virtual have kept me going though grim political times. It is to all, past and present, who struggle for better times, building solidarity across borders, that this work is dedicated.

Introduction

Enemies of Empire

Nowhere within the British Empire were black people passive victims. On the contrary, they were everywhere active resisters.
Peter Fryer, *Black People in the Empire: An Introduction*

On 4 August 1857, some three months after the commencement of the insurgency in India, though it is unlikely he was aware of it at the time, the former slave and American abolitionist Frederick Douglass gave a speech in Rochester, in New York State, felicitating a different revolutionary moment. Nearly twenty-five years before, in 'one complete transaction of vast and sublime significance', slaves in the British West Indies had finally been deemed human beings, restored to their rightful stature as free men and women.[1] Three decades after the 1807 abolition of the British slave *trade*, often confused with the Slavery Abolition Act of 1833, Britain's human chattel on the vast sugar and cotton plantations of the West Indies had officially ceased to be slaves, though they would remain compulsorily apprenticed to their owners for another five years. In the United States, however, slavery still flourished – as indeed it did in other parts of the world such as Brazil, where it carried on to the end of that century. Douglass was speaking to fellow abolitionists, gathered in Rochester to commemorate the West India Emancipation, and he took pains to contrast Britain's significant achievement with the 'devilish brutality' he saw around him in a formally democratic and republican land. The act of abolition, deriving though it did from 'the moral sky of Britain', had universal ramifications since, Douglass insisted, it 'belongs not exclusively to

England and English people, but to lovers of Liberty and mankind everywhere'.[2]

Douglass's speech paid due homage to the august ranks of British abolitionists. For those who had claimed that only Englishmen could 'properly celebrate' the West Indian Emancipation, he had a message: in that case *all* those who love freedom can 'claim to be Englishmen, Englishmen in the love of Justice and Liberty, Englishmen in magnanimous efforts to protect the weak against the strong and the slave against the slaveholder'.[3] Thereafter, however, his speech took a curious turn. Douglass had also to counter the charge, made by some of his fellow American blacks, that to commemorate the West Indian Emancipation was to celebrate the achievements of others, specifically the deeds of white people, 'a race by which we are despised'. In a two-pronged response, Douglass noted that, while in the North American struggle against slavery, 'we, the coloured people' had not yet played a significant role, this was not the case with Emancipation in the British West Indies. To the extent that they had been able to, the 'rebellious chattel' in Britain's Caribbean colonies had strenuously resisted their oppression, and so 'a share of the credit of the result falls justly to the slaves themselves'. It is this insight that then leads Douglass to make his famous pronouncement: 'The whole history of the progress of human liberty shows that all concessions yet made to her august claims, have been born of earnest struggle … Power concedes nothing without a demand. It never did and never will.' With an irony he was probably unaware of at the time – news of the Indian 'Mutiny' was only slowly making its way to and around Europe and America – Douglass quietly observed that some white abolitionists actively discouraged black initiative, expecting black abolitionists to 'fight like the Sepoys of India, under white officers'. This, Douglass says, must not deter him and others who would struggle for their own freedom; it is 'no part of gratitude to allow our white friends to do all the work, while we merely hold their coats'. As he was speaking, of course, the 'sepoys' had, in fact, risen against their white officers in a bloody insurgency that would alter the shape of the British Empire for good, ending the rule of the marauding East India Company in the subcontinent as the Crown took over full governance of British India.

Well over the century and a half since Douglass gave that speech, the notion that freedom from both slavery and imperial rule emerged

thanks to the benevolence of the rulers continues to exercise a tenacious hold within certain influential strands of British imperial history
and in the popular imagination. Both abolition and decolonization
– twin outcomes of Britain's expansionary colonial project over three
centuries – are all too frequently regarded as deriving chiefly from the
campaigning consciences of white British reformers or as the logical
outcome of the liberal and liberalizing project that empire ostensibly
always was, conquering in order to free. Despite an abundance of
histories of resistance, and not only from a nationalist perspective,
which make clear the constitutive role of resistance to the imperial
project, 'imperial initiative' – colonies 'given' their freedom when
they were deemed ready for it – as the motive force of decolonization
remains stubbornly entrenched in much political and public discourse in Britain. Where, for Douglass, the story of Emancipation
specifically, and freedom more generally, was one of universal
aspiration and shared struggles, in its most influential and popular
versions it continues to be figured as a capacious British, or now
Anglo-American, franchise generously extended to peoples across
the globe. Edward Said observed correctly that 'a standard imperialist misrepresentation has it that exclusively Western ideas of freedom
led the fight against colonial rule, which mischievously overlooks the
reserves in Indian and Arab culture that *always* resisted imperialism, and claims the fight against imperialism as one of imperialism's
major triumphs'.[4] Writing in the 1930s, G. M. Trevelyan, Regius professor of history at Cambridge, understood such extensions to be
'pre-eminently a result of our free institutions, our freedom of speech
and association, and all that habit of voluntaryism and private initiative'.[5] Today, where imperial initiative is not actively given the
credit for decolonization, we are offered the claim, here articulated
by David Cannadine, that the Empire was 'given away in a fit of
collective indifference'.[6] John Darwin, meanwhile, paraphrases that
school of thought in terms of the notion that 'the British colonial
empire was liberated more by the indifference of its masters than the
struggles of its subjects'.[7] In either event, the 'granting' or 'giving' of
independence to British colonies once they were deemed 'ready' for it,
remains a cause for national self-congratulation; it fits neatly into an
equally familiar establishment mythology about 'English capacities
to reform without violence or rejecting valuable past practice'.[8] Like

all mythologies, this too relies on the selective elision of key strands in the story.

Such accounts – which, of course, draw on a longer tradition of Whig historiography – typically figure the geopolitical West as rolling on inexorably towards greater freedom, the darker nations taught to follow in its wake. Influential popular right-wing historians such as Niall Ferguson have coined clunky neologisms like 'Anglobalization' which enshrine the pre-eminence of the British Empire as a positive force leading the world towards this hypothetical state of total freedom, an epic in which the Empire rises and falls, only to open out onto greater vistas of liberty.[9] As the historian Victor Kiernan has observed, the word 'freedom' carries a racialized inflection, 'easier made into a parrot-cry than defined, and Westerners boast now of being free very much as not long ago they boasted of being white'.[10] In actuality, freedom from British rule was the end result of hard-fought struggles and different kinds of negotiation, historical processes which unfolded over a long period of time. As the Empire expanded from the slave colonies of the Caribbean to encompass the settler colonies of North America, Australia and New Zealand, the Indian subcontinent and large swathes of Africa, it was met with different kinds of resistance, both peaceful and violent, sometimes taking the form of mutinies, revolts and wars, and at others of civil disobedience and passive resistance.[11] This much is not in question outside the most retrograde circles, even if there is disagreement about the extent to which such events actually had an impact on or effected eventual decolonization. While the work of such counter-historians of slavery and empire as Herbert Aptheker, Michel-Rolph Trouillot, C. L. R. James, Robin Blackburn, Terence Ranger, Hilary Beckles, Gelien Matthews, Richard Gott, John Newsinger, Stephen Howe and Antoinette Burton, to name just a few, has shown comprehensively that the history of the British Empire is also the history of resistance to it, and – importantly, from both beyond and within Britain – such resistance is still not central to the writing of British imperial history. 'The trouble with British imperial histories', Burton has noted recently, 'is that they are not written with dissent and disruption in the lead', even though 'the very character of imperial power was shaped by its challengers and by the trouble they made for its stewards.'[12] The familiar 'rise-and-fall' model is indeed misleading, suggesting a long period of stability followed by a sudden end, whereas the maintenance of imperial rule in fact required constant vigilance and frequently forceful responses to resistance.[13]

On the other side of the coin, much attention, within both imperial historiography and postcolonial literary studies, has been paid to the ways in which colonial subjects took up British ideas and turned them against empire, 'writing back' or 'striking back' when making claims to freedom and self-determination – the now well-worn 'Caliban' model, as it were, of a language learned from and deployed against the colonizer. Originally theorized by the Latin American critic Roberto Fernández Retamar, the idea has now been generalized beyond recognition and its original historical usage.[14] As an abstract paradigm it is vulnerable to being read as a version of an idea familiar to imperial historians whereby anticolonial nationalism was the result of 'the tendency of the colonial rulers themselves to construct political institutions which could then be captured by local politicians and used against their masters'.[15] Also invoking the figure of Caliban – Shakespeare's slave who learned language from his master, Prospero, and then used it to curse his enslavement – Jan Nederveen Pieterse notes: 'The most commonly observed form of dialectics of imperialism is the *dialectics of assimilation*, particularly as regards education ... [This] reared a colonial intelligentsia who absorbed the Western ideals of liberty and patriotism and put them in the service of national awakening.'[16] However, while Pieterse himself is attuned to it, in general the possibility of reverse impact – including reverse appropriation and reworking – either has been curiously sidelined or is, at best, invoked notionally. In fact, read carefully, a substantial archive points clearly to the existence of such reverse influence, particularly in relation to the emergence of British criticism of empire – too often read, in Whig mode, as a simple outcropping of a home-grown liberalism.

What would happen if, in something akin to the 'spirit of dialectics' which informs Susan Buck-Morss's exploration of the Haitian Revolution's influence on Hegel, we explored the possibility that Britain's enslaved and colonial subjects were not merely victims of this nation's imperial history and subsequent beneficiaries of its crises of conscience, but rather agents whose resistance not only contributed to their own liberation but also put pressure on and reshaped some British ideas about freedom and who could be free?[17] We might even ask whether the idea of Britain's uniquely liberal Empire, which was humanitarian in conception and had the liberation of its conquered subjects as its ultimate goal, might itself have been, at least in part, a response to the claims to humanity, freedom and self-determination made by those very subjects. One axis, though not the only one, along which this question can be explored is that of dissent around the question of empire in Britain, with dissidents variously referred to as 'critics of empire', 'imperial sceptics' or British 'anticolonialists'. We know, of course, that not only was there significant diversity in attitudes to the Empire within the metropole, but also, at various moments, interrogation of and even opposition to the imperial project itself. In recent decades, a small number of distinguished historians have produced an important body of work fleshing out the activities and impact of imperial dissidents.[18] They include, most importantly, Stephen Howe, to whose foundational *Anticolonialism in British Politics* this work, particularly the later chapters, is indebted. Significant additional contributions to scholarship detailing the nature of domestic criticism of aspects of empire have also been made by Gregory Claeys, Nicholas Owen and Mira Matikkala. While between them these works offer an impressive and substantial account of the existence and importance of British dissent on the question of empire over the nineteenth and twentieth centuries, they do not examine in any depth the vital *relationship* between anticolonial resistance in the periphery and the emergence of such dissent in the metropole. In his unsparing account of colonial repression and violence, John Newsinger has discussed the ways in which 'radicals and socialists in Britain organised, demonstrated and protested in solidarity with … resistance movements' in the colonies, noting rightly that the likes of Ernest Jones, the Chartist leader, are part of a proud British anti-imperialist tradition.[19] But it is important to account also for the ways in which that tradition was influenced and shaped by anticolonial insurgency and anticolonial agents (including campaigners and intellectuals). As we shall see in Chapter 1, the Indian uprising of 1857 fired Jones's imagination, distinctly shaping his criticism of the imperial project, and leading him to go as far as to urge British working people, whose own struggles were flagging, to learn from the Indian rebels. The emergence of metropolitan dissent on colonial questions alongside liberation struggles in the colonies, *Insurgent Empire* argues, was a dialogical and, at times, dialectical process in which the lines of influence can be seen to go in both directions.

To examine the extent to which awareness of rebellion and resistance in the colonies, and in due course contact with anticolonial figures, shaped British domestic criticism of empire, which eventually grew from occasional dissent into a more full-throated anticolonialism, is to overturn the still prevalent emphasis on political and intellectual influence as radiating outwards from the imperial centre towards the periphery. It is to interrogate the tenacious assumption that the most significant conceptions of 'freedom' are fundamentally 'Western' in provenance, albeit open to subversive appropriation by the colonized. A closer look at the archives indicates that, in the contexts of both antislavery and anticolonialism, 'freedom' was a contested concept, its content emerging dialogically, determined through experience and struggle. The rebels of Morant Bay in 1865, for instance, challenged the notion that they were being 'emancipated' from slavery into wage labour, insisting instead on different labour practices. Nearly a century later, for many Kenyan resisters and insurgents in the period following the Second World War, self-determination involved not individualism but collective land-ownership as manifested in a struggle for 'Land and Freedom'. Such contestations, I suggest, were not without impact on metropolitan ideologies and practices. Without merely replicating the inversions of nationalist histories, *Insurgent Empire* shows how specific states of subjection and struggles against them were fundamental to how freedom – and cognate concepts like 'liberation', 'self-determination' and 'emancipation' – were understood and asserted both by insurgents on the ground and by their interpreters in the diaspora, influencing, in turn, how it was understood and reframed in the imperial centre. As Timothy Brennan notes of anticolonial thought in the peripheries, the very fact of colonialism entailed that the ideas at hand would 'include (inevitably, though not exclusively) those from Europe'.[20] Without pretending that the field could ever have been level or the lines of influence simply reciprocal given the constitutive power differential, this book suggests that there was *also* an anticolonial impact from outside Europe on metropolitan thought – specifically, though not only, on British dissent around and criticism of the colonial project. Resistance to the colonial project in several parts of the British Empire in the nineteenth and twentieth centuries helped shape criticism of and opposition to the imperial project within Britain itself. That influence was not necessarily always ideational, best assessed using the tools of intellectual history; it was often exercised through struggle and by crises occasioned by insurgency.

Insurgent Empire argues that there were heterogeneous but not unconnected arcs of criticism of empire that can be said to constitute a dissident and, frequently, outright anticolonial inheritance in Britain forged over more than a century. It examines, first, some nineteenth-century critical engagements with empire in the wake of rebellions and unrest; and, second, the emergence of more explicitly left-wing and internationalist anticolonialism in the twentieth century. Two major nineteenth-century crises of rule – the 1857 uprising in India and the 1865 rebellion of former slaves in Morant Bay – had important consequences for many of a liberal or radical bent in Britain. Through the fog of racialized imperial righteousness that enveloped the public sphere, these crises and the controversies they generated allowed for a rebel consciousness to be discerned, acknowledged and interpreted, even if only through newsprint and parliamentary papers. Having troubled liberal hierarchies of 'freedom' in which elite white Englishmen were its most ardent and deserving devotees, these crises then cleared the ground for common cause to be made with some radicals, like Jones, drawing parallels between colonial insurgencies and working-class resistance. In the case of the Positivist Richard Congreve, it formed the basis for a working-class (and interestingly also female) rejection of the imperial project. At the *fin de siècle*, several politically inclined travellers to antique lands under British rule arrived into milieus of 'unrest', finding themselves not the dispensers but the subjects of political tutelage, learning from what they witnessed, shifting their views, and even being radicalized in the process. From the years following the First World War, this process of what I call 'reverse tutelage' was furthered by the presence of strong anticolonial black and Asian voices within the metropole, who took on the function of interpreters between British dissidents and the millions who were resisting being governed by Britain.

The 'interdependence of cultural terrains in which colonizer and colonized coexisted and battled each other', to use Edward Said's formulation, is examined in this study through the lens of resistance and response – specifically the response of those inclined to interrogate the imperial consensus.[21] British national self-conceptions, particularly those to do with a love of liberty, certainly drew on existing domestic traditions; but as the Empire expanded through the long nineteenth century into the first half of the twentieth century, these conceptions were also subject to the pressures created by resistance to that Empire. When these moments of discernment are set alongside the growing contact between domestic critics of empire and anticolonialists from Britain's vast sphere of colonial possessions and influence, it becomes clear that the development of ideas of freedom in the context of empire did indeed involve lines of influence in both directions, if unevenly so, since 'it was not the struggle of same with same'.[22] Said rightly notes that without 'metropolitan doubts and opposition, the characters, idiom, and very structure of native resistance to imperialism would have been different'.[23] Those doubts and opposition were moulded in turn by native resistance – a point Said makes but does not elaborate in any detail: 'Opposition to empire in London and Paris was affected by resistance offered in Delhi and Algiers.'[24] In assessing this relationship, both British imperial historiography and postcolonial literary studies have left work to be done.

Colonial Insurgency and Historical Silences

It was we ourselves who had supplied to our subject-races the materials which were now being used to weave the imperial winding-sheet. We had done this deliberately, not swerving from the stance adopted by Macaulay in the 1830s when he had pressed for the adoption of an English education system in India, under whose discipline Indians should be trained to become fit to take responsibility for their own affairs.

A. P. Thornton, *The Imperial Idea and Its Enemies*

Our Empire has grown into a Commonwealth of free nations,
because of Britain's deliberate policy towards her Imperial respon-
sibilities. What has happened today, therefore, is not a retreat but a
direct fulfilment of the noble work done by our fathers and grand-
fathers in taking our traditions of liberal law and material progress
to every quarter of the globe.

Lord De La Warr, upon the Royal Empire Society substituting
the word 'Commonwealth' for 'Empire' in its masthead

In his important assessment of the historiographical place of the
Haitian Revolution of 1791, the anthropologist Michel-Rolph
Trouillot has argued that it is not so much active suppression as
powerful silences that determine the process of writing histories.
Trouillot is not simply suggesting here that there are areas of silence
in individual historical accounts, as there might be in any narrative,
but that 'cycles of silences' pre-exist specific histories 'to fit a world
of possibilities' already deemed to be the only ones.[25] In the case
of European historiography, what he calls a 'bundle of silences' has
emerged specifically around the resistance of the colonized and the
enslaved to the colonial project.[26] For Trouillot, the turning into a
'non-event' of the Haitian revolution is emblematic of the way in
which racism, slavery and colonialism have themselves been marginalized, for in spite of 'their importance in the formation of what we
now call the West ... none of these themes has ever become a central
concern of the historiographical tradition in a Western country'.[27] In
these traditions, the period from 1776 to 1843 is generally taught
as an 'age of revolution' while essentially maintaining a silence on
'the most radical political revolution of the age' – that which took
place in Haiti.[28] Trouillot's point about the elision of black agency
can be generalized, I believe, to struggles against colonialism and
slavery more generally, where we see 'archival power at its strongest, the power to define what is and what is not a serious object of
research and, therefore, of mention'.[29] Thus, the narratives that continue to circulate and make sense to a majority of Western observers
and readers, Trouillot suggests, is one where the West – and elite
white men in particular – are the prime movers of history, taking the
initiative and the action necessary to propel humankind inexorably
towards freedom. The rest of the world inevitably figure as passive

beneficiaries of this impulse. Resistance to European imperialism fails to 'make sense', and, like conceptions of freedom not determined by capitalist definitions, becomes quite literally 'unthinkable'.[30] It is an understanding of history that continues to have decisive – and deleterious – consequences in the spheres of British, American and NATO foreign policy.[31]

Trouillot's point about the extent to which the archives are both constructed *and* interpreted so as to foreground the agency of white, Western, male actors is manifest in much of the British historiography of decolonization.[32] Within the 'imperial initiative' paradigm, decolonization emerges ab nihilo, the magical consequence of imperial policies developed in a vacuum immune to anticolonial pressures. It is manifest in the ongoing use of 'Commonwealth' as a euphemism for regions once colonized by Britain, enshrining as it does the cherished mythology of an Empire that ruled in order to free. The Whig politician and historian Thomas Babington Macaulay would famously say of Britannia's Empire: 'it is to her peculiar glory, not that she has ruled so widely – not that she has conquered so splendidly – but that she has ruled only to bless, and conquered only to spare'.[33] Harold Macmillan, presiding over post-war decolonization over a hundred years later, 'claimed self-government had been the intention behind colonial rule from its very beginnings'.[34] When it comes to critiques of imperial activity, there has been a tendency to privilege empire as a 'self-correcting device' rather than one that was forced to respond not just to 'enlightened opinion' in Britain but to the enslaved and colonized who asserted themselves.[35] These notions remain part of British common sense, along with a tenacious belief that the imperial project was, on the whole, for the good, a few blips and mishaps notwithstanding. The securing and consolidation of 'liberty' across the globe eventually became the official rationale for a Britannic empire that, over time, spread across swathes of North America, Asia, Africa, the Pacific Rim and the Caribbean. This would be a 'moral' and liberal empire with a humanitarian core, which enjoined 'improving' subject peoples until they were fit to receive their liberty. Making the globe and colonized peoples suitable for the spread of (capitalist) freedom would mark official British colonial and foreign policy throughout the nineteenth and twentieth centuries. As the 2003 invasion of Iraq on the basis of similar claims showed, this posture would continue to inflect foreign policy in the twenty-first century as well.

The treatment of resistance as episodic, even exceptional, has consequences for the wider public sphere. Historical studies that do emphasize dissent and disruption have not 'made their way into commonsense perceptions of the British empire'.[36] What Burton describes as the absence of 'grand synthetic counter-narratives of protest, resistance and revolution' allows for the continued salience of imperial apologetics in the public sphere, as well as a sense – even more prominent in the wake of 'Brexit', or the 2016 referendum vote in favour of Britain's leaving the European Union – that this country's imperial role and post-imperial influence continue to be valued in the postcolonial world, or the so-called Commonwealth.[37] This glow of post-imperial achievement sits alongside claims that the wider British population was largely indifferent to the fate of the Empire – the 'minimal impact thesis'.[38] Despite scant evidence, Stuart Ward has written, a 'broad consensus that British culture and society were in the post-war era insulated against the periodic shocks that occasioned the demise of British power and prestige abroad' has taken on the contours of 'historiographical orthodoxy'.[39] Ward argues that, on the contrary, 'the stresses and strains of imperial decline were not safely contained within the realm of high politics'.[40]

Insurgent Empire examines how such stresses and strains – generated over several decades throughout the period of colonial rule rather than during formal decolonization alone – made their impact felt in periodic crises of empire, which in turn cleared the ground for more critical assessments of the imperial project. If, as Ward argues, it is 'precisely the imperial context that underpinned contemporary perceptions of national degeneration' and cast doubts on Britain's place in the world, the various challenges to that supremacy throughout the centuries of imperial rule caused repeated crises of rule and of national identity.[41] Anxieties about national degeneration were often occasioned by the repression deployed against those colonial others who laid claims to their own humanity and freedom. Many of the ideas of 'British character' that Ward enumerates as progressively weakened by the imminent end of empire – they included notions of 'duty', 'loyalty', 'service', 'self-restraint' and 'gentlemanly conduct' – were in fact thrown into crisis each time insurgency was followed by repression.[42] The edifice of colonial rule was subject throughout its duration to implosions – and explosions – when confronted with resistance, and these registered in public and political discourse in Britain. If decolonization was a 'complex and intermittent process that ebbed and flowed over time', so too was the consolidation and continuance of colonial rule, punctuated as it was by resistance and repression.[43]

If, as John Mackenzie has argued, the 'notion of the utterly indifferent British' when it came to the fate of empire 'is something of a self-justificatory and consolatory travesty',[44] it is worth asking how this obsessive insistence on indifference also contributes to the entrenchment of the 'cycle of silences' with regard to the agency of colonial subjects more generally. The mythology of a managed decolonization which owed little to anticolonial resistance also resonates more generally with what Joanna de Groot describes as a familiar 'liberal wish to find acceptable and safe stories of reform (the theme of progressive change without conflict, going back to Macaulay)'.[45] Much the same impulse would seem to animate an insistence on the marginality of British critics of empire: it is not necessary to suggest that British dissidents on imperial questions ever had the dominant hand, still less hegemony, to argue for the importance of examining connections between dissidence in a society that did not, in fact, speak with one voice on the matter of the Empire, and insurgencies which took place in distant outposts of Empire. To examine the dissident, even in the margins, is to move away from what Andrew Thompson describes as an emphasis in much imperial history-writing on 'the official mind', or the policy-making elite, rather than considering 'an array of external forces working upon government'.[46] This is not to say, of course, that opposition invariably had a determinate effect upon government; lines of influence are, in any case, never easy to disentangle. If, as Thompson asserts, imperial politics 'was pre-eminently an extra-parliamentary activity', then opposition to empire with the agitation and activism that accompanied it should also not be assessed purely in terms of effects or numbers.[47] At the same time, we shall see that anticolonialism in Britain sometimes did decisively shape parliamentary and media debates.

Postcolonial Studies and Anticolonial Insurgency

While the field that has come to be known as postcolonial studies is assumed, in theory, to take a more than passing interest in the question of resistance to empire and imperialism, in its most influential incarnations it has emphasized the post- over the anti-colonial. In spite of its emphasis on analysing colonial discourse, the field as a whole has failed to challenge the tenacious assumption that ideas of 'freedom' – not just individualist or liberal renditions of liberty, but freedom in the broadest sense – are fundamentally Western (meaning European and American) in provenance, albeit available for appropriation. (I will come to more recent elaborations of the 'decolonial' later in this introduction.) In part, ironically enough, the focus on 'Eurocentrism' has resulted in a fixation on rejecting European thought generally – and the Enlightenment in particular – without a consideration of multiple lines of cultural and political engagement in the making of the entity called 'Europe'. Rather than properly considering the Enlightenment as at once historically and culturally situated, drawing on resources that are not in fact just 'European' but are potentially universal in some of their aspirations, intersecting with ideals theorized outside Europe, the field's most influential scholars, as Neil Lazarus suggests, 'have written at length to condemn as naive or, worse, tacitly authoritarian, any commitment to universalism, metanarrative, social emancipation, revolution'.[48] The notion of the universal – in the sense of ideas and values that might have a certain supple applicability across cultures – is itself assumed a priori to have only ever been thought of in Europe, which is guilty not only of having abused the idea – which its ruling elites certainly did – but of having come up with it in the first place. Such a sweeping repudiation of principles that might be held in common across contexts, indeed might have been forged through contact, flies in the face of the multiple historical and cultural sites where notions such as universal rights and social justice have been theorized. It also ignores a global history of human resistance to tyranny and exploitation of various kinds. Where theories of resistance are offered, the dominant wisdom of postcolonial studies has stressed what Homi K. Bhabha describes as 'affective ambivalence and discursive disturbance'.[49] Bhabha's transmutation of the putative ambivalence of colonial elites into a general theory of imperial undoing – which posited, as Lazarus puts it, 'a certain slippage at the heart of the colonial episteme' – has been persuasively subjected to critique, and need not detain us unduly here.[50] We may, however, wish to register the ways in which theories of psychic ambivalence shade without too much difficulty into a sanctioned, at times mandatory, ambivalence towards the brute reality of imperialism itself; this ambivalence in turn underlies and enables the popular apologetics for and defences of the British Empire, not least in the popular, and usually fatuous, 'balance sheet' assessments of empire's pluses and minuses. This privileging of 'ambivalence' – not a million miles from 'equivocation' – may account for why, nearly thirty years into its disciplinary consolidation, postcolonial studies has not succeeded in definitively dislodging imperialist apologetics. In turn, this failure entrenches a narrow – indeed, triumphally capitalist – understanding of 'freedom' when, in fact, the history of empire is also a history of contesting interpretations of the term.

By way of situating some of this book's own concerns, I want to pause briefly on some significant – and representative – recent work that has drawn on postcolonial approaches. (Readers who wish to proceed with the historical episodes should feel free to skip straight to Chapter 1 now.) Lisa Lowe's *The Intimacies of Four Continents* (2015) locates itself within the wider critique of European liberal thought developed by scholars such as Uday Mehta, Walter Mignolo and Dipesh Chakrabarty, among others, to argue that 'liberal philosophy, culture, economics, and government have been commensurate with, and deeply implicated in, colonialism, slavery, capitalism, and empire'.[51] Lowe herself seeks to make visible in this context global connections that bring together aspects of the imperial project (including indenture and enslavement) as they unfolded in Europe, the Americas, East Asia and Africa. Her aim is to provide an 'unsettling genealogy' that 'examines liberalism as a project that includes at once both the universal promises of rights, emancipation, wage labor, and free trade, as well as the global divisions and asymmetries on which the liberal tradition depends, and according to which such liberties are reserved for some and wholly denied to others'.[52] Exclusion, in other words, is built into the structure of liberalism. Concepts such as 'reason', 'freedom' and 'civilization' work to effect colonial divisions to which the subordination of colonized and dispossessed peoples, and the appropriation of their land and labour, are fundamental. This insight is unexceptional – indeed, familiar.

But what of those who resisted dispossession and expropriation? They do not loom large in Lowe's study. Lowe notes that, in the case of settler conquests in the Americas, 'native resistance to European intrusion was regularly cast as a threat to the security of settler sovereignty' (which, of course, it was!), and that black abolitionists such as Ottobah Cugoano, Mary Prince and Olaudah Equiano were 'often persuaded' to use the same terms of appeal as white abolitionists – against 'cruelty' and 'immorality', and to the ideal of a 'just, humanitarian English society'. Elided from the discussion, somewhat paradoxically, are the challenges offered by the colonized to the regimes that confronted them, including liberalism.[53] Without romanticizing such agency or proposing that insurgent consciousness is easily accessed, it is nonetheless possible to assess the ways in which liberalism was in turn thrown into crisis by, and often responded to, the resistance of the colonized, in sometimes unexpected ways, including appropriating and domesticating it. The example Lowe herself gives is a case in point: drawing on the distinguished work of Thomas C. Holt, she rightly notes that ' "emancipation" clearly did not establish freedom for Black peoples in the British West Indies, many of whom were still confined to the plantation, and others were left bound in economic servitude and poverty'.[54] At the same time, we may wish to pay attention – drawing both on the extant archives of counterinsurgency and the work of Holt and others – to the ways in which the 'emancipated' did not take the condition of continuing subjugation lying down; indeed, in the case of the West Indies, they were often the first to articulate, through their words and actions, a refusal of the condition of wage-slavery, insisting on the right to own and farm small plots of land over working for planters. As we shall see in Chapter 2, the Morant Bay Rebellion of 1865 both enacted resistance to a post-Emancipation regime deemed to be exploitative and, through the unfolding of the 'Governor Eyre' controversy back in Britain, enabled this resistance to generate debate and effect deep divisions among the metropolitan *bien-pensant*, who had to find a way to deal with the reality of black insurgency.

In the necessary process of challenging its premises, it is vital not to repeat the elisions and silences of European liberalism, particularly those that emerged historically around the agency of the enslaved and the colonized. Otherwise, at the very moment of interrogating liberalism's elisions and exclusions, we rehearse the ways in which it renders nugatory the agency and actions of those who put pressure on it, questioned it, or rejected it outright. Despite its formally adversarial stance, the focus of colonial discourse analysis, much like that of imperial history, has largely been on the imperial centre – ironically, to the detriment of a consideration of those who were subject to these regimes, but not necessarily (indeed, hardly ever) silently so. Colonized or enslaved people did not just create 'the conditions for liberalism' – they often also forced open its premises and challenged its exclusions, drawing not just on Caliban's learning of Prospero's language but also on their own existence, experiences and cultural resources to do so. Similarly, while their exclusion may have been constitutive of European humanism, the insistence of the colonized on their own humanity demanded, and often obtained, a reconstitution of humanism itself. An emphasis on the official mind, often made inevitable by the slant of the archives themselves, should not lead us to enact our own forms of forgetting, making black agency invisible or rendering resistance 'unthinkable' in Trouillot's sense of the term.

Certainly, the kinds of resistance explored in *Insurgent Empire* – from the legendary Indian uprising of 1857 to the Egyptian revolution of 1882, which was fomented in part within a milieu of radical Islamic intellectualism; from the Swadeshi movement in India, with its Hindu iconography; to the Mau Mau uprising in Kenya, which drew on Kikuyu cultural beliefs and practices – at once asserted cultural specificities and made insistent claims upon shared humanity. In this regard, we might recall Susan Buck-Morss's suggestion that, if 'the historical facts about freedom can be ripped out of the narratives told by the victors and salvaged for our own time, then the project of universal freedom does not need to be discarded but, rather, redeemed and reconstituted on a different basis'.[55] Similarly, the archives yield the sense that, even as colonial narratives of universal freedom were challenged and queried, the project of something like universal freedom was reconstituted and reframed, rather than discarded. Witnessing or interpreting resistance, British critics of empire read against the grain of colonial discourse's insistence on immutably sharp cultural differences or radical alterity, recognizing possibilities for forging common cause in cultures of resistance, as well as what Satya P. Mohanty describes as 'the kind of agency that is so crucial to defining practices and, collectively, cultures'.[56] In Said's words, rebellious 'natives' were able to 'impress upon the metropolitan culture the independence and integrity of their own culture, free from colonial encroachment'.[57] This does not necessarily imply either the elision of cultural differences and historical particularities, or the de facto imposition of a grand scheme of European Reason; indeed, the very nature of encounters in the face of anticolonial resistance made such elision difficult even where it might have been wished for. Uday Mehta is right to point to the impulse within British liberalism, when confronted with the unfamiliar, 'to hitch it to a more meaningful teleology', to annex difference, and render it a subset of more evolved European modes of thinking.[58] Yet, as we shall see, liberalism was affected not only by empire but also by anti-empire as idea and praxis. For British dissidents of a liberal-reformist bent, encounters with resistant colonial subjects often entailed learning that not all that was deemed 'European' was in fact solely European – that, when it came to ideas of freedom and justice, as Gurminder Bhambra puts it, 'the concepts and traditions are not European; what is at stake is the claiming of these concepts and traditions *as European*'.[59] Unlearning paternalism, for many British dissidents, involved interrogating and working through the seeming 'Otherness' of the colonized, and the 'sentimental charity' that a sense of difference called for, as well as working with the possibilities – radical in context – offered by the often difficult practice of equality. Far from neutralizing the other within a safe mode of 'difference', resistance brought home the fact of a commonality that could not be contained by the familiar disposition of benevolence. What was required was solidarity.

Human Affinities, Political Communities

A revolution which does not aim at changing me by changing the relations between people does not interest me; what's more, I doubt

*whether a revolution which does not affect me enough to transform
me is really a revolution at all.*

Jean Genet, 'The Palestinians'

For some time now, historians and literary critics who have made
use of postcolonial approaches have been excited by the 'utopian'
conceptual possibilities embedded in what they regard as profound
otherness. In her important and influential 2006 work *Affective
Communities*, Leela Gandhi reflects on the concept specifically in
relation to the emergence of British anticolonialism, arguing that
British radicals in the nineteenth century undertook border-crossings,
'visible in small, defiant flights from the fetters of belonging toward
the unknown destinations of radical alterity'.[60] Inasmuch as theirs
were 'flights from imperial similitude', the imperial dissidents of
Gandhi's study were radical, she argues, in their refusal of 'the exclusionary structures of instrumental binary reason'.[61] This refusal, for
Gandhi, is contiguous with what she sees as fundamental to postcolonial critique: 'the impulse against imperial binarism'. Gandhi does,
however, dissent from the tendency in postcolonial studies to figure
the dissolution of such binaries as inevitable; Homi Bhabha famously
theorizes 'ambivalence' always already inscribed 'at the very origins
of colonial authority'.[62] As I have already argued, such 'ambivalence'
would seem to be little more than a theoretically fashionable version
of Whig imperial history's own rendering of imperialism as a self-
correcting system that arrives at emancipation or decolonization
without regard to the resistance of its subjects. In other words, the
theory of ambivalence produced through mimicry also suggests that
there is always 'a kind of built-in resistance in the construction of any
dominant discourse – and opposition is an almost inevitable effect
in its construction of cultural difference'.[63] Gandhi rightly calls for
attention to be paid to more active dissidents, those 'from within the
imperial culture' who are 'unwilling to wait for its eventual hybridi-
zation, actively renouncing, refusing, and rejecting categorically its
aggressive manicheanism'.[64] For all that its use of 'anti-imperialism'
is expansive to a fault – 'troped as shorthand for all that was wrong
and iniquitous in the world' – Gandhi's study offers us a refresh-
ing return in our jaded times to a subculture of utopian aspiration
embedded in a longing for 'ideal community'.[65] Certainly, it is the

case that the late Victorian moment she examines – and to which *Insurgent Empire* also turns, if somewhat differently – was redolent with the promise of radical transformation on a global scale.

Ultimately, however, Gandhi too fails to break with the dominant elisions of postcolonial studies – a field that, despite her claims, is not for the most part predicated on the binaries between colonial power and anticolonial resistance, favouring as it has precisely the grounds of 'hybridity' and 'ambivalence'. Her welcome, if excessively cautious, critique of the conceptual inadequacies of Bhabha's rendering of colonial ambivalence notwithstanding, and despite a salutary emphasis on the 'aspirational energy' of metropolitan anti-imperialism, Gandhi's rather limited understanding and hostile repudiation of 'historical dialecticism' impoverishes her account. While it is gently critical of Bhabha's elision of agency, Gandhi's own rendering of metropolitan anti-imperialism in the mirror of postmodernism – diffuse, unorganized, even ludic – is appealing to contemporary literary sensibilities but performs several occlusions of its own. Foremost among these is the figuring of metropolitan dissidents as in some sense intrinsic exiles who responded to local pressures, rather than as evolving subjects who were often in dialectical engagement with insurgents and movements in the colonies that can be caricatured neither as simply nationalist nor as being in thrall to invented traditions. Even assuming that it might be possible or desirable to glean 'one paradigmatic narrative of metropolitan anti-imperialism' – a diversely unwieldy phenomenon – it is unlikely that such a narrative could be merely character-driven, simply a story of fascinatingly eccentric outliers whose actions constituted 'the disaggregated forms of a dissent engaged for its own sake, bearing no practical investment in the *telos* of the anticolonial nation-state and certainly gaining no apparent material advantage from the economic and political diminution of imperial power'.[66]

As we shall see, for many of the figures discussed here, 'intolerable domestic pressures' were less the cause of a conversion to anticolonialism for them than a useful point of comparison, a way of drawing connections between domestic forms of oppression and those being exercised abroad. Certainly, they allowed for common cause to be made. Characters such as Ernest Jones, Wilfrid Blunt, Nancy Cunard and Fenner Brockway may have been unique personalities with distinctive life-stories, but the point is not that they were somehow ontologically less 'immune to the ubiquitous temptations of empire'. What is more significant is that their critical positions developed out of a concatenation of factors in which their contact with or consciousness of insurgent movements and actors was significant. Anticolonial insurgency often inspired these personalities to call for parallel domestic resistance to tyranny. The elision of agency that emerges in theories of ambivalence resurfaces in Gandhi's attribution of these processes to 'cultural osmoses occasioned by colonial encounter' and 'the irremediable leakiness of imperial boundaries'.[67] In the face of the theoretical condescension that afflicts our present view of such movements, it is worth noting that not all anticolonialists – indeed, not even all nationalists – naively embraced 'purity' or 'edenic premodern antiquity'. On the contrary, they were all too aware of the strategic nature of the binaries they deployed against empire; these, moreover, often took the form not only of subject nation against imperial nation but of the powerless against the powerful, the just against the unjust, and right against might. Crucially, those ranged against power, injustice and oppression were not defined in exclusively racial or communal terms but could comprise alliances across the boundary between metropole and periphery. Imperial binaries could not simply be 'dissolved'; they had to be fought strategically with differently constituted ones not unlike those implied by the 'new and better forms of community and relationality' which Gandhi writes about with verve. The 'unsatisfactory theoretical choice between the oppositional but repetitive forms of cultural nationalism on the one hand and the subversive but quietist discourse of hybridity or contrapuntality on the other' may, in fact, exist only in the writings of contemporary critics.[68]

While profoundly attuned to its psychological dimensions and representational mechanisms, the metropolitan critics of empire and their anticolonial interlocutors discussed in *Insurgent Empire* rarely saw imperialism as, in the first instance, 'a peculiar habit of mind', or 'a complex analogical system' that could be disrupted simply through aestheticized versions of disorder, chaos or unruliness. Nor was anticolonialism simply a volitional matter of 'opting out from the idiom of their own colonizing culture' for an 'other-directed ethics'.[69] If the periphery did give rise to 'a new politics of unlikely conjunction and conjuncture', it was one that took hard work, reciprocal un-learning and learning, and collective organizational efforts. It was a politics, in short, not so much of friendship (though that was not absent) as of difficult solidarities forged through dialogism, in which both parties found themselves being transformed in just the way suggested by Genet above. The story of British metropolitan anticolonialism is not one of the growth of 'affective communities' alone, but also of shifting of affective dispositions, from that of the paternalist humanitarian to one of solidarity defined as a 'transformative political relation', or 'the active creation of new ways of relating' – one in which both sides might shift and evolve their dispositions in response to the encounter.[70] This transformation is traced here through thickly historicized textual readings in which the individual voice, distinctive as it is, was necessarily inflected by the collective, in a relationship that at its best is at once interrogative and representational. The effort – particularly in the twentieth century – was to create *political* communities that were not devoid of affect, or even of conviviality, but cognizant of challenges, disagreements and power differentials; a solidarity characterized neither by homogeneity nor by shared national belonging, and where contiguity of interests had to be argued for and forged rather than taken for granted. Indeed, to recall the famous closing scene from Forster's *A Passage to India*, Aziz and Fielding, the Indian and the Englishman, would have to be allies in the project of driving the English out of India before they could be friends. The resistance of the colonized was key to this process, in which the political and the affective were mutually constitutive.

Culture, Universalism and the Anticolonial

The word in language is half someone else's. It becomes 'one's own' only when the speaker populates it with his own intentions, his own accent, when he appropriates the word, adapting it to his own semantic and expressive intention.

Mikhail Bakhtin, *The Dialogic Imagination*

The relationship between the political and the affective as manifested in the relationship between anticolonial insurgency and British
dissent on questions of the Empire was a dialogical one in the broadest
sense, where each term influenced the other, if not evenly or equally.
The kinds of British oppositional discourse examined here can be
seen as manifest responses to the voices, insights and consciousness of insurgents, incorporating them in a transformative process.
Bakhtin's insight that the word 'lives, as it were, on the boundary
between its own context and another, alien, context' is helpful here.[71]
The actions, utterances and, in complicated ways, 'voice' of insurgency inhabited the discourses of British criticism of empire, so that
they embody what Bakhtin describes as a hybrid of 'varying degrees
of otherness or varying degrees of "our-own-ness"'.[72] The 'process of
interaction and struggle with others' thought' inflects the genres and
utterances of these texts, from speeches and manifestos to memoirs,
petitions and editorials. The emergence, at first, of 'sympathy', and
subsequently of variants of 'solidarity', as a metropolitan response
to resistance and crises of insurgency, can be broadly located in the
intersubjective space of communication. It is a space that can be
simultaneously conflictual and reciprocal, in which meaning is made,
and in which the fact of cognized difference does not preclude, and
may indeed facilitate, the emergence of shared ground. Inasmuch as
'a relation is never static, but always in the process of being made
or unmade', the dialogism of the anticolonial encounter, as much as
that of the colonial one, enabled the reconstitution of both selves
and relations in more radical directions.[73] If we might regard anticolonialism as a very specific form of address through self-assertion,
it can be seen to generate a sense of 'answerability' in imperial dissidents. To the extent that dialogism 'argues that sharing is not only an
ethical or economic mandate, but a condition built into the structure
of human perception, and thus a condition inherent in the very fact
of being human', I make the case for both something like a reconfigured critical humanism and an expansive universalism as central to
the anticolonialism of the texts examined here.[74]

The space of 'sharing' that emerges through the dialogism of the
encounters discussed here – also one in which universals make their
claims felt – does not necessarily entail the elision of difference or
the assimilation of it into the cunning of European 'Reason'. On the

contrary, as we shall see from the intellectual journeys of Wilfrid
Blunt, Henry Nevinson, Nancy Cunard and Fenner Brockway,
among others, the space of anticolonial encounter is also a field of
moral inquiry, in which different cultures functioned as 'laboratories
of moral practice and experimentation' for all concerned.[75] Satya P.
Mohanty's argument that cultural differences (and, arguably, historical specificities) are not necessarily at odds with moral universals is
useful here. He points out that it is perfectly possible for 'a nonrela-
tivist understanding (and defense) of diversity and pluralism' to be
developed if interaction between cultures (as 'fields of moral inquiry')
can be seen as a form of 'epistemic cooperation'.[76] This would mean,
as it did for many of the metropolitan figures I discuss, that the practices of 'other cultures', particularly in the crucible of resistance,
showed themselves to 'embody and interrogate rich patterns of value,
which in turn represent deep bodies of knowledge of humankind and
human flourishing'.[77]

As I will show, these encounters frequently generated a pedagogical process I call 'reverse tutelage', in which metropolitan dissidents
came to learn something from their anticolonial interlocutors and
the movements they represented. In the crucible of these pedagogical encounters which 'widen[ed] the fields of historical inquiry' and
enabled 'a fuller range of human possibilities', notions of human
good or a just global order were unsettled, challenged, expanded
and reconstituted.[78] The likes of Keir Hardie, travelling to an India in
'unrest'; Raymond Michelet, writing about various African cultures;
and even C. L. R. James and George Padmore, teaching themselves
about Africa in order to be able to better interpret and represent
black resistance, would come to a recognition of the narrowness of
their own frames of historical and epistemological reference. They
would seek to expand and deepen these through studying both
resistance itself and the various cultural resources which African and
Asian resistance to empire drew upon. There was certainly an operative sense in most cases that there were 'features of human nature ...
shared by all humans across cultures' and some 'minimal require-
ments for human welfare', but these were insights that were acquired
through reading the texts of resistance rather than an a priori claim,
often *conceded* rather than imposed.[79] Human commonality – and
equality – were reclaimed by the colonized, not bestowed by the

colonizer, much in the spirit of the black man who stands upright in the frontispiece to abolitionist and feminist Elizabeth Heyrick's magnificent 1824 polemic, *Immediate not Gradual Abolition*, who does not ask whether he should not be treated with common humanity, but asserts defiantly: 'I AM A MAN, YOUR BROTHER'.[80] Rejected here was the mendicancy and petitioning that many anticolonialists from the colonies would also take pains to repudiate.

If, in addition to the 'language' of force, anticolonial rebels also deployed the 'language of conscience', their purpose was 'breaking down the strategy of *dehumanization*', or the 'thingification' that Aimé Césaire so bitterly ascribes to colonialism.[81] In forcing a moral confrontation, insurgents were not merely claiming a shared humanity, but also pushing open the boundaries of what it meant to be human in a global frame: 'In thus creating political facts, setting limits, and placing beacons, emancipation movements recreate our collective environment and collective awareness, in a process of social creation from below.'[82] They were, in other words, participants not just in what Lloyd and JanMohamed call 'a viable humanism ... centered around a critique of domination' but also 'a utopian exploration of human potentiality'.[83] Here it is worth noting that while the subjects of resistance often drew on cultural resources and social practices of their own that were not derived from the regime of the colonizer or his language, these rarely translated in any simple sense into radical difference, or what the influential theorist of 'decoloniality' Walter Mignolo calls 'other epistemologies, other principles of knowledge and understanding and, consequently, other economy, other politics, other ethics' – or 'pluriversality'.[84] Claims to radical alterity are, in fact, rarely to be heard in the language of resistance, even as there is often a fierce insistence on cultural specificities. Even as the vocabulary of some forms of resistance drew on spiritual and religious frameworks that were clearly situated outside the European Enlightenment, there was no self-evident repudiation of 'reason' (in the lower case). The capacity for reason could be conceded to the colonizer no more than 'freedom' or 'humanity', whatever the claims he made for their provenance. Challenging the 'pretended universality' and the pseudo-humanism of the colonizer involved enriching and reconstituting universality through multiple strands of experience and engagement, rather than conceding the logic of absolute difference. Indeed, it might even be regarded, in the face of the dehumanizing gestures of colonialism, as a *rehumanizing* of the metropole. For anticolonial insurgents, there was no simple opposition between the logic of 'emancipation' (which for Mignolo belongs to 'Europe') and the claims of 'liberation' (the 'decolonial' option); Europe had to be forced to make good its moralizing claims even as the struggle for self-liberation pressed inexorably on. 'De-centering the universal emancipating claims in the projects grounded in the liberal and socialist traditions of the European enlightenment' did not, contra Mignolo, always entail a rejection either of emancipation per se or of the possibility of universally applicable values.[85] Mignolo is right to suggest that 'emancipation', as it was figured in European liberal discourse, is different from 'liberation' as it is conceived of in 'decolonial' discourse, deriving as it does from the provenance of revolutions in France, Britain and the United States. Events such as the Haitian revolution and the decolonization of Africa and Asia – two examples Mignolo uses – brought different dimensions to both liberalism and Marxism/socialism. At the same time, a disproportionate emphasis on radically different 'categories of thought' obscures the extent to which many 'liberation' struggles were committed to universalism – and not only because they were part of the dominant language or the colonizer's categories of thought. Indeed, rather than offer sutured, self-contained alternatives to the idea of universal freedom, resistance often deliberately showed up the colonizer's version of universalism to be anything but universal. Universals had to be embodied through experience and resistance, not refused as 'European'. This often entailed working with the 'logic of modernity', decolonizing rather than repudiating it, teasing out its revolutionary promises.

If, as Edward Said has argued in his posthumously published set of lectures, *Humanism and Democratic Criticism*, we would do well to be attentive to the ways in which all language 'exists to be revitalized by change', then the dialogical role of struggles for liberation in enacting that revitalization needs to be taken seriously.[86] They did so, not least, by forcing a process of 'self-definition, self-examination, and self-analysis' in the metropole. It is in that sense that Britain today is itself as much the product of anticolonialism as it is of the imperial project. Many of 'the achievements of emancipation enter into the mainstream by being assimilated by elites', Pieterse has argued; this turning of yesterday's struggles into 'today's institutional frameworks' holds true not only for postcolonial contexts, but also for Britain.[87] The making of an empire that was forced over time to make concessions, offer reforms, attend to human rights (if only notionally), embrace 'humane' considerations, and even regard itself as an emancipator in the first instance, must be read as a response to resistance. We know that history records 'the achievements of empires and imperial civilizations more than it does the humanizing and civilizing contributions of emancipation movements'.[88] It is now something of a commonplace that a certain kind of narrow, self-regarding and narcissistic humanism was exported to the colonies by the colonial project. Yet it is also the case that the resistance of the colonized expanded the scope of humanism in the metropole. As Paul Gilroy notes in his eloquent case for reconsidering the scope of 'humanity' and 'human rights', historical struggles in the 'Black Atlantic' against racial hierarchy have come up with radical understandings of the category of the 'human' and developed 'twentieth-century demands for a variety of humanism that would be disinclined to overlook Europe's colonial crimes'.[89] He notes too that the formation of transnational 'moral communities' – which registered in European cultures – often relied on 'the dissemination and refinement of an idea of the human which was incompatible with racial hierarchy'.[90]

Resistance and the Archive

Insurgent Empire is written with Said's insight in mind that what makes cultures and civilizations interesting is 'not their essence or purity, but their combinations and diversity, the way they have of conducting a compelling dialogue with other civilizations'.[91] This means returning to 'what has long been a characteristic of all cultures, namely, that there is a strong streak of radical antiauthoritarian dissent in all of them'.[92] Dissent, when it has an effect, often becomes invisible once absorbed into institutional frameworks.[93] Part of my effort here is to make it – and its dialogic nature – visible again. The materials examined here are not unknown to historians; I make no claims to unearthing an entirely new archive – though some materials

are perhaps less well known than they might be. Rather, to a rich set
of historical materials that have yet to be fully interpreted, this study
brings some of the tools of literary criticism – in particular, attention
to voice, allusion, quotation, influence, intertextuality and translation. The word in British anticolonialism, I suggest in a Bakhtinian
spirit, was half that of those who rose up against the Empire and of
those who sought actively, as anticolonial writers and intellectuals,
to 'manipulate the self-understanding of the oppressor'.[94] The effect
of non-European strands of thought – Hindu 'theosophy' and *l'art
nègre* on art, music and spirituality on *fin de siècle* and modernist
avant-garde cultural formations – has largely been documented. I
want to suggest that attention also be paid to the effect of anticolonial resistance from outside Europe and America on British dissident
discourse.

To study the texts of British imperial dissidents and critics of empire
in relation to the texts of anticolonial resistance is, in one sense, to
study a *minoritized* literature – that is, to reflect on them as texts that
'have been and continue to be subjected to institutional forgetting',
to borrow Abdul JanMohammed and David Lloyd's words once
again.[95] Through close textual analysis of an assemblage of texts –
accounts of trials, speeches, manifestos, journalism, essays, memoirs
– *Insurgent Empire* tracks the different ways in which resistance
in colonial contexts was variously received, refracted or reframed,
and allowed to revise and radicalize existing dissenting tendencies
in the metropole. Works by individual metropolitan figures such as
Wilfrid Blunt, Frederic Harrison, Nancy Cunard, Fenner Brockway
and Arthur Ballard are examined in relation both to the anticolonial insurgencies (and rebel voices) they read and assimilated into
their work, and, where relevant, to their personal engagement with
such oppositional figures who emerged from milieus of 'unrest' as
Jamal-ud-din al-Afghani, Colonel Ahmad Orabi, Aurobindo Ghose,
Claude McKay, George Padmore, C. L. R James and others. Even as
the emphasis here is on close textual reading, in such a way as to cast
light on influence and engagement, the account which follows insists
on the *worldliness* of oppositional discourse, whereby individual
voices and texts of insurgency and dissent are not only profoundly
imbricated with each other but also shaped by the practice of struggle
and the *collectivities* forged through it. If the tale here is told through

texts and individual authors, it is with a deep awareness of the wider collective context that produced these utterances. In the language of dissenters and opposers, we frequently see something like the creative 'process of *assimilation* – more or less creative – of others' words' that Bakhtin describes.[96] The metropolitan language of liberty and justice often manifested, I suggest, an assimilation, reworking, and re-emphasis of the languages – in the broadest sense – of anticolonial insurgency.

Examining how their actions, their voices and their words were in fact assimilated and refracted in metropolitan oppositional discourse, we can re-vision colonial subjects as agents whose actual resistance put critical transformative pressure on British claims to cherishing freedom, and on those Britons who spoke and campaigned in its cause. In doing so, these subjects may themselves have drawn, as Haiti's rebels had done, on the languages of revolution and emancipation that came to them from Europe (although there was arguably a difference between appealing to French republican values and to the benevolence of the British monarch). However, they also drew on other cultural resources, as well as on their own historical and material circumstances. 'Freedom' and 'equality' were not abstractions derived from the Enlightenment (itself hardly a homogeneous intellectual formation) – they were real and present aspirations shaped by the condition and experience of subjection and exploitation. If we take seriously, as we surely must, the testimonial insights of a campaigner like Douglass, who combines a clear admiration for British abolitionism with an unequivocal sense of the contribution of the enslaved to their own liberation, then it seems necessary to think somewhat differently about the emergence and circulation of emancipatory ideals in the context of slavery and colonialism. It would necessitate focusing more centrally than the British historiographical tradition has done on the shaping influence of struggles against British rule, and on the role played by rebellious slaves and colonial subjects in fomenting dissensus at the heart of empire. 'Opposition to a dominant structure', as Said observes, derives from an awareness 'on the part of individuals and groups outside and inside it that, for example, certain of its policies are wrong'.[97] *Insurgent Empire* seeks to elucidate the relationship between 'outside' and 'inside' in opposing empire.

One of the first scholars to work on British 'critics of empire' was the historian Bernard Porter, who noted rightly that 'in Britain the imperial theme had always had its counterpoint of protest'.[98] Porter's important early work examines what he calls a 'body of disaffection', and covers a range of contributing factors including pacifism, internationalism, humanitarianism, free trade, the 'rule of morality' and arguments about economic unprofitability. Symptomatically, however, the role played by anticolonial insurgency in inspiring some of this disaffection is missing. Take, for example, Porter's discussions of the Positivist Richard Congreve, and the Labour politician Ramsay MacDonald, both of whom explicitly engaged with anticolonial resistance at different points in their careers. While noting that Congreve called for a sympathetic and respectful approach to India, Porter speculates that this might be due to the philosopher's 'cultural relativism' and a related 'dissatisfaction with European civilisation'.[99] As we shall see in Chapter 1, Congreve's position on India also had much to do with his reading of the events of the summer of 1857, which, by his own admission, caused him to shift from an earlier, more supportive, position and criticize British rule on grounds that were far from relativist. Similarly, Porter reflects on MacDonald's travels to India as simply confirming the politician's existing 'ethical' viewpoint, whereby it was wrong to force native races into British thought and perspectives. While he does acknowledge that MacDonald's *Awakening of India* spoke of England having 'as much to learn from Asia and Africa as they from her', Porter again attributes this to the Labour leader's personal disposition of 'humility' rather than to the pedagogical process to which the latter explicitly alludes. By his own account, the evolution of MacDonald's critical views on the imperial project in India owed something to his encounters with Indian anticolonialism in the political travels he undertook just before the First World War, as I show in Chapter 4.[100] The vital significance of such pedagogical engagements throughout the latter half of the British imperial era, where the direction of teaching was from insurgent colony to imperial metropole, is one of the central concerns of this book.

From the eighteenth century onwards, runs Said's argument, there was a lively European debate on the merits and defects of colonialism drawing on earlier positions to do with the rights of the native peoples and the abuses of those rights by Europeans. During the nineteenth century, with some rare exceptions, there emerged a much more limited discussion on profitability, management and misman-agement, and on free trade versus protectionism. There are two things to say here. The first is that his correct assessment of J. A. Hobson's very limited critique of empire notwithstanding, those whom Said terms 'liberal anti-colonialists' were also a rather more diverse group than it may seem at first glance.[101] Secondly, what is interesting about many of these liberal critics of empire – say, Henry Nevinson or Frederic Harrison – is that where they might have begun with a simple 'humane position that colonies and slaves ought not too severely to be ruled or held', their positions did not remain static. They could be radicalized by anticolonial rebellions such that some, like Wilfrid Blunt (Chapter 3), did in fact come to seriously chal-lenge European domination of non-Europeans, and precisely 'dispute the fundamental superiority of Western man' or white supremacy.[102] Even Ramsay MacDonald, whom Said correctly describes as 'a critic of British imperialist practices but not opposed to imperialism as such', would come, albeit only for a brief period, to have more serious doubts about its viability.[103] These individuals, and earlier moments that entailed crisis and connection, certainly do not have the weight we might more justifiably accord to anticolonial struggles and inter-national coalitions in the era of decolonization. Yet they constitute, I believe, a vital strand of the larger story not just of anticolonialism in a global frame, but also of the 'overlapping and intertwined' histo-ries of some forms of British dissidence and global resistance. In that sense, they form an important part of the backstory to the twentieth-century 'common anti-imperialist experience' which enabled 'new associations between Europeans, Americans, and non-Europeans', transforming disciplines and giving voice to new ideas in the process, as Said suggests.[104]

While I hope that, in the course of this study, the importance of certain forms of dissent in their own right becomes clear, it is also worth noting that the question of 'significance' or 'influence' is a necessarily circular one when it comes to dissident traditions. Dissent from regnant ideologies and discourses is, of course, never in and of itself marginal; it emerges as (often, constitutively) margin*alized* dis-course that must articulate itself against the grain of the dominant.

We must also be alert to the ways in which sidelining dissent involves
the circular argument that such dissent was only to be heard from the
sidelines, and must therefore be consigned to insignificance. There are
also other compelling reasons to study dissent independent of what
'impact' it may or may not have had on the mainstream. For one, we
do learn that not everyone 'back in the day' thought that the imperial
project was unproblematic, as is widely believed – hence the charge
of 'historical anachronism' when imperial depredations are judged by
what are wrongly claimed to be only present-day moral yardsticks.
John Darwin is correct to suggest that we might think about empire
as 'a cockpit or battleground where different versions of Britishness
competed for space', but he seems curiously resistant to the idea that
those versions were themselves shaped by the imperial encounter –
an engagement which necessarily included resistance to the imperial
project.[105] What we are left with is a curiously abstracted and ahis-
torical British heterogeneity which is hermetically sealed from reverse
influence: 'It was in the end the protean nature of empire as a political idea, the extraordinary range of interests and purposes to which it
could be rhetorically harnessed (including preparing colonial peoples
for self-rule) that allowed its demise amid a mood of public indifference.'[106] What if it was, in fact, the resistance of the colonial peoples
which prepared Britain 'to relinquish or modify the idea of overseas
domination'?[107] Here, the narratives produced by British dissidents
and critics of empire have something to teach us.

Chapter Overview

In the archives that *Insurgent Empire* examines, capturing exemplary moments rather than recounting a narrative history, insurgency
variously registers with, reanimates and radicalizes dissenting individuals, tendencies and groups in Britain. In the first section, 'Crises
and Connections', I discuss two exemplary nineteenth-century crises
of rule, in which insurgencies of 'sepoys' and freed blacks impacted in
different ways upon British oppositional tendencies. While each crisis
– the 1857 'Mutiny' in India, and the 1865 'Governor Eyre affair' – had
specific resonances back in Britain, awareness of these early insurgencies, and interpretations of them, broadly prepared the ground for

the dialogical expansion of the moral imagination of British dissent to incorporate the consciousness of the rebel as 'an entity whose will and reason constituted the practice called rebellion'.[108] In these early crises, the 'voice' of anticolonial resistance could only be accessed, of course, by reading what were essentially hegemonic representations of rebellion, either in the form of dispatches or what Ranajit Guha famously termed 'the prose of counter-insurgency'.[109] From the outset, as we shall see, insurgencies within the Empire threw gradualist narratives of freedom into crisis. They helped to create the understanding among liberal campaigners in Britain that that people share a *human* tendency to resist injustice, whatever their context; *self-emancipation* itself then entered the frame of discussion as a precondition for real liberation, though at this stage more as distant counterpoint than distinct keynote.

The mid nineteenth century, bookended by two Reform Bills extending the franchise, is also typically read as a period of intense domestic opposition, with social movements for greater internal democracy necessitating a turn inwards. In fact, insurgency in the colonies was not infrequently referenced in domestic discussions, even if it was often by way of redefining internal protest, as Ernest Jones did, in terms that made explicit comparisons to the 1857 uprising in India. Even for less radical figures like the Positivist Richard Congreve, the rebellion would force open an understanding of the scope of 'humanism', as we shall see in Chapter 1. Chapter 2 shifts to post-Emancipation Jamaica and the events in Morant Bay in 1865, when an uprising of freed slaves and their descendants resulted in a controversial crackdown and the hanging of an opposition politician by the name of George W. Gordon. The summary execution of Gordon and the brutality with which the uprising was suppressed generated a huge controversy back in England which came to be known as the 'Governor Eyre affair', famously dividing well-known politicians and intellectuals along ideological lines. While this episode is often read as a very English crisis to do with the rule of law, what is overlooked is the ways in which the positions taken were based on contrasting readings of rebel voices. Central to the controversy was the reality of black people demanding a more meaningful, self-defined freedom than the notional 'Emancipation' that had been bestowed on them. Chapters 3 and 4 examine the effects of contact between opponents of empire in milieus of anticolonial ferment and British political travellers of a humanitarian or liberal bent, such as Keir Hardie, Ramsay MacDonald and Henry Nevinson. What is noteworthy here is how those travels had the effect of unsettling, and in some cases transforming, an unexamined paternalism or benevolent humanitarianism into something rather more radical. Frequently, travels to areas of 'unrest' turned into unexpected pedagogical journeys (the case of Wilfrid Blunt and the 'Urabi Rebellion' in Egypt, discussed in Chapter 3, is only one instance) in which the traveller learned something about the nature of resistance and the cultural resources it drew upon. As Frederic Harrison, influenced by Blunt, would observe, the strength of Egyptian anticolonialism was 'not military, but civil. It lies in the great university or school of Cairo, the intellectual centre of the Mussulman world.'[110] Even Donald Mackenzie Wallace, the otherwise establishmentarian *Times* foreign correspondent who was broadly supportive of the occupation, would find it necessary to pose the question: 'Is our position in Egypt a legitimate one? – How long have we the right to remain there?'[111]

In the twentieth century, the volume of travel in the other direction – into the heart of the Empire – increased, and this had determinate effects on metropolitan anticolonialism. The third and largest section of this book, 'Agitations and Alliances', considers the energizing presence of black and Asian anticolonial campaigners and intellectuals in the imperial metropolis as part of a tripartite dynamic. As Brennan notes,

> From 1880 to 1939, artists and social theorists in the European metropole, many of them foreigners, brought a new attention to the non-Western world. These regions were no longer simply artistic raw material or an ethical site for expressing sympathy with the victims of various invasive business enterprises, but an array of emergent polities populated by colonial subjects rising in arms and pressing their demands.[112]

This was part of a wider process taking place in Europe, in which 'European intellectuals learned from those outside its orbit in the colonial encounter'.[113] Insurgent movements in India, Africa and the West Indies galvanized African and Asian campaigners, who in turn functioned as what I call 'interpreters of insurgency', putting pressure upon British criticism of aspects of empire to develop in more comprehensively radical directions. These figures played a key role in facilitating links and networks between resistance movements in the colony and dissidents in the metropole. An important consequence of this contact was the attempt to form global anticolonial networks and, within Britain itself, to foster anticolonial movements and dissident institutions which could offer a platform for radical criticism. Chapter 5 examines the influence and role of Shapurji Saklatvala, the Labour and then Communist MP, as an interpreter between Indian radicals and the British political establishment. Chapter 6 takes up the labour insurgencies in India to which Saklatvala repeatedly drew attention in the House of Commons, and the impact of the notorious Meerut Conspiracy Case in fomenting and developing an anticolonial British internationalism inspired by struggles in the colonies. An important development here is the formation in 1927 of the League Against Imperialism, which put anticolonialists from the colonies in active partnership with British and other European critics of imperialism. The emphasis on self-emancipation and the need for Western liberals and leftists to register and respond to voices from the colonial periphery is also the subject of Chapter 7, which also looks at figures such as Sylvia Pankhurst, editor of the *Daily Worker*, and Nancy Cunard, editor of the pioneering anthology *Negro*, in the interwar period, and at the partnerships they formed with black intellectuals. Both Cunard and Pankhurst made strenuous efforts to educate a Western readership about what was taking place in the colonies.

Labour uprisings in the Caribbean form the background to the emergence of figures such as George Padmore, C. L. R. James and Amy Ashwood Garvey, among others, who would become enormously influential in the emergence of pan-Africanism. Engagement with them and with pan-Africanism more broadly – particularly in the wake of Italy's invasion of Ethiopia in 1935, which galvanized black anticolonialism in Africa, the Americas and the Caribbean – would shape the views of many British liberals and radicals with whom the former had close but often contentious relationships. The formation of the International African Service Bureau in the wake of the Italian invasion of Ethiopia in 1935 is at the heart of Chapter 8, which examines the powerful anticolonialism articulated in the pages of its

journal, *International African Opinion*. Another British journal, the
New Leader, which would become distinctly more radical on colonial matters under the influence of George Padmore, is the subject of
Chapter 9, which also examines Padmore's work and its impact in the
years immediately leading up to and following the pioneering Pan-
African Congress held in Manchester in 1945. Chapter 10 explores
the impact of one of the last major anticolonial rebellions, the so-
called Mau Mau uprising and the Kenyan Emergency, in fomenting
public controversy and crisis in Britain; nearly a hundred years after
the 1857 uprising, the British political and intellectual milieu was
once again torn between denouncing the barbarism of the insurgents
and supporting brutal repression, on the one hand, and, on the other,
blaming the colonial government and settlers for causing the unrest.
This chapter also considers the Movement for Colonial Freedom,
established in London in 1954 with Brockway at its helm, which
connected anticolonialism to movements across the world for the
rights of ordinary people.

Insurgent Empire does not aspire to achieve anything like comprehensive coverage of anticolonial insurgencies, bearing in mind that
the Empire was subject to almost constant challenge. It also does
not attempt to survey the whole terrain of British dissent on imperial
matters. The maps of anticolonial insurgency and dissidence are vast
and varied. Instead, my focus is on what I identify as exemplary *crises*
of rule and engagement that helped create a tradition of dissent on
the question of empire, looked outward to the colonial world, and
sought to effect transformation as much in Britain as beyond. This
book seeks to be capacious without pretending to be comprehensive. Even so, certain lacunae require explanation – in particular, the
Second Anglo-Boer war (1899–1902), which fomented a great deal
of anti-war sentiment (and a certain kind of criticism of imperialism),
and was most famously denounced by figures such as J. A. Hobson
and Gilbert Murray. I have also not engaged with the many important crises generated by Irish resistance through the nineteenth and
twentieth centuries. Apart from the fact that the impacts both of the
Boer War and of Anglo-Irish engagement have been worked on extensively, my interest here, for reasons already discussed, is in the specific
impact of resistance that emerged from non-European contexts – of
black and Asian subjects – on metropolitan dissent. There are also,

of course, gaps even where these are concerned: events and engagements I simply did not have the time or space to incorporate. These include Queen Victoria's 'little wars' (the Afghan, Opium, Ashanti, Zulu and Maori wars); the revolt in Palestine in 1937; the crises of decolonization in Suez, Malaya and Cyprus; and resistance in West Africa in the first half of the twentieth century.[114] The relative absence of black and Asian women is also a matter of justifiable concern – and, for me, great regret. They are very much there, of course, in the form of both organizers and foot-soldiers, active participants in resistance. When it comes to *voice*, the connecting strand of this study, however, unsurprisingly the most prominent and influential are gendered male. The recovery of marginalized non-male voices in this context is work that lies ahead of us. Gandhi and Indian nationalism, including the Quit India movement, are not discussed in any depth; they too constitute an overrepresented topic in discussions of anticolonialism, often at the expense of other conceptions and strategies of resistance (see Chapter 6).[115] While my aim has not been to offer a comprehensive overview of all relevant figures and ideas, my principles of selection may of course be subject to debate. I make no claims to writing a history; indeed, the methodological principles that have guided my research and writing are enthusiastically generalist. The book is structured as an ensemble of accounts, disparate in many ways yet vitally connected in others, gaining in its amateur 'sense of excitement and discovery', I hope, what it might not offer in specialist terms.[116] Its guiding literary model, similarly, is more akin to the short story than to the novel; but these are stories that emerge, of course, from an epic canvas. My hope is that this book will contribute to and advance lines of enquiry and discussion, including in other imperial contexts, to which other scholars will also contribute in future.

PART I

CRISES AND CONNECTIONS

1

The Spirit of the Sepoy Host: The 1857 Uprising in India and Early British Critics of Empire

Our rule has been that of the robber and the bandit and we are suffering from the natural result – insurrection.

> Malcolm Lewin, Judge in the East India Company

Despite the enduring myth of a nineteenth-century Pax Britannica, British rule in India and across the empire was punctuated by revolts, rebellions, insurrection and instability. So endemic were such challenges to British imperial rule that the events of the so-called Indian Mutiny of 1857 have been described as 'unique only in their scale'.

> Andrea Major and Crispin Bates, *Mutiny at the Margins*

In 1925, nearly three-quarters of a century after the event, the writer Edward Thompson addressed the topic of what he called 'Indian irreconcilability' – the 'unsatisfied, embittered, troublesome' attitude that marred Britain's relationship with the jewel in the imperial crown.[1] Like almost any other colonial writer, Thompson was confirmed in his belief that British rule had done India a great deal of good. Yet it was impossible to deny that in that country the British name aroused a great deal of hatred, a 'savage, set hatred' that could only be accounted for through widespread popular memories which, at any time, could flare up again in the face of resurgent discontent with colonial rule in India.[2] What accounted for 'the real wall, granite and immovable', which the Englishman encountered in India?[3] The answer, for Thompson, lay in the 'Mutiny' of 1857, a fountain that was 'sending forth a steady flood of poisoned waters':

> This case, unfortunately, is that of the one episode where we were really guilty of the cruellest injustice on the greatest scale. If we desire to eliminate bitterness from our controversy with India, we certainly have to readjust our ideas of this episode – the Mutiny … Right at the back of the mind of many an Indian the Mutiny flits as he talks with an Englishman – an unavenged and unappeased ghost.[4]

While Thompson repeats the familiar colonial canard that 'Indians are not historians', adding for good measure that 'they rarely show any critical ability',[5] he also notes that the English interpretation of the events of 1857 has had an unjust sway on history; no other significant episode had been 'treated so uncritically or upon such one-sided and prejudged evidence'.[6] He was largely right, of course, about the dominance of one-sided readings of the two-sided brutalities of 1857, and the powerful hold they exercised upon the British imagination well into the twentieth century. The vast majority of British accounts of the revolt in its aftermath were steeped in sanguinary patriotism, a sense of imperial destiny saved from peril. Public opinion was, we know, similarly shaped by retaliatory bloodlust and outrage, fuelled by a ceaseless raking up of Indian brutalities. Thompson, no 'extreme' critic of the imperial project as he repeatedly stresses, nonetheless reads the uprising as 'another of the world's great servile revolts',[7] on par with those in Demerara (1823) and Jamaica (1865), and one which drew an equally harsh retaliatory response that has never been subjected to critical historical scrutiny. For him, subsequent colonial severities were a consequence of this lamentable failure.

We know that Thompson was also correct about the overwhelmingly racialized British response to the 1857 uprising that told the story in the Empire's favour. A 'great crisis in our national history', as one of its earliest and most famous historians put it, the uprising in 1857 produced, in the first instance, conflicted and diverse responses in Britain, often along party lines.[8] Relatedly, there was plenty of criticism of the follies and failures of the rule of the East

India Company, which of course ended after the uprising and the takeover of India by the Crown in 1858. There was also a substantial amount of public agonizing on causation – on what had gone wrong and whether the unexpected scale and bloodiness of the uprising spoke to a lethal failure to understand India and Indians. One consequence of the uprising – and the crisis of rule that it undoubtedly provoked – was a debate about how best to undertake and manage the project of empire in India so as to minimize the possibility of revolt. The sanguinary horrors routinely evoked by accounts of the 'Mutiny' were not generally warnings against imperial rule, but cautionary notations about its dangers. Jill Bender has noted that the uprising in India also came to constitute a master-narrative, providing 'a model for understanding and responding to subsequent crises'.[9] Explicit comparisons were made between, for instance, the rebels of Morant Bay eight years later, and the 'treacherous' sepoys of north India. It remains, then, an unavoidable starting point for any examination of nineteenth-century crises of rule and their implications for Britain.

Much of the historical scholarship on 1857 appears to agree that the moment 'would mark the decisive *turning away* from an earlier liberal, reformist ethos that had furnished nineteenth-century empire its most salient moral justification'.[10] The distinguished historian Rudrangshu Mukherjee, among others, has argued that one of the consequences of 1857 was that the 'velvet glove of liberal rhetoric had to be abandoned for the mailed fist'.[11] Certainly, relations between British colonial representatives and Indian subjects on the whole manifested a hardening of racial, religious and cultural boundaries, with extreme otherness re-inscribed on the bodies of the 'fanatical' insurgents. In place of liberal policies, 'the principle of complete non-interference in the traditional structure of Indian society' would be enshrined alongside a clear racial hierarchy.[12] After the uprising was brutally crushed by early 1858, the British in India 'were able to dictate a settlement from a position of unquestioned mastery, and to enforce their will upon a subdued and chastened people'.[13] At the same time, not least for fear of further insurrection, they would, in the words of Queen Victoria's 1858 Proclamation, 'disclaim alike the right and the desire to impose Our convictions on any of Our subjects'. Post-rebellion unease, Christine Bolt has argued, produced 'a new awareness of the difficulties involved in understanding the Indian mind'.[14]

The 'Indian' or 'native' mind' was of course at the very heart of the question of the future of British India, and relevant too to the more general question of how the multihued subjects of the Empire were to be dealt with. The liberal and humanitarian position – steeped in principles of paternalist tutelage or 'improvement' – was that Indians, while not exactly equal, could be educated into self-government, or at least the native elites could be. For others, the mistaken view of political liberals – 'that all men were alike, entitled to identical rights and fit to be governed identically' – was itself culpable of having inspired the revolt, and had to be decisively repudiated in the post-1857 era.[15] There was, however, a third possibility, explored by a small number of thinkers, which came into view for a time. Reading the rebellion as a text, against the grain of discourses of counter-insurgency that dominated the British public sphere, this minority asked a different set of questions. What if neither the racial alterity touted by the hard-line approach nor the assimilative paternalism of the liberal tutelage model constituted the right response? Might there be a way to think about relations with India and its inhabit-ants that steered a course outside of this binary? For some in Britain, the rebellion presented itself as a text that necessarily asked for a different kind of reading, one that threw open other, more dialogi-cal possibilities. If the dominant political shift, as Karuna Mantena has it, was from 'a *universalist* to a *culturalist* stance', those who undertook more self-reflexive and critical assessments of the British presence in India did not so much reject universalism as express their sense that the relationship between the universal and the particular was a complex one.[16] Could it be that universals were not so much for export from Britain to its colonies as necessarily and already embedded in the particular? Moreover, what might Britain (or, more frequently, 'England') learn from, and how might it reconstitute *itself* in response to, the rebellion? In some of the most thoughtful met-ropolitan engagements with the rebellion, resistance was read as self-assertion, which opened up possibilities for a more reciprocal – and incipiently egalitarian – form of engagement with distant peoples who were making claims upon and against Britain. In these readings, Britain's subjugated Indian subjects could neither be relegated to pure otherness, as they were in the absolutist conservative response, nor simply yoked to the project of reformist improvement, in the liberal mode. For dissident English writers like the Chartist Ernest Jones and the Positivist Richard Congreve, the rebellion prompted a rethinking of their own premises and manner of engagement with the non-European; they invited their readers to think through the possibility that the cultural-particular and the humanist-universal were not entirely at odds with each other. The text of insurgency, in other words, threw open the problematic of engaging with subjugated others with whom common ground might be forged without eliding differences. If, for the official mind, one consequence of the uprising of 1857 was that a professed universalism 'easily gave way to harsh attitudes about the intractable differences among people, the inscrutability of other ways of life, and the ever-present potential for racial and cultural conflict', for some of a more dissident bent, it opened up rather more dialogical possibilities.[17] The native-in-revolt, as we shall see, was not always figured as inscrutable or irrational, but rather as staking claims upon a history they intended to make themselves, if in circumstances not of their own choosing. Partly in response, a small but distinct body of dissident discourse developed in Britain which sought to invoke a degree of sympathetic understanding for the rebellion, as well as a critical disposition towards the imperial project.

Beyond the Sepoy War

Since our interest is in how the events of 1857 in India shaped an emergent critique of empire within Britain, I will not devote much space here to discussing the uprising itself. An historical episode that has received a great deal of scholarly attention from the late nineteenth century onwards, the uprising continues to be revisited and debated in salutary ways.[18] In a volume produced by the Indian Council to commemorate the 150th anniversary of those events in 2007, Sabyasachi Bhattacharya notes rightly that the literature on the subject is 'dauntingly large' and includes important new revisionist work examining formerly overlooked aspects such as gender, the role of tribal and Dalit communities, and its representations in popular culture, making use of Indian-language sources as well.[19] Initially a point of contestation in British debates, it became clear that the insurgency was more than a military mutiny, and involved 'considerable participation by the civilian population', and diverse elements of that population.[20] It is also clear that a complex chain of causation extended well beyond the legendary 'greased cartridges' for the Enfield rifle, and indeed beyond religious identities and sentiments alone, even if those certainly played a determinate role. Our interest here is in how an understanding of causes and causality – and the predictable ferocity of the counterinsurgency – shaped dissent around the imperial question back in Britain.

The briefest of overviews then: the uprising – or the 'Ghadar' as it is known in Urdu – formally broke out on 10 May 1857. The ostensible 'last-straw' provocation for it has traditionally been attributed to the controversial cartridges for the new Enfield rifle, which had been provided to the native regiments of the East India Company's army, greased, it was rumoured, with pig and cow fat – thereby violating the religious sensibilities of both Muslim and Hindu infantrymen. The iconic cartridges, as Jill Bender has noted, 'provided a convenient explanation for the rebellion, one that did not openly challenge the legitimacy of British colonial control or validate Indian unrest'.[21] Rumour itself, of course, played a key role in the fomenting of the uprising, often acting, as in the instance of Meerut, as the match which lit a dry haystack. There were manifold other problems which caused soldierly discontent, including poor pay, loss of allowances, and insistence on overseas service. We know that soldier violence, one element of the uprising of 1857, was not in itself unprecedented; a contemporary observer notes that there 'had previously been several mutinies in the native army ... but they had been suppressed with little difficulty'.[22] Troubles had in fact been rumbling from February 1857 onwards when in May, the troops at Meerut rose against their officers, shot them dead, freed imprisoned fellow troopers and set off for Delhi. (One of the most famous figures associated with the rebellion, the infantryman Mangal Pandey, had already been executed on 29 March for firing at and wounding his commanding officer at his barracks near Calcutta.) Once the rebels reached and captured Delhi, they were joined by the 54th Bengal Native Infantry, which, ordered to fire at them, had refused to. Violence then spread across northern India into other cantonments as well as civilian areas, with government officers, telegraph lines, post offices, treasuries and local courts – the apparatus and infrastructure of colonial rule – unsurprisingly being targeted for destruction, in addition to books in English, maps and instruments.[23] As more than a dozen cantonments fell over that hot summer, hundreds of British officers and civilians perished in the rampage; their violent deaths, in particular those of women and children, would become the stuff of broadside and ballad. Among the fatalities were also 'Anglo-Indians' or 'Eurasians', as well as Indian Christians. In one of the most infamous incidents, in June 1857, after being promised safe passage by Nana Sahib, an entire garrison was ambushed and killed near Kanpur, on the banks of the Ganges at Satichaura Ghat, while 200 women and children were butchered, quite literally, in the equally infamous Bibighar incident after being confined there, their bodies thrown into a legendary well. The latter story would electrify British newspaper readers when it reached London two months later, becoming emblematic of 'native' treason and treachery.

In an attempt by the rebels to unify multiple interests which were set in opposition to the British, and to provide a direct oppositional sovereignty to the British colonial order, the King of Delhi – the aging and somewhat reluctant Mughal, Bahadur Shah Zafar – was proclaimed emperor of India. Both Hindus and Muslims were enjoined to participate in the rebellion as a religious duty. As Kim Wagner notes, those who fought under the banner of the Mughal emperor 'became the honourable defenders of *deen* and *dharma*, of faith and social duty and obligations. The rebels, in short, fought to preserve the moral order and fabric of north Indian society'.[24] Some other princes and feudal aristocrats – most famously, Tantia Tope, leading the forces of Nana Sahib; Rani Lakshmi Bai of Jhansi, the famous warrior queen of nationalist lore who died in battle; Khan Bahadur Khan; and Firoz Shah – also provided rallying points and leadership, while some stayed out of the fray or allied with the British. In August 1857, a famous proclamation issued in Bahadur Shah Zafar's name adumbrated some of the reasons for the uprising. These included land seizures from zamindars; trade monopolies 'of all the fine and valuable merchandise, such as indigo, cloth, and other articles of shipping, leaving only the trade of trifles to the people'; the treatment of natives employed in the civil and military services with 'little respect, low pay, and no manner of influence'; the casting into unemployment of 'the weavers, the cotton dressers, the carpenters, the blacksmiths, and the shoemakers ... so that every description of native artisan has been thrown into beggary'; and, finally, 'the Europeans being enemies of both the religions', Hindu and Mohammedan.[25] A multiplicity of causes fomented resistance, some of it directed against indigenous elites such as moneylenders and landlords.[26] Attacks on and the seizing of the property of the rich were a frequent feature of the uprising, as was the releasing of prisoners from gaols and the ransacking of treasuries and Kutcheries (law courts).[27] As Mukherjee notes, 'Two overlapping structures of domination – one native and the other foreign – were simultaneously attacked by the subordinated.'[28] Some of these elites, like moneylenders and traders, were also perceived to be collaborating with the British.

From a large number of historical studies and popular accounts, we are now familiar with the overwhelming sense of national distress and hysterical racial outrage generated back in Britain by rebel violence. Atrocities such as those which took place in Kanpur ('Cawnpore') and Lucknow have attained legendary status and continue to be obsessively revisited in British popular history; the mutilation of – and alleged sexual violence against – British women became central to British imaginings of the uprising. As one historian notes, the very use of violence against the British itself constituted a startling reversal of direction, a challenge to the conquering power. To the extent that authority arrogates to itself a monopoly on exercising violence, its return in the opposite direction is a transgression, an assertion of autonomy: 'The right to violence is everywhere a privilege that authority enjoys and refuses to share with those under it.'[29] A challenge to this monopoly was also, of course, a direct challenge to legitimacy of rule. As *The Times* would put it on 31 August 1857, the sepoys had 'broken the spell of inviolability that seemed to attach to an English man [*sic*] as such'.[30] The ferocity of the British counterinsurgency, observed John Lawrence, the governor of the Punjab, sought to 'make an example and terrify others' who might be tempted to undertake similar challenges to the right to violence.[31] The exemplary punishment by an 'army of retribution', as it came to be known, included shooting, hanging or blowing Indian suspects from the mouths of cannons. One British eyewitness wrote home thus:

> The prisoners, under a strong European guard, were then marched into the square, their crimes and sentences read aloud to them, and at the head of each regiment; they were then marched round the square, and up to the guns. The first ten were picked out ... and they were bound to the guns ... The potfires were lighted, and at a signal from the artillery major, the guns were fired. It was a horrid sight that then met the eye, a regular shower of human fragments of heads, of arms, of legs, appeared in the air through the smoke.[32]

Fragmenting bodies, including by guns 'peppering away at niggers', was a way of ensuring that there could be no appropriate funerary rites – a final humiliation.[33] In some cases, Hindus were deliberately buried and Muslims cremated, contrary to each religion's code. Boastful letters dispatched back to England spoke of terrified civilians hunted down and killed, their hutments razed to the ground or burned down. Two sons and a grandson of the Mughal were also scandalously shot in cold blood, *after* they had surrendered, unarmed. Bahadur Shah Zafar was himself imprisoned and put on trial 'for his treasonable design of overthrowing and destroying the British government in India', though he was spared execution.[34] Though it took some time – nearly two years in the end – the uprising was ultimately put down decisively, though this did not spell an end to the periodic emergence of insurgencies, mutinies and other forms of resistance. The violence of 1857–58 had seen hundreds of Britons slain and tens of thousands of Indians slaughtered. In November 1858, the Crown proclaimed its sole control and constitutional authority, and the East India Company's rule came to an end. In July 1859 the viceroy declared a 'state of peace'.

How and why the uprising of 1857 failed does not concern us here. Among the reasons historians have advanced are the very heterogeneity of the various interests involved and the absence of a coherent ideology and centralized leadership. There was, of course, also no matching the British when it came to strength in munitions and weaponry as the counter-insurgency, which saw thousands of troops in the shape of the 'army of retribution' shipped out from

Britain to assist, would brutally illustrate. Significantly, however, despite the ultimate victory, 'the rebellion and its aftermath embedded itself in the British national consciousness in a way unmatched by previous colonial confrontations', though some slave insurrections – not least the 1823 Demerara uprising – had generated public controversy, and, not many years before, the Second Afghan War had featured in public discussions.[35] Nonetheless, 1857 was undoubtedly the first major crisis in the post-Emancipation era to be relayed with relative immediacy to the British newspaper-reading public – news taking weeks rather than months to arrive – and to have generated such a vast amount of political, literary and cultural engagement, which continued into the next century. Before a degree of consensus emerged in the decade following the uprising – one in which Britain was figured as a benevolent and liberal colonial power disloyally attacked by reactionary native elites keen to preserve their own feudal and caste interests – the initial British responses to news of the uprising were in fact divided. Much scholarly work has been undertaken on mapping these fractures and debates, not least that between the Whig interpretation of the 'Mutiny' as a limited military insurrection and the Tory claim that interventionist reforms had caused the rebellion.[36] Famously, Disraeli declared: 'The decline and fall of empires are not the affair of greased cartridges. Such results are occasioned by adequate causes and the accumulation of adequate causes.'[37] Most of those subscribing to this theory 'were critical of the government and EIC, although the nature of their critique of colonial rule varied', writes Salahuddin Malik, noting that there then began 'a searching public exploration' of what these causes might have been.[38] Few, of course, challenged the legitimacy of British rule itself, focusing instead on specific policies and Company misdemeanours. On the contrary, Gautam Chakravarty has suggested, resistance in this case and others, including the 1865 Morant Bay rebellion and the 1882 Egyptian war, both of which I will examine in subsequent chapters, produced 'sophisticated forms of metropolitan counter-mobilisation structured around themes of race, religion, "pacification", imperial identity and a forthright binary of civilisation–savagery'.[39] Yet 1857, like the other crises, also produced myriad forms of dissent, ranging from a radicalized liberalism that placed the agency of colonial subjects at its centre to outright condemnations of the colonial project that went so far as to call for the complete withdrawal of Britain from India. While these do not quite add up to what Christopher Herbert rather hyperbolically terms 'a voluminous discourse of dissent', certain distinct species of unease and critique did emerge out of the intellectual and political churning that took place 1857.[40] I will explore some of the more uncompromising and interesting ones presently, and examine how they were directly shaped by the fact of rebellion read as a pedagogical text.

Although a vast body of British writings on 1857 is indeed marked by what Herbert describes as a 'hallucinatory stylistic register', evoking a sense of 'traumatic expulsion from a known world into a frightening new historical era', very little of it actually took on the imperial project directly.[41] The 'profoundly traumatic cultural crisis' generated by the conflicted responses to the retaliatory bloodshed suggests to Herbert that the imperial project was itself plagued by crises of 'that vital constituent of mid-Victorian culture, the national conscience'. This, he avers, shows up the fundamental wrongness of 'studies informed by Said's ground-breaking *Orientalism*', which have taken as their 'first commandment the premise of the monolithic, always self-consistent nature of imperialism'.[42] Quite apart from the patently absurd caricature of Said's work, what is really telling here is Herbert's own regurgitation of the axiom that imperialism was a self-correcting system, constitutively plagued by a sense of its own wrongness. If it was indeed the case that a constantly uneasy conscience redeems Victorian culture, then we must ask why it took events entailing violent anticolonial insurgency for a 'faculty of searching self-scrutiny' to be awakened, and for Britons to be 'afforded a deeply disillusioning view into the national soul'.[43] Why did this 'national conscience' emerge only in the face of resistance to the imperial mission and the brutal counterinsurgencies required to suppress it? Why would a value system inherently 'fatally at odds with itself' worry about 'shocking perversions' only when challenged by an opposite force making its own demands upon it?[44]

My own argument here turns away from the hypostatizing pieties of a presumed national conscience towards an examination of rebel agency as a catalyst for serious criticism of the imperial project. Looking at three very different readings of 1857 perceived as a revolutionary moment, I want to draw out some aspects of dissident engagement with India. The first is the way in which the rebellion itself functions as a text upon which is impressed the voice and will of insurgents. The second is the manner in which this text functions as a pedagogical enterprise in which the direction of tutelage is reversed: it is the colonizers who must learn from the colonized. The last – and perhaps most important for a longer narrative account of the emergence of British anticolonialism – is the emergence of possibilities for forging fellow-feeling between denizens of the metropole and inhabitants of the periphery, a shift that would replace paternalism with dialogism, thus creating new affective and political dispositions. John Bruce Norton, an 'India hand' of a critical bent, called for a radical reconstitution of relations between rulers and ruled in the direction of equality and, in a remarkable inversion, for the British to assimilate with the Indians. The Chartist leader and poet Ernest Jones would explicitly celebrate revolutionary 'contagion', whereby the Indian rebels might inspire domestic resistance. Finally, there is the unexpected radicalism of Richard Congreve, the Positivist leader who was one of the few to call unambiguously for a full British withdrawal from India and the forging of working-class solidarity with those under British rule.

'We may learn much from them as well as teach': John Bruce Norton and the Illuminated Text of Rebellion

Among those Britons of a liberal disposition who did not take 'the fact of resistance ... as evidence of a derisive and perverse rejection by Indians of the civilizational benefits proffered by imperial rule', but sought instead to engage with its implications for the Empire as a whole, was the Madras lawyer and jurist John Bruce Norton.[45] Norton is important for our purposes not only because he dissented from government policy and practice – well before the insurgency, which, he tells us, he predicted – but because his own conflicted view about the continuance of British rule in India begins to indicate the emergence of an attitude towards the colonized that was neither just paternalist nor simply relativist. What Norton's lengthy account of causation does make clear, however, is the need for a certain kind of reverse tutelage, whereby it would be the British who learned from the Indians.[46] Here, the actions of the rebels – rather than 'an explicit intellectual discourse', to use Trouillot's phrase – would be the primer.[47] In a resonant metaphor, Norton describes the rebellion as a text – indeed, an illuminated manuscript, wherein 'the same truth is thrust forward in a more startling and authoritative form … written in the blood of our murdered countrymen in India, illustrated by rebellion, and illuminated by the conflagrations at Meerut and Delhi, and Lucknow, and Allahabad'.[48] The reversal of textual *authority* is not insignificant: it is the rebellion that puts flesh and blood, so to speak, on the Englishman's words. Norton himself might not have been heeded when he warned of impending trouble but ignoring the claims 'written' in blood by the rebels would be catastrophic. 'We' have something to learn from 'them', and here Norton's drawing on the voices of rebels mouthing profanities is telling. He recounts an exemplary incident, 'a glimmering of the truth' relayed in the *Bombay Times*: 'At the slaughter of Neemuch, when the officers said to their native troops … "You have eaten the Company's salt, why are you not faithful to it?" The answer, as the sepoys shot down and bayonetted them, was, "You Banchats! have you been faithful to the King of Oude?"'[49] This moment of moral dialogism – where the sepoy, in turn, poses a question to the colonizer, asking him to examine his own betrayals and ethical violations – has pedagogic value, but for the British, not the natives. It is the British who need to learn to be consistent and loyal:

> Peruse the dying speech of the traitor at Sattara, as we call him – hero and martyr as the people regard him, and as we should ourselves regard him, were the fable narrated of ourselves and invading Russians – and reflect, whether his brief address to his country-men does not throw light upon the feelings which prompted the rising at Sattara.[50]

Norton – a known critic of the East India Company's courts who would become advocate-general for Madras in 1863 and who had served on the famous Torture Commission of 1855, which investigated claims that agents of the Company had tortured persons in the process of revenue extraction – begins his pointedly titled work *The Rebellion in India: How to Prevent Another* by noting that the gag orders preventing the press, both 'Native' and 'European', from covering most aspects of the uprising were 'intended to screen the cowardice and incapacity of the real authors of the revolution'.[51] Writing hot on the heels of the uprising – the book was published in London in the autumn of 1857 – Norton posed one central question: 'Shall we throw away or shall we preserve our Indian Empire?'[52] Norton was very clear that it would be a calamitous mistake to hold to the belief that 'the origin of the present crisis is *purely* military disaffection', and that 'the masses took no share in it'.[53] The widespread existence of negative feelings towards the British in India has to be taken on board as a central issue: 'There is indisputably a very large and influential population who hate us cordially.'[54] What is of real significance in Norton's sense of grim vindication is his emphasis on *engagement* with the ruled – on listening to those who, contrary to dominant assumptions, had a clear sense of their own needs. His own unheeded prognostications of trouble had been based on conversations with those he encountered in the course of his administrative work. Simply observing matters with 'ordinary intelligence' had shown that 'there was disaffection enough in the land for half-a-dozen rebellions', and that any failures these might meet with were due less to Britain's popularity and strength than to diversity and discordance among its inhabitants.[55] Given the overwhelming emphasis within the British community in India on severe retribution, repression and separation of communities, Norton's call for active engagement and listening was remarkable.

Norton had another valuable insight: the widespread Indian antipathy was to a *system* of rule, not simply to a few rotten apples, for it was 'a hatred not of obnoxious individuals who have given offence to their immediate inferiors; not a class feeling of the soldiery against their officers; but a general antipathy to the European race'.[56] Listing district after district which had become scenes of hostile outbreaks, Norton also denied that it was possible 'to limit the cause of outbreak to the offended religious prejudices of any particular caste … I believe there is no one so weak as to fancy, that had there been no greased cartridges there would have been no rebellion'.[57] Religion and cultural differences would not suffice as an explanation of causation, and any consideration of the 'feelings of the Natives' would have to be less facile.[58]

It is worth pausing on the 'actual feelings of the people', variations of which phrase Norton repeatedly uses.[59] His interest in that affective realm – and the recently manifested agency of those who act upon their emotions – enables his own criticisms of the self-serving discourse deployed by colonial administrators: 'They are so puffed up with an overweening idea of their own excellence, that they cannot believe the people disaffected under their superintendence; they are so wedded to the perfections of the Indian Government, that they cannot conceive it distasteful to the people'.[60] Equally significant is Norton's insistence that these negative feelings ought to be entirely legible in their specificity, rather than mechanically dismissed as fanaticism: 'They make no allowance for the existence among the Natives of those feelings which actuate themselves. They cannot believe that the Natives look with reverence, or affection, or respect to old institutions, old associations, old names, old dynasties. They look only to what they conclude their system ought to produce.'[61] Norton contended that this denial of parity was a significant part of the problem underlying the rebellion.

Since, taken to its logical conclusion, respect for the feelings of the governed might enjoin the withdrawal of a resented external power, Norton admits to a sense of his own contradictions: 'It may seem paradoxical, and I confess, I feel it difficult how to reconcile my statement of belief in discontent on the part of the masses with the admission that our Government is an improvement on any form which has preceded it.'[62] (He does, however, note that the previous form of government being 'worse' does not make this one 'good'.) This admitted paradox is important, as it is one that would continue to dog British critics of empire into the next century: the clash between acknowledging the wishes of the ruled and an inability to relinquish fully the liberal principle that it was possible to govern benevolently and responsively. Norton is conscious that his disquisition on the deep-rooted and widespread causes of disaffection here fails to follow through on its own conclusions about widespread disaffection, with a call for the withdrawal of Britain from the colony. Norton's declaration sits at odds with his analysis: 'It is not possible to conceive a greater calamity to the people of India, than the present dissolution of the bands between them and us.'[63] But, even so, Norton's conception of a reconfigured rule is radical in its insistent inversion of the direction of assimilation. If, on the one hand, the familiar liberal trio of 'justice, prudence, and benevolence' must be deployed to 'reconcile the Natives to our rule' until, on the other, they are 'fitted to take their own government peacefully and powerfully into their own hands', the very definition of benefaction had changed.[64] It was important for the British in India to change their behaviour to the point where the natives would come to regard them less as benefactors than 'as a portion of themselves'.[65] This seemingly throwaway exegetical phrase is important, for here is neither a radical othering nor a simple assimilation of native lives and cultures to European mores. It is the British outsider who must strive to become part of the Indian self; and, for this to happen, the wishes of those whom Britain rules had to be foundational: 'We have governed too much for ourselves, too little for the people.'[66] Rather than calling for Indians to be 'lifted to the heights of Victorian liberalism', Norton was calling for the ruling British to bend their ear low to their subjects – to listen and integrate.[67] They would, of course, do the opposite, withdrawing into the enclaves of power from which rule would be undertaken carefully, but enacted upon an inferior people who did not know what was good for them.

Norton's sudden shift – and it is self-consciously, even sheepishly, sudden – from articulating a trenchant attack on the failings of British rule, including charging it with being primarily concerned with revenue extraction, to producing an equally impassioned entreaty for a reformed continuance of it, is contradictory. Yet it also embodies a wider truth: calls for reforms, especially in colonial contexts, were generally responses to pressures from below rather than initiatives from above. 'Any government of ours in India must be one of opinion,' Norton insisted, meaning not only that it must be responsive but that it must be seen to be responsive to *native* opinion.[68] Rather than waiting to bestow self-government once Indians were deemed ready for it, British rule in India must become immediately accountable to the ruled. Norton was explicitly refusing authoritarian liberalism and benevolent colonial despotism as the answer to 1857. His counter-discourse – which is based, as he repeatedly stresses, on an attention to the spoken words of the subjects of British rule – points towards the possibility of a relationship between the inhabitants of India and the British that could be dialogical. At one level, Norton's reformism may be simply pragmatic; physical force might prevail now but will not suffice in the long run: 'When once combination among them becomes feasible, and a determination to combine is persevered in, the greater force must prevail over the lesser. When a hundred million combine, writes Sir Charles Napier, the game is up.'[69] But that would be to miss Norton's repeated emphasis on the ethical centrality of the views of the ruled and the way in which he insisted on treating the 'Mutiny' as a text that invited reading and dialogical engagement. Norton was raising the startling possibility that the ruled could be the authors of their own futures, agents of change rather than wedded to 'Oriental stagnation', and that the rulers might benefit from working collaboratively with them.[70] We should note here the acknowledgement that the greater power ultimately resides with the ruled and not the occupiers, and renders all projects of 'improvement' fraught with danger: 'May it not all end in the contempt of Caliban for Trinculo!'[71] Norton is not quite suggesting that it is the British who have taught Indians self-assertion, but rather that English education has afforded natives a means, by giving them knowledge of their rulers, of assessing and puncturing British imperial mythologies: 'Those whom they mistook for gods, they discover to be mere men.'[72]

Much of the remainder of Norton's text is a damning list of annexations ('thefts'), especially of the kingdom of Oude, treaty violations, and revenue extraction that 'have had no small share in causing the suspicion with which we are now universally regarded'.[73] Indians are capable of speaking up – and Norton stresses both the existence of these voices and their elision in colonial discourse – against those crimes, and it is to Britain's disadvantage that they are not heeded when they do. The state in which Lord Dalhousie left India is evidenced by 'the crowds of Indians now to be seen in London on every side, who have come to petition the throne of England against his acts'.[74] Norton anticipates and dismisses the apologetics that will inevitably be trotted out: 'No doubt we shall have the brilliancy of the electric telegraph and the railway flashed across our eyes; but I say these measures ... were forced upon him by the pressure of public opinion; and both were measures calculated immeasurably to increase the centralizing power of government, as well as to benefit the people.'[75] It is Britain's double standards which have been shown the mirror by the 1857 uprising, for 'we do in India precisely what we will not allow Russia to do in Europe ... our palpable, transparent violation in the East of principles by which we profess to be guided in the West'.[76] Seizing lands by doctrine of escheat, 'this vast universal effort to make ourselves the sole landlords of the soil ... is ample cause for the general disaffection of the people'.[77] Norton emphasizes the salience of native voices – relaying accounts of conversations with Indians full of 'vehemence and passion' and the ability to speak up in self-interest. This is why, 'if we retain India, a representative form of Government must sooner or later be introduced'.[78] The spirit of such reforms, in Norton's mind, applies as much to the British as to the ruled: 'We must drop the habit of regarding ourselves as mere exiles, whose first object should be to escape from a disagreeable climate with the greatest possible amount of the people's money in the shortest possible time.'[79] Norton again goes against the grain of the ascendant insistence on radical separateness in asking whether 'it is worthy of consideration whether the era has not arrived for striving to establish friendships between ourselves and the educated Natives? There are few people, however repulsive their natural antipathies, who do not come to esteem each other when familiarity has been established between them. We may learn much from them as well as teach.'[80] He notes, moreover, that the 'native mind' is not stationary and both parties can change in response to each other:

> But we must go further; we must admit them socially to our conversational circles. They are not to be regarded as an inferior race, unworthy of, and unfitted for, polite society. They have, of course, their peculiarities and *mauvaise honte*; perhaps we also have our peculiarities in their eyes; but it is by the constant collision of friendly intercommunications that the angles of difference are broken off and polished down.[81]

In a later book, *Topics for Indian Statesmen*, Norton would return to the theme of the British needing to be educated by India a year into the rebellion: 'But one of the gravest lessons ever read in history lies open before us, and it behoves us to read it right.'[82]

How, though, was it available to read? Norton wrote his warning narrative in his capacity as a 'man on the spot', but one with a very different sense of what was unfolding 'on the ground' than those who were formulating post-1857 policies of rule. Back in Britain, news was of course only available through dispatches, letters and the published accounts of those, like Norton, who had witnessed the rebellion. These made the text of the rebellion – and the rebellion as text – available for metropolitan reading and had provided the basis for the widespread outrage at Indian atrocities. Certainly, in the first several months after the outbreak of violence, these dispatches were heavily official in character, of the sort Guha describes as written 'by those who had the most to fear' from rebellion.[83] In due course, there were also accounts by administrators and historians (or administrators-turned-historians, as Guha puts it) who also wrote from the perspective of counterinsurgency. But these were also read – and differently interpreted – by those Britons who were inclined to be more critical of the British establishment and its 'organs', such as *The Times*. In Ernest Jones's readings of news dispatches and accounts of the rebellion, we see once again a sense that the Indian revolt was a primer from which a reverse tutelage was possible, and from which lessons could be learned not only about the limits of imperial rule but also about the relationship between the universal and the particular. In his engagement with the 1857 uprising, as also Richard Congreve's, there was an effort to 'break away from the code of counter-insurgency' and understand, even adopt, 'the insurgent's point of view'.[84] Where Jones's reading anticipated a reframing of domestic politics in terms made visible by the situation in India alongside calls for identity of purpose, in Congreve's case it prompted both a call for the immediate abandonment of the imperial project – astonishing, given his quintessentially liberal preference for gradual change – and an exploration of how common ground might be forged, rather than assumed in the face of manifest cultural differences.

'The spirit of the sepoy host': Ernest Jones and Revolutionary Contagion

In a useful article referencing the 1857 uprising, Tim Pratt has argued rightly that while historians have acknowledged that the episode elicited criticism of aspects of imperial policy and administration in the imperial metropole, 'the possibility that the rebels were actively supported in their struggle has been almost completely ignored'.[85]

He notes that one of the people to conspicuously offer such support was the Chartist leader, Ernest Jones: 'Rather than joining the chorus of horrified condemnation of the Indian insurgents, Jones actively sought to identify the causes of the rebels and Chartism by attempting to elide the political, racial and cultural differences between the British and Indians being highlighted in parliament and the mainstream press, instead stressing the linkages between their respective causes.'[86] Chartism – the movement which emerged from the publication of the People's Charter in 1838 – was itself headed for decline by the late 1840s, when Jones entered it, and working-class radicalism in general was an increasingly marginalized force in mid Victorian Britain.[87] As Miles Taylor, drawing on John Saville, notes: 'Ernest Jones and Chartism became synonymous in the mid-1850s.'[88] Already a reasonably well-regarded poet and a journalist of some note, Jones would give Chartism one last lease of life, lecturing widely, and editing as well as writing large portions of the weekly People's Paper.[89] The latter fact is important, because 'it was at precisely this juncture that the press assumed an overriding significance in the annals of the Chartist movement'.[90] Jones's engagement with – and championing of – the cause of India through that period would, apart from anything else, bring a non-European and more strenuously anticolonial dimension to Chartist internationalism, which, while it had sympathies with Polish nationalism and the Irish struggle, had been largely focused on domestic matters.[91] By the time Jones came out of prison, where he had been serving a sentence for 'sedition' until 1851, Chartism as a mass movement was over, though its influence would be felt in other reform initiatives and movements. Jones would try valiantly after his release to resurrect it, and as he did so, he found inspiration from an unexpected quarter. Framed as a stimulus to action in England, the Indian revolt allowed Jones to try to expand the language of a movement in decline.

Although better known for writings on European affairs, including the Crimean War, Jones had long taken an interest in Indian affairs, writing stinging polemics in the People's Paper about the management of the East India Company in 1853, when its charter came up for renewal before parliament. In these, he had described a 'mighty and magnificent country' turned into 'a nest for the most profligate nepotism' by the greed of a 'race of harpies'.[93] Critical as those pieces are of British rule, there is little sense in them of the presence of colonial subjects – still less of any resistance on their part. Jones's focus is squarely on misrule. News coming out of India in the late spring of 1857 initially appeared to interest him less for its implications for the subjects of East India Company rule than for what it meant in terms of securing British lives and commercial interests. As news of regimental mutinies started to pick up in frequency during late June 1857, the *People's Paper* began by analysing them in generally familiar terms, as an all-too-understandable soldiers' rebellion born of disaffection with poor working conditions which included reduced pay and pensions, onerous terms of enlistment, and lengthened marches. Given this situation as well as the sharpening of the lines separating the races, 'is it unreasonable', one excerpt from another newspaper asked, 'that they should exhibit symptoms of discontent?'[94] While speculating that slighted religious feelings and the racial divide between ruler and ruled might be at work, the paper's initial reports did little more than note that the Indian populace was 'held at bay only by the bayonet's point'.[95] Eventually, Jones wrote of the existence of wider discontent generated by the tax regime of the 'Permanent Settlement', noting accusingly that 'the ryot was thrown into destitution – the universal confiscation of the soil was your great crime, and you are beginning to taste the fruit of retribution'.[96] Though within weeks he would deem it a 'patriotic assertion of a gallant people's rights, against the vilest usurpation that polluted the black page of history', Jones seemed initially unsure whether the Indian rebellion would indeed grow.[97] He did, however, provide his readers with extended essays on the 'vast land', in which he delineated its many features, including a 'mighty gathering of races', diverse resources, and historical and artistic achievements; terra nullius, it was not.[98]

When by August, however, it had become clear that what was unfolding in India was indeed a large-scale uprising, Jones's tone would change quite dramatically, as he set himself the task of deciphering the text of the rebellion against the grain of the interpretation provided by *The Times* and other organs on the side of the East India Company. He found in the rebels' actions not only vindication of his earlier critique of Company rule, but also evidence of a will to resist, an insurgent consciousness exhibiting an 'internal drive' to transform historical circumstances.[99] This story had to be deployed against the emerging consensus: 'The organs of the Government are trying to represent in their blackest colours the conduct of the Hindhus, Mahommedans, and Brahmins.'[100] In ways that are reminiscent of Norton's story of the sepoys who counter-accused those who charged them with treachery, Jones tells his readers that the actuality was the opposite: those who 'now talk of loyalty and truth – of faithlessness and treason' to describe rebel actions – were doing so 'as though every hour of complicity in their ill-gotten sway, were not disloyalty and falsehood, treachery and guilt, against all that man holds holiest in his individual and aggregate capacity'.[101] His position at this stage was that of a principled patriotic dissident: 'When a war of extermination is being waged between two mighty nations, the one oppressed by the other – and when the vital interests of business-life/are [sic] at stake – those who aim at higher morals, those who desire the prosperity of their country on the basis of justice, those who profess the sacred principle of liberty and truth, should not be silent.'[102] He had already cautioned against consuming the news coming in from India uncritically: 'The reader must recollect he hears one side of the question only.'[103]

More questionable perhaps is Jones's casting of the 'retributive agency' of the rebels as a struggle for an independent nation by a 'patriot army' – though he was not alone in countering claims that this was merely a military mutiny by pointing to a wider project that might be understood in 'national' terms.[104] As he read more deeply and extensively into the reports coming in, Jones advised his readership that, in the British press generally, they were only hearing one side. He went on openly to attack *The Times* – the 'dishonest' and 'unprincipled' 'organ of the Leadenhall Moneymongers' – for parroting the line that events in India constituted a military mutiny rather than a national insurrection.[105] It was clear to him that the 'independence' of India had to be recognized, and rule by the 'merchant-robbers of Leadenhall St' ended, if things were not to get even bloodier.[106] Was this a discursive annexation in its own right, then – India functioning as little more than an elaborate metaphor? For Pratt, Jones's attitude to the uprising in India, even as it shifted, was relentlessly opportunistic, involving the manipulation of news and events to mould it in the image of the renewed Chartist movement he now hoped to revive and lead. This meant that he also 'began to configure India and the rebellion in an increasingly European image ... refracting the image of India and her people through the prism of English political culture to dissolve the boundaries of race and religion, asserting the justice of the rising'.[107] Ultimately, it would seem, the 1857 uprising had been little more than an 'effective motif' through which 'Jones could construct and manipulate bonds of identity between the reform movement and both sides in the conflict to suit his purposes'.[108] Pratt's argument here resonates with Guha's own assessment of socialist readings of peasant rebellions as a species of 'assimilative thinking' which seeks to 'arrange it along the alternative axis of a protracted campaign for freedom and socialism'.[109] There is some truth to the argument that Jones, at least initially, registered and interpreted events taking place in India in ways that confirmed and validated his own vision for a renewed Chartist struggle. It is certainly possible to see in the blatant transformation of a poem written for the New World into an encomium to the 'revolt of Hindostan' evidence of the Chartist leader annexing 1857 to 'a broader narrative of the coming of democracy across the world'.[110] It is also fair to say that, in early articles on the insurgency, Jones's invocation of the 'jewel' of Indian independence had something abstract about it: a will to bestow equality of aspiration upon these faraway denizens of a strange land, and command on their behalf the solidarity of English democrats and working-men as votaries of 'liberty and truth'.[111] Any hope of 'securing' the Indian empire, by no means assured, would necessitate a radical reform programme not entirely unlike what was being demanded at home – land given back, just laws, readjusted taxation, abolition of torture, respect for local laws and an improved judiciary. This was, of course, a familiar Chartist recipe.

Once the full scale of the bloody uprising became clear, however, Jones would begin to read events more in terms of their own implications – clearly enthused, even surprised, by what seemed to be an even more powerful rebellion than he claimed to have anticipated. This made him far more cognizant of difficulty; reform now was too little, too late, since the claims of the insurgents themselves would have to be central: 'It is all very well to talk now about remedying the state of things in India – about redressing grievances. The natives are not waiting for us to redress them – they are beginning to take the question of redress in their own hands.'[112] This is the insight which militates against reducing the entirety of Jones's engagement with India in 1857 to 'self-interested political calculation', a charge which obscures the fact that events served to shape his understanding of anticolonial resistance in more supple ways than is suggested by simple opportunism.[113] It is true, of course, that Jones was positing, in Guha's terms, 'an ideal rather than the real historical personality of the insurgent', as was true of most British attempts to read the rebellion against the grain in the absence of direct contact with rebels; the insurgent's consciousness was mediated by the dissident's.[114] When it comes to the past, as Guha also suggests, it is necessary 'not to deny the political importance of such appropriation'.[115] But Jones was also doing important work in relation to his present in actively rereading – and reframing – the information that came to him and the rest of Britain via the government and *The Times*, the main source of reportage about the uprising, rather than simply 'min[ing] them for evidence'.[116] Reprinting these sources in the paper, Jones constructed an archive of sorts, comprising, in addition to *The Times* (which he would attack directly in stinging editorials), government dispatches, telegrams, private correspondence, articles from the Indian press, eyewitness accounts, placards and proclamations. The *People's Paper* also carried reviews of books critical of the East India Company and British rule in India, which frequently alluded to native discontent and simmering resistance. As Jones read vast quantities of 'the prose of counter-insurgency', he discovered Guha's insurgent, the 'entity whose will and reason constituted the praxis called rebellion'.[117] That which can be dismissed as appropriation may also be evidence of a growing sense that the impulse to liberation was indeed to be found beyond familiar spaces, and in particular beyond Europe's boundaries.

What makes Jones's reading of the rebellion more active and dialogical than a mere annexation of events to a pre-existing framework would invoke is the way in which he repeatedly identifies the rebel as a speaking subject with a voice who can be heard in sundry texts, and who, as such, ought to be heeded. Engaging with and interpreting these utterances enabled Jones to elaborate a discourse which ran counter to the one being forged in the British public sphere. Once it became clear that the 'mutinies' were picking up in frequency, Jones began to republish his densely informed articles from 1853, giving his readership more contextual knowledge. There he had cited the unheeded petitions and complaints made by subjects under East Indian Company rule, to which Norton also refers. Rather than immediately annexing early dispatches about the insurgency to the Chartist cause, Jones in fact appeared disinclined to see what was happening as genuinely revolutionary. As more detailed reports of the actual mutinies came in, the paper criticized the colonial regime's failure to listen; ignoring symptoms of disaffection in people who knew their rights had been a big mistake on the part of the British India government. The sanguinary events of the summer of 1857 should not have come as a surprise, for 'the native press [had] openly revealed' the possibility of an uprising.[118] Parliament had ignored 'the complaints of the injured' in the form of petitions, as well as 'seditious journals' brought to its attention, and so: 'The result is before us.'[119]

These voices, and this result, would now need to be heard as inspiration in the other direction. 'Now is the time to shew the Hindhus that we are prepared to reform, not them, but ourselves'.[120] The argument that Jones is merely annexing a distant rebellion to an English cause is complicated by the trouble he takes to invert the direction of influence; events in India became more a textbook than a motif. 'Democracy must be consistent', he insists, noting that he has not concealed the fact that he is 'avowedly … on the Indian side'.[121] It is Indian action that casts light on Englishness, demanding that the latter clarify and assert *itself*; one form of national assertion makes claims upon the other: 'If it is "un-english" to be on the side of the Hindhu, it is more "un-english" to be on the side of tyranny, cruelty, oppression and invasion.'[122] If the Indians are to reclaim their country from their rulers, so too do the English need to reclaim their country, or rather, 'England, as misrepresented by her rulers'. Jones was crystal clear about where transformation was required and it was not in India: 'It is time that England change – or rather, that England make her veritable voice be heard – the voice of the English people – and cry, "right is right, and truth is truth."'[123] The much-vaunted pedagogical enterprise of empire had rebounded on the British: 'If they massacre us, *we taught them how*'.[124] In several articles, Jones uses striking metaphors of corporeal transmission to draw out the reverse direction of influence, especially with regard to unity of purpose. 'Suppose the spirit of the Sepoy host (without its barbarity) were infused into English Democracy', he writes, 'where then would be class government?'[125] Two weeks later, as news of cholera outbreaks came in, he would exhort fellow Chartists with characteristic trenchancy: 'Do you not see that the Asiatic East can send us something better: – yet more terrible than cholera; the glorious contagion of successful revolution?'[126] The language here is, of course, distinctly reminiscent of David Hume's elaboration of sentiments, passions or manners spreading between people like a 'contagion' – a word Hume uses along with its cognates, 'sympathy' included, 'to refer to the *process* by which people enter into the sentiments of others'.[127] It was also a deliberate reframing of the ruling elites' anxiety that rebellion could spread across the colonies. So, for instance, the Duke of Cambridge: 'I cannot forget the observation made by the Emperor Napoleon, who said, in alluding to our Indian affairs, that we should keep an eye to all our colonies, and on no account think of reducing our force in them, as a mutiny was a very catching thing, and nobody could foresee how other localities might take the infection.'[128]

Rather than just point to the English love of liberty spread into the colonies or the happy coincidence of national aspirations, Jones seeks to chide and galvanize a dispirited, defeated people's movement by drawing its attention to a resistance that does not appear to be futile – and one which has implications for their own democratic futures: 'Indian mismanagement will be felt in our mines and mills, our farms and factories.'[129] The biblical series of corporeal and fleshly metaphors of revitalization here enable Jones to pronounce prophecy: 'Do you not see, the "dry bones" are shaking all around, putting on the full flesh of a new life, and rising up in glorious resurrection, to fight once more the old–old fight of freedom?'[130] Beyond the figurative, the revolt in India has salutary material consequences: 'Do you not see that our false system of exchange and credit, the golden crust on which our oligarchy stands, is breaking like the ice-floes at the April-thaws, before the hot breath of that Hindhu revolt?'[131] Note the acknowledged shift in emphasis from deeds of (mis)rule to acts of resistance: indeed, the first such essay is titled, with simple significance, 'The Indian Struggle'.[132] As 'one of the most just, noble, and necessary ever attempted in the history of the world' (unlike many,

Jones regards India as part of world history), the struggle for liberty in India cannot justifiably be seen as different from those European struggles his readership – and others – would have sympathized with: Poland against Russia, Hungary against Austria, Italy against the Germans and the French. He thunders: 'Was Poland right? Then so is Hindostan. Was Hungary justified? Then so is Hindostan. Was Italy deserving of support? Then so is Hindostan. For all that Poland, Hungary, or Italy sought to gain, for that the Hindhu strives. Nay, more!'[133] It is easy to underplay the radicalism of this insistence on parity at a point in time when ideas of freedom were considered distinctly European in provenance: 'The wonder is, not that one hundred and seventy millions of people should now rise in part; – the wonder is that they should ever have submitted at all.'[134] The rhetoric is no longer that of 'slumbering millions' who must awaken into the dawn of a taught freedom, but of people who would not have submitted in the first place had it not been for the betrayals of their 'kings, princes, and aristocracies', a shared curse with Britain – indeed, 'the enemies and curses of every land that harboured them, in every age'.[135]

With due attention to his emphasis on 'sympathy', necessarily an act of imagination catalysed by 'contagion', Jones's yoking together of the Indian anticolonial and English democratic causes is plausibly read as an attempt to construct solidarity in the face of differences: 'We bespeak the sympathy of the English people for their Hindhu brethren.'[136] As if unsure that this will be forthcoming – 'Their cause is yours', he urges – Jones suggests an elaborate exercise of the imagination in which his readers find themselves conquered slowly through intrigue, betrayal, confiscation, pillage and attack by various groups from Europe who had first arrived and asked permission merely 'to build a factory on Woolwich Marsh'.[137] What would they, the English, do? 'You would rise – rise in the holy right of insurrection, and cry to Europe and to the world, to Heaven and earth, to bear witness to the justice of your cause'. This 'sympathy' derives, unlike contagion, not 'so much from the view of the passion, as from that of the situation which excites it', in Adam Smith's terms, with fellow-feeling deriving from 'changing places in fancy with the sufferer'.[138] Both are distinct from benevolence, breaking from the paternalism of reform. Of course, Jones makes a leap of faith here – that a common standpoint will emerge from the imagination of a common condition. As Knud

Haakonsen notes, however, the emphasis on imagination is embedded in Smith's famous elaboration of 'sympathy', of which Jones
cannot have been unaware: 'The act of sympathetic understanding
is a creation of order in the observer's perceptions by means of an
imagined rationale for the observed behaviour. As agents or moral
beings, other people are, therefore, the creation of our imagination
... the same can be said of ourselves; as moral agents we are acts
of creative imagination.'[139] Jones is also vulnerable to the charge of
romanticizing what he calls 'one of the grandest and most justifiable national wars ever waged by an oppressed people'.[140] Yet, to
leave it at that would be, firstly, to grossly underestimate the radicalism of insisting at this point in time that 'Indians have as good a
right to govern India, as the English have to govern England'.[141]
It also minimizes the extent to which Jones's readings of the crisis
were clearly responsive to events, and to the increasing emphasis
he placed on the assertiveness of the rebels. The *People's Paper* also
carried letters by Indians, such as one on 23 January 1858, headed
'Importance of the Study of the Indian Language' and signed by one
'Syed Abdoolah', calling for daily spoken communication between
British and Indians.[142] Jones commented in this regard, 'There can
be no greater proof of the iniquity of our rule' than that colonial
officials 'are not even expected to understand the tongue of those
whom they are sent to govern.'[143] It is also worth noting that Jones
attended and spoke at public meetings on India, with, for instance,
the paper carrying prominent front-page notices of such events. 'An
Important Exposure of our Government of India', on 17 February
1858, was to be attended by MPs John Townshend, Charles Gilpin
and H. Ingram. His ideas were not without means of circulation
beyond the *People's Paper* and were articulated within earshot of the
influential.

By the late autumn of 1857, Jones appeared to switch from cheering on the insurgency to assessing the flaws and strategic mistakes
of the counterinsurgency, including poor planning: 'Thus imbecility
is losing a great colonial Empire.'[144] This, Pratt suggests, exemplifies
'his proclivity to switch between identification with rebel or counter-
insurgent as the likelihood of a successful rebellion receded'.[145]
While it is clear that, as the insurgency was put down over several
months, Jones manifestly revised his vision of where things would

go, deflated perhaps after his bout of raucous cheerleading, and also explicitly sickened by the bloodshed he wanted stopped, it is certainly not the case that he simply reneged on his commitments to popular resistance: 'The national character of the Indian insurrection can be no longer truthfully disputed', he wrote. 'No matter whether it be the Anglo-saxon or the Hindhu, the American or the Celt ... the people are ever the only saviours of imperilled nations, the cradle and the home of all great thoughts and truths. It is the people who conceive; it is the people who realise, the greatness of every age.'[146] Indians were setting a 'noble example'. The failures of counterinsurgency largely provided Jones with a weapon with which to continue his relentless attack on the incompetence and blunders of the ruling elites. Indeed, after a few weeks' silence, as 1857 drew to a close Jones would title an article 'How to Secure India', but almost immediately issue a caveat: 'Let not the above title mislead our readers ... We do not believe that the British can prove a rightful claim to one solitary acre of ground ... of Hindostan.'[147] But, he says, with the knowledge of where things are headed, it would be another half-century or so before English rule could be undone, in which case, the only recourse was to make English-ruled India 'as happy as you can; do as much justice as circumstances admit'.[148] To this end, British rule had to be democratized, and treaties honoured in the name of the English people, with princes restored to their thrones and their subjects treated on terms of honourable equality.[149] One of the last articles on the topic in the paper, which would itself fold in 1858, would note categorically that, in the final analysis, given that the insurgency was not quite fully crushed, 'the development of Indian greatness will be found most consistent with India's freedom from British rule, and its thorough, uncontrolled, and unshackled independence'.[150]

Marx and 1857: A Brief Note

What of Jones's friend and comrade, Karl Marx? In an interesting essay Thierry Drapeau argues that, while scholars have 'long established the intellectual ascendancy Marx had over [Jones], they have failed to track the opposite direction of influence'.[151] Drapeau contends that, while it may be that Marx's eventual 'multilinear perspectives' on anticolonialism derived from intensive study of non-Western societies, 'Ernest Jones was inextricably linked to the unfolding of those efforts in the early 1850s ... adding nuance and deeper understanding to them'.[152] There is some merit to the argument that Jones and Marx influenced each other during the early 1850s, when their friendship took root, and certainly Marx would move away over time from the 'Eurocentric, unilinear, and determinist model of historical development' he had cleaved to in 1848.[153] But there is less evidence to suggest that Marx made huge strides in that direction in the 1850s as a consequence of Jones's influence. For one thing, Jones himself would not really relocate 'the initiative of revolutionary transformation ... to the oppressed peoples of the British Empire' until after 1857; his 'The New World, a Democratic Poem' was only reworked as a tribute to the Indian uprising several years after its first publication.[154] It was in the wake of 1857 that the 'vantage point of the colonized' became a manifest reality outside the text for Jones. The other fact is that, for all its deprecation of the brutality of British rule and condemnation of the exploitation of the Indian peasantry, and notwithstanding a sense that a national insurrection of sorts could be discerned in events, Marx's famous dispatches on the Indian uprising for the *New York Tribune* did not particularly interest themselves in that vantage point – one reason that I have not engaged with them here. His suggestion that it was conceivable that the Indians could throw off the English yoke remained abstract, something for the distant future. But it is true that, by this point, Marx was markedly less inclined to view colonialism as a beneficial force – and this, as well as his passing concession that what England 'considers a military mutiny is in truth a national revolt', may well have had something to do with Jones's analysis.[155]

It is fair to say that, even if 1857 was not the occasion for the immediate production of revolutionary anticolonialism in Britain, some important political and intellectual seeds had nonetheless been sown, including in Marx's case. While proletarian internationalism of the domestic variety may have always been integral to Jones's engagement with colonial questions, there seems little doubt that the historical actuality of the 1857 uprising caused him to shift markedly in the direction of seeking 'contagion' from that source of revolutionary agency. Given that Marx and Jones were estranged by that point, it remains open to question whether Jones in fact influenced his friend after 1855, but it is not inconceivable that engagement with Jones in the first half of the 1850s, and then subsequently studying the 1857 rebellion, were part of Marx's developing understanding of anticolonialism in the long run. Pranav Jani has argued eloquently that it took the events of 1857 'to force Marx to develop a better understanding of the agency of the colonized subject', and that there is to be discerned 'a more dialectical relationship between the development of Marx's ideas and the 1857 Revolt' than scholars have identified before.[156] While this dialectical understanding is not, I think, immediately visible in his famous articles on the Revolt itself for the *New York Tribune*, which focus largely on British mistakes and military manoeuvres, Marx does evoke even here 'the secret connivance and support of the natives' given to the sepoys, while cautioning against expecting 'an Indian revolt to assume the features of a European revolution'.[157] He notes too that the imperial project in India is one that benefits individuals, and as such increases the national wealth, but is also offset by the very great costs involved in 'endless conquest and perpetual aggression'.[158] Agreeing that some of the outrages committed by the sepoys were 'hideous' and 'appalling', Marx was inclined to see them as mirroring colonial atrocities: 'the reflex, in a concentrated form, of England's own conduct in India'.[159] Jones too noted trenchantly: 'The conduct of the "rebels", throughout the mutiny, has been in strict and consistent accordance with the example of their civilised governors.'[160] He would repeatedly point out that the 'wild, wanton, and wicked demand for native blood' would only make sense if it weren't the British who had, in the first place, 'sowed the seeds of that sanguinary harvest which is but now being reaped in British India'.[161] Certainly Marx, like Jones, was inclined to read the discourse of counterinsurgency critically, as one in which it was supposed that 'all the cruelty is on the side of the sepoys, and all the milk of human kindness flows on the side of the English'.[162]

No 'Patient Acquiescence': Richard Congreve
and 'Common Human Feeling'

If Jones appeared to back down on his revolutionary fervour for
the Indian cause in favour of an interim amelioration of grievances (which Marx regarded as a turn to the right), a rejection of
reforms aimed at keeping Indians as happy as possible came from an
avowedly non-revolutionary quarter: the leading English Positivist,
Richard Congreve. In a pamphlet published in November 1857, even
as national outrage in Britain was reaching a high point, Congreve,
aware that he might be charged with 'reckless opposition to the feelings of the majority', launched an attack on what he called 'the better
language now adopted' to justify continued British rule in India:

> We occupied India under the impulse of commercial and political
> motives; we have governed it as a valuable appendage, commer-
> cially and politically. That is the broad truth. When our Empire is
> tottering to its fall, then to step forward with moral or Christian
> motives for holding it, which have never influenced our previous
> policy, is a very questionable course.[163]

His own response to the uprising is 'simple in the extreme': 'that
we withdraw from our occupation of India without any unnecessary delay'.[164] Two years later, as the country prepared a national
Thanksgiving ordered by Queen Victoria for 1 May 1859 to commemorate victory over the rebels, Congreve released the pamphlet
again, along with what he called a 'Protest Published as a Placard', in
which he pleaded with his fellow English to 'reflect' on the rebellion
as 'the legitimate effort of a nation to shake off an oppressive foreign
yoke', and not, therefore, to commemorate 'the triumph of force over
right'.[165] At one level this position was of course entirely consistent
with Congreve's doctrinal allegiance to Positivism. In the preceding
year, he had published an article on Gibraltar where – in accordance
with the views of the Positivist guiding spirit, the French philosopher
Auguste Comte – he had laid out the case for a foreign policy driven by
moral rather than political considerations, whereby England would
do the right thing in relation to 'weaker' entities. Why, then, had he
not spoken of India in this context? Only, he claims, because he had

detected no native resistance: England's dominion in the subcontinent was '*apparently* unquestioned' and the *seeming* acquiescence to arbitrary English actions had suggested that there was 'no probability of an immediate agitation of the Indian question'.[166] Thus, while clear as to the wrongness of the acquisition itself, he 'had accepted it as a fact'. Indeed, he had himself partaken of the rationale of the 'improvement' mission, accepting that any withdrawal from India could be adjourned for some time while the government redeemed itself and offered compensation for conquest to its Indian subjects 'by the enforcement of order, the furtherance of material improvements, and by the lessons of Western punctuality and honour'.[167]

Why so dramatic a change in position, then, from one whose doctrinal allegiances to Positivism also committed him to order and gradualism, evolution not revolution?[168] Quite simply: 'The recent revolt has dispelled all such ideas of patient acquiescence in a recognized evil.'[169] For Positivist principles to be fully activated in relation to India, eliciting parity with weaker European nations, the emergence of native resistance was vital. Like Jones, Congreve read the revolt in India as making specific claims of England (for him, too, it was 'England' rather than Britain) and as having, in turn, distinct implications for this nation's conception of *itself*. In his assessment of Congreve as one of a very small minority who did indeed advocate full withdrawal from India, distinguished historian of empire Bernard Porter notes that the Positivist philosopher insisted that withdrawing from India would in fact be in Europe's interest, and that, contrary to the standard view, the country 'would not lapse into barbarism and anarchy once the imperial grip were relaxed'.[170] Such a 'sympathetic approach to alien civilisations was something new in English colonial criticism'. Speculating on the reasons for Congreve's unusual attitude, Porter argues that at work here was not so much 'the mass of information about those civilisations which had been accumulated in the recent past by travellers and scientists', but instead 'cultural relativism' – meaning, in this instance, a standpoint that simply chose not to be ethnocentric, and to regard other 'cultural systems' as different but not inferior to that of Western Europe.[171] This, it seems to me, is to overlook two determining aspects of Congreve's meditations on the future of India. The first is the admitted centrality of the 1857 uprising in getting him to abandon the reformist position. The second is the extent to which Congreve emphasizes the need for the English working classes and women generally to extend 'sympathy' to the ruled, sympathy defined here not merely as commonality of feeling but as a means of thinking together with Indians.

Richard Congreve was Britain's foremost exponent of the influential ideas of Comte, the Positivist founder of the 'Church of Humanity' whose values appealed to the nineteenth-century British middle classes: 'upholding morality, providing a means of controlling social change, and providing a sense of identity to the individual by defining his place within the community'.[172] There was to be no revolution, but order and progress were to be reconciled through social reconstruction. While both liberal individualism and class society were to be shunned, 'the dominant values of this society would be largely those of the middle class' and capitalism could have a 'moralized' form.[173] Congreve – who founded the English Comtean organization, the 'Religion of Humanity', in January 1859 – lectured on Positivism, and his lectures were attended by, among others, George Eliot (though she apparently found him dull). It is this commitment to a moral, ordered and controlled social change – he would reiterate that his 'whole notions are alien to disorder' – that makes the impact of the 1857 uprising on Congreve all the more remarkable for its undoubted radicalism in getting him to call for immediate, not gradual, withdrawal.[174] (Half a century later, his pamphlet 'India', responding to the uprising, would be republished and disseminated by the London-based Indian radical and editor of the *Indian Sociologist*, Shyamji Krishnavarma.) While Congreve was something of an outlier, he matters for any study of British dissent inasmuch as Positivism's scientific and humanist tenor was one of the tributary strands of mid-nineteenth-century British radicalism. Both as a high-profile Oxford don until 1854, and later as a Comtean, Congreve also influenced a later generation of critics of empire, most importantly Frederic Harrison. A distinctive contributor to what might be regarded as the nineteenth-century legacy of imperial scepticism, Congreve would become a supporter of trade unions, as well as an advocate of Irish independence. Even as a smaller voice, however, he was among the first to bring into view three dimensions of British criticism of empire which would become increasingly salient: the need to listen to and make central the wishes of those at the receiving end of colonialism; the ways in which resistance to the imperial project called upon the metropole (in Congreve's case, England) to reflect on and reconstitute itself; and finally, perhaps most importantly, the need to forge 'sympathetic' bonds that at once recognized differences and identified points of commonality.

There are a great many things to be said about this slim but powerfully articulated work – not least about the ways in which it prefigures Thompson's critique of the one-sided writing of the history of the uprising in calling for justice (not 'military vengeance') to be dispensed in all directions without national or racial superiority determining the outcome: 'Not alone the white woman, or the child of English parents, but Hindoo women and children, should be fearfully avenged.'[175] What is of most relevance for our purposes, however, is the way in which Congreve appears to break not only from gradualism, but from *benevolence* as the driving force of reforms, advocating instead a 'sympathy' with the ruled that is conceived very differently from paternalism. Indeed, Congreve was in many ways an early theorist of 'solidarity' – not a word that he would have had available to him, but certainly a concept he seemed to understand fully. He dispenses very quickly, for instance, with the idea of imperial rule as a form of 'trusteeship' – a concept and term that would recur in arguments for the Empire well into the twentieth century, when it would also be challenged by black and Asian anticolonialists on grounds very similar to those Congreve articulates. Confronting Gladstone's argument that the mode of acquisition of India mattered less now than the 'obligations ... contracted towards the nearly 200 millions of people under our rule in India', Congreve noted that the rebellion had made one thing abundantly clear in relation to the former's claim that the British occupy 'the condition of trustees' between God and the Indians: this 'trusteeship has not hitherto been *recognised*'.[176] Rebellion is thus a forceful reminder that the colonized share the right to recognize and be recognized – but also, crucially, to *refuse* recognition. Given the importance of the act of 'recognition' to international law, to which Congreve explicitly alludes in his questioning of the British right to hold India down by force, his insistence on the right of Indians to recognize or refuse recognition of the colonial presence is of no small import: 'Is there in the East Indies a different international law from what exists in England?'[177] Thus, rather than call for reforms, 'solutions which to me are incoherent and immoral', he preferred to pose the question that he believed the revolt itself was posing of England: 'Shall we set to work to re-conquer India?'[178] It is the basis on which he offers his resounding negative that is most significant: the ruled did not wish to be ruled.

At the outset, still defending his own inaction on the question of India and his past endorsement of the 'improvement' mission, Congreve suggests, perhaps a little disingenuously, that he had been waiting 'patiently for the day when ... the energies of the native population should make our further hold impossible', even as he hoped that England would, on the basis of a 'purer moral feeling', voluntarily relinquish its hold on India.[179] The revolt changed all that, showing clearly that the ruled, not the rulers, would be the prime movers of both India's immediate present and distant future. 'Recent events' had demonstrated that the only way for the English to keep India was by force. Whatever their own problems, Indians appeared to 'prefer the chances of less settled government to the certainty of an alien despotism'.[180] Principles of trusteeship, Congreve pointed out, prefiguring anticolonial thinkers of the next century, could not be imposed on a reluctant people, but were 'valid only with those who accept them'.[181] The revolt could be read then as the future of the Empire in India writ large: 'For, either they expel us, or we retire.'[182] The other justification for colonial rule Congreve had to deal with was precisely a relativist one: 'that what holds good of independent States in Europe is not binding in the East'.[183] It was unclear that this claim was defensible: 'What are the limits of this difference, and on what rational basis does it rest?' Admitting frankly that he was 'not deeply versed in the literature and religious antiquities of India', based on a 'mass of information', Congreve insisted on the right of Indian civilization not to be subjected to English rule.[184] As other liberals had done, he cited Burke copiously on the difference between savages in the Americas (whom it was, presumably, acceptable to conquer) and the Indians, 'cultivated by all the arts of polished life, whilst we were yet in the woods'.[185] Ultimately, however, Congreve's own argument, while it drew on the Burkean critique of empire, rested less on India's civilizational achievements than on the fact of ongoing resistance, which had made clear that there was no probability of amalgamation (of the sort Norton wanted) and 'a genuine union being at last effected'.[186] Given that 'the different manners of the East' were not, to his mind, grounds for a relativist application of international law or moral principles, the fact was that the rebellion pointed to the impossibility of common cause under British rule.[187] With the right kind of imaginative labour, common cause could, however, be *forged* between English working-men and Englishwomen, on the one hand, and Indians under British rule on the other. If colonial conquest had resulted in such a 'want of sympathy' with conquered societies, that even 'instructive forms of civilisation' were destroyed, it could be attributed to a distinctively class-based attitude.[188] Congreve was clear that the end of colonial rule was specifically 'alien in conception and results to the thoughts and wishes of the upper classes of England'.[189] But he was more hopeful of others' attitude to Indians, the 'large numbers in England who, if my opinions could reach them, would sympathise with them in spirit at least, if they could not wholly accept them'.[190] This was a necessarily dialogical process, involving cognition and recognition, imaginative labour that the English people could undertake, even in the absence of actual contact with Indians. Adam Smith's cognitive model of 'sympathy' as denoting not just pity or compassion but 'our fellow-feeling with any passion whatever' is useful here.

Congreve's appeal to women was brief and relatively predictable in its gendered assumptions: since they hold aloof from the strife and personal ambition that mar men's politics, women can bring vital moral considerations and a moderating power to political questions. Here, too, in 'the court of moral feeling', Congreve stressed the need to pose questions, then listen for and keep in the foreground the wishes of the ruled in India: 'Is it with the consent of its people that we persist in trying to rule it, or solely by virtue of a favourable judgement on our claim pronounced by none but ourselves?'[191] It is really, however, with his appeal to 'the Working Men of England' that Congreve came up with a theory of common condition that enabled him to make the case for the 'keenest political sympathy' not just between himself as philosopher and the proletariat, but between them and the subjects of British India.[192] Here Congreve enunciated a claim about the intertwined structures of empire which would be articulated by other critics too in the decades to come: 'The question is two-fold. It is an Indian one, but it is also an English one. The interests of both countries are at stake. You may take them apart for convenience, but you cannot really separate them.'[193] The working-men were in a unique position to listen to and sympathize with the aspirations of the ruled, not least because they lacked the upper classes' material and personal connections to India and 'derive no advantages from its possession'.[194] They too were ruled and lied to by the same class: 'You will not be deceived by the assertions that the mass of the Hindoo nation wishes us to continue its ruler', not least because of the 'similar ones made at home by your own state of feelings'.[195] The extent to which Congreve stressed the similarity (rather than congruity) of condition, as well as the resulting capacity to interpret the feelings of the ruled, is striking: 'You know that your own state of feeling is misinterpreted or entirely neglected by those who administer your Government; is it likely that they would be successful in interpreting that of the distant and alien population of India?'[196]

Congreve is not suggesting that the standpoint of the working Englishman is the *same* as that of the subject of rule in India – or not quite. He is instead calling for this man to recall at once his own condition and 'sympathise' – as he already does with those in Hungary or Italy who ask for independence and justice – 'with the Hindoo in his struggle for the same objects'.[197] This did not, as he had already made clear, imply an *identity* of culture or belief systems. It did, however, mean that those at the receiving end of exploitation were in a better position to conceive 'what we ourselves should feel in the like situation', to use Smith's elaboration of 'sympathy'.[198] The working-men of England, by contrast with the English upper classes, were in a unique position to undertake the imaginative labour that could bridge some of that distance and difference:

You can judge of the bearing of the English in India by the bearing of the same classes at home, by the bearing of your aristocracy, whether commercial or landed, by the bearing of your middle classes. The hard indifference of the latter, the haughty neglect of the former, the reckless way in which both satisfy their personal tastes and feelings, and take no care of yours, the strange display of almost fabulous wealth and luxury, in vivid contrast with the extreme of poverty and suffering, all these you can appreciate at home. You watch them with mingled feelings, for those who so act are your countrymen, and have some points in common with yourself, some points of friendly contact, some common feelings. Take away all that softens the relation; let the conduct be the same, and let the men be conquerors of another colour, another language, and another religion, and let them add the contempt such difference too naturally inspires: you may then have the measure of the feelings of the subject Hindoo or Mahometan towards his European masters. You may understand their vengeful spirit; you may not palliate their mode of vengeance.[199]

I quote this passage at some length because of its extraordinary emphasis not only on 'feelings', but also the bold equation Congreve makes between fellow feeling and the capacity to judge not only the causes but the ferocity of – and the means deployed against – the Indian rebellion. Common ground, even shared human feeling, is not a given, but is arrived at through imaginative work. The relationship between English working-man and distant Indian subject is one that has to be dialogical in some form, entailing the work of interpretation, comprehension and reconstitution. The form of 'sympathy' that Congreve calls for entails, then, emphatically not charity, benevolence or compassion, but 'common human feeling',[200] or what Smith would call 'fellow feeling', which is 'an analogous emotion ... at the thought of his situation, in the breast of every attentive spectator'.[201] Women and the working classes are more likely to be 'attentive' interpreters in this mode.

There is also, of course, a sound material basis for, and indeed self-interest in, identifying analogous aspirations. Like Jones, Congreve emphasizes to the working classes he addresses that the disadvantages of an exploitative domestic order and those of colonial rule are part of the same formation: 'India is the keystone of the existing system of Government.'[202] It is they, the English working classes, who will foot the bill as well as provide the cannon fodder for holding down India by force:

On all grounds, then, so far as India is concerned, I fearlessly appeal to you for a verdict, given by the light of your common English experience, and by the light of your common human feeling; and,

as you would rise, to a man, to prevent your country from being
the victim of foreign oppression, so I call on you to raise your voice
no less unanimously in protest against her being the oppressor.[203]

There could be no change in the domestic social order without an
end to the Indian empire, and the result could be salutary: 'a dominion narrower in extent but better wielded'.[204] It is precisely in the
light of this relatively modest proposal for the domestic benefits – 'in
no revolutionary spirit' – of letting go of empire that we must read
Congreve's pamphlet on 'India' less as a Positivist assimilation of a
far-off uprising than as an exemplar of Positivism pushed to more
radical analysis by a rebellion with distinct domestic resonances.[205]

The Afterlife of 1857

'The events of 1857 forced all of us to consider the whole question of the Empire', recalled another Positivist, Congreve's former
Oxford tutee, and lawyer, Frederic Harrison, some years later. 'From
that day I became an anti-Imperialist'.[206] Harrison, a figure we shall
meet again, initially appears to have been divided between seeing
the uprising, like Congreve, as necessarily universal in its assertion
of righteous resistance, and deeming it a consequence of 'savage
instincts', the insurmountable alterity underpinning 'the inevitable
struggle of black man against white – native against European'.[207]
Yet, in that same autumn of 1857, Harrison found himself accepting that this was 'a long-expected inevitable rebellion of a keen race
against their conquerors and masters'.[208] Now he credited the rebels
with greater thoughtfulness and agency than he had before, arguing
that the soldiers who had mutinied were 'the *élite*, the leading class,
the most spirited, the most intelligent, the most thoroughly Hindoo.
They lead and represent the rest, as much as Cromwell's Ironsides
were the marrow of England.'[209] It is the emergence of this resistance
that makes a 'phantom' of British rule, a simulacrum of conquest.[210]
Clearly, the mission to 'Europeanise' was not successful, even if much
had been imparted, for 'no respectable native class ever identifies itself
with us'.[211] If the British in India were to be overthrown in the course
of an insurgency, there could be no re-conquest, for then the British

working classes 'would not allow their lives, their money, and their claims to be sacrificed in an object they would feel to belong wholly to the commercial classes'.[212] What is striking about Harrison's meditations, in contrast to Congreve's rather more surefooted insistence on the wrongness of colonial rule, is that they are shot through with doubt. 'We are indeed a nation of colonists; and India is the fairest of our possessions', Harrison concedes; but what if, in fact, all such conquests do, other than enhance commercial interests, 'is to wrap round Britannia a useless purple' which will enable historians of the future to 'show how the imperial pomp blinded both English and Europeans to the real position of this country on the map'?[213] In the end, 1857 had shown that India resisted incorporation and could only be governed now as a 'temporary possession', one which it was futile to attempt to Europeanize or Christianize. From this vantage-point, Britain's empire was at best folly, and at worst a catastrophe that did nothing for 'national existence'.[214] Though he prognosticated that the century 'long before its close – will see the last of British rule in India', within a few weeks of writing these words Harrison would find himself once more doubtful, as it became clear that the uprising would be suppressed.[215] Now, not unlike Jones, he suggested he would support a reformed project 'to govern India, but *solely from the point of view of an intelligent and patriotic native* – if it can be done. If not – marchons!'[216]

For all that it created both uneasiness and public anguish, the Indian uprising of 1857 did not constitute a crisis that forged anything like a critical consensus on the downsides of empire. As others have noted, it undermined the liberal pedagogical mission to raise the inhabitants of the subcontinent to higher civilizational standards. It is also widely accepted that lines of difference were hardened, confirming 'the mutual distrust between rulers and ruled'.[217] Yet, as I have argued here, some responses to the uprising laid the ground for a different interpretation of such crises of rule – one that undermined attitudes of paternalism and benevolence in favour of dispositions that emphasized fellow feeling, reciprocal engagement and reverse pedagogy. Such interpretations may have been a minor key against the upsurge of emotions that marked the response to the uprising, but they constitute, nonetheless, a bookmark which kept different political possibilities open. These included modes of relating to non-Europeans that both acknowledged the variety of the ways in which the 'human' expressed itself in cultures and sought to forge common ground. The idea that Englishness, or Britishness, also needed to reconstitute itself for the better in the face of resistance, learning from it in the process, was also put into play at this time.

Let us return, finally, to Edward Thompson, writing not quite seventy years later, convinced that another Indian struggle was once again imminent, but hoping that it would not be necessary, and arguing that it need not be embittered. If there was 'irreconcilability' between white and brown in India, its roots lay far back in the events of 1857: 'But from Bihar to the Border the Mutiny lives; it lives in the memory of Europeans and of Indians alike. It overshadows the thought and the relations of both races ... Those memories have never slept, and now they are raising their heads as never before.'[218] The shadow of accepted accounts of the 'Mutiny' thus fell over events that followed, from the second Afghan War to the 1919 massacre at Jallianwala Bagh, by enshrining harsh retribution for any resistance. On the British side, General Dyer could not be pilloried as the sole villain of the horrific massacre in Amritsar, but needed to be seen instead, in Thompson's view, as the embodiment of a national delusion generated by a fatal mythology: 'It was our inherited thought concerning the Mutiny and Indians and India that drove him on. The ghosts of Cooper and Cowan presided over Jallianwala.'[219] If relations between the British in India and Indians were not to escalate into a final, irrevocable clash, then it was for the British, not the Indians, to 'face the things that happened, and change our way of writing about them'.[220] The process of changing the way the Empire was written about would take a very long time; indeed, it remains incomplete. Events that made such a rewriting imperative, however, would take place with determined regularity across British colonial possessions: the next one would be less than a decade after the Indian insurgency, in faraway Jamaica. It too would put questions of empire and the imperial project back into the public consciousness in Britain.

2

A Barbaric Independence: Rebel Voice and Transnational Solidarity, Morant Bay, 1865

The rebellion of the negroes comes very home to the national soul. Though a fleabite compared with the Indian Mutiny, it touches our pride more and is more in the nature of a disappointment.

The Times, 18 November 1865

What have the English people done that the irrepressible negro should make an interruption into their daily press, disport himself at their dessert, chill their turtle, spoil their wine, and sour their pine-apple and their temper? ... Are we henceforth to be separated, as a nation, into negrophilites and anti-negroites?

Saturday Review, October 1866

Constitutionally considered, it makes no difference in the question, that what Governor Eyre did was done in Jamaica and not in England. For this purpose, the two islands are one and the same.

The Bee-Hive, 1 September 1866

On a cloudy Monday morning in October 1865, a few hours after the end of the Sabbath, George William Gordon, a forty-five-year-old man, stood beneath the arch of a burned-down courthouse in the Jamaican town of Morant Bay. His hands and feet had been pinioned and a halter was draped around his neck. After the drop fell at 7.10 a.m., the corpse, dressed in a borrowed white coat, was

kept suspended and swinging on public view in inclement weather
for a full twenty-four hours and then thrown into a felon's grave.
It was, however, far from being consigned to anonymity. Gordon's
name would soon reverberate 4,500 miles away on another island,
one which, by that point in history, was more habituated to rainy
days than to summary public executions of opposition politicians.
From late November 1865, when news finally reached London of
Gordon's execution under martial law and of the extra-judicial
deaths of many others – mostly black or Afro-Jamaican men deemed
part of a conspiracy to overthrow white rule – a controversy raged
in England for nearly three years. The so-called 'Jamaica Affair'
would shake the English intelligentsia and political classes, creating fresh and bitter divisions while widening existing cleavages. It
would also be discussed at working-class meetings held in the run-up
to the Second Reform Bill, which was coming up for parliamentary
debate.[1] For nearly three years, the English public sphere would
concern itself with what also came to be known as 'the Eyre controversy', as attempts were made by some of England's best-known
political and intellectual figures to bring to book the colonial governor under whose administrative aegis Gordon and over 500 others
had met their untimely deaths.

Breaking out eight years after the Indian uprising, Morant Bay has
long been recognized as the other mid-nineteenth-century national
crisis which contributed to 'new ways of categorising racial difference'.[2] 'After the Morant Bay Rebellion', writes Marouf Hasian, Jr,
'the belief in racial hierarchies also ossified, and Afro-Jamaicans were
re-characterized as unruly and untrustworthy colonial subjects.'[3] The
profound effect of this uprising on metropolitan discourse has also
been discussed in terms of the fundamental questions it raised 'about
the nature of Englishness itself'.[4] Tim Watson reminds us of the 'disproportionate significance' accorded to Morant Bay at the time,
arguing that the event presaged the re-emergence of 'the modern
notion of the British Empire as a single conceptual, territorial, and
political unit'.[5] Consequent upon the controversy was nothing less
than the consolidation of the British Empire 'as an imaginary unit
soldered together by modern humanitarianism'.[6] Within the British
historiographical record, the Governor Eyre controversy functions
as a *locus classicus*, a characteristic moment of internal moral crisis

Contemporary etching of rebels being hanged at the Morant Bay Courthouse

leading to self-correction – in this case a more responsive, liberal and reforming colonial government, with Jamaica passing to direct Crown rule in 1866, when its Legislative Assembly dissolved itself. 'The moral perils of empire', writes R. W. Kostal, situating the controversy in a historical frame, 'were quintessentially English pre-occupations, and they had surfaced many times before.'[7]

What happens, though, to the insurgent Jamaican subject who instigates the crisis in the first place? While there is little doubt that the whole controversy was 'appropriated and reconstructed as a means of contesting political positions and propositions in *England*' itself, it is a mistake to view the Eyre affair as only as the *mise en scène* for a very British debate about rights and constitutionality, the Jamaican elements rendered secondary to the process.[8] Even where connections have been touched on, discussions of the Morant Bay episode have in general tended to emphasize *either* events in Jamaica *or* the famously divided high-profile response in Britain. In fact, not only was the Jamaican insurgent instrumental in fomenting debate and division but black agency – and what was to be done with it – was, in many ways, at the heart of the controversy. The positions taken by British domestic parties to the controversy were profoundly inflected by an awareness of both the reality of black Jamaican self-assertion and, crucially, the fact that 'ex-slaves chose to define the content of their freedom in apparent opposition to market forces'.[9] Their words and actions fomented division in Britain, and in doing so also formed the basis for the emergence of criticism of post-Emancipation white rule in the West Indian colonies, as well as something very like the transnational working-class solidarity envisioned by Congreve and Jones in the wake of the Indian rebellion.

Once again, the question of 'voice' is central – indeed more so, for, unlike the 1857 crisis, this time the documents of counterinsurgency provided a channel for the voices of black Jamaican rebels – as well as Gordon himself – to resonate more fully in the British public sphere. Mimi Sheller notes that, even prior to the rebellion, 'the numerous two-way ties between freed people and the British government made both sides adept at addressing the other', leaving a more extensive documentary trail than was often the case.[10] Thus, the historical record shows very clearly that Jamaican dissidents and rebels made demands of Britain and British rule while challenging its rhetorical contradictions. Their specific post-slavery understandings of what freedom should mean were frequently distinct from, and in conflict with, those generated by the imperial centre. The multiple speech acts through which the black Jamaican peasantry and their political leaders communicated, both leading up to and following the rebellion, registered upon and were interpreted by various interests back in Britain and should be regarded as significantly tributary to the controversy that subsequently unfolded. It is not just that when Jamaica 'reappeared on centre stage of British public life in late 1865, it also found itself at the centre of a new set of political and cultural beliefs'.[11] Afro-Jamaican insurgency helped shape those beliefs in very fundamental ways, giving them genuinely transnational dimensions and thickening the meaning of democratic rights. In his excellent legal history of the controversy and the various attempts made by the Jamaica Committee to prosecute Eyre for 'murder', among other misdeeds, Kostal has suggested that the 'controversy arose from the tectonic stresses generated by the collision between global imperial ambition and bedrock moral and legal sensibilities'.[12] This familiar reading of the controversy largely in terms of 'Burkean qualms' elides a constitutive third party: the Afro-Jamaican peasant rebels who, in ways their Indian counterparts could not, offered to a metropolitan audience engagements with their own condition.[13]

One of the reasons that the Morant Bay uprising created much more pronounced and high-profile divisions than we saw in the case of India 1857 is the extent to which the voices of Jamaican discontent were heard – and speaking in English – back in the metropole. The British press across the spectrum reported assiduously on the insurgency and its repression, often carrying copies of dispatches and reports from the Jamaican press. The views and aspirations of black Jamaican peasants were available for metropolitan understanding in a striking variety of forms: petitions, memorials, speeches, addresses, resolutions, letters, placards, and leaflets. These embodied genres ranged from complaints, lamentation, deposition and testimony to plea, threat, demand, accusation and claim. Even Edward Underhill, whose famous letter to the colonial secretary detailing the condition of the Jamaica peasantry became a flashpoint for Jamaican organizing, would recall in his memoirs that the Royal Commission of Inquiry itself drew on a wide variety of evidentiary texts, from pieces by 'editors and writers in newspapers' to 'the loose talk of the nursery', 'the jokes of friends', 'the vague rumours which accompanied or followed the political meetings' and 'the exasperated language of men smarting under fresh acts of injustice'.[14] Underhill's memoir details the manifold ways in which black Jamaican peasants voiced their discontent, his own controversial letter having drawn on their articulated grievances rather than 'authoring' them, as was charged. One response to such self-assertion was, as Holt observes, a redefinition of black people themselves as 'a different kind of human being', so that hardened racial lines became a means of fending off the threat of resistance to the demands of political economy.[15] Studies of such 're-characterization' have tended to focus, as in the case of India in 1857, on this sharpening of boundaries and racial 'othering', which undoubtedly testifies to the ultimate triumph, as it were, of the Eyre camp's racism. Those responses which sought, in contrast, to insist on the need for parity of treatment for white Briton and black Jamaican, have largely been read in terms of anxieties about the British constitution and the rule of law, rather than as an engagement with the question of racial equality. (Holt is one of the few to suggest that this might have been strategic, given a post-1857 milieu of tremendous racial hostility to non-white peoples.) My own argument here is that the self-assertion of the Jamaican blacks and their insistence on shaping their historical condition were key not just to the vitriolic racism of those like Carlyle, Dickens and Ruskin, who counted themselves supporters of Eyre and were open about the dangers of black agency; they also put pressure on those liberals and radicals who came together to hold the governor accountable, making for the emergence of more racially inclusive and egalitarian conceptions of rights. If John Stuart Mill's leadership of the Jamaica Committee was impelled by an 'imagined community [which] was one of potential equality', it is necessary to acknowledge the role of the Jamaica rebels in pushing open the racial and geopolitical borders of that community.[16] Here, as elsewhere, agitation and insurgency from below served to radicalize liberalism in ways that need to be made more visible – or audible.

A recognition of black agency also inflected an incipient British labour internationalism which began to stress class 'sympathies' or solidarity over racial differences. The 'Jamaica affair' was one of the few Victorian crises of empire in which there is a record of expressed British working-class sympathies for victims of violent colonial repression. The parallels between domestic struggles and those of the Jamaican peasantry were not invoked simply out of generosity or a colour-blind egalitarianism, but in response to a self-assertion which made claims upon working-class solidarity. We know, for instance, that in early September 1866, by which time the Royal Commission had reported back very fully on events leading up to the rebellion, Eyre was burned in effigy on Clerkenwell Green.[17] Funerary decorations used in some condemnatory working-class protest meetings hailed Gordon's death as that of a martyr. As the controversy over Eyre's conduct heated up, the question of according parity to the struggles of both the white working classes and the black peasantry itself became a flashpoint, Dickens complaining in a letter to a friend: 'So we are badgered about New Zealanders, and Hottentots, as if they were identical with men in clean shirts at Camberwell, and were to be bound by pen and ink accordingly.'[18] Others, however – labour leaders and trade unionists – called for common cause to be made, not least because the Tories could do to the English working classes what they had done to Jamaicans. Indeed, the question of who had the right to be accorded 'sympathy' was central to the arguments for and against Eyre's actions. But it is misleading to view this

simply as an exercise in the expression of existing political dispositions; it was, at least partly, a dialogical response to the claims put
forward by rebellion. In the context of the Hyde Park riots of 1866
and the Habeas Corpus Acts in Ireland, 'political reformers did not
take long to see similarities between the Jamaican episode and their
own struggle for parliamentary reform', Douglas Lorimer rightly
observes, though insisting that these 'simply reconfirmed existing
beliefs'.[19] Such an assessment overlooks the ideological and rhetorical tensions that became evident in progressive engagements with the
moment and afterlife of the Morant Bay rebellion. If, as Catherine
Hall suggests, the Eyre debate 'marked a moment when two different
conceptions of "us", constructed through two different notions of
"them", were publicly contested', it is worth examining how it was
black insurgency that made space for the construction of a radical
'us' that crossed both racial lines and the boundary between colony
and metropole. This was less about the 'potential of Jamaican blacks'
to become like a transnational 'us' through a civilizing process, but
rather the active forging of 'us' out of a fellowship of ongoing struggle.[20] In what follows, I first explore the content of the uprising; then
the role played by Gordon, and his death, as a vehicle for controversy;
and, finally, the responses of British liberal reformers and working-
class radicals to the claims made by the Jamaican insurgency.

A Most Serious Insurrection

John Edward Eyre had been first lieutenant governor then governor
of Jamaica for about three years when he faced the uprising that
would eventually result in his immense notoriety. Though it has now
receded from the popular memory in Britain, the general outline
of the story is a familiar one to scholars of British imperial history.
On 11 October 1865, an organized procession of several hundred
black men and women entered the town of Morant Bay, converging
from different roads leading into town. They were blowing shells
and horns or beating drums, and many were armed with sticks
and cutlasses. While their destination was the town courthouse, en
route they stopped at the police station where, by all accounts, they
beat up at least one policeman before divesting the building of its

weapons (though, as it turned out, the guns were missing parts and there was no ammunition to be had).[21] When the crowds reached the town square, they were addressed by the Baron von Ketelhodt, the 'custos' or chief magistrate of the parish of St-Thomas-in-the-East in which Morant Bay was located. In front of him stood a line of 'volunteers' from the island's militia, which had been summoned as a precaution. Ketelhodt asked those gathered not to come into the square and, when they proceeded to do so, read out the Riot Act. The crowd's response was to fling stones at the militia, at which point the latter began firing, killing several. Instead of backing down, many of those present then rushed the militia. Outnumbered, the volunteers retreated into the courthouse to join the custos and other officials. Ignoring the truce flags, the insurgent crowd then set fire to the court-house.[22] As the custos and other officials came running out, some of them, including Ketelhodt, were set upon and killed.[23] Some accounts suggest that the latter's fingers were deliberately cut, with one person 'observing that they would write no more lies to the Queen'.[24] After setting another building on fire and releasing some fifty prisoners from the district gaol, the crowd left the area.[25] By most accounts, the protesters retreated to a Native Baptist chapel run by their leader, Paul Bogle, in the settlement of Stony Gut, and spent some time in prayer.

The unrest spread to a handful of settlements and sugar plantations in the parish of St-Thomas-in-the-East the following day as crowds entered them, plundering some stores and houses. One threatening chant hinted that that the area would be cleansed of 'buckras', or whites:

> Buckras' blood we want
> Buckras' blood we'll have
> Buckras' blood we are going for
> Till there's no more to have.[26]

Despite some pillaging and taking of prisoners, there was in fact only one killing – that of the attorney of the Amity Hall Estate plantation, Augustus Hire, who had been directly involved in a conflict with some of the rebels over land tenure. As official reports would later take the trouble to note, no white women or children were harmed;

some had been taken to safety by loyal black servants. By the next day, Governor Eyre had sent troops to regain control of the area, and within three days the outbreak had been completely suppressed, the troops apparently meeting with little resistance. Martial law was nevertheless declared in the whole county of Surrey excepting the town of Kingston, which was the seat of government. Over the next several days, as troops rampaged through the eastern portion of the island, hundreds of actual and presumed rebels were summarily shot, while others were executed after cursory military trials. Additionally, over 600 men and women, many of whom had nothing to do with the uprising, were subjected to brutal floggings, and some thousand dwellings were burned to the ground in what would later be described by a Royal Commission of Inquiry as a 'wanton and cruel' manner.[27] Some military officers would write back to friends and colleagues in England describing the killings and floggings with a 'levity' deprecated by the Royal Commissioners.[28] Meanwhile, in Kingston, after hearing that a warrant for his arrest had been issued, George William Gordon, who had been unwell, voluntarily turned himself in to the governor. Eyre promptly loaded him on board the naval sloop *Wolverine*, and personally conveyed him to Morant Bay to face a military trial. This would turn out to be a disastrous misstep on Eyre's part. After a trial that

lasted barely a few hours, Gordon was hanged after having been deemed – according to Major General O'Connor who presided over the clearly flimsy proceedings – 'to have been one of the principal instigators of the people to rebellion, and the primary cause of the miserable massacre of Europeans and native inhabitants at Morant'.[29] The creak of that scaffold would resonate in England for the next three years.

When news of the uprising reached England in early

George William Gordon (1820–65)

November, there was immediate consternation: memories of 1857 were still fresh in the public mind, and familiar racial anxieties were swiftly rekindled as snippets of news about atrocities against whites came off the ships arriving from the Caribbean. *The Times* reprinted a bulletin from Major General O'Connor claiming the rebels' plan was 'to murder all of the white and coloured men first, then the children, and to keep the women as servants and for their own pleasure'.[30] As the week went by, however, more reassuring news indicated that the situation was in fact under control, and that the white community of Jamaica was now safe.[31] Speculation about the causes of the rebellion began, with some fingers pointed at Baptist missionaries for 'authoring' discontent, and others at colonial officials and the planters of Jamaica for poor governance and deteriorating social conditions. By the time Governor Eyre's first official dispatch, dated 20 October, arrived in London on 16 November 1865, news had already started circulating about the questionable manner in which the uprising had been put down. The dispatch itself would set off a flurry of sceptical responses, inaugurating the 'Governor Eyre' or 'Jamaica' affair. Opening with news of the 'great loss of life and destruction of property' entailed by what it termed a 'most serious and alarming insurrection of the negro population', Eyre took self-regarding cognizance of his own 'promptitude and vigour of action' in suppressing the uprising.[32] His swift imposition of martial law and dispatch of troops to the troubled region, he asserted, had spared the mother country the loss of Jamaica, the alternative to which might have been an 'almost interminable war and an unknown expense' to keep the colony.[33] Instead, those responsible had been brought swiftly to military courts and executed after trial to prevent the outbreak spreading further. While outlining troop movements and suppression measures in a matter-of-fact tone, Eyre's dispatch is unable to resist a touch of post-1857 sensationalism pertaining to what he describes as black atrocities against whites: a victim who 'is said to have had his tongue cut out whilst still alive' as attempts were made to skin him; another who was set on fire; and still more who 'are said to have had their eyes scooped out' as 'heads were cleft open, and the brains taken out' (these were later shown to be unsubstantiated rumours). Indeed, Eyre pointed out cannily that 'the whole outrage could only be paralleled by the atrocities of the Indian mutiny', before going on to add that, 'as usual', the women 'were even more brutal and barbarous than the men'.[34]

It is only towards the end of his dispatch, however, that Eyre finally reveals his hand. As he toured the affected region in the days following the outbreak, he writes, he had 'found everywhere the most unmistakable evidence that Mr George William Gordon, a coloured member of the House of Assembly, had not only been mixed up in the matter, but was himself, through his own misrepresentations and seditious language addressed to the ignorant black people, the chief cause and origin of the whole rebellion'.[35] After briefly outlining what he identifies as additional provocateurs and provocations responsible for the uprising – primarily a letter by the Baptist missionary Edward Underhill that, earlier that year, had detailed the multifarious distresses suffered by the majority of islanders – Eyre somewhat defensively alludes to the 'just severity' of the measures that had been exercised under his personal approval and instruction.[36] Then, in a terse postscript dated 23 October at the bottom of the letter, Eyre finally informs the colonial secretary that Gordon 'has been tried by court-martial at Morant Bay, and sentenced to be hung' that morning.[37]

An outbreak of some seriousness contained by proportionately serious measures: Eyre's dispatch unfolded a story that had been told many times before. As the activist lawyer Frederic Harrison would note sardonically, 'the oft-recurring tale of insurrection' was a familiar one,

> a tale of wonderful sameness – one unbroken weary round of horror. A riot; much agitation; a good deal of plunder; a little bloodshed: then an ominous pause. Soon an organized reign of terror by the planters, martial-law, burnings, floggings, torturings, and indiscriminate massacre of an unresisting and cowering people, protracted for months, until the very executioners become exhausted. Afterwards a murmur of indignation at home, defiance from the planter interest, a craven Government, and public apathy.[38]

The Colonial Office published Eyre's unmistakably defensive dispatch in short order, three days after it arrived, on 19 November 1865, and it was carried by the country's main newspapers, with unhappy consequences for the colonial governor. From the early perception that he had done an admirable job in so swiftly quelling a catastrophic uprising against colonial rule, the tide now turned to concern that Eyre might have presided over a brutally disproportionate response to a small, localized insurrection. As newspapers began to carry other letters and reports, it became apparent that there were many questions to be asked of Eyre and his officials in Jamaica. Why had suppression of the uprising necessitated the gruesome deeds, including the vicious flogging and shootings-on-sight of which some military officers were boasting in letters? Why was martial law imposed for so many days after the insurrection had been put down? Had the brief military trials been just and based on clear evidence of complicity? Why had Gordon – now revealed to be a political opponent of Eyre and other legislators – been swiftly transported from Kingston, where civil law prevailed, to Morant Bay for military trial and execution? By the beginning of November, in just two weeks, as one historian puts it, 'the Jamaica affair had been transformed from a narrative about the salvation of Jamaican colonists into a narrative about the destruction of the English constitution'.[39] As various representations criticizing Eyre's actions were made to the Colonial Office and to Downing Street, with British antislavery activists leading the charge, the government announced the formation of the Jamaica Royal Commission to investigate what had happened in Morant Bay.[40] On 19 December 1865, the newly constituted Jamaica Committee – which included members of various existing antislavery advocacy organizations, including Exeter Hall – also met for the first time.[41] A number of luminaries agreed that, pending further investigation, Eyre could face prosecution. They included the politician John Bright, the philosopher and politician J. S. Mill, the academic Goldwin Smith, the Positivist Frederic Harrison, and the scientists Charles Darwin, Thomas Huxley, and Herbert Spencer ('all the leading evolutionists ... besides others less known', as the last would note).[42] It was around this attempt to hold Eyre to account that a bitter controversy would unfold over the next several months, leading the Tory *Saturday Review* to complain that every dinner party and tea party was 'worried and wearied' by arguments as to the 'brutal inferiority or the angelic superiority of the sons of Ham'.[43] The culture wars brewing from the 1838 Emancipation onwards had finally come to a head.

In her influential work on the Eyre controversy, Catherine Hall has suggested that slave emancipation itself provoked a hardening in the typologies of racial difference, inasmuch as it 'raised the spectre of black peoples as free and equal'.[44] In fact, the Morant Bay uprising manifested the feared *reality* of subjects of the British Empire willing to struggle – just as their slave forebears had rebelled – for rights, justice and opportunities beyond the nominal freedom which was bestowed on them.[45] It is this embodied reality – of what the *Spectator* magazine correctly described then as 'the demand of negroes for equal consideration with Irishmen, Scotchmen, and Englishmen' – that underpins much of the British response to the Morant Bay uprising, and shapes the ideological fault line that became visible in its wake.[46] It elicited a range of reactions, all of them to do in one way or another with the implications – for Britain and the colonies – of realized black freedom. The presence of colonies, writes Linda Colley, made inescapable the question of whether colonial subjects, 'those millions of men and women who were manifestly not British, but who had been brought under British rule by armed force ... have any claim on those vague but valuable freedoms so many Britons considered to be peculiarly their own'.[47] What if the Morant Bay rebellion also pointed to a *clash of freedoms* – one in which, rather than be forced to concede ground to a wholly different conception of political economy where workers had considerably more control over what to do with their labour power, it might be wiser to concede, in response to a claim, certain limited shared rights precisely as joint 'British subjects'? 'The case of Governor Eyre', as Bernard Semmel observes, 'was perhaps the first in which it might be said that the realities of a heavy-handed imperial rule were confronted by the growing acceptance of democracy in the homeland'.[48] That confrontation, however, was itself facilitated by the voices of G. W. Gordon – whose language had been so central to the charges against him – and those his judicial execution had brought to metropolitan attention.

'A sanctimonious bearing and a brown skin'

> *Wild, east and west, he roams and raves,*
> *Against the Church and State,*
> *Seeking to idolize the small,*
> *And demonize the great.*
>
> W. Hosack, describing G. W. Gordon[49]

In the late autumn of 1865, as arguments began to rage (again) over whether 'strong white government' was the only way to control the black man, or whether Britain had been dishonoured by the violation of the rule of law, from beyond the grave came the sobering voice of George William Gordon, whose last letter to his wife, written on the morning of his death, was published by British newspapers on 1 December 1865.[50] In the letter, which was later distributed by antislavery activists and cited in a great deal of writing around the incident, Gordon's tone was calm but disconcertingly firm:

> My beloved Wife – General Nelson has just been kind enough to inform me that the court-martial on Saturday last has ordered me to be hung, and that the sentence is to be executed in an hour hence; so that I shall be gone from this world of sin and sorrow.
>
> I regret that my worldly affairs are so deranged; but now it cannot be helped. I do not deserve this sentence, for I never advised or took part in any insurrection. All I ever did was to recommend the people who complained to seek redress in a legitimate way; and if in this I erred, or have been misrepresented, I do not think I deserve the extreme sentence. It is, however, the will of my Heavenly Father that I should thus suffer in obeying his command to relieve the poor and needy, and to protect, as far as I was able, the oppressed. And glory be to his name; and I thank him that I suffer in such a cause.[51]

For all that it is written by a 'truly devoted and now nearly dying husband' who accepts his fate with faithful calm, Gordon's last letter is also unflinching, indeed defiant, in naming the injustices he has been subject to. The judges appear to have been against him from the outset, he notes, even determined to have him 'sacrificed'.[52] He had hoped that the governor would give him a fair trial, but witnesses had changed their testimony, judges retaining the version that was to his disadvantage. The 'rigid manner of the court' meant that he had been silenced and could not 'get in all the explanation I intended'.[53] What he is very clear about is that neither his wife nor other members of his family should be ashamed of his death: 'I have fought a good fight, I have kept the faith.'[54]

It is tempting to suggest that Gordon became the focus of moral outrage and anti-Eyre sentiment in England because he was essentially regarded as an almost white Christian English gentleman. This, however, is to overlook not only the extent to which the Jamaican politician was explicitly racialized as an ungrateful 'incendiary mulatto', but also his open espousal of the interests of the black poor.[55] Gordon also practised a form of Christianity – Native Baptism – that was wholly connected with black life and African influences, a fact used against him politically. As Abigail Bakan has noted, the 'political leadership of the producing classes was associated with self-styled Baptist preaching'.[56] While it is certainly true that Gordon exuded a certain establishmentarian respectability – he was a man of property who was also educated and articulate – it would have taken a degree of wilful evasion for his supporters in England to overlook both his close connections to the black peasantry and his consistently antagonistic relationship to the white planter establishment. Underhill, for instance, describes Gordon as 'a staunch and unfailing advocate of the interests of the negro, to which race, by his birth he was allied'.[57] One British politician described Gordon as possessed of the 'fanatical earnestness of the field-preacher', likely referring both to his religious observances and his political style.[58] While Gordon undoubtedly used a politician's calculus in setting up a large support base among the black peasantry, it seems clear that he was also genuinely 'willing to confront the wrong-doings of men who hold a position of public and important trust', and that this earned him great malice from his foes.[59] The *Spectator* clearly grasped the importance of Gordon's connections to Jamaican blacks, as it criticized Eyre's acquittal in a private prosecution brought by the Jamaica Committee:

> We remark that Mr Justice Blackburn uses the phrase, 'general belief in the colony' – which he says was all against Mr Gordon – as synonymous with general belief *amongst the whites* of the colony … That Mr Gordon had plenty of warm friends who thoroughly disbelieved in his guilt amongst the mulatto and native population, and who were utterly aghast at the violent measure taken, no one disputes.[60]

It is likely that Gordon, in fact, posed something of a problem for detractors and admirers alike, since he was at once recognizable as someone 'rather eccentric in his views and notions of the people's rights', a familiar prototype in mid-Victorian Britain, but also insistently different by virtue of his own skin colour.[61] His insistence on what he called 'the stern obligations of a sense of justice and common humanity' would have struck a chord with English liberals; but they were rather more used to calling for the benevolent deployment of humanitarianism towards the 'weaker races' than having the claims of common humanity articulated as a *demand*.[62] In the face of inhuman treatment and lack of redress, Gordon apparently agreed that 'the people would be quite right to break out into open rebellion. If an illegality is permitted in the Governor, an illegality may be permitted on the part of the people.'[63] Described by fellow assemblymen as habitually thwarting their goals, Gordon was 'a sort of constitutional Opposition in himself', speaking up persistently and urging his constituents to do the same, and insist to their employers on their rights as waged labourers.[64] Testimony before the Royal Commission described his 'language and deportment' as 'anything but what it ought to have been'; his personality was obdurate – he refused to leave the vestry even after he was stripped of his position as a churchwarden and physically lifted in his chair out of the room.[65] At the same time, he appears to have exhorted his Afro-Jamaican electors to self-improvement: 'Educate your children, and in time they will be able to take the leading posts in the country.'[66] In a letter to the colonial secretary shortly after Gordon's execution, Eyre claimed that a few educated persons were stirring up the ignorant and illiterate: at meetings 'language of the most exciting and seditious kind was constantly used, and the people told plainly to right themselves, to be up and doing, to put their shoulders to the wheel, to do as the Haytiens had done, and other similar advice'.[67] He was referring to Underhill and other Baptists, but clearly also to Gordon and his allies.[68] Whether or not Gordon could be held 'morally guilty and legally innocent', as one of Eyre's later biographers had it, he certainly minced no words, and was clearly aware of rebellious sentiments fermenting among Afro-Jamaicans.[69] In Jamaica, Gordon was both disliked and feared by white politicians, including Eyre, who – referring partly to Gordon's ownership of the newspapers the *Watchman and Jamaica Free Press* and the *Sentinel* – complained to the Colonial Office that the newspapers were mostly owned by 'either Jews or coloured persons – classes that have been generally for the last two years in violent antagonism to me from one cause or another'.[70]

It was the black vote in a restricted franchise that, in 1863, saw Gordon elected to the Assembly; his political agent was Paul Bogle, a prominent figure in the uprising to come. Gordon also established his own 'Tabernacle' as a Native Baptist preacher. 'That he was an agitator, I will not dispute; that his agitation was invariably measured and prudent I may not affirm', wrote one of his white supporters.[71] It is inadequate to claim, as a sympathetic British politician did, that Gordon simply represented the best of representative politics within an English constitutional system, a politician who 'out of his very restlessness and troublesomeness often does good ... representing the check of perpetual opposition'.[72] But it is very likely that 'his employment of the usages of British political agitation in so heated an atmosphere, probably contributed to store up combustible elements'.[73] Indeed, he seemed fully aware both of the level of discontent on the island and of his own power to harness it, observing frankly to one white interlocutor: 'If I wanted a rebellion I could have had one long ago. I have been asked several times to head a rebellion, but there is no fear of that.'[74] At the same time, he believed that a popular 'great movement' was afoot and that, unless changes were secured, 'in six months there will be a revolution in this country' – apparently noting too, according to witness testimony that was taken by some to be damning: 'As I have always stood by the people, I will stand by them then.'[75] A report of a meeting chaired by Gordon indicates that he actually cautioned his constituents against terrorizing and abusing white residents, but urged them to 'speak out boldly as to the state of the Island' and claim their rights as British subjects.[76]

'It was never made clear to me how a rich brown man and a poor black man came to share the gallows at the Courthouse in 1865', remarked a commentator in the Jamaican newspaper the *Sunday Gleaner* in 2004, reflecting on Gordon's death.[77] The answer has to do with the milieu of political ferment, in which alliances between the coloured middle classes and the black peasantry were integral. Although Gordon knew how to put pressure on the constitutional system within which he operated, it is important to recognize that Jamaicans – who were, in any case, not fully enfranchised – did not merely '"learn" democratic political culture from British tutelage', but seized opportunities 'to push forward their own vision of freedom' in ways that were sometimes constitutional and, at others, possessed of 'more violent undercurrents'.[78] By the middle of 1865, in conditions of extreme poverty and deprivation, and the widespread resentment that resulted, there had emerged a remarkable political confluence: investigative missionaries from Britain like Underhill, Jamaican political agitators of colour (of whom Gordon was only the most literate and prominent), and, most crucially, a black population in dire straits willing to organize and take risks. Emancipation had both enabled this concatenation of factors and created a need to make *claims* on freedom as a state of being, and expand it into a more meaningful condition; in this sense, the end of formal slavery in 1838 had posed a beginning rather than an ethical and political end-point.

If Gordon is a key figure in thinking about the implications of the Morant Bay rebellion for dissent in Britain, it is not only because he himself was extraordinarily articulate, but also because the manner of his detention, unjust military trial and subsequent execution excavated a channel through which voices other than those of English missionaries, planters and colonial administrators could be heard back in the imperial homeland. The Reverend Henry Clarke, an Anglican rector in Jamaica who wrote to the Anti-Slavery Society, noted of Gordon's power-in-death:

> G. W. Gordon is at this moment speaking more loudly, more persistently, more effectively for the people of Jamaica than ever he did in his life time, and the time is not far distant when amid the grateful tears of a free and prosperous people a glorious monument shall be erected over his grave inscribed to him as the self-sacrificing martyr whose blood sealed the Magna Carta of the black man's liberties.[79]

As in many other colonial contexts, our knowledge of what happened at Morant Bay comes largely from the written accounts and archived documents provided by British officials, travellers, missionaries and journalists. Embedded within these, however, are the copious communications of those Jamaicans involved in some way with the uprising, particularly those who attended the infamous 'Underhill meetings' called by Gordon and his allies, using the English missionary's critique of conditions in Jamaica as a basis for speaking up and organizing. These included, according to one disgruntled editorial in the *Colonial Standard and Jamaica Despatch*, 'the stump orator, the little agitator, the small speechifier [and] the disappointed scoundrel, the embryo cut-throat, the ambitious leader of illicit trainbands and secret associations'.[80] One of the organizational roles that Gordon had played successfully was the 'bridging of oppositional middle-class and black smallholder networks', and this meant that the archives contain a combination of formal registers and constitutional and 'gentlemanly' as well as more untutored and colloquial forms of speech.[81] These also reflected a range of oppositional activities which realized what Sheller calls 'peasant economic agency', from organized work stoppage and strikes to cooperative labour, self-help societies, collective landholding and credit associations.[82] It was precisely this level of organization and the concomitant 'spectre of ... increasing black control of the legislature' that had caused anxiety for Eyre and his supporters well before the Morant Bay episode:[83]

> The negroes were for the most part uneducated peasants, speaking in accents strange to the ear, often in a phraseology of their own, with vague conceptions of number and time, unaccustomed to defi-niteness or accuracy of speech, and in many cases still smarting under a sense of injuries sustained.[84]

The report of the Jamaica Royal Commission and the related papers laid before parliament, for instance, enable us to hear – as many Victorians would have – the voices of Gordon, his political allies like Paul Bogle and James McLaren, and many ordinary and poor Jamaican blacks.[85] Some are refracted – and undoubtedly distorted – by second-hand accounts, while others emerge through copies of anonymous letters and accounts of meetings and resolutions taken. They speak in varied registers and tones but are strikingly devoid of simple postures of suffering – the passive, imploring and benev-olent black figures that had become familiar to a British audience through abolitionist discourse. If the answer to the 'world-renowned' question 'Am I not a man and a brother?' was in some doubt, as one British newspaper argued, it was perhaps now being posed as a statement rather than a plea.[86] As illustrated in several threaten-ing letters to colonial officials collected and placed before the Royal

Commission, there was growing anger and a spirit of self-assertion
among the Jamaican peasantry:

> Your swords we do not care about. Your firearms we don't care
> about. It must be life or death between us before we should live
> in such a miserable life ... We are yours disobedient subjects [sic].
> (Anonymous, sent to the Custos of St Mary)

> We not to be dread of anything ... By the time you send for man-
> of-war and soldiers all you white fellows will be sent to a flight and
> all you who call yourself men in laws that will try to oppress us
> because we are poor. (Signed 'Thomas Killmany, and intend to kill
> many more', sent to Messrs J. B. Goffe & Co.)[87]

We can hear in this untutored speech growing awareness of both what
freedom from slavery has meant and what it has not yet achieved;
discontent at the limitations that still govern the lives of former
slaves and their descendants, 'disaffection' with a government that is
perceived to be not on their side and, increasingly, a sense that little
will change without some form of action and assertion undertaken
by those who feel themselves exploited. 'Remember that, "he only
is free whom the truth makes free"' exhorts the 'State of the Island'
placard that circulated in the wake of the 'Queen's Advice': 'You are
no longer slaves but free men.'[88] Freedom – and this is an insight
repeated in a variety of ways – will have to be fleshed out and given
meaning through some form of action by the 'freed': 'We advise you
to be up and doing; and to maintain your cause; you must be united
in your efforts.'[89] As Underhill himself recollected: 'An opportunity
had now come for the despised negro to give utterance to his complaints. The oppressed and down-trodden people were not without
able expounders of their rights, men risen from their own ranks'.[90]

Many of these expounders 'were able public speakers, and could
express themselves in forcible Saxon speech'.[91] Immediately prior to
the outbreak, Bogle and nineteen other black men had also sent an
articulate collective statement of their position to the governor:

> We, the petitioners of St Thomas-in-the-East, send to inform
> your Excellency of the mean advantages that has been taken of

us from time to time, and more especially this present time, when on Saturday, 7th of this month, an outrageous assault was committed upon us by the policemen of this parish, by order of the Justices, which occasion an outbreaking for which warrants have been issued against innocent person, of which we were compelled to resist. We, therefore, call upon your Excellency for protection, seeing we are Her Majesty's loyal subjects, which protection, if refused to will be compelled to put our shoulders to the wheel, as we have been imposed upon for a period of 27 years with due obeisance to the laws of our Queen and country, and we can no longer endure the same.[92]

While this missive has been read variously – as indicating, according to Eyre's critics, a willingness to follow a constitutional path, or, according to the Royal Commissioners, 'the character of a manifesto preparatory to and attempting to justify a recourse to violence' – what is really significant is its insistence that resistance in the face of governmental intransigence is not so much a right as a moral compulsion on the part of otherwise law-abiding subjects. The freed blacks who are signatories to this manifesto are, like many slave rebels before them, 'purposeful subjects aware of their own voices', clearly cognizant of and insightful about their political situation and the possible need for forceful action to remedy it if other avenues remain closed to them.[93] We know, for instance, that, in August 1865, Bogle had headed a delegation to take grievances to Eyre, only to be turned away.[94] The above address, sent to the governor on 10 October 1865, refers to having endured injustice but also makes clear that the time of endurance is over. Whether or not the Royal Commissioners were correct in suggesting that the primary purpose of the letter was to justify violence, they were certainly right in detecting a note of 'scarcely concealed defiance'.[95] This kind of knowing self-assertion – which even in its early stages manifested itself in 'impertinent' body language, 'insolent' back-chat and deliberate idling at work – could not ultimately be entirely ignored by debates and commentary in the imperial capital, though it could be either demonized as Carlyle's famous 'miserable mad seditions' or minimized by some missionaries as 'a proneness to petty quarrelling and a love of litigation'.[96]

Exactly two months before the riots outside the courthouse, on 11

August, a placard was posted on a cotton tree on the main road in Morant Bay. It was an exhortation:

People of St Thomas ye East, you have been ground down too long already. Shake off your sloth, and speak like *honourable* and free men at your meeting. Let not a crafty, jesuitical priesthood deceive you. Prepare for your duty. Remember the destitution in the midst of your families, and your forlorn condition. The Government have taxed you to defend your own rights against the enormities of an unscrupulous and oppressive foreigner. Mr Custos Ketelhodt, you feel this: it is no *wonder you do*. You have been dared in this provoking act, and it is sufficient to extinguish your long patience ... it is your duty to speak out, and to act too![97]

The language of the lengthy notice, titled 'State of the Island', is clearly erudite and sophisticated, and evidence indicates that Gordon, even if he was not its sole author, had contributed substantially to its formulation. This short extract reprises the themes that would be rehearsed both in private and public communications by Gordon and others: the fact of widespread poverty across the island, a flat tax that weighed disproportionately on the poor, and a judicial system which was seen, with good cause, to be skewed in favour of the white planters who also, scandalously enough, comprised the magistracy. Such causes for disaffection had already been elaborated in Underhill's letter.[98] But unlike the letter, which highlights suffering, the emphasis here is on the unavoidable *duty* of claiming freedom and working to give it meaning by being 'up and doing'.

The insistence of the Jamaican peasant petitioners on taking responsibility for their own futures is relevant to the contest over the meanings of Emancipation. Following the 'Underhill meetings', a petition or 'Memorial' signed by 108 persons was sent to the queen in April 1865 by the 'poor people of Jamaica and Parish of St Ann', laying out their grievances and asking for due redress.[99] The petition spoke of 'great want and distress for want of employment' and lack of land to cultivate to ameliorate this situation.[100] High prices and heavy taxes caused further impoverishment; many poor blacks had committed themselves to prison in consequence. If rendered some initial assistance – that is, if the queen would rent them land to work at a low rate – the petitioners would 'put our hands and heart to work, and cultivate coffee, corn, canes, cotton and tobacco, and other produce. We will form a company for that purpose'.[101] Where missionaries read the document as a cry of distress from a suffering people, it was treated by Eyre's government as a political demonstration. In fact, it had elements of both. Described later by the Jamaica Committee as an 'insult', the widely circulated reply from the Colonial Office and Cardwell, in the form of 'The Queen's Advice', would come as a huge blow to the petitioners, greatly increasing disaffection and laying the ground for the more radical steps that some of them would advocate and take. Implicitly upholding the white plantocracy's view of black labour as lazy and uncooperative, the letter informed the petitioners that the prosperity of Jamaica depended 'upon their working for wages, not uncertainly or capriciously, but steadily and continuously, at the times when their labour is wanted, and for so long as it is wanted'.[102] Put simply, the petitioners would not be assisted in their modest goal of farming their own small plots of land, but were patronizingly urged instead to become the reliable wage labourers sought by planters. By endorsing the planter view that the main problem affecting Jamaica was the lack of steady black plantation labour, this royal 'advice' refused to acknowledge the widespread desire among freed slaves and their descendants to control their own economic destiny through farming smallholdings rather than be shackled to low-wage labour on terms laid out by the planters.[103] What had emerged, therefore, was a stark ideological clash about what freedom meant. One view, touted by the planters and endorsed by the colonial government, insisted that freedom consisted of the 'option' of selling labour to a capitalist entity for prices determined by the latter. The other refused anything resembling the contractual and compulsory extraction of labour in favour of controlling the output of a smallholding. This disagreement paved the way for the events in Morant Bay on 11 October 1865.

The Uses of Freedom

What God Almighty make land for? You have plenty; we have none.
                                                    A Morant Bay peasant

The personal cultivation and ownership of land was fundamental
to the post-slavery Jamaican conception of freedom. Well before
1865, rumours had begun to circulate that, along with freedom, the
queen had bestowed lands upon ex-slaves to cultivate, linking 'the
idea of liberty of the person with liberty of the land', as the Royal
Commission would put it.[104] The owner of an uncultivated estate,
Wellwood Maxwell Anderson, testified before the Commission that
his tenants refused to pay ground rents, arguing 'that the Queen had
given them the place when she gave them freedom; and *freedom
would be of no use if they had not their lands and houses*'.[105]
Although Gordon himself became the subject of rumours in which
he says that peasants were entitled to get land or fight for it, such
claims appear to have emerged autonomously. As James C. Scott
notes, oppressed groups 'often read in rumors promises of their
imminent liberation'.[106] A plot of land, however small, 'symbolized freedom, personhood, and prestige among the descendants of
former slaves'.[107] The Royal Commission concluded that 'a principal
object of the disturbers of order was the obtaining of land free from
the payment of rent'.[108] The bone of contention was access to what
was known as the 'back lands' – lands that lay on the perimeters
of cultivated or plantation land which had fallen into disuse by its
tenants and owners. One witness's account of a September meeting
in Paul Bogel's chapel in Stony Gut illuminates matters clearly.
Addressing the meeting, McLaren, who would be one of the leaders
of the October uprising, explains 'why cause me hold this meeting',
given that, although his parents were slaves, he himself had been
born free:

> But now I am still a slave by working from days to days. I cannot
> get money to feed my family, and I working at Coley estate for
> 35 chains for 1s., and after five days' working I get 2s.6d. for my
> family. Is that able to sustain a house full of family? ... Well, the
> best we can do is to come together, and send in a petition to the
> Government; and if they will give up the outside land to *we*, we
> shall work with cane, and cotton, and coffee like the white. But
> the white people say we are lazy and won't work ... if the outside
> land was given up to them to work, they should pay the taxes to
> the Queen, and if the land was given up to them they did not want

anything from the white people, they would try to make their own living themselves.[109]

In former slave colonies, ownership or use of land at reasonable rent was more than an alternative means of sustenance; it was tied to a deeply felt resistance to working for plantation owners, owing not only to a clearly inadequate, indeed unviable, economic return, but also a suspicion that wage labour under those conditions was too close to, and might entail a return to, slavery. In the months leading up to Morant Bay, a popular rumour held that slavery was to be reinstated.[110] There was something of a panic about this, one clergyman maintained in his testimony: 'a settled belief gaining strength from the time it arose' which, to his mind, paved the way for potential rebellion. Importantly, the curate is firm in his insistence that the black peasantry are no more credulous 'than England or other places', taking seriously 'only such reports as that which peculiarly affect their own position, such as that of being made slaves'.[111]

Another element of the organized mobilizing that appears to have emerged independently of either Gordon or his 'seditious language' was a call to black unity by some agitators. The rhetoric of race and racial unity in Morant Bay was most apparent as a form of collective self-assertion, one underpinning a claim to land through a reversal of the existing racial hierarchy of ownership and use: 'Hurra! Buckra country for us.'[112] For the white propertied class of Jamaica and their supporters in Britain, the perceived refusal of freed blacks and their descendants to submit to the regimes of plantation labour in favour of tilling their own plots of land threw their self-serving idea of 'freedom' into crisis. The liberty of black Jamaicans to sell or withhold their labour power as they pleased was as much an economic problem as a political one. In this regard, an observation offered to the Royal Commission by a planter on his relations with the freed black peasantry is illuminating:

> I should be very glad if they would be dependent on my capital; but they are not, and that would be the great difficulty in Jamaica with regard to agriculture; the negroes are not like those in Barbadoes, they are not dependent upon estates for their livelihood ... their very independence is an evil.[113]

Another critic of the Morant Bay rebels, who describes himself as a 'A Thirty Years Resident', concedes that, at Emancipation, planters 'rather resembled madmen than reasonable beings; deprived of the unrequited labours of the slaves, their great object seemed to be to assimilate [the slaves'] freedom as nearly as possible to slavery'.[114] This included concerted action to keep wages as low as possible and charge enormous rents for cottages and provision grounds.

Their unacceptable resistance to a regime of wage labour within the plantation economy is a salient theme in Victorian broadsides against ex-slaves and their insurgent descendants. It is not so much the discursive spectre of an existentially free black human being that occasions indignation here as the material refusal of Jamaican peasants to comply with the economic imperatives of mercantile capitalism. The *Times* editorial of 13 November 1865, just after news of the Jamaica insurrection came in, mulls over what it regards as the colonial failure to 'eradicate the original savageness of the African blood' by turning slaves into wage labourers: 'The negro has been able to live with little or no work, he has been able to get a patch of land readily, and to subsist by a wretched cultivation of it.'[115] Necessitating the importation of coolies, or indentured labour, from India and China to do the plantation work instead of them, black Jamaicans are uncivilized to the precise extent that they refuse to accede to the demands of capitalism or 'the laws of industry and labour, which naturally regulate all well-managed communities', as one critic of Emancipation puts it.[116] In frustrating the demands of political economy, the emancipated black is 'freer than ... the white man'[117] – and so prosperous that 'no peasant in England, Scotland, France, or Belgium could compete with him in his command of the comforts of life'.[118] In his later, more measured reflections on the matter, Charles Roundell, who had acted as secretary to the Jamaica Royal Commission, would ask in a hopeful vein whether the perceived 'failure' of Emancipation might not be 'an economical question of capital and labour, supply and demand, which, like all economical questions, is capable of being grappled with, of being understood, and successfully surmounted'.[119] The right restrictions on labour and employers alike could ensure a controlled liberty that would result in more plentifully supplied capital, a consistent labour supply and better returns.

For supporters of Eyre, the resistance to the claims of political economy, which culminated in the Morant Bay violence, could easily have led to a repeat of the nightmare of the Haitian Revolution – an obsessive preoccupation for many critics of Emancipation. Gordon was repeatedly accused by planters of exhorting his electorate to 'do as they do in Hayti'; he was equally insistent that he had never thought of it. 'The vicinity of Hayti and its barbaric independence', *The Times* editorial of 20 November 1865 pronounces, almost triumphantly, 'have fostered [the black man's] dreams of vengeance and his dreams of aggrandizement ... He dreams of the glorious island in which he lives being owned in perpetuity by himself and his posterity.'[120] That version of freedom, to be avoided at all costs, is 'the erection of a semi-barbarian Sovereignty in the West Indies', along the lines of Haiti.[121] Freedom, in other words, was divisible into the putative universalism of capitalist political economic imperatives and the unacceptable particularism of refusing them. The real issue at stake for those who denounced the Jamaica rebels emerges more explicitly in a well-known polemic titled 'The Negro in Jamaica', given before the Anthropological Society of London in 1866. In it Commander Bedford Pim would state the case for 'moderate control' in baldly honest political-economic terms:

> The negro in a state of freedom continues powerless to advance himself in civilisation, and he is most improvable when under moderate control. It is no longer expedient to make a slave of him; he has performed his part in the world's history in that capacity ... He has no right, however, and civilized man has no right to allow him, to pass his existence without in any way contributing to the advancement of mankind.[122]

It is not until the ex-slave has been fully incorporated into this economic regime, having proved his title, that 'he can be admitted into the fellowship' of the free, and therefore the fully human. In the ensuing discussion, many of Pim's audience would repeat a familiar grouse: that the Afro-Jamaican limited 'his husbandry to the satisfaction of his daily wants', and that as a group they refused to 'apply their knowledge for their own gain in life or for the benefit of their employers'.[123] As the writer J. A. Froude, a friend of Charles

Kingsley's, would put it, looking back on the events of 1865 some two decades later, if self-government of any kind was to be granted in the West Indies, it would be impossible to take black allegiance for granted, or to remain confident 'that the liberties which we concede will not be used for purposes which we are unable to tolerate'.[124]

Reframing Rebellion: The Jamaica Committee and the Problem of Freedom

What purposes should underlie liberty, and who should have it? These were indeed the questions at the heart of the disagreement over Eyre's actions, as English intellectuals broke ranks and formed two opposing committees to determine the governor's future after he was recalled from Jamaica in 1866. Once, in August 1866, it became clear that the Jamaica Committee would pursue a private prosecution of Eyre, as the government had declined to charge him, an organization to champion Eyre's cause came into being. The Eyre Defence and Aid Fund felt it to be 'a solemn public duty on the part of all those who believe that Governor Eyre quelled the insurrection in Jamaica, and saved the island, to come forward and boldly proclaim such to be their opinion'.[125] Its constituent members included many well-known writers and intellectuals, such as John Ruskin and Thomas Carlyle, as well as John Tyndall and Charles Kingsley; it would receive support from the likes of Charles Dickens, Alfred Lord Tennyson and, later on, J. A. Froude. Equally revealing are the self-descriptions given by those who anonymously sent subscriptions to the fund; they include, among others: 'One whose sister was massacred at Cawnpore', 'One who perceives the necessity of firmness and vigour in those in authority', 'A lady who has suffered by insurrection', 'A soldier who has not forgotten Cawnpore', 'A lady who was in India during the Mutiny' and 'A lady ashamed of her country's ingratitude'.[126] For Eyre's defenders, the rebellious blacks whom he had contained were an imminent threat, above all, to the political economy of empire. In a letter to the Jamaica Committee, some of whose members he was friendly with, the scientist John Tyndall lambasted 'a tendency on your part to tone down the crimes of the negro and to bring his punishments into relief'.[127] Objecting to the Committee's downgrading of the Morant Bay uprising to a mere 'local riot', Tyndall pointed to 'the spirit of rebellion' born of widespread disaffection that could only have been quelled, as Eyre had done, by 'making the name, power, and determination of England terrible throughout the island'.[128] Like many others, Tyndall saw this insurgent flame as originating from and nourished by the historical and spatial proximity of Haiti's success in overthrowing the power of France. Gordon, he said, had to be read as, at the very least, a 'taproot' for insurgency, rather than the bland constitutionalist that the Jamaica Committee had made him out to be.[129] Moreover, attempts to universalize liberty and identify black and white resistance were illegitimate: 'We do not hold an Englishman and a Jamaica negro to be convertible terms, nor do we think that the cause of human liberty will be promoted by any attempt to make them so.'[130] Also writing a letter on the topic, to the *Daily Telegraph*, was John Ruskin, an active member of the Eyre Defence Fund, noting that the difference between him and the Jamaica Committee was not just that he was for lordship and they for liberty, but that he believed 'that white emancipation not only ought to precede, but must by law of all fate precede, black emancipation'.[131] In a lecture on 'Liberty', also given in 1865, Ruskin uses a tellingly vivid metaphor of the dangers of excessive freedom illustrated by the housefly, 'free in the air, free in the chamber – a black incarnation of caprice – wandering, investigating, flitting, flirting, feasting at his will, with rich variety ... what freedom is like his?'[132] Carlyle, who drafted a Petition from the Eyre Defence Fund to the House of Commons, spoke similarly of the Morant Bay incidents as a 'frightful and immeasurable kindling of black unutterabilities' – a telling phrase, seeking to render the voices of black rebellion literally unspeakable.[133] Famously, of course, Carlyle also described the Jamaica Committee's observations as less than human, relegating them to the same level of speech as those they defended, 'nothing but a group or knot of rabid Nigger-Philanthropists, barking furiously in the gutter, and threatening one's Reform Bill with loss of certain friends and votes'.[134]

For the Jamaica Committee, which included no fewer than nineteen members of parliament headed by John Bright, the questionable deployment of martial law by Eyre raised the possibility of repression coming home to roost: 'What is done in a colony to-day may be done in Ireland to-morrow, and in England hereafter', as Fredric Harrison had it.[135] 'Men became members of that committee who had never taken part in public agitation of any kind before', wrote the MP Justin McCarthy many years later.[136] The 'members of the Jamaica Committee', Bernard Semmel averred, were 'men of the new middle classes, sober, respectable, pious and serious'.[137] For those who came to Eyre's defence – largely 'King's men', in Ruskin's terms – the Jamaica Committee represented what would today be called 'political correctness gone mad', or as Dickens would put it, a 'platform-sympathy with the black – or the native, or the devil – afar off, and platform indifference to our countrymen at enormous odds in the midst of bloodshed and savagery'.[138] Ironically, of the two parties, it is those who backed Eyre who accorded to the Jamaica rebels, albeit with outrage, the status of full-fledged black insurgents whose actions and views might, in the long run, portend full independence from white rule, along Haitian lines. The Jamaica Committee's deliberations, in contrast, stressed the right to constitutional forms of agitation. Though they denied that events at Morant Bay amounted to outright rebellion, the right of those in British territories to *agitate* – 'as men must ever be allowed to do in every free country' – was nonetheless central to the case the committee made against Eyre.[139] Their principal goal, insisted these campaigners – who came to include the veteran antislavery figures from Exeter Hall, Louis Chamerovzow, Charles Buxton MP, and Frederick Chesson – was constitutional: the absolute 'defence of those legal and chartered rights which protect the lives and liberties of all'.[140] The language of its public documents and deliberations was therefore self-consciously 'moderate' and, perhaps also reflecting its composition, carefully parliamentary. As Mill, who had spent a career with the East India Company, and had just been elected to parliament, in July 1865, put it: 'There was much more at stake than only justice to the Negroes, imperative as was that consideration. The question was, whether the British dependencies, and eventually perhaps Great Britain itself, were to be under the government of law, or of military license.'[141] Events in Morant Bay indicated, the Jamaica Committee argued, rioting rather than outright rebellion, so that the imposition of martial law was not only legally questionable but also strategically unnecessary. Even if 'resistance did occur in the riots', they argued, there was, nevertheless, no 'rebellion', in the sense not only of 'forcible resistance to lawful authority, but a resistance that is concerted, and, to some extent at least, organized'.[142]

There was undoubtedly a certain doubleness to the Jamaica Committee's formal position, which at once insisted on the right of colonial subjects of the Crown to resist, as domestic subjects could, and attempted to mitigate the extent of that resistance as it had unfolded in Morant Bay. The rebellion in Jamaica was, in other words, recast by the Jamaica Committee in terms that would be familiar to British constitutionalists and advocates of gradual change, annexed to the rhetoric of liberal constitutionalism. In its advocacy of Gordon as a semi-heroic and peaceable figure, the Committee insisted that any 'popular agitation as revealed in the Jamaica press was of a constitutional kind', deriving from a situation where 'a large portion of the people believed themselves to be under a system of government in which the interests of the many were sacrificed to the desires of the few'.[143] There was 'no evidence that revolutionary measures were contemplated'.[144] While reminding 'their fellow-citizens that hopeless wrong is the sure parent of rebellion, and that its best antidote is the hope of constitutional redress', the Committee also insisted that, in sending their representatives to Jamaica to investigate matters, they had 'no desire to abet resistance to lawful authority or to weaken the arm of the magistrate in preserving public order', and intended to 'lend no assistance or countenance to those persons who had suffered for real'.[145] Collating evidence and assessments into a series of pamphlets, the Committee believed that these showed not only

> the necessity for an official inquiry into all the circumstances of the so-called 'Rebellion' in Jamaica, and into the legality of the sanguinary measures of repression, but ... the need of a powerful organization to assist in the collection and examination of evidence, and to demand, on behalf of the British nation, the impartial application of the law in any well-authenticated cases of cruel excess of power.[146]

This doubleness has to do with the fact that, in significant ways, what the Jamaica Committee was also doing was channelling into more

parliamentary language the emergence of a more radical solidarity
with Jamaican resistance.

There was an important third force which, like Eyre's defenders,
chose to read events and actors in Jamaica as indeed constituting
a radical resistance to political economy; unlike the Eyre party, it
considered the resistance desirable. British working-class and labour
movement engagements with the Jamaica controversy were direct
and polemical in defending the right of Jamaican labourers to resist
an exploitative system with all their might. This third approach
manifested a process of recognition in which the voiced resistance
of the Jamaican peasant resonated with attempts to give voice to
working-class men in Britain through the franchise. Radical British
polemics on the Eyre controversy cautioned against seeing the violent
repression of resistance in Jamaica as singular, for what the Jamaican
rebels had exposed was a system of exploitation so red in tooth and
claw that it was unlikely to take any more kindly to being substantially challenged in the metropole than in the colony. Such a system
necessitated a resistance that would cut across the racial divisions of
empire. The popular *Reynolds Newspaper*, founded by novelist G.
W. M. Reynolds with a largely working-class circulation (350,000
by 1870), covered the Jamaica controversy extensively. One of its
regular columnists, writing under the pseudonym 'Northumbrian',
sounded the keynote for an oppositional approach at the outset,
reading dominant rhetoric – purveyed by the likes of *The Times*
– against the grain, and identifying points of commonality with
the rebels. 'Somehow or other', observed Northumbrian sardonically, 'British arms are always engaged in fighting Kaffirs, Maories,
Hindoos, or negroes. Now, this policy may be necessary, but certainly is not glorious.'[147] Race and racial discourse are engaged with
directly: 'Excesses and atrocities of the most fiendish kind have been
committed', announced an article in late November 1865 satirizing
the hysterical high notes of *The Times*'s coverage of the insurrection
as an attack on whites. 'The most lawless, malignant, and diabolical of these atrocities have been perpetrated, not by the blacks, but
by the whites ... men of British blood, who arrogate to themselves
an immeasurable and unapproachable superiority over the despised
African.'[148] Identifying similarities in the workings of power across
colonial contexts helped allies of the Morant Bay insurgents to make

the argument that what happened out in the Empire was likely to come home to roost by stages: 'Our rulers have not used the Jamaica negroes in a more unlawful manner than they have the Irish Fenians. The difference in the treatment of these two is one of *degree*, not of principle ... Let Englishmen think of these things; for, although Irishmen and negroes are the present victims, who knows who may be the next people exposed to the tender mercies of the Hobbs's, the Eyres, and the Wodehouses?'[149]

Reynolds was clearly drawing on sentiments expressed in working-class and other public meetings held to discuss the Jamaica business, lengthy accounts of which were also carried in the paper. A report of a meeting in Manchester notes that 600 signatures had been requisitioned to call it. 'A riot was a rising of the people against authority for the time being,' said one speaker, as a resolution introduced by T. B. Potter MP – who also edited the smaller-circulation trade union paper the *Bee-Hive* – invited listeners to make connections between violence against colonial subjects and repression at home.[150] Manchester too had faced an 'attack upon the people by the authorities [which] gave the signal for great changes in this country', he reminds his listeners, referring presumably to the Peterloo massacre of 1819.[151] The trouble taken to make these parallels and to urge audiences to see the historical resonances cannot be simply dismissed as discursive annexation, for a great deal of effort goes into identifying and illuminating points of connection. Similarly, Potter's insistence on Gordon's and his allies' right to be seen as Englishmen is clear-sighted in reframing national identity as a fellowship of common cause rather than a matter of racial essence: 'When one looked at the case of Mr Gordon, he (Mr Potter) confessed it made his blood run cold to think that an Englishman – for though coloured men these were Englishmen – (cheers) – our fellow-subjects, whose rights were our rights, as ours were theirs – (renewed cheers)' had been subjected to a court martial as the Jamaican civilian opposition politician had been.[152] The language is deliberately reciprocal, locating both parties in a mutually reinforcing relationship of struggle against a common enemy, rather than one 'bestowing' rights on another. Indeed, most of the writing on the controversy in *Reynolds Newspaper* is marked by a distinct lack of paternalism and contains strikingly few references to the 'inferiority' of other races. Speaking at the same meeting, Jacob

Bright, brother of the famous Liberal politician John, would apostrophize Gordon thus: 'And if there could be fifty such men, there might be a Government in Jamaica (applause).'[153]

From several articles and summaries of speeches at public meetings, it is clear that the recognition of common cause was, in fact, based on an informed engagement with the issues at stake, including the fact that the blacks of Jamaica had articulated their needs only to be denied redress. In its very first report on the insurrection, *Reynolds* was swift to note that the blacks of Jamaica laboured under very real injustices, and had cause to be 'dissatisfied' with the results of their applications for relief.[154] A later article observed that the whites of Jamaica had 'never yet reconciled themselves to the emancipation of the blacks', despite the hefty compensation paid out by the 'plundered and impoverished' working classes of Britain.[155] It is understandable, however, that the 'freedmen' (printed with scare quotes) might not have found wage labour on plantations a congenial prospect, and would wish to make their 'freedom' more real than the planters intended it to be:

When the negroes obtained their nominal freedom, they very naturally preferred to work for themselves. They desired to be their own masters ... But, because they have done this – because they declined to work for the white planters as slavishly and cheaply as when they were slaves – they have been denounced as lazy, sensual, and insolent creatures, unfit for freedom and incapable of sustained industry.[156]

The piece quotes extensively from various depositions, as well as the 'St Ann's Address', which it attributes to Gordon, offering a different reading from that articulated by the British authorities. 'Phrases deemed inflammatory and exaggerated' such as '"Naked people of St Ann's"! ... "Starving people of St Ann's!"' were, it argued, 'words descriptive of facts which are not less terrible than true'.[157] Any form of speaking out by Jamaicans came up against a pernicious interdict: 'If the negroes complain of this treatment, they are at once charged with rebellious and murderous designs.'[158] This suppression of voices found a direct parallel in Britain, noted the chair of another public meeting, held to protest the welcome banquet held for Eyre upon his return to a country where 'the working men could not make themselves heard in the House of Commons because unrepresented'. The 'only way left to them to show that they took an interest in the affairs of the nation was to hold public meetings'.[159]

The struggles of the Jamaican blacks and the violent repression they subsequently faced not only found expressions of identification or outrage back in Britain, but also offered opportunities for the practice of democracy. The meeting alluded to above took as its purpose not just expressions of solidarity with blacks struggling for their due, but also distancing the English working classes from the white ruling classes, for 'it behoved the people of England to demonstrate ... that they did not identify themselves with acts which had disgraced the British name'.[160] This reclaiming of nation was in stark and deliberate opposition to Charles Kingsley's bombastically imperialist and much-resented ruling-class encomiums to Eyre at his welcome banquet as an embodiment of 'the English spirit of good-nature, of temper, of the understanding of human beings, of knowing how to manage men ... that English spirit which had carried the Anglo-Saxon tongue round the world, and which had made us the fathers of the United States and the conquerors of India'.[161] If the Jamaica controversy had indeed set into motion a struggle over the very meanings of Britain/England, it was one to which the question of democracy and economic justice as posed by the Afro-Jamaicans was central. The expropriations of land and labour were, in fact, issues that resonated for both white and black working classes, as 'the chief end and object of all royal and aristocratic governments is to enslave the masses of mankind' – an insight from 'Northumbrian' that directly echoed Jamaican peasant views of wage labour on plantations as slavery in another form.[162] Gordon's death was deemed exemplary of the lengths to which the ruling classes would go to preserve this state of affairs. Wearing a black armband like the others, and standing on a wagon draped with a flag bearing the name 'G. W. Gordon' in white letters surrounded by wreaths, one speaker pronounced:

> George William Gordon ... was murdered without a trial, although the charges brought against him were inquired into by the foppish striplings of an odious and dangerous aristocracy. (Hisses) And, need he say that the same aristocracy would treat John Bright

– (loud cheers) – and Edmond Beales – (cheers) – in a similar manner to-morrow if they had the chance? (Cries of 'They would if they dare.')[163]

Another speaker would note that 'it had always happened that the aristocracy of England were opposed to the rights and liberties of the people'.[164] The common condition of exploitation, and not race, had to be the basis of kinship.

Even as these radical responses, and the distinctly more moderate line taken by the Jamaica Committee, differed in their approach to the question of how resistance should be undertaken, there are clear lines of connection between them. One can be traced through Edward Beesly, a Positivist like Harrison, and also a member of the Jamaica Committee. A student of Richard Congreve's at Oxford, a labour campaigner and close associate of Karl Marx in the run-up to the First International, Beesly, also a London university professor, became a familiar voice speaking and writing on the Eyre controversy. He was one of the few writing in the pages of *Reynolds* to maintain a racial hierarchy in discussing the Jamaicans: 'The treatment of uncivilized races by Englishmen is a subject that demands far more attention from workmen than it gets.'[165] Beesly's racial hierarchy finds a parallel in his delineation of a class order in which the working classes must be represented by educated middle-class men. For him, Gordon's death was not so much a story about the Jamaican poor as one of the disciplining of those more elevated individuals who spoke for the margins: 'Every one [*sic*] who makes himself … conspicuous by pointing out to the lower orders the political and social evils under which they suffer will do so at a terrible risk.'[166] Here too, however, Gordon is a cautionary tale for what might just as well happen in England with liberal leaders:

> Take care of Mr Bright or Mr Beales. They have both of them repeatedly used much stronger language than any that was proved against Gordon. If the reform struggle should become more embittered; if the Tories, by their insane management should bring about a riot, attended with loss of life … what will there be to prevent Mr Bright and Mr Beales from being treated as Mr Gordon was? The cases would be exactly parallel.[167]

Beesly shares with his radical working-class readers a developed sense of the implications for democratic agitation in Britain of allowing repression in the colonies to go unchallenged. Indeed, he suggests, the key bone of contention in Jamaica may also have an exact parallel:

> But political privilege is not the dearest possession of the upper classes. Touch their monopoly of the land and you will see their teeth. When Mr Bright said in Glasgow that half Scotland belonged to a dozen proprietors, and half England to a hundred and fifty, he put his finger on one of the most frightful blots on English civilization.[168]

There is no reason to assume, he points out, that the violence exercised against a different race in Jamaica will not be reprised at home should the same kinds of challenges to power – and land-ownership – be issued by white working people. To allow 'the Jamaica precedents to remain unchallenged' is to 'furnish our oligarchy with a weapon' that can be turned against white Britons.[169]

Beesly was writing this in a letter to *Reynolds*, as he puts it, because 'your journal is read by a very large number of workmen who never look at any other'. He himself was a more regular contributor to the *Bee-Hive*, the trade union journal for the 'industrial classes' which also covered the Morant Bay uprising extensively – though slightly differently from *Reynolds*, in that its emphasis was on the consequences of the repression for organized British working-class agitation against systemic exploitation. In the pages of the *Bee-Hive* on 25 November 1865, Beesly argued that the punishments inflicted on the Jamaicans were self-evidently severe, but that the real point was 'that they have been inflicted to maintain an abominable system which it behoves our working men here to do their best to tear up the roots'.[170] At stake were the relations between labour and a parasitical planter class, eager to sit on its hands doing nothing, 'a burden on the land', that prioritized profits at the cost of both wages and the public purse. Beesly is at his polemical best when, in a series of reversals, he attacks those in power, using the same terms Thomas Carlyle famously deployed when polemicizing against freed blacks as 'lazy': 'The emancipation of the blacks left all the land in the possession of the whites, a lazy, vicious, bankrupt class, filled with hatred for their late slaves; too proud to work, though not ashamed to beg in a genteel way'.[171] The charges of 'laziness', he observes, are also deployed at home against strikers. Beesly notes that, in response to demands for better wages from black workers, white Jamaican planters 'sent half round the world for shiploads of "Coolies" to do the work cheap – a trade which, if the truth be told, is not much better than the old slave-trade'.[172] He was, of course, referring to indentured labour. While Beesly famously distances himself from the black man as such – 'I protest I am no negro-worshipper' – and remains unshaken in his assumption of black inferiority, it is precisely this protestation that makes his call for solidarity and parity of rights worth examining.[173] Indeed, it is because he shares a wider liberal sense of racial hierar-chies that Beesly's call for 'vigorous and indignant' cross-racial and international solidarity is striking. His advice is that the trade unions draw up a petition to parliament which would make it clear that the petitioners as 'labourers look on the cause of the labourers in Jamaica as their own'. Thus, 'when the upper classes see how such injustice to labour, even in a distant colony, is resented by the working men of England, they will be careful how they trifle with similar interests at home'.[174] Comparing events in Morant Bay to the Hyde Park riots, he notes in another piece: 'In both instances wealth and respectability employed the executive apparatus to put down the lower orders.'[175]

Other articles in the *Bee-Hive*, however, did engage directly with the question of race. A regular columnist, 'Plain Dealer', would put it with absolute clarity: 'Yes, there are working-men in Jamaica. Though their skin is black, their hair woolly, their noses flat, and their lips thick, they are entitled to the same consideration and sympathy as working-men of fair complexion.'[176] For Plain Dealer, Morant Bay was a case of outright repression in response to legitimate agitation where, he would write a year later, 'agrarian discontent and political aspiration among the people of Jamaica were extinguished in their own blood and in that of good men who acknowledged to them that they had cause for complaint and did well to speak up for them-selves'.[177] Again, speech is the key issue, the writer observing that repression along the lines of what took place in Jamaica 'would be an excellent device ... for silencing the voice of the working men of England claiming the rights of industry, and soliciting a share in the constitutional franchise of their country'; they too could be 'hunted down or hanged up or shot as the negroes were'.[178] Race hierarchies are operative, but whiteness will not in itself protect English agitators. Sympathy for Eyre, he opined,

> may be attributable to the habit of setting a lower value upon the lives of black or coloured men than upon those of the white. But, while no such distinction is to be for an instant allowed, neither must we delude ourselves with the vain imagination, that it makes, in the minds of those who entertain it, the least difference in favour of the working men of England over the field negroes of Jamaica.[179]

Where Beesly relies on a certain abstraction to emphasize that the same system operates in both metropole and colony, which leaves agitating labour vulnerable across the board, Plain Dealer warns against allowing sympathy and solidarity to emerge solely on race lines: 'Those of our countrymen who, in any dispute between white and black, confine their fellow-feeling to that side where they find complexions like their own, are not to be trusted, let them protest ever so loudly their devotion to the cause of public freedom and to the interests of the community'.[180] Racists, in short, cannot be depended upon for solidarity along class lines either, Plain Dealer cautions, also denouncing *littérateurs* like Kingsley for failing to develop sympathies with their fellow humans of a different hue.[181] The *Bee-Hive* columnist is clearly attuned to the clash of freedoms in Jamaica, warning that the whites of the West Indies are the 'sworn enemies' of all liberty 'but that which would give them license to work out their own will'.[182] Real freedom is necessarily universal, so that its violation in one place constitutes its violation in another: 'Most certainly the only way to preserve the liberties of our country is, to assert and vindicate them wherever they are assailed and violated.'[183] In the killing of Gordon and the harm visited upon the Jamaican blacks, 'our rights as Englishmen, the rights of every one of us, have been outraged and endangered'. If the Jamaicans stood up for their rights, so must Englishmen, duly inspired – shades of Ernest Jones here – 'make a stand for your rights' rather than sitting 'quiet with our hands before us and our mouths closed'.[184] The test to which Emancipation was put by the Jamaicans is not irrelevant in

England, for the 'time has come when we must make it seen whether English freedom is a real fact or a mere fancy'.[185]

Another prominent member of the Jamaica Committee writing in the *Bee-Hive*, the Oxford classics don Goldwin Smith, also picked up on the distinction between 'public liberty' and the planter class's liberty to oppress at will by warning that, for the plantocracy, race bonds did not actually extend across class: 'Do we flatter ourselves that the Eyre party would regard the English workman or peasant as their own flesh and blood, and that they would not ... do to him what they glory in having done to the negro peasantry of Jamaica?'[186] Noting that Gordon's lighter skin had not ultimately protected him, Smith also suggests that if an agitation similar to that in Jamaica were to arise in England and create class 'panic', a sense of racial kinship would not stop 'the planter party here' from implementing 'Jamaican measures of oppression', referencing once again the Peterloo massacre and bloodshed in Ireland. For Smith, the violence visited upon light-skinned, chromatically liminal figures like Gordon and the Irish is evidence that race is no ring-fence when it comes to 'oligarchic vengeance'; resistance must therefore also be forged across race lines. 'Startling' and 'extravagant' though it may sound, the prospect of a real war is 'a hard struggle between the enfranchised and the unenfranchised, between capital and labour'.[187] The most developed account of the wider implications of the 'fatally chronic' exercise of arbitrary power 'to maintain our vast unresting empire', however, came from Harrison, who, though he had declared himself to be politicized by the Indian uprising, really emerged as an oppositional voice on colonial issues with his work for the Jamaica Committee, in which he clearly drew on the emergent identification of the Jamaican peasant with English working-class causes.[188]

For Harrison, whose *Martial Law: Six Letters to 'The Daily News'* was collated and published by the Committee as a single work with their imprimatur on it, there could also be no impermeable border which would prevent the wave-like contagion of a repressive counter-insurgency from rebounding on the colonial motherland. 'We cannot make rules for negroes', he would note pointedly of the 'reign of terror' in Jamaica, 'without baiting them like traps for Europeans ... Whose turn, be it colony or citizen, might not come next?'[189] His comparison of the Jamaica insurgency and those historical rebellions in England is explicit: 'The sacred principles for which the English people once fought and struggled we now invoke for the loftier end of checking the English people themselves from imitating the tyranny they crushed.'[190] For all that Harrison repeatedly invokes the principles of English 'liberty', his language also evinces an acknowledgement that, in the face of a struggle for rights, the 'rebel' and 'repressor' are shifting subject positions, one capable of turning into the other. At the time he was writing, the place where these liberties were being asserted was the colonies, and the person who had become the symbol of that assertion was the executed Gordon, now carrying 'in himself all the acts of wrong which his race has endured'. With the end of slavery, Harrison notes, 'all separate rights of colour' have been 'utterly extinguished'.[191] Empire and motherland, imperial subject and domestic subject, are now inextricably linked: 'Every citizen in that empire, black or white, is perilled by the sanction of outrage on any other.'[192] For Harrison, it is 1857 which is in danger of becoming a precedent: 'It called out all the tiger in our race. That wild beast must be caged again.'[193] In a metaphor familiar from the rhetoric of antislavery, he expresses a particular disquiet at the civilizational inversions implied by the exercise of absolute power and arbitrary violence: 'We know that African slavery has bred in white men a spirit more devilish than any that has ever defiled human nature – cannibalism only excepted. That spirit is yet rampant. It mastered the late governor.'[194] The idea that whereas rebellion humanized, power bestialized, was given more blunt polemical force at a working-class meeting where an effigy of Eyre was burned, one placard suggesting he should be thrown to the lions in the London Zoo to devour.

Given the existence of this range of radical readings of the Morant Bay uprising, how do we situate the relatively cautious – if nonetheless controversial – response to it of the Jamaica Committee? In her assessment of J. S. Mill's engagement with Eyre and the Jamaica Committee, Jennifer Pitts has speculated that 'Mill's motives in avoiding public mention of the racial and colonial context were in part strategic: he feared that he would lose the sympathy of the British public if he were to insist on the racial aspect of the crimes.'[195] Pitts notes rightly that, despite his efforts to bring Eyre to book representing 'his most determined criticism of the British Empire … Mill's

response fell short of a thoroughgoing interrogation of the premises and systemic failures of British rule over populations that Mill,
like most of his countrymen, considered civilizationally inferior'.[196]
Mill, of course, had famously defended the East India Company's
rule and denied that the British had provoked the 1857 uprising. My
own argument here is not that Morant Bay 1865, any more than
India 1857, resulted in a discursive rejection of the imperial project
as such. There can be little doubt, however, that it constitutes a significant moment of ground-clearing in which oppositional tendencies
emerged, not least from within working-class and labour movements,
which in turn put pressure on political liberals. In 1865, this took the
form not so much of a rejection of empire, but of what might be
regarded as an incipient internationalism – one in which there was a
self-conscious identification of the causes of black and white *people*
against the depredations of the ruling classes. Given the dominant
and increasingly polarized view of non-whites as inferior, and therefore not deserving of parity, these early forms of theorized solidarity
– in response to black resistance – are both radical and remarkable.

What emerges in Mill's and the Jamaica Committee's contentions
as a bland constitutionalism insisting on equality for all the 'Queen's
subjects' (not to be treated lightly, either, in an atmosphere inclined to
justify colonial and racial violence) should be understood, in crucial
ways, as a distillation and reframing of a more thoroughgoing criticism from below. It is possible in one sense to read the more careful
phrasing of John Stuart Mill, quoted below, and his colleagues on
the Jamaica Committee as translations (with due elisions) of radical
outrage into parliamentary discourse:

> If officers of the Government are to be allowed to take the lives of
> the Queen's subjects improperly – as has been confessedly done in
> this case – without being called to a judicial account, and having
> the excuses they make for it sifted and adjudicated by the tribunal
> in that case provided, we are giving up altogether the principle of
> government by law, and resigning ourselves to arbitrary power.[197]

Nonetheless, 'the people', an entity which emerges as a constitutively transnational, cross-racial collectivity in radical working-class
discourse on Morant Bay, is also invoked in Mill's speech when he

notes that the 'great public duty' of holding the executive to account was ultimately a democratic one; it 'may be discharged without the help of the Government: without the help of the people it cannot'.[198] As Pitts suggests, while Mill's contributions on the Jamaica affair stressed the importance of upholding the rule of law there, two weeks after news of the rebellion reached England, he expressed his support for black enfranchisement through suffrage in America, observing: 'What has just taken place in Jamaica might be used as a very strong argument against leaving the freedmen to be legislated for by their former masters'.[199] Certainly, after 1865, Mill appeared to have moved in more radical directions, even without repudiating the colonial enterprise per se, beginning in 1866 to reflect on the 'universal colonial question' and the consequences of Britain's treatment of its colonial subjects, including in India during the 1857 uprising.[200] The Eyre episode may have prompted Mill to struggle 'with concerns about colonial violence towards non-European subjects as he never had in his Indian career'; his faith in colonial benevolence was no longer unquestioning.[201] But the question is, why? Could it have at least something to do with the ways in which the voices of the oppressed and the rebellious resonated in parliament through the Royal Commission's report, among other documents, in a far clearer way than had occurred during the 1857 uprising? Were they becoming, not least through Gordon's representations, recognizable as political subjects voicing unanswerable claims? As Semmel observes, Goldwin Smith too had been a votary of British paternalism in the colonies; news of Morant Bay would change his mind.[202] Eyre had to be brought to book to 'vindicate humanity', and 'to prove that all British subjects, black or white, were under the protection of British law'.[203] In this, Goldwin Smith tellingly notes, echoing the assertions made in public meetings, they were 'defeated by the sympathy of the Tory upper classes with arbitrary and sanguinary violence'.[204]

My father died in a morphia-dream, the subject of which was the high-handed action of Governor Eyre in Jamaica ... the Eyre-prosecution, then pending, greatly occupied his mind. His last audible words concerned the controversy which was raging at the time.

So wrote Herbert Spencer in his memoirs. In the end, Eyre successfully faced down attempts at prosecution by the Jamaica Committee,
but lived out his days quietly in the Devonshire countryside, in possession of a government pension attained after some campaigning;
his career as a civil servant, to the outrage of his defenders, was over.
Jamaica passed to direct Crown rule as its Legislative Assembly –
fearful of an eventual black majority – fell on its sword and dissolved
itself in December 1865. It was an action that many, including the
Jamaica Committee, saw as a public admission, if an honourable one,
of 'incapacity to rule'.[205] But the reverberations of both the Morant
Bay rebellion and the Governor Eyre controversy would be felt in both
colony and imperial motherland for several decades to come, provoking debate and analysis well into the twentieth century. Thomas
Huxley, who joined the Jamaica Committee, in opposition to friends
of his like Kingsley and Tyndall, was right to say that 'men take sides
on this question, not so much by looking at the mere facts of the
case, but rather as their deepest political convictions lead them'.[206]
He also pointed out that the affair acted as a clarifying lens to 'help a
great many people to find out what their profoundest political beliefs
are'.[207] I have argued here that this moral crisis, engendered by the
rebellion and suppression, cannot be read in isolation from the figure
of the rebel who instigates it in the first place. G. W. Gordon, Paul
Bogle and many others made their voices heard in the metropole
through the documents of insurgency and counterinsurgency and
elicited in response both deep hostility and a sense of common cause.
Like the uprising of 1857, but far more intensively and explicitly, the
Morant Bay uprising raised questions and concerns which, in causing
debate and self-reflection, formed the seedbed for oppositional discourse on imperial questions to emerge. In the next two chapters, I
will explore how travel and contact opened up fresh modes of dialogical engagement between anticolonial movements in Egypt and
India and British travellers of a dissident bent. While it was not until
well into the twentieth century, during the interwar period, that
something like transnational anticolonial alliances would emerge,
these several chords of criticism and crisis in the nineteenth century
constitute a vital backstory which teaches us that it is out of a struggle over the meanings and scope of freedom that solidarity emerges.

3

The Accidental Anticolonialist: Egypt's 'Urabi' Rebellion and Late Victorian Critiques of Imperialism

In the year 1876 I too, as I have said, was a believer in England, and I shared the common idea of the beneficence of her rule in the East, and I had no other thought for the Egyptians than that they should share with India, which I had not yet seen, the privilege of our protection.

Wilfrid Blunt, *Secret History of the Occupation of Egypt*

Surely, on the contrary, we should hide our heads in shame, if we had any national conscience after these hundred years of violent fraud and crime? You will say, Sir, that out of all this good will come! But good to whom? Not surely to the nations we have devoured!

Wilfrid Blunt, *The Shame of the Nineteenth Century*

The British diplomat, traveller and poet Wilfrid Blunt was somewhat anxious as he set out from his Cairo lodgings to the Kasr-el-Nil barracks on a delicate mission. His brief was to convince the popular Egyptian leader, Colonel Ahmad Urabi, that the 'Joint Note' issued by Britain and France three days before, on 6 January 1882, far from being hostile to the Egyptian nationalists, was in fact a favourable missive.[1] Blunt was on excellent terms with Urabi, and it had made eminent sense for the British consul, Sir Edward Malet, to entrust him with the job. The problem was that Blunt himself was unconvinced by the interpretation he was supposed to advocate.

The note had made abundantly clear that the two European powers would back, not the Egyptian representatives in government, led by Urabi, but Khedive Tewfik, the Turkish viceroy, through whom Britain and France exercised controlling power in Egypt. Tewfik was in conflict with Egyptian nationalists in the government, and the note was categorical and deliberate in stating its commitment to him:

> The two Governments, being closely associated in their resolve to guard, by their united efforts, against all causes of complication, internal or external, which might menace the order of things established in Egypt, do not doubt that the assurance publicly given of their fixed intention in this respect will tend to avert the dangers to which the Government of the Khedive might be exposed and which would certainly find England and France united to oppose them.[2]

Clearly, there was not much room for ambiguity here. Convincing Urabi that what the British government *really* meant was that it would not permit Egypt to be harmed by either the Turkish sultan or the khedive would take some doing.

Blunt was right to be worried about being the 'bearer of such rubbish', as he himself put it.[3] He writes that he found Urabi, also the Egyptian under-secretary for war, alone in his office and angry, his face 'like a thunder-cloud' and a 'peculiar gleam in his eye'.[4] Blunt delivered his message, but the colonel's response was scathing. 'Sir Edward Malet must really think us children who do not know the meaning of words', he thundered. 'In the first place … it is the language of menace. There is no clerk in this office who would use such words with such a meaning'.[5] Urabi carried on parsing the note, pointing to sentences he interpreted, quite correctly, as threatening his government. He noted that the unanimity of France and Britain on the matter could mean little other than that they would invade Egypt in much the same manner as France had recently annexed Tunis. Urabi then spoke for his countrymen: 'Let them come … every man and child in Egypt will fight them. It is contrary to our principles to strike the first blow, but we shall know how to return it.'[6] Dismissing Blunt's services, Urabi took the Englishman by the arm and, in a softer manner, invited him to come home for a visit. Blunt, promising to return with better news, reported to Malet that the note had seriously damaged Anglo-Egyptian relations; instead of frightening the Egyptians, it had enraged and united them. His warnings were of little avail: the British government did not provide the kind of clarification or reassurance that might have calmed tensions. Within six months the British invasion and occupation of Egypt would commence, and by the following year Urabi would commence a long exile from his homeland, after a trial which found him guilty of treason.

I begin with this anecdote, taken from Blunt's memoirs, because it tells us something about the nature of encounters between a certain kind of British 'political traveller', and anticolonial figures who emerged from the crucible of late-nineteenth-century resistances to imperial incursions in Asia and Africa.[7] While, on the face of it, there is little in this scene that signifies much more than another failed informal attempt at rapprochement in the months leading up to Britain's invasion of Egypt, we might note here an inversion of familiar prototypes: it is the white man, emissary for the colonial powers, who remains silent as the Arab leader offers a lucid critique of his message and the infantilizing discourse that underpins it. Blunt represents himself in his own account as a silent interlocutor who takes the lesson back to his fellow Britons to try to persuade them to act otherwise; in this he would fail. The significance of this brief encounter also derives from a compelling backstory that tells us something not only about the age of British imperialism in North Africa, but also about how resistance to that imperialism emerged, and in turn influenced criticism of empire in Britain. If the occupation of Egypt inaugurated the modern phase of British high imperialism – the infamous 'scramble for Africa' would begin shortly thereafter – Egyptian resistance to it also generated early and important British counterpoints to anthems of empire. Blunt's would be one of the loudest voices, but by no means a lone one, in a growing chorus of dissent from within Britain. The resistance in Egypt, which came to be known as 'the Urabi revolt', was integral to the development of his critique – as well as those articulated by the likes of Fredric Harrison, A. M. Broadley, J. S. Keay, William Gregory and Wilfred Lawson, a learning process in which British liberals found their assumptions and ideals challenged, complicated and reshaped by witnessing anticolonial rebellion and engaging with Egyptians involved in it. The story of Blunt's relationship with Urabi, and with other significant figures on the scene of

Egyptian resistance to both Turkish and European incursions – and the manner in which he changed over time from champion of English benevolence to a self-professed Egyptian nationalist – constitutes, I argue, a key strand in the story of the development of British anti-colonialism partly as a critical dialogue between anticolonial figures in the periphery and their metropolitan interlocutors.

In this and the following chapter, I examine the role played by travellers to 'antique lands' in forging critical perspectives on imperial rule, as they journeyed through outposts of empire during the last phase of European imperial consolidation, from the 1880s onwards. Travelling with the intent of trying to understand what was going on in Egypt and India, these were explorers who sought to map geopolitical rather than geographical terrain, but found their categories and assumptions disrupted and reframed in the 'contact zone' of insurgency; indeed, as in Blunt's case, they themselves often underwent quite dramatic political transformations.[8] Episodes of insurgency such as those in 1857 and 1865 were read largely through news reportage, letters and the documents of counterinsurgency, which yielded glimpses of affinities and connections. By the last decades of the nineteenth century, however, some Britons sought to understand the growth of what was called 'unrest' – anticolonial and nationalist movements – through personal engagement and witnessing. While 'contact zones' involve the establishment of relations between peoples with very different histories and cultures in a context of 'radically asymmetrical relations of power', the narratives I examine here and in Chapter 4 frequently speak to a performative role reversal in which it is the traveller who becomes a tutee, sometimes willingly and at others more reluctantly, while insurgency itself becomes a teaching text of sorts.[9] The act of reverse tutelage, in which the disparities of power were not ignored but their abolition imagined, would itself become significant in the emergence of metropolitan anticolonialism. The 'seeing man' was seen, and the tutor became taught. Moreover, the political landscape is not yielding or available for possession: it must be engaged with and allowed to transform. As the self-activity of the colonized becomes more visible or audible, the Empire itself comes under scrutiny.

Six months after Blunt and Urabi met in the latter's offices – they would continue to correspond after Blunt returned to England and resumed his efforts to mediate between the British and Egyptian governments – the fateful British bombardment of the Egyptian coastal city of Alexandria began. Shortly after dawn on 11 July 1882, ten ironclads and several smaller gunboats belonging to the British Mediterranean Fleet began firing at Egyptian forts. It took just over ten hours for them to decimate the latter, which were struggling with their obsolete weaponry and returning weak fire. Nine days later, the British cabinet authorized the arrival of an expeditionary force under the command of Sir Garnet Wolsey. His troops met Urabi's forces at the famous battle of Tel el-Kabir on 13 September 1882, after violating the neutrality of the Suez Canal, honoured by Urabi and accordingly left undefended, and seizing it at both ends.[10] Striking without warning at 4.30 a.m. on 13 September, Wolsey's infantry routed Urabi's irregular forces, slaughtering ill-clad Bedouins by the thousands. By 6 a.m. the British forces had declared victory. Two days later, Colonel Urabi surrendered and was imprisoned pending trial. The formal British occupation of Egypt, which would last well into the twentieth century – longer than anyone had anticipated – had begun. Urabi, along with several others, was charged with acts of mutiny and rebellion. He was accused of exciting the Egyptians to arm against the khedive (who changed sides and sought the protection of the British halfway through hostilities), fomenting civil war, and overseeing the conflagration in Alexandria pursuant to the bombardment in July.[11] The British government, now headed by Liberal prime minister William Gladstone, hoped that the tricky matter of Colonel Urabi's fate – rebellion carried the death penalty – would go away quickly and quietly once he was handed over to Khedive Tewfik, who remained under British counsel.[12]

Matters did not unfold quite that way. While there had been a sustained negative campaign against Urabi in the British political sphere and newspapers over the months leading up to the invasion – he was painted as a fanatical military despot – the bombardment of Alexandria did not go unchallenged, and Urabi's fate generated some debate, with a few strong voices raising questions on his behalf.[13] Had there in fact been a rebellion in the strict sense of the term, an uprising against a legitimate head of state? Had there been a national movement which had been widely supported with cries for Urabi's triumph ringing across the streets of Cairo? In other words, who represented Egyptian popular feeling, and could that feeling be described as 'national'? With Britain now an occupying power, should Urabi not be afforded a fair trial rather than the summary court martial that had been planned? In the end, a reluctant British government gave in. There was a nominal but highly publicized trial, albeit with the outcome negotiated ahead of time, Urabi having agreed to plead guilty to the charge of rebellion in return for having his death sentence commuted to exile on the island of Ceylon – a location of the British government's choosing. The key to Urabi's reprieve was not, in fact, the belatedly awakened conscience of British officialdom, but Blunt's decision to mount a legal campaign on the Egyptian leader's behalf. The Englishman would champion Urabi's cause with extraordinary passion and tenacity, putting not only sharp words but also large sums of his own money into the cause. Thanks to Blunt's efforts, Urabi would be defended by the British barrister A. M. Broadley, who would also articulate the case against the British presence in Egypt in his published account of the trial. The collective defence of Urabi was itself the culmination of a longer campaign by Blunt and a small handful of allies and sympathizers to make the case for Egyptian nationalism in Britain, an endeavour – and it is important not to underestimate the importance of this – in which they were not entirely unsuccessful.[14] His own radicalized position inspired by Egyptian resistance to both Turkish and European control, Blunt was a significant contributor to fomenting metropolitan dissent from British foreign policy. He and others associated with events in Egypt helped forge a language of critique that not only ran determinedly against the ascendant ideology and rhetoric of imperialism, but also put Egyptian resistance to foreign rule at its centre. The trenchant critiques of imperialism which emerged out of the Egypt crisis of 1881–82 – early versions of colonial discourse analysis – would be voiced only in a distinctly minor key for many years to come, but were important in paving the way for the eventual development of a more pronounced criticism of empire within Britain. The crisis was arguably one of the first in which the terms of criticism were very distinctly shaped by direct personal interaction between some British dissenters and forces of resistance within the Empire; indeed, by the witnessing of a revolution at close quarters.

Some historical scholarship has dismissed Blunt as an 'anti-imperialist British gadfly', even as many scholars of that period of Egypt's history have drawn on his copious notes on what unfolded during the Urabi uprising.[15] Yet no study of British anticolonialism can ignore this figure who, as Gregory Claeys notes, 'produced over the course of some thirty years an exceptionally detailed, critical narrative of British imperial policy, more sweeping in its scope and relentless in its condemnation than anything outside Positivist circles'.[16] Indeed, I would argue that Blunt's criticism was frequently more radical and textured than that produced by Positivists, including Harrison, and that this was in no small part due to his regular contact with anticolonial figures from the Arab world. While it is certainly true that Blunt had a self-important air about him, and tended to overestimate his ability to influence individuals and events, there is also little doubt that he had both a ringside view of events and extraordinary access to the corridors of power and key players both in Britain and in Egypt, being regarded by some in government as 'a considerable authority on Asiatic matters'.[17] Certainly, many of the Egyptian actors in the revolution were fulsome in their praise when recollecting his role. Blunt sought in turn to provide an alternative voice to British establishment discourse on empire, and self-consciously construct a counter-history delineating 'the true condition of things'. This he opposed to what he called the 'manipulation of the organs of public news in the interests of our diplomacy', including the presence in Cairo and elsewhere of what we might today call 'embedded journalists' – a fact he cautions future historians to bear in mind when consulting newspaper files in search of information.[18] My argument in this chapter is that what Claeys rightly describes as the 'subtlety and complexity of his anti-imperialist outlook' was directly shaped by Blunt's witnessing of the Urabi revolt, and by engagement with some of the most renowned thinkers of that moment and milieu.[19] Blunt's campaign on behalf of Urabi also provided a structural space that drew others into the fray. In this sense, the revolt in Egypt and Blunt's engagement with it can be said to have inflected British dissidence on empire in that moment very profoundly.

An Unlikely Anticolonialist: The Education of Wilfrid Blunt

Wilfrid Scawen Blunt was not born to be an imperial sceptic, let alone the forceful anticolonialist he would eventually become, even going to jail for his efforts on behalf of Ireland in the late 1880s. This is precisely what makes him important. The milieu of landed gentry into which he was born was conducive neither to political radicalism nor even to the sort of persistent dissent on imperial questions which would become something of a vocation for him in the wake of the events of 1882. Described by a recent biographer as a 'West Sussex country squire, society darling, ladies man [sic], horse fancier and middling poet', Blunt was a political Conservative (he had even regarded the Liberal Gladstone as 'an ignoramus and fanatic' on 'Oriental questions') who came into some wealth upon the death of his older brother, prior to which he had spent ten unremarkable years as a bored career diplomat in Europe and South America.[20] The money enabled him to leave the service and, along with his wife, Lady Anne, also a writer of some note, to indulge a passion for travelling in the Middle East from the mid 1870s onwards.[21] During these sojourns, the couple purchased Arabian horses that were shipped back to England to establish what would become a well-known stud farm at Crabbet, their estate in Sussex; the lineage of most British racehorses today can still be traced back to the Crabbet Stud. It appears to have been during these travels – along with time spent in India – that Blunt, the gentleman of leisure, became something of a professional Orientalist, developing a lifelong interest in Islam and Arab culture, as well as an antipathy to what he deemed to be repressive and brutal Turkish Ottoman rule. Although it was Lady Anne who wrote the two compendious travelogues detailing their journeys through Arab lands, Blunt claimed to have had a heavy editorial hand in them.[22] His own career as a writer and self-described Arab expert began with articles he contributed to the journals *Nineteenth Century* and *Fortnightly Review*, where he expounded his views on Arab people and culture, Islam and politics in the Middle East. These were remarkable works inasmuch as they both drew on established Orientalist frameworks for understanding the Middle East, and combatively challenged many widely espoused assumptions generated by those very frameworks. Such early intimations of dissident tendencies notwithstanding, it would not be until Blunt spent time in Egypt and came to know – and learn from – many of the chief players in the making of the Egyptian revolution that he would come into his own as one of the earliest and most powerful voices of British anticolonialism. Blunt's own trajectory of change presages aspects of British criticism of empire that would emerge more distinctly in the decades to come, his own learning curve representing, in some ways, the evolution of dissident discourse. Blunt came to unlearn a habitual paternalism and understand that there were substantive cultural resources available to non-European subjects for thinking about emancipation and change which did not preclude engage-ment with other cultures. With these insights in hand, Blunt began to formulate a textured humanism which was not about the 'abstract promise of a shared humanity' available to the colonized 'if they embraced Western values, customs and practices'.[23] The ideas Blunt began to espouse were more akin to what Edward Said describes as 'critical humanism', a practice not restricted to any particular culture or civilization, which recognizes that all human beings and cultures are capable of 'a continuous process of self-understanding and self-realization'.[24] Starting out with something like the abstract promise of inclusion on European terms, Blunt's experience of the revolutionary milieu in Egypt, and the cultural resources it drew on, brought him to acknowledge, in Said's terms, 'what has long been a characteristic of all cultures, namely, that there is a strong streak of radical antiauthoritarian dissent in them'.[25] It was this streak that could provide the basis for solidarity between Britons of a dissident inclination and Egyptian anticolonialists.

'Islam does move'

The profound change that Blunt underwent over the course of his engagement with Islamic intellectuals and his experience of the milieu of the

Wilfrid Blunt and Lady Anne with Crabbet stud

Urabi revolution can be mapped through his writing on both the Arab world and Islam in a short period between 1880 and 1882 in the *Nineteenth Century* and the *Fortnightly Review*. After a piece based on his long-standing equine expertise, which compared English and Arabian thoroughbred horses, Blunt began to explore Bedouin life and Arab culture.[26] He offered a counterpoint to the wearying 'tale of Oriental corruption and Oriental tyranny', in an idealized account of the Arab as practical, physically vigorous, and prone to despotic rule, in which 'popular feeling' nonetheless exerts its influence.[27] With familiar Orientalist benevolence, Blunt suggested that the Arab was exceptional, and thus 'fully entitled by his intellectual and moral powers to political freedom'.[28] (Later, he would note that, while liberty, equality and brotherhood were 'three blessings' that Europe liked to boast about, 'we do not in truth possess them'.)[29] Certainly, in Blunt's early forays into thinking about Islam and the Arab world, the keynote was benevolence. It was still a time, he would recall, when he 'clung to the thought that England in the East might yet ... be made an instrument for good'.[30] Accordingly, he stressed points of equivalence between Europe and Central Arabia, where he had spent some time in 1879, suggesting that liberal values prevailed there: 'Englishmen should rejoice to hear that there is at least in one corner of Asia a state where life and property are absolutely secure, where justice is impartial, taxation light, military service voluntary, and where a prosperous and happy people cheerfully acquiesce in the established forms of law.'[31] Charting that period later in his memoir, Blunt notes that his thoughts were not then especially political, though he was struck, in Algeria, by the 'spectacle' of 'an Eastern people in violent subjection to a Western', and felt a certain 'sympathy' with the former.[32] Of his early travels to 'Arabic-speaking lands', Blunt also confessed: 'I heard their voices, but knew neither their language nor their ways of thought'[33]; Egypt, to begin with, was 'another pleasant travelling adventure'; and though he noted the abysmal condition of the fellah, or Egyptian peasant, as the upper classes feasted on plenty, he assumed the former not to have any thoughts of revolt in their nature – though he would later acknowledge he had been wrong.

Blunt's personal encounters during his lengthy travels in the Middle East were clearly an important element of his evolution from poet-squire to, first, advocate of benevolent British imperialism, and then vociferous critic of British rule in Egypt, India and Ireland; but they do not in themselves explain his trajectory. Other such travellers and 'experts' on the Middle East during this period were to be found, after all, including the likes of Richard Burton and Edward William Lane, each believing, in Said's classic terms, that 'his vision of things Oriental was individual, self-created out of some intensely personal encounter with the Orient, Islam, or the Arabs'.[34] All such Orientalists also typically 'expressed general contempt for official knowledge held about the East'.[35] Yet Blunt was different – and not only because he did not express what Said described as 'the traditional Western hostility to and fear of the Orient'. What is more significant is the way in which he ended up bearing faithful witness to the unfolding of one of the first major anticolonial revolutions in Africa and Asia, and learning from it – moving from an early Orientalism with idealizing tendencies to studying Islam in more substantive ways, and then finally being politicized by anticolonial Egyptian thought. Where British imperialism may have turned Burton into an 'imperial scribe', resistance to British imperialism turned Blunt into an anti-colonial voice of some distinction.[36] This was due in no small part to his intentional efforts to understand Egypt and Islam from the standpoint of those who were resisting Europe's incursions. Blunt's evolution was ultimately not about experimenting with alternative Oriental identities, as it was for some travellers to antique lands, but something rather more substantial and enduring. Neither posture nor performance, Blunt's transformation into an advocate for Egypt was deeply influenced by a sense of voice – both those voices he heard raised in Egypt against Europe's incursions, and his own as a vehicle for carrying them over to the heart of the Empire.[37]

In 1880, Blunt was thrown into a 'chaos of ideas, literary, social and political'.[38] Inspired by intense discussions with scholars of the religion, Blunt found himself thinking about Islam in both its spiritual and political dimensions. He wrote retrospectively that these conversations 'affected me profoundly, and to a certain extent revolutionized my ideas'.[39] Beset by the feeling 'that in all my thought of freeing and reforming the East I had begun at the wrong end', he decided to study Islamic thought properly (he was already being tutored in Arabic).[40] This study would be parlayed into an eloquent and informative set of essays, published under the characteristically magisterial title *The Future of Islam*.[41] Blunt's authorial persona in these essays – published serially in the *Fortnightly Review* – was still very much that of an Orientalist who sought to understand how the past of an entity can teach us something about its future. With the overweening confidence in the importance of his own views to matters of state that marked much of his political writing, Blunt claims that he had set out his disquisition on the question of Islam 'in the hope that it may be instrumental in guiding the national choice'.[42] By this, he meant that Britain's responsibility as a power governing a very large number of Muslims could be better discharged if there was a more informed sense of what Islam had to offer. Nothing in *The Future of Islam* indicates anything less than faith in the imperial project, with England (Blunt rarely uses 'Britain') maintaining a 'position as the guide and arbiter of Asiatic progress'.[43] The last essay ends with a classically paternalistic image, Blunt calling on England to 'take Islam by the hand and encourage her boldly in the path of virtue' – a path preferable to 'a whole century of crusade'.[44]

Yet, even as he was completing these essays, Blunt's thinking was beginning to shift in critical directions. For all that he maintains a position towards Britain's imperial reach that is loyal and hopeful (he would, with the benefit of hindsight, in a tellingly religious register, call it a 'failing faith'), *The Future of Islam* nonetheless carries within it intimations of a different set of possibilities that would underpin Blunt's transformation into a sharp-voiced antagonist of empire in the wake of the Egyptian revolution. He had started to identify cultural and social dynamics that would lead him to abandon thoughts of assimilating Arab societies to British liberal values, having found 'new worlds of thought and life in an atmosphere I had fancied to be only of decay'.[45] Mapping the beginnings of a significant personal transformation, he writes: 'if I had not exactly come to scoff, I certainly remained, in a certain sense, to pray'.[46] If there was one formative insight that changed Blunt's perspective, it was that Islam and Islamic cultures were no less capable of introspection and change than any other – just as Christian societies were as capable of stagnation and reaction as any other. 'I know', he writes, 'that it is a received opinion ... that Islam is in its constitution unamenable to change, and by consequence to progressive life.'[47] For all that, there is plenty of evidence to marshal in favour of this assertion: 'The fact is, Islam does move'.[48] It is around this insight that any considerations of the past and the future of Islam and Islamic polities must necessarily arrange themselves. While he acknowledged that equivalences should not be strained beyond credibility, Blunt recognized, in a way that Frantz Fanon would also do decades later, that the capacity to change is not unique to particular cultures and societies. For Fanon, this is a capacity which is put into abeyance in the face of colonization, a 'tragic labyrinth' in which 'the truth objectively expressed is constantly vitiated by the lie of the colonial situation'.[49] Blunt too was coming to understand what Fanon articulated so clearly well over half a century later: until it is distorted and arrested by the fact of colonialism and its insistence on 'successful integration' to the supposedly superior values of the colonizing entity, cultures have a healthy dynamic that includes engagement with new ideas and other cultures.[50] Reason and faith coexist as much in Muslim societies as in Christian ones, so that Islam ought to be treated on par with Christianity as 'a true religion, true inasmuch as it is a form of the worship of that one true God in whom Europe, in spite of her modern reason, still believes'.[51]

Towards the end of his set of essays on Islam, much of which is devoted simply to explicating Islam in an historical frame and delineating differences within it and between Muslim societies, Blunt also reverses his own initial emphasis on European influence in the Middle East – a gesture at once historically sound and polemically powerful. Now he notes that European thought itself has long been influenced by Arab ideas: 'We have seen in Europe, even in England, a land never brought physically into contact with Arabia, how long Arabian thought, filtered as it was through France and Spain to our shores, has dominated our ideas'.[52] If it has survived so far away, 'Who shall fix the term of its power, and say that it cannot renew itself and live?'[53] Still in a moderate and reformist vein, Blunt's goal in this work was to find a modus vivendi for Islam and Christianity to coexist. Yet, in less than a year, Blunt would again come to see his own position as well-intentioned but naive, not least in its belief that England had a special relationship with the Muslim world, 'seeking of them practical advantages of trade rather than conquest'.[54] Now he saw himself, schooled by the Egyptian revolution, as 'a single voice against a multitude, the voice of one man who had lived inside the house of liberty against the many voices of men who had only stood outside'.[55] In September 1882 he would announce himself to his countrymen as one who was in 'violent sympathy with the enemy', Egypt, and the country's devout Muslim leader, Colonel Urabi.[56] The 'violence' of this sympathy spoke of a dramatic wrenching of self from the Englishman's benevolent interest in Egyptian Arabs as the subjects of Britain's informal empire to complete solidarity with the Egyptian resistance. The conversion to 'so strange a state of feeling', as he put it, was one in which he would fulfil a promise to 'return and throw in my lot with [the Egyptians] in a campaign for independence'.[57] What had happened? Two strands of Egyptian life had become Blunt's touchstones for speaking up against the doings of the British in that country: one was that the restless fellahin, already 'despoiled of everything', were willing to rise up, and Urabi represented this strand. The other was represented by a man who was, for a time, a pivotal figure in providing the intellectual scaffolding for the rebellion. By the time the 'Urabi revolt' broke out, Jamal al-Din Al-Afghani had been banished from Cairo for his role in fomenting it. In what Blunt described as his 'courageous teaching', Afghani had told his Egyptian audiences that their choice was either to 'live like free people or die as martyrs'.[58] Between them, the conjoined movements represented by Urabi and Afghani transformed Blunt's political views.

'So strange a state of feeling': The Making of a British Anticolonialist

When Blunt and the Egyptian leader met for the first time on 6 December 1881, the conversation began with Urabi referring to Lord Byron, Lady Anne's grandfather. Familiar already, via the Azhar, or Islamic university of Cairo, with Blunt's reputation as a 'friend of the fellah cause', Urabi told his new English acquaintance that, while he knew nothing of Byron's poetry, he was an admirer of the poet's contributions to the campaign for liberty in Greece. Fresh from putting together *The Future of Islam*, Blunt himself was focused on Arabia as 'the cradle of Eastern liberty and true religion', not having realized that 'in the National movement in Egypt the chief interest for me in Islam already lay, as it were, close to my hand'.[59] This, he notes, was because he had himself accepted the British establishment's line that what was taking place was purely military and sinister: 'I share with most lovers of liberty a distrust of professional soldiers as the champions of any cause not that of tyranny.'[60] And indeed, in ways that will not be unfamiliar to the twenty-first-century reader, both press and official sources had taken a virulent pleasure in painting Urabi as a 'military oppressor' and 'dictator', who had placed a 'military yoke ... around the neck of Egyptians' while also fostering religious fanaticism.[61] Blunt noted not only that there was 'nothing in him of the fanatic, if fanaticism means religious hatred', but also that his unmistakable piety did not prevent Urabi making transnational and cross-religious alliances 'with Jew, Christian, or infidel'.[62] Pious though he was, Urabi was no fanatic, but, in the first instance, a class warrior of sorts, representing the fellahin – the tillers of Egyptian land: 'It cannot be too strongly emphasized that the National movement of 1881 was essentially a fellah movement, having for its object the emancipation of the fellahin ... and only incidentally against the Anglo-French control when this last declared itself openly the ally and supporter of that tyranny.'[63]

Urabi's nationalism was focused on land rights and economic grievances rather than on excluding racial or religious outsiders. On the contrary, the fellah leader exuded an open attitude to 'humanity at large without distinction of race or creed'.[64] It is really at this point that Blunt's growing understanding that freedom from bondage could be thought of as a shared human aspiration rather than one unique to European thought appears to have crystallized into a clear insight. His subsequent letter to Gladstone cut against the prevalent political rendering of 'freedom' as a gift from Britain to Egypt – a notion that was already being bandied about as a possible military intervention to end Urabi's putative despotism was considered. 'The ideas he expresses are not merely a repetition of the phrases of modern Europe', Blunt said of Urabi, 'but are based on a knowledge of history and on the liberal tradition of Arabian thought, inherited from the days when Mohammedanism was liberal'.[65] Blunt also insists that Urabi was no mimic man, and that his words were markedly different from the usual language used by Eastern politicians when talking to Europeans. There was no developmental teleology, no 'nonsense about railroads and canals and tramways as nostrums that could redeem the East'.[66] Blunt's assessment was shared by another of Urabi's defenders, Lady Gregory, who noted in her demystifying account *Arabi and His Household* (based on visits, with Lady Anne, to Arabi's wife and mother) that the Egyptian leader was distrusted by the authorities precisely as a 'man with ideas'.[67]

The son of a fellah headman who had received schooling in the village and then some education at the Azhar in Cairo, Ahmed Urabi al-Hussaini had risen rapidly up the ranks in the army under Khedive Said. The khedive had put in place a controversial policy of fellah advancement in the army, to the dismay of the Turko-Circassian officers who had traditionally enjoyed preferment. They were returned to dominance after Said's death, thereby laying the groundwork for the fellah military discontent. By the time Blunt heard of him in Cairo, during the autumn of 1881, Urabi had become fairly well known as one of the authors of a petition to redress fellah officers' grievances. These included withheld pay and the preferential treatment given to Turko-Circassian officers. Fellah soldiers were being made to undertake non-military hard labour, but Urabi had refused to let his men dig canals. The eventual consequence of this affair was an attempt by Khedive Tewfik, on 1 February 1881, to arrest Urabi and two of his fellow officers by summoning them to the palace under a false pretext. The officers were famously and dramatically rescued by their regiments, who forced open the doors of the royal edifice. Consequent to this episode, Blunt writes, Urabi had been invested with the mantle of 'champion of fellah wrongs against the Turkish ruling class', a role he appears to have embraced: 'It must be remembered that in all Egyptian history, for at least three hundred years, no mere fellah had ever risen to a position of any political eminence in Egypt, or had appeared in the light of a reformer, or whispered a word of possible revolt.'[68] Blunt had grasped that, in important ways, this was not simply a national struggle in the attenuated sense of 'natives' against 'foreigners', but an insurgency to reclaim Egypt that had vital class dimensions to it. The second incident took place a few months later, in September 1881, when a series of events led to a direct and dramatic face-to-face confrontation between Khedive Tewfik and Urabi, whose troops had occupied the square in front of

Abdin Palace. After dismounting and handing over his sword, Urabi placed three demands before the khedive, whose reply was: 'I am Khedive of the country and shall do as I please.'[69] Urabi's reply has gone down in legend, entering Egyptian school textbooks: 'We are not slaves and shall never from this day forth be inherited.'[70]

Though educated, Urabi was not an intellectual; he appears to have been driven by a deeply felt sense of class injury as a non-Turkish fellah officer in the Egyptian army, and by a willingness to channel the wider resentment of the fellahin at material inequalities. 'He seems to be a man', Lady Anne wrote, 'who has set himself a task and who never loses sight of the main object of his life, considering himself the servant of that object – the welfare of others and not his own ... He may be mistaken in details as to some things, from want of knowledge, but that this does not materially signify.'[71] Urabi's memoirs of the revolution that came to be named after him were published in 1925, after he returned from exile to live and die in obscurity. While not a treatise on the meaning of nationalism, or even the titular 'awakening' (*nahda*), Urabi's account nonetheless situates his mutinous actions within a wider context of discontent and dissent.[72] Land – and the arbitrary grant of land titles to Circassian khedivial favourites, often involving land grabs – were at the heart of the conflict, as were debt and taxation, both of which disproportionately affected the fellahin. In his account, the army and intellectuals came together to protect the rights of the *umma* – a term that eludes easy translation, but in context clearly refers to the non-Europeans and non-Turks, that is, native Egyptians, as a national community that comes into being precisely through shared subordination and connection to land, rather than necessarily through race or religion.[73] There is little here that suggests the demands Urabi made in the name of the *umma* in January 1881 – including equal, non-discriminatory, non-racialized treatment for native Egyptians and a Majlis Nawab, or Council of Representatives – were developed mainly through contact with Western ideas. Urabi also appears to have gone out of his way to emphasize that equal treatment for Egyptians did not mean hostility to other races, including the Circassians. Indeed, in a speech he gave at the Hussein mosque in central Cairo, he took pains to distinguish the expansive Egyptian sense of freedom from its expansionist European counterpart: 'Those who read history know that the European nations have achieved freedom through extravagant impetuosity, spilling blood, ravishing honour and perpetrating acts of destruction but we have achieved freedom in an hour without spilling one drop of blood, without terrifying one heart and without touching any one's honour.'[74] Urabi sought precedent for his political claims in Arabic-language works, including histories and chronicles, giving examples of events in the past where demands for individual or collective rights had been asserted. He was not alone in this; a raft of terms and concepts situated in indigenous traditions and texts were in circulation at the time. In his assessment of the poetry of emergent Egyptian nationalism, for instance, Mounah A. Khouri observes that these terms included *adl* (justice), *hurriya* (freedom), *qawm* (folk, people, nation), *shura* or *mashura* (consultation, deliberation).[75]

As Juan Cole has noted, discontent and resistance had been germinating for considerably longer than the events associated with Urabi himself would suggest.[76] Several different interests and grievances underlay the revolution which finally unfolded in 1882. These included 'the desire to end the extraordinary privileges of the dual elite (coded as foreign) and to ensure more consultative involvement of the middling sort (coded as indigenous) in governance'.[77] Fellah and military discontent turned the mixture combustible. In his essay 'The Egyptian Revolution', published in September 1882, Blunt attested to his final conversion in this milieu not just to 'sympathy' with the Egyptian, but to something rather more fundamental, indeed visceral. He distinguished his own feelings from those of other critics of the invasion, like Harrison and the MP Wilfrid Lawson, distancing himself from paternalism in the process: 'Their sympathy is not as that of a man for his own kin, rather as of a man for some ill-treated beast. They do not love the Mussulman "Arabs" of Egypt as I do.'[78] Back in Cairo in late 1881, Blunt came to the conclusion that he had wronged the movement in Egypt by being initially suspicious of it: he now found a country united and confidently open in talking the 'language of religious and political liberty'.[79] It was a living, moving exemplar of the ideas that he had only grasped in the abstract in *The Future of Islam*. Witnessing the struggle had turned his ideational world upside down: 'During the last few weeks of my stay in Egypt I retired from the European world of Cairo to the world I had learned to love better, that of the Egyptians. I had learned too to respect it.'[80]

When he did visit the European quarters it was, he claimed, 'with the feeling that I was descending from a higher to a much lower moral and intellectual level'.[81]

The Blunts returned to an England in the spring of 1882 where the political landscape had changed significantly and for the worse. The Liberals, now in power, had abandoned their 'enthusiasm for Eastern nationalities and Eastern liberty', and were full of ideas of 'imperial coercion' in relation, not least, to Ireland.[82] Answering hostile parliamentary questions put to him after the bombardment of Alexandria, Gladstone insisted that, without European intervention, Urabi 'would have become dictator of the country'. He, in turn, had been told by Edward Malet that 'the University, the Chamber, and the nation are anxious for the termination of the military despotism which now terrorizes them'.[83] At one level, Blunt's work was cut out for him: to undo the myth-making of imperial self-justification alongside the concomitant demonizing of Islam and Muslims, itself a legacy of the 1857 uprising, which the British authorities blamed largely on Indian Muslims. 'Fanaticism' was 'a convenient word which began now to be freely used in describing the National movement'; even the proposed reduction of the budget of the European Opera House in Cairo, not to mention criticism of wasteful expenditure, became proof of 'fanaticism'.[84] While Urabi was keen 'to restore good Mussulman government in his country', he was 'evidently the reverse of a fanatic', Blunt pointed out, not least given that his was primarily a movement against the supremacy of another Muslim power.[85] 'Fanaticism' had become convenient European shorthand for what Blunt described quite simply as 'the patriotism of the people, to protest against the presence of the French and British fleets'.[86] To his mind, the only extant fanaticism was that evident in the efforts of English agents 'to bring about a revolution counter to the will of the people'.[87] Influenced by Blunt, some parliamentarians also enquired why Britain's way of showing regard for the Egyptian people 'was to go out and shoot them'.[88]

Blunt's other task, as he saw it, was to persuade the British political classes to take seriously and empathize with what was going on in Egypt in terms of self-assertion, including demands for more consultative rule and better conditions for the fellahin. Translating these into the legitimizing language of nationalism was at once true to how many in Egypt themselves viewed matters – through the lens of *wataniyat*, or 'feeling for one's native land' – and strategic in relation to British political discourse. Barely four years before, when in opposition, William Gladstone MP had himself sharply criticized calls for intervention in Egypt, although mainly on grounds of inexpediency.[89] The gap between the politician's rhetoric in opposition and his practice in power was one that gave Blunt ammunition in a letter he wrote to Prime Minister Gladstone on the question of Egyptian national feelings:

> I think the lovers of Western progress should rather congratulate themselves on this strange and unlooked for sign of political life in a land which has hitherto been reproached by them as the least thinking portion of the stagnant East. You, sir, I think, once expressed to me your belief that the nations of the East could only regenerate themselves by a spontaneous resumption of their lost national *Will*, and behold in Egypt that *Will* has arisen and is now struggling to find words which may persuade Europe of its existence.[90]

His own project, then, would be to help find those words by interpreting the texts of resistance and change. It is worth recalling here, given our own dominant post-national theoretical sensibilities, that in the context of late-Victorian Britain's imperial world order, nationhood was not usually conceded to societies outside Europe. Recall, for instance, J. S. Mill's firm pronouncement that 'barbarians have no rights as a nation', though they could eventually be made fit to become one.[91]

Blunt's interventions making the case both for Egyptian 'nationalism' and for Islam's 'liberal' traditions naturally raise questions for the postcolonial reader. If, on the one hand, Blunt identifies a British failure to accord equality of aspiration to Egyptians resisting foreign rule and demanding representative institutions, is he, on the other, culpable of grafting European political categories onto a distinctly non-European and very different cultural context? Is he simplistically turning Egypt's singularities into a variation on familiar categories for the purposes of European comprehension?[92] In his incipiently modernist way, Blunt as mediator may have committed that most postmodern of crimes: the denial of difference. Yet, to level this charge is to overlook the ways in which Blunt's Eurocentric liberal abstractions had been, first, undone by his study of Islam, and then reconfigured by a milieu of revolutionary ferment. The Englishman may have set himself the task of interpreting his countrymen and the Egyptians to each other; but in the process it was he who found himself learning new languages. A somewhat theoretical insight into how Islam was not lacking in ideas of liberty and consultative governance was given heft and texture when Blunt witnessed a largely Muslim society in historical turmoil around questions of class, nationality and rights. Part of Blunt's rationale in using the language of democratic constitutional nationalism was to counter the pernicious Orientalism of British colonial claims, such as that made by Edward Dicey: 'In Egypt – as, for that matter, in any Mussulman country – parliamentary government is an impossibility.' Dicey believed that representation and taxation should both be considered as 'incomprehensible to the Oriental mind as the differential calculus would be to a ploughboy'.[93] Where questionable assertions of alterity were made the basis of rule, the assertion of common capacities could be a form of resistance.

The Intellectual Background

A few weeks before the Joint Note sent waves of indignation across Egyptian shores, Blunt, after consulting with Urabi, had drafted a 'studiously moderate' memorandum detailing the nationalist agenda, which was sent to Gladstone and published in *The Times* on 3 January 1882.[94] It was an attempt to persuade politicians and the broadsheet-reading classes of the existence of a coherent nationalist programme in Egypt under Urabi in terms that would render it legitimate to them.[95] The 'Programme' made clear its commitment to pan-Islamism in reiterating an allegiance to the sultan of Turkey as the caliph, but insisted that the khedive, as his representative, must reign 'in accordance with justice and the law', and with the help of a Majlis Shoura or Council of Deputies. It attempted to soothe European bondholder and Dual Control sensibilities by declaring that Egypt accepted the entirety of the foreign debt as a matter of national honour, though a matter-of-fact bitterness underlay the adjacent observation that the debt was 'incurred not for Egypt's benefit, but in the private interests of a dishonest and irresponsible ruler'.[96] It called for special privileges for Europeans, including exemption from general taxation, to cease. Becoming more forceful as it went on, the Programme was plain-spoken in stating the vision of Egyptian nationalists: 'Their object is some day to see Egypt entirely in Egyptian hands'.[97] The text was not, despite Malet's claims, an inauthentic confection drawn up by Blunt on his own. While it is clear that this document was attempting to articulate various Egyptian aspirations to liberty and justice, com-municating them to a British readership in the recognizable language of national sovereignty, it manifestly drew on rich resources specific to the Egyptian context, not least the intellectual milieu of Islamic 'reawakening' and reform.

The late nineteenth century in Egypt had seen the emergence of several circles for intellectual debate and political engagement, including the Mahfil at-Taqaddum (Circle of Progress), Jamiyat Muhibbi al'Ilm (Society of the Lovers of Knowledge) and Misr al-Fatah (Young Egypt). Dissident journalism had become an important part of the Egyptian scene, with newspapers such as *Misr*, run by the Syrian Christian Adib Ishaq, taking strongly anti-imperialist lines while still engaging with European ideas. Ishaq, among others, did not see 'liberty' as deriving from the West, but as having an ancient home in the East to which it was now returning.[98] Blunt had come to know influential figures like the wandering and determinedly enigmatic Islamic scholar Jamal-ud-din al-Afghani, describing him memorably as a 'wild man of genius' who was able to make the case for reform and progress 'from below', showing how these were wholly com-patible with Islamic law and the Koran. Blunt also became lifelong friends with Afghani's disciple and Urabi's ally, Muhammad Abdu (sometimes spelled Abduh), who would eventually become grand mufti at Cairo.[99] Both men were acutely concerned with the need for Muslim societies to respond robustly to the West's claims to civiliza-tional superiority – and thus political dominance – through scientific learning and social progress.

Accordingly, Afghani and his milieu sought to revivify critical prac-tices of reading, interpretation and epistemological inquiry within Islam. Nikki R. Keddie has argued that Afghani's appeal to the Islamic tradition 'was strengthened by a desire to avoid identification with the Western oppressors or feelings of inferiority toward them'.[100] It was also, however, a genuine process akin to what Said has described as 'restlessly self-clarifying' critique 'in search of freedom, enlightenment, more agency'.[101] Describing his time in Cairo as a student 'seeking Mohammedan instruction', Blunt attests to a sense of joy in encountering through his teachers Islam's most expansive and ecumenical manifestations – 'the larger and purer school of thought', as he saw it.[102] This he attributed largely to Afghani's influence, which 'taught that Sunnite Islam was capable of adapting itself to all the highest cravings of the human soul and the needs of modern life' (it is worth noting here Blunt's emphasis on articulating both material needs and more ineffable human aspirations).[103] Afghani's influence in Egypt extended to institution-building; himself a fixture in Cairo's café culture, which provided spaces for intense debate, he encouraged the setting up of newspapers and secret societies, including Freemasonry, which facilitated political organization.[104] Sometime in 1879, Afghani also called for the establishment of *hizban watani-yyan* or a patriotic ('homeland') party.[105] His circle at the Azhar included Christians like Adib Ishaq and Louis Sabunji (who worked very closely with Blunt during the 1882 crisis and Urabi's trial) and the Jewish writer Yaqub Sanu (or James Sanua), all of whom played a role in emerging nationalist political and public activities. For disciples like Mohammed Abdu, Afghani played a crucial role in enabling opinions critical of the regime to be voiced openly by encouraging the establishment of newspapers which combated the tendencies of the older, more subservient ones. By 1879, when his once-friendly acquaintance, Khedive Tewfik, alarmed at the extent of Afghani's anticolonial preaching, would expel him from Egypt, even the correspondent of *The Times* noted that Afghani and his followers showed that 'a native opinion exists, has means to find expression, and therefore is not to be utterly ignored'.[106]

It is not necessary to overstate the correlation between Afghani's teachings and the rise of Egyptian nationalism to note the significance of his presence in Egypt for nearly a decade in the run-up to the revolution. Astonishingly, as Pankaj Mishra has noted, 'Afghani is barely known in the West today, even though his influence ... at least in its longevity, almost matches Marx's'.[107] Afghani, a notoriously evasive and shape-shifting figure, would go on after his Egyptian sojourn to become perhaps the most influential political theorist of pan-Islamism as an anticolonial strategy and ideology. His fierce anticolonialism, with a particular animus against the British, is thought to have developed in India at the time of the 1857 rebellion.[108] In Cairo, the wandering intellectual's speeches calling for Egyptian independence invoked the ways in which 'they, the Egyptians, had submitted to centuries of despotism and submission and their oppressive governments had taken from them what they had created with the sweat of their brows'.[109] Emphasizing what would be theorized in the twentieth century as 'self-emancipation' or 'self-liberation', their choice, he told his listeners, was either to 'live like free people or die as martyrs'.[110] Afghani also addressed the fellah directly: 'You break the heart of the earth in order to draw sustenance from it and support your family. Why do you not break the heart of your oppressor? Why do you not break the heart of those who eat the fruit of your labor?'[111] By advocating resistance both to 'egotistical Sultans' and the forces of European colonialism, Afghani appears to have anticipated many anticolonial arguments that 'were generally brought forth only some decades later'.[112] His copious, very diverse body of work – and the way in which it changed over time – merits further study in its own right, for which there is insufficient space here. I do, however, want to pause on a couple of lectures that give us some sense of the 'new critical spirit' Blunt saw as integral to the wandering teacher's influence in Egypt. The lectures were given in India, where he returned shortly after he was expelled from Egypt and give us a flavour of his thinking in that period.

A powerful commitment to the pursuit of knowledge, as well as a sense of epistemological inquiry as a *human* rather than culturally specific endeavour is evident in Afghani's thought. Afghani's speeches frequently suggested that knowledge necessarily involves the transmission of ideas across borders, so that they could not be said to 'belong' to any single culture – even if, reversing the colonial order of things, he cannily told his Indian audience: 'Human values spread out from India to the whole world.'[113] The recovery and revivification of hermeneutic traditions in the face of stagnation did not mean that colonized peoples were thereby acceding to the West; it was to return to something that was already embedded in their own traditions and histories. For Afghani, scientific thinking was part of a political explanation for the West's *current* domination and prosperity but not an inherently Western mode. In a speech in Alexandria, Afghani noted that present-day Egyptians were the descendants of peoples who had 'made major breakthroughs in engineering and mathematics, and who had taught writing, agriculture and philosophy to the Greeks'.[114] Equally, those countries – including India and the Muslim polities of the Middle East – which had neglected their scientific traditions were now paying the price for intellectual dereliction. Afghani's own investments are in philosophy or *falsafa* – a comprehensive mode of inquiry that subsumes the other sciences because, he says, 'its subject is universal'.[115] Hence, those Muslim scholars 'who forbid science and knowledge in the belief that they are safeguarding the Islamic religion are really the enemies of that religion ... and there is no incompatibility between science and knowledge and the foundation of the Islamic faith'.[116]

Reclaiming knowledge as an ineluctably human endeavour, Afghani defines the provenance of philosophy as 'the wide arena of human feelings', and its goal as 'human perfection in reason'.[117] In another essay probably written around the same time (*c.*1882), addressed explicitly to Indian Muslim clerics or *ulema*, Afghani figures 'Reason' not as a particular mode of thinking, but as part of the 'light of natural intelligence' which all human beings have necessarily deployed to know and shape the world around them, 'to cultivate, to plant trees, preserve fruits, procure animals, protect rivers, bring forth waters, dig canals, dikes, and dams, to spin and weave, in an agreeable and appropriate way'.[118] All of this requires knowledge through the spirit of inquiry, whether this be of 'the nature of soils' or 'the action and reaction of the elements'.[119] Knowledge by definition is limitless, which is why those Muslim scholars who seek to narrow its scope, closing 'the doors of why and wherefore to pure minds' and wearing the 'garment of infallibility', are 'defective and incomplete'.[120] As he would note in his famous rebuttal of Renan's condemnation of Islam, all religions have it in them to be intolerant and stifle learning and all have done so at different points in their history.[121] For Afghani, the 'Precious Book' or Holy Koran itself, however, makes clear the importance of 'knowledge, wisdom, learning, reflection, thought and insight', and clarifies the laws of civic and domestic relationships so as to prevent 'the harm of oppression and injustice'.[122] Equally,

knowledge cannot be culturally bounded, for 'to be proud regarding learning is to be satisfied with ignorance'; humbly learning from
other cultures is vital to the natural progression of ideas.[123] Many
ideas that are seen as Greek or Roman have travelled there, Afghani
tells his audience, through India, Babylonia and Egypt, in each move
acquiring 'a new form, and in each migration ... fresh adornment'.[124]
Spirituality and science are neither closed nor mutually exclusive
systems. 'No end exists for this great Book', which is open to infinite
study and interpretation, he writes of the Koran, and anyone who
either claims to have fathomed it or attempts to close off its meanings
'is suffering from compound ignorance or madness'.[125] In closing, he
urges the *ulema* of India to give up defective scholarship, to cast their
glance on the 'wide world' around them and ask why Muslims are
afflicted by 'poverty, indigence, helplessness, and distress'.[126] To do
this, they will need to engage with science, technology, indeed modernity itself: 'Is it not a fault for a percipient sage not to learn the entire
sphere of new sciences and inventions and fresh creations ... when
the world has changed from one state to another?'[127] Keddie suggests
that Afghani was drawing here on a longer Islamic philosophical
tradition in which 'when scripture apparently contradicted reason or
science, scripture must be reinterpreted'.[128]

An Egyptian Nationalist Returns to Britain

When, in early 1882, Blunt left Cairo, radicalized by the ferment,
his sense of himself as a mediator who was, in the final instance,
loyal to the British crown had been badly shaken. He wrote that
the three months he had recently spent in Egypt had felt like a life-
time, 'so absorbing had been the interests they had brought me'.[129]
In a marked reversal, he began to think of key British officials in
Egypt such as Malet as former friends, 'gone over to the enemy's
camp, and ... now no longer to be trusted', and himself described
the Joint Note he had set out to advocate to Urabi as an attack on
the national movement.[130] This attack was taking place under the
cover of 'a crusade of civilization' which was in fact 'a support to the
established order in Cairo of financial things'.[131] As his visit to Urabi
in December on behalf of Malet had so clearly demonstrated, the

Egyptians were not credulous and passive recipients of his attempts to translate imperial intentions. He himself, meanwhile, had turned from being a mere sympathizer – he would now subject 'romantic sympathy' to critique – into a man who would see himself as an Egyptian nationalist, who perhaps felt the betrayal of Britain and its messianic rhetoric of spreading liberty more sharply than any other. Leaving for England on 27 February 1882, a bare four months before the bombardment of Alexandria which led up to Urabi's defeat, he noted another inversion, in which it was not the colonized who assimilated to English values: 'I looked upon Egypt already like a second *patria* and intended to throw my lot in with the Egyptians as if they were my own countrymen. I was estranged from those of my countrymen in blood, except Gregory, who formed the then little English colony at Cairo.'[132] This was not the romantically Orientalist Blunt going native, like many before him, including his acquaintance Richard Burton, or toying with his admitted attraction to Islam (he would, later in life, consider converting).[133] What Blunt had undergone by the time Alexandria was shelled and Urabi put on trial was, as it were, a Cairene conversion to anticolonialism. He would bitterly distinguish the genuineness of his own identification with the cause of Egyptian liberty from the fraudulence of the Liberal, Gladstone, who 'like the tragedian in Dickens, when he had to act Othello … began by painting himself black all over'.[134]

Despite the efforts of Blunt, Sir William Gregory and others to sway Gladstone's government, in the end the British occupation of Egypt (the French bowed out early on) was indeed the result. Ably assisted by Malet and other colonial administrators, Gladstone succeeded in his efforts to portray Urabi as a military dictator who would usurp rather than represent Egypt's national aspirations, which both the Liberal Party and the liberal press continued to claim to respect. Although

Lady Anne and Wilfrid Blunt

attempts were made to obtain the consent of other European powers to the invasion, Britain ultimately went it alone. The sleight of hand did not go unremarked by the *Annual Register*:

> Up to this time, and indeed for a long time afterwards, Arabi Pasha was regarded by the English Foreign Office as a mere military adventurer – the national support which his programme gradually received was altogether ignored, and a deaf ear was turned to those warnings which came from even official sources; whilst those addressed to the public by Sir William Gregory, Mr Wilfrid Blunt, and others who were conveniently classed together as dreamers or partisans, were put aside as unworthy of a moment's attention.[135]

Blunt was incredulous: 'I could not believe that England had an interest in crushing liberty anywhere', he wrote in an article after Urabi's defeat at Tel-el-Kabir.[136] He had been wrong: 'It has been to prevent a crime that I have laboured – alas, in vain!'[137] His experience of colonial myth-making around Egypt gave him a fresh perspective on other situations, such as Ireland, of which restive colony it was also being said that 'agitators' were at work, 'that the Irish fellahin are not really with the National Party, and that armed intervention would set things right'.[138] Despite Gladstone's having labelled him the 'one unfortunate exception' among Englishmen with Egyptian experience in opposing the war, Blunt was not exactly a 'single voice against a multitude' (as he described himself) even if he had been the most vociferous.[139] There was even one high-profile resignation over the intervention – that of the Liberal MP John Bright, who had been very active with the Jamaica Committee. 'I think that in the present case there has been a manifest violation both of international law and of the moral law, and, therefore, it is impossible for me to give my support to it', Bright maintained in his resignation address, the day after the bombardment.[140] Most questions, unlike Blunt's, Harrison's or Gregory's, were asked after the event. Had 'the bombardment of Alexandria … been undertaken to protect British subjects and British interests, or to protect the interests of British and French bondholders?' Had parliament 'been drifting into war with their eyes open … carrying fire and sword into the country on behalf of usurers'?[141]

Gladstone's government held the line even as it declared that it was not at war with Egypt at all. Invoked in a trope that will be all too familiar to present-day readers, Egypt was represented as a land of 'lawless military violence, aggravated by cruel and wanton crime', while 'Arabi was a military oppressor; whose success would revive the worst abuses of old Egyptians' misrule; and our troops were engaged not in a war with Egypt, but in freeing Egyptians from oppression'.[142] Furious at criticism in the House, Gladstone insisted that the bombardment had been undertaken in 'self-defence'.[143] Less credulous Liberals demanded of their leader: which party in Egypt had invited Britain to rid them of the despot? And how could the arrival of the fleet well before the riots be construed as 'self-defence'? The answer was not precisely satisfactory, but it came in the form of Sir Charles Dilke's groundless assertion that, had action not been taken, it 'would be to put the lives of Europeans throughout the East absolutely at the mercy of a fanatical mob of Mahomedans'. What was at stake, he noted, with greater honesty perhaps as he appealed to the working-men of Britain, was not only 'the sanctity of European life' but the right of British traders not to be 'completely debarred from operations in the East and driven out'.[144] Although Dilke went on to insist that the protection of British trade was not the reason for bombardment, the revolution had portended significant changes to the way in which Egypt would be governed, in particular, with regard to labour and finance. What cantankerous British parliamentarians referred to as 'bondholders' backed by military force were in fact an expandable tribe in the service of international capitalism, 'a foreign stratum of investors, merchants, workers, and diplomats [with] extraordinary leverage over the indigenous state'.[145] There is little doubt that this was a class whose interests were firmly in the sights of the revolution, and that their privileges would have been significantly undermined if Urabi and his allies had not been stopped. One of the first – and, for the Anglo-French alliance, more alarming – acts of the Urabi government was the cancellation of fellah loans contracted from foreigners. Whatever changes may have been forthcoming, they were certainly not conducive to the maintenance of the advantages of powerful foreign commercial and financial interests.

Once Urabi had surrendered and been taken prisoner of war, on 13 September 1882, his trial and presumed death sentence would

bring together a small but articulate group of British campaigners, including the anti-war Radicals Wilfrid Lawson MP, Frederic
Harrison and John Seymour Keay.[146] The Gladstone government did
not look upon the prospect of a fair trial in open court with equa-
nimity; too much might come out in the wash, putting their carefully
constructed version of events in jeopardy. Neither, of course, did the
khedive and his advisors. It took extraordinary persistence on Blunt's
part, combined with a shift in British public opinion, for an agreement to emerge that Urabi could, after all, be represented by the
barrister A. M. Broadley, who had already been working on behalf
of apprehended rebels in French-occupied Tunis. Upon Broadley's
advice, Blunt (reluctantly) and Urabi accepted the compromise offer
that, if the latter pleaded guilty to the charge of rebellion, other
charges would be dropped and his sentence commuted to exile. Once
the initial flush of military success died down, Blunt thought, 'reasonable people were beginning to ask themselves what after all we were
fighting in Egypt about'.[147] The aftermath of war and the highly publicized attempt to save Urabi's life certainly made way for increased
domestic criticism in Britain of the annexation of Egypt. Urabi's trial
and all the various components of 'the Egypt crisis' would become
the point of departure for writing alternative histories of the annexation, which in turn were also 'secret histories' of British imperialism
itself. What is common to this small but significant body of work –
which would provide a historical resource for the development of a
more sustained body of anticolonialism within Britain – is the way
in which it both takes native Egyptian resistance seriously and finds
points of cross-cultural identification with it.

Sulking at 'Civilization'

One of the most trenchant voices to articulate a position critical of
both the motivations for such imperial incursions and their impact
on Britain was not that of an iconoclastic 'Tory Democrat' like Blunt,
or of an avowed socialist, but rather of the Positivist intellectual and
writer Frederic Harrison, briefly discussed in Chapter 2. Harrison
did not share Blunt's Oriental enthusiasms, his travel experience, or
his personal engagement with Egypt and Egyptians, but had studied

the situation extensively in addition to discussing it with Blunt. Regretting that they had not met earlier, Blunt described Harrison as 'the soundest and most courageous man on foreign policy then in the Liberal Party, and by far their most vigorous pamphleteer'.[148] Harrison had, of course, been a relatively young member of the Jamaica Committee, and had produced the six 'Letters' on martial law which, as we have already seen, were particularly concerned with the question of the rebounding impact on the British psyche and body politic of violent suppression in the further reaches of the Empire. This concern resurfaced in his powerful indictment of 'Englishmen fighting to rivet on a weak people the chains of a debt-slavery' in Egypt.[149] Delivered first, as a speech to the Anti-Aggression League, in 1882, just before the bombardment of Alexandria, Harrison's essay 'Egypt' also provides a succinct counter-history of events leading up to that fateful moment. The forensic critique he laid out in it is marked by an unsparing scrutiny of the language used to justify the unjustifiable, but the thrust of the argument focuses on Egyptian resistance born of 'the irritation of the native mind at the European exploitation of their country'.[150] If the colonial enterprise was indeed to be understood as one based on spreading liberal values, as Gladstone was claiming, how strange was it that 'the Egyptians grew sulky at so much civilisation'?[151] Perhaps the answer lay in more grossly material realms:

A native pays tax of 12 per cent annual value on his house; the European lives tax free. The native fly-driver pays a heavy tax on his carriage; the European banker drives his pair tax free. Next, the civilisers having obliged the country with some 115 millions sterling at 7 and 10 per cent, obtained 'concessions' for about thirty-five millions more. Then they kindly exempted themselves from taxation, were good enough to set up local courts in which they had the right to bring their civil and criminal affairs to a judge of their own nation. An army of European judges, and secretaries, and assessors, and barristers were called in at very liberal salaries, who kindly undertook to do the law for the Egyptian people.[152]

Even 'the worst exactions of his native Mahometan tax-gatherers never imposed on him so hopeless a burden as the cool, scientific, book-keeping sort of spoliation of his European civilisers', Harrison observed, in direct contradiction of the claim that European rule was less exploitative of the ordinary Egyptian than native despotism.[153] As the despoiled Muslim population 'conceived what is called a "fanatical" objection to the foreigners; they even blasphemed the value of the civilisation; they murmured it was rather too dear'.[154]

In a trenchantly sardonic style, Harrison drew out a feature of the Egyptian rebellion that had been deliberately obscured in official accounts of the Egypt crisis: shifting loyalties and complicated internal relations notwithstanding, it was fundamentally a polarized struggle between the agents and allies of European commercial and financial interests, on the one hand, and the diverse indigenous forces which came together to resist them, on the other. It suited 'the European ring' to reduce this challenge to a military mutiny which, Harrison scoffed – far less uncertain than he had been in 1857 – was simply 'a wild and silly calumny'; Egypt was hardly, he noted pointedly, the first place where a 'national rising' had been headed by soldiers.[155] On the contrary – and the link to Blunt's advocacy of the Egyptian cause is clear here – its inspiration could be found in the great university of Cairo, 'the intellectual centre of the Mussulman world'.[156] Instead of being cowed by the bombardment of Alexandria, the Egyptians 'were roused to fury by it'.[157] Rather than crush such justifiable resistance, Harrison wonders (in inevitably gendered language) whether it ought not to be possible, instead, to 'honour the Egyptian people that they were capable of such manly indignation'.[158] The emphasis on the feelings and consequent actions of the Egyptians is of no little significance; much as Ernest Jones once did in his editorials on the Indian uprising, Harrison asked his readers to reflect on the feelings that might arise in their own breasts if French and Russian fleets sailed up the Thames to serve an ultimatum on the queen to exile Gladstone to Australia and dissolve the House of Commons. Far from being evidence of a strange fanaticism, Harrison suggested, the fury of the Egyptians was evidence of shared sensibilities and values: 'Well, the Egyptians have feelings, and they resented, as was natural, this insolent and impotent menace'.[159] As he had in his letters on martial law, Harrison was able to map the topoi of colonial apologetics deftly, in a plea to Gladstone not to betray his earlier avowed Midlothian principles:

India, the Empire, British interests, commerce, our countrymen in personal danger, English capital sunk in Africa, the large financial interests at stake, our international obligations, the harmony of Europe, the cause of good government, the emancipation of the slaves, the amelioration of the lot of the fellah, the jealousies and ambition of France, with a general background of 'civilisation' ... It is the old story; the same grand phrases which so often did duty on the Danube and the Bosphorus, on the Vaal and the Indus.[160]

'Sonorous' and self-serving civilizational discourse, Harrison was perhaps one of the earliest to articulate, was deployed in the interests of 'certain rich men in London and Paris' with determinate financial interests in Egypt, India and beyond, so that war became 'a shallow and shameless pretext' to protect 'one hundred and fifty millions or so of Western gold trembling for its dividends and interest'.[161]

That it was Egyptian resistance, rather than just his own allegiance to a species of English Liberalism which inspired these reflections on commonality is evidenced by the fact Harrison was not at all immune to the racial hierarchies of his time. Initially protesting only Britain's assumption of the governance of what he himself called 'semi-civilised nations', Harrison certainly did not arrive at his reflections on Egypt through a presupposition of cultural equality, but found himself *conceding* parity of aspiration by coming to an understanding of the aspirations and claims that drove the rebellion. Given that he did not have personal experience of engagement with other cultures, Egyptian resistance appears to have had a significant role in shaping Harrison's critical asseverations on empire. This human tendency to self-assertion in the face of attack, he even tried to tell Gladstone in an open letter, would render any civilizational mission inevitably incendiary: 'You can always produce anarchy anywhere by goading a people to frenzy where any spark of courage or independence is left them.'[162] There can ultimately be no such thing as a cooperative and accommodating colonialism; the forces it unleashes are necessarily polarized: 'The ascendancy of a foreign race, even where they have much to offer the natives ... cannot be permanently secured without conquest; and it must be maintained by a protracted struggle for supremacy'.[163] For Harrison as for Blunt, this was a marked shift in perspective. In relation to Afghanistan and Jamaica, Harrison was more concerned with the exercise of imperial terror, which, in its illegality, undermined the English as a 'civilised and honourable people'.[164] The 'Egyptian imbroglio', in contrast, impelled Harrison to experience something like shared indignation, and no small degree of identification, with the Egyptian rebels. It appears to have been a sensation akin to 'solidarity'.

That what had emerged in Egypt was both natural and universally legitimate – and ought to be treated as such – was also the insight that drove the Scottish–Indian businessman, administrator and politician John Seymour Keay's *j'accuse*, uncompromisingly titled *Spoiling the Egyptians*. Keay, a supporter of Indian native claims to a greater share in government, and later a member of the British Committee of the Indian National Congress, noted that suppressing the fact of Egyptian resistance to spoliation was vital to the myth-making of the colonial mission. Colonial discourse had routinely to deny the existence of indigenous conceptions of rights in order to make the case that justice was the gift of colonial rule. In fact, colonialism resulted in the forced abrogation of those customary rights:

> Among all the Eastern races ... a great variety of different customs, tenures, and privileges have grown up connected with the land, all of which, however ill-defined, have, among the people, the force of absolute rights. We may imagine, then, the feelings of those people, when a corps of aliens appears, and spreads itself abroad over the country, placing in every village its representative, *whose express duty is to dispute and confiscate those rights*.[165]

Colonial officialdom, in Keay's critical view, had

> made most determined efforts to convince the English nation that nobody in Egypt dislikes them, or has raised any issue with them, except a few mutinous soldiers ... It would never do for those who existed only for the Bondholders to admit that a really National feeling had arisen against their organized extortions, whereby one half of the income of the Nation was expropriated.[166]

Like Harrison, Keay identified emergent colonial mythologies, such as that the 'Egyptian peasantry were formerly more grievously oppressed under Native rule than they have been since European dictation began'; that the country itself had now 'been raised from misery to unalloyed happiness by the *Deus ex machina* of the European Control; and that 'there existed a real longing for its beneficent presence among all classes'.[167] All these colonial fantasies rely on a chilling moral relativism: 'The Egyptian eel was a reptile so accustomed to be skinned, that it rather enjoyed the process!'[168] For both Keay and Harrison, this colonial denial of parity through a deliberate refusal to imagine the lives and feelings of others had disturbing moral implications. Urabi, who ought to be seen 'as a political liberator' and 'a political leader of the people', had himself appealed to England in her capacity as a slave-freeing nation '*to sympathize with the Egyptians in their attempt to obtain liberty*'.[169] This liberty had been denied because the first use Egyptians would make of it 'would, no doubt, be to check the wholesale depletion of their country by the foreigner'.[170]

Charged with being unpatriotic, Harrison too would counter that criticism of empire was continuous with antislavery – an idea that would surface periodically in British anticolonial thought:

> What slavery and the slave trade once were to our grandfathers here, what a slave industry and a slave society were to the Americans of yesterday, that empire is becoming to Englishmen to-day. A cry of emancipation, as of a religious duty to redress the sufferings of humanity, is rising up here too. Our people have no share in this guilt, as they have none in the gain or the glory.[171]

Unsurprisingly, it was Harrison who was most exercised by the implications for his country of crushing political self-assertion in other lands: 'England is not herself, whilst she is forced thus to keep anxious and suspicious watch across Africa and Asia over her huge and precarious prize.'[172] The 'hard mechanical pressure' it would take to secure and hold the Empire in the face of resistance would only work for a limited time, 'breaking every now and again into further seas of blood, more conquests, more vengeance, ever sliding down the slope of tyranny, cruelty, and panic'.[173] Much as Congreve had done with the Indian uprising, Harrison would suggest to working-class listeners that the energies consumed in repressing resistance elsewhere provided a subterfuge for avoiding a legion of domestic problems; they needed to tell their politicians that 'civilisation' which 'is making the tour of the world on board ironclads with eighty-ton guns ... is terribly wanted in the three kingdoms at home'.[174]

The opposition was eloquent but offered in vain, Harrison would note: 'The party system, the financial interests, and the thirst of Empire are forces that do not listen to the voice of reason and of justice.'[175] Urabi and others tried with him for 'rebellion' received commuted death sentences and 'perpetual exile' to Ceylon; he himself would eventually return to Egypt to live and die quietly. Within days of the verdict, the deposed leader would write to *The Times* a letter dated 4 December 1882, included in full in Broadley's memoir, in which he would note that he could 'leave Egypt with perfect tranquillity and confidence in the future, because I know that England cannot any longer delay the reforms which we have struggled for'.[176] Despite protestations of gratitude, a quiet but unmistakable defiance – astonishing given that he was virtually a British prisoner at this point – also marks the deposed leader's insistence that any reforms undertaken by England in Egypt would have derived ultimately from native initiative. They would include, he predicted correctly, the abolition of the Anglo-French Control, legal and judicial reforms, more representative government 'with a voice' for the Egyptian people, and the end of foreign domination of gainful employment: 'Egypt will be no more in the hands of a myriad of foreign employees filling every available post, to the exclusion of the Egyptians'.[177] It is not, however, a narrowly anti-Western declaration; on the contrary, 'Arábi the rebel' addressed himself, across national boundaries, to a commonality of understanding and, amazingly enough, urged the English to 'complete' the work he had commenced: 'The English people, when they see all these things, will then be able to realize the fact that my rebellion had a very strong justification.'[178] His words and the movement he led were only temporarily defeated; that resistance would once again find expression in the 1919 revolution that would eventually force the British out of Egypt.

In his letter, Urabi also thanked those, including members of parliament, who had 'often and nobly spoken on [his] behalf'.[179] The most stentorian of these voices was, of course, Blunt's. He would continue to speak out on Egypt and on colonial issues for the next four decades, until his death in 1922. The Egyptian revolution had been as much a baptism of fire for him as it had been a watershed historical passage for Egyptians. Gone was the naively benevolent writer of *The Future of Islam*, with an unexamined sense of empire's liberalizing potential. Travelling in India after the Urabi Rebellion (he was not allowed to disembark in Egypt), Blunt wrote uncompromisingly in the *Manchester Guardian*: 'That Asia is awake and politically self-conscious and desperately in earnest for self-government cannot any longer be denied … The vast millions of Asiatics denied their aspirations under British rule must in the end break the strength to coerce them of the British empire.'[180] In *The Wind and the Whirlwind*, a long and angry poetic jeremiad of disputable quality, Blunt would lay out the case against imperialism in Egypt in copious verse. What is of interest about the poem is the emphasis it places in its opening on the uses (and abuses) of voice, the first line repeated throughout the text:

> I have a thing to say. But how to say it?
> I have a cause to plead. But to what ears?
> How shall I move a world by lamentation –
> A world which has not heeded a Nation's tears?[181]

How can the case against imperial power be made? Blunt's sense of himself as a lone voice, 'unthanked' and 'unhonoured', veers into bombast, of course; but, once again, his target is, in part, the selective apostrophizing of freedom in English verse. Why should the cause of 'freedom / Lost on the Nile' be any less worthy of a poet's hymning than the liberty Milton or Dante might have sung of?[182] The language of freedom was not English alone: 'Its utterance / Was in that tongue divine the Orient knew'; the Egyptians – 'Jew, and Copt, and Moslem' – join the chanting chorus, catching and echoing words that speak to shared aspirations.[183] Though his plan to bring Urabi himself to London to plead the Egyptian case failed, Blunt would also continue to facilitate engagement with anticolonial figures such as Afghani and Abdu, hosting them in London and introducing them to political players such as Randolph Churchill. While staying with Blunt in 1884, Abdu gave a startlingly frank interview to the *Pall Mall Gazette* in which he rubbished all English claims to benevolent influence in Egypt: 'Your liberality we see plainly is only for yourselves, and your sympathy with us is that of the wolf for the lamb which he designs to eat.'[184] After the invasion of 1882, Egyptians 'know that there are worse evils than despotism, and worse enemies than the Turks ... There is no Mohammedan in Egypt so oppressed as to wish for any more of your help.'[185] Calling for British troops to be withdrawn from the country and for Urabi to be returned to Egypt from exile, Abdu closes the interview with a devastating pronouncement: 'But do not attempt to do us any more good. Your good has done us too much harm already.'[186]

On Christmas Eve, 1899, looking back on the century just gone, Blunt penned a short but magnificent polemic from his Cairo home in the form of a letter to *The Times* titled 'The Shame of the Nineteenth Century'.[187] It is worth quoting at some length not only because it shows how far he himself had come from his days as an Orientalist traveller and aristocratic horse-trader, but because it cuts sharply through the narratives of empire that, at the turn of the century, held Britain in their grip:

We have come to the last week of the glorious Nineteenth Century, and your columns and those of every other great London newspaper will, I know, be full of its praises, and especially for the part we Englishmen, in the character of sons of the Empire, have played in it. We shall be told of our imperial expansion, of our glories, of our mission of freedom and justice, and of our claims on the admiration of the world and of ourselves. We shall be called on to fall down as a nation and worship our own golden image revealed in a splendid record of heroic deeds and noble impulses, and, if any dissent, it shall be counted to him for envy and uncharitableness or wilful blindness to the sun at noon-day. It is against this self-worship I would raise my voice, however feebly, against this shameless self-praise, this painting in every gaudy colour of the imperial idol in which Englishmen, each day of the week, behold the image of their own imperial faces. Is it possible that we do not see the folly of it all, the childishness of concealing terrible facts known to all the world, the huge vulgarity of pretending to be other than the miserable sinners we are, fulfilling a destiny half chosen by ourselves, half thrust upon us by the disease of our world-hunger, of devouring peoples more beautiful and better than ourselves?[188]

If 'imperial scepticism', to use Gregory Claey's term, runs like a skein through the dramatic canvas of the second half of the nineteenth century, it would find its apotheosis in Blunt's persistently raised voice which, as the new century began, was beginning to speak the language of full-fledged anticolonialism. It entailed anti-capitalism too: 'free labour' under capitalist imperial rule, where complete destruction is avoided only because labouring hands are needed for the enrichment of the employer, Blunt notes baldly, can spell degradation 'far worse than slavery'.[189] Like Harrison, Blunt points to the dangers of 'moral and mental decay corresponding very closely with the ruin we have inflicted on others' rebounding on Britain.[190] He deprecates a growing international division of labour whereby Englishmen expect others to work for them, just as in the colonies indentured workers, 'the black or yellow races, labour in the sun and the white man sits idly in the shade'.[191] If the Urabi revolution constituted Blunt's initiation into the language of anticolonial resistance, he would continue to learn from its later manifestations in various local contexts, not least Ireland. It would be a very long time before anything like the 'change in the public mind' with regard to empire which Blunt hoped for would begin to emerge in Britain; he would not live to see it happen.[192] But the curtain of the twentieth century opened on a rapidly enlarging theatre of protest and resistance. The best efforts of its politicians and propagandists notwithstanding, Britain could not shut out the echoes.

4

Passages to Internationalism: The 'New Spirit' in India and Edwardian Travellers

There is no empire lost by a free grant of concession by the rulers to the ruled. History does not record any such event.

Bal Gangadhar Tilak

They had in the House itself the constant co-operation of a small but active group of members, who constituted themselves into an 'Indian Party', and were ever ready to act as spokesmen of Indian discontent.

Valentine Chirol, *Times* correspondent in India

In the spring of 1882, Wilfrid Blunt returned to London from Egypt deeply critical of British foreign policy, but he was not yet the wide-ranging anticolonialist that he would become over the next decade. It would take his very personal involvement with the Irish struggle during the late 1880s to complete his radicalization on questions of empire. In 1883, en route to Ceylon to see Urabi, he broke his journey in India, a country he had previously visited in 1879. Blunt's diaries record that the suggestion he spend a few months in India came from Afghani, but also that, as a consequence of what he had learned in Egypt, he himself was keen on understanding Indian Muslims as a 'living force in Islam'. As a 'Home Ruler', he also wanted to ascertain 'what the true feeling of the country was towards its English masters, and what the prospect of India's eventually gaining her freedom'.[1]

The immediate result was *Ideas about India*, whose constituent essays, previously published in *Fortnightly Review*, Blunt grandiosely billed as 'the first complete and fearless apology of Indian home rule which had been published'.[2] The short volume was also a defence of his friend Lord Ripon's rule as a liberal viceroy; without further reforms in the direction of home rule such as Ripon had made, Blunt warned, the prospect of revolution was real. Curiously, perhaps, for the reader of the decidedly more militant *A Secret History*, Blunt's language in this text is that of a defender of British rule in India, albeit one who wishes for it to continue only until such time as India has 'worked out her salvation' under the protection it offers.[3] Such mellow paternalism was very much in accordance with the views of other late Victorian and Edwardian critics of empire for whom the horizon of full independence was as yet unimaginable, or certainly very distant. They would voice critiques of British rule (rather than of the imperial project as a whole) predicated on a paternal concern for its subjects, and issue fraternal warnings to politicians and colonial administrators about the dangers posed to the well-being of the British Indian empire by their policies and practices. The assumption, in Annie Besant's words, was that India had no wish to 'break her link with England, but she desires so to transform it that it may be a tie honourable to both and prized by both'.[4]

Blunt and 'India for the Indians'

Even so, Blunt's account of his Indian sojourn towards the end of the nineteenth century registered intimations of the agitation that would break out more fully in the wake of the 1905 partition of Bengal. His Egyptian experiences fresh in his mind, he believed he could see signs of 'the dawn of that day of unrest which is the necessary prelude to full self-assertion in every subject land'.[5] He had arrived in India, politicized by his experience of the Egyptian Revolution and taken with Islam, but admittedly ignorant about 'Hindu life', as he put it. As a guest of Viceroy Ripon, Blunt was inclined, in a somewhat unexamined manner, to enthusiastically endorse the liberal reform-based approach to ruling India which his host was propounding. That enthusiasm was quite quickly moderated. In a curious comment

in a later memoir, based on his journals from that period, Blunt noted
that when accused of stirring up trouble where all had been well he
had been compelled to ask: 'Who are the satisfied natives? I have not
met a single one since I came to India.'[6] He was disconcerted by the
extent to which he found 'everywhere distrust of the Government, fear
of the officials, and a certain vague disquiet which is an unmistakable
sign with nations that all is not well'.[7] Accordingly, his assessment
of the British Empire's prospects in India vacillates – as would the
memoirs of those who followed him – between insisting that there has
been no irreconcilable breach between ruler and ruled, and gloomily
noting: 'There is no love lost whatever between the Indians and ourselves, whether they be Mohammedan, or Hindu, or Parsi, or native
Christian.'[8] While characteristically centred on Blunt's own acumen
and insight, *Ideas* is nonetheless strikingly concerned with the extent
to which radical analysis and ideas are already thickening the air in
native circles. The post-Egypt Blunt is swift to dismiss the colonial
canard that the only Indians holding forth on self-rule are mimic men
who are not representative of India: 'It has constantly been pretended
by English writers that it is only what are called "Babus" of Calcutta
who are sufficiently educated to have advanced ideas on the political
regeneration of their country; but nothing is less true'; this too was
an insight later political travellers would reiterate.[9] Blunt recounts
encounters with a wide variety of people, including peasant farmers
or ryots with whom he converses through interpreters. For all that
Blunt cleaves to a teleology which finds its apotheosis in the nation
form, much of his analysis is taken up with criticizing the destruction
of existing resources of governance which had served India well, if
not perfectly, in precolonial times.

Ideas about India is structured by a set of parallel tensions,
between reform and overthrow, and between insistence on native
loyalty to imperial rule and acknowledging dissatisfaction with it.
The text is shot through with the sense that, even in India, different
though it is from Egypt, cataclysmic revolt is not an impossibility;
Blunt had 'no doubt whatever that if things continue in their present
groove a revolution is the necessary end', though 'by timely reform
that catastrophe might be averted'.[10] While colonial rule may have
acted as a catalyst for a cultural reawakening, Blunt writes, it was
time for his fellow Britons to admit to 'the destruction of much that

was good and noble and of profit in the past by the unthinking and
often selfish action of Western methods'.[11] Faced with the realities
of the situation, Blunt's own vision of India's future is dialectical: he
does 'not wish the past back in its integrity', but would nonetheless
'save what can still be saved of the indigenous plan, and ... use in
reconstruction something of the same materials'.[12] The 'sound' reasoning of 'native economists' looms large in this narrative as Blunt
recalls his most recent experiences: 'We have seen the results of an
unsound finance in Egypt: and we shall see them repeated in India
before the world is many years older.'[13] In the end, however, it was
the potentially intractable racial divide fostered by British rule which
put Blunt in mind of General Gordon's warning which he cites to end
his narrative: 'You may do what you will. It will be of no use. India
will never be reformed until there has been there a new revolt.'[14]
In averring that, if things continued as they were, revolution would
be the inevitable and catastrophic consequence, Blunt may not have
been quite imagining self-emancipation, but was certainly confronting the limits of well-meaning reformism: 'I am convinced that if
at the present moment any serious disaffection were to arise in the
native army, such as occurred in 1857, it would not lead to a revolt
only. It would be joined, as the other was not, by the whole people.'[15]

Twenty-five years after the 1857 uprising, concerted and widespread resistance to colonial rule in India had, on the face of it, been
eliminated from the wider horizon, although several significant localized uprisings took place, including the Indigo Rebellion in 1859.
Two years after Blunt's visit, the Indian National Congress (preceded
by an organization that called itself the Indian Association) would
constitute itself under the guidance of the Scotsman Allan Octavian
Hume, as a project of tutelage in which Indians would learn to ask
for a share in governance. For 'sympathizers' like Hume, the language of nationalism, presumed to have universal reach, nonetheless
had to be taught to Indians, against the grain of their habitual fatal-
ism, as this verse suggests:

> Sons of Ind, why sit ye idle
> Wait ye for some Deva's aid?
> Buckle to, be up and doing!
> Nations by themselves are made![16]

From Theosophist Congress member Annie Besant's perspective, 'responsible Englishmen have declared that England desired to give to India the liberties enjoyed by her own people, so soon as India was ready to possess and utilise them'.[17] Accordingly, for its first two decades the Congress would undertake modest lobbying for a larger native role in the administration of British India, in order, as two early twentieth-century historians would put it, 'to consider how best they could influence the foreign government under which they and their children were fated to live'.[18] In this project, Indian campaigners received support in Britain from 'prominent individual Whigs or liberals who raised their voices in defence of India'.[19] These defenders of India would include, in addition to Besant, former colonial civil servants Henry Cotton and William Wedderburn. In the main, however, such voices were raised in the interests of amelioration and reform rather than as critiques of the imperial project per se. This was as true, in the first instance, for socialist figures such as the relatively militant H. M. Hyndman of the Social Democratic Federation, and J. Keir Hardie of the Independent Labour Party (and, later, one of the founders of the Labour Party) as it was for those of a more liberal disposition, such as Besant and Cotton. As Gregory Claeys has noted in his study of 'imperial sceptics' in the last years of the nineteenth century, while there was 'considerable socialist antagonism towards imperial expansion', this too was 'increasingly balanced by a desire to improve rather than dispense with Britain's colonial possessions … broadly conceived in terms of a co-operative commonwealth ideal rather than an exploitative capitalist model.'[20]

A will to reconfigure rather than abandon was also manifest in the views of the most famous critic of empire during that period, J. A. Hobson, whose own critique of imperialism drew on the Cobdenite idea that imperialism violated free trade and was harmful for national prosperity. The Boer War at the end of the nineteenth century shaped Hobson's view that imperialism need not be repudiated but had to be forged as a 'higher' ideal in which jingoism had no place. At any rate, the views of the subjugated did not particularly impinge on his critique:

Finally, the government by force, not by consent, of another people, and the chronic temptation hypocritically to feign that the dominating motive in our rule is their good, not our own gain, may react so powerfully and so insidiously upon the mind of an Imperialist nation that it loses the capacity not merely to recognise the advantage of leaving lower peoples to follow their own paths of progress or regression, but to perceive the fatal injuries which domineering practices abroad inflict upon the efficiency of national self-government at home.[21]

To the extent that 'sanction' mattered to Hobson, it was not that of the ruled but that of 'a society of nations' in which all were represented, and which 'delegated England or France in the interests of civilisation to take under tutelage some backward or degraded people which lay on their borders', so that there would be some 'moral basis' for imperialism.[22] In other words, the distinction between a moral and a 'parasitic' imperialism would largely rest upon the former's assumption of the role of tutor.[23] Stephen Howe has also argued that for most Victorian and Edwardian radicals self-determination was an idea that extended only to the white settler colonies; as both 'a minority current and a limited and conditional stance', critiques of empire in Asia and Africa were generally made on the basis of calling for 'good government rather than self-government'.[24] Those Britons who did celebrate rebellion against other empires – the Haitian uprising against the French, for instance – rarely 'extended similar sentiments to revolts against British rule'.[25]

Most early socialist engagements with empire in Britain, however critical, were also limited, taking for granted a civilizational hierarchy within which colonies like India would need to be tutored into political maturity. It is worth pausing briefly, however, on the controversial figure of Henry Mayers Hyndman, who has largely been regarded, not entirely without justification, as 'having nationalist and imperialist tendencies', and certainly ones in which anti-capitalism was folded into anti-Semitism.[26] We know that Hyndman started out as a believer in the beneficence of British rule in India, even supporting the suppression of the 1857 rebellion and calling for 'a wise, firm, economical, and liberal rule' so as to avoid disaffection.[27] As Claeys notes, however, Hyndman did become a prominent and quite unsparing critic of British rule in India, condemning what he saw as deliberately manufactured famines, impoverishment and the 'drain' of Indian wealth – a theory elaborated most famously by Dadabhai Naoroji and William Digby. Hyndman also corresponded quite extensively with Blunt, among others, also producing an 1882 pamphlet titled *Why Should India Pay for the War on Egypt?* Where Claeys argues that Hyndman never envisaged full independence for India, embracing a 'Home Rule' position, Marcus Morris has suggested that he did over time become far more radical and actively anti-imperialist more generally. While there is a debate to be had about Hyndman's shifting and evolving position on imperialism, and that of his Social Democratic Federation, what is most relevant to my present purpose is the question of whether resistance to empire in India shaped Hyndman's views in any way. Here it becomes clear that, although Hyndman warned of the consequences of stoking the disaffection of the colonized, it was really in 1907 that he became more fully attuned to the possibility that colonial rule would be overthrown before it might be withdrawn.

In a well-known 1907 pamphlet titled *The Unrest in India*, Hyndman's emphasis shifts from his repeated denunciation of British 'ruin' inflicted on this subcontinent to the Indian refusal to allow the despoliation to continue. A verbatim report of a speech Hyndman gave to a packed Chandos Hall in London, the pamphlet opened with the motion that would be approved by the meeting held on 12 May 1907, sending 'cordial greetings to the agitators all over India, who are doing their utmost to awaken their countrymen of every race and creed to the ruinous effect of our rule'.[28] Sympathy and admiration were expressed for Lajpat Rai and others on trial at that point for their agitation in Punjab. Hyndman then spoke explicitly about his previous belief that 'our rule had substituted order for disorder, and amity for discord', and was a 'great service to humanity'.[29] While several paragraphs return to the drain theory, with damning figures and statistics about the extent of Indian impoverishment, this time Hyndman's point was one about resistance:

It generally happens, however, that at periods of very great misrule comparative trifles produce the really dangerous crisis. It is the last straw, again, that breaks the camel's back. All over Hindostan to-day we have got what is called 'unrest.' People are not satisfied.

(Laughter) Just think of that! (Laughter) They are beginning not to like it! (Laughter and applause)[30]

Here, Hyndman makes a point that would be made repeatedly in the interwar period in relation to the 'unfitness' of some peoples to govern themselves, and their apparent need for colonial tutelage. How could it be that a people (he does refer specifically to 'Hindus' here) with such a great history of art, architecture, industries and 'all that goes to make greatness' behind them now find themselves so deeply impoverished by an apparently beneficial rule which contends that 'these people are not capable of managing their own finances today?'[31] Quite simply, had India not been wealthy when they arrived there, the British would have 'scuttled out' quickly. Beyond that – and there is no mistaking the contextual radicalism of Hyndman's position here – the direction of tutelage was the other way around: 'We owe much of our science, much of our mathematics, much of our religion, and much of our laws to these people who cannot govern themselves!'[32] For Hyndman, the scale of the resistance now would make its effects felt: 'We have kept India to a large extent because Indians have let us do so.'[33] He was referring to the agitation that is the subject of this chapter – the movement which gathered pace in the wake of the Partition of Bengal in 1905, an event which 'brought home to the people of India the fact that the British government was a despotism'.[34] Confronted with repression in the face of perfectly legitimate objections to misrule, Indians 'do not altogether appreciate the beauties of injustice, even when committed by Englishmen'.[35] Hyndman would also make the point that Englishmen too had been involved in the agitation for India's rights against its rulers, rulers who 'if you were at all dangerous, my dear fellow-countrymen ... would play exactly the same game with you'.[36] He would end with a cautionary allusion to the Haitian leader Touissant Louverture – an 'early and terrible disaster' might yet fall upon British rule in India.

Thus, it is not wholly true that, in the decades before 1914, arguments about empire were 'conducted with minimal attention to the desires or rights of the colonised'.[37] It was also the case that debates whose participants sought to conduct themselves without attending to the views and the 'rightful aspirations' of the colonized themselves were, in some instances, disrupted and reconfigured by the assertion of those rights and desires.[38] When some who were prone to advocating benevolent tutelage in a liberal vein travelled to colonial contexts, witnessed unrest on the ground, and engaged with the militantly disposed, it was they who found themselves being tutored instead. Re-reading the travel memoirs of progressive Edwardians who visited India before the First World War, in the wake of the Swadeshi agitation, this chapter suggests that the seeds of a more sustained and equal engagement between British and Indian critics of empire from the late 1920s onwards were sown during this period of politicized encounters on travels.[39] For all that late Victorian and early Edwardian critiques of empire can be read in terms of the familiar liberal posture of insisting that imperial pledges be fulfilled, it is impossible to miss the extent to which 'the embers of unrest which are always smouldering there' become ever more salient in the dispatches and memoirs of sympathetic political travellers to colonial contexts.[40] Where India in particular was concerned, aspirations to benevolence were tested and disrupted by 'the undercurrent of bitterness and discontent' which ran through the last decades of the nineteenth century and which would take radical form as the 'Swadeshi' movement gathered pace in the early years of the twentieth century.[41] Indeed, even some of those who very much believed in the model of Britain 'teaching freedom' and imparting 'national aspirations' to its Indian colony would, through their travels in India, come to a less one-sided understanding of how resistance to colonial rule was evolving. It is at this point that the idea of self-emancipation begins to come more determinedly into the frame of discussion, albeit in nascent form, paving the way for the more evolved internationalism which would emerge in the post-war decades. While, as Nicholas Owen suggests, British anti-imperialist work could often be structured unequally, 'seeking to alter the relationship between the Indians and the *raj* without much altering the relationship between the emancipating sympathiser, and the emancipated Indian', these roles were not stable, and in the context of the Swadeshi movement, broadly understood, could also undergo pedagogical reversal with the colonial subject becoming the tutor.[42] These moments of disruption and reconfiguration are a necessary part of the longer story of the development of British criticism of empire and metropolitan anticolonialism.

The Line of Most Resistance: Edwardian
Dissenters and the 'Unrest in India'

In his important and illuminating work on the British left and India in the context of metropolitan anti-imperialism, Owen makes a series of useful observations about the terms of engagement between British liberals and leftists on the one hand and, on the other, Indian nationalists of different stripes.[43] He argues that anti-imperialist work in Britain was constantly hampered by a basic tension 'between linked-up agitation and sustaining a liberal in office'.[44] While it had proved a useful shared tool between British and Indian constitutional campaigners who could call for reforms on the basis of the gap between 'liberal professions and imperial practices', liberalism of the sort which drove the British India Committee, for instance, was hamstrung by serious weaknesses. It was inherently asymmetric, tending to 'collapse into endorsement of Western positions', and predicated on the idea that 'Indians had much to learn and little to teach'.[45] Its professed values were not 'commonly owned' by Indians and Britons, since it was presumed to be taught to the former by the latter. For those on the more radical side of the new movements in India, 'the need to reverse these flows of authority and power' was becoming more urgent.[46] Once the Labour Party entered the picture in the early years of the twentieth century, more radical figures in the Indian movement, such as Lala Lajpat Rai, were optimistic about the prospects of an alliance with them and other socialists. Owen notes, however, that this prospect 'had its own difficulties', including the fact that Swadeshi tactics like boycotts had an impact on British working-class interests, as did Indian protectionism.[47] There was also doubt on the Labour side as to whether Congress aspirations were compatible with Labour ideals. Nonetheless, when thirty Labour MPs were returned for the first time in the 1906 election, Keir Hardie 'promised their "strenuous backing" for the Indian cause'.[48] In order to study this cause and the ongoing 'unrest' in India, some Labour figures visited India, and Owen argues that their 'differing perceptions and recommendations' give us a good sense of Labour responses to the 'new nationalism'.[49] Another traveller of significance was H. W. Nevinson, a well-known journalist who was also a member of the Liberal Club, but not unsympathetic to the Labour cause.

Taking a slightly different route from Owen, I want to suggest that, in at least some cases, something like a 'reversal' of the flows of authority and knowledge took place, if only provisionally and partially. The encounter with the unfamiliar which Owen highlights as a point of difficulty for Labour sympathizers with the Indian cause could also work to push the boundaries of understanding, getting them to think against the grain of colonial paternalism. For these Edwardians who travelled to India, ambivalences about whether the Raj or nationalists would be better for this country were disturbed, we see, not so much by what Homi Bhabha famously termed 'sly civility' but by being confronted with the much more active agitation that followed in the wake of the Partition of Bengal in 1905.[50] As the retired colonial administrator Henry Cotton would put it, deprecating the British 'fashion of deriding the Indian movement as a mere schoolboy agitation':

> There is now a party of Indian nationalists who despair of constitutional agitation, and openly advocate the establishment of an absolutely free and independent form of national government in India. Their aim is to sever the connection between India and England altogether and at the shortest notice. Their object is to propagate a violent anti-British agitation, and, by any means in their power, to make British rule impossible in India.[51]

Cotton's main interest was in ensuring that change was as gradual as possible, or 'without disturbance'.[52] While Owen rightly notes that people like Hardie and Nevinson were puzzled by the relative passivity and acquiescence of many adherents of the Congress, they also encountered severe fractures within that body, and a milieu of turmoil and ferment in which self-reliance and self-emancipation were being theorized and propounded. It is not quite the case that it was only among the 'Extremists' that these travellers encountered figures who met with their approval; they were as much disconcerted as illumined by their conversations with the likes of Ghosh and Tilak, whose fierce assertions of self (religious and Hindu) were not always modulated or rendered palatable to Western consumption. These engagements, I suggest, did shape their thinking, and cannot be irrelevant to what Owen describes as the 'more confrontational approach in Parliament' taken by Hardie and others upon their return to England. Tellingly, when presented with an address by Tilak during his tour, Hardie replied: 'My sympathies were always with India, but now they've grown a hundredfold.'[53]

Theorizing Self-Rule

What we have to reckon with, especially in Bengal, is the revolt of the younger generation, and this revolt draws its inspiration from religious and philosophical sources which no measures merely political, either of repression or of conciliation, can reach.

Valentine Chirol, *Indian Unrest*

As a consequence, throughout Bengal, there were meetings that proclaimed that this partition was wrong, improper, and altogether despotic, and contrary to the interests of the people.

H. M. Hyndman, *The Unrest in India*

Although the twentieth century had begun with the Congress still in the hands of reformist campaigners such as Gopal Krishna Gokhale and Sir William Wedderburn, the Swadeshi movement in Bengal threw up a decisive ideological fault line within the Congress, signalling the first turn to radicalizing and consolidating anti-colonial resistance in the Indian subcontinent. The bitterly opposed Partition of Bengal in 1905, aimed at diffusing growing militancy in the region, resulted instead in the emergence of the figure of the 'Extremist' whose militant agitational tactics were the counterfoil to the more traditional petitioning mode of those deemed 'Moderate'. Swadeshi translates to 'of one's own country', the *swa-* derived from the Sanskrit prefix denoting 'self'. While the term 'self-emancipation' would not explicitly appear on the rhetorical horizon of British anti-colonialism until the 1930s, the idea that the governed would claim the reins of governance for themselves – and not just wait for them to be offered – would from this point on become an increasingly significant dimension of critiques of empire in Britain. With its rhetoric of non-cooperation and people's rule (as opposed to the Congress's more traditional requests for a larger share in government), Swadeshi

set the stage for anticolonialism in India to grow into the mass movement that it would fully become under Gandhi's canny tutelage in the
interwar period. The cognate notion of *swaraj*, or 'self-rule', which
translates as 'self-government', could either be deployed to suggest
self-government as British subjects or, as in Tilak's famous interpretation, point to the more radical version of full independence from
colonial rule.[54]

By the time the distinctly authoritarian viceroy, George Curzon,
undertook the fateful division of Bengal that would set off a whole
new chain of events, 'memories of rougher times had grown dim'.[55]
Curzon had taken over from the more liberal Ripon, determined not
to yield to pressure from below: 'If we are weak enough to yield
to their clamour now, we shall not be able to dismember or reduce
Bengal again; and you will be cementing and solidifying, on the
eastern flank of India, a force already formidable, and certain to
be a source of increasing trouble in the future.'[56] In the Partition of
Bengal that was announced in late 1903 and effected in mid 1905,
there had admittedly been 'an unfortunate disregard for local sentiment and public opinion', Lord Minto would concede some years
later, when he took over as viceroy from Lord Curzon.[57] Nonetheless,
given the indisputable existence of political agitation, he too would
agree that the Partition was a wise move – one that would lower
the volume of militant voices and contain 'the growing power of a
population with great intellectual gifts and a talent for making itself
heard'.[58] He could not have been more wrong. As the historian Sumit
Sarkar – whose book on the Swadeshi movement in Bengal remains
a foundational work on the subject – notes, 'with startling rapid-
ity after July 1905, the movement broke away from all traditional
moorings, developed new techniques of militant action, and broadened into a struggle for swaraj', or self-rule.[59] Aware that the Indian
peasantry and poor 'could not be mobilised by appeals couched in
the language of Western progressives', militants sought to develop
an indigenous, if mainly Hindu and manifestly upper-caste, grammar
of resistance, 'expressed in an enormous variety of causes and campaigns, in opposition to rent rises, in defence of customary rights and
religious observances, and so forth', and deploying methods such as
demonstration, boycott and 'the attempt to enforce collective action
through the use of religious sanctions'.[60] As the administrations in

East Bengal and the Punjab responded with repressive ferocity, violence erupted across these regions; 1907 also marked, of course, the fiftieth anniversary of the 1857 uprising. Although the stated objectives of the division of territory were administrative, it is clear that other, more political motives were also at work, including the need to undermine militancy and exploit religious-communal divisions by establishing separate Muslim-majority areas. The resistance to the division was spun by colonial administrators as merely the attempts of various elite interest groups to protect their own zones of power and influence. In fact, as Keir Hardie would also note, disquiet was far more widespread, the partition 'coming as a kind of last straw in a long series of humiliations' accompanied by entrenched governmental indifference to modest requests.[61] Moreover, the much-disliked Curzon had, in the space of a few short years, managed to put in place legislation curbing press freedom and tightening imperial control over education.

While ideas of self-assertion and self-reliance were not, as we have seen, absent in British India in the late nineteenth century, by the early twentieth century a series of events had won them wider adherence and, importantly, a pan-Asiatic frame of reference – particularly through Japan's military victory over Russia in 1905, and the Chinese boycott of American goods in response to discriminatory immigration laws. Theorists of Swadeshi like Aurobindo Ghose and Bipin Chandra Pal explicitly referenced these events in calling for constructive work which would ignore colonial bureaucracy, and for full-blown passive resistance which would 'refuse to render any voluntary and honorary service to the government'; this extended to an economic, judicial and educational boycott.[62] The revolution in Egypt, as well as the Mahdi uprising in the Sudan in the mid 1880s, had demonstrated the power of unifying appeals to faith, and this would inspire what was, in the case of Swadeshi, Hindu revivalism. The Swadeshi movement constructed itself very centrally around the Sanskritic idea of *atmashakti*, which is generally given the loose translation of 'soul force' – a concept that would be central to Gandhi's later theorizing of *swaraj* as freedom. Forging a rhetoric of belonging and pride in cultural heritage, Hindu revivalism, which had begun to gather force towards the end of the nineteenth century, 'served as a major stimulus for radicalism even while creating serious problems for the future' by further alienating Muslims.[63] Muslims were not entirely absent from Swadeshi activism, however, and some played an important part in it even as, over time, its militantly Hindu rhetoric exacerbated communal divisions.[64] Despite the existence of Muslim agitators like Liaqat Husain, who was active in organizing strikes, fundraising and boycotts, and the support of journals like the *Mussulman*, Swadeshi was hamstrung by its Hindu revivalism, as Rabindranath Tagore would make clear in his famous *The Home and the World*, an early and powerful critique of the limitations of nationalism.[65] This context of constructing the Indian national 'self' by deploying some of the resources of Hinduism was the one that would be encountered by three progressive Edwardians with different political affiliations – the journalist Henry Nevinson, and the Labour politicians James Keir Hardie and Ramsey MacDonald – when they arrived to study the 'unrest in India'; this would necessarily involve an engagement with Hinduism.

'The limits of endurance': Keir Hardie's Seditious Journey

In November 1907, Aurobindo Ghose wrote a piece that began in characteristically implacable fashion, noting that, while quite happy to hear tales about Russian tyranny, Englishmen were utterly impervious to hearing 'home truths about England's dominion in Hindusthan'.[66] There were, he believed, a few exceptions to this rule, 'some truly noble men who hold humanity far higher than Imperialism', but who are either refused a hearing or 'contemptuously ignored' in the councils of the Empire.[67] Yet one voice now had 'the ear of the civilised world', breaking through the unspoken moratorium: that of the Labour politician James Keir Hardie. He was, therefore, received with Anglo-Indian dismay:

> The hasty, hideous, indecent, savage yell that has been raised by the whole of the English Press against Mr Keir Hardie because he has dared to tell the truth about the present situation in this country is a striking confirmation of what we have said above ... They are bursting with rage because their long and unscrupulously kept-up fiction of a just and benevolent Indian rule has been exposed in all

its ugliness at last by one who happens to be an *Englishman* (Oh
the sting of it!) and an Englishman of power and prestige too, who
easily has the ear of the civilised world.[68]

Aurobindo was referring to the stir caused in Britain by statements
made by Hardie, the working-class Scot who was one of the founders of the Labour Party, in the wake of his visit to India in 1907; the
Times reported him as 'Fostering Indian Sedition'.[69] Long associated
with a small group of more radical voices on India in parliament,
Hardie had already garnered some notoriety for his views on India.
In July 1906, coached by the visiting Congress leader, G. K. Gokhale,
Hardie had made a speech in the House of Commons attacking
conditions in the Raj, from the rising death rate to low wages in
textile factories and the exclusion of Indians from administrative
posts. When he finally visited India in 1907, the Labour leader toured
Bengal under the guidance of Tilak and other Swadeshi campaigners, giving supportive speeches to their followers. One biographer
notes: 'Exactly what he said in his speeches there was the subject of
fierce dispute; but there is little doubt that he gave every encouragement to the Congress movement's campaign for Indian home rule.'[70]
Hardie was blamed for the outbreak of riots, and there were calls for
him to be deported, leading Vladimir Lenin to comment happily that
'the whole of the English bourgeois press raised a howl against the
"rebel"'.[71] It is in this uproar that Aurobindo finds vindication for
his own uncompromising stance against mendicancy, noting that the
attempts to drown out Hardie's 'disengaged' voice make clear that
'England *will not* give us anything unless we can force her to her
knees, this is the only moral to which the present outrageous clamour
of the English Press points'.[72]

Based on articles he wrote for the Independent Labour Party's
paper, the *Labour Leader*, Keir Hardie published a volume entitled
India: Impressions and Suggestions, which, despite its indeed impres-
sionistic mode, embodies some of the shifts and tensions I am talking
about here. Though a socialist, this Labour Party pioneer was not – as
indeed most British socialists at the turn of the century were not – a
natural-born critic of the British imperial project. *India: Impressions
and Suggestions* moves symptomatically between a deep-seated
paternalism which urges liberal treatment of colonial subjects in the

interests of empire, vouching repeatedly for their loyalty, and a more sombre sense that the disaffection with imperial rule is deep-rooted enough to warrant greater convulsions. Published jointly by the ILP and the Home Rule for India League, the book was influential, one of Hardie's biographers notes, making 'a considerable impact' and playing 'a major role in educating British liberal opinion on Indian affairs'.[73] Contradicting the colonial claim that only the educated Indian middle-classes were challenging the Empire, Hardie quickly came to the conclusion that resistance was not confined to any particular class or community, and that there was in fact a widespread dissatisfaction with British rule underlying the boycott movement. 'Everything in India is seditious', he noted accurately, 'which does not slavishly applaud every act of the Government.'[74] The extent of agitation also becomes clear through the depth of repression. Publishers were convicted of sedition for merely noting that Europeans who murdered Indians were given very slight sentences, and the likes of Lajpat Rai, the 'agitator who voiced the grievance of the heavily-burdened peasants', deported without trial to Burma.[75] In this siege-like context, 'The Swadeshi movement grows and spreads on every hand.'[76]

If Hardie also propagated the familiar colonial claim that Indians were largely loyal to the Empire – it remains unclear what he based it on, unless he was deliberately misled by the Swadeshi activists who guided him through his travels – the agitation he witnessed was serious enough for him to understand the situation in terms of the breaking of 'limits even to Hindu endurance' among the 'loyal, patient, and long-suffering'.[77] (We might recall here Douglass's famous assertion that the limits of tyrants are prescribed by the endurance of those whom they oppress.) A great deal of Hardie's narrative is taken up with registering what he had perhaps not anticipated: the breadth of 'resentment, deep and bitter, against the partition'.[78] Criticizing the familiar colonial canard that only the anglicized 'Babu' was involved in agitation, Hardie points to the long-suffering tenant farmers or ryots who had been agitating against unfair revenue settlements and taxes and the conscription of labour. Although Hardie ostensibly offers his suggestions towards India being pacified and kept loyal to the Raj, a great deal of his narrative is in fact devoted to showing 'that the condition of the Indian peasant has worsened' under British rule, and that, despite being 'slow to anger', the rural poor have been agitating against their conditions.[79] Travelling in India – from Bengal and Madras to Bombay, Poona, Delhi and the Punjab – and witnessing disaffection at first hand brought Hardie to the realization that the situation had little to do with individual colonial administrators or their goodwill, which he never doubts. It was 'the system now at work' which had produced grinding conditions: 'Everywhere these kindly, simple people are full of discontent; they find themselves in the grip of a set of circumstances which they do not understand and which they cannot break through.'[80] Scandalously, for colonial bureaucrats, 'the people of India are but so many seeds in an oil mill, to be crushed for the oil they yield'.[81] As Jonathan Hyslop notes, Hardie's early Christianity had sown in him a 'profound moral commitment to a sense of human equality' which underlay his ethical socialism, but it is clear from his narrative that the scale of both suffering and resistance in the Raj was not something he had reckoned with.[82] Like Blunt some years earlier, Hardie avers that the answer to the 'gathering volume of unrest' must lie in self-government – 'the solvent to which we must look for dissolving a difficulty rapidly becoming unbearable'.[83]

In the final analysis, Hardie's narrative does not resolve the tension between insisting that India and Indians (Hindus in particular) have 'no higher ambition in life than to live loyal under the British flag' and, given the wider context of insurgency in Asia, worrying that 'if unrest spreads throughout India a conflagration may one day break out in China, Japan, or even nearer home, which will set India ablaze and burn up the last vestige of British rule'.[84] In other words, although the idea of a full and immediate break for India from the British Empire eluded him, as it did other metropolitan critics of empire, it certainly took the form of a violent possibility. Hardie ends his narrative with a clear sense that there can be 'no real pacification, no allaying of discontent', failing some effective form of self-government, and it was this partisan conclusion to his dispatches from India that had *Punch* satirizing Hardie wearing a Scottish miner's suit and waving a firebrand labelled 'sedition'.[85] In the wake of Hardie's visit, one biographer avers, 'public attention had been focussed on the question of the government of India as it had never been since the days of the Mutiny.'[86] In his limited and somewhat muddled way, Hardie also brought into the frame the question of India's long history of achievements – indeed, its 'historical precedence over Western civilization'. This, despite some patently absurd 'racial nonsense' on shared Aryan heritage, did 'put him firmly at odds with the emphasis on Indian incapacity which permeated contemporary British political discourse'.[87] Those who followed him to India, like Nevinson and McDonald, would pick up the question of India's *capacity* for ruling itself, identifying the cultural resources the nation-in-waiting could draw on to do so.

'In politics there is no benevolence': Tilak and Empire

For over a generation we were groping in the dark, begging at the bureaucracy's doors, beseeching England to grant us what no nation can grant to another, what every nation must achieve for itself – Swaraj ... A People must work out its own salvation! That is the meaning of the New Movement, as I understand it.

T. L. Vaswani

The most significant aspect of the post-1905 fracture in Indian nationalism was the emergence of a new type of leader who would theorize and more widely propagate the idea of India as a nation with a distinct 'national self'. *Swaraj*, or self-rule, in this paradigm was to be based not on 'an Indian use of the British forms of the state', but on a 'revolutionary recasting of those forms to accord with Indian civilization's value system'.[88] What is important for our purposes is the corollary insistence on a very different mode of engagement with the British presence in India. Prominent among its key theorists was Bal Gangadhar Tilak, who was one of the organizers of Hardie's journey. Tilak told Hardie that his side of the Congress – the 'New Party', as it was known – 'is not going to depend any longer on the Liberals or other political parties in England to achieve its objective of Swaraj', even as he urged the British politician to make the case for Indian self-rule to his electorate.[89] A monumental 1907 speech by Tilak in Calcutta gives us a flavour of the views he is likely to have communicated to the political travellers who engaged with him. In it he laid out with clarity the radical break from past modes of resistance, while noting that the terms 'Moderates' and 'Extremists' were necessarily subject to change over time. The idea of benevolent imperial rule was itself contradictory, for 'in politics there is no benevolence'.[90] This meant that appealing to and depending on liberal politicians for concessions were inherently futile, not least because empire routinely turned political liberals into de facto conservatives. Entirely new methods were now called for: 'The Old party believes in appealing to the British nation and we do not.'[91] In words reminiscent of Afghani's call to the fellahin, and indeed the admonitions of the Morant Bay agitators to their fellow blacks, Tilak defined freedom as an act of agency, entirely constituted by the actions of those who would be free: 'What the New Party wants you to do is to realise the fact that your future rests entirely in your own hands. If you mean to be free, you can be free; if you do not mean to be free, you will fall and be for ever fallen.'[92] Words were not to be dispensed with entirely, but wielded differently than by those who would plead, pray and petition; this time, the 'self' asserted itself by withdrawing cooperation, refusing to be 'willing instruments of our own oppression in the hands of an alien Government'.[93] In one sense, Tilak's point was sharply materialist: only attacks, like boycott, directly on 'their pocket or interest' would have any impact on a British electorate, for it 'must be a fool indeed who would sacrifice his own interest on hearing a philosophical lecture'.[94] At another, it was that freedom constitutively required self-liberation. Empire was a machine, he would note in another speech, this time given in Marathi, in which he reminded his audience of their own role in sustaining the Raj as 'the useful lubricants which enable the gigantic machinery to work so smoothly'.[95] Economic force could give radical words their bite, rendering them less easily dismissed as the 'howl' of 'a few agitators'.[96]

The Justice of Indian Disquiet: Henry Nevinson's 'New Spirit'

Not long before he was sentenced to transportation in 1908 for 'sedition', Tilak was also one of the first major Extremist figures whom the journalist Henry Woodd Nevinson met after he arrived in India in late 1907. Nevinson was a well-known war correspondent who had achieved a measure of fame for his reporting from the Graeco-Turkish war in 1897, and then the Second Boer War. His brief for the *Manchester Guardian* and the *Glasgow Herald* was to examine and report on the Swadeshi agitation and 'the movement in India known as "unrest" [which] was becoming continually more urgent or more dangerous in its demands and actions'.[97] Once in India, he would travel extensively, covering famines and plagues, and talking in depth with Moderate leaders like Gopal Krishna Gokhale – who introduced him to others as a sympathizer – as well as the Extremists, Tilak, Aurobindo and Bipin Chandra Pal. In addition, Nevinson attended, and sometimes gave speeches at, several political meetings, and was present with Rutherford at the eventful annual Congress conference in Surat that year, which resulted in an historic fracture that would not be mended until 1916. Uneasy at the extent of his engagement with oppositional figures and his presence at 'seditious' political events, the British Indian government became progressively colder to Nevinson, Viceroy Minto describing the fifty-one-year-old as 'a dangerous sort of young gentleman'.[98] Nevinson's account of this insurgent conjuncture in India, collated in his book *The New Spirit in India*, makes for absorbing reading as a combination of travelogue, political history, colonial discourse analysis and memoir. Illustrated with arresting photographs of both high-profile figures and ordinary people, as well as landscapes, the evocative narrative takes Nevinson's reader across vast tracts of the country that he traversed over a few months. Its accounts ranging from personal conversations, interviews and private encounters to public meetings, religious processions and Congress conferences, with hefty doses of historical and geographical information stirred in, the book ends with a summary of the political situation and a series of recommendations for remedial measures.[99] Along the way, it develops a sharp critique of British rule in India, drawn substantially from what Nevinson witnessed and learned during his journey – which was also one of witnessing, appalled, how his fellow Britons behaved with their pith helmets on. If, at one level, *The New Spirit* is an attempt to render the adversarial Indian 'new spirit' legible to a British readership, at another it is also an acknowledgement of the difficulty of doing so given both the recalcitrance of this spirit itself and, to no small extent, the unfamiliarity and opacity of its Hindu moorings.

Even as Nevinson appears to come up with a set of legible measures
to address the situation, his narrative is unable to shake off the sense
that the Empire is up against intractable opposition that will, in due
course, bring it to an end. It is likely that Nevinson approached the
task of writing *The New Spirit* with 'distaste' and 'uncertainty' not
because he was repelled by the rise of Extremism, as his biographer
Angela John infers, but because he found himself unable to deploy
familiar liberal categories with customary surefootedness.[100] It is certainly of some significance that a book originally to be titled *India in
Unrest* (from the Raj's point of view) would change its title to reflect
instead how many in India now felt about the Raj.

Although, as Owen argues, Nevinson was uneasy from the start
with the acquiescence and 'over-politeness' he perceived in Indians,
he did not in fact arrive in India ready, 'from a comfortable position
of invulnerability to the *raj*, to urge defiance upon those in a much
weaker position'.[101] There is little in this memoir to indicate that
Nevinson toured India with a prefabricated radical position which
he then enjoined upon his interlocutors. What took place, firstly, was
that Nevinson saw for himself the manifold problems and resent-
ments generated by the Raj's misrule: 'It is difficult to define how far
the most paternal of Governments is responsible for the excesses of
its children, to whom it refuses the common rights of grown men.'[102]
He also noted that paternalism, indeed even mere 'sympathy', would
no longer cut it: 'It might be that, in old days, the Englishman found
it easier to be sympathetic with natives whom he could treat as dear
good things. But educated Indians had come to detest such sympathy
as only fit for pet animals, and both races were beginning to notice
the change.'[103] Secondly, not least but not only as a consequence of
pondering the religious grammar and iconography of the Extremists
via Tilak and Aurobindo, Nevinson engaged with everyday Hinduism
and Hindu worship traditions. He did not study them in the way that
Blunt did Islam, or come to consider himself either an Indian or a
Hindu, but he did find himself pondering both identity and difference
at the intersection of political ferment, religious revivalism and bitter
divisions on the question of resistance. He experienced no dramatic
political conversion in the manner of Blunt, departing India as the
leftish liberal he had arrived as, but one whose sense of where change
would come from had been nonetheless reconfigured.

Nevinson's account of his own passage to India, not unlike his friend E. M. Forster's novel of that title, is a narrative about encountering and attempting to come to terms with difficulty in a milieu shaped by resistance.[104] Both texts end with the aspiration to conciliation undermined by an awareness of present intractability. Nevinson's delineation of a spirit that is both new and notably difficult is considerably more thoughtful, and at times more radical, than his memoir's ending might suggest. Indeed, Nevinson's titular phrase and central insight is one that Forster appears to echo a few years later when writing his justly famous novel of India, in which the narrator observes that 'a *new spirit* seemed abroad, a rearrangement, which no one in the stern little band of whites could explain'.[105] Here we must distinguish the inability to 'explain' from the ambivalences and uncertainties that are familiar to us from much colonial discourse analysis. Neither Forster nor Nevinson uphold uncertainty for its own sake (indeed, Nevinson does his best, clumsily, to override his). Rather, what emerges is a radical disruption of liberal pieties without an abandonment of the imperative to learn – to know more and know better. Benita Parry's illuminating reading of Forster's text argues that *A Passage to India* is a novel which exceeds its generally cautious critique of empire and basically liberal politics in a more profound dissidence. This emerges specifically in the novel's reconfiguring of India 'as a geographical space and social realm abundantly occupied by diverse intellectual modes, cultural forms, and sensibilities'.[106] It is fair to say that *The New Spirit*'s 'dissident place' also lies less in its critique of the colonial situation – though that is not insignificant – than in its recognition of the existence of 'cognitive traditions … inimical to the British presence'.[107] This mainly takes the form of grappling with the difficulties of understanding Hindu religious thought, for, like Forster, Nevinson sidelines India's 'long traditions of mathematics, science and technology, history, linguistics, and jurisprudence'.[108] Unlike Forster, Nevinson gives Islam and the Islamic presence in India short shrift, restricting his interviews to just one Muslim nobleman. Both Nevinson and Hardie are culpable of engaging somewhat uncritically with the Hindu chauvinism of Tilak and some of his adherents, particularly their claims about Hindu victimization at the hands of Muslims. Nonetheless, Nevinson's apprehension of the political possibilities embedded in certain forms of (more egalitarian and ecumenical) everyday Hinduism identify these as providing the adversarial basis for a more complete resistance to colonial rule and its corollaries. His is a text which engages, like Forster's, with colonial India 'as an agent of knowledge and an adversary to imperial rule', disrupting British colonial self-representation in the process.[109]

Tilak was one of the first Extremists Nevinson spent time with. The most orthodox Hindu among the nationalist leaders the British journalist met, Tilak did not come across as especially radical. While he comments on Tilak's implacable observance of caste restrictions, which extended to not eating or sharing a roof with a European, and describes him as one whose orthodox Hinduism 'often reacts against the forces of progress',[110] Nevinson's report of Tilak's political views suggests that the leader was not seeking to sever connections to the British Empire as such, at least not in the present, but was holding out for 'colonial self-government'.[111] His differences with the Moderates, Tilak appears to have told Nevinson, were largely those of tactics: where the former sought to influence British public opinion, the Extremists had 'determined on other methods'.[112] The two Tilak-ite ideas that Nevinson would reiterate in his own account were that Indian unity was itself a consequence of resistance to British domination, and that the ignorance and indifference of the British public towards the Indian situation had led to the present impasse. Citing extensively from both 'The Tenets of the New Party' and 'The Shivaji Festival', Nevinson engaged with Tilak's critique of colonial benevolence: 'He did not believe in the philanthropy of British politics. There was no instance in history of one foreign nation ruling another for the benefit of the other and not for its own profit.'[113] This insight had implications for tactics of resistance, and Nevinson would grasp this fully, citing from Tilak's essay 'The Shivaji Festival': 'An appeal to the good-feeling of the rulers is everywhere discovered to have but narrow limits.'[114] While Nevinson readily acknowledged the difficulty of trying to 'understand' Tilak's beliefs in themselves, the 'strange significance' of the Maratha leader, with his enthusiasm for Shivaji and Hindu mythologies, was nonetheless legible to his British interlocutor, certainly insofar as Tilak appears to have couched his observations in the eminently comprehensible language of demands for self-government and a right to representation.[115] 'Our motto is

"Self-reliance, not Mendicancy"', Tilak told Nevinson, reprising the formulation that Aurobindo had turned into the Swadeshi mantra.[116]

Nevinson seems to have been at least as impressed by the speakers and attendees at a public meeting called by the Extremists on Madras's Marina beach. With a certain lyricism, Nevinson describes 'a line of white-robed students carrying a yellow banner' against the backdrop of the 'deep and ominous colours' of a monsoon sunset, telling his British readers: 'But there was no wild gesticulation, no frantic excess, such as we might imagine in a fanatical East. A Trafalgar Square crowd is more demonstrative and unrestrained.'[117] Though he was deliberately countering stereotypes of the agitation prevalent in Britain, Nevinson appears also to have been genuinely moved by the sights and sounds of the demonstration, including a little boy singing the nationalist song 'Bande Mataram' in Tamil. Providing the reader with a full translation (as does Hardie), he notes that its content is different to that of a stirring European anthem, but that 'the tenderness, the devoted love of country, and the adoration of motherhood are all characteristic of the Indian mind'.[118] Nevinson speaks of a sense of 'quiet reasonableness' in the speeches he hears, 'so different from our conception of the Oriental mind'.[119] The claims made in these speeches, at least as Nevinson interpreted them, were not hard to relate to: 'the simple human rights that other peoples enjoy – the right to a voice in their own affairs, and in the spending of their own money'.[120] These were reassuringly liberal in their tenor, of course. It was only when he met Aurobindo a few weeks later that Nevinson at last encountered the fully uncompromising face of the new nationalism:

> His Nationalists would let the Government go its way and take no notice of it at all. They hoped nothing from reforms; all the talk about Legislative Councils and Indian members and the separation of Judicial and Executive functions was meaningless to them. They did not spend a thought upon it. In fact, the worse the Government was, the more repressive it became, and the less it inclined to reform, so much the better for the Nationalist cause. He regarded the Partition of Bengal as the greatest blessing that had ever happened to India. No other measure could have stirred national feeling so deeply or roused it so suddenly from the lethargy of previous years.[121]

It is then that Nevinson's own understanding that 'a deeper spirit was at work' begins to crystallize.[122] Reading Aurobindo's work in the coming days, he would note and cite from the young Bengali political philosopher's call to fellow Indians to relieve the administration of its duties and immediately enact self-governance in as many ways as possible. 'No growth is possible under perpetual tutelage', Aurobindo wrote.[123] Contrasting it with Tilak's canny pragmatism, 'the shrewd political judgement of Poona Extremists', Nevinson writes of 'a religious tone, a spiritual elevation', in Aurobindo's writings that eluded simple translation into liberal categories: 'Nationalism to him was far more than a political object or a means of material improvement. To him it was surrounded by a mist of glory, the halo that mediaeval saints beheld gleaming around the head of martyrs.'[124] Compelled though he is by Aurobindo's brand of Extremism, it is also hard to miss the slight recoil from 'what the irreligious mean by a fanatic'.[125]

While he had been primed by Tilak for a rejection of petitioning as a political tactic, it was really with Aurobindo that Nevinson saw British liberalism comprehensively challenged. In a series of editorials written for the English-language nationalist daily *Bande Mataram* between 1906 and 1908, Aurobindo expounded his own theory of 'the new spirit which has gone out like a mighty fire from Bengal lighting up the whole of India' as constitutively unavailable to compromise or moderation.[126] (Nevinson's book title arguably alludes directly to Aurobindo's phrase.) In these editorials he would insist that, in thinking about the future of India, reference to British views or British interests was a fundamental hindrance; there were ample other resources Indians could draw on to think about a destiny independent of Britain. 'The new movement is not primarily a protest against bad Government', he would observe, but 'is a protest against the continuance of British control; whether that control is used well or ill, justly or unjustly, is a minor and unessential consideration.'[127] Glossing 'Extremism' as 'Democratic Nationalism', Aurobindo describes Moderates as a hybrid species who thought they could 'arrive at a compromise between subjection and independence – a half-way house between life and death'.[128] Aurobindo's sardonic analysis of why imperialism found it necessary to speak the language of liberalism is compelling. Once an openly aggressive ideology of 'might is right', colonial rule was impelled in the nineteenth century, the era of nationalism, to justify itself 'by pretending to be a trustee of liberty, commissioned from on high to civilize the uncivilized and train the untrained until the time had come when the benevolent conqueror had done his work and could unselfishly retire'.[129] The colonial subject was 'obliged to accept Englishmen on their own valuation'.[130] Yet thirty years of engaging English liberals such as Lord Morley through patient supplication had only brought in its wake refusal, rejection and, with regard to colonial subjects, the continued insistence that 'they are not fit to receive' political reforms.[131] To the extent that liberalism engaged with the subjects of rule, it was not in order actually to listen, redress grievances or allow such engagement to influence administration, but because its wary practitioners knew: 'A despotism out of touch with the people is a despotism continually in danger.'[132] Indeed, to Aurobindo's mind, acquiescence or 'the slave's politics', as practised by Loyalists and Moderates, only served to heighten the English sense that Indians were unfit for freedom – which, he reminds his reader, necessitates struggle.[133] Where Europe fought for liberty 'through a welter of blood after her struggles of centuries', the disapproval and resentment of Indian Moderates 'find expression only in weeping and sobbing', or 'persistent mendicancy'.[134]

Foreign rule was, above all, incompatible with nationalism for the masses, rather than for an elite few – another dig at those Moderates who only sought a place at the table. While Aurobindo determinedly includes Mughal rule under the rubric of the 'foreign', he does note that 'it immediately naturalised itself in India', unlike that of the British, and so did not either centralize power or destroy 'existing organs of national life'.[135] (This was a point that Ernest Jones had also made in his editorials fifty years earlier.) Everything now depended on getting both Hindu and Muslim common people to join with the middle classes for a 'common salvation'.[136] The 'new spirit' itself was one of mass mobilization in which, for the first time, 'the man in the workshop and the man in the street have risen in revolt'.[137] Echoed in this by Nevinson and others, Aurobindo pronounced: 'The distinction, which Anglo-India has striven to draw between the "Babu class" and the people, has in the Punjab ceased to exist.'[138] Importantly, Aurobindo sets emergent Indian national self-consciousness within a larger spectrum of international insurgency in Japan, West Asia, China, North Africa and semi-Asiatic Russia, all in the same year, 1906–7; there were also indications of forthcoming disturbances in other parts of the Far East. But since the greatest kindred 'awakening' had been in the Muslim or 'Mohammedan' world – in Afghanistan, Persia and Egypt – India could also draw inspiration from the Islamic world, becoming part of a wider 'Asiatic revival'.[139] Indeed, Aurobindo describes the foreign textile boycott strategy of Swadeshi as 'a *jehad* against foreign yarn'.[140] The 'Asiatic', for Aurobindo, encompasses both early Christianity and Islam, the Prophet Mohammed being one of those who 'tried to reestablish the Asiatic gospel of human equality in the spirit'.[141] Responding partly to the critique of those, like Rabindranath Tagore, who warned presciently against the exclusionary and aggressive aspects of Swadeshi, Aurobindo argued that the call to boycott British goods had to be seen not as a 'gospel of hatred' but as an attempt to create the conditions of equality without which 'there can be no real love and good feeling except such as exists between man and some of the lower animals' (a metaphor also used by Nevinson, as we have seen).[142] Aurobindo's rejection of 'insulting patronage' and 'degrading loyalty' is unequivocal.[143] However, both caste hierarchies and Hindu dominance were undoubtedly blind spots for Aurobindo, who would counter colonial apologetics by asking in a somewhat limited and limiting way why, if England's aggressive social divisions were no bar to its enjoyment of liberty, caste divisions should debar Indian freedom.

About halfway through his account, Nevinson, whom Forster described as possessed of the temperament of a soldier and 'the outlook of the saint', suddenly poses a question with something of the esoteric about it: 'But what if all this so-called unrest is only the beginning of another great humanistic reform, another incarnation of that "Lord of the World" whose attribute is equality?'[144] This reflection was inspired not by his meeting with Aurobindo, but by a visit that Nevinson had made to the Jagannath temple at Puri. This is, in many ways, the most remarkable chapter in his book, akin perhaps to the 'Temple' section of Forster's novel of India, the narrator at once bewildered and compelled by witnessing unfamiliar religious rituals. Deftly invoking common ground with a Chaucerian allusion, Nevinson observes that late in middle age is when Indian 'men and women long to go on pilgrimage', for 'the field has been sown and reaped, the buffalo fed, the taxes paid, the children tended, the cotton garment daily washed'.[145] Nevinson also deliberately undermines the cultural 'othering' of the Hindu, this time taking on the fearsome colonial image of 'our old friend Juggernath, of childhood's stories and journalistic tags – the God in the Car, before whose bloodstained wheels the benighted heathen were driven by deceiving priests'.[146] As against this familiar rendering of a fearsome despotic deity, Nevinson draws out an alternative possibility, that here sits a unique shrine. Influenced perhaps by the Buddha's egalitarian preaching, Nevinson speculates, 'the unaltering rule of Juggernath's worship' is 'that before his sight all castes and ranks and riches are equal, and the woman is equal with the man'.[147] Inside the temple walls, caste distinctions are abolished as 'Brahman may eat with sweeper' and the warrior with the butcher: 'It is the sacrament of equality, the consecration of mankind.'[148] Nevinson suggests that the missionaries who first came up with the story of the abominable Juggernath were incapable, he implies, of understanding a 'divine passion' for union with the eternal. A possibly dialectical relationship between equivalence and unfamiliarity, or between commensurability and alterity, also emerges in his reflections on the idols 'upon which no alien may look'.[149] Conceding that it might be too much to identify the main deity's sister as 'Liberty' and the brother as 'Fraternity', he insists nonetheless that Jagannath himself 'has beyond question the attribute of Equality, and it seems possible that it is just this glorious attribute, and no deeper metaphysic reason, which gives his temple its place as the most worshipped fane of India'.[150]

This curious dialectic is significant not just for the interesting tensions it generates – those, for instance, between ineffable faith and secular ethics, or between untranslatability and comprehension – but because it is clear that such things as liberty and equality are to be found embedded in this most non-European of contexts. Like Blunt, Nevinson does not see 'humanistic reform' as the unique provenance of the West.[151] He does not romanticize Hindu practices here; indeed, in a striking parallel he notes: 'Many people worship what most they fall short of, just as in England we struggle to worship Christ, whose character and manner of life differed so entirely from our own.'[152] Indian society is deeply unequal, and in that very fact might lie an explanation for the ease with which colonial rule has taken root there. Yet, as he has discovered, Indians also share a 'longing for equality'.[153] In an extraordinary meditation, Nevinson then synthesizes the (Hindu) religious and (Indian) political, neither erasing cultural specificity nor assigning irreducible otherness:

> Throughout India we are witnessing the birth of a new national consciousness, and with it comes a revival of dignity, a resolve no longer to take insults lying down, not to lick the hand that strikes, or rub the forehead in the dust before any human being, simply because he wears a helmet and is called white. Like pilgrims bound for the shrine of Juggernath in an ecstasy of devotion, the leaders of India are inspired by that longing for equality which is always springing afresh in human minds. If any one chooses to say that equality is like Juggernath's Car, crushing everything equally flat, he is welcome to his little jest. But as I saw the white-robed pilgrims passing into the temple, there to partake of equality's sacrament, I knew that these outward things were but the symbols of an invisible worship, which may renew the face of the Indian people, and save ourselves from a threatening and dishonourable danger.[154]

The identification here of a *human* 'longing for equality' which renews itself periodically in the face of sclerosis is in telling contrast to his earlier, more familiar suggestion that the British have sown the seeds for their own removal by offering an education in equality. Indians – at least the Hindus (and Buddhists) he has in mind here – may, in fact, have cultural and spiritual resources of their own out of which to develop a philosophy of equality, and may not require tutelage at all. In the final analysis, Nevinson would attribute the 'unrest' to multiple causes, including the Partition and Japan's victory over a great European power, in addition to British influence. Though he would tell a wandering ascetic with whom he sat in meditation in Banaras, 'Yours is the Order I belong to by nature', Nevinson never considered himself more than a tourist and a sympathizer of India's.[155] Even so, he was quick to observe when asked by a group of Indians to intervene against Swadeshi strictures that, if he had been an Indian, he 'would have done my utmost to dissuade my countrymen from buying any foreign goods at all till grievances had been redressed'.[156]

The outraged British charges against Nevinson of disloyalty are, of course, hardly surprising.

How, then, are we to understand Nevinson's summative recommendations, which, like Hardie's, have a distinctly reformist flavour – somewhat at odds with the rest of the text – and certainly speak of a sense of 'benevolent western influence'?[157] Owen suggests that, for Nevinson, 'as for other British observers, western liberalism, confronting the new Extremist spirit in India, had hit the buffers of its understanding'.[158] This is true, but only partially so. What Nevinson did accept, particularly after witnessing the fisticuffs and fractures of the Surat Congress of 1907, in which Moderates and Extremists literally came to blows, is that what had arisen in the country was indeed 'a different and difficult spirit'.[159] Yet he concludes, albeit with negative reasoning: 'When the very worst that can be said against our rule has been said, the substitution of Russia's rule for ours would be an incalculable disaster.'[160] Offered towards a temporary continuance of rule based largely on negative reasoning, Nevinson's proposed reforms are also formulated as a corrective to unacceptable British colonial behaviour: 'Our indifference to the Indian peoples, from whom we are continually sucking so much of our wealth, is universal and invariable.'[161] Any changes in metropolitan attitude could be elicited 'only at long intervals after outbreaks of bloodshed and threatenings of revolt'.[162] The Extremist case is echoed in Nevinson's assertion that pleadings based on 'constitutional propriety' and order have had 'no influence upon the action of the Indian government, and no influence upon English opinion at home'.[163] The 'unrest' of Swadeshi, by contrast, had ensured that 'England during 1907 and 1908 has probably paid more attention to India than at any time since the Mutiny'.[164] The fact remained, too – and here Nevinson was prescient about Gandhi and Gandhi's methods – that religion and politics could not be kept separate, for 'the events of the last few years have given to national politics the place once held by theology'.[165] There is little to suggest that Nevinson either disapproved of this turn of affairs or believed it to be a danger to India's future, but he did certainly suggest that a degree of moderation – that of a Gokhale, for instance – might be the way forward for the present.[166] It is as though, having read the writing on the wall, Nevinson's imagination stops short of envisioning a final break between India and the

Empire.[167] This is not unlike the situation Conrad, according to Said, found himself in when writing *Heart of Darkness*; he maintains an ironic and critical distance from the imperial project but 'does not give us the sense that he could imagine a fully realized alternative to imperialism' beyond European tutelage.[168]

By the end of his account, Nevinson stands in the reconfigured space between the liberal humanitarian framework with which he had arrived in India and the insights he has gleaned from his sojourn there, including the fact that the 'difficult' spirit and 'the line of most resistance' have made thoughts of imperial benevolence obsolete.[169] While he can never quite relinquish the British colonial idea that the quests for liberty and equality are now deep-rooted 'plants that we ourselves have generously set in India', he also observes quite categorically that the Swadeshi movement had expanded into a 'much wider movement in self-reliance ... quite independently of our influence'.[170] Gone is the absolute certainty that Britain is the sole fountainhead of political thought; Nevinson's rhetoric on where aspirations to liberty derive from is now far more qualified: 'Many things have combined to create a new spirit, and we have ourselves contributed much.'[171] This means that the usual question posed by critics of empire – what should Britain do? – must now be inverted, with the agency of Indians at its centre: 'The question immediately before India now is, which of two courses with regard to ourselves the new spirit as a whole will take.'[172] To ask India to continue to acquiesce in the British presence for the common good is, he acknowledges, a long shot, requiring 'a sweet reasonableness and a strength of character which few men in any nation possess'.[173] It is not for Indians to cooperate; Britain must ask itself 'whether we are to hold the new spirit fairly on our side, and to co-operate with it'.[174] It is Britain, too, which must undertake Burkean remedial measures, and give up vulgar, extenuating relativism, particularly the 'weary ineptitude that "East is East, and West is West"'.[175]

Nevinson never became an anticolonial radical in the mould of Blunt, with whom he shared the combination of conservative aesthetic tastes and liberal political inclinations, but it would be churlish and dishonest not to recognize the extent to which his dissidence on the Indian questions was, like his friend Forster's, at a considerable distance from the regnant notions of his time. Indeed, reviewing *A*

Passage to India in 1924, Nevinson offered a strikingly trenchant takedown of colonial discourse:

> It is unfortunate that the very name of India arouses despair or indifference in British hearts. Our average citizen thinks vaguely of a vast country inhabited by hordes of brown or blackish 'natives', who worship strange and improper gods, are given to atrocious mutinies and massacres, and would fight horribly among themselves if the controlling power of England were withdrawn ... There have been stages in our knowledge or our ignorance. There was the stage of the 'Nabobs,' when India was a dream of diamonds and gold and pearls ... the stage when India was to us the scene of widows burnt alive, madmen swinging themselves by hooks from poles as an act of sanctity, and worshippers flinging themselves beneath the bloody wheels of Juggernaut; from which abominations only English missionaries could save them.[176]

Adding to this list the 'Kipling stage' of the British Empire, in which he had been brought up and which he had had to think against, Nevinson deprecates the falseness of all of these conceptions, but notes that there have been some shifts in opinion since the 'widespread horror' generated by both the Amritsar massacre and 'the growing insistence of Indians themselves' on taking control of their destinies.[177] He may have formally opted for gradualism, as both Owen and John note, but, along with that of Hardie, his work in the press also 'helped inform the public from radically different perspectives from those generally promulgated by the British Raj'.[178] Nevinson's project, in the end, was really about fostering a degree of self-awareness and self-reflexivity among his fellow Britons when it came to the Empire. Modest as this achievement may have been, it helped create the ground for more far-reaching criticism.

The Brief Awakening of Ramsay MacDonald

Another fact-finding traveller who went to India two years after Hardie and Nevinson, in 1909, to examine the 'unrest' and report back on it was the former's parliamentary colleague, the Labour politician Ramsay MacDonald, who in the 1920s would become Britain's first Labour prime minister. Aurobindo, not hostile but sceptical, had this to say about him:

> Mr Macdonald belongs to the new thought, but he is, we believe, one of those who would hasten slowly to the goal. He has not the rugged personality of Mr Keir Hardie, but combines in himself, in a way Mr Hardie scarcely does, the old culture and the new spirit. He has as broad a sympathy and as penetrating an intelligence as Mr Nevinson, but not the latter's quick intensity. Nevertheless, behind the slow consideration and calm thoughtfulness of his manner, one detects hidden iron and the concealed roughness of the force that has come to destroy and to build, some hint of the rugged outlines of Demogorgon, the claws of Narasingha ... So far as an Englishman can help India, and that under present circumstances is hardly at all, he certainly wishes to help. It is not his fault that the blindness of his countrymen and the conditions of the problem in India make men like him, perforce, little better than sympathetic spectators of the passionate struggle between established privilege and a nation in the making that the world watches now in India.[179]

Like Hardie, MacDonald had been born into a Scottish labouring milieu; his own engagement with imperialism began with debates around the Boer War (1899–1902), which he and many others of a liberal persuasion opposed. As Peter Cain has noted, MacDonald was critical of aspects of imperial policy, but was no anticolonialist; on the contrary, he had 'some strong leanings towards what can be regarded as conventional imperial sentiments'.[180] His narrative account, *The Awakening of India*, which is based on reports he wrote for the *Daily Chronicle*, was also the most conventional of the travelogues examined here in terms of its narrative structure, replete with the obligatory account of the sea voyage and short ethnographic portraits of various 'types' of Indians he encountered during his visits to princely courts, and so on. It is also perhaps the most literary of these otherwise political narratives. MacDonald's expressed views on British rule in India, formed before he arrived there and not entirely dislodged by the time he left – his trip interrupted by a general election – are taken straight from the chapbook of liberal imperialism;

'the historical fact remains that England saved India', he notes, also trotting out the familiar claim that 'the warring elements in Indian life need a unifying and controlling power'.[181] Given so strident a view on the need for British rule, we must ask, what then led MacDonald to the conclusion that, in the end, 'the house in which we are sheltering our official hopes is built on the sand'?[182] What accounts for the sense of imperial doom invoked at the very beginning of a narrative which also insists on the British desire to do the right thing?

> If any one reading these pages detects in them an unhappy sugges-
> tion that all is not well in India, that unsettlement is getting worse,
> that we have not yet found the way of peace, that the West might be
> more hesitating in asserting the superiority of its materialist civil-
> isation, I confess he will only have detected what is actually my
> feeling.[183]

Read carefully, *The Awakening of India* is an account of how a liberal imperialist's journey through India disrupted some of the cherished tenets of liberal imperialism. This is what makes the text less of 'an easy afternoon's work for a theorist of colonial discourse' than might be expected, or at least one which requires more than either denun-ciation of colonial stereotypes or the familiar resort to claims of ambivalence as always already embedded in the colonial.[184] If it is an account of the prototypical 'awakening of India', a much-favoured colonial trope at the turn of the century, MacDonald's is also an awakening *by* India. Towards the end of his account, MacDonald would opine, perhaps surprising himself as much as anyone else: 'On the whole I therefore regard the future as belonging to Nationalism.'[185]

Upon arrival in the country, MacDonald finds it less amenable to explanatory narration than he might have liked. About a third of the way through his account, after several lyrical passages that provide a tourist's view of India – with evocative descriptions of minarets, temples, palaces and narrow lanes, and finding impenetrable 'their mysteries of devotion and deceit, of holiness and blackguardliness' – MacDonald suddenly announces: 'I have written of India; but before one has been here a week, one doubts if India exists.'[186] This is partly an admission of the difficulty of narrating the India of multitudinous

singularity within a liberal paradigm of comprehension and equivalence. It is, to use Edward Said's words, a familiar acknowledgement
of the difficulties of codifying in writing India's 'vastness, incomprehensible creeds, secret motions, histories and social forms'.[187]
It is also, however, a comment on the complexities of Indian politics, which elude both British administrators and the well-meaning
British supporter of Indian causes. Is there even such a thing as an
Indian nation-in-waiting? 'At first sight, and on the surface', writes
MacDonald, 'India appears to be a land where people live side by
side but do not form a national community. The hope of a united
India, an India conscious of a national unity of purpose and destiny,
seems to be the vainest of vain dreams.'[188] Such observations were
not unfamiliar, of course – they routinely underpinned arguments for
the unifying importance of British rule. But MacDonald would use
them as a point of departure to investigate both the diversity of aspirations he encountered and the challenges faced by those who sought
to give those aspirations national form.

While, like Nevinson and Hardie before him, he believes that
Britain has given Indians 'the spirit which craves for nationality' and
'taught' them the principles through which that craving can be translated into definite political demands, much of Macdonald's argument
is actually taken up with what he has learned from his encounters
– that Indian nationalism in the wake of Swadeshi has found imaginative, spiritual and political resources of its own.[189] Having studied
a variety of Indian newspapers of different political shades, including the nationalist *Swaraj* and *Karmayogin*; having met a range of
figures, from Aurobindo to Gokhale (both of whom he cites); having
read novels like *Anandamath* and listened to Tagore's poetry being
sung, Macdonald is moved to recognize that there is a spirit abroad
which 'is living. It is independent. It is proud of itself. It challenges
the foreigner and draws inspiration from its own past.'[190] The issue
is how the British in India deal with it, and here the blustering 'I
know' of the colonial administrator will simply not suffice; this spirit,
though 'blurred by blackguardism, dulled by indifference, coarsened
by deceit, is nevertheless in its purity the spirit which we have to
understand'.[191] It is too reductive of this narrative to suggest that
'MacDonald has little time for the notion that India's past provided
any bases for building democratic institutions', or that he came

away from India convinced that only 'gradualism and compromise would work'.[192] He was undoubtedly critical of much that he saw, including the ways in which Hinduism relegated vast swathes of the population 'to a life little removed from that of the beasts that perish' – people whose lives were less sacred than that of a cow.[193] The only one of the travellers of this moment to be pertinently and presciently critical of the 'hard and bigoted' Hindu chauvinist and upper-caste moorings of Hindu revivalism, MacDonald also asked pertinently whether a certain kind of nationalist was really seeking a united India or simply 'the dominance of his own kind'.[194] He points out trenchantly and with some acuity that, as far as many of the oppressed castes were concerned, 'Indian Nationalism means Brahminism'.[195]

Even so, MacDonald argued, as Nevinson had, that it made no sense to insist that religion and politics be kept separate in a context where they never had been. The 'significance of this deification of India' in the 'unconstitutional' movement that rejected petitioning had to be grasped in its specificity in order to understand the present moment, but it was not entirely without a British parallel: 'The Indian assassin quotes his *Bhagavad Gita* just as the Scottish covenanter quoted his Old Testament', and inspires youths to 'cast constitutionalism to the four winds'.[196] Swadeshi – and its hold on the Bengali imagination and beyond – had to be understood for what it was because 'on the shores of its enthusiasm it will throw up the bomb-thrower as a troubled sea throws up foam, and from it all will come India – if India does ever come'.[197] His advice to his fellow Britons with an interest in India is simple: acknowledge that there is as much hostility to and 'insane suspicion' of British rule as there was before the Mutiny.[198] To overlook this seething resentment is to be 'like the inexperienced summer boatman who trusts himself to a sea subject to angry storms which arise without warning and apparently from all the quarters of heaven at the same time'.[199] Making a point of visiting women's clubs and reading papers and magazines edited by Indian women, MacDonald also observed, against the grain of stereotypes, that the strength of Swadeshi was due to Indian women who were active protesters, so that it was 'sheer blindness to overlook the women's influence as a factor in the unrest'.[200] For all that he appreciated what Swadeshi means both for India and for British rule in India, Macdonald notes, not inaccurately, that its economics are in fact based on capitalist and Western thinking, and thus are 'not going to carry India very far', since Indian capitalists simply want to exploit India themselves.[201] 'Individual capitalism', he notes, 'is proving itself to be even more destructive of the best that is in India' than it has been in the West, where it is 'less alien' in civilizational terms.[202] Another pernicious aspect of colonial rule is the erosion of the agency of colonial subjects, the Pax Britannica in India having been 'bought at the price of her own initiative ... The governed are crushed down. They become subjects who obey, not citizens who act.'[203] Colonial rule has undermined cultural resources, rendering Indians into copyists and 'hewers of wood in their national industrial economy'.[204]

Towards the end of his narrative, MacDonald offers a more quali-fied assessment of Britain's role in India, insisting, like Nevinson and Hardie before him, on its continued importance but acknowledging that its benevolent aspects might be a corollary to less edifying ones: 'Under our protection India has enjoyed a recuperative quiet. If we cannot say that our rule has been a necessary factor in the devel-opment of Indian civilisation, we can say that in view of historical Indian conditions it has been a necessary evil.'[205] Yet, MacDonald is beset by the sense that the India he witnesses in 'living' struggle will not yield to such liberal certainties and equivalences: 'You feel insignificant before it, just as a decently minded prize-fighter would feel insignificant before a saint. The difference which separates you from it cannot be bridged.'[206] At one level, this is close to what Benita Parry describes in her reading of *A Passage to India* as 'the time-honored topos of a mysterious land'; as Forster would ask: 'How can the mind take hold of such a country?'[207] In MacDonald's case, the insistence on 'the difficulty of getting a mental grasp of what India is' serves to undercut and leaven his own attempts – and those of the 'Anglo-Indians' he both sympathizes with and criticizes – to assimilate Indian nationalism to a ready-made explanatory frame-work in which it is simply the legatee of British pedagogy.[208] And so, MacDonald's narrative ends with a dual gesture: the first, like Nevinson's, a normative call to British administrators to liberalize their rule and make it more consultative with the ruled, in order to secure 'the fulfilment of our work in India';[209] and the second, a reiteration of the admission made in the narrative preface of India's recalcitrance, of 'something hidden in its heart which you will never know ... Thus, your attempts to understand, thwarted, laughed at, denied every time, become maddening. India eludes you to the last.'[210] He would go so far as to invert a familiar binary to suggest that India was communist and pantheistic, 'centred in the universal', while the West, 'centred in the particular, is theistic and individualist'.[211] Having offered a recipe for improving administration, MacDonald ends with a long, impassioned peroration on the temporariness of any rule; his assurances that the expulsion of the Raj, of 'our good government', from India is a long way off are also undercut by the contrapuntal insight that 'a revolution could bury it in its own dusty ruins'.[212] Strikingly, for what is intended as an account of a political engagement between two nations, the last lines of the memoir ask much more fundamental and distinctly un-pragmatic questions of the imperial (and capitalist) project: 'Are the pursuits we have taught India to follow anything but alluring shadows? Is the wealth that we are telling her to seek anything but dust and ashes?'[213] The riddle, MacDonald says, is troublesome, while the last lines of his narrative are curiously redolent of the devotional Hindu rhetoric of Swadeshi as MacDonald calls for Britain to welcome India's rise: 'Her Destiny is fixed above our will, and we had better recognise it and bow to the Inevitable.'[214] For a politician – indeed, a future prime minister – this is a formidable concession about the power of anticolonial agitation. Certainly he had come to a clear recognition of the existence of other historical experiences and trajectories which challenged the British assumption of exemplary status, placing themselves 'on a pedestal as the one example for men': 'At the root of most of our mistakes is the assumption that India should copy us.'[215] MacDonald would comment again on Swadeshi activists in a later work: 'They believed in India and did not believe in Europe. They believed in their own civilization and not in ours. Their ideal was an India sitting on her own throne, mistress of her own destiny, doing homage to her own past. They shook the Government more than it has been shaken since the Mutiny.'[216]

The Sense of a Beginning

I have argued that the quarter-century or so spanning the years leading up to the formation of the Indian National Congress in 1884 and the aftermath of the Partition of Bengal in 1905 functioned as a kind of pedagogical watershed for many British liberals and radicals with an interest in the Indian empire. The votaries of imperial tutelage in nationalism also became the beneficiaries of an education in anticolonial resistance. Reformist assumptions were deepened, challenged or unsettled by their encounter with 'unrest' and the cultural resources and possibilities it drew on. Back in Britain, these Edwardian political travellers remained a dissident minority, but their interventions in the media and in parliament, and, in the 'level-headed' MacDonald's case, as 'intermediary between the Indians and the British Government', were not without effect.[217] MacDonald was even invited to take up the presidency of the Indian National Congress in 1911, which he was unable to do because of his wife's illness.[218] Moulton also observes that 'without persistent Radical prodding the constitutional reforms of 1909 would probably have had fewer liberalizing features'.[219] What matters more than the undoubtedly circumscribed impact such dissidents may have had on policy was the insight that figures like Hardie, Nevinson and MacDonald brought back from their travels – that there were imaginative, political and spiritual resources, drawn from South Asian traditions, 'that might provide meaningful correctives or alternatives' to those put in place by colonialism or offered by Britain and the West'.[220] Hilda Howsin, who did not travel to India, but who wrote in defence of the Indian cause in her 1909 work *The Significance of Indian Nationalism*, would describe this as the presence of the West not so much teaching as helping regenerate and renew 'in India the consciousness of her ancient ideals, of her latent powers, of her own traditions of liberty, of justice, of self-ordained constitutionalism'.[221] The spectre of 'self-determination' now certainly haunted even modest and conditional discussions of a greater share in rule for colonial subjects. As V. H. Rutherford, who also visited India during this period and would become a prominent parliamentary advocate of the Indian nationalist cause, would pointedly observe in his 'Introductory Note' to Howsin's work: 'Great Britain, the boasted home of Freedom, is face to face with a national and patriotic demand for Freedom on the part of India, and the awful question arises: Will the British people exhibit sufficient moral courage to decide for Freedom, or, driven by a cowardly and selfish Imperialism, plunge deeper into the Dead Sea of Despotism?'[222] Interestingly, for Rutherford, the answer to this question would determine not only whether Britain could take credit for tutoring 'a sublime and bloodless revolution', but also whether Britons were in fact the 'slaves' that the anthem to Britannic rule denied they were.[223] Howsin ends her own tract with the ominous warning that, if Britain does not seize the moment to recognize India's claims, 'in wresting from our grasp that which is rightfully her due, India will achieve at once her own emancipation and the disgrace and downfall of the British Empire'.[224]

The moment of Swadeshi, then, needs to be seen here as part of a global moment of questioning European hegemony, one early contributing strand of 'a geography of political affinity that was resolutely anti-imperial and anti-capitalist' which emerged in both metropole and colonies in the first quarter of the twentieth century. Dilip Menon notes correctly that, rather than assume Swadeshi met an untimely end by 1910, 'we need to conceptualize the after-life and indeed the afterglow of Swadeshi in the first two decades of the twentieth century within the worldwide insurgency against empire involving anarchists, socialists, Sinn Feinians in a geography that extended from Mexico to the Phillipines'.[225] As others have noted, London would become an important node in this network in the wake of the First World War, functioning as a 'junction box' which brought together critics of empire from across the globe. While modulated by the political travels of its imperial sceptics and dissidents, Britain's education into anticolonialism would also continue at home.

PART II

AGITATIONS AND
ALLIANCES

5

The Interpreter of Insurgencies: Shapurji Saklatvala and Democratic Voice in Britain and India

From him British Labour, sometimes a little inclined, I am afraid, to be too parochial, has learned more clearly and definitely than ever before of the real conditions of India's toiling millions, and of how Britain's labour standards can never really be secure while there exists the menace of a great mass of underpaid and sweated labour in the East.

Herbert Bryan

As Indian activists travelled, some basing themselves outside India, in the years leading up to the First World War, Swadeshi acquired international dimensions. 'Activists in London, Paris and New York, led by Shyamji Krishnavarma, Bhikaji Cama and Lajpat Rai, respectively, set up centers for anticolonial agitation and pamphleteering, and they coordinated their efforts with Swadeshi radicalism in India,' notes Kris Manjapra.[1] The Swadeshi movement can itself be situated 'in the context of growing identification by Indians with a world-wide belt of insurgencies in the first years of the twentieth century to oppose European and American imperial power'.[2] At the very beginning of the century, Krishnavarma, who was a friend of Richard Congreve's and in close contact with Henry Hyndman, had already established the Indian Home Rule Society in London, and the controversial journal the *Indian Sociologist* (which would be banned for import to and sale in India) to espouse a more radical position than that of the Congress Moderates. Though he was not able to make the substantial inroads into British political discourse or public opinion that he had hoped to, not least because he moved to Paris in 1907, Krishnavarma's idea was one that would be espoused by larger numbers of colonial intellectuals in the years following the First World War. He believed that 'interpreters' of political relations between Britain and its colonies were needed, people who would be able to show, as in the Indian case, 'how Indians really felt and fared under British rule'.[3] Krishnavarma's writings in the *Indian Sociologist* also made clear that colonial peoples had to take charge of their own liberation – an idea that would come more prominently into view during the interwar period. His most material contribution, however, may have been the setting up of fellowships to enable young Indians to come and study in London, and India House, in Highgate, which would become a political nerve centre for Indian revolutionary nationalists. Unsurprisingly, Krishnavarma was pilloried in parliament as 'undesirable and dangerous', a target for expulsion, quite possibly one of the reasons he felt obliged to leave Britain.[4] He had also made contacts with Irish and Egyptian nationalists, and written about those freedom struggles in his journal, again foreshadowing the more extensive anticolonial networks that would emerge in the interwar decades.[5] Even as such networks which drew inspiration and strategies from each other sprang up across the globe, creating transnational connections, a 'wide spectrum of opinion now came to accept the nation-state as the universally normal and legitimate form of the modern state'.[6] The espousal of 'self-determination' by both Woodrow Wilson and Vladimir Lenin (the former drawing on and reframing the latter) only strengthened this position. Where the likes of Congreve, Jones and Blunt had had to make a relatively lonely case for the right to nationhood of non-European polities, with the contradictions and double standards more visible in the years following the Great War, the right to self-determination could be pointed to with greater confidence in making the case against imperial rule. Once it became clear, however, that Wilsonian proclamations did not extend, in practice, to the sovereignty of most non-European peoples, anticolonial nationalism, stiff with disillusionment, emerged 'as a major force in world affairs'.[7] As we shall see, even as nationalists 'incorporated his principles into their rhetorical arsenal', the gradualism of Wilson's view of self-determination for the colonies would also be challenged, along with the idea that colonial rule might also continue with his much-touted 'consent of the governed'.[8]

If the war had diminished the power and prestige of the major European empires in the eyes of many colonial subjects, an even more seismic event had taken place over its course: the Russian Revolution of 1917. The revolutionary overthrow of an authoritarian monarchy – a project with an explicitly egalitarian programme at its heart – would have a galvanizing influence on resistance to imperial rule in many parts of the world. The Communist International (Comintern) established in 1919 was a significant catalyst in this process, although the vacillations of its position on 'the Colonial Question' would sometimes become part of the problem. As we shift now from the early years of the twentieth century to the interwar period, the networks, groupings, solidarities and influences which emerged in the wake of the 1917 'October Revolution' are the *mise en scène* for the emergence, in Britain, of a more distinct form of anticolonialism. Technological advances in communication and travel brought far more traffic between colonial contexts, as well as between these contexts and various metropolitan centres; this movement, which included labour migrations, was naturally reflected in greater political and intellectual traffic. Certainly, developments in communication 'allowed colonized subjects around the world unprecedented access to information about conditions in other colonies'.[9] As a result, anticolonial activists recognized that 'the problem of empire was not specific to single nations but instead a global problem requiring global resources and solutions' – though, at the same time, the national would retain its specificity and power as a legitimizing category for emancipatory aspirations.[10] The global or transnational was never a stark alternative to the local or the national; these terms were frequently seen as intertwined, even in a dialectical relationship.[11] Global alliances between anticolonial groupings could, however, take on different political complexions. As some historians of 'the internationalist moment' between 1917 and the beginning of the Second World War have noted, 'although in retrospect a number of classificatory labels suggest themselves – socialist, communist, fascist, Pan-Islamic – the sentiment (and it was often a sentiment) was far less differentiated, more amorphous than these labels can describe'.[12]

The Bolshevik revolution, however, set many such broadly dissident tendencies in dialogue in a 'qualitatively different' way.[13]

Integral to the process was the presence of black and Asian anticolonial intellectuals and campaigners as an active nodal link between resistance movements in the colonies and metropolitan dissidence; many were engaged, in complex ways, with both Marxism and nationalism. As is now well known, in the 1930s London (like Berlin and Paris) became a kind of 'junction box' for oppositional black and Asian figures from various parts of the British Empire – not least because, ironically enough, it was possible to articulate criticism of that Empire in the city that was its beating heart without being subjected to repressive colonial anti-sedition legislation. London therefore 'provided a unique incubator for radical black internationalist discourse'.[14] Although some lived in other British cities, it was London which seemed to have made it possible for colonial subjects – writers, intellectuals, labour activists, campaigners and journalists – to encounter each other, and to organize away from more repressive contexts. The internationalism of anticolonialism emerged, as Marc Matera, among others, notes, 'through the initiative of non-European thinkers and activists'.[15] Importantly, these thinkers and activists placed non-European initiative at the centre of their anticolonial thought. With Indian radicals shifting base to Paris and other European capitals, the presence of black (African and Caribbean) radicals and revolutionary leftists became increasingly crucial to putting pressure on and radicalizing groups and individuals broadly belonging to the British left.[16] The notion of colonial tutelage, as we have seen, had already been challenged by nineteenth-century insurgencies. In the interwar period there would be an even more explicit rejection of the idea that colonial government was necessary in order that backward races might be taught to govern themselves, not least because of the attempt to rehabilitate colonial rule in the form of 'mandates' and 'trusteeship'.[17]

A different kind of tutelage, however, would take place in the heart of the metropolis. As Asian and black anticolonial figures collaborated with progressive British critics of empire, they frequently interrogated the latter's tendency to endorse gradualism and such notions as 'trusteeship', guiding 'backward' regions to self-government. In the process they not only internationalized British opposition to empire, but also pushed it in more radical directions. The relationships between these anticolonial figures and white British dissidents are an important part of the story, but these were not always a simple matter of affinities or friendship, textured as they were, like the city's own agonistic encounters, as much by friction, disagreement, tensions and negotiation as by sympathy and goodwill. Black and Asian antagonists of empire served as important conduits of engagement between crises of insurgency in the colonies and British critics of the imperial project, as well as contributing, where possible, to mainstream public discourse and parliamentary forums. As interpreters between British dissidents and the millions who were asserting themselves in far corners of the Empire, they 'appropriated the practices of liberal civil society – speaking to crowds at political rallies or in Hyde Park, petitioning the Colonial Office, and publishing books, small tracts, and journals – performing citizenship in advance of its formal achievement'.[18] They themselves were often simultaneously students and pedagogues, learning from insurgent movements and sharing their knowledge with British domestic dissidents – not always, it must be said, with complete success.

What emerged out of these encounters were cultural and political formations, movements and organizations – the League against Imperialism, with its very active British branch, being only one example – that were substantially dialogical in nature; black, Asian and white British dissidents learned from and shaped each other's politics while forging alliances that took work on all sides. As we shall see in the following pages, what figures – the most prominent voices were, unsurprisingly, male – such as Shapurji Saklatvala, George Padmore, Claude McKay and C. L. R. James brought to the table, in addition to an uncompromising rejection of gradualism and tutelage, was an insistence on self-representation and self-emancipation. While all these figures were closely engaged with collectivities of resistance, each also had a distinctive personal voice that they impressed upon their work. At all times they sought to bring a sense of the live and urgent collective struggles taking place across national borders and in distant parts of the Empire. All of them launched powerful attacks on paternalism and gradualism, on tutelage and trusteeship, drawing on these struggles to illustrate the futility of these cherished imperial concepts. We begin in this chapter by looking at a very unusual figure, one of the few left-wing radical critics of empire who made it to the House of Commons, and was able to use that position of prominence over seven years to craft powerful attacks on the imperial project from the very heart of Westminster. Even more significantly, Shapurji Saklatvala was able to pick up the links that had been made by earlier critics of empire, such as Ernest Jones and Frederic Harrison, and insist on the necessity of solidarity between those who were at the receiving end of exploitation by capitalism and class in Britain, and those who suffered a racialized manifestation of that exploitation in the colonies. Solidarity, he would explain, was not a matter of proffering charitable feelings, but essential to survival itself – both in the colonies and in the heart of the metropole.

The Impatient Communist

There are not two ways of ruling another nation. There is not a democratic and sympathetic way, and also an unsympathetic way.
                                                            Shapurji Saklatvala

On 17 June 1927 a heated debate was underway in the House of Commons on a controversial proposal to send to India a commission that would review the provisions of the India Act of 1919, with a view to possible further limited constitutional reforms. To be headed by the right-leaning Liberal Sir John Simon, a cautious proponent of gradual changes, the proposed consultative body would have no Indian representative. The Simon Commission's blatantly racist composition – especially egregious given that it was a body set up to discuss the issue of political representation for Indians – was manifestly inflammatory, and the protests that rocked India a few months later surprised many political observers by their 'sheer ferocity'.[19] When the commissioners did arrive in India, they were greeted by a sea of black flags and placards reading 'Go back, Simon'. In Britain itself, however, it would be left to the member for North Battersea to voice outright criticism of the commission, in an indignant and characteristically direct parliamentary peroration:

It is absolutely impossible for one country to hold another in subjection and pretend to offer them measures of reform giving them a

partnership in the commonwealth. That is all humbug. I see that a
new Commission is going to be appointed, and I would like to ask
what is going to be the scope of that Commission and its terms of
reference. Everybody knows, whether it is put in black and white
or not, that the first thing that will be put in the terms of reference
is how this country can keep a stranglehold over India.[20]

A fellow MP had had quite enough. Launching into an ad hominem
attack on his prolix colleague's personal history, George Pilcher,
member for Penryn and Falmouth, noted that, while the honourable
member for Battersea had 'made some very cruel and unjustifiable
charges against the European population in Bombay' in relation to
poverty, low wages and slums, he himself belonged to the wealthy
community 'most responsible' for Mumbai's industrial development.[21] It was 'high time', Pilcher sneered, for parliament to 'know
who the hon. Member for North Battersea is and what is his relationship with that great industrial community in Bombay'.[22] During
another fractious debate on the Simon Commission that autumn, it
was the turn of the Tory under-secretary of state for India to get personal about his Battersea colleague, who had once again attacked the
mission. No one with 'the remotest knowledge of India', snarled Earl
Winterton, 'could possibly accept the hon. Gentleman as an exponent
of Indian opinion. As far as I know, he has absolutely no authority of any sort. He is repudiated by every responsible organisation
in India.'[23]

The focus of this sniping was Shapurji Dorabji Saklatvala, the
lone Communist member of the House. Saklatvala was a Parsi from
Bombay, who had first come to Britain in 1905 in his late twenties for
medical treatment. After marrying an Englishwoman, Sally Marsh,
he had settled down in London, where the couple would raise a large
family. Saklatvala was indeed related to the great industrial dynasty
inaugurated by Jamsetji Tata, and had worked for several years in
the family concern.[24] He was not quite culpable of being an 'heir
of the industrial system which he attacks', however, having been a
paid employee and a poor cousin rather than a direct descendant
of the main branch of the business dynasty. Responding to Pilcher's
broadside, Saklatvala replied simply that he had no greater stake
in defending his own natal community than he had in attacking

Bombay's elite European milieu: 'The Parsee capitalist class is just as abominable and as much to be avoided as the class to which the hon. Member and his friends belong in this country'. Responding to Winterton's charge that he was not taken seriously by any Indian organizations, he pointed out that he, who had been officially welcomed in nine Indian cities during a recent tour, could speak of matters Indian with far greater legitimacy than the 'unrepresentative Indian Princes on the League of Nations' placed there by the earl in his capacity as colonial secretary. At this point, Saklatvala had been in the House for three years, elected first in 1922 as a Labour MP, and then again in 1923 as a Communist (after the Labour Party expelled Communist members). So he noted that while he spoke in this debate as 'one of the conquered and enslaved subject races', he was also 'representing the interests of the British electors who sent me'.

It is this sense of carrying a dual but intertwined representational responsibility – and his persistence in identifying common ground between the two sides – which makes Shapurji Saklatvala a figure of transnational significance in thinking about the relationship between colonial insurgencies and British anticolonialism in the interwar period. Deemed 'one of the most violent anti-British agitators in England' by state espionage agencies, Saklatvala sought actively to forge a language of opposition to empire that would at once undo the pretences and prevarications of gradualist reformism and make clear that resistance to empire was in the interests of both the Indian and British working classes.[25] Where Hardie, MacDonald and others who visited India during the Swadeshi years came back to make the case for reforms that might defuse the 'unrest', Saklatvala was arguably the first MP to make a sustained case in parliament against reformism and 'liberal' approaches to colonial governance in themselves. His biographer, Marc Wadsworth, argues that Saklatvala was also responsible for putting empire and anti-imperialism firmly into the view of liberals and progressives at a time 'when the British left was by no means committed to anti-imperialism'; he invited campaigners from the colonies to speak at meetings and wrote on the topic in such organs as the *Labour Leader*.[26] At meetings of the Independent Labour Party, which he joined in 1909, 'Saklatvala raised the issue of Indian independence and chided the ILP on the need to be more internationalist'.[27] The subject of three biographies – one by his daughter, Sehri – Saklatvala, Britain's third Indian MP after fellow Parsis Naoroji and Mancherjee Bhownagree, is usually mentioned only in passing in studies of early twentieth-century relationships between English dissenters and Indians, which have tended to focus on more reformist figures such as Annie Besant, C. F. Andrews and Mirabehn (Madeleine Slade), who appear less Manichean in their approach to colonial questions.[28] Yet Saklatvala – who described the likes of Besant as 'white men and women' who 'pass as India's friends and pretend to be almost Indianised' – himself emerges in some ways as the consummate hybrid, deeply rooted in British political and social life while equally committed to the Indian anticolonial struggle. To the later dismay of the British Communist Party, he was also committed to retaining something of his Parsi cultural and religious heritage.[29] Described later by George Padmore as the 'most independent-minded Communist ever', during his parliamentary career Saklatvala produced the first truly uncompromising refutation of imperialism in the House, one which put in place an unbridgeable antagonism between empire and democracy, refused to accept that reforms or 'trusteeship' were possible in the context of political subjugation, identified the centrality of capitalism to the imperial project, and stressed the revolutionary agency of the oppressed out of which common ground would emerge.[30]

In doing so, 'Comrade Sak' crafted a unique political voice for himself, at once Indian and British, speaking out candidly and passionately on many causes, but most especially against imperialism, which, for him, was inextricable from capitalism. Known for 'a striking and original manner of speaking', he would tell his British audiences that 'he could not help it that his accent was a little foreign but his heart was not foreign'.[31] One contemporary, the journalist Herbert Bryan, described Saklatvala as possessed not of 'the mock eloquence of the demagogic wind-bag, but the deep sincerity of the man finding expression in flaming words', also noting: 'His command of English is infinitely superior to that of the average Englishman.'[32] The over 500 interventions he made in the House of Commons during a relatively short but packed parliamentary career certainly ranged over domestic issues such as housing conditions, unemployment, wages and trade unionism, but the majority were on India and imperial matters, earning him the sobriquet of 'Member for India'.[33]

While it is true that he 'was only one of many personalities operating in the West from a variety of Indian political tendencies', few were able so deftly to negotiate – and make a polemical virtue of – colonial subjecthood as a form of dual citizenship.[34] The fact that Saklatvala was at once influential and reviled had much to do with his ability to navigate artfully – though never without integrity – between the pronouns 'you' and 'we' when addressing British politicians and lawmakers; the 'you' was a source of irritation to his political opponents. Unsurprisingly, not a little racism came his way, with some on the 'pink' left allegedly wanting to get 'this bloody nigger off our backs'.[35]

Saklatvala's synchronic identification with both fellow Indian colonial subjects and ordinary British citizens appears to have been completely sincere; certainly there is nothing in either his private communications or his public pronouncements to suggest otherwise. Indeed, the insight that subjects of the British Empire and ordinary Britons had more in common with each other than with their respective ruling classes was one that he attempted to elaborate from his earliest years in British politics, and which he later parlayed into the language of communist internationalism. Intervening in Commons debates and playing an active role in organizations ranging from the British Socialist Party and the Independent Labour Party to the Workers' Welfare League of India and the League against Imperialism, Saklatvala made significant public contributions that tell us something about how British criticism of empire was shaped and reformulated, particularly after the October Revolution, by the growing presence and pedagogical impact of Asian and African campaigners and intellectuals in the imperial metropolis. Certainly, he was responsible for adamantly bringing resistance to the imperial project – particularly, though not only, in India – firmly into both parliamentary view and public hearing, which was no mean feat. Close readings of his speeches and writings indicate the extraordinary extent to which Saklatvala was preoccupied with the project of channelling a democratic 'voice', both for the subjects of colonialism and for ordinary Britons; he also wanted each of these constituencies to hear the other. Later in his political career, Saklatvala, with what fellow MP Philip Snowden described as 'volcanic eloquence', would also become a prominent spokesman in Britain for another juridical crisis of empire that became a cause célèbre in Britain – the infamous

'Meerut Conspiracy Case'.[36] Both Saklatvala's political career and the Meerut campaign, which are explored in Chapter 6, are significant moments in the history of metropolitan anti-imperialism in the interwar period.

India in Britain: The War Years and Beyond

The war years, from 1914 to 1918, had not been especially active campaigning years in relation to imperial matters in Britain. They witnessed an unfolding tussle – between the Congress in India, which would come under Gandhi's leadership after the war, and the British Committee of the Indian National Congress – over who would speak for India and control the direction of agitation on Indian matters in Britain. Wartime powers had enabled the colonial government in India to ban political demonstrations and repress the Home Rule agitation, Besant herself being imprisoned in 1917. In Britain, the British Auxiliary to the Home Rule Leagues undertook some activism, which included meetings, petitions and court cases that brought in supporters including 'many of the organisations dedicated to socialism, democratic control and the protection of civil liberties which the war had thrown up and which had responded vigorously to Besant's arrest'.[37] Certainly, this form of engagement had worked to garner more British public support for a moderate and gradualist programme, whereby India would be 'given' Home Rule and perhaps dominion status. Meanwhile, a bitter divide between Besant and Tilak also emerged, the former calling for the Congress to accept the extremely modest 'Montagu–Chelmsford reforms', while the latter adhered to the more advanced insistence on dominion status. The spectrum of options nonetheless remained relatively narrow, and on the whole reformist rather than radical. In the immediate post-war period, partly due to Gandhi's reluctance to encourage foreign propaganda, campaigners for Indian freedom in London were a muted voice.[38]

Saklatvala would be something of an exception, and an important one, as he positioned himself assertively as an interpreter between India's resisting colonial subjects and Britain's governing classes. A prolific campaigner for the causes he espoused, Saklatvala did not leave behind a collated body of work. His views, analyses and arguments have to be reconstructed from his frequently lengthy parliamentary speeches and interventions, addresses to rallies, and journalistic contributions to a range of political organs, including the *Labour Leader*, the *Labour Monthly*, the *Daily Worker* and the *Anti-imperialist Review*.[39] The focus in this chapter will be largely on his parliamentary years and the powerful critique of the British Empire in India that he articulated in his Commons interventions. Even before he took up democratic office, however, Saklatvala challenged paternalism both in the usual imperial quarters and on the left of the British political spectrum. In July 1919, when he submitted a statement to the India Office on behalf of the Workers' Welfare League of India, established in 1917, Saklatvala commented on the assumption that the franchise had to be withheld from Indian workers on account of their illiteracy. Noting that many illiterate Britons had in fact been enfranchised in the course of the Reform Acts, he observed:

> The Indian village worker, though illiterate, is far from being uncultured. The latest revolution in Russia proves at least one thing, that an illiterate Asiatic when given a vote and voice in State affairs, is capable of appreciating and enjoying it to the extent of living up to it, fighting for it, and dying for it, as ardently as his literate European comrade.[40]

The league's 'Statement of Principles' also notes that, where the Labour Party was concerned, 'instead of a voice from India we are confronted by a dumb people'.[41] Saklatvala's influence is unmistakable in this document's observation that such a constructed 'dumbness' makes it possible for all manner of reformist declarations to be made in India's name, including assertions that 'this or that trifling change is not only necessary but sufficient to satisfy India's needs'.[42] Repeatedly invoked in his writings, this emphasis on 'voice' was clearly derived from the exposition of the national 'self' as it emerged in Swadeshi and *swaraj* ideologies of self-determination – Saklatvala would refer to himself at one point as 'a Tilakite extremist' – but, over time, it took on a more specifically communist dimension.[43] Indian resistance, much like Indian opinion, was not homogeneous, and resistance took varied forms. Similarly, Saklatvala repeatedly underlined the fact that all countries and cultures had traditions of resistance embedded in them: 'You have had your struggles, and we have ours, and shall still have them.'[44]

In post-war India, some of these struggles took the form of labour rebellions. As the Royal Commission on Labour in India pithily put it, by the late 1920s there had grown a reasonably widespread 'realization of the potentialities of the strike'.[45] From 1925 onwards, left-wing and communist activities in trade unions – and trade union membership itself – began to increase, as a wave of strikes once again paralysed the country. Where 'Gandhi preached a philosophy of class peace and collaboration and opposed any appeal to class interest', communists were able to address a lacuna, appealing to 'the self-consciousness and organization of the proletariat or the peasantry'.[46] For all its power as a mobilizing force, then, the Congress in the 1920s was 'not without a certain vulnerability to political ideologies not its own', and the question of class and labour, which it generally evaded under Gandhi, was brought firmly into view by socialists and communists. Beyond that, of course, Lenin, in oppositional debate with M. N. Roy, had famously arrived at a formulation for colonial policy to be adopted by the Second Congress of the Communist International in 1920: 'All Communist Parties must give active support to the revolutionary movements of liberation, the form of support to be determined by a study of existing conditions, carried on by the party wherever there is such.'[47]

The background of British interwar communism is important here. Saklatvala left the Independent Labour Party in 1919 after joining the Communist Party of Great Britain (CPGB), which was constituted by the merging of various small left-wing groupings, the most consequential of which was the British Socialist Party. He became a member of the CPGB's Colonial Committee as well as a group calling itself the Indian Bureau, both set up to follow the Comintern's directive that there should be close collaboration between the CPGB and emergent communist movements in various parts of the British Empire, including India and Egypt. There has been considerable debate about the extent to which the CPGB did in fact engage with the question of colonialism.[48] Certainly there is some merit to the argument that India was something of an exception to a wider CPGB indifference to, or at least ineffectiveness on, colonial questions. In a very critical but important article, the historian Marika Sherwood has claimed, for instance, that the CPGB ignored black workers and issues of racism despite instructions from the Comintern to engage with colonial matters. Claims that the party 'pioneered the analysis of and sponsored discussions of imperialism in colonial and semi-colonial lands', she argues, were exaggerated, as was the insistence that the 'party stressed the growth and importance of the anti-imperialist struggles of the working peoples of the countries of the British Empire'.[49] Sherwood cites Saklatvala himself as expressing disappointment as late as 1934 with the CPGB's record on colonialism:

> the fundamental sense of the Party members' duty towards colonial problems [does] not exist ... the Party as a whole has not been keenly live to it ... There has been a tendency to treat the colonial problem as a mere side issue and nobody's problem in particular ... the condition of indifference and suspicion between the Party and their colonial nationals is deplorable.[50]

This is not the place to revisit the frequently bitter discussion about the role of the CPGB as a whole in relation to imperial questions, but it is worth noting that Saklatvala was certainly the most prolific and noteworthy of high-profile figures associated with the CPGB to speak on them. While not the only party member who wrote on empire per se – Rajani Palme Dutt's writings on India come to mind – he was certainly the most committed to attacking reformism and gradualism, while emphasizing the insurgent agency of the colonized masses.

'Does a communist have to *witness* oppression in order to take up the struggle?' Sherwood has asked in the context of her analysis of the CPGB's treatment of colonial issues and its inadequacies in engaging with anticolonial resistance movements in the Caribbean and Africa.[51] Even as the answer must be in the negative, there seems little doubt that the power animating Saklatvala's speeches and writings on colonial matters drew significantly upon his experiences of life in the Raj, as well as his continued close engagement with real struggles there after he had moved to Britain. Even where India was concerned, Saklatvala was distinctive not only in the extent to which he engaged with colonial questions, but also in how he approached them. He was, for one thing, direct in identifying the pressing need for the British labour movement to engage with colonial issues: 'If by any chance continued unwisdom, apathy or arrogance on the part of British Labour drives the Indian Labour or mass movement into open hostility against them, British Labour will have to be prepared for evil days.'[52] As Saklatvala would note on many occasions, the resistance to British imperialism in India both exceeded and challenged the limits of bourgeois nationalism. Genteel parliamentary discussions about 'reform' served to obscure far more fundamental questions about empire which were being posed by resistance on the streets and in the factories of India. Saklatvala would put them to parliament.

'In the people's voice': Saklatvala and the Commons

Admittedly, the task of a solitary Communist member in a hostile capitalist House of Commons is a difficult one.

Shapurji Saklatvala

A refusal to register the voices – still less the resistance – of colonial subjects was built into the very structure of colonialism, Saklatvala argued, as he made it his task to voice that resistance in the House of Commons. He would remind his colleagues repeatedly that their discussions on India evaded the fact that the Raj was being resisted fiercely, and was only able to perpetuate itself through intense repression:

We are debating here as if the Bengal ordinances were never promulgated, as if the shooting of Bombay operatives during the cotton strike had never taken place, as if a great strike of thousands of railway workers is not even now going on in the Punjab, with men starving ... as if all these things had not happened, as if a great controversy is not raging, not only with the people of India but with people all over the world, whether British Imperialism, whatever its past history, is at all permissible to exist now for the benefit of the citizens of Great Britain herself.[53]

It is this refusal that enabled the myth of the liberal empire to persist, along with the notion that 'true' Indian opinion was 'moderate' – an adjective that simply denoted views in accordance with those of the Colonial Office. In an astonishing maiden speech as a Labour MP in the House of Commons on 23 November 1922, Saklatvala brought together a range of themes he would develop and finesse – often at stupendous length – in the seven years he spent there. Foremost among these was the right of ordinary citizens to be heard and represented, rather than have 'reforms' imposed from on high. Opening with an apology for not speaking in 'the traditional manner of the House of Commons', he insisted with courteous firmness that it betokened no lack of respect for his colleagues if 'we of the people shall now require that the people's matters shall be talked in the people's voice'.[54] The speech was long and covered substantial domestic ground, but moved swiftly enough to Saklatvala's signature project – illuminating the workings of empire as inextricably tied to the workings of capitalism, thus tying together the fates of all those at the mercy of the 'spread of the cult of private enterprise'.[55] It was a theme to which Saklatvala would return over and over again: imperialism was not simply about forcing nations under foreign subjugation and thus violating British values – though it was that too – but also about putting in place systemic inequalities and exploitation that rebounded as damagingly on British workers as on colonial subjects. From this perspective, anti-imperialism – a rejection of the economic workings of empire – was as essential to the health of British society as it was to colonized ones. Colonialism's 'seductive tale' full of 'glamour' became an altogether different narrative when it registered high unemployment figures in Britain: 'It is the growth of this private enterprise, of these large corporations and trusts, these huge industrial concerns in India, which is beginning to tell its tale upon the workers of this country.'[56]

The constitutive futility and bad faith of colonial 'reforms' undertaken on the assumed wishes of colonial subjects, while they were simultaneously rendered 'dumb', would become one of Saklatvala's parliamentary and campaigning preoccupations. It would also underlie his unflagging insistence on the need for constant *democratic* contact between the working peoples of Britain and subjects of the Empire – necessary not just for the colonized, but in order that the former too might understand their own historical circumstances. In February 1923, with the House debating the Indian States (Protection against Disaffection) Act of 1922, which limited criticism of native rulers of states, Saklatvala offered a fierce critique of the 'mock Debate' and even his own Labour colleagues' attempts to have royal assent withheld from the Bill:

> By our very effort to save the Government from rushing into a mad act, we are liable here on the Labour Benches to be surreptitiously drawn into an Imperial policy, as if we wanted Imperialism to be run more correctly than they desire, but though there is such a danger, there is no reality in it.[57]

There can, Saklatvala repeats, be no mitigated, reformed or 'democratic' version of imperialism – a danger even Indian nationalists court when they parlay with the British government, 'tacitly accepting the right of this country to send a Viceroy at all'.[58] The war had made clear that there could be no halfway house, 'that no country and no nation can now live at peace and in prosperity by crushing other nations economically'.[59] The only 'reforms' that would make sense would obviate any requirement for imperial rule, and 'start a scheme by which the workers and peasants of India enjoy the same standard of life as the workers and peasants of Europe and of America'.[60] Saklatvala also repeatedly emphasized the paradox of *petitioning* for reforms in a colonial context: either a country had the right to rule another without being told how to do it, or it had no right to do so; anything else was just 'little details in the art of governing another nation by a sort of hypnotisation'.[61]

Saklatvala's criticisms enshrined the insight that, for all their humanitarian pretensions, reformist approaches to empire were devoid of a genuine universalism which ought to be, by definition, indivisible. If 'the same principles of life are in every European or Asiatic nation', then it was constitutively impossible to 'bestow' such things as freedom and sovereignty in a 'gradual' manner. The routine elision of anticolonial resistance in favour of negotiation and petitioning obscured the simple fact, Saklatvala took pains to point out, that no British man or woman or any person in Europe would 'tolerate for one day a power so despotic and arbitrary as the Crown ... is insisting upon enjoying in India'.[62] And so – and this was the point which bore repetition – it was far from a uniquely British habit to resist tyranny; theories emphasizing ineluctable difference in order to argue, for instance, that Asians venerated despotism were themselves, Comrade Sak pronounced damningly, a consequence of 'Western ignorance' and self-regard: 'It is an untruthful statement to say that the people of the East are tolerating high privileges in monarchy and in their ruling castes and classes. It is a false notion. It is the Western conceit; it is the Westerner admiring himself, as though the Westerners have the highest consciousness of human life.'[63] Pointing to examples of rebellion by the Chinese, Turks and Persians, the last having 'overthrown completely one monarch after another', Saklatvala tore apart fraudulent theories according to which 'Asiatic people always allow a good deal of latitude to their monarchs' as enacting a self-serving and willed 'Western ignorance' of histories of Asian resistance.[64] In fact, he averred with a touch of malice, the opposite was true: 'No Eastern country would tolerate as the British people have tolerated the humbug and nonsense from the governing classes.'[65] Equally, 'schoolboyish' British theories of India as a country always ruled by a foreign monarch appeared to overlook the fact that Britain had routinely sourced its own rulers from abroad: 'A few families supply monarchs to Europe just as a few biscuit factories supply biscuits all over Europe.'[66] Saklatvala rejected reformism because it inscribed the right of an imperial 'higher consciousness' to extend its generosity and intelligence towards a consciousness figured as less advanced. As a result, it was fundamentally antithetical to the principle of human equality, and led inevitably to double standards even in progressive rhetoric: 'You call the Indians seditious when they protest against these things, but when you rise in revolt in this country against the ruling classes it is called the spirit of democracy.'[67]

Saklatvala was unabashedly universalist even as he insisted on the need for historical specificity. Given that 'human feeling, the human heart and the human mind are just the same in India as here or elsewhere', he deemed appeals to absolute cultural difference and relativism an elaborate ploy, deployed selectively and self-servingly.[68] It enabled the absence of consistent principle from imperial practice – 'Sometimes one thing is right and at another moment it is wrong'.[69] Such selectivity invariably worked in favour of the ruling imperial class by allowing factories, mines or dockyards to be set up as universally beneficent, but suddenly generating culturally sensitive apologetics when it came to fair working conditions, equal labour rights or minimum wages: 'We cannot do it, because India is cut up by caste, or because of Hindu and Mohammedan hatreds, or because there are depressed classes.'[70] Spreading the benefits of modernity was given as an excuse to colonize, 'to start cotton factories, jute factories, steel works, engineering works, post offices, railways and telegraphs'; but the same modernity was deemed far too much of an experiment when it becomes the basis of demands for social justice and decent working conditions.[71] Saklatvala's own insights about the need to radicalize both Indian nationalism and the British response to it were shaped by the growing industrial unrest in India. They prompted him to observe trenchantly in parliament that any progress on wages for Indian workers had not so much been 'granted' as 'extorted by the workers fighting inch by inch against you'.[72] Such pieces of progressive legislation as existed in India, too, had only come to pass after some nominal powers were extended to Indians. The much-vaunted role of imperial trustee had generally only been exercised with machine guns and soldiers, 'with bayonets ready' on behalf of industrialists, in the face of protests like those demanding an end to brutal conditions in the Bengal mines.[73] Why, he asked his colleagues pointedly, did those claiming to have gone to India 'because *suttees* were being burnt' have nothing to offer factory women facing an infant mortality rate of 600 to 700 per thousand?[74]

In 1927, the beneficent delusions, as Saklatvala saw them, of the gradualist camp took the form of a 'great British blunder' – the all-white and all-British commission headed by Sir John Simon. As one historian notes: 'In one stroke the British had achieved the very thing that had eluded Gandhi since the end of non-cooperation – nationalist unity ... Boycotts and protests against the Simon Commission's stately progress across the subcontinent reawakened the excitement of direct action. It also coincided with an extremely alarming level of workers' strikes and communist and terrorist activity.'[75] As Gandhi launched his famous Salt Satyagraha, and finally called for 'Purna Swaraj' or 'Complete Independence', seeking to regain greater control of a movement split between agitators and constitutionalists, Saklatvala once again bore the mantle of 'the member for India' in the House of Commons, and challenged not only its terms of reference but its most fundamental assumptions. The arguments he had made against imperialism and the philosophy of reform on the basis of the right to voice and self-determination now came together in the form of a powerful and sustained polemic:

> Just as this country would not allow Chinamen or Germans to write a constitution for this country, it is equally absurd for this country to appoint a Committee to write a constitution for the people of India, on whatever basis. The only point of discussion in this Chamber should be whether this country is still to be a tyrant over India, or whether it will be courageous enough to say 'no' and cease to be a tyrant. There is no gradual process about this.[76]

The only kind of commission that would make any kind of sense would be one whose brief was to 'investigate as between Imperialism and anti-Imperialism', one which consisted not of dissembling reformers who traded in ambiguity, but rather of 'honest imperialists' and 'candid, open-minded, outspoken anti-Imperialists'.[77]

On 17 June 1927, Saklatvala put to the House that the commission's purpose of looking into reforms while holding India down in subjection was 'humbug'.[78] Once again, he distanced himself from the reformist position of his Labour colleagues, like the Labour MP George Lansbury, noting that none of this was 'a question of reform, or gradual or quick reform'; what was at stake was 'a question of the possible relationship between two nations on the basis of one nation deciding what is good for the other'.[79] Saklatvala spelled out for his fellow parliamentarians the fundamental paradox of reformism: 'Between slavery and freedom there is no middle course, and a transition from slavery to freedom can never be attained by gradual measures.'[80] Freedom was indivisible: 'When you make up your minds that there shall be no slavery, then the bond must break, and it must break completely ... There is no such thing as gradual freedom.'[81] It was a point he would make again and again in the course of the Simon Commission debates, 'that there is no such thing as Committees and Commissions being appointed, granting stage by stage freedom to conquered nations from their conquerors'.[82] The 'antiquated, savage system of rule of another country and another people' quite simply had to end.[83]

It is all nonsense to say that for the benefit of the Indians the British nation has got to be there, and is performing some benevolent action. For goodness sake be honest, and say you are a nation of enterprise, and, in seeking for enterprise to seek your own good, opportunity placed you in a strong position to throttle the country and the people of India ... It is no use pretending as though a deputation had come to you from the Indians, as though a section of the moderate opinion of India came to Great Britain and said, 'Come and protect us; come and give us military protection; come and teach us civil administration', and so on.[84]

In nonetheless proposing an amendment later that year which would require Indian legislative consent to the Simon Commission, Saklatvala was making an important philosophical and political point about voice and the recognition of widespread resistance to British rule in India. His amendment would 'compel the Government to take notice of the existence of the second party to the contract, and not to move in the matter as if they alone count, and India does not exist at all'.[85] In the absence of such minimal consent, an already compromised process simply elided the other party which, he noted pointedly, having 'heard of our one-sided activity ... is objecting as strongly as possible and in whatever manner it can against this proposal'.[86] This modest amendment was rejected, as was an even more minimal one in which Saklatvala proposed simply that Pandit Motilal Nehru of the Indian National Congress be invited to speak to the House so that it might 'listen to the voice of India through another Indian and then judge for yourselves whether you are not doing a most criminal thing to-day in appointing this Commission'.[87] Due in no small part to Saklatvala's campaigning leadership, and inspired by the fluttering black flags of the Indian protests, Britain too witnessed demonstrations: 'To hell with the Simon Commission' read placards in Hyde Park rallies at which Saklatvala and others spoke.[88]

It was precisely such attempts to represent the forces of Indian anticolonial resistance in Britain that led to the spiteful personal attacks from parliamentary colleagues on Saklatvala's own position as a Parsi from a wealthy community who was in no position to speak for Indian interests. Saklatvala was unfazed by the criticism,

Shapurji Saklatvala speaking to crowds at Speakers'
Corner, Hyde Park, September 1933

noting trenchantly that the question of 'voice', when it came to colonized people, was in any case tendentiously invoked:

> And we are told here that that Commission which will be appointed in India will express the voice of the people of India. A little while ago the Under-Secretary told us that it is impossible for any representative to express the voice of the people of India; but when it is the mill-owners, and the industrialists, and the magnates, and the landlords, and the zemindars, and the princes, then they represent, not only the voice of the people of India, but all that is perfect in democracy, all that can be imaginable in the world as expressing the sorrows and grievances and sufferings of the people.[89]

It is of some importance that Saklatvala insistently extended the same arguments he made for democracy and self-determination for India to Britain and the British people. The hierarchical division between those who were considered properly representative and those whose voices did not count applied to Britain as well: 'Anybody who would try to speak of Great Britain as one homogeneous nation is wrong;

anybody who is trying to speak of India as a homogeneous nation is wrong. Both the British nation and the Indian are sharply divided into two classes.'[90] This is what enabled him to make perfectly clear that he was no more a votary of the Indian capitalist classes than he was of their British counterparts, and to keep on repeating, given his responsibility to his electorate in England, Scotland and Wales, that it was a curse for all, 'for the workers of Britain, for the workers of India and for the peasants of India, to have these Imperial ties'.[91] Most valuably, he made clear that a failure to understand the workings of empire in fact hurt the British working classes: 'The neglect of the British working-class to study British imperialism in its proper light is leading to the accomplishment of two processes, namely, a rapid Britainising of a capitalist master-class in India and a rapid Indianising of the large working-class in Britain' – a race to the bottom for both working classes in the long run.[92] These were points that had been heralded in different ways by Jones and Congreve in the wake of 1857. Even as he urged a coming together of campaigning interests, writing in the *Labour Monthly*, Saklatvala reminded the British labour movement that it was really in India that the ugliest face of contemporary capitalism could be seen – a face that would reveal itself at home in due course if not resisted:

> Take your worst slums, your most congested lodging-houses and yet you cannot conceive of that broken-down mud hut, to enter which even a stature of 5 feet of humanity has got to nearly double up. There is no other ventilation or opening for light, and there is even nothing to see inside these huts, which are invariably completely unfurnished. I am not talking now of villages; I am talking of large industrial centres like Nagpur and Cawnpore where exist cotton mills more flourishing than most cotton mills in Lancashire, and where several thousand workers are still consigned to these death-traps.[93]

Comrade Sak did not hold back in telling British labour they were wrong not to have seen that their 'immediate task lay in levelling up the conditions of … fellow workers in India'.[94] There was a tendency to act as though the Empire did not exist at all. 'An almost conceited view was taken that the low level of the Indian was well deserved and that the higher level of the British worker was something that was

permanently secure by his own merit.'[95] The British labour movement had failed signally to look at 'securing a world standard' for
labour as an act of solidarity rather than 'an act of secondary charity
from the stronger to the weaker group'.[96] This, he said, would prove
to be a mistake.

For all the hostility with which he was met, Saklatvala was
not without support from some parliamentary colleagues, one of
whom observed that, as 'the only Indian-born native in the House',
Saklatvala provided his fellow MPs invaluable perspective on the
question of Indian opinion in India that could not be ignored any
longer.[97] Another pointed out that every effort had been made by
the government to prevent Saklatvala from 'visiting his own country
to get in touch with Indian opinion'.[98] It was indeed after much
trouble getting a nervous British government to endorse his passport
for travel back to his country of birth (he had already been banned
by the US government from travel to that country) that Saklatvala
arrived in India on 14 January 1927, for what would be his last visit.
He received a hero's welcome, with throngs gathered to see him disembark in Bombay, welcoming him with enthusiastic speeches and
garlands – which he refused to wear, but deposited at the statue of
Tilak on Chowpatty Beach. Whatever their reservations about his
affiliation to the Communist Party might have been, Indian nationalists of various stripes clearly recognized that he 'was a member of
the British parliament fighting for them'.[99] Saklatvala himself viewed
the trip, rather grandiosely, in terms of an attempt to 'pull the two
working-class brotherhoods together'.[100]

A British Comrade in India

*I want India to be a country where one man lives with another and
not upon another.*

                                                      Shapurji Saklatvala

During the war years, India had also witnessed something of a pacification of the anticolonial energies unleashed in the first years of the
new century, during which the young Saklatvala had himself initially
been politicized. Wadsworth suggests that his 'increasingly outspoken

views on home rule for India had come to the attention of the colonial authorities', and that he was sent out of the country by displeased senior family members for that reason, recuperation from malaria providing the perfect excuse.[101] The official line of the Congress was to offer support to British war efforts; there was, of course, an expectation that such assistance would bring with it the quid pro quo of large strides towards self-government. The minimal nature of the reforms which did finally come in 1919 was perceived as a particularly outrageous betrayal given the high-minded rhetoric of national self-determination that had driven British war propaganda. The treatment of the Ottoman Empire and its 'khalif' ('caliph') united subcontinental Muslims in hostility to Britain under the aegis of the pan-Islamic Khilafat movement, while inflation, famine and an influenza epidemic (nearly six million died) stoked discontent across the Raj. By the time Britain saw fit to roll out the bitterly resented and repressive Rowlatt Acts in 1919, intended to curb protests, tensions had already been stoked high, preparing the ground for a reinvigorated, sustained and far more radical resistance to the British Empire than had been seen since 1857. The infamously brutal response of General Dyer in opening fire on an unarmed and corralled crowd holding a public meeting in Jallianwala Bagh to discuss the Rowlatt Acts threw stark light on a gaping imperial divide; the response in Britain played down Dyer's actions as isolated, while Indian public opinion read the incident as emblematic of deep structural racism and endemic colonial brutality.[102] Nobel Laureate Rabindranath Tagore famously returned his knighthood in May 1919, writing: 'The accounts of the insults and sufferings by our brothers in Punjab have trickled through the gagged silence, reaching every corner of India, and the universal agony of indignation roused in the hearts of our people has been ignored by our rulers – possibly congratulating themselves for imparting what they imagine as salutary lessons.'[103] In introducing the Rowlatt Acts, the government of India had overplayed its hand, attempting to extend permanently wartime provisions, such as trial without juries for certain political cases and internment of suspects without trial.

Onto the stage of empire now entered Mohandas Karamchand Gandhi, coordinating non-violent direct action in the form of the Non-Cooperation movement. While Gandhi propounded

satyagraha – the 'offering of truth' – as the core of his theory of
passive resistance, events frequently exceeded his control in the years
following the commencement of the Non-Cooperation movement.
Rallies and demonstrations called in his name were often 'charac-
terised by the rowdy, undisciplined energies of the peasantry and the
rural poor', fleshing out anticolonialism beyond the colonizer–colonized binary to ask questions of other forms of oppression.[104] Some of
the many struggles during this period that exceeded Gandhi's initiatives included the famous Mappila ('Moplah') Rebellion of 1920–21,
when Muslim peasants took control of parts of the Malabar Coast
away from the British – and Hindu landlords – to declare 'Khilafat
republics'. Some took the form of 'depressed-class' and oppressed-
caste mobilizations that were critical of Gandhi's paternalist vision,
papering over a serious caste hierarchy, of a seamlessly united Hindu
community. Anti-landlord rent boycotts and no-tax campaigns were
no part of Gandhi's vision, but such mobilizations were frequent and
often undertaken in his name. As Sumit Sarkar has noted, while economic deprivation was key to the several food and agrarian riots that
took place from 1918 onwards, 'what was happening in India was
in the broadest sense a part of a world-wide upsurge, anti-capitalist
in the developed countries and anti-imperialist in the colonies and
semi-colonies'.[105] The Russian Revolution of 1917 played no small
part in influencing events from afar, having taken place in another
largely agricultural economy; it was all the more appealing to Indian
insurgents for the patent unease it was causing their British rulers.
In the early 1920s, directed partly by M. N. Roy, who was based in
Mexico and then Europe, the Indian communist movement began to
gather strength, choosing in the first instance to work as a pressure
group with the Indian National Congress. Historians of India have
tracked the myriad ways in which Gandhi and the Congress were
both subject to pressures from below and adept at containing, mar-
ginalizing or compromising with radical energies.[106]

In 1922, as Roy would note bitterly, Gandhi accomplished in one
fell swoop what the British government, with its huge repressive
apparatus, had not been able to achieve, simply because of his 'dread
of the popular energy'.[107] Following the burning down of a police
station in Chauri Chaura by protesters in February of that year,
Gandhi abruptly and unilaterally suspended the Non-Cooperation

movement, which proceeded to collapse. What followed, and continued for the better part of the 1920s, was a scenario of fragmentation
and multiplicity with episodic bouts of popular militancy and the emergence of a range of political organizations – not least the Communist
Party of India. Several organizations and individuals in the Indian
diaspora in Europe and the United States also worked diversely for
the Indian cause, among them the Home Rule Leagues, of which
Saklatvala was a member; the Ghadar Party in the United States;
the Berlin Committee, led by the communist Virendranath 'Chatto'
Chattopadhyaya and other groups associated with the Comintern.[108]
It was out of this energetic, often fractious, Indian and global context
that Shapurji Saklatvala had emerged as one of the most stentorian
voices of Indian anticolonialism in Britain, representing not the
Gandhian brand of nationalism but rather the many 'disillusioned
revolutionaries', including peasants and labour activists, who were
critical of Gandhian methods, and 'sought new roads to political and
social emancipation' that might, in some cases, involve revolutionary violence.[109] In the latter part of the 1920s, several British trade
unionists and labour leaders, including Saklatvala, also arrived in
India to assist with organizing (though these were also resented by
some Indian communists – most famously M. N. Roy, who saw their
participation as continued imperial control from London).

Shapurji and Sarah Saklatvala (née Marsh) profiled in a British newspaper article,
1922, titled 'The Indian MP and His English Wife'. Also included was his election
manifesto.

Just as he had in parliament and other political arenas in Britain, in India too Saklatvala assumed the pedagogue's mantle in his public addresses. Freely describing himself as an 'extremist' and an 'agitator' at the nationalist and trade union meetings that he addressed, Saklatvala called on young activists to go to agricultural and industrial areas to do the same hard and unpleasant work as peasants and workers and share their precarious existence, but then lead them to self-assertion. His tone friendly but often didactic, Saklatvala returned in these speeches to his favourite themes: the futility of reforms in the context of imperialism, and the folly of engaging with British politicians and officials in a spirit of negotiation or compromise. Just as he had explicated India to his parliamentary colleagues, he would explain to his Indian audiences the need to read 'the West' in differentiated terms: 'There are two distinctly separate, contrary Wests – one dominating, commanding, exploiting, monopolising West, and the other suffering, dictated, exploited and dispossessed West.'[110] If, back in the metropole, he was an interpreter of anticolonial resistance to the British governing classes, in India Comrade Sak positioned himself as exponent of revolutionary communism to the nationalist leadership. He was not unaware of the awkwardness, or even hostility, with which this might be received: 'I can hear your voices now. "We like Saklatwala [sic], we approve of so much that he says and does, but of course we totally disagree with his politics, and condemn his party, if not from our hearts, from our sense of political expediency."'[111] His speeches prefigured a point now familiar to us through Frantz Fanon, among others, who cautioned against simply replicating the structures of colonial rule, as he urged the Congress not to 'copy phrases' from the statute books of the self-governing dominions, which enjoyed very different conditions:

> Mere change of political names and legislative phraseology do not constitute a communal self-rule ... These conditions are absent in the association of Great Britain with India, China, and other Eastern countries. You cannot remain blind to these differences and pretend there is a parallel association by printing a law book in which you copy phrases taken from the constitutions of self-governing dominions.[112]

In being inveigled by the putative virtues of dominion status, established Indian nationalists were potentially being misled by 'advice from sentimental and emotional British friends'.[113] Their own duty, meanwhile, was also to democratize the nationalist movement, and to become accountable to masses rather than individuals.

In rehearsing this point in India, Saklatvala was also walking knowingly onto a minefield upon which Gandhi's authority had been stamped. The British-Indian communist sought to chide Gandhi – now firmly back in the driving seat – into radicalizing the nationalist movement. Unlike Roy, India's most prominent communist, whom he managed to annoy by hobnobbing with less than revolutionary sorts, Saklatvala viewed Gandhi, for some time at least, as a necessary ally – one who had obviously succeeded in forging a mass movement of sorts, for all its doctrinal deficiencies.[114] This view of a necessary alliance was of course consistent with the Comintern's 'united-front' thinking at that juncture. Saklatvala attempted valiantly – perhaps even somewhat foolhardily – to engage with Gandhi publicly on the question of self-assertion and democratization. The agonistic engagement – in which he was more or less bested by Gandhi, a cannier rhetorician – was based on Saklatvala's not unjustified apprehension of the ways in which, as one historian puts it, 'Gandhian restraints inhibited the process of mobilisation for the anti-imperialist cause of large sections of the poor peasantry, tribals and industrial workers'.[115] In his famous open letter to Gandhi, published in the *Amrita Bazar Patrika* newspaper, unyielding, cranky and unusually humourless in tone, Saklatvala called on the national eminence to abandon an 'injurious' method of campaigning which encouraged submission to his own influence:

> You now complain that the masses are not ready for any such self-assertion, but even if that were so, your whole procedure is certainly not making them more ready for it … You are preparing the country not for mass civil disobedience but for servile obedience and for a belief that there are superior persons on the earth and Mahatmas in this life at a time when in this country the white man's prestige is already a dangerous obstacle in our way.[116]

There was, of course, a tension between Saklatvala's insistence that the people needed to be approached 'on terms of absolute equality' and his own emphasis on the need for more knowing organizers to take charge of the project of 'developing' political consciousness. Even so, he was able to lay bare the contradictions of Gandhi's own positions, with a view, certainly naive, to persuading the older leader to change both his tactics and his allegiances in more radical directions. Saklatvala wanted Gandhi to abandon his hostility to labour organization: 'You actually and deliberately fraternise and cooperate with the master class, so as to make the task of labour organisers not only difficult but almost unjustifiable in the eyes of poor workers.'[117] Using the pronoun 'us' now with reference to India and Indians, Saklatvala did, in a later missive, identify points of agreement, such as the insight that 'labour should be so organised as to remain self-conscious, self-reliant and self-existing, evolving its own leadership and aim'.[118] Given this, Gandhi's 'confusion' in refusing to help with trade union organization and 'timidity' in defining the rights of labour were betrayals.

The charge against Gandhi of undermining mass movements was not, of course, unique to Saklatvala; it had been made by other justifiably disenchanted anticolonial campaigners in India. Referring to Gandhi's controversial decision to call off the Non-Cooperation movement in 1922, Saklatvala asked the Indian leader why he sought to create a psychology of resistance 'if you did not intend immediately to form men and women into an organisation for a definite material object ... before that influence passes away'.[119] He noted too that a move away from liberal mendicancy towards open resistance had preceded Gandhi's mobilization: 'By the year 1900 the masses of men got tired and sick and their hearts began to burn with fire.'[120] Gandhi, he acknowledged, was able to 'express boldly and fearlessly the unexpected voice of the people', but he had allowed a mystical cult of 'the Mahatma' to develop around him that was in danger, paradoxically, of eclipsing that voice.[121] Like other radical critics of Gandhi, including the Dalit leader Dr B. R. Ambedkar – whom Saklatvala singled out for praise – he was forceful in his attack on what he clearly saw as Gandhi's own problematic paternalism, a damnable 'touchability' with regard to the 'uplift' of 'Untouchables'.[122] Gandhi needed to halt the cult of worship and 'servile obedience' surrounding him: 'a man of the depressed class worshipping the feet of his deliverer is a more real individual depression and degradation of life ... I must call upon you to stop this nonsense'.[123]

Gandhi's reply to Saklatvala, written in a tone that characteristically embodied both self-deprecation and an adamantine insistence on his own rightness, yielded nothing to the younger man. While sharing a commitment to 'the good of the country and humanity', Gandhi agreed, they differed widely in their approach to modernity, defined as 'the multiplication of wants and machinery', which, to the Indian leader's mind, was 'satanic' and 'baneful'.[124] While agreeing with Saklatvala's critical analysis that he, Gandhi, did not 'regard capital to be the enemy of labour' and believed that the interests of both could be harmonized, he was not hostile to labour organization per se, but rather wanted it, in a telling conflation, to be 'along Indian lines or, if you will, my lines'.[125] While Gandhi's response was predictable, he was able to suggest, not entirely without justification, that Saklatvala had failed to appreciate the specificity of the Indian context in his patently urban bias, unexamined advocacy of a Western model of trade unionism, and unwillingness to examine 'modern civilization' critically as it functioned in India. The 'impatient communist' whose model was explicitly derived from what he called 'the advancing and powerful countries of the world' had indeed clearly underestimated, at the very least, the symbolic power of spinning and self-sustaining cloth manufacture.[126] Saklatvala also did not appear to recognize, as Gandhi pointed out, that spinning provided a concrete means of organizing politically around a traditional cooperative activity. As Wadsworth, a sympathetic biographer, also notes of Saklatvala, there was in his assessment of Gandhi 'an impatience with the moral/cultural dimensions of Gandhi's appeal to a traditionally minded peasantry' which obscured some of the organizational possibilities inherent therein.[127] In their exchanges, neither Gandhi nor Saklatvala was willing to concede an inch, but each was able to cast some critical light on the weaknesses of the other. Unlike his more unyielding comrade, M. N. Roy, Saklatvala did, however, see that Gandhi might in theory use his influence to 'render easier the otherwise stupendous task of organising an illiterate, overawed and semi-starved population'.[128] In his belief that Gandhi and the Congress needed not to be rejected but radicalized, Saklatvala was in line with Comintern thought at the time but at odds with some on the Indian communist left, whom he also criticized in the course of his journey there. As we shall see in the next chapter, it was from within this left that the next great crisis of empire would emerge – one that would also galvanize British anti-imperialism and recharge Saklatvala's crusading energies.

Conclusion: Civilizing the Civilizer

> *What on earth is a British Commission to find out in India in regard to whether Indians should rule in their own country, any more than if you had the impudence to send a Commission to France tomorrow to see whether that country should be run by Frenchmen or whether the British should go there to take care of the minorities in Alsace–Lorraine?*
>
> Shapurji Saklatvala

Let us return, in closing, to Saklatvala's fierce, indeed frequently rebarbative, parliamentary interventions on the Simon Commission, after his return from India. In a lengthy, unsparing, brutally condemnatory speech in November 1927, Saklatvala laid out (and into) the multiple hypocrisies, elisions, falsehoods and sleights of hand that comprised official British discourse on India. The speech was a testament to Saklatvala's sense of a necessarily cross-national representational responsibility. He began by noting that he preferred, when expressing the feelings of those who were 'crushed' and 'oppressed', to use plain speech.[130] The emptiness of parliamentary language, the tendency to 'weigh and choose words which mean nothing', was a recurrent theme with him. Almost at once, however, Saklatvala insisted that he spoke not from a 'narrow nationalist point of view' with regard to India, but as a British MP 'representing the vital interests of the workers of this country, who show sufficient confidence in me, not one electorate alone, but all over England, Scotland, Wales and even Ireland'.[131] For Saklatvala, at times, the pronoun 'us' could simultaneously refer to both Indians and Britons. He would repeatedly return in this speech, as in others, to the assertion that an 'injury' upon the Indians was also 'treachery' to British workers. The speech was also a sustained attack on justifications for colonial rule based on a 'hideous picture' of the colonized and a 'virtuous picture' of colonizers – particularly the familiar claim that India was full of chaos and division, which necessitated a unifying British presence. Saklatvala's point of comparison was well chosen: 'There was the Kaiser in Europe. He also felt the same thing, namely, that among the European communities there was such a welter and chaos that one strong man was required to rule the whole of Europe. He also felt like coming forward as the trustee and guardian of the small nationalities in Europe.'[132] The claims of the German Kaiser and the British imperial Kaisers were 'equally preposterous from the ethical standpoint and the point of view of national rights'. British rule in India, far from making 'less religions', would 'only make one more' – hardly a basis for 'trusteeship'.

Saklatvala was scathing about the 'bunkum and nonsense' justifications for the Raj which claimed that its *raison d'être* was the safeguarding of minority rights. Exposing these claims as at once internally incoherent, hypocritical and simply untrue, he spoke of his own experience in being prevented as a young man from entering a white club in Bombay: 'Yet a representative of that race to-day talks nonsense about the untouchability among the Hindus.'[133] As we have already seen, Saklatvala was not denying the existence of untouchability, but noting that, apart from the fact that the British practised their own form of deep discrimination in India, they had also done materially little for the rights of oppressed Indians and minority communities. Indeed, the British Empire sought refuge in a hands-off relativism when it came to such matters: 'What is this Commission going to do? If it was going out tomorrow to abolish untouchability I would assist it, but the Government say, "No, that is not our business." Then why keep on "chewing this rag" about untouchability and depressed classes?'[134] Even more damningly, these were sections of society in India that remained politically disenfranchised and illiterate, precisely on the basis of a pernicious relativism: 'They are an Asiatic people, full of religious superstition.' In fact, it was not religion or religious customs that constituted the problem: 'What is wrong is the presence of British rule, which prevents the introduction of modern thought, modern evolution, modern education and scientific methods of evolving a people's political, economic and

social rights.'[135] For Saklatvala, imperialism was not a party political affair, and Labour's accord with their political opponents on the
Empire was 'disastrous to the Labour movement, although it may be
all right in a Parliamentary Debate'.[136] Comrade Sak reiterated here a
point he had made throughout his parliamentary career: that British
workers were adversely affected by 'that abominable competition of
exploited labour in the East by British Imperialism'.[137] It is why both
the colonized and the British working classes were at the receiving
end of ruling-class paternalism, a connection the latter needed to see:

> The leaders of the Labour movement say to the Indians and the
> Chinese, 'We are ruling you; we are sending Commissions to your
> countries because you are less experienced and we are more experi-
> enced, and we want to be kind to you and tell you how you should
> live your lives.' That is exactly what the capitalist masters and
> bosses are saying to the workers in this country. They say to them,
> 'We are more experienced in directing industry than you are, and
> we keep an Army, a Navy, and an Air Force to protect you, because
> you are less experienced than we are.'[138]

Over the course of his hundreds of interventions in parliament,
Comrade Sak succeeded in articulating a full-fledged critique of
empire and imperialism which covered cultural, psychological,
economic and political terrain. He invited Britons who espoused a
sentimental attachment to the Union Jack to think about the effect
that same flag had on those who saw it as one with 'an alien, historical, religious and social condition attached to it'. Many of his
speeches laid out at great length the specific economic consequences
for both the Indian poor and the British working classes of cheap
labour toiling in India for British capital:

> So long as British financiers open coalpits in other parts of the
> Empire and compel miners to work at 8d. per day, so long will the
> British miners and their Continental competitors be driven down-
> wards and downwards … so long as this slave labour exists in the
> Empire, so long the economic position of the British miner will be
> one of continual danger.[139]

Attacking the idea that correctives could be provided from within empire, Saklatvala had already brought together the literal and the metaphorical in a trenchant image, saying that it made no sense 'to create a death rate and then to appoint doctors to cure it'.[140] He turned civilizational discourse on its head, suggesting (to much mockery from some of his listeners) not just that the 'great civilising revolution in Russia' should be the model to follow, but also that it was only with the end of empire that 'a great advanced movement for the civilisation' of Britain and Europe could be imagined. This, of course, earned him opprobrium, one MP charging him with violating 'the hospitality of this country' and showing his ingratitude by doing everything he could to bring 'red ruin'.[141]

Although Saklatvala lost his parliamentary seat at the 1929 elections, he continued to write and give speeches, returning repeatedly to the parallel questions of democratizing India by making the concerns of labour more central to anticolonialism and internationalizing the British labour movement in specifically anticolonial directions. In an election address delivered when he contested a by-election in 1930, he noted that the 'hypocritical promises' of the Labour government concealed a reality in which British workers were still facing violence, while also pointing out that he had supported anticolonial struggles everywhere, including in Ireland, 'for whom alone in the House, I did not fail to expose the fraud of the Irish Free State Treaty instead of a genuine Irish Workers Republic'.[142] He grew increasingly critical of the mainstream of Indian nationalism as well. As Gandhi arrived in London for the Second Round Table Conference in 1931, the veteran communist reminded his readers that many in the Indian National Congress would be quite happy to have conservative rule by the feudal and capitalist elites of India; their objection was not to plutocracy, but to diarchy or sharing rule with the British elites. The conference itself, he wrote, returning to the theme of 'voice', would aim 'to give a megaphonic expression to the right of privileges and interests' while the 'completely ignored majority' continued to face down bombs, bullets, bayonets and poison gas.[143] Much like British Labour leaders who 'had so successfully let down the 1926 General Strike' (during which Saklatvala was arrested and imprisoned for two months on charges of making a 'seditious' speech at Hyde Park), the Congress leadership hoped to neutralize the Indian

masses, persuading them that they could be led to 'national independence one fine day without molesting the millowners or landowners or
Indian princes'.[144] Saklatvala was correct to note that extraordinary
state violence had been exercised against a populace exhorted not to
retaliate: 'Almost ten thousand of the common people have been shot
and killed, eighty thousand have been batoned and incarcerated, the
brave Gharwalli troops and heroic Trade Union leaders are in gaol,
young brave lads have been executed or imprisoned.'[145] These were
people, he acknowledged, whose 'legitimate militancy' had indeed
come together under the Congress flag, for better or for worse, but
whose spirit and determination were in the cause of goals that were
much more radical than that of their leadership.[146] In Gandhism,
he insisted, 'I still see the prolongation of British imperialism and I
will continue to say so even though many of my best friends in the
Congress camp get angry with me for so doing'.[147] In the decade he
had left before he died suddenly in 1936, Saklatvala's most prominent work was firmly internationalist in tenor, as he participated
in campaigns and movements that sought to bring together radical
anticolonialists from across the world, and to put liberation movements in dialogue with each other. Two of these – the Meerut Defence
Campaign and the League against Imperialism – are the subject of
the next chapter.

6

The Revolt of the Oppressed World: British Internationalism from Meerut to the League against Imperialism

On our platform in Hyde Park we must remember that three English comrades are among the thirty-one prisoners of British Imperialism now awaiting trial in Meerut in India. These British and Indian comrades are threatened with twenty years' imprisonment in barbarous conditions, for no more heinous a crime than that of openly and legally organising workers and peasants in India ... Let May Day be a pledge of our determination to rid the world of Imperialism, breeder of war, poverty and pestilence.

Shapurji Saklatvala, May Day speech in Hyde Park, 1929

On the morning of 20 March 1929, the young British journalist and labour organizer Lester Hutchinson was disturbed twice: the first time, as usual, by his tiresome milkman, and then by 'a *posse* of armed police headed by a European inspector and an Anglo-Indian sergeant in occupation of my front garden'.[1] Hutchinson, who would shortly become editor of the left-wing journal the *New Spark*, after the Indian editor of its predecessor, *The Spark*, was arrested that day, only had his house searched that morning – an experience he described as a rather romantic one; he too would be arrested a few months later. But, that same morning, no fewer than thirty-one labour activists were detained and imprisoned across half a dozen towns in British India, as the Warwickshire Regiment spread out all over Bombay – where the majority resided – to avert any trouble. They included twenty-nine Indians and two Britons, Philip Spratt and Ben Bradley. All were transferred to a jurisdiction none of them resided in, and twenty-four of them had never even been to: the cantonment town of Meerut, which would lend its name to the most infamous colonial 'conspiracy case' of the time. Charged under Section 121A of the Indian Penal Code with conspiring to 'deprive the King of the sovereignty of British India', the detainees would controversially be refused bail and subjected to trial without jury.[2] In addition, Section 121A carried a proviso whereby no actual illegal act had to take place in order for a conspiracy charge to be levied.[3]

The arrests had been in planning for several months, as a rattled imperial government assessed the threat of the Soviet Union to the British Empire and attempted to stem intensifying waves of labour unrest and increased violence by groups such as the Hindustan Republican Association (modelled on the IRA). Early in 1929, protesting the Public Safety Act and the Trades Disputes Bill, the association's Bhagat Singh and two accomplices threw bombs onto the floor of the Indian Legislative Assembly; he would be caught and hanged, becoming a *shaheed*, or martyr.[4] The Public Safety Act would have also prevented foreign communists from coming to India and working there with Indian labour organizers. Part of a wave of colonial repression, the arrests of the Meerut defendants also took place – not by accident – as the government braced for the release of the Fawcett Report, commissioned in the wake of the Bombay General Strike of 1928, which was expected to be unfavourable to worker demands, and therefore to generate more militancy and strikes. As Saklatvala had been warning in his parliamentary speeches, 'reforms' as a response to genteel petitioning were no longer going to staunch the colonial wound. Indeed, a note to senior government officials, sent in June 1927, warned that among 'the lower classes in India', both in town and rural areas, post-war inflation had 'induced a feeling of restlessness, making them discontented with conditions which previously they bore patiently'.[5] In turn, repressive legislation which had been put in place to pre-empt and punish resistance was routinely invoked – and wound up producing the long-running international drama that became the Meerut Trials, described by one prisoner as 'a war of attrition, a trial of endurance'.[6] Their aim was to staunch the spread of communism in India – certainly a major contributing factor to the strikes in the textile mills; the Girni Kamgar Union for millworkers was a hugely successful communist-led endeavour, and the Millowners' Association had petitioned the British government 'to rid them of the nuisance'.[7]

News of the arrests spread immediately, and the ensuing protests encompassed work stoppages in fourteen Bombay textile mills, public meetings, demonstrations, and processions which resulted in clashes with the police. Many Indian leaders – eight of the accused also held posts in the Indian National Congress – spoke up immediately against the arrests, arguing quite rightly that the real motive of the colonial government was to kill the labour movement at an early stage, and so obstruct the growing momentum towards full independence.[8] Rather than attempt to make the case for the existence of an actual conspiracy, in his lengthy opening statement prosecutor Langford James notoriously dwelt on the dangers of the Russian Revolution, Soviet politics, the perniciousness of communism, and the manifold problems with Marxism, using his readings of various general left-wing texts as 'evidence' against the accused. James averred that these were relevant to those in the dock because their object was 'to replace the Government of His Majesty King George in India, and in its place to put the Government of the Third Communist International'.[9] Irrespective of whether Bolshevism was 'a cruel and tyrannous autocracy' or 'a paradise on earth', James claimed: 'The hard fact still remains that if Bolshevism and that system is to be introduced into India the government of His Majesty must as a preliminary be smashed in pieces. There is no room for both of them'.[10] The incompatibility between capitalism and communism – on which the defendants agreed with the prosecution – was in itself deemed to prove 'conspiracy' on the part of the accused, who criticized capitalism. Partly to drive a wedge between the defendants and the mainstream nationalist movement, James would later insist that his problem was with 'perpetual revolution' and not with 'a national revolution'. The defendants, he pointed out with alacrity, were in fact deeply critical of the 'leaders of Nationalist thought in India', and 'stigmatised' the Indian National Congress 'as a misguided bourgeois body'.[11] The first half of his speech took great pains to insist that 'there is no question of their being nationalists'; the professed internationalism of the defendants was, in effect, anti-nationalism.[12]

As the Bolsheviks he deemed them to be, they shared certain char-
acteristics: 'You do not love your country, you are anti-country, you
are anti-God, and you are anti-family.'[13] Meanwhile, the magistrate,
R. Milner-White, argued that those nationalists who sought to petition the king through the 'usual civil channels' to 'give independence
to India' were not, unlike the defendants, in breach of Section 121A,
which only punished those who would forcibly deprive the monarch
of sovereignty.[14] Mendicancy was acceptable; even imagining alternative possibilities, on the other hand, was punishable. Most Indian
nationalists were not, however, fooled, or easily available for sowing
dissension on this basis – at least not immediately. Gandhi – no
communist sympathizer and himself the frequent subject of communist criticism – was prompted to note that the 'farce of a trial'
had exposed the British colonial government's 'red claws which
usually remain under cover'.[15] Nehru, who would become involved
in the international Meerut campaign, observed trenchantly: 'this
cry of communism is meant to cover a multitude of sins of the
Government'.[16] Hutchinson noted that serious riots broke out, and
that 'the peasants became restive and began to demand the initiation
of a movement for refusing to pay rents and taxes, a movement that
would have changed the whole basis of Indian nationalism'.[17]

What had perhaps not been anticipated, however, was the scale of
the negative reaction to the trials in Britain itself over the course of a
case that lasted four years – one defendant, D. R. Thengdi, even dying
in jail over that needlessly protracted period. (The accused endured
especially uncomfortable conditions, including nine hours of manual
labour a day.) The Meerut episode served to amplify and embody the
two points that Saklatvala had repeatedly been making in and out of
parliament: that there was serious resistance to the Raj, and that it
was being crushed on a regular basis. It therefore provided the first
major interwar colonial flashpoint around which efforts to mobilize
criticism of empire more widely in Britain were undertaken – criticism based on solidarity with protests rather than on paternalism. It
was also, of course, a test case for international anticolonial alliances
in more than one sense. With three Britons among those targeted
by the prosecution, the dragnet of state persecution had been deliberately thrown around 'those who linked India with a wider world
and with solidarities beyond the boundaries of India or the British

Empire'.[18] The dogged judicial persecution of the Meerut defendants also constituted, of course, official recognition that anticolonial networks were spreading beyond the boundaries of specific colonies. With the Trades Union Congress and the Labour Party often, though not always, on board, the League against Imperialism (LAI) and the Meerut Defence Committee organized hundreds of public meetings and demonstrations. Saklatvala spoke at many of these, using the occasion – as the defendants also did – to stage 'a form of political theater'.[19] If the Meerut Conspiracy Case was an attack on left-wing internationalism from the perspective of the state, it paradoxically provided internationalists with a real opportunity to organize and proselytize in the cause of making cross-border alliances against imperialism. In that sense, the Meerut Defence Committee and allied activities mark an important moment in the history both of British anticolonialism and of internationalism more broadly. In more systematic and illustrative ways than in the past, perhaps, it allowed for the case to be made that what happened to British subjects in the colonies – punishment for ordinary activities like trade unionism and demands for labour rights – could boomerang, and have equally sinister consequences at home. This chapter explores one significant episode in the internationalizing of British anticolonialism – that of the global defence campaign for the Meerut prisoners – and an important institution in the history of internationalism – the League against Imperialism – which participated in the Meerut campaign. Both were part of the ongoing unlearning of paternalism as an anticolonial disposition in favour of constructing working solidarities.

In parliament, questions about the length of the trial, its unsound basis, and the treatment of prisoners were routinely raised by many MPs, including Fenner Brockway, Joseph Kenworthy, Philip Oliver, Peter Freeman, David Kirkwood and John Kinley. Some suggested that it was the labour movement as a whole that was being attacked in the name of fighting global communism.[20] Certainly, as Hutchinson – whose mother, Mary Knight, a British communist, campaigned vigorously on behalf of the prisoners – noted with satisfaction, 'statesmen in foreign countries made sarcastic comments on British justice in theory and in practice … and the much-vaunted traditions of British justice were shown to be hollow and public opinion was alarmed'.[21] The Independent Labour Party also voiced bitter parliamentary

criticism of the trials through Brockway, while condemnatory statements were issued by a diverse range of public figures. As Harold
Laski would note in his preface to Hutchinson's memoir, the Meerut
prosecution pointed to the continuity of imperialist repression across
party lines, since 'the responsibility for undertaking it lies at the door
of a Tory viceroy, that for its continuance ... to a Socialist Secretary
of State', with the greater moral culpability upon the latter for
betrayal of principles.[22] Protest resolutions flooded the India Office,
particularly once the draconian sentences – years of imprisonment
and transportation for most of the defendants – were announced in
January 1933. The *Daily Herald* described the trial process itself as
'one of the greatest judicial scandals in the history of the Empire',
while the *Manchester Guardian*, though typically scornful of the far-
left politics of the defendants themselves, noted the tenuous nature of
the evidence presented for the existence of a conspiracy, and deemed
the affair 'a long-drawn scandal of British justice in India'.[23] Even as
it deprecated the fact that this extended 'unpleasant episode in the
history of British justice' was 'giving Communism an unexampled
advertisement', it was, the liberal newspaper also opined, 'an evil
thing to prosecute men for their opinions' – or to be seen to be doing
so.[24] A critical statement calling for justice for the prisoners was
issued by a joint council representing the Trades Union Congress,
the Labour Party and the Parliamentary Labour Party.[25] Indeed, the
pressure of British public opinion – particularly after the sentences
'raised a storm of protest' in both India and Britain – did eventually
lead to the sentences being reduced considerably.[26] As one historian
of the episode has remarked, the Meerut Conspiracy Case has no
parallel in Indian history; given the relative anonymity of the defendants, 'the extraordinary amount of international attention which
the case received puts it into a special category of historical significance'.[27] Meerut, much like the Scottsboro case of a few years before,
and through overlapping activist circuits, 'became a global passion
among the committed, the presence of three Englishmen among the
defendants eliciting special curiosity and sympathy among anticolonialists in the metropole'.[28]

The moment of Meerut also takes on significance as yet another
colonial juridical crisis – arguably the first in the twentieth century –
which provided a means for the voices of anticolonial resistance, this

time also inflected by international communism and communist internationalism, to be heard in the British public sphere. Developments in travel and communication technologies enabled both the swift dissemination of news and propaganda and actual communication links between metropolitan and colonial activists. The letter in the *Manchester Guardian* co-signed by H. G. Wells, Harold Laski, R. H. Tawney and Walter Walsh had urged that the prisoners be given the 'elementary rights of British citizens on trial', such as bail and trial by jury, and, equally significantly, suggested that the views of 'the leaders of Indian political opinion', calling for amnesty, be heeded.[29] Such views – and the more militant ones of other sections of the Indian political spectrum – were, indeed, registering on the British political scene. In producing its pamphlets, the Meerut campaign deliberately used the Meerut prisoners' individual testimonies, less perhaps to 'humanize' the defendants through eliciting sympathy, as Pennybacker argues, than to allow for more radical anticolonial voices in India to emerge in the British public sphere on their own terms, making claims upon human solidarity.[30] The articulate and defiant statements of the Meerut accused became central to the British Meerut Defence Committee as voices that could and would represent themselves. These were voices and views that also resisted cooptation by the more acceptable face of nationalism speciously lauded by the Meerut prosecutors. As Gandhi toured England during the Second Round Table talks in 1931, to considerable adulation in liberal circles, voices from Meerut also made clear that politics in India went beyond the remit of Gandhian nationalism, and that other questions were being asked, not just of the colonial government, but also of the Indian capitalists, landlords, upper castes and political elites. Once again, it became clear that the colonized, a heterogeneous group, were in fact capable of representing themselves robustly in more than one sense.

One of the more audacious such acts of self-representation was that undertaken by Shaukat Usmani, the journalist (he edited an Urdu working-class paper) and trade unionist who, from his jail cell in Meerut, contested British elections twice as a candidate for the Communist Party of Great Britain – once in Spen Valley in 1929 against John Simon himself, and once in St Pancras in 1931 (where he won 75,000 votes). Like Saklatvala, Usmani sought to make himself a presence in the British public sphere with the help of the CPGB, drawing attention to both British misrule in India and the injustices of the Meerut case. Sharp and cogent, Usmani's statement, an explicit defence of communism, was the first extracted and included in a section called 'The Prisoners' Reply' in *The Meerut Prisoners and the Charge against Them*, a pamphlet published by the Defence Committee that carried extensive extracts from the prisoners' defence statements.[31] His electrifying inaugural gesture queried the very terms of the charge of attempting to undermine the 'sovereignty' of the king-emperor:

> There is nothing like a sovereign under the sovereignty of capitalism. The sovereignty of the British Empire to-day belongs to the omnipotent Big Five (Banks), who not only forge methods of exploitation in India but are as ruthless in Britain, too. The British working class, which is our ally, is as much their victim as the Colonial peoples.[32]

If there was any 'conspiracy', Usmani averred, it was that instigated by finance capital 'against the rising forces of revolution throughout the colonial world', which included those in China, Indonesia, Iraq, Syria and Morocco.[33] Dharni Goswami, a member of the Workers and Peasants Party (WPP), was another of the Meerut accused who evinced a remarkable defiance of tone in his defence statement.[34] He had become a member of the party, he notes, almost scornfully, for self-evident reasons: 'the WPP is the only party in India that stands for complete independence from British Imperialism and the thorough democratisation of India based on economic and social emancipation and political freedom of men and women'.[35] Goswami's experience as an organizer with jute workers gave him unique insight into an industry that had begun as a heavily colonial enterprise, but now saw Indian capitalists also 'appropriate the huge profit that comes out of this industry', at the expense of the sweated and the starving.[36] While refusing to distance himself from the work he himself had done, for instance, in organizing a Scavengers Union, Goswami pointed out that collective resistance also had been undertaken independently of him and other labour organizers, when its members went on strike without waiting for a formal decision. This was one instance among many of the oppressed castes undertaking resistance independently of both Gandhi and the Communist Party, which was itself heavily populated by members of the dominant castes, like Goswami himself.[37] His point was partly that the resistance was organic and self-sustaining even in the face of constant repression and punitive action; he and other communists only sought to give it organizational form.

One of the most striking aspects of the Meerut detainees' statements is the combination of their willingness to criticize both imperialism and the limits of the mainstream nationalist response to it. While the language of Marxism explicitly facilitates and anchors such analysis, one defendant noted that it was the experience of being a colonial subject that had led him to Marxism, rather than the other way around. 'It was my studies and experiences and the objective conditions in a colonial country that made me a Communist by conviction', insisted Gopal Chandra Basah of the Bengal Textile Union, a youth organizer, 'and I am sure that any radical young man given the same chances and conditions would develop similarly'.[38] In other words, in the context of imperialism's constitutive entanglement with capitalism, Marxism and communism provided a common global language in which both the identification of oppressive structures and liberation from them could be articulated. Another organizer in the jute industry, R. R. Mitra, announced that he saw no contradiction in claiming to be at once an internationalist and a nationalist, the latter as a necessary vehicle of anticolonialism: 'As an internationalist I stand for a free federation of all the peoples of the earth, but that cannot be achieved unless all are freed from the yoke of subjection and all stand on a free and equal footing.'[39] The point of the conspiracy charges, Mitra averred quite rightly, was not so much to remove thirty-one individuals from the field of action as 'reading a lesson to all who would follow the line of the mass revolutionary struggle in future'.[40] His point was further fleshed out by Gopendra Chakravarty, an official of the East India Railway Union, who noted that the conspiracy case mounted by the British government of India was also a warning shot across the bow of the bourgeois nationalists about 'the dangers of appealing to the masses, owing to the risk it involved of letting loose the class struggle'.[41] 'Red Scares', he observed shrewdly, had already shown their electoral utility in Britain. Meanwhile, Gautam Adhikari, a scientist by training, in fierce words that would be repeatedly cited in pamphlets, quite simply turned the charges against the imperial government, boldly accusing the prosecution benches of representing class crimes:

> Who are the social criminals? I ask the bloodthirsty imperialists who carried fire and sword through entire continents, who have instituted a colonial régime of blood and terror, who have reduced the toiling millions of these continents to abject poverty, intolerable slavery and are threatening them with mass extinction as a people; or the Communists, who are out to mobilise the revolutionary energies of the toiling masses of the whole world and hurl it against this wretched system based on ruthless oppression and brutal exploitation, smash it and create in its place a new one ... ?[42]

Such analysis – and the repeated insistence that the enemy was British finance-capital rather than the British people – enabled the Meerut campaign in Britain to make connections between an apparent crisis of Britishness and Britain's own traditions of vernacular radicalism. It was a point, as we have seen, that Saklatvala had repeatedly emphasized in trying to forge common cause between British and Indian labour. 'The complaint is essentially that of "incitement of antagonism between capital and labour," a phrase carrying us back to the old anti-combination laws in Britain 100 years ago', the preface to *The Meerut Prisoners and the Charge against Them* pointed out, again stressing that the attack was a more general one against all anti-capitalist organizing.[43]

Picking up on these connections, in *Meerut*, a Workers Theatre Movement play that toured Britain in 1932, the players-as-prisoners warn their audience: 'Those who have jailed the workers in India are the men who cut your wages and enforce the Means Test in Britain.'[44] The play itself is perhaps, like much agitprop, more powerful in the performance than read, taking the form of a mass declamation. What is striking in the directions for actors is the emphasis on voice as the vehicle for expressing solidarity, also symbolized by extended 'hands across the sea': 'Inflection of the voice is most important.'[45] The guidelines are, perhaps somewhat predictably, gendered, the emphasis on muscularity: 'Pretty girlish voices must be cut right out, but a strong feminine voice vibrating with the conviction of the message can be just as effective as a masculine one.'[46] The directions are specific as to when whispers, staccatos, mass speaking, contrasts, inflections and crescendos are to be deployed. 'This sketch offers most unusual opportunities for voice-acting', the directions note, going on to suggest: 'Get the utmost out of words – these and your faces are your only means of expression.'[47] Of the play itself, which began with the shout, 'Murder! Murder! MURDER! MURDER!', one actor recalled: 'At the time, it was quite the most exciting bit of theatre I had ever seen and, looking back over the fifty years that have slipped by since then, I find it still has the power to move and excite me.'[48] With a handful of actors using 'poles' dexterously – vertically and horizontally – to represent prison bars, the play also relied on powerful visuals. The attempt was to offer a swift education in ideologies of colonial rule and labour exploitation: 'They foster our religious differences in order to divide us, so that they can extract their millions yearly in profits and taxation … They tell you we are religious maniacs.' In a sign of the official jitters occasioned by the Meerut protests in Britain, performances of the play, which lasted only five or six minutes, often commanded a strong police presence, and some were proscribed entirely.

The most powerful words on Meerut from the camp of Western critics of imperialism eventually came from the pen of French anti-fascist writer and Gandhi's biographer Romain Rolland, who wrote a short polemic for the British Meerut campaign after draconian jail and transportation sentences were announced for the majority of the Meerut convicts in 1932.[49] For Rolland, who was clearly influenced by the Meerut testimonies, the moment had universal import; the protests around the Meerut trials and sentences presented a challenge to those who 'renounce the struggle in advance' by contenting themselves with 'the miserable excuse for not acting, that what is has always been and that one cannot change it'.[50] While oppression may always have been a feature of human life, the last half-century had also been unique in the 'degree of deliberate organisation' with which nine-tenths of humanity was being crushed by the 'imperialism of money': 'Menaced by the trembling of the capitalist economy, which in its difficulties plunges to madly destructive courses, shaken by the revolts which to-day like earthquakes stir the enslaved peoples, this hideous oppression manifests itself yet more brutally, employing

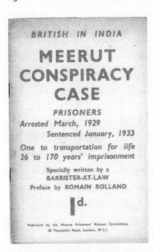

BRITISH IN INDIA

MEERUT CONSPIRACY CASE

PRISONERS
Arrested March, 1929
Sentenced January, 1933

One to transportation for life
26 to 170 years' imprisonment

Specially written by a
BARRISTER-AT-LAW
Preface by ROMAIN ROLLAND

1d.

Published by the Meerut Prisoners' Release Committee,
38 Theobald's Road, London, W.C.1.

Cover of Romain Rolland's
pamphlet for the Meerut case

to an extent and with a rigour unexampled, the most monstrous means ... By terror it was established and is maintained.'[51]

If British India offered an exemplar of most 'gigantic proportions', the phenomenon Rolland described extended well beyond it and Britain to the Dutch Indies and French Indo-china – and that was not counting Italian, Belgian, Portuguese and US imperialism, not to mention the instances of South Africa, South America and Japan. What had changed with Meerut? As long as the oppressed responded to exploitation 'only by intermittent and piecemeal spasms of revolt', coercion was able to prevail 'swiftly and noiselessly'.[52] Gandhi's large-scale organization of the masses saw the colonial system begin 'to lose all measure of restraint', but it was reassured nonetheless by the way in which 'the genius of one man' was able to hold back the wave.[53] But with the moment of Meerut, in which the rebellion of labour exceeded the 'magnanimous opposition' of those like Gandhi, Rolland contended, a 'new era has opened in the revolt of the oppressed world', met of course by repression, 'immediate and implacable'.[54] Rolland's analysis here, startling in some ways coming from so well-known a partisan of Gandhi, was explicitly inflected by that of prominent Meerut prisoner R. S. Nimbkar, whom he cites on the English brand of liberalism, as 'not only powerless to repair the verdict' but 'incapable of conceiving either the illegal proceedings which have become current or the exceptional laws which the imperialist terrorism of Great Britain applies to six-sevenths of the people of its Empire, to one-sixth of the population of the world'.[55]

Ultimately, Rolland pronounces, the Meerut Conspiracy Case – not least because of the fierce attacks on it by the accused – had ended up becoming 'the trial of the system of government which has passed judgement on them'.[56] Meerut was also a call to British workers to stop being passive accomplices in the oppression of Indian workers:

They are for us the living symbol of those thousands of victims
in the great combat which to-day is being fought throughout the
world to break the yoke of imperialism. All those victims make
a victory, for they bear witness to the iniquity which is crushing
them, and to the irresistible rising of the new revolutionary forces
which are awakening mankind.[57]

In the end, the Meerut Conspiracy Case, with its protracted unfolding, volumes of testimony, and draconian sentences followed by
commutation, resulted not in the extinguishing of either protest or
communism in India, but a greater surge in both, 'a sudden revival
of interest and activity', as one police report in 1934 put it.[58] It certainly provided both a national and an international platform for the
articulation of anticolonial views – which was openly used as such
by the defendants.[59] 'What had been intended as propaganda against
communism', observed Hutchinson, 'had turned into propaganda for
communism', the government of India not playing the role of saviour
it had hoped for, but rather 'unexpectedly [finding] itself actually
playing the part of the villain of the piece amid hisses and boos of the
audience'.[60] Whether it made clear to a British public the truth that
'the whole of Asia was seething with revolt', the Meerut case clearly
brought home the fact of imperialism being challenged, as the prisoners' general statement put it, 'from the dock'.[61]

Like Saklatvala, many of those involved in the Meerut Conspiracy
Case were deeply influenced by the seismic impact of the October
Revolution in 1917; the testimonies of the Meerut accused make
clear how compelling it was to find a language of emancipation that
both enabled a critique of empire and offered a vision for restructur-
ing decolonizing societies in radically egalitarian ways. We also know
that communists in Britain brought to 'metropolitan anti-imperialism
a level of commitment, intellectual consideration and organisation
that it had usually lacked, even if this fell considerably short of the
task and their own ambition'.[62] British communists like Bradley and
Spratt, among the Meerut accused, were less successful as organizers
in India faced with a political terrain of enormous and shifting complexity, a radically unfamiliar social order in which the agrarian was
key, and a repressive colonial administration.

Nonetheless, it is necessary to situate the moment of Meerut in relation to the specifically communist idea of a revolutionary international alliance against both capitalism and imperialism. It was an idea that caught on, laden with the 'contagion' dreamed of by Ernest Jones and denounced by the Meerut prosecutors, exercising enormous power and imaginative reach not always fully realized in organizational efforts. Founded in March 1919 with the aim of fomenting world revolution, the Comintern, before it fell into notorious disarray, 'was a significant force in inter-war politics, able to command the loyalty of millions of militants and sympathisers'.[63] The aim, as Lenin put it, was 'a repetition, on an international scale, of what has taken place in our country'.[64] The First Congress of the Peoples of the East, held in 1920 in Baku, brought together representatives of Asian communist parties with Soviet leaders; acknowledging the upsurge of anticolonial struggles across Asia, it would assert the need for 'united action against British imperialism'.[65] As has been noted by others, the 'unprincipled zigzags of Soviet and Comintern policy' (see Chapter 9) should not entail a wider forgetting of the latter's many accomplishments before it was disbanded.[66] Even when it took the form of dissent and disagreement, anticolonialism in the interwar period was ineluctably shaped by dialogues, real and imagined, with communist internationalism. At the Comintern's Second Congress in 1922, Lenin and M. N. Roy famously debated colonialism, resulting in the 'Theses on the National and Colonial Questions', which incorporated the latter's 'Supplementary Theses' as amendments.[67] Roy succeeded in enshrining the analysis that the fight against colonialism was key to 'the downfall of the capitalist order in Europe' not least because the 'super-profits' from colonialism enabled the 'labour aristocracy' in the metropole to be given concessions.[68] In essence, then, the Comintern committed to extending its field of activity through alliances with 'revolutionary liberation movements' in the colonies while keeping in view the need to organize peasants and workers 'in common revolutionary struggle to overthrow the landowners and bourgeoisie'. Although Lenin's theses were modified by Roy so that the Comintern was urged to support 'revolutionary movements of liberation' rather than 'bourgeois-democratic liberation movements', in practice, uncertainties and differences on this question would emerge periodically.

In trying to contain the implications of the Meerut case, colonial officials frequently described events in terms of machinations of Western communists causing trouble where there would otherwise have been none.[69] In fact, it was often the other way around, as Hutchinson's lively and witty memoir attests:

> I had come to India five years before full of romantic illusions and a
> novice in the game of life. I had lost these illusions, but had gained
> many things in their stead. I had been caught in a wild current of
> conflicting forces and had managed to keep my head above water;
> I had been given the opportunity to study India from a new angle;
> and I had shared the misfortunes and slavery of a great people.
> And all my experiences are the grim realities of the everyday life of
> a vast and oppressed population ... Experience provides a certain
> cure, and as we learn by experience to face and even to appreciate
> realities, the further we are away from the self-deception of roman-
> ticism. I was leaving India definitely cured.[70]

One of the insights that Hutchinson, the son of communists who was not himself a party member, had gleaned from witnessing both resistance and repression in various contexts was that imperialism had perforce to use different tactics in Britain and India, even though the 'same oligarchy' ran both countries: 'But this oligarchy employs methods in India, which it does not dare employ as yet in Britain'.[71] The latter elicited greater open brutality, 'white terror', because of what was at stake: 'A single spark in India may cause a conflagration which might well be the end of Imperialism altogether'.[72] With the Meerut Conspiracy Case, the oligarchy's ways had been exposed in India, where it was forced to make use not just of fraud and deception, as it did in Britain, but also of 'the Iron First of open terrorism'.[73] Given that young men were in jail 'for doing nothing more than holding opinions distasteful to the Executive', asks Hutchinson, in what respects did 'the legislation of British Imperialism differ from that of Fascist Terrorism in Italy?' His answer is bald: 'In no respect.'[74]

British communists like Robin Page Arnot were among those who observed that the severity of the Meerut sentences had more than a little to do with the fact that the activities and beliefs of the defendants betokened a degree of class-political solidarity between empire and metropole, breaching a racial cleavage that usually benefited colonial rule. Arnot, clearly drawing on Roy's Supplementary Theses, also noted in his essay on the Meerut sentences that the Indian working classes, being themselves the 'source of super-profits', could not be 'bribed as were sections of the English working class in the later nineteenth century by crumbs from the rich man's banquet'.[75] In some sense, the Indian working classes, as an organized force, were thus British imperialism's 'deadliest enemy'.[76] Arnot was scathing about those elements of the British trade union movement who, he claimed, 'would not raise a finger to release the men who were organising trade unions in India'.[77] He may have been making a point that was familiar not least from Saklatvala's parliamentary speeches, but it was one on which the Meerut campaign based its call for solidarity:

> Not only is it true that a nation that oppresses another cannot itself be free; but the same Imperialist class that is oppressing India, is oppressing and robbing the workers of this country by wage-cuts and speed-up, tariffs and taxes, is taking the bread out of the mouths of the workers' children, depriving them of the benefits of education, insurance and all other social services, and casting into gaol Tom Mann or any other leader of working-class revolt. The railwaymen facing a wage-cut, the busmen on strike against speed-up, the Lancashire workers suffering under the Midland Agreement, are fighting the same class that would deny the Indian workers the right to organise.[78]

This is perhaps the real significance of the Meerut controversy as it played out it in Britain. Pointing to Englishmen and Indians standing in the dock together and all articulating vehement critiques of both capitalism and imperialism, it was possible, as Arnot did, to call time on 'the jingo picture of "black men" versus "white men," of "Asiatics against Europeans"' which worked in favour of the powerful who peddled it.[79] This would, as it turned out, be no simple matter in the face of tenacious cleavages. But attempts would be made from this point on to organize across racial and national boundaries, and it is to one such attempt that I now turn.

'A parliament of mankind': The League against Imperialism

*It was attended by delegates from all over the world, who com-
prised a sticky conglomeration of Hindoo students and intellectuals,
American 'parlour' Bolsheviks, Chinese Nationalist Generals,
British Socialists and Communists, discontented French bourgeois,
German professors, coloured agitators from all parts of Africa, and
Mexican and South American nationalists.*

> John Baker White, president of the anti-socialist
> Economic League, in a letter to the *Morning Post*

*While I was in Berlin, I came into contact with the Head Office of
the League Against Imperialism. I did not, as the Prosecution allege,
do any work for the League nor was I a member of it. I was merely
there as a sympathetic observer, because I realised that the League
Against Imperialism – which, by the way, is not a Communist body
– was doing splendid work on behalf of the oppressed millions in
the colonial and semi-colonial countries.*

> Lester Hutchinson, *Meerut, 1929–1932*

The end of the Meerut trials, and the handing down of 'savage sentences of transportation' for what were essentially thought crimes
deemed a 'conspiracy', had the effect of disquieting more than a few
in the mainstream of British politics and opinion-making.[80] For some
on the British left, however, it came as bitter vindication of an analysis they had been advocating for some time. The Communist Party
of Great Britain's organ, the *Daily Worker*, opined that, while the
punishment of hurling the convicted into 'living death' by transportation to a penal island was clearly intended to squash the ongoing
labour unrest, it had generated a 'wave of indignation' among British
workers that would lead to a sense of common struggle.[81] Whether
or not that was the case, the unease around the Meerut sentences certainly enabled the case for joining the cause to be made more widely
in Britain. One of the organizations most active in campaigning for
the Meerut prisoners was the British Section of a recently formed
international organization known as the League against Imperialism
(LAI), which had published the pamphlets discussed in the previous
chapter. In an interview with the *Daily Worker*, Reginald Bridgeman,

who was one of the LAI's principal organizers in Britain and who in 1922 spent some time in India, where he would have witnessed labour unrest, explained that the LAI in Britain would, in its campaigning work on behalf of the Meerut prisoners, 'couple the arrest of the leaders of the unemployed in Britain with the conviction of the workers and peasants on India'.[82] He wrote to the German communist Willi Münzenberg, who promised 'a large campaign ... in support of the arrested in Europe while London would be the centre for campaigning'.[83] Sunday 19 April 1931 was designated 'Meerut Day'. Demonstrations were organized across Britain, and money raised for the Prisoner Relief Fund; a demonstration was also made in the House of Commons on 4 May 1931, from which one demonstrator was ejected.[84] Questions were prepared for the House of Commons, and MPs associated with the LAI, including Fenner Brockway, posed them from the floor.[85]

A member of the Labour Party who would be expelled from it in 1930 for working with the LAI – though he would later rejoin – Bridgeman had fought tenaciously, if unsuccessfully, to get the party's rank and file to oppose the Labour government's complicity in the Meerut prosecution as vigorously as they might oppose Labour

The League against Imperialism canvassing at
Trafalgar Square in London in August 1931

'effecting national economies at the expense of the unemployed'.[86] 'The British people', Bridgeman wrote in an open letter to party members, 'were given to understand that the régime of brutal exploitation of the colonial peoples would cease with the assumption of office by a Labour Government in 1929'; in fact, repression, with 'the buckshot, the batonings and the deliberate destruction of food and private property', had worsened.[87] Throughout the Meerut campaign, Bridgeman addressed meetings, lobbied the influential, wrote frequent letters in the press, and collected material support for the prisoners.

We do not know very much about Reginald Francis Orlando Bridgeman, or what led to his conversion to passionate and lifelong anticolonialism. The grandson of an aristocrat, with aristocratic cousins who were high-level Tory politicians, Bridgeman, like Wilfrid Blunt (with whom he also apparently shared sartorial panache – 'the greatest dandy in Europe', sniffed the *Evening Standard*, which also described him as 'Byronesque'), started off as a diplomat, and conducted his career on traditional lines, becoming known as a 'glutton for work'.[88] According to John Saville, the author of Bridgeman's entry in the *Dictionary of Labour Biography*, while it is unclear what brought about his conversion to left-wing socialism, the change appears to have taken place between 1919 and 1922 – a period which saw him posted in the British embassy in Tehran and visiting India, Muscat, Bahrain, Kuwait and Iraq.[89] During this period, in the heady wake of the 1917 October Revolution, Bridgeman, already drawn to socialism during his time in Vienna, maintained friendly relations with the Russians, much to the disapproval of his Foreign Office superiors. Recalled from Tehran, Bridgeman was retired on 1 July 1923. Getting involved in local Labour politics, and later standing unsuccessfully as a parliamentary candidate for Uxbridge, Bridgeman (who had been a Gold Staff Officer at the Coronation of George V in 1911) excited a certain amount of interest in the British press not least because of his aristocratic political family connections; his cousin, Viscount Bridgeman of Leigh, was a dedicated empire man serving as personal secretary to the secretary for the colonies, Lord Knutsford. Much was made of Bridgeman's personal style – 'His tastes are decidedly aesthetic', pronounced the *Star*, while the *Daily Record* and *Daily Mail* claimed that he wore red gloves as a political signifier.[90] Bridgeman also engaged with Chinese affairs through the London Trades Council and the Chinese Information Bureau, which investigated working-class conditions in East Asia. While never himself a member of the Communist Party of Great Britain, and emphatic, as were many others, that the LAI was not affiliated to them, Bridgeman did not tend to voice public criticism of the Comintern or the CPGB, though he did occasionally challenge officials on specific strategies. Bridgeman's activities around Meerut were quite clearly the most impactful of his career with the LAI, while later on he would become a vigorous critic of Zionism and an advocate of justice for the Palestinian Arabs; he would be re-admitted to the Labour Party after the LAI folded in 1937.

Any engagement with Britain and anticolonialism must necessarily pause on the LAI, a relatively short-lived but symbolically important formation which signalled, in one sense, the formal institution of a collective politics of solidarity between European (including British) and colonial critics of empire, as well as between various anticolonial movements.[91] Bridgeman's writings and notes, now preserved at the University of Hull, make clear that he had come to understand anticolonialism as a shared enterprise with the common interests of both colonial and metropolitan people at its heart, rather than one of philanthropic humanitarianism. (Bridgeman's personal copy of Stafford Cripps's *Empire*, issued by the India League, underlines with a question mark the phrase 'whereby a true trusteeship of such colonial territories is carried out during their minority'.)[92] He would also write to Labour MPs like Philip Noel-Baker expressing concerns that the party was supporting the implementation of the Mandatory system in India and Burma without the consent of those who would be subject to it.[93] Both personally and in his capacity as secretary to the British Section of the league, he would attempt to disseminate such anticolonial insights more widely. Bridgeman himself gave a prodigious number of talks on a variety of topics, including empire and anticolonialism, in forums as diverse as the St Clements Political and Social Council, the Marx Memorial Library, the St Michael Men's Discussion Group ('The Empire – Whose Responsibility?'), the Association of Engineering and Shipbuilding Draughtsmen, the St Albans Labour Party, the Hendon Central Women's Co-operative Guild and the 4th Harrow Rover Crew.[94] The recognition that the principle of 'tutelage' had to be erased on the left as much as in the mainstream was also articulated by Clemens Dutt, the British communist who had been active in the Meerut campaign and was a member of the LAI. Dutt vociferously criticized the Labour and Socialist Second International's own reformist paternalism: 'A large section of the colonial peoples are not considered to have "reached the standard" for self-government, they are not fit to be free and they must be educated and led for their benefit by the kindly tutelage of the superior civilising imperialist power.'[95] As resistance was met by 'bloody repression, hangings, shootings and air-bombings' in places such as Syria, Palestine, Mesopotamia, Samoa and New Guinea, it was possible to assess 'what an invaluable experience in imperialist tutelage their inhabitants are receiving'.[96]

Tutelage, of course, had been enshrined as a core principle in Article 22 of the Covenant of the League of Nations:

> To those colonies and territories which as a consequence of the late war have ceased to be under the sovereignty of the States which formerly governed them and which are inhabited by peoples not yet able to stand by themselves under the strenuous conditions of the modern world, there should be applied the principle that the well-being and development of such peoples form a sacred trust of civilisation and that securities for the performance of this trust should be embodied in this Covenant. The best method of giving practical effect to this principle is that the tutelage of such peoples should be entrusted to advanced nations who by reason of their resources, their experience or their geographical position can best undertake this responsibility, and who are willing to accept it, and that this tutelage should be exercised by them as Mandatories on behalf of the League.[97]

The League against Imperialism, in name and in conception, offered itself as a conscious counterpoint to the League of Nations and its complicity in revitalized structures of post-war imperialism – in particular through the Mandates system that gave various European 'mandatory powers' continued control of overseas territories without the appearance of direct annexation.[98] Colonialism, in other words, was made more legitimate and 'humane' for the twentieth century,

or, as Bridgeman described the Mandatory system, 'an imperialist
system exercised collectively ... without any previous consultation
of the opinion of the mandated people'.[99] As one LAI document
described it, the word 'mandates' was arrived at because 'the Great
War had been fought by the Allies on specific pledges against all
annexations'.[100] The pretence now was that 'the "trustees" [were]
seeking only the welfare of backward peoples'. Whatever purpose
the Mandates system served, 'extending the right of national self-
determination was not one of them', Susan Pedersen observes, and,
as a result, populations placed under it 'responded by resisting its
imposition'.[101] If the Mandates system was 'the site and stake of a
great international argument over imperialism's claims', as Pedersen
has it, the LAI sought to become the terrain on which anticolonialism would coalesce and challenge those claims.[102] In the years to
come, both tutelage and the idea that it could underpin a more gently
paternal and 'humane' form of colonial rule would be fiercely challenged both within the colonies and by exilic intellectuals in imperial
metropolises, with self-emancipation placed at the ideological centre.
The LAI and its offshoots can be seen as a preliminary attempt to
make an an international anticolonial field of sorts; within it, the
colonized did not just 'stand by themselves', but seized the initiative.

   The league itself had been initiated by a German communist by
the name of Willi Münzenberg, along with the peripatetic Indian
communist Virendranath Chattopadhyaya ('Chatto'), initially as
the 'League against Colonial Oppression' (Liga gegen koloniale
Unterdrückung). The actual organization of the first conference in
the Palais Egmont, Brussels, which took place on 10–15 February
1927, involved the efforts of a vast number of individuals and organizations belonging to the broader left, including, from Britain, the
Labour Party, the CPGB, the Workers Welfare League and the ILP.
A truly astonishing range of politicians, intellectuals and campaigners from the colonial world also attended the conference, including,
most famously, Jawaharlal Nehru (India), Lamine Senghor (Senegal),
James La Guma (South Africa), Sukarno (Indonesia) and Diego
Rivera (Mexico). The league's own statistics recorded nearly 200 delegates representing 134 organizations from thirty-seven countries. To
give just a small sampling, affiliated organizations included the San
Francisco–based revolutionary Hindustan Ghadar Party, the Indian

National Congress, the Workers' and Peasants' Party of Punjab, the Persian Socialist Party, the Egyptian National Party, the National Radical Party of Egypt, the African National Congress, the Arab Workers' Union, the Jewish Workers' Party, the Étoile Nordafricaine, the All-America Anti-Imperialist League, the Anti-Imperialist Federation of Ireland and the All-Russia Federation of Trade Unions. The LAI 'was a network which, in turn, twirled around a complex set of other networks', its principal constituents sharing a belief in the struggle against imperialism, with many (though not all) also committed to communism.[103] Other global luminaries associated with the LAI included Romain Rolland, Albert Einstein and Madame Sun Yat-sen. The idea was to bring together 'the friends and sympathisers of the oppressed peoples' with the delegates of mass organizations involved in anticolonial struggles, some numbering several thousand members.[104] It was not a communist, but the Labour politician George Lansbury, who was elected the league's first international chairman, and when he resigned, he was succeeded by the Independent Labour Party MP James Maxton. When a British Section was formed at a meeting in the House of Commons a few weeks later, Brockway was elected to the chair and Bridgeman made secretary, while Saklatvala

Members of the British Section of the League against Imperialism. Middle row (left to right), James Maxton (second left) and Shapurji Saklatvala (third), Reginald Bridgeman (sixth). It is not clear who the two women are.

was one of the Executive Committee members, along with fellow communist Harry Pollitt. In 1930, the National Meerut Prisoners' Defence Committee transferred its work to the LAI, and asked local Meerut committees to form league branches.[105]

It would be easy to dismiss the LAI – and most histories of the period do give it relatively short shrift – as an organization of little consequence that died a swift death as a result of internecine left-wing battles and the Comintern's own vacillating colonial policies. While that is certainly one aspect of the story, and a tragic one, the league's emergence internationally, as well as its British operations over the next decade, nonetheless remains a 'significant event in the history of anti-colonialism'.[106] At its best, the league functioned in its early years and for nearly a decade after, albeit mainly in Britain, as a terrain of debate on the question of how to organize more effectively against empire. It was terrain on which the Comintern sometimes prevailed, but at other times was more marginal. Michele Louro, for whom the emergence of the league and the Meerut campaigns were deeply intertwined, has argued that the league 'attracted a robust and equally balanced membership of communists and noncommunists who sought alliances to challenge imperialism'; indeed, Münzenberg 'failed to garner much attention or financial support from Moscow until after the Meerut case began, while noncommunists took up the lead in the formative years of the LAI's existence worldwide'.[107] The league's establishment was widely reported in Indian newspapers, and the British Indian government was quick to proscribe its literature; its documents were also produced as evidence of 'conspiracy' by the prosecutor in the Meerut case.[108] The league certainly worried authorities enough for Saklatvala, Bridgeman and James Maxton to be intercepted and detained overnight in Ostend, Belgium, as they were travelling to the league's Frankfurt conference in 1929; the incident caused a mini-scandal. (When they returned, Bridgeman and Saklatvala addressed a meeting in London at which an effigy of Lawrence of Arabia was burned – another incident reported in the British press.) It is perhaps more helpful to think about the moment and afterlife of the LAI less as a failed or short-lived institutional achievement than as an acknowledgement from within the heart of the metropole that, in the wake of the last war, something had shifted globally in relation to the imperial project, and demanded networked action. The centre of gravity had shifted to the colonies, and the agency of the 'darker races' would henceforth be integral to conceptualizing the end of empire; freedom would be the result of pressures from below, and not freely bestowed from above.

The most important aspect of the LAI's early congresses and constitution was the extent to which it showcased nationalist and left-wing leaders from Asia and Africa; in doing so, the LAI put both resistance movements in the colonies and international networks of solidarity at the heart of its vision of decolonization. Several of the speeches made at the Brussels Congress, which remains a landmark occasion in the history of global anticolonialism, made clear that the era of paternalism was definitively over. The fiery Senegalese campaigner and intellectual Lamine Senghor, who had previously set up the Comité de défense de la race nègre (CDRN) on explicitly self-emancipating grounds, spoke of it as 'not a minstrel show managed by some humanitarian white politician, but a universal race movement'.[109] At the first LAI Congress, where Senghor represented the CDRN, he also warned in a resonant metaphor: 'The Negroes have slept too long. But beware, Europe! Those who have slept long will not go back to sleep when they wake up.'[110] Josiah Tshangana Gumede, the ANC leader and delegate to the congress, hailed the event as a 'new era for the oppressed peoples'.[111] Read as an aspiration rather than an achievement (though it is all too easy to diminish the latter), the LAI embodied the growing understanding in the metropole that colonial subjects should not be seen as a humanitarian 'problem' to be rescued from their situation, but as partners in a struggle that was necessarily collective, and the outcome of which would have resonances for ordinary citizens of Europe as well. As the British communist J. R. Campbell would put it some years later, while introducing an anti-war resolution at one of the British Section's conferences, and noting that repressive legislation was now rife in dealing with great mass movements of resistance,

it is not a question of treating India as a problem or Africa as a problem, it is a question of asking ourselves, what are we, the British working class, going to do in relation to those living movements which are struggling for independence for the colonies at the present moment ... The same capitalist class which is holding down

India is holding us down here. And the stronger the Indian people's struggle, the stronger we become in this country ... It is not for us to determine whether the Indian people are ripe for self-government. Who are we that we should set ourselves up to judge?[112]

The Labour MP and chairman of the International League, James Maxton, described the LAI's view of itself as an organization 'within which the peoples of the oppressing and of the oppressed nations can meet on common ground and pursue in common the task of emancipation'.[113] This call for common ground was also met by an insistence – and there is no reason to believe it was not made in good faith – on cooperation between different political tendencies that shared a belief in anticolonialism. And so, Münzenberg again:

Every Communist or Syndicalist who joins the League today must be prepared to cooperate with the Socialists of the British Independent Labour Party. But every Socialist or bourgeois intellectual who enters the League must remember that he can only do so, if he is seriously prepared to work together with Communists.[114]

It is fair to say the LAI did indeed briefly succeed as a forum 'enabling actors holding different political points of view to stand on the same political platform around a common cause'.[115] Solidarity rather than charity, and common cause rather than paternalism, would be the order of the day.

Integral to the emergence of this understanding was the presence of large numbers of delegates from Asia and Africa, who voiced an uncompromising refutation of paternalism, striking an anticolonial keynote for the decades to come. These numbers certainly made a great impression on British delegates to Brussels; both Lansbury and Brockway came away from the founding LAI conference profoundly impressed, clear not only about the need for a global anticolonial partnership but also that the fulcrum of 'freedom' had moved eastwards. As Brockway would enthuse in an editorial he wrote for the *New Leader*, it was an 'extraordinary association' for its potential to 'lead to a worldwide movement of significance' which was not dominated by white campaigners. The new leaders were people of colour: 'I have attended many conferences which have been described as "International," but only one of them was international, in fact. The white peoples do not represent, I suppose, more than one-fourth of the human race. Yet at most international conferences one looks almost in vain for any but white faces.' This lamentable situation, however, changed in early 1927: 'But one international conference, in my experience, placed the whites in their proper place. It was held at Brussels last February. From the platform the conference hall was a remarkable sight. Every race seemed to be there ... in proportionately greater numbers, the races of Asia, Africa and America.'[116]

But beyond the 'Parliament of Man' that Brockway excitedly hoped would emerge out of this gathering, the congress had made crystal clear that it was now 'coloured workers' who were at the helm of a struggle for political and economic equality, which might unfold as 'the biggest human event of the next 20 years'.[117] No communist himself, he was nonetheless justifiably impatient with anti-communist sectarianism in the organizations he was affiliated to, the Socialist International and the Labour Party, warning strongly later that same year that it would be 'suicidal' for socialists to stay away from the LAI on grounds (spurious, in his view) that it was funded by 'Moscow gold'.[118] He urged fellow British socialists in the Independent Labour Party and Labour Party not to lose an opportunity to bring together 'all sincere anti-Imperialists in Europe with the rising Liberation Movement of the subject races of the world [which] may easily prove to be one of the most significant movements for equality and freedom in human history'.[119] In an unsigned editorial, Brockway suggested that the league also provided a forum in which nationalist movements might themselves be radicalized: 'Some Nationalists are as Capitalist as the Imperialism which they oppose; all they seek is the right freely to exploit their own peoples'; here was a chance to weave nationalisms into 'a wider Internationalism'.[120] Brockway would reiterate the insight that 'economic emancipation' was as vital as political freedom, noting too that the league's twenty-six associated organizations representing national or working-class movements across the globe made for a historic network of 'rapid international links'.[121] He also chided fellow Labour Party members 'suffering from the Communist complex' and being 'careful' about association with the LAI:

Of course Scotland Yard has its eye upon it. A movement which sets out to unite and strengthen the subject peoples of the world in their struggle against Imperialism is not likely to be overlooked by the Secret Service of the most powerful empire in the world! But we are in a bad way indeed if such attention deters us from sympathy and activity.[122]

The transformative impact of an organization not driven by white leadership is evident even in the observations of progressive, but not radical, Labourites like George Lansbury MP. To him, the league represented both actual historical resistance and an imaginative political possibility 'for the final and complete emancipation of all those races in the world which capitalist governments pleasantly label as subject races'.[123] In an article titled 'A Great Weekend at Brussels', Lansbury, no communist by a long shot (his tenure as international chairman of the LAI would be brief thanks to a Labour whip which debarred members from working with communist organizations), was vociferous about defending what he called the 'spontaneity' of the gathering in Brussels against charges of following a Comintern line.[124] Going so far as to call it the only conference he had attended that was not dominated by a 'machine-made cast-iron set of resolutions pushed down the throats of delegates', Lansbury, like Brockway, apostrophized the enormous diversity of the 'anti-imperialist international', listing not only the multifarious nationalities present – 'men and women speaking in various languages and divers tongues' – but also describing a wide political spectrum, from nationalists and communists to trade unionists and socialists: 'Negroes and Riffis, Indians and Japanese, Chinese and Egyptians, Italians and French, Russians and Germans, British and Irish, Mexicans and Dutch, Belgians and Scandinavians'.[125] For Lansbury, the LAI was distinguished from all prior organizations by being the first 'specifically and without qualifications [to challenge] the right of the white races to dominate, control and exploit the races which are described as backward'.[126] The organization's constitutive repudiation of paternalism was clearly pivotal here – with a remarkable degree of self-reflexivity, Lansbury acknowledges that, even among socialists, the historical tendency had been to go along with the claim that 'white men organise and control coloured people for the good of those controlled'.[127]

This unexamined belief shored up the idea that imperialists were ultimately 'philanthropists, bringing the blessings of civilisation and religion to the uncultured, uncivilised heathen'.[128] The league, on the other hand, 'does without reservation challenge that whole doctrine'.[129] That so self-reflexive an insight had something to do with the influence of Asian and African anticolonialists is made clear by Lansbury's reference to the prominent presence of China, Japan and India at the conference, which had the effect of 'making every one understand that these great nations were determined to throw off the yoke of Imperialism and band themselves together in defence, not merely of Nationalism, but Internationalism'.[130] The dawn, he pronounced, citing Edward Carpenter, regarded by many as a critic of empire, was rising in the East. Europe would not, could not, lead a global movement towards freedom.

Lansbury's and Brockway's acknowledgement of the importance of non-European and non-white voices and leadership is especially significant against the backdrop of the League of Nations' elision of those very voices. We know, for instance, that there were 'very few black delegates at the League Assemblies between the wars', and that this was a time when only Liberia and Abyssinia were free of white rule in sub-Saharan Africa.[131] The haphazard petition process which had 'brought the voices of the system's subjects – albeit muted, ventriloquized, and distorted – into the rooms in which their fates were determined' and allowed for claims to be made, ultimately foundered on the paradox that these had to be made through government channels; complainants had to 'communicate their grievances to the very persons of whom they complain'.[132] The LAI, in complete contrast, attempted to level racial hierarchies, putting resistance at its core and calling for engagement rather than petitioning. As Pedersen notes, the League of Nations' petitioning process failed partly because the founding assumption of the Mandate system was that the petitioning parties could not 'stand by themselves', which meant that nationalist claims or those based on self-determination were not sustainable under its terms.[133] Those making the complaints or claims had already been deemed childlike and 'incapable of knowing their own minds'.[134] The LAI, on the other hand, was founded on the fact of the right to equality, and on taking resistance to imperialism as a historical given. The League of Nations sought to preserve the Mandatory powers;

the LAI put on the table a vision of the end of empire, signalling the eclipse of an apparent consensus around the durability and legitimacy of European power. If, in decades past, and certainly in the nineteenth century, the episodic metropolitan crises generated by the resistance of the colonized had only hinted at the eventual end of European supremacy, the moment of the League against Imperialism was one that signalled a decisive fracture in the hegemon.[135] It was a fracture that would be enlarged and deepened by the decade of actual rebellion – and repression – that would follow.

Spurred by these new insights, the British Section of the LAI drew them out in several magnificently trenchant analyses of imperialism itself, some produced and distributed as pamphlets and tracts. One of the most brilliantly pithy and powerful, probably written in 1931, was authored by the 'Red Vicar', Father Conrad Noel (1869–1942), a Christian socialist who was chairman of the LAI for some time, and 'whose place has always been in the thickest of the fray'.[136] Noel's elegantly written fifteen-page tract, *The Meaning of Imperialism*, is a brilliantly pithy yet concrete but far from abstract distillation of the workings of empire, specifically Britain's.[137] As his damning account sweeps across various geographical and historical moments, Noel proffers a forensic analysis of 'humanitarian cant' or the mythology that an empire of this magnitude can be 'based not on force but on goodwill'.[138] To Noel, the clergyman, the development of British self-regard based on the notion that the nation held paternal sway over humanitarian empire was a form of 'collective pharisaism'; just as the biblical Pharisee thanks God he is not like the others, imperialists of every political persuasion insist 'that our Empire exists not for the purposes of conquest or exploitation or power' but with liberty as 'its binding principle'.[139] Noel was only too happy to remind his readers that, from the Roman to the German, and from the American to the League of Nations–sanctioned Belgian one, all empires declared themselves for 'humane and benevolent purposes'; such 'moral apologies are as old as the hills'.[140] Indeed, the bullish vicar headed straight for the mother lode of humanitarian myth-making, the story told on each Empire Day, that 'the British Empire has the proud distinction of being the first to abolish slavery', a story that has much to say about abolition and a lot less to say about slavery:

You would hardly gather from that that till almost within living memory the British Empire was the largest slaving association in the world; that the cities of Bristol, Glasgow and Liverpool were built upon the colossal profit of the trade in the human flesh; that from the sixteenth to the middle of the nineteenth century not thousands, but millions, of people have been torn from their homes, transported under conditions of unspeakable devilry to other parts of the Empire, there to provide cheap labour for the dominant race.[141]

In fact, Noel asserts, the facts are against the British abolition myth: Denmark abolished slavery in 1792, and the Northern States of America in 1794, while in 1807 only the trade was abolished by Britain, and not slavery itself. Nor, when compensation made abolition effectual after 1833, were the slaves themselves compensated in ways that might have given them some 'economic freedom', so as to avoid 'the meshes of slavery of another kind'.[142] The latter was a fate, as we have seen, that the Morant Bay rebels were determined to avoid.

The other noteworthy emphasis in Noel's tract – one very much of the LAI moment – is on the relationship between imperial exploitation in the colonies and the condition of working people at home. If the celebrations of the much-vaunted British abolition of slavery took no cognizance of 'English slavery', or the pauperized conditions in which many worked in the mines and factories of England, it took still less interest in how much worse were 'the conditions of the coloured people whom we own and exploit' in the colonies.[143] While evoking the land-grabbing and forced labour in regions like Southern Rhodesia and Kenya – which, he notes, even some of the least Bolshevik and most imperialist of figures have themselves deprecated – Noel returns to the question of how exploitation in the colonies is inextricably entangled with the undermining of British labour. In ways that are evocative of Saklatvala's speeches and writings, Noel (drawing on the work of the communist Rajani Palme Dutt) observes that the half-starved and ill-paid workers of the Bombay textile and Calcutta jute mills are wretched on their own terms, but also that 'when labour can be had for next to nothing', it 'will drive down the British workers to increasing slavery and starvation'.[144]

He then makes a compelling observation: 'You cannot be a patriot and a capitalist imperialist. You must either love Scotland and hate the Empire which is ruining it, or fight imperialism for the love of England or Scotland, and put an end to the Empire which is ruining the home people body and soul'.[145] The argument that 'without her Empire, Britain is nothing', which an Empire Day pamphlet propagated, is in fact the most unpatriotic of claims.[146] Noel also takes heart from the fact that Britain is heir to a tradition of truth-telling about empire, pointing, among other texts, to Edward Thompson's *The Other Side of the Medal* and Justin McCarthy's *History of Our Own Times*, in addition to those criticizing Britain's depredations in Ireland, such as G. K. Chesterton, and even Gladstone in his time. At the heart of British anticolonialism, as Noel delineates it, is the demolition of self-regarding cant. He cites the Indian historian Professor Panniker, as cited by Noel's fellow churchman, C. F. Andrews: 'Great Britain ... certainly does not stand for freedom and national life for the great majority of non-European people. What it stands for is a white oligarchy exploiting coloured nations.'[147] The failure to recognize this is puts Great Britain in danger of becoming 'a kind of riviera [*sic*] for the plutocrats', where 'such English workers as are lucky enough to find any work at all [will be] engaged in parasitic employments, tending the rich masters as "slaves of the palace"', while the 'extortion' of workers in the colonies continues apace.[148]

Peppered throughout the LAI's documents are insights that would gain traction in the run-up to the Second World War. Introducing a resolution on war and imperialism during the British Section's conference in 1934, the communist J. R. Campbell noted that only two things were considered 'above party' in Britain, seen as unquestionably good: the monarchy and the British Empire.[149] Out in the Empire, meanwhile, great mass movements were being met with fierce repression of the kind – and here is a nod to Meerut – that would have made ordinary trade union activity illegal. The existence of such mass resistance to colonial exploitation would be a running theme in league discussions. In 1931, another league document (issued by the International Secretariat and influenced at this point by the Comintern line) would speak of its own development as contingent on 'the tremendous wave of struggle for national freedom in the colonies ... gradually reaching its culmination and shaking the foundations of imperialist dominance'.[150] Citing insurrections taking place in Egypt, Syria, Palestine, China, India, Indo-China, Morocco, Africa and Latin America, a resolution passed at a meeting of the LAI's Executive Committee in Berlin in June 1931 noted that repression in the British Empire – now, ironically, under Ramsay MacDonald's Labour rule – was ferocious and bloody:

> The so-called 'Labour' Government under the leadership of MacDonald uses every possible method of oppression against the Indian national-revolutionary struggle for freedom. It bombs Indian villages slaughtering men, women and children, it arrests and hangs Indian revolutionary leaders, it sends punitive expeditions to Burma to exterminate the native revolutionaries, it sends British warships up the Chinese rivers to bombard the Chinese revolutionary forces. MacDonald's government is doing its best to drown the revolutionary struggle of the Egyptian and Arabian peoples in blood. Slavery in South Africa finds a powerful supporter in Macdonald and his friends.[151]

The resolution records struggles by Indian workers and peasants 'in spite of bombing, machine-guns, police violence, shooting, floggings and innumerable imprisonments'; 'shooting down of Nigerian peasant women', strike-breaking in the Gambia and armed attacks on miners on the Gold Coast, as well as peasant revolt in the Tharawaddy district of Burma.[152] In 1932, the British Section's annual conference passed a resolution describing the Scottsboro case as an exemplar of the desire 'to crush the growing spirit of revolt among the Negro toilers', but once again the emphasis was on the 'fighting spirit' of black Americans, to which the league would offer its fullest support, as also to 'the struggles of the Negro workers in Africa, and the West Indies for complete freedom and self-determination'.[153] It would also contribute to domestic struggles against racial discrimination, such as 'the alien registration scheme which deprived coloured British-born seamen of the right of British nationality'.[154]

While the LAI did not ultimately make the transition from a sympathizing organization into the centre of a mass global movement – ultimately becoming a victim of its own central fracture corresponding to that between the Comintern's changing imperatives and those of various non-communist anticolonial and socialist organizations – it nonetheless symbolized a decisive shift in how anticolonial organizing was conceptualized as necessarily transnational.[155] It is possible to regard the LAI as a 'failure', but it is important to acknowledge that it was a symptomatic embodiment of both the possibilities and difficulties inherent in the attempt to forge internationalism within a crucible of diverse political affiliations.[156] Despite the promising coalitional beginnings, it would not be long before both the ILP and the Labour Party expressed hostility towards and refused to affiliate with the LAI, on the grounds that it was a communist front organization. In turn, the LAI's British Section expelled Maxton, and Lansbury would also resign eventually. The 'harsh radicalism' of the Comintern's 'new line' was, of course, detrimental to wider international and internationalist linkages, advocating as it did the 'class-against-class' doctrine instead of 'collaboration outside the communist movement'.[157] In November 1933, the league's international headquarters moved from Berlin, where the Nazis were now in power, via Paris, to London. Bridgeman became its international secretary, and its chief guiding force. The league itself would fold within the decade; Bridgeman proved unable to carry on without sufficient resources, and the organization was plagued by internal Comintern politics, policy vacillations and attempts to make ideological 'corrections' to the course of anti-imperialism – an impossible task given the diversity of actors. Many of its prime movers – not least Münzenberg, who was found dead in France in 1940 – would also fall victim to Stalin's Great Terror of 1937. For all its failures and tragically short life, the LAI, particularly the Brussels conference, would remain a key symbolic point of reference for anticolonial campaigners and Third World leaders in the years to come and following decolonization. From this point, however, linked-up agitation, networks and alliance would be the hallmark of anticolonialism in Britain and beyond.

7

Black Voices Matter:
Race, Resistance and Reverse
Pedagogy in the Metropole

When viewed through the lens of race, the thesis – advanced by
many labour and socialist historians – that this period marked
some kind of universalist class awakening that had brought Britain
to the 'brink of revolution' requires considerable revision. A more
nuanced explanation is required that can help us understand both
the rising tide of working-class industrial and political struggles,
and working-class deployment of racism, including violence and
discrimination against Jewish migrants, as well as those from the
British colonies.

Satnam Virdee, *Racism, Class and the Racialized Outsider*

If the League against Imperialism was a metonym for the making
of international anticolonial coalitions based in the metropole
but fuelled by resistance in the colonies, the *idea* of transnational
opposition led by the colonized had in fact arrived on the global
stage in a modest but significant way nearly thirty years before. In
1900, the initiative was taken by a group of campaigners describing themselves as 'men and women of African blood'.[1] The first of
several pan-African conferences then took place in London at the
instigation of the African Association – an organization founded by
Henry Sylvester Williams, a Trinidadian lawyer who was determined
that 'the association would act on its own, draft its own rules, and
not be led by Europeans'.[2] The British Anti-Slavery Society expressed

its good wishes but, despite explicit requests from the association, refused further involvement, leading one historian to remark trenchantly: 'Perhaps the humanitarians found a world conference of blacks too frightening a project as the time got nearer for the delegates to meet.'[3] In the wake of the division of spoils by colonial powers, the notorious 'scramble for Africa' in the late nineteenth century, pan-Africanism had emerged first 'not as an organised movement but as a widespread sentiment of solidarity among Africans, West Indians and African Americans'.[4] The idea behind the conference of 1900 was that, without rejecting the assistance of white allies, people of African blood were capable of and ought to be standing up – and speaking – for their own interests with 'our own chroniclers' and 'our own libraries and organizations'.[5] The succinct 'Address to the Nations of the World' on behalf of 'the darker races of mankind' is worth pausing on, for its role in laying out some of the rhetorical terms for twentieth-century black anticolonialism.

A Habit of Democracy: The African
Background to Internationalism

Issuing from 'we, the men and women of Africa in world congress assembled', the address, famously drafted and delivered by W. E. B. Du Bois, and co-signed by Williams, Henry B. Brown and Alexander Walters, opens with two preliminary gestures which, at first glance, draw on the language of mendicancy.[6] There is an appeal to shared Christian values as the basis for extending 'the opportunities and privileges of modern civilization' to all, regardless of colour.[7] This is followed by a call for the work of white champions of 'Negro Freedom' such as Wilberforce, Clarkson and Buxton to be 'crowned' by Britain, an act which would include giving 'the rights of responsible self-government to the black colonies of Africa and the West Indies'.[8] Beneath the appeals to European decency, however, the address contains uncompromising notes of black self-assertion, putting into play themes that would be reprised and amplified in the decades to come. It begins by noting that much-vaunted differences of race are based on the most superficial markers, showing themselves 'chiefly in the colour of the skin and the texture of the hair'.[9] While the 'darker races' may at present be 'the least advanced in culture *according to European standards*', this 'has not, however, always been the case in the past'; both ancient and modern history provides many instances of African ability and capacity.[10] Then, in a more implacable tone, the address reminds the world that, in the century to come, great influence will be inevitably exercised by 'the millions of black men in Africa, America, and the Islands of the Sea, not to speak of the brown and yellow myriads elsewhere'.[11] Human progress itself will suffer if, instead of being given 'the largest and broadest opportunity for education and self-development', the black world is further exploited and degraded. Even as it appeals to the followers of 'the Prince of Peace' to take the black cause seriously, the address calls uncompromisingly for the removal of the 'cloak of the Christian missionary enterprise', which hides 'the ruthless economic exploitation and political downfall of less developed nations'.[12] The concept of self-emancipation surfaces gently but distinctly in this text, which, while saluting both white and black abolitionists from Wilberforce and Garrison to Sharpe and Douglass, also insists on the need generously to recognize and honour the ordinary 'American Negro' and 'the great work he has accomplished in a generation toward raising nine millions of human beings from slavery to manhood'.[13] And in a final determined gesture which would turn out to be a prescient warning, the address calls for the sovereignty of black nation-states to remain inviolate:

> Let the nations of the World respect the integrity and independence of the first Negro States of Abyssinia, Liberia, Haiti, and the rest, and then let the inhabitants of these States, the independent tribes of Africa, the Negroes of the West Indies and America, and the black subjects of all nations take courage, strive ceaselessly, and fight bravely, that they may prove to the world their incontestible [*sic*] right to be counted among the great brotherhood of mankind.[14]

As the century progressed, so did the strength of black challenges to empire.

Manifestos were among the genres which proffered a platform for such challenges and self-assertion, expressing as they did 'a structure of feeling of an empire in crisis'; they produced narratives of modernity which often made 'central the racial margin'.[15] By the time of the London Manifesto, produced twenty years later by the second Pan-African Congress, held in 1921, black self-emancipation was an idea that had gathered heft. The first Congress, under W. E. B. Du Bois's leadership, had taken place in 1919, and had issued a set of demands on behalf of the 'Negroes of the world' calling for the Allied and Associated 'trustee' powers to ensure that the land, capital, labour, education and political rights of 'the natives of Africa and peoples of African descent were safeguarded. What is striking about the 1921 text, particularly in comparison to the more reformist resolutions contained in its predecessor, is a determined insistence that self-government involves not the concession of a new right but the 'recognition' of an existing one. It is a right already inscribed in history and made manifest by resistance and struggle: 'The independence of Abyssinia, Liberia, Haiti and San Domingo is absolutely necessary to any sustained belief of the black folk in the sincerity and honesty of the white. These nations have earned the right to be free, they deserve the recognition of the world.'[16] Indeed, the document goes so far as to suggest that these nations, for all their faults and mistakes, 'compare favourably with the past and even recent history of most European nations and America', which continue to invade and overthrow free institutions.[17] It then issues a robust challenge to the idea that some nations had to be looked after by others – an idea that would find its apotheosis in notions of 'trusteeship':

> The insidious and dishonourable propaganda which for selfish ends so distorts and denies facts as to represent the advancement and development of certain races as impossible and undesirable should be met with wide-spread dissemination of the truth; the experiment of making the Negro slave a free citizen in the United States is not a failure; the attempts at autonomous government in Haiti and Liberia are not proofs of the impossibility of self-government among black men; the experience of Spanish America does not prove that mulatto democracy will not eventually succeed there; the aspirations of Egypt and India are not successfully to be met by sneers at the capacity of darker races.[18]

This manifesto references earlier pan-African appeals, but recasts them as more far-reaching *demands*, the boldest of which is a return to the 'ancient common ownership of the Land and its natural fruits and defence against the unrestrained greed of invested capital'.[19] Africa must be a 'co-ruler' of the world along with other peoples, and there can be no compromise on 'absolutely equal' political, civil and social power for Africa's citizens, both black and white.[20] In a striking inversion of the usual terms of argument, it is not so much justice that must be bestowed on the oppressed but *injustice* that has to *cease* on the part of those who 'lynch the untried, disenfranchise the intelligent, deny self-government to educated men, and insult the helpless'.[21] There is also a scathing dismissal of the ways in which the time lags of inevitably uneven development in human societies form the basis of 'adventitious and idiotic' race hierarchies populated by demigods and apes, rather than accepted as part of the 'richness and variety of human nature'.[22]

The London Manifesto is not without its own biases in favour of what it calls 'cultured black citizens', insisting that leaders from the black 'intelligentsia' are needed because the millions they sought to represent 'have not even what we have; the power to complain against monstrous wrong, the power to see and know the source of our oppression'.[23] At its ethical heart, however, is what it resonantly calls a 'habit of democracy' that must be 'made to encircle the earth' not least because there was nothing uniquely European about a capacity for democracy.[24] Like liberty, democracy is not racially or culturally specific, as the colonizers would have it, 'the secret and divine Gift of the Few'.[25] In reality, 'no habit is more natural and more widely spread among primitive people or more easily capable of development among wide masses'; indeed, it could be implemented 'tomorrow', though some 'general control and guidance' might be needed.[26] Notably, in comparison to the more specifically Christian tone of the document of twenty years before, this text alludes to the twentieth century not just as that of the 'Prince of Peace' but also as 'the millennium of Buddha and Mahmoud' [*sic*], as well as 'the mightiest age of Human Reason'.[27] The real 'shame of the world' derives not from racial differences or developmental time lags, which are accidents of history, but from that which allows 'the majority of mankind to be brutalised and enslaved by ignorant and selfish agents of commercial institutions whose one aim is profit and power for the few'.[28] Capitalism and capitalist 'world organisation', in which 'the favoured few may luxuriate in the toil of the tortured many', are quite simply indefensible, the true blot on human civilization exacerbated by 'the outrageously unjust distribution of the world income between the dominant and suppressed peoples'.[29]

Here, in its closing paragraphs, the London Manifesto made visible a fault line that would haunt metropolitan anticolonialism and debates on the left over the next decades. In the execution of capitalist crime, where the project of empire was inextricable from the project of capital, could it be that white labour 'is *particeps criminis* with white capital'?[30] The authors and endorsers of the manifesto were not claiming that white labour was not exploited, as is clear from the proximate declaration that the wealth and well-being of the rich 'rest on a pitiful human foundation of writhing white, yellow and brown and black bodies'.[31] They also refuse to claim 'perfectness of our own', assigning black people responsibility for what the text calls 'failure to advance'.[32] Instead, it places a more challenging question on the table: how could and should white labour assess its role in the project of imperialism given the extent to which, both consciously and unconsciously, not least through its share of the vote in modern democracies, it had 'been cajoled and flattered into imperialistic schemes'?[33] The manifesto is clear that this complicity, far from benefiting them, has had fatal consequences for white workers, as they 'are themselves today bound and gagged and rendered impotent by the resulting monopoly of the world's raw material in the hands of a dominant, cruel and irresponsible few'.[34] How could the problem of race in the context of global imperialism be addressed in its specificity and as it intersected with the question of class and the exploitation of labour? This question, as we shall see in the following chapters, became a lightning rod for debate.

A Rebel Sojourner in London

Anticipating points that would be made at the first LAI congresses, and then developed in the years to come, the London Manifesto put forward a difficult proposition.[35] The problem of labour versus capital would not be solved in England, it ventured, as long as a parallel dynamic 'mark[ed] the relations of the whiter and darker peoples'.[36] The exploitation of black, brown and yellow labour through imperialism – and the dangers of white working-class complicity in that exploitation – was not a topic being addressed frontally or consistently on the British left in the immediate post-war years. Indeed, as Satnam Virdee has pointed out, the much-vaunted British working-class insurgency in the post-war period, manifested in strike waves, was accompanied by race riots. Racism and xenophobic nationalism were frequently intertwined with labour militancy.[37] In an episode that encapsulates this intertwining, the well-known anti-slavery campaigner and anti-war activist Edward Dene Morel, famed for his exposure of Belgian atrocities in the Congo, wrote a shocking and sensational article titled 'The Black Scourge in Europe'.[38] A member of the left-leaning Union of Democratic Control, and later a Labour MP, Morel claimed sensationally and with crude suggestiveness that France was 'thrusting her black savages still further into the heart of Germany' by sending troops from the colonies into the area.[39] He was referring to the presence of black troops. There, he averred, far from policing the area as they were supposed to, 'primitive African barbarians' with their unique 'well-known physiological' traits were 'over-running Europe' and busy raping or otherwise satisfying themselves on the bodies of white women, who consequently suffered particularly grave injuries often with 'fatal' consequences.[40] The article, written for the most widely read left-wing newspaper in Britain, was a mix of deep racism and breathless righteousness as it bemoaned the fate of white women at the hands of the 'black menace': 'Sexually they are unrestrained and unrestrainable. *That is perfectly well-known*'.[41] Whatever else Germans might be willing to let go, the article argued sympathetically, this rapine could never be forgiven. Insisting hysterically that the 'abundance or otherwise of specific reports' was 'immaterial', Morel's argument was made in anti-capitalist and anti-militarist terms as it invoked the possibility of 'black mercenaries being used against trade union and revolutionary movements'.[42] Significantly, Morel repeatedly brought his unproved assertions back to the fate of the white working classes against whom this black weapon was being deployed. The casual slide from capitalist 'lusts' to the black slaking of those lusts is not especially subtle:

For the working classes the importation of negro mercenaries by the hundred thousand from the heart of Africa, to fight the battles and execute the lusts of capitalist Governments in the heart of Europe is, as I have said elsewhere, a terrific portent. The workers alike of Britain, France, and Italy will be ill-advised if they allow it to pass in silence because to-day the victims happen to be German.[43]

Morel's fevered article invoking 'a terror and a horror unimaginable to the country', facilitated by white degradation in the face of war, would also be developed into a pamphlet, *The Horror on the Rhine*, which found wide international circulation and went into no less than eight editions.[44]

In the first instance, however, it was carried by the *Daily Herald*, the Labour Party newspaper edited by George Lansbury, then a serving MP, as a 'revelation so horrible' that it had no choice but to carry it. A subsequent article on the front pages of the newspaper lauded its own courage in publishing Morel's article, adding: 'The Labour movement and all other people with a remnant of decent feeling demand the immediate withdrawal of the black troops and their return to Africa.'[46] While defending the newspaper against the idea that it was 'encouraging colour prejudice' and insisting, in a preface to Morel's article, that it championed 'the rights of the African native in his own home',[47] Lansbury nonetheless wrote a supportive (unsigned) editorial titled 'Brutes in French Uniform' and subtitled 'Danger to German Women from 30,000 Blacks' in which he reiterated Morel's claim that black troops with 'primitive sexual passions' were rampaging through Germany.[48] Later that year, following the publication of the pamphlet version, around which women's organizations held meetings, both the Independent Labour Party and the Labour Party passed resolutions condemning the use of black troops by France. (Morel himself was a member of the Labour Party's think tank on colonial issues, the Labour Party Advisory Committee on Imperial Questions.) The matter was also discussed in the ILP's official journal, the *Labour Leader*, now under Fenner Brockway's editorial hand. Morel's salaciously overheated accusations, however, went largely unchallenged on the British left. As Robert C. Reinders has noted, Morel was known as a man who, to quote one co-worker, 'had "agonies of sympathy with his beloved black man"' and unimpeachable 'liberal credentials'.[49] The *Herald* also urged British women to rise up in support of their German sisters – a call enthusiastically taken up, among others, by the socialist women's campaigner Ethel Snowden, as well as several women's organizations.[50] Histories of the Labour left in Britain make little of the episode if they mention it at all, and it is not part of general knowledge about Morel, who is largely known as a champion of black rights and kindly defender of Africa.[51] With Morel strenuously denying that his protest had been inspired by 'racial bitterness', the *Labour Leader* also gave space to him and others to discuss the issue without questioning Morel's version.[52] The pamphlet's eighth edition carried endorsements from the Danish modernist writer Georg Brandes, the French communist writer Henri Barbusse, and Karl Marx's grandson, the French socialist and editor Jean Longuet.[53]

There was, however, one important dissenting voice and, importantly, it was that of a black man originally from the colonies. In early 1920, the poet and journalist Claude McKay, who would become a major figure of the literary and cultural phenomenon known as the Harlem Renaissance, had arrived in England from the United States (where he had relocated from his native Jamaica a few years before). At the time, McKay was a 'scribbler' who had also worked manual jobs for several years, including on the American railroad, before joining the staff of the left-wing magazine the *Liberator*. In the famous 'Red Summer' of 1919, which signified 'at once the political repression of leftists and the bloody suppression of black rebellion', McKay – shocked into bringing together his growing radical politics and his passion for verse – burst onto the scene with one of his most famous poems, the sonnet 'If We Must Die'.[54] With its compelling last line envisioning defiance to the bitter end in the face of racialist pogroms – 'Pressed to the wall, dying, but fighting back!' – the poem was a recitative paean to black insurgency in the face of all-encompassing oppression. Having already witnessed white mobs in the United States launching brutal attacks on African-Americans, when McKay read Morel's attack on the 'black scourge' in the *Daily Herald* shortly after arriving in London, his immediate response was to write a letter to the editor in which he asked that his rebuttal be published. Lansbury, with great disingenuousness, reiterated that neither the paper nor Morel subscribed to racial prejudice, but nonetheless declined to publish McKay's riposte. McKay then contacted Sylvia Pankhurst, the suffragette, communist and anti-war agitator, who immediately agreed to carry it in her weekly, the *Workers' Dreadnought*, which at that time was functioning as the organ of the British Section of the Third International. In the pointedly titled 'A Black Man Replies', McKay was bullishly con-frontational, determined to hold the British left to account, noting that it was thoroughly inadequate for an ostensibly progressive newspaper like the *Herald* to claim not to be 'encouraging race prej-udice' and to 'champion native rights in Africa' while carrying the 'obscene, maniacal outburst' of Morel, who otherwise 'peddles his books and articles on "the poor suffering black"'.[55] The line between the acknowledged 'odiousness' of race prejudice and Morel's legiti-mized brand of paternalism was thin, he suggested, and hardly likely to take forward the urgent task of helping 'white and black peoples to a better understanding of each other'.[56] Professing complete igno-rance of the ostensibly 'well-known physiological reasons' that made the white women in question particularly prone to injury, according to Morel, McKay noted with stark simplicity: 'Any violent act of rape, whether by white, yellow or black, civilized or savage man, must entail injury.'[57]

McKay's intervention – which, astonishingly, remains the only major rebuttal of Morel's manifestly outrageous and unsubstantiated accusations – was important not only as a clear and direct exposé of the latter's unpardonable and absurd racism, but also in exposing the broader British left's persistent blind spot on race.[58] The whole truth, McKay was obliged to point out, was that white men also rape, black men can control their sexual proclivities as well as any other men, white men have fathered thousands of disowned children among the 'colored races', and the syphilis Morel accused the French black troops of carrying had been contracted by sexual contact with whites. Socialists might indeed do well to stop the French exploi-tation of North African conscripts (not 'mercenaries'), but not by peddling harmful racial generalizations:

> During my stay in Europe, I have come in contact with many weak
> and lascivious peoples of both sexes, but I do not argue from my
> experience that the English race is degenerate. On the other hand,

I have known some of the finest and cleanest types of men and women among the Anglo-Saxons.[59]

With the memories of the American pogroms fresh in his mind, McKay was insistent that his rebuttal derived less from the fact of his being a black man himself than from well-founded anxiety at the inevitable 'further strife and blood-spilling between the whites and the many members of my race, boycotted socially and economically', that such propaganda would help incite.[60] In fact, the poet's powerful voice did bring to bear upon his intervention vital insights shaped by the experience of being a black man in a colonial and white-supremacist order. These enabled him to illuminate the British white left's racial and national biases, implicating it in the structures of white domination. They also helped him make the case for a serious and genuine universalism that was predicated not on white humanitarianism, but on taking seriously the fact of an unequal global order in which the black experience of racial-capitalist oppression had to be integral to an understanding of world history. McKay's use of the 'lens of race' was not one that segregated black working-class experience as incommensurable with others; it allowed for common cause to be *made* in the face of racial stratification, rather than the identity of working-class interests being simply assumed. McKay was grappling with problems that retain urgency in our own times: how is it possible to come up with a shared vision of emancipation and social justice that has universal resonances and scope, but does not lose sight of vastly different historical experiences which often come into conflict with one another? How can an identity of class interests be constructed when the experience and operation of class also rely on a racial hierarchy? My argument in the remainder of this chapter, which looks at McKay's work for the *Workers' Dreadnought* and at the pioneering collaborative anthology *Negro*, edited by the poet Nancy Cunard, is that there were serious attempts during the interwar period to 'teach race' and make blackness matter on the British left, which, in tandem with the growing pan-African presence in Britain, are an important part of the story of metropolitan anticolonialism (and anti-racism). These pedagogical projects often took the form of collaboration and collective publishing in which radical white allies (both women in this instance) encouraged and facilitated the emergence of radical black anticolonial voices into the metropolitan public sphere, using their institutional and social networks to this end and often emerging as notable anticolonial figures themselves. These collaborations allowed for difficult, often awkward, conversations to take place, and were a vital part of the attempt to undo paternalism and replace it with a politics of radical, if often uneasy, solidarity. The universal would be aspired to through an understanding of the particular; world-historical knowledge would be accessed through the epistemology of the margins.

A 'race man and a class man'

In 1919, when McKay arrived in London, he found a scenario of labour militancy without labour unity. There was tension on the London docks as unemployment rose, and impoverished white workers, a few disenchanted ex-service personnel among them, were encouraged to turn their wrath upon foreign seamen, many 'dumped down on the English docks since the ending of the European war'.[61] There had been race riots, many taking place in different British seaports, spurred by the belief that foreigners, particularly blacks and Asians, were taking jobs that white seamen should have; renewed attempts were made to enforce a union colour bar.[62] In turn, various organizations of black and Asian workers and residents were formed to protest and challenge racist discrimination. In a few cases, 'black British sailors protested about the employment of foreign white sailors'.[63] Not least due to the now extensive presence of black workers, including those who had served Britain in the war, race became a potent issue in the wider discussion of labour conditions and workers' rights. 'Amidst these racist riots', Virdee reminds us, 'no section of British society saw fit to recall how the British state and employers had scoured the four corners of its Empire in search of labour to fill the gap' left by war-volunteer seamen.[64] Recalling the moment in his memoirs, and noting that it was a period of 'great labor unrest' in the Rhineland as well, McKay writes that his aim in 'A Black Man Replies' was to remind Lansbury of the duty of 'a radical organ to enlighten its readers about the real reasons why the English considered colored troops undesirable in Europe, instead of appealing indirectly to illogical emotional prejudices'.[65] He also warned the politician and editor that 'his black-scourge articles would be effective in stirring up more prejudice against the negroes', to which Lansbury predictably replied that 'he was not personally prejudiced against Negroes'.[66] McKay rightly saw this as irrelevant, since what was at stake was not a 'personal issue', but the 'public attitude' of the Labour journal. He did, however, acknowledge that the Labour MP had 'energetically denounced' the situation of the previous summer, 'when colored men were assaulted by organized bands of whites in the English ports'.[67] He would note later that, while he was 'not sentimental' about his own race, 'I hate oppression of subject races and peoples'.[68]

Already host to several campaigning South Asian organizations, including the India League, run by the redoubtable V. K. Menon, London in the era after the end of the First World War would also witness a steady inflow of intellectuals and campaigners from its West Indian and African imperial possessions. By the 1930s, frequently facilitated either by white allies or through black-run organizations and journals, radical black voices became more powerfully audible. Black sojourners like McKay would, as Cedric Robinson has argued, learn from the radical left milieu they encountered in the great imperial capital, but they would also bring to it their own experiences of anticolonialism and struggles against racial oppression, including pan-Africanism. It is tempting, given the brevity of his stay, to suggest, as Robert Reinders and Wayne Cooper do in their useful overview of McKay's year in England, that, if there is a broader significance to that sojourn of otherwise 'limited importance', it is as a 'case study of the disillusioned colonial'.[69] He is arguably deserving of more than 'a footnote in modern British history as the first Negro Socialist to write for an English periodical'.[70] In one sense, McKay stands at the head of a long line of West Indian and African intellectuals – among whom C. L. R. James and George Padmore are only the best known – who formed productive, if sometimes fraught, alliances with radical figures on the British left, and helped shape the contours of interwar British anticolonialism. McKay (who was prevented from travelling to any colonies other than Jamaica after his spell in England, where he was put under surveillance by Special Branch) also brought a vital transatlantic dimension to bear on questions of race, colonialism and radical politics. While he may not have viewed himself to be speaking 'as a black man', McKay indisputably articulated a perspective honed by the experience of both colonialism and metropolitan racism. His partnership with Pankhurst was vital to that understanding being disseminated into a broader progressive and left-wing milieu. In inviting McKay to her printing office in Fleet Street and offering him a job as a reporter at the *Dreadnought*, where she also asked him to 'dig up something along the London docks from the colored as well as the white seamen',[71] and to 'write from a point of view which would be fresh and different', Pankhurst appears to have recognized the pedagogical value for the British left of a powerful voice which could speak eloquently on race and empire.[72] She tasked him also with reading newspapers from the colonies and marking items to bring to the attention of *Dreadnought* readers. McKay first got to know Pankhurst at an international club, which he described somewhat ambivalently in retrospect as a place full of 'dogmatists and doctrinaires of radical left ideas: Socialists, Communists, anarchists, syndicalists, one-big-unionists and trade unionists, soap-boxers, poetasters, scribblers, editors of little radical sheets which flourish in London'.[73] Later he would tell Nancy Cunard that, living in 'uncongenial' London, the club 'was altogether a foreign milieu' in which he had found refuge.[74]

While the political partnership between McKay and Pankhurst was to last just about a year – she would be arrested later in 1920 over an 'inflammatory' article McKay had commissioned from a young sailor sent undercover to investigate conditions 'below decks', while he would return to the United States – it has both a symbolic and a material importance. Through Pankhurst's connections within 'the nest of extreme radicalism in London', McKay met figures such as Saklatvala and Lansbury, describing the latter contemptuously as symbolic of all that was 'pious and self-righteous in the British Labor movement'.[75] In each other, Pankhurst and McKay recognized constitutively dissident sensibilities, a willingness not only to challenge the establishment but also to put pressure on and transform their own oppositional milieus. Such partnerships and affinities, even when brief and sometimes uneasy, were the warp and weft of metropolitan anticolonialism. McKay wrote of his feminist employer: 'And in the labor movement she was always jabbing her hat pin into the hides of the smug and slack labor leaders. Her weekly might have been called the Dread Wasp. And wherever imperialism got drunk and went wild among native peoples, the Pankhurst paper would be on the job.'[76] McKay also described the *Dreadnought*'s relationship to the more established *Daily Herald* as that of 'a little cat up against a big dog' and 'always spitting'.[77] Pankhurst's employment of McKay on clearly equal terms is particularly significant in a milieu where race feeling was far from absent, whether that took the form of hostility, paternalism or curiosity (George Bernard Shaw, for instance, would ask McKay why he preferred writing to pugilism).[78] What is very clear is that, despite occasional disagreements with Pankhurst – not least over her refusal to publish a 'scoop' revealing Lansbury's employment of strike-breakers in his sawmills – McKay left an impression on her and an imprint on the journal. Issues of the *Workers' Dreadnought* after McKay left show a determinate rise in international and imperial coverage, with particular attention paid to Ireland, South Africa and India.

McKay would also open up the fraught question about the relationship between race and class in the crucible of the Empire. In the very first piece that he wrote under his own name for the *Dreadnought*, in early 1920, McKay made the case for left-wing Britons to engage with anticolonial nationalism. Taking issue with some English communists who had remarked to him that they were not sympathetic to 'nationalistic' movements in India and Ireland, McKay, who would soon go on to a triumphal tour to the Soviet Union, opined that 'for subject peoples, at least, Nationalism is the open door to Communism'.[79] English revolutionaries ought not to be 'unduly concerned' about the manner in which blows against imperialism – and, thereby, capitalism – were struck.[80] McKay's short piece was itself structured by productive tensions: on the one hand, he criticized organizations like the National Association for the Advancement of Colored Peoples (NAACP) for failing to recognize that 'the Negro question is primarily an economic problem' that would not be solved by admitting a few chosen ones into white society through wealth and attainment.[81] On the other, McKay conceded, such efforts did develop 'race-consciousness in the Negro and made him restive'.[82] Here he was drawing on his own fraught experience with Garveyism, where, despite disagreements with Marcus Garvey and the Universal

Negro Improvement Association, he could see that black people 'oppressed by the capitalists, despised and denied a fighting chance under the present economic system by white workingmen', could find means of self-assertion through black nationalism.[83] In making the radical case for nationalism, McKay argued, somewhat optimistically, that people 'who are strong enough to throw off an imperial yoke' would not 'tamely submit to a system of local capitalism'.[84] What McKay had begun to theorize was the necessarily dialogical relationship between race and class in the post-1917 era, in which European empires still held global sway.

One of McKay's recurrent concerns, evident in both his response to Morel and his later writing for the *Dreadnought* under the pseudonym 'Leon Lopez', was the way in which divisions between white and non-white workers were instigated by and played into capitalist and imperialist hands: 'The whole plot is so obvious and yet the nicely fed and clothed labour officials play the capitalist game to perfection, by stirring up the passions of the workers against aliens (and need I add Jews?)'.[85] The roving reporter 'Leon Lopez' describes going down to the docks and seeing the devastation wrought by unemployment with 'scores upon scores of seamen, white, brown and black, waiting wistfully for an undermanned ship'. As Lopez wonders what will unfold as a consequence of these conditions, his question is answered by a screaming headline in a local newspaper: 'CHINATOWN SCANDAL. WHITE GIRLS AND YELLOW MEN'. After a few sharp words for the 'kept press' and its disingenuous fascination with what 'our English girls find in these foreigners', McKay/Lopez proposes this: 'The dockers, instead of being unduly concerned about the presence of their coloured fellow men, who, like themselves are the victims of capitalism ... should lead the attack on the bastilles, the bonded warehouses along the docks to solve the question of unemployment.'[86] Only a year later, McKay would publish, in Russia, *Negry v Amerike* (The Negroes in America), which is described by one critic as arguably 'the first ever black-authored monograph theorizing the relationship between race and class', and criticizing the left-wing elision of the race issue.[87] In turn, McKay's class radicalism was not always congenial to those who believed that organizing around race was the way forward for black Americans. He did, however, write to Marcus Garvey urging contact and alliances between 'radical Negroes' and 'white radical movements': 'To me they are the great destructive forces *within* while the subject races are fighting without ... We have a great wall to batter down, and while we are working on one side, we should hail those who are working on the other.'[88] As Winston James notes, McKay was ultimately dialectical, 'a race man and a class man'.[89]

While clearly committed to colonial freedom even during the *Dreadnought* years, Pankhurst herself would become a full-time anticolonialist by the late 1930s, in the wake of Italy's invasion of Abyssinia – an event which would galvanize both pan-Africanists and British critics of empire (see Chapter 7). During the attacks on black workers in London, she had challenged those who were justifying them, making the connection between imperialism abroad and racism at home:

> Do you think the British should rule the world or do you want to live on peaceable terms with all peoples?
>
> Do you wish to exclude all blacks from England?
>
> If so, do you not think that blacks might justly ask that the British should at the same time keep out of the black peoples' countries?[90]

While some of Pankhurst's *Dreadnought* editorials before 1920 were clear in their commitment to Irish and Indian self-determination, the latter achieved 'either by taking it herself, or by a British Revolution extending it to her', something of McKay's influence can be seen not only in the increased coverage of international issues in the wake of his tenure on the weekly, but also in an even greater emphasis on colonial insurgency as itself inspirational to the working classes of Britain, requiring not just solidarity but also emulation.[91] In early issues, unsigned *Dreadnought* pieces (likely to have been written by Pankhurst as editor) deprecated the 'colour bar' in South Africa, and took issue with moderate reformers like Annie Besant being seen as representatives of Indian aspirations. The influence of Saklatvala – who also contributed several articles to the *Dreadnought* around this time – is clear here. Later issues of the journal, however, took pains to point to the growth of 'great insurgent movements in Ireland, in India, in Egypt', suggesting, as Jones had once suggested to the Chartists, that they should 'cause Communists to consider deeply:

why are these movements so flourishing and so capable of action, whilst the working-class movement is languishing in apathy and ineptitude?'[92] An editorial noted that Britain too needed 'a movement that is moving', as was the case in India, where a 'vast revolt' was in the making; India would also give confidence to Ireland's anticolonial movement. Pankhurst would also deprecate Labour's weakening of its internationalist inheritance in not offering 'strenuous opposition' to the weakly reformist 1919 Government of India Act, and accuse the party of lacking in 'the sturdy democratic fibre of the Chartists'.[93] After a tussle with the newly formed Communist Party of Great Britain over control of the *Dreadnought* when she was released from prison in 1922, Pankhurst ran the paper for two more years before it folded. She would not return to journalism and public life again till the early 1930s, though she did write a book on India in 1926. While the book itself is not especially remarkable – one among many overarching histories of the region that seek to understand it in historical context – it does attempt to delineate the manifold ways in which colonial rule has had to resort to repressive measures for its survival, including legislating against 'disaffection'. Pankhurst also considers the resources for democratic and egalitarian government already embedded in Indian vernacular traditions, comparing the village *panchayats* to the Russian *mir*. To the extent that empire attempts to render subject populations 'dumb' through the force of the machine, the claims of the civilizing mission are rendered void: 'Civilisation must indeed be written down as a failure, if it could find no better means of spreading knowledge than is provided by the sword, and no nobler motive for doing so than that of exploitation'.[94]

'Though still white': Black Voice and the Extraordinary Dreams of Nancy Cunard

YOUR BOOK IS MARVELOUS. LANGSTON.
Langston Hughes, cablegram to Cunard, April 1934

Voices crying in the wilderness
At so much per word
From the white folks:

> *'Be meek and humble.*
> *All you niggers*
> *And do not cry*
> *Too loud.'*
>
> Langston Hughes, 'To Certain Negro Leaders'

In 1931, McKay, now an established figure on the cultural landscape of Harlem, wrote an enthusiastic letter to a woman who had invited him to contribute to an anthology she was putting together:

> We poor Negroes, it seems to me, are literally smothered under reams of stale, hackneyed, repetitious stuff done by our friends, our moral champions and ourselves ... We most of us live in fear of <u>the fact</u> of ourselves. And can hardly afford to render even the artistic truth of our own lives as we know and feel it; but it is unimaginable that you could be handicapped or allow yourself to be by the social-racial reactions that hamper us sometimes unconsciously even. And so I hope the stuff you are going to put out will be a revelation and inspiration to us.[95]

Given a literary context where black voices – his own and those of Langston Hughes and Countee Cullen, among others – were in fact expressing the 'artistic truth' of black lives with increasing vividness and power, McKay was being more than a little self-deprecating. He was right, however, to suggest that his addressee could potentially make good use of her cultural capital as a white author to put into the public domain a collaborative piece of work which would be fresh and revelatory. She was Nancy Cunard, a British aristocrat descended from the shipping baron Samuel Cunard, though by no means the wealthy 'heiress' the media sensationally portrayed her as. Already something of a celebrity as a poet, writer, journalist, art collector, artistic muse, music aficionado and publisher, Cunard had written to McKay to solicit a contribution for her anthology, *Negro*, originally titled *Colour*. The owner of the Hours, a small press which published European avant-garde work, and also a discerning collector of African artefacts, Cunard wanted to curate a panoramic work that would at once function as a cultural history of African and African-American life and as a forum for black liberation globally.[96]

The case which had galvanized her, as well as many others in Britain and continental Europe, to think about the problem of racism and white supremacy was the that of the so-called Scottsboro Boys, the nine young black men in America who had been tried and summarily sentenced (eight of them capitally) for purportedly raping two white women. As was obvious to many, there was no evidence of their guilt; the prosecution was based on the testimony of the two women, one of whom recanted. The League against Imperialism was one of the key constituents of the European Scottsboro campaigns, and Cunard was alongside, operating in Paris, London and New York. Her involvement and networks brought high-powered figures to the international defence of the Scottsboro nine, including Ezra Pound, Albert Einstein (a patron of the LAI who had also come out in support of the Meerut detainees) and Charlie Chaplin.[97] The communist-led Scottsboro front also represented, not least through its transatlantic dimensions, the yoking together of anti-racism and anticolonialism in a global frame. In Britain, the campaign drew on the momentum generated by the smaller Meerut campaign, attracting many of the same key figures, including Saklatvala and Bridgeman. As a response to that moment, the *Negro* anthology constitutes a declaration that the raced voices of the colonized-in-struggle would henceforth have to be central to the project of decolonization. Symptomatic of this centrality was the change of the anthology's title from *Colour*, with its emphasis on racial oppression, to *Negro*, with the agency and voices of black people in the foreground.[98] The anthology not only produces 'blackness as an inescapable presence', but places the historical condition of blackness as a necessary particular through which it would be possible to think in world-historical terms.[99]

Cunard's personal motivations for putting together this monumental volume have been the subject of much salacious and excessively psychoanalytical speculation; these need not detain us, not least because they detract from the importance of the anthology's insistently collective dimensions. While it is certainly true that her romantic relationship with the African-American jazz musician Henry Crowder, to whom she dedicated the volume, and concomitant alienation from her viciously racist mother, Emerald (Maud) Cunard, were shaping factors in Cunard's life at the time she undertook the project, these factors, or theories of 'self-abnegation', are

Nancy Cunard in her print studio in France

less interesting and significant than the work's own intellectual contours, both as Nancy Cunard conceived of them and as they actually
emerged in a volume of quite remarkable collective genius. Testimony
to the coalitional nature of resistance itself, the book emerged as
necessarily collaborative. It was rooted in Cunard's friendships with
black musicians, writers, artists and photographers, and her sense
that any resolution of the 'Negro question' would require engagement with the histories and struggles of black peoples across the
globe. In later correspondence with Dorothy Padmore, Cunard

would recall that George Padmore, who would become a close friend, was 'the principal and most important of the many contributors to the large African section of the work', and would declare her own indebtedness to his 'stupefying' knowledge of Africa, 'with its great complexity of conditions in all the diverse colonies, the comparisons to be drawn between them, the knowledge of local laws and circumstances, and how much more'.[100] Cunard has been justifiably described as herself a living black internationalist network; equally, the text, and Cunard's editorship of it, were made possible by the black internationalist moment, one in which learning about and from the lives of others was constitutive of solidarity.[101] As one critic has noted of *Negro*, drawing on Walter Benjamin, 'assembling, collecting, and curating as a cultural and aesthetic practice can make occluded and excluded histories visible'.[102] Cunard described her own 'arduous anthological road', to which sustained study was integral, as one that 'held many surprises'; before commencing it, she had asked herself whether she could 'not learn a great deal in Africa, of the Africans themselves, they in their endless diversity'.[103] Certainly, Cunard's personal papers make clear that an enormous amount of work went into the making of the anthology, with copious notes, drawings, maps and letters among the preparatory materials for it. Signing off letters of solicitation addressed to a 'Dear Collaborator' with 'Yours for the freeing of the innocent Scottsboro boys and the true emancipation of the Negro peoples', Cunard worked into the anthology a unique combination of harrowing accounts of oppression and exhilarating portraits of black music, art and literature. The latter spoke to the existence of plentiful cultural and political resources for liberation and reconstruction. Scholarship has sometimes been befuddled by a text that is collaborative on a global scale, moving between representations of oppression and resistance, and attempting, despite the strong editorial presence of Cunard, to facilitate black self-representation in all its diversity. With photographs of jazz musicians and African art interleaved with visual depictions of lynching, *Negro*, some critics have suggested, is hampered by the lack of 'an overarching narrative' and 'relies on the juxtaposition of many unrelated or loosely related materials'.[104] But this is to overlook the volume's explicit investment in heterogeneity as both content and form, setting itself as it does against monolithic and flattening narratives of blackness. The eminent African-American academic and critic Alain Locke wrote to Cunard after receiving his copy, describing it as

> the finest anthology in every sense of the word ever compiled on the Negro. When I saw the announcements, I feared a scrap book, but by a miracle of arrangement, you have built up a unity of effect and a subtle accumulative force of enlightenment that is beyond all contradiction and evasion. It is just the kind of thing needed at this time; and all of us are grateful.[105]

As Jane Marcus has argued, the relative neglect of Cunard, 'an auto-didact, a self-made intellectual and political organiser', in literary scholarship is striking.[106] She suggests that the absence of Cunard in histories of both modernism and the Harlem Renaissance has been made possible by either dismissing her contribution to various fields of knowledge or belittling her as 'an English heiress slumming in search of sex with black men'.[107] (When Cunard arrived in the United States to commence research for the book, she received voluminous amounts of horrifyingly racist and misogynist hate mail suggesting that sex with black men was her main aim.)[108] It could be argued that it is precisely Cunard's deliberate undoing of the lines between modernist aesthetics and political engagement with race and empire, as well as the emphasis she placed on the raced black voice, that accounts for why she has, 'until recently, been culturally and histori-cally marginalized or ignored'.[109] The story of *Negro* is one in which Cunard occupies the position of an auteur, but one who makes clear the importance of colonized and oppressed black people represent-ing themselves. Cunard's own interventions in the volume are better situated as part of the project of constructing solidarity through the anthology's form, rather than 'hierarchizing the interpretation of its contents'.[110] Similarly, there is little sense of Cunard's 'refusal to acknowledge her race and class privilege as a white vanguard poet and activist'; if anything there is an insistence that, while white sup-porters must use their connections and resources, it was imperative for blackness to be central.[111] Indeed, it was a question not of 'includ-ing' black voices, but of reconfiguring the understanding of world history to make black experience central to it – what Robin Kelley calls 'the quest to situate black and brown peoples at the center of world history'.[112] Throughout her writing career, privately and publicly, Cunard was insistent on the need for the colonized and oppressed to speak for themselves: 'It is very good to have a book on Africa by an African', she wrote of *Africa Answers Back* by Prince Akiki K. Nyabongo.[113] 'Permit me to ask', she ventured in a scathing letter to the *Spectator* magazine on the topic of race and racism, sent sometime in 1931, 'if you have ever discussed the subject with the person best qualified to speak on it: with the Negro himself?'[114] In preparing the anthology, Cunard positioned herself as both a student of black life and a curator of its enormous diversity – succeeding, as one interlocutor noted, in bringing together its many dimensions in a 'variegated and comprehensive' volume. 'What a marvellous, magnificent piece of bookmaking it is!' noted another correspondent.[115] She freely sought and received the advice and assistance of writers like McKay, who put her in touch with various Jamaican contacts, and Hughes, who regarded her as 'one of my favourite folks in the world'.[116] The volume was not easy to place with a publisher; in addition to carrying an explosive combination of radical politics and a direct confrontation with racial and colonial ideologies, it would require hundreds of pages of typesetting. The expensive printing (£1,500 – a small fortune) of the volume, published by Wishart in London after being turned down by publishers like Jonathan Cape and Victor Gollancz, was ultimately, and with a degree of poetic justice, funded by libel suits brought by Cunard against publications which had carried stories about her supposed liaisons with black men, such as the radical singer and actor Paul Robeson. Marcus is right to suggest that Cunard was 'very much aware of the form of the anthology as cultural capital', deliberately producing 'a weighty and dignified tome' that would materially represent the weight of black contributions to art, politics, letters and music. It was 'necessary' not only to make this book, but to make it 'in this manner', Cunard notes in her foreword.

Negro is regarded, even by some of its detractors, as a stupendous textual achievement, motivated by what Cunard described as 'the longing to fight'.[117] As early as 1932, McKay had told Cunard that, since her book 'is so different in spirit and plan from anything that had been done before ... it might become when it was published the rallying-point for a strong new expression'.[118] Introducing an abridged version in 1970, Hugh Ford noted pithily: 'One of the most astonishing facts about *Negro* is its existence; another is its author'.[119] Famously weighing eight pounds and nearly three inches thick, it brings together 250 articles written by 150 different people, the large majority black – from the United States, the West Indies and various African countries – but also several white authors from the United States, France and Britain.[120] Samuel Beckett undertook many of the translations from the French, as did Cunard's cousins, Victor and Edward.[121] Other already famous names who contributed to it included Ezra Pound, Langston Hughes and André Breton; a significant number of authors included were black women. Within its 855 pages – which cover the United States substantially, but also Africa, the Caribbean, South America and Europe – 385 illustrations are to be found, including photographs of artworks. Manifestos, photography, sculpture, political analysis, historical retrospectives, ethnography – the volume covers a remarkable breadth of non-fictional genres, in addition to several pages of poetry and music, all aimed at elucidating not only the diversity and significance of black cultures, but also the history of enslavement, colonization and resistance. It was constitutively heterogeneous, a contrapuntal ensemble showcasing black voices of different political stripes. One contributor, Eugene Gordon, observes: 'In general, the anthology is excellent, because it has brought together in one volume the opinions of persons who think about the negro in *different ways*'.[122] At the same time, the common condition of oppression, from 'the docks of Sierra Leone' and 'the diamond mines of Kimberley' to the 'banana lands of Central America' and the 'streets of Harlem', made blackness not just one political standpoint among others, but one vested with an epistemic privilege out of which a transformative critical analysis might emerge on a global scale.[123]

Certainly, part of Cunard's motivation, described in her satirical broadside against her mother and her friends in the London intelligentsia, 'Black Man and White Ladyship', was to address those willed gaps in historical understanding that gave enslavement and colonialism their justification – the lack of written records, super-cities and machines:

'In Africa,' you say, 'the Negro is a savage, he has produced nothing, he has no history.' It is certainly true that he has not got himself mixed up with machinery and science to fly the Atlantic, turn out engines, run up skyscrapers and contrive holocausts. There are no tribal Presses emitting the day's lies and millions of useless volumes. There remain no written records; the wars, the kingdoms and the changes have sufficed unto themselves. It is not one country but many; well over 400 separate languages and their dialects are known to exist. Who tells you you are the better off for being 'civil-ised' when you live in the shadow of the next war or revolution in constant terror of being ruined or killed? ... How come, white man, is the rest of the world to be re-formed in your dreary and decadent image?[124]

In her own initial planning notes for the volume, even as she knew that music, art and photography might be central, Cunard would explic-itly solicit 'outspoken criticism, comment and comparison from the Negro on the present-day civilisations' across continents.[125] Cunard wanted the anthology to be one among many correctives to what she regarded as the prejudiced and paternal handling of African topics by so many white writers. One of the most innovative and politically significant curatorial principles governing *Negro* is the illumination of connections between languages, art, music, literature, folklore and customs, on the one hand, and resistance, organization, movements, achievements, leadership, protest and self-assertion, on the other. Thus, the 800-odd pages give us not a seamless but a textured, some-times unwieldy, constellation of writers, genres and themes, from Zora Neale Hurston on black forms of 'expression' to short biog-raphies of Harriet Tubman, Sojourner Truth and Phillis Wheatley; from harrowing descriptions and photographs of actual lynchings to memoirs of racism, accounts of starvation in Cuba and labour conditions in Jamaica; from poetry by Langston Hughes to sheet music for songs to Barongo proverbs and polemics on the state of Africa and the West Indies by Hughes, George Padmore and Nnamdi (Ben) Azikiwe. Far from being articulated from the perspective of a European understanding of universalism, the anthology sought to understand universalism itself differently, as articulated from multi-ple sites, and as a rather more textured ideal than had been rendered by colonialism.[126] To put it in Aimé Césaire's resonant words, what was being mooted was 'a different idea of the universal. It is a universal rich with all that is particular, rich with all the particulars there are, the deepening of each particular, the coexistence of them all'.[127]

Irina Rasmussen Goloubeva has observed that 'Cunard's anthology ventures into ideologically treacherous ground', risking accusations of 'the European appropriation and re-contextualization of African art'.[128] Cunard has not been immune to such charges. Yet, these would only have traction if the authorship of the anthology could be defined as solely Cunard's, or its main purpose an exercise in European modernism. Accusers would, however, need to overlook the extent to which the anthology aspired to produce an understanding of the universal that was precisely not reducible to the European, or even to modernism. As Goloubeva indicates, it is necessary to be attentive to the 'world-historical' dimensions of the anthology – but also, I think, to its iterative interest in the black contribution – African, African-American and West Indian – as *constitutive* of 'world history'.[129] In this light, it is, as Warren Friedman suggests, 'remarkable that *Negro* has largely disappeared as a cultural and historic document', if nonetheless symptomatic of how the privileged archives of anticolonialism have been so partially and patchily put together.[130] Forged in a crucible which brought together avant-garde culture, communism, anticolonialism, jazz and anti-racism, *Negro* is anything but a footnote. Rather, it is a collective document – or, as Raymond Michelet, Cunard's collaborator on the anthology, saw it, a *livre collectif* of anticolonialism as necessarily constituted by contending voices from the colonial and transatlantic peripheries.[131] Peter Kalliney suggests that *Negro* 'constitutes one of those very special sets of circumstances in which white and colonial intellectuals were almost, but not quite, equal partners in an institution of cultural production'.[132] While it is the case, as McKay's comments also make clear, that white allies like Cunard had access to more powerful networks and institutional resources than black writers, for Cunard herself the equality of participants in the *Negro* project was key; white contributors to the anthology were not paternalist mentors but 'honest defenders, admirers of the Negro on an exactly equal footing'.[133] The anthology itself, in other words, enacted solidarity through cross-racial alliances. It was, in many ways, as Hugh Ford suggests, an effort to bypass the discourses of 'extending' rights in favour of the assertion of something like 'black power'.[134] What Cunard was trying to avoid for black voices is, ironically, what happened to her in the end – written out of cultural history, 'marginalized by being transmuted into an iconic figure', and thereby converted into a containable 'cultural footnote'.[135] The relative neglect of *Negro* is not, then, simply a signifier of missing individual pieces in a modernist puzzle, but also part of the larger and even more consequential elision of crucial dialectical strands in the history of anticolonialism.

While some attention has been paid to its place in the history of modernism, and, via Brent Hayes Edwards's important work, to its role in 'recording' black internationalism, the *Negro* project has been largely overlooked as a central text in its own right in the annals of anticolonialism and in the history of specific endeavours to form transcontinental and cross-racial alliances of resistance.[136] Its importance really lies in its unashamedly exploratory and reverse-pedagogical aims – Africa teaching Europe, colony teaching metropole, and, in some cases, black teaching white. With resistance as its central thematic, *Negro*'s subversive potential can be gauged from the fact that it was banned as seditious by colonial administrations in parts of Africa and the Caribbean. As Cunard makes immediately clear in her foreword, the most important aspect of the anthology of some 150 black and white voices (although two-thirds are of African heritage) is its emphasis on 'spirit and determination' in struggle as a response to oppression. Throughout, there is a sense of black life as fundamentally shaped by resistance to oppression and attempts to crush that resistance; the anthological 'panorama' which documents both phenomena is for the 'recording of the struggles and achievements, the persecutions and the revolts against them, of the Negro peoples'.[137] In this sense, the scandal of Scottsboro is metonymic, 'part of the effort to force into the dumbest and most terrorised form of subjection all Negro workers who dare aspire to live otherwise than as virtual slaves'.[138] Seriously engaged as it is with music and art (sheet music is included), the *Negro* anthology has its own keynote; 'the chord of oppression, struggle and protest rings, trumpet-like or muffled, but always insistent throughout'.[139] Black art, education, letters and music are important as documents of a 'diverse genius', and a 'spirit of determination … to break through the mountain of tyranny', even as some black people cleaved to the idea that 'justice will come to them from some eventual liberality in the white man'.[140] Writing in 1932, when the glittering hopes of 1917 remained a beacon for many, Cunard is open about her own conviction 'that it is Communism alone which throws down the barriers of race as finally as it wipes out class distinctions'.[141] As one critic has noted, 'far more important than speculations about what the Soviet Union may have accomplished (and did not) in terms of race relations, is the appeal of revolutionary rupture to open the present moment to alternative visions and possibilities outside of European cosmopolitanism'.[142] Although Cunard was never herself formally allied with the Communist Party and many of her contributors were not communists, the anthology was put together at a historical moment when communism clearly provided a compelling vision of internationalism and cross-racial solidarity. In one sense, then, the anthology puts black and white voices in engagement not only with each other, but also with communist internationalism. At the same time, the anthology's dialogical attempt to bring together multiple voices across national, racial and political lines sets itself within a longer history of alliances of solidarity between Europeans and non-Europeans: 'From the beginning of the Anti-Slavery struggle to the present-day official and social obstructions of the Colour-bar there have been voices to protest against the infamous treatment of coloured people.'[143] It is with a black fellow-traveller's voice that the volume opens – Langston Hughes's 'revolutionary voice of liberation' insisting famously: 'I, too, am America.'[144]

While there is not the space here to discuss the entirety of the *Negro* volume, one recurrent feature demands our attention. In the context of the emergence of twentieth-century anticolonialism as a decisive rejection of theories of tutelage and trusteeship, the shared critique of paternalism common to many otherwise diverse essays is striking. In one of the first essays in the volume, a mock-anthropological polemic against segregation and racism shot through with barely concealed anger, the African-American singer Taylor Gordon amplifies Cunard's own introductory repudiation of the idea that the white man was in Africa for the black man's good: 'The caucasians [*sic*] are queer people. They think that any other people that can't see things as they do are to be pitied and cared for. That if there's ever

an eternal peace among men, it will be because of their generosity.'[145]
It is almost impossible, given the way the literary sphere is segregated, to 'read what the Negro really thinks'.[146] Other writers, like the African-American scholar of Romance languages John Frederick Matheus, are no less stringent about the structural absences that facilitate both racism and paternalism: 'European ignorance of the African Negro is monumental, and misinformation concerning the American Negro ridiculous, but in most cases not a bigoted prejudice, but sheer lack of knowledge.'[147] Many essays in the volume seek to correct this ignorance, not least around black agency and the ways in which black struggle exerted pressures upon and elicited transformations in Western polities. An unsigned article, taken from the left-wing journal *The Liberator*, notes that while abolitionists like William Lloyd Garrison often took fright at the thought of slave rebellions, believing words and pleas would suffice, actual rebellions often had the effect of furthering the cause of freedom: 'Anti-slavery sentiment flared up even in the Southern States immediately after the Nat Turner rebellion. A number of petitions were circulated in Virginia, to the effect that, since the slaves had proved themselves so ready to fight for their liberty, it was hopeless to try to keep the Negroes enslaved.'[148] The fact that slave revolts had essentially been written out of histories accounted for the undue prominence given to gradualism and petitioning in the abolitionist tradition. An article by Du Bois, taken from his journal *The Crisis*, also speaks of a long history of slave revolts, going on to observe with calm audacity that, quite apart from the black role in Emancipation, black agency had forged America itself. Democracy in America 'has been developed because of the pressure of the slaves for freedom and recognition'; American women as a whole gained more status because 'the Negro woman was a working woman before she was a housewife', whose example spread to white working women; Negro art – music, literature, dancing – made a 'permanent contribution to American civilisation'; and public schools were an 'accepted institution, primarily because of the insistence of Negroes on free education'.[149] Black labour had, of course, been fundamental to the making of America. Noting that black people had always 'reacted and reacted sharply' to their surroundings, Du Bois invokes a tradition of 'many strong individual Negro thinkers' across the Americas, as well as the success

of the Haitian revolt.[150] Yet Western thought routinely played down black agency, preferring instead the 'widely held assumption that there is no inner reaction among the Negroes; that you are dealing with a people who, while they are swayed by certain primitive feelings and instincts, are not thinking and planning or moving in any self-motivated ways'.[151] Michel-Rolph Trouillot makes a similar point when he notes that the Western historiography of the Haitian Revolution routinely trivializes 'the slaves' independent sense of their right to freedom and the right to achieve this freedom by the force of arms'.[152]

Du Bois's essay was prefaced by a critical and somewhat crude demolition job from Cunard which both rehearsed the hostility of the Communist Party towards him and the NAACP and insisted that 'the Communists are ... *the only* defenders of the oppressed Negro masses'.[153] Given Cunard's leanings, and despite its undoubted political diversity, the weight of the volume comes down on the side of communism as the only social form which would end both racial and class exploitation. James W. Ford, an erstwhile vice-presidential candidate fielded by the Communist Party, wrote an essay for the volume called 'Communism and the Negro', which also attacked the NAACP as 'petty bourgeois Negro reformists'.[154] While accusing reformists (with more than a touch of purple prose) of attempting 'to hide and destroy the revolutionary traditions of the Negro masses', Ford too – ironically, in much the same vein as Du Bois – paid homage to slave rebel leaders like Denmark Vesey, Gabriel Prosser and Nat Turner, as well as to the Haitians; all of these examples illustrated that liberation was not 'something to be handed down, or denied, from above'.[155] Reformism is the enemy, whether offered as 'a favour from above' or solicited by the 'boot-licking diplomacy' of the 'Negro petty bourgeoisie', whose 'misleaders' both make use of and hinder the liberation struggle by winning petty concessions from power without insisting on radical change.[156] Liberalism too is identified as a problem, shamelessly peddling illusions 'such as the "possibility" of liberation without a struggle against imperialism, of real democracy under robber capitalism, of emancipation from the skies'.[157] Cunard picks up on this theme in her own comprehensive essay on the history of Jamaica with an assessment of the importance, but also the limitations, of Marcus Garvey's back-to-Africa movement: 'He does not see that the white imperialists will never *give*, but that they must be *forced*, and for this that the actual condition, the system itself, must be revolutionarily changed.'[158]

Frequently illuminating the connection between imperialism abroad and racism at home, the anthology as a whole is also unstinting in its criticism of the 'colour bar' in both Britain and the United States. In a damning account of how the colour bar operates in British hotels, Cunard attacks the 'vicious and scandalous actions of the English against people of colour', many of whom are subjects of the British Empire or 'other white capitalist nations'.[159] Her angry account here includes a letter by Reginald Bridgeman on behalf of the LAI to the British Home Office protesting racial discrimination in hotels, but to no avail, leading Cunard to observe bitterly: '"Teach niggers their 'place'" is as much the government view as it has ever been.'[160] Domestic metropolitan fights against racism were connected to the global anticolonial struggle, as an article taken from the *Negro Worker*, edited and probably authored by George Padmore, observed: 'The British ruling class, frightened by the growing revolts of the colonial peoples for national freedom and self-determination on the one hand, and the solidarity struggles of white and coloured workers in England on the other, are intensifying racial and national chauvinism.'[161] Once again, liberalism, with its petitioning advocacy of 'better' race relations – the reference here is to the League of Coloured Peoples – acted 'to put a brake upon the growing resentment of the coloured workers and students against the shameful way in which they are being treated in this so-called democratic country'.[162]

The historical example of free Haiti runs through several essays, underscoring the history and relevance to the present of black resistance and self-emancipation. But it is Ethiopia which provides a contemporary focal point for discussions of black self-assertion and independent governance. As we shall see, within two years of the publication of *Negro*, the invasion of Ethiopia would also become a rallying point for anticolonial organization. In 'Ethiopia Today', a piece which would later cause him to be pilloried by some communists as supporting a feudal reactionary emperor, Padmore observes that the huge symbolic importance of that nation derives from the fact that Ethiopians are 'the first non-European peoples since the Haitian Revolution to defeat the white race at arms'.[163] Ethiopia's closest contemporary in this regard was the republic of Liberia, which, however, suffered from a heavy US capitalist presence, and was 'mortgaged to the Firestone Rubber Company, thanks to the machinations of Yankee dollar diplomacy'.[164] The very fact of Liberia, 'that a Negro republic exists in Africa' at all, writes Ben N. Azikiwe (Nnamdi Azikiwe), the prominent Nigerian nationalist and later first president of independent Nigeria, 'naturally makes the white man conscious of the psychological effect of this on the self-determination of other indigenous natives'.[165] That in itself explained the several incursions made upon Liberia's sovereignty by European powers, including Britain. Liberia also gave the lie to another cherished colonial idea: that the black man had no 'political capacity' for self-rule. Azikiwe is defensive about the charge that Liberia was guilty of forced-labour practices, admitting that these must be eradicated but pointing to the hypocrisy in singling the black republic out when other African colonial possessions were guilty of the same, including 'the incompetent semi-sovereign state of the Union of South Africa'.[166] Ultimately, the republics of Haiti and Liberia 'withstand the buffets and assaults of imperial countries' to show that 'the Negro ... is capable of directing his political destiny and that 'the African is a natural statesman' with plenty of institutions of governance to draw on: 'If his past history reveals such genuine evidences of political capacity, then his future needs no further comments or conjectures ... Take it or leave it.'[167] On the same topic, the Harlem writer George S. Schuyler notes that the exploitation of labour is hardly unique to Liberia, for in 'the richest country in the world', the United States, millions 'were absolutely dependent upon grudging charity for their few crumbs of daily bread. No one was secure.'[168] In the hinterland of Liberia, on the other hand, in village after village, all denizens work, eat and have shelter because 'the land, on which all depend for a living, cannot be bartered or sold by a few individuals but belongs to the tribal collectivity, and therefore cannot be disposed of'.[169] The future Kenyan leader Johnstone (Jomo) Kenyatta would also observe in his contribution to the anthology that 'forced labor has no limits under the rule of British imperialism', which liked to call it 'communal labor'.[170] Africa had its flaws, but the imperial powers were in no position to call themselves superior.

If the project of *Negro* was to lay out a panoramic history of black life and struggle across continents, using the tools of ethnography, among others, it was also a counter-history of Western imperialism and, relatedly, of 'whiteness'. The last sections of the book prefigure later modes of 'colonial discourse analysis' in offering scathing and detailed examinations of the discursive modes and justificatory narratives of imperial apologetics – a kind of reverse ethnography. The Surrealist Group in Paris, for instance, contributed an essay translated by Samuel Beckett, resonantly entitled 'Murderous Humanitarianism', which observed: 'The white man preaches, doses, vaccinates, assassinates and (from himself) receives absolution. With his psalms, his speeches, his guarantees of liberty, equality and fraternity, he seeks to drown the noise of his machine-guns.'[171] Inverting the usual terms of both ethnography and the civilizing mission, the pioneering Nigerian educationist T. K. Utchay undertakes to examine 'the most barbarous thing in modern civilisation'; 'white-manning', he writes, is 'a technical word to describe one of the world's strangest actions ever in existence' whereby one set of human beings think themselves superior to another simply by accident of a 'white skin'.[172] The term can be extended to those not of a white skin who, nonetheless, defer to white supremacy. 'White-manning' is, by definition, an identity politics focused on the entitlements of a particular racial type; it enables a person, 'by virtue of his white skin, to ask and claim first consideration in every walk of life, in health, in position, in comfort and in luxury'.[173] This includes, of course, a far greater cut of the material pie – wages twelve times those of the black man, for instance. 'White-manning' is not an inherent quality, Utchay stresses, but in fact an historical *response* to resistance at the point when 'the black man wants to share in the natural and unlimited liberty enjoyed by the white'.[174] For practitioners of 'white-manning', paternalism met with gratitude was acceptable: 'The picture used to be the figure of a white boy stooping over his willing black pet. The white man pitied and determined to raise the black man's condition to that of a civilised being, and set himself to work.'[175] However, a black person's claims to being equal were deemed insupportable: 'How can he be? To me this is insolence.'[176]

Negro's interest in universalism as constituted by thick particulars means that the tendency of the anthology is to reject both positivism and radical alterity. The anthology's critique of colonial discourse is paired with extensively researched and detailed accounts of diverse African cultural resources and political institutions, some of which have been decimated by the colonial encounter, while others could provide the basis for independent polities to draw on. Especially interesting here are the contributions of Cunard's collaborator on the volume, the young Frenchman Raymond Michelet, whose work features prominently towards the end. In 'African Empires and Civilisations', Michelet delineates at great length the tremendous diversity of various African polities and political institutions, taking pains to note, without unduly romanticizing them, that many states 'enjoyed genuine prosperity' as well as indigenous industries, several of which were now gone forever.[177] '"Primitive" Life and Mentality' takes on Western colonial renditions of black thought in order to demolish the 'extenuating' notion of the inferior negro whose modes of thought and living are utterly different: 'The system of forcing people to work for the exclusive benefit of their masters, on lands that have been stolen from them and under conditions verging on slavery, if not worse, very soon creates its own ideology, namely, that these people are, by definition, inferior and only receive the treatment they deserve.'[178] It is an ideology facilitated by the complete lack of interest in understanding how the indigenes of these stolen lands actually think, since the travellers and colonists who wrote accounts of these cultures were 'less interested in what a thing meant than in how it looked and how they looked beside it'.[179] At best, there is some cursory acknowledgement of the picturesque and the beautiful, but 'the white men on the spot are in no way concerned with understanding the natives, but only with extracting from them the maximum'; 'imperialists of learning' are represented by the likes of one major intellectual who holds forth on the supposed 'pre-logicism' of the 'black mentality', but 'has never spoken with an African in his life':[180]

In this system the savage appears as a kind of dismantled creature, bound to his environment, his group, food, dwelling, wife or wives, law of his clan, etc., by a variety of 'mystical participations', which are presented with the utmost extravagance by M. Lévy-Brûhl and his school. It is on this account, we are informed, that the behaviour of the Negroes is inexplicable and unreasonable ... so

that it is really nothing, but the old legend dressed up to the latest
nines.[181]

Only by working expropriated land for the European and learning
Christian morality is the black person deemed to emerge 'from their
vale of folly and ignorance into the light of pure reason'.[182]

It is not just Michelet's attack on questionable stereotyping that
is of significance here. More valuable is his refusal of both absolute
difference and total equivalence in approaching black cultures – or
what Césaire describes as the Western ethnographic 'insistence on
the marginal, "separate" character of the non-whites'.[183] Even as he
rejects 'the model white rationalist ... as the archetype of truth and
practical wisdom', Michelet charges existing inquiries into black life
and thought with making

> no attempt to understand how these 'strange' thoughts and actions
> may be an integral part of life itself, profoundly human and often
> evincing, what is more, an acute perception of reality and an ability
> to harness its most hidden resources – so acute indeed that it cannot
> immediately be apprehended by the narrow, cocksure brain of the
> European (or American) positivist.[184]

Rather than compare degrees of closeness to or difference from 'the
model white rationalist', Michelet advocates studying specific historical and ecological circumstances in which, for instance, some people
'were at liberty to develop in themselves to a high degree certain
modes of perception and of action, apparently extra-scientific, but
symptomatic in effect of reality quite as real, if not more so, as [sic] the
positivist world of the European'.[185] Michelet is talking here of that
which is deemed to be 'magical' and 'bizarre', pointing out through a
series of examples that many beliefs that seem 'strange have only to
be examined with a little attention to become perfectly human and
normal'.[186] It is possible to identify historical specificities and cultural particularities without taking them to be 'the sign of a singular
mentality'. The mind, in certain circumstances, can relate differently
to the magical or the ineffable without therefore being incapable of
reason or ratiocination. Scientific and experimental modes of thought
are not absent in Africa, as shown by the existence of everything

from metal-works and medicine to weapons and weaving looms. Michelet anticipates something of Césaire's famous polemic against Eurocentric assumptions here: 'That the West has invented science. That the West alone knows how to think; that at the borders of the Western world there begins the shadowy realm of primitive thinking, which, dominated by the notion of participation, incapable of logic, is the very model of faulty thinking.'[187] Significantly, Michelet diagnoses the widely held colonial belief in the African's 'positively chronic *inaptitude* to learn or receive fresh vigour from any alien source whatsoever' as a *colonial* failure – a failure to read resistance to 'European importations' as a reasoned and deliberate choice, a failure 'to realise that their refusal to abandon their way of living does not arise from an inability to assess for what it is worth the substitute proposed to them, but on the contrary from a definite act of preference and with full knowledge of what they are doing'.[188] The European Positivist, however, is so hampered by his own pompous imagination and determination to impute inferiority that all evidence, including that of 'a particularly rapid and accurate ratiocination', ceases to matter.[189] Here, Michelet draws on the example of African languages, both the specific 'richness of their vocabularies, forms, locutions' and the existence of equivalents for European terms.[190] Given their inability to grasp the complexities of African thought, Michelet asks, could the truth be the inverse of the standard claim – that the real 'arrested mentality' is, in fact, that of the European anthropologist? Michelet's alternative reading of Africans refusing to be treated by a white doctor, frequently cited as 'another example of Negro stupidity and fastidiousness', suggests that, once again, it is black resistance that is at stake.[191] Drawing on the work of M. Leroy, Michelet points out that many Africans repudiated white doctors because they justifiably associated European medicine with brutality and violence. This was a point Fanon would also make years later in his essay 'Colonialism and Medicine': 'It is necessary to analyze, patiently and lucidly, each of the reactions of the colonized, and every time we do not understand, we must tell ourselves that we are the heart of the drama – that of the impossibility of finding a meeting ground in any colonial situation.'[192] In his closing essay to *Negro*, 'The White Man Is Killing Africa', Michelet lists, alongside a comprehensive index of colonial crimes, multiple colonial insurgencies, from French West

Africa to British Gambia, and from the Gold Coast to Nyasaland and South Africa, and observes acerbically: 'THE NATIVES ARE EVIDENTLY SO WELL SATISFIED WITH THE NEW RÉGIME OF PEACE AND HAPPINESS BROUGHT IN BY THE EUROPEANS THAT AMONG THE RISINGS WHICH EACH GOVERNMENT ATTEMPTS TO KEEP DARK MAY BE ENUMERATED ...'.[193] A long list of uprisings follows, from French Guinea and the Ivory Coast to Nigeria, Cameroon and Madagascar.

Towards Ethiopia: Re-centring Africa

McKay pulled his piece from *Negro* when Cunard told him she could not afford to pay for the work, at which point an extensive correspondence appears to have come to an end along with a budding friendship.[194] In a stern penultimate letter, McKay informed Cunard that his own romanticism about literature was 'different from those nice people's who ask and expect artists to write, sing and perform in other ways freely and charitably for a cause while they would not dream of asking the carpenter, caterer and others who do the manual tasks to work for nothing'.[195] Both Pankhurst and Cunard would go on to become stentorian and committed voices on the British anti-colonial left, and both would speak out forcefully against the Italian invasion of Abyssinia, as well as against fascism in Germany, Italy and Spain. Pankhurst would excoriate Britain for standing by while 'Ethiopia was vanquished', attributing this failure to colonial thinking whereby 'this is only Africa, this is not a White Man's country'.[196] She would repeatedly insist that the rank and file of the British labour movement had to understand that 'imperialism is intimately bound up with its own enslavement to the capitalist system. International solidarity is a sentiment which only attains a sturdy growth among those who are convinced that capitalism has had its day.'[197] For her, there were clear continuities between anticolonialism and anti-fascism, both of which involved the exercise of violence, governmental and extra-governmental, in the service of the capitalist state. In May 1936, after the invasion of Ethiopia/Abyssinia, Pankhurst launched the *New Times and Ethiopia News*, which remained in circulation for twenty years and would be a prominent campaigning organ against fascism and colonialism. It provided an important forum for black nationalism, not least in the form of a regular column titled 'Africa for the Africans'.[198] Like Cunard, Pankhurst grasped the value of African history being written by Africans. From the time McKay had been involved in it, her paper provided a forum for black academics and journalists; unlike many on the white left who dismissed Haile Selassie as a feudal relic, she developed a friendship with the emperor, understanding his positive symbolic value for black anti-colonial campaigners.

'Poets are the trumpets that sing to battle.'[199] With this in mind, Nancy Cunard hoped to put together another volume after *Negro*, this time 'a short symposium of poetry' that would 'make a record of the Negro's rising spirit against oppression'. To be titled 'Revolution – the Negro Speaks', the book never materialized, although she drafted and sent out a call for contributions for a collection of poems which, as far as possible, should be 'inspired by some revolutionary event, some phase of the struggle in Negro history, past and present'.[200] Her aim was to commemorate insurgency, revolutionary events and resistance struggles in black history, once again emphasizing the black subject not as 'slave' or 'victim' but as a 'revolutionary-born'.[201] Cunard would remain heavily involved in the Scottsboro case in the decade that followed, having already launched the Scottsboro Defence Fund in London. She would work as a journalist, like Pankhurst – whose *New Times and Ethiopia News* she wrote for – frequently filing pieces for the Associated Negro Press, as well as various West Indian newspapers, on topics such as the invasion of Ethiopia, the Spanish Civil War, black intellectuals in Britain, and 'race relations'. After she died in 1965, alone, depressed and ill, T. K. Utchay would note that he had named a school 'Cunardia' after her, and that she would always have a place in African hearts as one who 'suffered slander, ostracism and loneliness because of us'.[202] Whether or not it became, as Mckay hoped it would, 'the rallying-point for a strong new expression', *Negro* is now recognized as 'ahead of its time, bursting with ideas whose time had only come in the intervening years or have yet to come'.[203] Many of those ideas would be elucidated by black intellectuals in the decades that followed. The invasion of Ethiopia by Italy in 1935, involving the slaughter of 275,000 Ethiopians, would also bring together many London-based black intellectuals and their allies, including Jomo Kenyatta, C. L. R. James and George Padmore, who would join the likes of Pankhurst, Bridgeman and Cunard in another coalition, the International African Friends of Abyssinia, that would once again put blackness – and Africa – at the centre of its analysis.

8

Internationalizing African Opinion: Race, Writing and Resistance

Imagine what it meant to us to go to Hyde Park to speak to a race of people who were considered our masters, and tell them right out what we felt about their empire and about them ... and yet, as George Padmore would say ... 'Where else but in Britain would you get Lord Bridgeman's son heading the League against Imperialism, or the daughter of Lord and Lady Cunard – Nancy – associating with people like George Padmore??'

Ras Makonnen, *Pan-Africanism from Within* (1973)

No race has been so noble in forgiving, but now the hour has struck for our complete emancipation.

Amy Ashwood Garvey, speaking at a
Trafalgar Square rally in 1935

Walking down a London street in May 1935, the young student Francis Nkrumah was feeling dispirited and pondering returning home rather than continuing his onward journey to study in the United States when he 'heard an excited newspaper boy shouting something unintelligible'.[1] As the boy grabbed a bundle of the latest editions, Nkrumah caught sight of the headline on a placard: 'MUSSOLINI INVADES ETHIOPIA'. He would note famously in his autobiography that this shocking piece of news was all that he needed to overcome his malaise: 'At that moment, it was almost as if the whole of London had declared war on me personally. For the next few minutes I could do nothing but glare at each impassive face wondering if those people could possibly realise the wickedness of colonialism ... My nationalism surged to the fore.'[2]

Since Nkrumah was, of course, from the Gold Coast, present-day Ghana, what was being evoked here was something far more expansive and powerful than a nationalism of birthplace. He was not alone; there were others in London and beyond, black thinkers and campaigners from across Africa and the Caribbean, who would be galvanized by incidents in Ethiopia. In London they included figures who would, in many cases, become household names across the decolonizing world: C. L. R. James, Eric Williams, Jomo Kenyatta, I. T. A. Wallace-Johnson, T. Ras Makonnen, Nnamdi Azikiwe, Amy Ashwood Garvey, Chris Braithwaite and George Padmore. In many cases, notably Padmore's, they were socialists and communists disillusioned by the Comintern's vacillations on the question of imperialism during that period, seeking a way to align anti-capitalism to a serious engagement with questions of race, colonialism and culture. The result was what Brent Edwards has described as a 'striking shift from the institutions of international communism to a non-aligned effort at "international African" work'.[3] London at this historical juncture has been described by Minkah Makalani, in a resonant phrase, as providing 'a unique incubator for radical black internationalist discourse'.[4] In his excellent account of C. L. R. James's years in 1930s Britain, Christian Høgsbjerg observes that a critical mass of campaigning figures from the African and Caribbean colonies in London led to 'black, radical, anti-colonialist activists ... developing their own alternative counterculture of resistance in the imperial metropolis alongside more directly political campaigning in Pan-Africanist organizations'.[5] Crucial to this counterculture was a vibrant black press, a 'valuable source for understanding the roles played by Blacks in Britain' during the 1930s and 1940s.[6] As a 'wave of black publications rolled off the presses in the late 1930s' and 'harangued' the British government on a wide range of issues, from Ethiopia itself to the serious Jamaican riots of 1938, they also whetted and sharpened the cutting edge of British criticism of empire.[7]

Two events were vitally catalysing for that counterculture: the labour rebellions that shook the British West Indies from the 1930s onwards and 'forced themselves into the consciousness of the

C. L. R. James giving a speech at a rally for Ethiopia in London

people and rulers of the British Empire', and the Italian invasion of Abyssinia (later Ethiopia) which was met by fierce resistance from the Ethiopians.[8] Very different in their manifestations, and yet possessed of shared features, between them these struggles helped give a high international profile to anticolonial resistance in both African and Caribbean contexts. After the invasion of Ethiopia, black campaigners held anti-war rallies which were attended by people of various ethnicities, including a 'substantial crowd of English people'.[9] At one, Amy Ashwood Garvey, a dynamic force in the London scene, though lamentably ill-represented in its archives, spoke forcefully to European colonizers: 'You have talked of "the White man's burden"

... But now we are carrying yours and standing between you and fascism.'[10] While excellent work has been done on the contributions of black radicals in London and other European capitals, and on the development of transnational and diasporic networks, by Makalani, Matera, Edwards and Pennybacker among others, further attention needs to be paid to the extent to which this radical – and radicalizing – black counterculture in London drew on actually occurring resistances, learning vital lessons from insurgencies on colonial ground and interpreting them to a metropolitan audience. In doing so, black radicals, positioning themselves as both colonial and British in their London base, developed important tenets of anticolonialism, which in turn shaped the approach of their metropolitan allies. They also sought to create institutions and formal networks which would facilitate anticolonial thought and work in the heart of empire. The theory and practice of self-emancipation now emerged as a necessary corollary to an uncompromising rejection of paternalism, while questions of 'blackness', indeed of race itself, became much more salient.

This chapter considers the International African Service Bureau (IASB) and its journal, *International African Opinion*, as metropolitan institutional sites which facilitated the development of an anticolonial counterculture which, while drawing on Marxism, also sought to identify resources for resistance which were embedded in black colonial experiences. While insisting on the specificity of both black oppression and black resistance, this counterculture did not lay claim to incommensurable cultural difference; the task at hand was to reconstitute the grounds of the universal. Gary Wilder's suggestion that 'we now need to be less concerned with unmasking universalism as covert European particularisms than with challenging the assumption that the universal is European property' is relevant here.[11] The radicals of the IASB were doing both, calling European and American claims to universalism to account while re-centring Africa and the West Indies in a new cartography of liberation. Similarly, the diversity of lived experiences of race and global race hierarchies could not simply be reduced to epiphenomenal expressions of economic truths. As interpreters of Ethiopian and Caribbean resistance, the most important contribution of black radicals in London may have been to make questions of labour and capitalism central to black anticolonial thought, and, conversely, to make race and culture more fundamental to metropolitan discussions of labour and anticapitalism. Rather than just 'translating' communist categories into 'the idiom of Pan-Africanism', the task at hand was one of creating a new language that did not repudiate other vocabularies of critique, but sought to bring them in more strenuous engagement with each other.[12] Out of this, would emerge a revitalized collaborative anticolonialism. The collective work of the IASB pointed towards Africa and the West Indies as 'co-producers' of modernity, black intellectuals not just being influenced by European thought, but producing knowledge of the world.[13]

African Emancipation and Black Metropolitan Organizing

> *All this revolutionary history can come as a surprise only to those who, whatever International they belong to, whether Second, Third, or Fourth, have not yet ejected from their systems the pertinacious lies of Anglo-Saxon capitalism. It is not strange that the Negroes revolted. It would have been strange if they had not.*
>
> C. L. R. James, writing as J. R. Johnson

> *The whole history of British colonial rule has taught that native leaders and masses, be they Africans, Indians or West Indians, are only respected if they agitate for their rights and meet their rulers with courage and dignity. Cringing will get Africans nowhere. Let us stop it.*
>
> *International African Opinion*, 1939

On 5 December 1934 a shot rang out in a remote part of Ethiopia known as Wal Wal, where a border dispute was underway between the Italian military, which had occupied Somaliland, and Ethiopian soldiers. A heavy fusillade of fire in two directions followed. At the end of several hours, during which three Italian aeroplanes strafed Ethiopian lines, there were 107 dead on the Ethiopian side and thirty on the Italian. Overpowered, the Ethiopians withdrew, but the incident was the beginning of what came to be known as the 'Abyssinia crisis', an event that would shake up the tenuous peace then prevailing in Europe and cause a flurry of frantic diplomatic activity. Benito Mussolini, Italy's Fascist leader, would use the episode to clear the way for a full-scale invasion of Ethiopia, then the only country on the continent of Africa not under some form of European colonial rule or, in the case of Liberia, United States protection. Emperor Haile Selassie (Ras Tafari), crowned only a few years earlier, in 1930, would take the fateful but hugely important decision not to follow the path of appeasement urged by Britain, but to lay his case before the League of Nations, stating categorically that, as the maps showed, Wal Wal lay well inside sovereign Ethiopian territory.[14] In doing so, he was boldly staking Ethiopia's claim to equality of status with sovereign European nations and, equally significantly, challenging the league to show that its vaunted universal principles – collective security, peace and order – would be applied beyond Europe. His attempt to hold them to their stated universal commitments would fail signally, and that failure, which enabled Italy to invade his kingdom unchallenged, would reverberate across an outraged West Indies and Africa: 'Apart from the Kingdom of the Lord there is not on this earth any nation that is superior to any other', he pronounced firmly.[15] The failure was read, correctly, as a signal that Europe refused to recognize the independent status of a sovereign black African nation – and in doing so, was reifying the status of all of Africa as subjugated, not included in 'universal' rights.[16] Africans were once again marked as something less than wholly free, which was to be less than fully human. If that status had never been acceptable to the enslaved and the colonized, it was now beyond the realm of possibility, to be challenged unequivocally and by black people across continents.

European historians of the Abyssinia crisis have tended to discuss it as a preliminary act of appeasement on the road to fascism which was not 'an episode in the relations between European and African peoples', but rather 'a catalyst of the disintegration of international law and order in Europe, leading to a European and so to a World War'.[17] In contrast, for many colonial subjects in Africa and the West Indies, as well as black intellectuals resident in London, the incursions upon and invasion of the only sovereign and fully independent African nation by a European power was *precisely* about African people and their relation to Europeans. The Ethiopian resistance

represented a radical yet realizable possibility: defeating imperialism and seizing back the continent of Africa. James recalled that the
attack on Ethiopia prompted him and others to organize a campaign
and demand action against Italy, and even to consider forming a military organization to fight the Italians. An important cognitive shift
had taken place with the invasion and Ethiopian resistance to it: a
sense that 'the African revolution', as James termed it, was underway,
and that it was important for black intellectuals to identify themselves 'with those bands, hundreds and thousands of them, who are
still fighting, and for years are going to carry on the fight against
Imperialistic domination of any kind'.[18] The result of this recognition
among black radicals resident in Britain was the formation of the
International African Friends of Abyssinia, which was soon renamed
the International African Friends of Ethiopia. This significant black
presence and flurry of activity in the service of 'colonial emancipation in general and African emancipation in particular' meant,
James opined, that, 'As far as political organisations in England were
concerned the black intellectuals had not only arrived but were significant arrivals.'[19] It also brought black people from various parts of
the globe into alliance, as Makonnen recalls:

> It's very important to put the response of the black world to the
> Ethiopian War into perspective, especially since it is easy to get
> the impression that pan-Africanism was just some type of petty
> protest activity – a few blacks occasionally meeting in conference
> and sending resolutions here and there. But the real dimensions
> can only be gathered by estimating the kind of vast support that
> Ethiopia enjoyed amongst blacks everywhere ... It brought home
> to many black people the reality of colonialism, and exposed its
> true nature ... It was clear that imperialism was a force to be
> reckoned with, because here it was attacking the black man's last
> citadel.[20]

In 'Abyssinia and the Imperialists', a 1936 piece written for *The Keys*,
the journal of the League of Coloured People (LCP), James acerbically hailed the invasion as a salutary pedagogical occasion, for
'Africans and people of African descent, especially those who have
been poisoned by British imperialist education, needed a lesson'.[21]

Abyssinia posed a special challenge for all five imperial powers who
desired it, since the people 'are splendid fighters', making it less easy
for those powers to 'steal it as easily as they had stolen the rest of
Africa'.²² The lesson to be learned from this morass was applicable
across colonial contexts: 'The only thing to save Abyssinia is the
efforts of the Abyssinians themselves and action by the great masses
of Negroes and sympathetic whites and Indians all over the world, by
demonstrations, public meetings, resolutions, financial assistance to
Abyssinia, strikes against the export of all materials to Italy, refusal
to unload Italian ships etc.'²³ It is this recognition that makes the conflict, 'though unfortunate for Abyssinia … of immense benefit to the
race as a whole'.²⁴ What the Abyssinia crisis had indeed done was to
provide a concrete focus for black anticolonialism both in Britain and
beyond, opening up a horizon of imaginative possibility – one that
James would use, along with the ongoing labour unrest in the West
Indies, as an inspiration for the work he had already begun on *The
Black Jacobins*, his great historical ode to black self-emancipation.²⁵
The invasion of Ethiopia, seen as the 'final Caucasian victory', came
to stand in for European colonialism tout court – not least, of course,
due to Britain and France's reluctance to rein in Italy and the far-
from-suppressed admiration accorded by Britain's ruling elites to the
likes of Mussolini.²⁶ There was also material support in the form of
arms and war materials.

That the language of nationhood permeates what was a necessarily transnational endeavour is significant. In his important account
of the black presence in London during this period, Marc Matera
notes that black radicals shunned narrow racial and national chauvinism as 'dangerous illusions'.²⁷ While he is correct to suggest that
many studies of resistance to colonialism have reduced diverse
political imaginaries and struggles to 'a Wilsonian rhetoric of self-
determination', and that 'the nationalist plot occludes whole realms
of political imagination and struggle', the fact also remains that
a substantial amount of effort was put into demanding that principles of self-determination, articulated by both Wilson and Lenin
in very different ways, be genuinely universalized.²⁸ As the case of
Ethiopia suggests, national belonging and transnational affiliations,
nationalism and internationalism, were seen to have a symbiotic
relationship; it was certainly not quite the case that 'the majority of

these black intellectuals and organizations rejected nationalism as a divisive and obsolete paradigm for political community'.[29] In most cases, individuals from the Caribbean and Africa had no independent nations of their own to reject as 'obsolete', which is why tremendous importance was placed on Ethiopia and Haiti as the world's only two independent black nation-states (Liberia had a more ambiguous status). In a sense, the national had to be clawed out of the colonial before a postcolonial – or a postnational – future could be anticipated and imagined. We should be cautious about reading back into a very different political moment that sense of jaded obsolescence which is an affective disposition of our own theoretical present. For these black intellectuals, it was also not just a question of offering solidarity to Ethiopian nationalists; the sovereign statehood of this one country was felt to be vitally organic, its violation symbolic of the violence and injury inflicted upon Africans as a whole. In Cedric Robinson's words, 'Ethiopia' became a point of reference, 'a term signifying historicity and racial dignity in ways the term 'Negro' could not match'.[30] One nationalist newspaper in Sierra Leone went so far as to suggest that 'peoples of the African group will admit that the dictator has done a distinct service' in bringing them together into a united front with differences swept away by 'the magic touch of kinship'.[31] It certainly turned James into a fierce advocate of anticolonial alliances, enjoining 'sufferers from imperialism all over the world, all anxious to help the Ethiopian people', to 'organise yourselves independently'.[32] His metaphor was simple: prisoners broke their own chains – 'Who is the fool that expects our gaolers to break them?'[33] We know that, as a member of the politically moderate LCP in 1933, James was already inclined to advocate a 'spirit of nationalism' to liberate the West Indies from its colonial condition, making the case for 'a West Indian consciousness, and a pride in the matters that pertain to [West Indians]'.[34] With the invasion of Ethiopia, there emerged a clear sense that anticolonialism could therefore be necessarily at once nation-oriented (stressing independence from colonial rule) and determinedly transnational in organizational form: it would deploy the language of nation-states put in instrumental place by empire while defiantly exceeding its territorial and conceptual limits.

This insight made it both possible and necessary to demonstrate how there were or had been viable communities and collective entities which had pre-existed colonial states, and whose resources could yet be deployed in the forging of altogether different post-imperial polities. Part of the impetus here was to lay claim to an understanding of freedom and rights which sought simultaneously to expose the colonizer's version of the universal as in fact parochial, partial and self-serving, and to show that these were concepts with African roots of their own, hardly unique to Europe or the West. Already in 1934, when he had begun to study Africa in greater depth, James had spoken of the Bushongo of Kasai as an African people with 'a civilisation which showed what Africa would have been able to achieve had it remained free from foreign interference. In fact, their moral code might have served as an example to the rest of the world'.[35] Makonnen recalls: 'George and I spent a good deal of time in the British Museum digging out some of the ancient history of Ethiopia.'[36] Such research made it possible for them to 'discourse at Hyde Park' and to 'attempt to educate English public opinion' on the political possibilities deriving from anticolonial insurgency. It is important to resist the temptation to read this engagement with Ethiopia, even in James's case, as evidence of a pre-Marxist culturalism which would eventually be replaced by a properly economic analysis. The combined inspiration of the Ethiopian situation and labour uprisings (the protests over the former frequently fronted by the leaders of the latter in the West Indies) spelled the emergence of a black anticolonialism that managed to take seriously culture and economy, race and class, putting them in necessary and dialogic engagement. This was also the period, as Davarian L. Baldwin notes, when the term 'New Negro' returned to discourse in the United States and beyond, referring both to 'the assertiveness and defiance of the first generation of free black people' and to 'the more pronounced convergence of politically leftist and black radical internationalism'.[37] As the question of capitalism and its deep implication in the structures of empire became vitally central, questions of race, nation and culture would not, could not, be subordinated to the status of superstructure. If 'Marx and Engels did not see any revolutionary potential in non-Western peoples or their civilisations', as Anthony Bogues argues, what was taking place in Ethiopia, Africa and across the Caribbean would require that contention to be revisited.[38]

'We repudiate this imperialist benevolence ...':
The *International African Opinion*[39]

> *Of course we had people like C. L. R. James and Cedric Dover in*
> *the 1930s, but such few writers as there were had to enter a field*
> *that was predominantly white – white journals, white publishers,*
> *and nearly always white men writing about black. All right. But*
> *what this meant in even such a radical circle as the Left Book Club*
> *series was that your work had to be read by a white man to see if*
> *it had any merit.*
>
> Makonnen, *Pan-Africanism from Within*

> *You'd better join our group while you're here. We're a sort of brains*
> *trust behind the various colonial organizations in this country.*
>
> Peter Abrahams, *A Wreath for Udomo*

The first serious organizational attempt to create a global black coalition of resistance out of the Ethiopia campaign was made in Britain.
The International African Friends of Ethiopia (IAFE), the brainchild
of James and Ashwood Garvey, was the first prominent incarnation of these efforts; after the eventual defeat of the Ethiopians, it
would transform itself in 1937 into the International African Service
Bureau (IASB), a task which could be described in the terms Stafford
Cripps used for Padmore's work: a 'bare and courageous exposure
of the great myth of the civilizing mission of western democracies
in Africa'.[40] Disseminating anticolonial writing and critical analyses
specifically by black campaigners and intellectuals was central to the
work of the IASB, Abrahams's thinly fictionalized 'brains trust'. (That
they were overwhelmingly male was a fact that went unremarked by
them at the time, though, as Matera notes, the organizational labours
of women, not least of Amy Ashwood Garvey, were, in fact, fundamental.) Well connected within both black and pan-African circles,
Ashwood Garvey ran a restaurant and club, the Florence Mills Social
Parlour, which famously afforded a congenial space for many black
activists and intellectuals to meet. According to Ras Makonnen's
memoir, the explicit aim of the IASB was to direct anticolonial activity in Britain under black leadership and consciousness: 'we were not

going to have any European leadership' and the 'idea therefore was
to emphasize service to people of African descent in as many ways as
possible'.[41] The IASB's paper, *International African Opinion (IAO)*,
would note acerbically that 'European organisations tend to ignore
the African struggle and to use the colonial movement merely as a
decoration to their own for ceremonial occasions'.[42] As its general
secretary, I. T. A. (Isaac) Wallace-Johnson, remarked, the Ethiopia
episode and the failure of Britain and other League of Nations
members to curb Italy demonstrated one thing: 'that the world is still
dominated by the philosophy of might over right. It has also opened
the eyes of Africans the world over, that they have no rights which
the powerfully armed nations are bound to respect'.[43] In its own literature, the IASB described one of its primary purposes as helping to
'enlighten British public opinion about conditions in the Colonies,
Protectorates and Mandated territories in Africa, the West Indies
and other parts of the Empire'.[44] It would also campaign for democratic rights and freedoms in the colonies and against such things
as child labour, forced labour and the colour bar. A prolific flurry
of publishing activity by members of the bureau followed, including such works as *How Britain Rules Africa* and *Africa and World
Peace*, both by Padmore, followed by James's *A History of Negro
Revolt*, Eric Williams's *The Negro in the Caribbean* and *Capitalism
and Slavery* and Jomo Kenyatta's *Facing Mount Kenya*.[45] The one
work from this period which has been given any sustained attention in postcolonial literary scholarship is James's justly celebrated
Black Jacobins, although Williams's and Kenyatta's works have been
central to African studies over the years. Equally important are the
collective efforts embodied by the *IAO* and related publications,
emerging as they did out of a campaigning milieu of debate, discussion and organizational work.

It is not only possible but right to think about many of the Asian
and black intellectuals and campaigners resident in London in the
1930s as distinctively British figures, addressing British audiences
and laying claim to British political and ethical terrain; they brought
with them, of course, colonial histories and experiences, and sought
to integrate these into their analyses of both the British and the global
present. My point here is somewhat different from the way in which
the likes of James and Padmore, for instance, are routinely figured as

'Black Englishmen', steeped – as they undoubtedly were – in English (but also European) literary and political traditions. Cedric Robinson has suggested that many such figures felt that 'a part of their mission was to correct the errant motherland', and that even the most anti-imperialist among them found it difficult to shake off a Whiggish belief in the eventual triumph of English 'fair play and deep moral regulation'.[46] James's later, rather tongue-in-cheek, remark about his journey from Trinidad is, of course, widely cited: 'The British intellectual was going to Britain.'[47] Noting that even Trotsky considered James's 'cast of mind all too typically English', Howe suggests that James's 'central thrust remained that of the extreme, indeed shameful, chasm between the British values he genuinely cherished and their betrayal in the colonies'.[48] Schwarz notes of Padmore that he 'mastered the culture of the colonisers, having learned to inhabit Englishness at perfect pitch', and that for him, as for James, 'mastering the codes of England provided a way out from colonial Trinidad'.[49] None of this is untrue, but it is necessary to push beyond variants of Shakespeare's 'Caliban' as a generic symbol for these figures, with the attendant implication that their 'cursing' criticism and analyses were fundamentally made possible by their mastery of the colonizer's language. Something more interesting was going on during this moment of discernment, in which black campaigners and intellectuals found themselves undertaking a different kind of journey to Caliban's. For those who had travelled from the West Indies and parts of Africa, what came into focus was their own sense of self, individual and collective. As Ethiopia was bombarded, while Britain and the League of Nations stood by, urgent questions presented themselves. Who were 'we', the black sojourners in Britain who had arrived there from across the Caribbean and Africa? Was it even possible for that diversity of backgrounds and histories to coalesce into a collective identity, deeply felt as a shared experience in the attack on a sovereign African nation few of them actually came from but to which a shared affective allegiance united them? How could this collective African and black self, shaped by the colonial encounter but not reducible to it, be given voice – and, given the importance of self-representation to the act of self-emancipation, by whom? The black self in a historical frame became the object of study for these black intellectuals. Indeed, James appears to have said as much: 'I began to gain in England a conception of black people which I didn't possess when I left the Caribbean.'[50]

To 'close ranks' in creating black organizations like the IASB was, then, a necessary step in this process of self-study and self-understanding, which entailed crafting a voice that did not simply echo European intellectual insights, and then making it heard. If one of the most important reasons for doing so was to repudiate white leadership and European tutelage in order to act from a place of confident self-knowledge, equally vital was a sense that there were resources to be drawn on which were not simply reducible to Prospero's gift. These were, to some extent, provided by coming to grips with a history of ideas and achievements out of Africa – James confessed, for instance, that he had been completely 'unaware that Africa had artistic structures and traditions of its own' – but it was the resistance in Ethiopia and the insurgencies in the Caribbean which most inspired the insight that the language of black rebellion needed to be understood and espoused.[51] If the Caribbean had been a foundational agent of capitalist modernity through plantation slavery – an argument James, among others, would make – it was also the case that the descendants of those rebellious chattel were once again leading the way in challenging the depredations of capitalism and empire.[52] Now, as then, it was the metropole that had something to learn from the periphery, and the black radicals of the IASB sought to play a key role in this process. And so, while the organization was assertively black in composition and primary membership – and self-consciously more radical than existing black organizations like the LCP, which James had been involved with for a time – numerous sympathetic white Britons were listed as 'patrons' on its letterhead. They included Nancy Cunard; Sylvia Pankhurst, MP and future colonial secretary Arthur Creech Jones; the publisher Victor Gollancz; the Rev. Reginald Sorensen; the writer Ethel Mannin; the MPs Ellen Wilkinson, Noel Baker and D. N. Pritt (among others); and the radical journalist F. A. Ridley. James would edit the organization's journal, *International African Opinion*, which laid out the IASB's aims and guiding principles with admirable clarity: 'Educate – Co-operate – Emancipate: Neutral in nothing affecting the African Peoples'.[53] It would provide speakers to go to 'Labour Party branches, Co-operative Guilds, League of Nations Union branches, peace societies and religious organisations'.[54]

In his illuminating assessment of black internationalism in this period, Minkah Makalani has noted that the IASB's output was copious: 'One of the more striking aspects of the bureau's intellectual work was its sheer volume. In a span of just four years, a core group of roughly seven members produced nine books, a novel, a play, a score of pamphlets, and three journals and a news bulletin.'[55] Authorship ensured a hard-won authority; James himself noted that speakers from the bureau often spoke at public meetings where there were more whites than blacks, and that 'the fact that we had published books gave us some sort of status'.[56] The *International African Opinion*, which billed itself as 'a journal of action', explicitly aimed not only at consolidating the oppositional energies unleashed by the invasion of Ethiopia but, as its pointed title indicates, at foregrounding a black non-metropolitan understanding of global events. Its masthead featuring a black woman holding up a torch with a world map in the background, the journal offered 'the most wide-ranging and cogently argued articulation of the anti-imperialist position in the late 1930s'.[57] The fact that its run did not outlast the newsprint shortage in the months leading up to the outbreak of the Second World War should not lead us to overlook the importance of the terrain claimed by the journal. The collective efforts of the IASB executive and other *IAO* contributors gave clear and consolidated expression to the critical and analytical currents that had emerged from black resistance over the preceding years. Although the importance of the journal has been recognized in scholarship on black internationalism, a more detailed engagement is needed with its contents, and in particular its uncompromising delineation of a cogent, detailed anticolonialism.[58] For the first time, a number of vital points looking ahead to the era of decolonization were made within the pages of a single journal, and expanded on by other writings associated with it. These included the recognition of the extent of black and other anticolonial resistance, and the concomitant centrality of self-emancipation; the repudiation of notions of tutelage and trusteeship; the importance of solidarity across racial and national lines; and finally, perhaps most controversially, a radical challenge to the presumed opposition between fascism and 'democratic' imperialism that was central to colonial myth-making which will be considered in greater detail in Chapter 9.

The address of the *IAO* was determinedly global and cross-racial,
even as it sought to build on a pan-African consciousness of shared
racial oppression: '[We do not] believe that African emancipation is
to be achieved in isolation from the rest of the world. But the freedom
of the African or any other people can be won only by those people
themselves.'[59] Any engagement between white and black workers
would have to be dialogical, 'accomplished only by mutual confidence and respect on a basis of complete equality, learnt in discussion,
struggle and danger, honestly shared and reciprocal assistance generously given'.[60] While it stresses the necessarily racialized nature
of this 'awakened black political consciousness', the journal is clear
in its rejection of 'racial chauvinism' from any quarter: 'We repudiate the idea of substituting a black racial arrogance for a white'.[61]
Although African emancipation could not be arrived at in isolation
from that of the rest of humanity, organizational efforts would have
to be constitutively 'AFRICAN'.[62] In a pointed reversal of familiar
metropolitan gestures of inclusion, 'while jealously guarding our
independence', the journal's editors noted that the contributions of
white friends would appear in the journal. (Their financial assistance
was repeatedly acknowledged and thanked.)

Universal Blackness, Global Anticolonialism

The first editorial of the *IAO* deserves special attention as a collective
statement of aims which brought together several of these points. It
is important for its definition of shared 'black political consciousness' as deriving from 'a common bond of oppression' and 'scattered'
struggles which need to be brought together.[63] Conversely, it repudiated black middle-class petitioning or 'seeking crumbs from the
tables of their imperialist masters' as a dead end: 'No freedom will
ever be given by any other people or any other organisation, and
the black people must therefore shoulder their own burden.'[64] This
was also to reject in the most strenuous terms the 'constant subordination' that is a widely accepted tenet of imperial propaganda
among whites, 'that Africans can do nothing except under tutelage,
this desire even on the part of our so-called friends, that everything should be done *for* the blacks and nothing *by* the blacks'.[65]

While announcing its retrenchment into an organization based on ethnic kinship and cultural affiliation – 'membership of it is limited to Africans and to persons of African descent' – the IASB and the journal 'take no isolated view of our task'.[66] The 'common destiny of all the oppressed of whatever nationality or race' would guide the mission. The *IAO* would seek to learn, assist and facilitate with due intellectual modesty:

> We know our limitations. We know that we cannot liberate the millions of Africans and people of African descent from their servitude and oppression. That task no one can do but the black people themselves. But we can help to stimulate the growing consciousness of the blacks, to give them benefit of our daily contact with the European movement, to learn from the black masses the lessons of the profound experiences that they accumulate in their daily toil, to point out certain pitfalls that may be avoided, to co-ordinate information and organisation, to do an incessant propaganda in every quarter of Britain, exposing evils, pressing for such remedies as are possible, and mobilising whatever assistance there is to be found in Europe for the cause of African emancipation.[67]

Noting that it was a centenary year for the 1838 People's Charter in Britain, the editorial suggested that colonial black people would take forward the demands of the Chartists as an intermediate stage towards full independence.

Over its run, the *IAO* both identified aspects of colonial rule and showed, in counterpoint, how these were repeatedly contested and challenged. Padmore skewered the pretensions of the newly opened Empire Exhibition in Glasgow, which 'was informing their Imperial Majesties what a glorious contribution to the peace and prosperity of the people of the Empire this Exhibition represents', even as 'the working masses of the West Indian island of Jamaica were being shot and bayoneted for demanding betterment of their miserable working conditions'.[68] An essay on Ethiopia in this same first edition inverted the terms of civilizational discourse produced by the 'noble teachers of barbarous savages' to criticize 'the jungle-law, which is imperialist diplomacy, though wild animals at least do not justify their killings by references to Christ and international morality'.[69] Resistance by

Ethiopians and then on the part of West Indians was putting paid to such hypocrisy, however, creating 'disorder not only in the streets but in the calculations of the British Colonial officials, these men born to govern'.[70] The 'judicious management of the black intelligentsia, giving them jobs, O.B.E's and even knighthoods', would no longer suffice to control the 'explosions in island after island'.[71] All too often, imperial mythologizing was successful in masking resistance, a 'self-boasting' which, 'like all advertising which is insistent and continuous', had succeeded.[72] As the conquest of Ethiopia receded in British public awareness, the West Indian labour rebellions provided a focus of organization and agitation for black radicals in London, with many public meetings in Trafalgar Square and Hyde Park, working 'to build public support for the strikes in Trinidad and Barbados'.[73] Reframing what was being dismissed as disorderly 'hooliganism' in anticolonial terms, the *IAO* noted that Royal Commissions such as that sent to the island in 1938 were predictable and familiar responses from colonial authorities, ways of killing time so that reforms could be staved off. This gradualist reformism had to be repudiated for good.

The journal's direct attack on imperial mythologies immediately found its target. Shortly after the first issue of *International African Opinion* went into circulation, its editors received an irate letter from an Englishman who had read it and wanted to share a few 'home truths'. Dipped in spiteful ink, the trolling epistle offered its own version of the 'Caliban' theory of resistance, whereby 'sub-logical' black men first learned the arts of freedom from white rulers:

> In the first place, but for the beneficent rule of this country and its administrators (at whom you lose no occasion to sneer) you would not have such a paper. Far from being able to write such articles, you would be unable to even read them. In short, it is only from the rulers whom you so hate that you have received the education that has enabled you to bite the hand that feeds you.[74]

The letter found its way into print despite the author's stated supposition that the editors would not 'dare publish' it, but was accompanied by a remarkably full editorial response that deserves some attention. Inverting the premises of their critic's civilizational claims, the editors noted sharply: 'As far as we know, it is to the Babylonians, the Egyptians, the Jews, and the Greeks that Europe owes the foundations of its culture. The Arabs contributed heavily during the Middle Ages. But we have not noticed any special feeling of gratitude among the modern Europeans to either Arab or Jew, for instance.'[75] It is not just that all cultures owe something to their predecessors and to other cultures, the editors informed their bristling interlocutor; quite specifically, 'a very elementary knowledge of history would teach him that far from blacks owing anything to Britain, Western civilisation owes a debt to blacks which can never be repaid'.[76] Some of the greatest business houses and family fortunes in Britain were built on the slave trade and on the West Indian sugar plantations. As to the familiar claim that the journal itself would not exist were it not for British education, far from Africans needing to be grateful to Europe for teaching a small number to read and write in European languages, many more Europeans owed their entire 'standard of living and education' to the 'labour of generations of Africans'. In response to the claim that Britain was liberal enough to allow them to 'so vilify the Government', the editors noted that such freedom of speech as was available to them was a result of 'the devoted struggles of the British working-class movement through the centuries' and not the liberal beneficence of the Empire's ruling classes.[77]

A Question of Rebellions

As Roderick Macdonald has noted, the 1930s represented a definitive break from 'reformist and essentially élitist' approaches where criticism of empire was concerned.[78] To no small extent, this break was a result of 'a state almost of insurrection' that prevailed in the West Indies, which Padmore, along with others, gave several accounts of in the pages of the *IAO*:

Unarmed, the crowd took to throwing stones. A warning came from the police. The Riot Act was read and shots were fired over the heads of the strikers. More stones were thrown, and the next volley, lasting for ten minutes, was directed straight at the men, women and children, who by that time numbered over a thousand.

Many were wounded, and four workers were killed. One of them, an old Negro woman, was bayoneted to death. The crowd went wild, and, rescuing as many wounded as they could, they retreated into the fields, setting the canes on fire.[79]

In an episode uncannily resonant of Morant Bay, on an April day in 1937 a small riot had taken place outside the Frome Estate sugar plantation office – owned by a subsidiary of the gigantic Tate & Lyle Corporation in the parish of Westmoreland, Jamaica. Workers were angry about the dilatory payment of wages. The action soon escalated into a strike 'and then a large-scale violent confrontation'.[80] For a host of reasons to do with wages (subject to arbitrary and severe cuts) and working conditions, including security of tenure, a volatile situation intensified, culminating in a showdown with armed black policemen commanded by white officers facing 'about a thousand strikers who were armed only with bits of wood, iron pipes and stones'.[81] By the end of the day, three people had been shot and one bayoneted by the police, two of them women – one old and one pregnant. Several people, including five policemen, were wounded, and nearly a hundred arrested. Subsequently thousands attended protest meetings and marches to draw attention to the situation of the working poor, and soon sporadic strikes ensued. On 22 May 1937 the capital city of Kingston was shut down, disorder spread, public property was set upon, streets were blocked and mobs occupied public utility buildings. A crowd of thousands being addressed by trade unionists Bustamante and Grant refused to disperse, and met the inevitable baton charge with a return shower of stones and bricks. As similar scenes repeated themselves over the next few days, extending to rolling strikes, looting and the firing of cane-fields, during which Bustamante was jailed, police numbers were reinforced by troop battalions, and several civilians died during violent clashes. The rebellion, described by Ken Post as a 'counter-blow against capitalism',[82] finally calmed down when a 'New Deal' involving a large land settlement was agreed by the colonial administration under Acting Governor Woolley.[83] Labour militancy would continue in various forms, however, leading up to another violent confrontation in June the following year, with an emergency declared on the nineteenth of that month. As one historian notes, 'the economic foundations of slavery, especially in the general picture of land-ownership, had basically remained untouched' since Emancipation.[84]

In the necessary retelling of the history of black oppression as the history of black resistance, the Caribbean also came to occupy an increasingly important place for the intellectuals of the IASB. The arc that could be drawn from the moment of Ethiopia to the conflagrations that swept the British West Indies allowed precisely for the illumination of connections between the construction of pan-African solidarity and a conceptualization of resistance as necessarily rooted in the everyday struggles of black toilers. Both events could also be situated in the longer history of black resistance, which James, among others, saw as vital to the present-day struggle. In places like Jamaica, 'Ethiopianism' (also known as 'Rastafarianism') – in which all people of African descent identified as Ethiopian – already existed as a strong and vital force. The fate of Ethiopia came thus to stand in for the fate of all black people, not least those dispersed across the Caribbean. Tellingly, James ends his short treatise, *The History of Negro Revolt*, with an account of contemporary 'Negro movements' that includes an extended engagement with the Trinidad labour uprisings, beginning with Uriah Butler's agitation among oilfield workers. Recounting how labour organizing in Trinidad shifted from Captain Cipriani to Butler when the former refused to sanction strike action against Apex Oilfields in 1935, James appears to track the radicalizing of his own political trajectory, from his making the case for West Indian self-government before coming to England in 1932 to writing histories of black self-emancipation through revolt.[85] As revolts spread across the West Indies – to Barbados, St Vincent, St Lucia, British Guiana and Jamaica – James wrote: 'Consideration of the remedies is beyond us but they will need to be far-reaching.'[86] Like others, he 'had become aware of the existence of a more vigorous Black opposition than that with which he was familiar in his own class ... he had witnessed the capacities for resistance of ordinary Black people, the transformation of peasants and workers into liberation forces.'[87]

This is not the place for an extended review of the causes and consequences of the waves of unrest that spread across the Caribbean in the 1930s, and certainly accelerated the islands' progress towards decolonization.[88] As in the nineteenth century, multiple difficulties to do with land and labour were at stake. What we can note, however, in the historical light of Morant Bay, are the remarkable resemblances to earlier forms of resistance: refusal to work or harvest crops; occupations of factories; gatherings which invited the charge of 'riotous assembly'; the escalation of simple demands into active rebellion in the face of frustration; ringleaders identified and punished, unleashing further unrest; and, last but not least, frequent violent repression. All of these were followed by the decision of the British government to appoint a West India Royal Commission, which would submit a report of its inquiry. The Moyne Report, submitted in 1939, just over a year after the commissioners arrived in the islands, would in fact be suppressed until after the war, only its recommendations being published in the interim, for fear of further controversy. 'The labour rebellions of the 1930s', noted the labour organizer and historian Richard Hart, 'increased the self confidence [sic] of the workers in these colonies and convinced them of the influence they could exert by united action', where there had been none.[89] As Ken Post, another chronicler of the episode, points out, conditions on the island of Jamaica represented 'the essence of the colonial condition', a distinct mode of production that was nonetheless 'closely bound up with structures of exchange and distribution in the metropolis and was indeed determined in its own structure by the demands of British capitalism'.[90] This gave the resistance – generally agreed to be spontaneous, if reliant on strong leadership – an international significance of its own. However 'dimly visible', a 'tradition of popular protest, often violent, spanned the years back through Morant Bay to the slave revolts ... When other factors of consciousness, leadership and organisation were added to this tradition things of great importance could happen'.[91]

While 'Ethiopianism' was not the primary cause for the strength of this labour militancy, the return to the racial language that also circulated during the Morant Bay rebellion – 'skin for skin and colour for colour' – is striking.[92] As noted in the joint memorandum submitted by the Negro Welfare Association, the IASB and the LCP in London to the Moyne Commission (which, tellingly, was reluctant to receive evidence from them), Ethiopia had served to consolidate and channel existing consciousness of a material oppression that clearly had a racial basis:

In 1833 there was reason to apprehend a universal Negro rebellion
for freedom, and emancipation was granted from above to prevent
the cataclysm of emancipation from below, as had occurred in San
Domingo [*sic*]. Similarly today, when the rape of Ethiopia has given
a great stimulus to growing Negro consciousness, it is not a question of rebellions if, but rebellions unless, democratic government
is granted.[93]

In places like Jamaica, an eccentric mixture of Garveyism, Ethiopianism and Rastafarianism constituted 'an important part of the
political culture of resistance in Jamaica' which was marked by 'economic deprivation, social volatility and politicisation'.[94] Garveyism
had already spread a 'Black Nationalist message of racial dignity
and pride in an ancestral Africa' even as its economic programme
stressed 'racial development through private enterprise'.[95] Workers'
organizations in Trinidad staged agitations in which dockers refused
to unload Italian ships, and actively attempted to illuminate links
between issues at home and abroad. For the *IAO*, this rebellion had
been some time in the making: 'And in proportion to the tardiness of
their awakening they are now aggressive in their militancy.' Measures
such as instituting a Royal Commission would not suffice any more:
'There have been too many Commissions and too little action. This
is just a method of killing time, in the hope that the temper of the
masses may die down and the long-awaited reforms staved off.'[96]
Something had changed irrevocably in the West Indian colonies. 'Yet
to say that Quashee stood up in 1938', writes Post, referencing the
colonial stereotype of the happy and feckless black peasant made
famous by Carlyle, among others,

is to say both everything and nothing. It is everything because, for
once, the poor of Jamaica made their own history. It is nothing
because there was not one Quashee – he is a stereotype, a reifica-
tion, a device of the ruling class like shackles or wage labour. Rather,
there were many Quashees ... thousands of whom had come by
May 1938 to feel that the stereotype must be transcended.[97]

While full independence from British rule was still a long way
away, Quashee, it could be said, 'did not bend as low as before,

and after the middle of 1938 Jamaica was never quite the same
again'.[98]

'What are you going to do about it?' Solidarity as Imperative

Solidarity with such forms of resistance underway in the colonies
emerged as a keynote in many articles in the *IAO*. 'The great masses
of the British people', announced the first issue, 'must see what is
being done in their name'.[99] In an echo of Marx's famous observation to the effect that white labour could not be emancipated while
black labour was being oppressed, an article on the importance of
the Anti-imperialist Exhibition in Glasgow, which was set up to
counter the imperialist one (see Chapter 9), noted that 'while the
colonial workers are in bondage, the British workers labour but in
vain to free themselves from the burdening yoke of Imperialism'.[100]
It was therefore incumbent on British labour to support Caribbean
workers 'without reservation'.[101] One of the most striking editorials
in this vein was produced as an open letter from the executive of the
IASB to the delegates of the Trades Union Congress at Blackpool in
September 1938. Having offered to make blacks everywhere aware
of their common cause with British workers, the letter poses in turn a
series of not-quite-rhetorical questions to white British trade unionists: 'At the present moment Africans and West Indians are struggling
for their elementary democratic rights. What are you going to do
about it?'[102] Traditions of resistance must be honoured in their global
provenance without ignorance providing an alibi:

> You celebrated the centenary of the Tolpuddle martyrs not long ago.
> All politically conscious Africans celebrated it with you. But Ulric
> Grant in Barbados, for daring to organise the Barbados workers, is
> now serving a sentence of ten years' imprisonment. If you did not
> know it before, gentlemen, then you ought to have known it, and
> you know now. What are you going to do about it?[103]

From land- and cattle-grabs in Kenya to restrictions placed on
trade unions in Trinidad, British labour was imperilled if it was

not as 'vigilant in protest and action on these issues' as with its own concerns. Importantly, this call for solidarity was not only issued across race lines but, in another sharp open letter a few months later, directed at West Indian intellectuals and their own overlooked responsibilities.[104] The West Indian uprisings, this letter began by noting, 'have forced themselves into the consciousness of the people and rulers of the British Empire and the whole world, and the method by which this has been done is at once a reproach and a sign-post to the better-educated people of African descent in these colonies'.[105] Admonishing the intellectuals of the islands for not having undertaken any noticeable political activity in support of the labour cause, the letter reminds them that the demands of the workers are theirs to espouse too, that their own liberties are threatened when those of the workers are threatened. If equality is to replace racism globally, so too are West Indian intellectuals tasked with 'eliminating from their movement the reactionary discriminations that exist between those who differ in shades of colour'. Nor were the West Indian masses to be treated as 'raw material for the political activity of the few'.[106] The intellectual did have something to give to them, but 'they have more to teach him'.

Towards a Theory of Colonial Fascism

This letter returns to a recurrent theme in the literature of the IASB – the nature and scope of fascism and its relationship to forms of imperial rule:

> Fascism, which is the most brutal form of imperialism, puts a firm brake on all liberal ideas, all freedom, on every concept of human equality and fraternity. In Germany, it bases itself on a fanatical nationalism, and exaggerated racial arrogance. Its inhuman persecution of the Jews is a sop to national discontent and a convenient destraction [*sic*] from the real issues at stake. With giant strides it stalks all over the world. In Italy, Germany, Poland, Rumania, in diverse forms, it raises its foul head everywhere. It has appeared in Britain and in the British House of Commons.[107]

Unambiguous in its insistence that Hitler was an irredeemable entity, and crystal clear that both he and Mussolini had to be strenuously opposed, the journal raised a question which would become a point of discussion on the British left more broadly: what was the relationship between imperialism in its supposedly 'democratic' form and fascism of the German and Italian varieties? 'The British democrats of property are democrats', the open letter to intellectuals warned, 'just so long as democracy serves them'.[108] The treatment of trade unionists and workers in the West Indies rendered nugatory the frequent declaration by liberals, socialists, communists and Tory humanitarians – with regard to similar arrests in Germany and Italy – that this 'could happen only in a Fascist country'.[109] The term 'colonial fascism' was put into play by an unsigned article, possibly drafted by Padmore, to signify those authoritarian and violent practices of rule undertaken specifically in colonial contexts by the putatively 'democratic' powers.[110] Another *IAO* editorial made a point that would be picked up in British left-wing papers, such as the *New Leader*, in the run-up to the Second World War:

> We will not shed our blood to maintain the yoke around our necks. Let it be known that as far as we are concerned, the 'Democratic' imperialisms are fundamentally no different from the dictator Powers, for the conditions under which the vast majority of colonial peoples live savour of Colonial Fascism. For example, what rights have the natives in South Africa to lose? If we must fight, then Africans and peoples of African descent will fight for themselves, confident that in taking this course we, like the blacks of San Domingo, will be playing an historical role in liberating not only ourselves but other sections of oppressed humanity.[111]

To no small extent, this view drew on the bitter colonial experience of the previous war and a now deeply felt aversion to being used as 'cannon-fodder' in a war that aimed at a 're-division of territory' from which black people would 'gain nothing'.[112] As a black anti-war manifesto, probably drafted by Padmore, and reprinted in the *International African Opinion* (which had received several communications on the topic from across the colonial world) asserted: 'Black brothers, what do we know of democracy? This is just a bait to catch us. In 1914 they also talked to us about Democracy and self-determination. Millions of us died on Flanders Field, in Palestine, in East, West and South Africa. But what did we get? More slavery, more oppression, more exploitation.'[113] In another essay, the journal noted that blacks had 'a strong sympathy with the Jews' as a persecuted people, and that it was vital 'not to cease to point out in Africa the greed, savagery and brutality which distinguished the Nazi régime and its ignorant and insolent claim to racial superiority'.[114] At the same time, plans to resettle the Jews in East Africa constituted a way out of European capitalism's difficulties 'at the expense of Africans'. The *IAO* urged the pursuit of solutions that were 'unconnected with the mean subterfuges of imperialism', since that plan for resettlement also entailed ignoring the ways in which the Kenyans had been penned into reserves and deprived of their own lands.[115] But it was also clear that 'the struggle against anti-Semitism is an important part of the struggle against imperialism'.[116]

The situation in Kenya was also at the heart of a later editorial on the topic of 'Hitler and the Colonies', which delineated the practice of 'colonial fascism' even more unsparingly, 'closing the rhetorical distance European powers tried to create between empire and fascism'.[117] As plans were discussed for the possible 'return' of the East African 'protectorates' to Germany – another measure of appeasement – East African white settlers called for resistance to the proposals and solicited the support of black Africans in this. This situation was layered with rich historical ironies, as the *IAO* was quick to note. It was 'a new phenomenon for East African whites to acknowledge coloured races in the same breath with themselves', still less to allow them a voice in matters.[118] The white settlers were not objecting to fascist methods as such, the editorial observed astutely, but only to becoming themselves victims of fascist annexation; after all, they had already taken land and forced Kenyan blacks, paid miserable wages, to carry a *kipande* or pass-book 'like common criminals, register their finger-prints, live in filthy, stinking hovels. What further degradations could Hitler heap on them?'[119] The sudden concern about how white minorities might be treated under German rule ought to raise the equally pertinent question of how Britain had been treating Africans, and black labour in particular: 'Fascism is not a monopoly of Mussolini and Hitler, but is employed by the "democratic" nations throughout their colonies.'[120] The Africans, for their part, opposed the transfer of the protectorates to Hitler because they did not wish 'to be bandied about by one European Power to another', and 'not because they envisage any fundamental difference in treatment'.[121] Where the false war between fascism and imperialism was concerned, the only legitimate response was 'A plague on both camps!'[122]

Freedom's Backstory

> Consider the chronology of these fateful years 1935–1938. A sugar strike in St Kitts, 1935; a revolt against increase of customs duties in St Vincent, 1935; a coal strike in St Lucia, 1935; labour disputes on the sugar plantations of British Guiana, 1935; an oil strike, which became a general strike, in Trinidad, 1937; a sympathetic strike in Barbados, 1937; a sugar strike in St Lucia, 1937; sugar troubles in Jamaica, 1937; dockers' strike in Jamaica, 1938. Every governor called for warships, marines and aeroplanes. The torch had been applied to the powder barrel.
>
> Eric Williams, The Negro in the Caribbean

> With the transportation of the Negro from Africa to the Caribbean the germ of political revolt was transplanted to the New World. Contrary to the belief widely accepted among both whites and Negroes, the Negro slave was not docile and devoted to his master. The moment he was placed on the small tubs which made the Middle Passage, that moment he became a revolutionary, actual or potential.
>
> Eric Williams, The Negro in the Caribbean

The Caribbean rebellions and their mix of racial and class consciousness injected urgency into a series of anticolonial pamphlets which the IASB disseminated. One of these, The Negro in the Caribbean, written by the historian and future first prime minister of Trinidad, Eric Williams, who would also go on to write the hugely influential Capitalism and Slavery, also suggested that there was an arc of continuity to be drawn from slave rebellions to the present-day insurgencies, an understanding of which required a 'correct idea of the revolutionary role of the Negro slave' who fought for his freedom.[123] Explicitly referencing the Morant Bay rebellion, Williams notes the emergence and persistence, once again, of fault lines within black struggle. For the black middle classes in the Caribbean, 'it was a struggle for a share in political power, for extension of the franchise, for jobs', while for the working-classes, 'it was basically an economic struggle, a struggle for land-ownership, for better wages, for decent living conditions, for the right to organize in trade unions' – two sets of interests that nonetheless coalesced at times.[124] Inasmuch as they marked the passing of the initiative 'from the brown middle class to the black working class', the years from 1935 to 1938 were something of a revolutionary watershed: 'Rawle, Marryshow and Cipriani (a white liberal), gave way to Butler and Mentor, Payne and Grant.'[125] Like others, Williams noted that political democracy would be taken where not given: 'The explosions in the British West Indies indicate the danger of continued exasperation and continued repression: there is still time to heed the signals and so correct, by democratic reforms, an unsound economy and the present abuses of the sugar industry.'[126] It was a view Padmore had articulated even more bluntly in an article for the ILP discussion journal, *Controversy*, in 1938, calling for British workers and socialists to support their Caribbean brethren: 'This is the task which history has placed on the toiling masses of the West Indies – Indians as well as Negroes; for the West Indian bourgeoisie is one of the most reactionary colonial ruling classes and will never make any concessions unless forced to.'[127] Another IASB pamphlet, *The West Indies Today*, demanded universal adult franchise, federated constitutions, higher direct taxation, land settlement, labour legislation, industrialization and greater social services. It reiterated the centrality of self-liberation: 'West Indians know this. They know that unless they act for themselves they will get little; but they know, too, that if they are sufficiently well organised their rulers cannot but give in to their demands if unpleasant consequences are to be avoided.'[128] West Indians had 'taken the situation in their own hands … no longer prepared to acquiesce silently in their present intolerable conditions'.[129] In this the solidarity rather than the leadership of white British allies was sought.[130] To white British workers, there was a reciprocal offering of friendship on shared terrain in the face of the fight for real democracy, 'Though you have neglected us in the past, to-day in this hour of common crisis, we want you to know that we Blacks bear you no ill will ... Our freedom is your freedom.'[131]

'Whatever the future of tropical Africa will be', wrote James a few years later, 'one thing is certain, that it will not be what the colonial powers are trying to make of it. It will be violent and strange, with the most abrupt and unpredictable changes in economic relations, race relations, territorial boundaries and everything else.'[132] In his important comparative study of anglophone and francophone black internationalism, Brent Edwards takes this to mean that what James and Padmore were involved in producing was 'an other epistemology of blackness' altogether.[133] While it is certainly true that the milieu of the IASB sought to create something new which broke out of the dead ends of both race essentialism and mechanistic forms of Marxism, framing this black radicalism as epistemologically 'other' is to miss a crucial aspect of the work in question – indeed, the very source of its radicalism.[134] What emerges in the historically grounded polemics produced by the radicals of the IAFE/IASB milieu – in the wake of the Ethiopian invasion – is precisely an insistence on reclaiming and reframing universalism and humanism as neither singularly European in provenance nor (therefore) radically 'other'. The task they set themselves is radical in its very simplicity: to demonstrate that impulses towards freedom and equality can be seen to arise across multiple contexts and cultures, not least those of Africa, and as such would be impulses towards reclamation *from* rather than bestowal by Western benevolence. That multiple resources nourished such aspirations could be seen from the history of rebellion itself. Or, as Williams put it in relation to the Caribbean: 'Slavery was a state of war, a constant struggle for freedom on the part of the slave. Liberty or death!'[135] Freedom was not a discursive object to be passed down from a superior culture to a 'backward' one; rather, it was defined and forged precisely through the historical experience of oppression and resistance.

One of the first texts to make this case with some force was *A History of Negro Revolt*, James's exploratory companion to his monumental *The Black Jacobins*. It was a lengthy pamphlet produced in 1938 for Raymond Postgate's *FACT* magazine, in which James detailed the continuity of the many attempts of the Negro 'to free himself from his burdens' in Africa, America and the West Indies. 'Negroes have continually revolted', James notes, beginning his treatise with 'the only successful slave revolt in history', that in Saint-Domingue in 1791–1804: the Haitian Revolution.[136] While he attributes the success of that great rebellion, as he does in his later, more famous work, to the scaffolding provided by the French Revolution, here he makes a more controversial claim: 'The success of the San Domingo blacks killed the West Indian slave-trade and slavery.'[137] It is less the case, James suggests, that insurgent slaves 'embraced' a revolutionary doctrine from Europe, than that the French Revolution provided a ready-made language as well as material support for aspirations that were already there but had been kept in check by the degradation and violence of the slave system. With their revolution, 'these slaves, lacking education, half-savage, and degraded in their slavery as only centuries of slavery can degrade, achieved a liberality in social aspiration and an elevation of political thought equivalent to anything similar that took place in France'.[138] Rebellion itself, James stresses repeatedly, is rooted not in systems of thought but in a human response to intolerable conditions: 'First of all, as we have seen, the Negro was no docile animal. He revolted continuously.'[139] The persistence of this spirit could be documented in multifarious forms of resistance, from Sierra Leone and the Gambia to Nigeria, Nyasaland and the Union of South Africa. In the case of 'the extraordinary women's revolt' of Aba, Nigeria, in 1929, in which over fifty women were killed, the rebels were protesting taxes levied on their work by chiefs under so-called 'indirect rule': 'The women seized public buildings and held them for days. The servants refused to cook for their white masters and mistresses and some of them made the attempt to bring the European women by force into the markets to give them some experience of what work was like.'[140] It was only in the wake of this unprecedented uprising that a more widespread agitation ensued, other workers also refusing to pay taxes and demanding redress for their economic and political grievances. Another form of rebellion, James observes, was religious in form but deeply anti-European in nature: 'Such education as the African is given is nearly always religious, so that the leader often translated the insurrection into religious terms.'[141] As Walter Rodney indicates, James stressed that the language of religion which inflected such revolts 'should not obscure the fact that they sprung from such things as forced labour, land alienation and colonial taxation'.[142] One such was the Chilembwe uprising in Nyasaland (present-day Malawi), in which coffee estate workers rose up against syndicates that maximized profit and offered no development in return, whether in the form of schools or hospitals or missions. In the Belgian Congo, such resistance took the form of leaving European-controlled churches in favour of independent African ones under the leadership of Simon Kimbangu.[143] In Kenya, the movement named after Harry Thuku agitated in more secular terms against high taxation and forced labour, among other grievances, meeting with suppression at the hands of the King's African Rifles.

The value of James's work from this period, Rodney noted, was that it gave African freedom from colonial rule a backstory, allowing the resistant consciousness of contemporary Africans to be 'heightened by knowledge of the dignity and determination of their foreparents'; to 'give historical depth to the process of resistance'.[144] Silences in colonial history about the fact of rebellion proliferated through the first half of the twentieth century. Underscoring the significance of James's work, in an observation arguably applicable to the the IASB's output as a whole, Rodney reminds us that 'African resistance to European colonization was not supposed to have existed as far as colonialist scholars were concerned'.[145] For James, such silences were facilitated by omissions in the historical records: 'The British send out their punitive expeditions against revolting tribes and do not necessarily mention them in the annual colonial reports. But if the revolt awakens public interest, a commission will investigate and make a report.'[146] He compares the organization of South Africa's Industrial and Commercial Workers Union (ICU), which undoubtedly achieved great momentum in its first years, to the Haitian Revolution: 'There is the same instinctive capacity for organization, the same throwing-up of gifted leaders from among the masses.'[147] The dimension of self-emancipation, he suggests, might be even more relevant here given that there was nothing radical happening in Britain, like the French Revolution in the Haitian case, 'needing the black revolution, and sending out encouragement, organizers and arms'.[148] In the eventual – and, for James, inevitable – decline of its leader, Clements Kadalie, was the lesson that intellectual heft was needed for movements to succeed; what ultimately doomed the ICU was that Kadalie 'lacked the education and the knowledge to organize it on a stable basis – the hardest of all tasks for a man of his origin'.[149]

While he appreciated and drew attention to the indigenous dimensions of black revolt, James in this work was scathingly critical of Marcus Garvey's pan-Africanist movement. He nonetheless understood it in terms of a misdirected articulation of sincerely felt liberationist impulses. Though James dismissed Garveyism as 'pitiable rubbish' and demagoguery, he was able to concede that 'desperate men often hear, not the actual words of an orator but their own thoughts', particularly when they are looking for a leader.[150] For all that Garvey is a proto-fascist and chauvinist, and in James's acidic rendering a 'hare-brained' schemer and a 'dishonest' anti-communist 'reactionary', he has to be credited with creating 'for the first time a feeling of international solidarity among Africans and people of African descent. In so far as this is directed against oppression it is a positive step.'[151] The impulse to achieve human freedom runs deep and wide across Africa, James suggested – a fact obscured by misleading colonial representations of many revolts as merely labour strikes that had got out of hand. Reading a powerful 'native translation of the call for the strike' written by one G. Lovewey, James observes that its language goes well beyond a 'mere appeal to strike', being rather 'a summons to relentless struggle with mortal enemies':[152]

Listen to this all you who live in the country, think well how they treat us and to ask for a land. Do we live in good treatment, no; therefore let us ask one another and remember this treatment. Because we wish on the day of 29th April, every person not to go to work, he who will go to work, and if we see him, it will be a serious case.[153]

As surely as the Haitian blacks destroyed the French plantocracy, if world events were to give them a chance, many of the currently colonized, now too ready to resist to the death, 'will destroy what has them by the throat'.[154] Speaking of the influence of the secret religious movement, Watch Tower, on the Northern Rhodesian workers, James again stressed the ways in which religion had 'become a weapon in the class struggle', and was able to 'represent political

realities and express political aspirations far more closely than programmes and policies of parties with millions of members, numerous
journals and half a century of history behind them'.[155] The Executive
Committee summarized the situation in an open letter to the workers
of the West Indies:

> Writing in *The Tribune* (June 17, 1938), Mr Bevan said: 'A short
> time ago we had a discussion in the House of Commons on Labour
> in Trinidad. Tuesday we discussed Jamaica. Why? Because the con-
> science of Britain is disturbed at the sufferings of the natives in our
> colonies? No. It is because these natives have at last rioted against
> British masters. Even now, it is not their sufferings that are stirring
> us to laggard action. It is their protests. *If they cease their protests,
> we will cease giving redress.*[156]

If the work of the *International African Opinion* and its associated
writers in parsing African and Caribbean insurgencies was vital in its
own right, contributing powerfully to the anticolonial discourse of
the coming decades, it is worth noting that these uprisings were not
without wider metropolitan impact. Ken Post asserts: 'They shook
the whole colonial system so severely that it was never quite the
same again.'[157] For all that sections of the British media attempted
to explain away the convulsions as 'one of those sudden explosions
of excitement to which negro labour suffering from a sense of grievance is notoriously prone', it also became clear that imperial rule
would have to make significant changes in its mode of operation.[158]
Even the secretary of state for the colonies, Malcolm MacDonald,
would admit that the disturbances in Jamaica pointed to a 'condition
[which] constitutes a reproach to our Colonial administration'.[159]
Questions were raised in parliament by Arthur Creech Jones, an IASB
patron, and others (on 12, 16 and 25 May 1938), while the Trades
Union Congress created a colonial advisory committee to study conditions in the colonies.[160] Even Stafford Cripps, pilloried in the pages
of the *IAO* for advocating 'trusteeship' in Africa, would announce
in 1938 when he was a guest at the founding of Jamaica's People's
National Party:

I want to see the new peoples of the world rise in their power giving us a new and great and glorious, more humane civilization, and I hope that in the development of your new political life you will all develop the cultural life of the Jamaican people until here in the Caribbean there grows, perhaps small at first but gradually widening in its influence, a new culture, new people, a new humanity which can gradually take over the reins of government from the dying and decadent peoples of Western Europe.[161]

Others, like the British socialist Arthur Calder-Marshall, would warn that unless significant changes were enacted, 'troubles such as have occurred in Barbados, Trinidad, Jamaica and British Guiana will become more and more frequent'.[162] As the influential liberal economist from the Caribbean island of St Lucia, W. Arthur Lewis, remarked in a pamphlet he wrote for the eminently moderate Fabian Colonial Bureau, 'even before the emancipation of slavery the free coloured people were in constant conflict with the plantocracy, and throughout the nineteenth century that conflict continued'.[163] Workers had become 'very bitter and militant' over long periods of unemployment, wage cuts and increased taxation, and there was a tendency in official reports to describe them erroneously as 'hooligans'.[164] The political consciousness of West Indian workers had been increased by the Italian conquest of Ethiopia, Lewis tells his readers, making them 'more willing to take their fate in their own hands', and news of industrial action in France and America had also galvanized them.[165] Lewis's pamphlet remains a usefully succinct account of the unfolding of the rebellions, beginning with St Kitts in 1935, moving on to St Vincent, St Lucia, Barbados, British Guiana, Trinidad and Jamaica. He notes that the resultant formation of trade unions and labour legislation is less significant than the fact that 'on the political front nothing short of a revolution has occurred', with the working classes rather than the middle classes setting the agenda.[166] In addition to the British government being '*forced* to appoint a strong Royal Commission specifically to investigate social conditions', the concessions obtained were not insignificant: fixing minimum wages, making land settlements, expenditure on public works, slum clearances, old-age pensions, and workmen's compensation.[167]

If the British left were largely preoccupied by the growing threat of fascism and the Spanish Civil War during this decade, the political and intellectual stage was nonetheless being set for the rapid advance of decolonization in the post-war period. The criticisms of benevolence and gradualism would gather force in the 1940s, as would the rejection of such concepts as 'trusteeship'. The 'legend that the British Colonial Office patiently "taught" the Africans of the Gold Coast to govern themselves is a bubble which badly needs pricking', James would observe in his later reflections on George Padmore and his protégé, Kwame Nkrumah.[168] Indeed, James would go so far as to suggest that his own argument in *The Black Jacobins* had to be revised as it became increasingly clear that self-government and independence in Africa would come not from the metropolitan proletariat rising up against capitalism, but from 'struggle in Africa itself', led by black personalities.[169] The IASB merged with the newly formed Pan-African Federation, which hosted the famous Pan-African Congress of 1945 – an event that could be said to have closed one era in the history of Afro-Caribbean anticolonialism and heralded another. Looking back on the period, Ras Makonnen recalls: 'We were operating in the midst of a radicalism unmatched in Europe, but it was a gay period, a period of purposefulness. You had the feeling that the truth was being told once and for all. Britain was really in a ferment – seething, in fact, like an African pot.'[170] Determinate efforts at sustained campaigning and organized institutions of consciousness-raising and education would continue into the war years and beyond, with conscious endeavours to forge cross-racial and cross-political alliances. This involved an identification of common cause, but also an engagement with fractures and tensions. The next chapter explores more closely the role of *IAO* editor and centrifugal force George Padmore in London, not just as a catalyst for black radical organization, but also in putting pressure on liberal and left formations – specifically the British dissidents associated with the Independent Labour Party and its journal, the *New Leader*.

9

Smash Our Own Imperialism: George Padmore, the *New Leader* and 'Colonial Fascism'

It is only when there is some riot in Jamaica, or shooting in Palestine, or unrest on the North-West frontier, that the average Briton is made even remotely conscious of his responsibility toward the hundreds of millions of coloured people over whom the British ruling class speciously claim to be exercising a benevolent trusteeship.

George Padmore (1939)

Professor J. B. S. Haldane once asserted that he would rather be a Jew in Berlin than a Kaffir in South Africa. I can well believe him. It is no exaggeration to say that Hitler and his Gestapo sadists are merely applying, with the usual Germanic efficiency, in Poland and other conquered countries, colonial practices borrowed lock, stock and barrel from the British in Southern Africa.

George Padmore (1941)

Comrade George Padmore is a great intellectual force and the voice of our negro brothers.

Arthur Ballard (1939)

A few years after the publication of *Negro*, Nancy Cunard and George Padmore were involved in a second literary collaboration. Structured as a dialogue between them, *The White Man's Duty* was published in 1942 as a pamphlet in a series produced by the International African Service Bureau. The 'firm of Cunard and Padmore' had produced 'a bouncy half-caste' to set tongues wagging, Padmore joked.[1] Subtitled 'An analysis of the colonial question in light of the Atlantic Charter', the pamphlet invoked the manifold contradictions of an Allied document which made grandiose claims for a war of freedom against fascism without addressing Britain's imperial holdings and their claims to democracy and freedom.[2] Targeting a white British readership, *The White Man's Duty* drew attention to the implications of Winston Churchill's assertion that the charter's aims of restoring sovereignty, self-government and national life did not apply to 'peoples which owe allegiance to the British Crown' in quite the same way as it did to Europeans formerly under Nazi domination.[3] For those under British rule, the only option was 'progressive evolution' to self-government – in other words, gradualism. The conversation between Cunard and Padmore also highlighted two other aspects of anticolonial discourse that had been growing in visibility through the ferment of the 1930s. The first was that such tendentious claims about the provenance of 'freedom' did not go unchallenged by colonial subjects – a fact which comes 'as a shock and a surprise to the powers-that-be'.[4] The colonized, Padmore noted, were 'no longer satisfied with just the expressions of goodwill and the suggestions of better things in the by-and-by'.[5] The second point, articulated by Cunard, who extolled Forster's *A Passage to India* and Leonard Woolf's *The Village in the Jungle* as she did so, was that the time had come for those Britons 'hating all race complexes' and who 'don't get much of a hearing as yet' to make their voices heard.[6] They were those who genuinely sought exchange, espoused 'human values', and were willing to put 'a bit of love into things ... and a bit of humour'.[7]

In many ways, of course, Padmore and Cunard themselves embodied the subjects they invoked – he, the defiant and articulate black colonial who would not settle for sops, and she, the intelligent and critically engaged white Briton who sought to forge solidarity with the colonized beyond the distorting relations of imperialism. What would be needed in the post-war era, as Cunard wrote, was not just reconstruction but 'a new policy of life for humanity – for the whole of humanity'.[8] Despite its proto-Socratic form, the pamphlet comes across as a real dialogue, 'easy to follow and understand', in which Cunard acts less as a pupil than as an intelligent partner who seeks to learn from an equal.[9] Her extended preface to the text, written with an informed confidence, makes clear that her own grasp of the political terrain of empire and questions of race is derived from a clear sense of the experiences of those at the sharp end. Padmore, for his part, as a 'specialist in colonial matters',[10] speaks with practised authority as he responds to Cunard's question: 'What should be done for the peoples of Africa, of the West Indies, of India, and all British colonial possessions ... that the pledges given by our public leaders, if they be carried out, entitle us to expect after peace has been declared?'[11] If Cunard sets herself up as the voice of the white progressive, Padmore's job is to put critical pressure on the hope and goodwill represented in these views, but with an assumption that they are part of a shared endeavour to transcend the limitations of the present. The book addressed its readers directly on the cover: 'Does the "Colonial Question" mean anything to you? It is one of the most momentous issues of our times, and here, in dialogue form – easy to follow and understand – you will find the facts. It is your duty to know them.'[12]

Let us return to July 1929 as the League against Imperialism (LAI) held its second conference in Frankfurt. In attendance, representing American labour, was a young communist delegate from the United

George Padmore in London, 1943

States, George Padmore. We do not know much about Padmore's specific contributions to the event; most of the talking was done, Padmore biographer James Hooker avers, by his companion, the black American communist and one-time presidential candidate James Ford, who was also a contributor to the *Negro* anthology.[13] Padmore would forge some important connections in Frankfurt, meeting Reginald Bridgeman and others in the British section of the LAI, as well as members of the Labour Party and the Independent Labour Party, some of whom he would continue to work with in years to come. Another delegate at the conference was Tiemoko Garan Kouyaté, a West African labour organizer born in the French Sudan, and leader of the Ligue de défense de la race nègre and Union des travailleurs nègres in France, with whom Padmore would strike up an important political and personal friendship. Padmore himself would also become one of the most significant figures in both British and African anticolonialism in the decade that followed the conference, and it is his role in shaping and sharpening the rhetoric of criticism of empire in Britain that is the subject of this chapter. At the Second Congress of the LAI, in 1929, Padmore was among those delegated to organize a 'Negro workers' conference'; he would spend some time in Moscow, as a high-ranking party member and head of the Negro Bureau of the Red International of Labour Unions (RILU), also known as Profintern.[14] He would also become editor of the *Negro Worker*, a Comintern journal aimed at organizing black labour globally through the International Trade Union Committee of Negro Workers (ITUC-NW).

The First International Conference of Negro Workers, held in Hamburg in 1930, was an important one, bringing together both black American trade unionists and, despite the denial of travel documents to most delegates from the colonies, a handful of attendees representing South African, Caribbean and West African labour. It was here that Padmore would articulate what would be an increasingly strong note of his interventions during the decades to come, 'the growing awareness of coloured peoples that they could control their own destinies', and the interconnectedness of black and Asian revolutionary movements in this regard.[15] Shortly after he was jailed by the Nazis and then deported from Germany, where he had been based, he found his relationship with the Comintern strained when it sidelined the ITUC-NW. After a painful and controversial break from the organization, Padmore would spend several years in Britain, where he became an influential and authoritative exponent of an anticolonialism which took inspiration from actually occurring resistance in the colonies, challenged false geopolitical divisions, and sought to make progressive transnational and cross-racial alliances. In the process, like his better-known friend and colleague C. L. R. James, Padmore also became a powerful presence contributing both to black organizing in Britain and to shaping the views of white British left-wing criticism of imperial ideologies and practices. As others have noted, Padmore consistently refuted the notion that imperialism was 'in any way concerned with welfare', though in this, as we have seen, he was part of a longer tradition rather than an entirely 'rare figure'.[16] What Padmore did bring to the table was an analysis which insisted on considering the relationship between fascism and colonialism in a global frame rather than, conveniently, depicting them as opposed geopolitical forces. As Robin D. G. Kelley, among others, has observed, the idea that fascism was not 'some aberration from the march of progress, an unexpected rightwing turn', but a 'blood relative' of European capitalism and imperialism, was shared by many mid-century black intellectuals, including W. E. B. Du Bois.[17] Padmore was the most indefatigable of them all, not only in ensuring that the analysis of 'fascism–imperialism' or 'colonial fascism' was brought home to the broader British left, but in suggesting that it was only such an intertwined and brutally honest analysis that could provide the basis for resistance and solidarity in both colony and metropole. The metropolitan left would have to understand the relationship of racial capitalism to fascism, rather than seek either to separate the phenomena or reduce their workings to class alone. Just as the defenders of empire could not demand the loyalties of the colonized in a putative war for freedom, the left could not demand solidarity based on a presumed homogeneity of class interests without recognizing the intertwining of racial, capitalist and colonial ideologies.[18] As we shall see, Padmore's analysis shaped the response of at least one British left-wing and dissident formation.

While George Padmore, 'not a dashing writer', as James would concede, has not received the kind of attention that the latter's own magisterial corpus has justifiably elicited, there is now a growing

interest in the work of this major figure in the history of anticolonialism.[19] Padmore's style does come across as information-heavy,
but it was not devoid of theorizing; as one recent biographer notes,
he was 'deeply engaged in political thought of his own'.[20] The broad
details of Padmore's political life have been elaborated in a slender
1967 biography by James R. Hooker, and a thoughtful, much fuller
subsequent account by Leslie James, who focuses on Padmore's
later work. Other scholars, such as Susan Pennybacker, Minkah
Makalani, Brent Hayes Edwards, Rupert Lewis and Carol Polsgrove
have also written illuminatingly on Padmore's work both as a political organizer and as a leading black intellectual.[21] Born Malcolm
Nurse in Trinidad to a schoolmaster father, whose own father had
been born into slavery in Barbados, Padmore had changed his name
after coming to the United States in 1924 for higher education at Fisk
and Howard universities, where he became a communist and radical
student organizer. Although he was never himself a votary of Marcus
Garvey, Padmore's teenage years had been spent in Trinidad, where
Garvey's United Negro Improvement Association (UNIA) had been
active and influential. As James would recall, what his childhood
friend brought to the table, while exiled in Britain – not least through
his experience working with the Comintern – was 'the courage, the
world-wide historical vision, the political knowledge and organizational skills'.[22] The break from the Comintern was just as vital; it
gave Padmore a keen sense of the specificity and irreducibility of
the question of race. Indeed, James would acknowledge: 'I then
was a Marxist and took the "black question" as part of Marxism
– but Padmore was the one who said no! I am a Marxist too but
this question needs special attention and he made me realise that the
"Black question" was an independent question of great importance
in historical development'.[23]

Unlike James when he had first arrived in London, Padmore brought
with him strong connections to labour organizers in the United States,
Europe, West Africa and the West Indies. He also had links to black
campaigners in North America, including W. E. B. Du Bois, with
whom he corresponded after arriving in Britain. One habitué fondly
recalled 'the political magnetism of Padmore's London flat which
drew young people from Africa and the Caribbean'.[24] As Leslie James
notes, 'Padmore's own network was massive. From his Cranleigh

Street base in London, he worked political contacts not only in Africa, the Caribbean, and the United States, but also in places as far apart as Denmark, Sri Lanka, Vietnam, and Singapore.'[25] As an organizer within London's black communities, Padmore also took seriously the task of shaping metropolitan opinion. He would be influential in putting pressure on and radicalizing at least one British organization until then only cautiously critical of empire;[26] like James and, before him, Saklatvala, Padmore became closely, if often critically, involved with the Independent Labour Party. Padmore's frequent contributions to the ILP's journal, the *New Leader* (originally the *Labour Leader*, and from 1946 the *Socialist Leader*), allowed for a wider dissemination of their views and, crucially, facilitated greater awareness of and engagement with insurgencies and resistance movements in Africa and the Caribbean on the British left more generally, and in the ILP specifically.[27] Of that period, James writes that 'the chief thing that we did, and George organised it and kept it going, was to keep in touch with the left wing of the Labour movement. We got into close touch with the Independent Labour Party ... We were in close touch with the left-wing members of the Labour Party and left-wing organisations. And whenever the Communists held a meeting or some kind of conference, we were there, presenting resolutions, making speeches'.[28]

If the *New Leader*'s line on empire became markedly radical in the mid 1930s, a good portion of the credit is due to Padmore's increasing involvement with it. One scholar gives him almost sole credit for explicating black resistance to a British readership: 'The growing consciousness both in Africa and the Caribbean became public knowledge through Padmore's expositions.'[29] 'How easy it is for an Englishman to forget that his country is the biggest land-grabbing nation that history has ever seen', Padmore observed, as he devoted his writing to explicating the British Empire to British readers.[30] James also recalled that Padmore's indefatigable correspondence and journalism on colonial questions 'kept the situation alive', and that when other media organs failed them, 'there was usually Fenner Brockway editing the *New Leader* to give us a helping hand. On every issue, when *The Times* and the big Conservative press, the Colonial Office, the Stalinists, the Labour Party put forward their side, we saw to it that the anti-imperialist case was put forward.'[31] (This was

despite the fact that Padmore had attacked Brockway's own moderation and gradualism in *How Britain Rules Africa*.) Padmore's prolific
journalism was described later by Peter Abrahams as a 'major early
version of a new, Third-World way of looking at the news', and it
is this way of seeing that, I argue, made an impression on sections
of the British left.[32] In his account of the rise of pan-Africanism in
England, Immanuel Geiss notes that Padmore also held weekly discussions to which *New Leader* contributors like Reginald Reynolds,
another noted critic of empire with a special interest in India, would
come.[33] Apparently Padmore repeatedly refused invitations to stand
for election to parliament as an ILP candidate, but spoke for many
years running at the ILP summer school, and was instrumental in
shaping the interventions of the party's MPs on colonial questions in
the House of Commons.[34]

In 1933, despite run-ins with the leadership on colonial matters,
Padmore, as chair of the ITUC-NW, was still an important member
of the Comintern executive, hewing to the Comintern's line as he
facilitated contacts between unions and activists in the African diaspora. But all was not quite well. Disheartened among other things by
what they saw as a failure to address white racism within European
labour movements, there was a sense among several black activists, including those like Arnold Ward in Britain, that the party used
'Negroes when they are wanted' but 'put them aside' when convenient.[35] Then, in the wake of Hitler's rise to power, the Communist
International changed course more sharply, telling Padmore: 'George,
you know, we have to change the line. We must say that the United
States, Britain and France, they are imperialists it is true, but they are
democratic imperialists; but Germany, Italy and Japan are the fascist
imperialists.'[36] Padmore refused, arguing that the new line made nonsense of what he and the Comintern had been preaching up to this
point; his analysis of fascism and colonialism as deeply intertwined
is surely in part a response to what he saw as an untenable separation. Later, he apparently told St Clair Drake that, when he received
orders to soften criticism of imperialism in the *Negro Worker*, he
decided that he was 'no Joe Stalin' but 'just a West Indian darkie out
here trying to help my African darkie brothers free themselves. And
so I decided I wasn't going to stop my agitation.'[37] From this point
on, Padmore would determinedly set fascism and imperialism within

the same analytical frame, identifying overlapping features, without eliding either their respective provenances or their differences.

When passing through London in 1933 – he would move on to Paris for a time – Padmore famously reconnected with his childhood friend, C. L. R. James, who had come to a talk Padmore was giving without realizing that the speaker was the boy whom he had known as Malcolm Nurse.[38] After a glad reunion with James, who described him as then 'tied up with Moscow' while 'I was headed away from Moscow', Padmore became better acquainted with London's socialist and Labour milieu.[39] Among others, he met the future chair of the ILP, C. A. Smith, editor of the journal *Controversy*, to which he would contribute in the coming years. Shortly afterwards, his break with the Comintern would be finalized; Padmore resigned, writing that to thus 'put a brake upon the anti-imperialist work of its affiliate sections' was to 'sacrifice the young national liberation movements in Asia and Africa. This I considered to be a betrayal of the fundamental interests of my people, with which I could not identify myself. I therefore had no choice but to sever my connection with the Communist International.'[40] A few months later, in a gesture at once symbolic and redundant, he would be formally expelled and duly vilified in print as 'A Betrayer of the Negro Liberation Struggle'.[41] In James's account, Padmore arrived at his flat one afternoon in 1935, looking dishevelled, telling his host: 'I have left those people, you know.'[42] As Padmore, who remained a Marxist, would always acknowledge, communism had been enabling, even as its limitations ultimately made staying on impossible: 'I stayed there because there was a means of doing work for the black emancipation and there was no other place that I could think of.'[43]

James was right that once unshackled from party affiliation, Padmore would live 'to become an even more powerful enemy of imperialism than when he had at his disposal the immense resources of the Russian state and the Communist International'.[44] The former Comintern member had already made his mark on anticolonial thought with *The Life and Struggles of the Negro Toilers*, remarkable for its condensed but sweeping account of black labour and labour resistance across continents. Banned immediately by colonial governments across Africa and the Caribbean, *Life and Struggles* makes the communist case for black labour to be organized by party activists into a revolutionary force, specifically through the Red International of Labour Unions.[45] The RILU, was, Padmore asserts loyally, 'the only international which conducts a consistent and permanent struggle against white chauvinism for equal rights for the labour movement in the colonial and semi-colonial countries, for the correct solution of the national-race problem'. Presaging the direction in which Padmore would go after his break with the Comintern, the book documents the breadth of anticolonial resistance by black people in various contexts, and the powerful repression that colonial governments had variously exerted in order to crush it. Strikes were of 'frequent occurrence' in Kenya, where the King's African Rifles were deployed to crush Kikuyu uprisings under the doughty early nationalist Harry Thuku; so also in Basutoland, where military planes were deployed to suppress peasant revolts led by Lakho La-Baffo (affiliated to the LAI). In Nigeria, 'over 30,000 women organised monster protest demonstrations against British imperialists and their agents' in 1929, breaking into bank and trade buildings and occupying them for days. As reprisal, martial law was declared, hundreds were arrested, huts were burned to the ground and fields were laid waste by troops. Information sent to the outside world was severely limited and censored. The story repeated itself, *mutatis mutandis*, in the Gambia, Sierra Leone and the Gold Coast, as well as French and Belgian African territories. In an extended section, Padmore reported that the British West Indies had become a site of febrile 'unrest among the natives' – struggles over wages and labour conditions were at the heart of the movements, which, predictably, were met with bayonets and rifles – and that nascent nationalist movements were crystallizing under the slogan 'The West Indies for the West Indians!' As Leslie James points out, Padmore's early experience of labour militancy, strikes and unrest in Trinidad in 1919 was of 'profound importance … he witnessed active revolt that sprang up among workers of different professions and races'.[46] Such revolt would remain absolutely central to his thought over the next decades. 'We rebels never surrender until we are buried', he wrote to a friend.[47]

While dutifully denouncing 'petty bourgeois reformists' among black activists (including Du Bois and Garvey) and calling for 'Negro workers [to] conduct a more relentless struggle' against 'disrupters and splitters of the working-class movement', *Life and*

Struggles nonetheless hints at Padmore's growing disquiet about the Comintern's inability and apparent unwillingness to tackle the matter of race and imperialism. 'Even in the ranks of the revolutionary workers', he observed, 'numerous examples of white chauvinism can be recorded.'[48] Once his departure from the Comintern was final, Padmore was free to develop his thinking in less constrained ways. Writing to his friend Cyril Olivierre, Padmore explained:

> Last August the Communist International wanted us to close down our activities in order to appease the British Foreign Office which was raising hell because the blacks in Africa were beginning to wake up ... Well, the Africans objected and I stood up loyally with them and resigned. Since then the 'Reds' ... are trying to slander me in order to cover up their betrayal.[49]

It is worth acknowledging that for all the bitterness of the break from the Comintern, 'the milieu of Third Period internationalism ... also allowed Padmore to move towards alternative views of black liberation' that still drew on Marxism.[50] In addition to his associate, Kouyaté, now in Paris, also now blacklisted by the Comintern as a 'renegade', Padmore's broader milieu in London would come to include, among others, C. L. R. James, then chair of the Finchley branch of the ILP; the 'moderate' founder of the League of Coloured Peoples (LCP), Dr Harold Moody; the Jamaican writer and broadcaster Una Marson; the Guyanan-born Ras Makonnen; the labour organizer from Sierra Leone, Wallace Johnson; and Amy Ashwood Garvey, an important campaigner in her own right.[51] West African students were also becoming politicized through the newly formed West African Students Union (WASU); Padmore was in contact with its leading members. 'We became so well-known', wrote James, 'that in time leftist labour groups and unions would write to us for speakers.'[52] A counter-discourse was developing – one that protested distorting stereotypes and 'everyday ridicule' in representations of Africa (during the British Empire exhibition, for instance) while insisting that analyses and understandings of empire be elaborated from black – Caribbean and African – perspectives.[53] While he wrote for British publications and was close to many members of the ILP, Padmore would not 'ever again join any European or worldwide organisation in which black or colonial peoples did not have the dominant and controlling role'.[54] He did, however, direct his energies towards influencing British dissent and calling for solidarity with colonial peoples, constantly seeking 'a manoeuvre with the Colonial Office, an avenue for some propaganda in the British press'.[55]

In the summer of 1934, shortly after *Negro* was published, Padmore was ensconced at the French country home of one of his fiercest advocates, Nancy Cunard, where she typed out for him the manuscript of what would become *How Britain Rules Africa*. Cunard later recalled her own deep upset at the way in which Padmore, 'one of the few people I reverenced for his integrity and very being', should be vilified by 'members of the ideology (communism) that I admired also entirely and wholly'.[56] She would note, however, in the face of this 'hideous, unjust crisis', that communism and an actually existing Communist Party could often be two different things. In the bucolic surroundings of a village near Paris, Padmore – still a Marxist, still committed to Lenin's analysis of imperialism, and insisting to Cunard that Russia remained 'the great example, the encouragement' – wrote the book with fierce concentration, shutting out the 'distress and disappointment' of his break from the Comintern and the subsequent vilification campaign against him.[57] He was supported by Cunard, who wrote to Nnamdi Azikiwe, a mutual friend, that she was 'enjoying the typing out of his new book' on the African colonies, and found it 'fine': 'What an indictment!'[58] In it Padmore would note that 'Blacks have no powerful press, control no broadcasting stations, sit in no parliaments of the world, and therefore have no means of voicing their grievances.'[59] That did not, however, mean that they were not 'thinking seriously about the vital economic, political and social problems which confront them'.[60] Why should this thinking not be central to metropolitan discussions? As though to prove its own point, the book had a hard time finding a publisher, and was rejected by several before it was finally taken on by Wishart. With Padmore's permission, a heavily bowdlerized German edition was also produced. Although it annoyed British reviewers, one of whom saw it as an unsparing and unfair attack on 'everything the white man has done in Africa', the book was, in fact, also a warning that what was done in the colonies was coming home to roost in the form of fascism:[61]

Habits once formed are difficult to get rid of. That is why we maintain that Colonies are the breeding ground for the type of fascist
mentality which is being let loose in Europe today. Therefore, the
working class of England and other defenders of the hard-won
democratic rights of the British peoples cannot beat back fascism at
home and at the same time continue to be indifferent to the intolerable conditions of the overwhelming majority of the coloured
people of the Empire who inhabit colonial lands. The fight against
fascism cannot be separated from the right of all colonial peoples
and subject races to Self-Determination. For any people who help
to keep another people in slavery are at the same time forging their
own chains.[62]

The point, which Padmore would make repeatedly in his journalism,
was that British capitalism was not and could not be 'hermetically
sealed up' in the British Isles: its global character meant that reserve
forces of labour were always available to it – a fact which also
worked against British labour.[63] Even as his book sought to influence
Labour's colonial reform policies, Padmore's aim was less to appeal
to the good sense of Labour politicians than to expose their 'indifference' and 'sabotage' as part of the problem. Transformation, he
suggested, would ultimately derive not from their initiative but from
the resistance that was being put up to colonial depredations.

Padmore's move away from party vanguardism towards enabling
'Africans to speak for themselves'[64] is perhaps most evident in his
engagement with the question of race and his probing of the ways
in which race was deployed to undermine class solidarity, which he
described unsparingly as 'the spectacle of the white working class
openly collaborating with the capitalists in helping to keep down
their black class brothers in return for certain economic advantages
and political and social privileges'.[65] White workers and mine-
owners were the ones, for instance, who demanded a colour bar
in that industry. Since, in some places, 'race is thicker than class',
Padmore made so bold as to say, the Marxian appeal to workers of
the world to unite 'finds no response among the white proletariat'.[66]
At the same time, a 'twofold burden – class and race' – was carried
by black workers in the colonies. This not only called into question
the claims of the British Empire to being ideologically different from

'the racial philosophy of Hitlerism', but also suggested that colonized black subjects had a different kind of war on their hands – one that had to be conducted on two fronts.[67] At any rate, it was indisputably the case that, from this point on, 'the coloured races do not intend to allow the white imperialist nations to trample over them as in the past'.[68] Italy's ongoing unhindered incursions into Ethiopia had been eye-opening in this regard: 'It has served to reveal before the black peoples of the world who are their friends, and who their enemies'.[69] Socialists and vaunted friends and champions of Africans, including ILP leaders like Fenner Brockway, were shown up when they declared that Ethiopian independence was 'no concern of the British working class'.[70] With or without the support of white allies, Padmore asserts bullishly, 'the Blacks will fight for their country's independence'.[71]

For all its insistence on the specific provenance and scope of black anticolonialism, *How Britain Rules Africa* is not a separatist document. Indeed, having thanked Nancy Cunard in his acknowledgements for being 'one of the staunchest and most trusted white friends of the black race',[72] Padmore ends the book by insisting that 'the fact remains, that all Whites are not our enemies'; many, like their abolitionist predecessors, were 'struggling against the new slavery – *Fascist-Imperialism*'.[73] He would even suggest that the minds of some in the governing classes might be changed – a prospect James, reviewing *How Britain Rules Africa*, found improbable: 'But, astonishingly, he welcomes the appeal of "enlightened and far-sighted sections of the ruling classes of Europe with colonial interests in Africa" to co-operate with Africans. That is madness.'[74] James and Padmore were in agreement, however, that the Africans would have to 'win their own freedom. Nobody will win it for them.'[75] Padmore would not have disagreed that cooperation with 'the revolutionary movement in Europe and Asia' was vital for Africa, and that 'each movement will neglect the other at its peril.'[76] His book itself is offered as a 'weapon in the struggle for the new social order', and 'to arouse the conscience of the British people, especially the common folks, who are being exploited at "home" by the same classes that oppress the Indians, the Africans, the Chinese and other colonial peoples'.[77] The key political shift, however, lay in the prominence of colonial subjects: it was the moral force of the aspirations and actions of the colonized which would serve to rouse white conscience, and not that conscience which would serve to uplift the colonized. If anything, it was the working classes of the metropolitan countries who would remain enslaved and unable, in another echo of Marx's dictum, 'to emancipate themselves without the fraternal support of the colonial and subject peoples'.[78] Rather than simply condemn as 'bourgeois-democratic' the nationalist form taken by the aspirations of colonized peoples, Padmore thought it necessary to make the distinction between 'colonial-nationalism' (meaning the nationalism of anticolonalism) and 'imperialist-nationalism'.[79] If a workers' dictatorship is not the same as a fascist dictatorship, which it is not, then it was 'stupidly' mechanical for communists to argue that 'all nationalisms are the same'.[80] Under the circumstances, racial chauvinism in an oppressing class had to be understood very differently from racial solidarity in an oppressed one. Padmore was clear that racial chauvinism was 'part and parcel of the capitalist system', and as such, despite his own experience with the Comintern, impossible in a place like the Soviet Union, where it was 'not in the interest of the new rulers to foster or encourage' prejudice.[81]

Towards the conclusion of *How Britain Rules Africa*, in a short section on anticolonial insurgency in Sierra Leone, Padmore offers some important reflections on the relationship between aspirations to freedom and Westernization. While Western education could reinforce an appreciation for democratic institutions, in this part of Africa the push for freedom itself derived not from Western influence but from a history of resistance. Sierra Leoneans were descended from North American and West Indian ancestors who had 'rebelled against chattel slavery' and, when they migrated to the region, 'brought with them not only their spirit of rebellion, but ideas of human liberty which they have since jealously safeguarded'.[82] The organizational forms used by anticolonial insurgency in the region, whether trade unions or parliaments, may have been Western, but their emancipatory content derived from a history of black rebellion. Where colonial governments proscribed institutions such as trade unions, insurgencies sprang up that were 'religious in form' but 'political and racial in content'.[83] (Recall James's parallel insight about West Indian slaves as 'the most rebellious people in history'.)[84] *How Britain Rules Africa* ends by explicating how Africa will rid itself of imperialism, citing Lamine Senghor's fiery speech at the founding Congress of the

LAI: 'The Negroes have slept too long. But beware, Europe! Those who have slept long will not go back to sleep when they wake up.'[85] Even if Africa did not yet have 'a Gandhi or a Sun-Yat Sen' – lacking, unlike India or China, a native bourgeoisie – Africans had rallied with 'a tremendous feeling of racial solidarity' around the flag of the besieged Ethiopian emperor, Haile Selassie, the Italo-Ethiopian conflict acting 'like dynamite in arousing and consolidating' this as never before.[86] The invasion of Ethiopia could act, Padmore avers, as a general clarion call to commence the final push against European empires. For Padmore, too, events unfolding in Ethiopia could constitute 'the turning-point in the future relationship between White and Black'.[87] He himself would put every effort into making it so.

'Smash our own imperialism': The Independent Labour Party and the Question of Empire

> But the ILP is in altogether a different state. Its apparatus is not homogeneous and therefore permits great freedom to different currents. The revolutionary rank and file of the party eagerly seeks solutions.
>
> Leon Trotsky

> The white natives are going through the same hell that has been the lot of the blacks for centuries.
>
> George Padmore

It is correct to say that, in the interwar years, criticism of empire in Britain outside the black radical circles already discussed was emphatically a minority discourse – albeit, on more than one occasion, one that was able to percolate through to and register itself upon public and parliamentary debates. One important forum for the emergence of such dissenting voices in the 1930s was the Independent Labour Party, a socialist formation committed to economic justice – some of whose most high-profile figures, such as Keir Hardie, we have encountered already. Founded in 1893 by a group of socialists including Hardie and Robert Blatchford, the ILP was a core member of the Labour Representation Committee, which became the Labour

Party in 1906. Functioning initially as a 'ginger group' – a radicalizing lobby – within the latter, the ILP, formally socialist, retained the
right to formulate independent positions, most famously taking an
anti-war stance in 1914 while the Labour Party voted for military
action. Tensions increased in the post-war years, followed by a split
and permanent disaffiliation in 1932. At the time of the split, the
membership of the ILP was 'over five times the size of the Communist
Party of Great Britain', and the party had returned five times more
candidates than the Labour Party in Scotland.[88] Before its influence
declined, the ILP had 'an extensive organisation at both national
and local level [and] a well regarded national journal supplemented
by many more local publications'.[89] These provided an interface, as
it were, between black anticolonialists and white British critics of
empire; certainly the *New Leader*'s coverage of foreign affairs, and of
colonial issues in particular, was possibly the most extensive among
British news media at the time. The ILP was also active in organizing a socialist contingent to fight in the Spanish Civil War on the
republican side. The most famous member of this brigade was, of
course, George Orwell, who, Christian Høgsbjerg reminds us, met
both James and Padmore upon his return from Spain in 1937.[90] The
editor of the *New Leader* at this time was Fenner Brockway, who
would become a notable figure in post-war British anticolonialism
(see Chapter 10). While it is true that, after its disaffiliation from the
Labour Party, the direct political influence of the ILP was weakened,
'the argument that the ILP was isolated and alienated in the 1930s
overlooks the intricate networks of collaboration and co-operation
between left-wing groups in this period'.[91]

Satnam Virdee has noted that in the early decades of the twentieth
century – during the race clashes of the post-war period, for instance
– the ILP was 'a party whose members often displayed a deep-rooted,
almost unconscious attachment to nationalism … within which they
located the struggle for working-class justice'.[92] Where it might have
challenged working-class racism, 'the ILP chose instead to accommodate to it'.[93] This was, of course, a racialized discourse in which
some workers were seen to 'belong' to the nation while others did
not. In the 1930s, however, a shift within the ILP became discern-
ible, and we must assume that the presence in its wider milieu of
black radicals such as James, Padmore, I. T. A. Wallace Johnson and

Jomo Kenyatta, writing for the *New Leader*, had more than a little to do with this change of direction. In the late autumn of 1941, the ILP's National Council passed four resolutions, the first of which had a dual aim: 'To establish social justice in Britain and national liberation in the Empire.'[94] As Leslie James has noted, though the ILPs membership was circumscribed, especially after its disaffiliation from Labour, 'it maintained a disproportionately high profile in British politics', not least through prominent members such as George Orwell and Kingsley Martin.[95] It was 'also the only party on the left willing to take an openly critical stance against Stalin's rule'.[96] From the 1920s onwards, the ILP had strong links with Indian nationalists through Fenner Brockway and Reginald Reynolds, who were close to Jawaharlal Nehru, among others; Nehru wrote occasionally for the ILP's weekly newspaper, the *New Leader*. While the *New Leader* gave substantial coverage to the invasion of Ethiopia in the mid 1930s, the ILP was famously divided on how to oppose it: James, Brockway and others called for workers' sanctions against Italy, while Maxton, McGovern and others in the party's parliamentary grouping insisted that there should be no intervening in a 'clash of imperialisms'. James observed bitterly in the pages of the *New Leader*: 'British imperialism will not fight Italy either for Abyssinia or for collective security. It will fight for British Imperialist interests and nothing else.'[97] Notwithstanding James's presence, a few pieces on the Scottsboro case, some dispatches on the situation in Palestine and some coverage of India via Nehru, Reynolds and V. Krishna Menon of the India League, the *New Leader* cannot be said to have engaged extensively with imperial issues until the late 1930s, with the arrival of Padmore and others associated with *International African Opinion*. Unsurprisingly, perhaps, much of its coverage in 1936 and 1937 concerned the Spanish Civil War and the threat of fascism. A piece by Kenyatta written in 1937 attempted to make the case for considering the links between fascism and imperialism, noting that such things as 'democratic rights and civil liberties' were 'things unknown' in British Kenya, where land-grabbing proceeded apace and detention camps were 'similar to concentration or labour camps in fascist countries'.[98] Kenyatta was clear: it was now 'necessary for British Labour organisations to give more attention to the struggles of the colonial peoples' if the latter were to 'be able to distinguish the difference between the imperialist forces and the anti-imperialists'; it was time to cry 'Down with Fascist rule in the Colonies'.[99]

This was a cry that would be amplified relentlessly by Padmore after his arrival in London. Between 1937 and 1945, Padmore wrote a large number of articles for many left-wing British papers, but most notably for the ILP's flagship paper, which rapidly became the main British weekly to carry articles on the colonial situation. Indeed, the correlation between Padmore's arrival and the *New Leader*'s increased, bolder, more sharply critical coverage of colonial issues is striking. Padmore would relentlessly reiterate the call for white working-class solidarity with colonized workers towards the necessarily twinned projects of undoing both capitalism and imperialism. 'To conceive of getting rid of the capitalists without smashing up the Empire is like trying to make the omelette without smashing the egg', he noted, urging British workers to see colonial peoples as allies, not competitors.[100] Providing painstakingly detailed accounts of events taking place across far-flung locations in the British Empire, Padmore repeatedly made the case for the British working classes to boldly support the claims of colonial peoples, in their own interest as much as anyone else's. He would frequently make comparisons between contexts, noting, for instance, that popular efforts to achieve political liberties and acceptable working conditions were being resisted by the British in more than one colony: 'The tragedy of India is being repeated in the West Indies.'[101] In the latter, too, constitutional reforms were attempts to deflect rather than resolve long-festering issues, attempts to 'bamboozle the West Indies, just as the East Indians, but they will succeed no better in one way than in the other'. Padmore's British journalism relentlessly reiterated a critique of gradualism, benevolence and the wilful refusal to acknowledge what he described as the 'quieter Fascist tendencies within the British Empire'.[102] He had no hesitation in pointing out that the leadership of the 'opportunist' and 'reformist' Labour Party was also deeply compromised in its relationship to imperialism, being as willing as the Conservatives to 'apply the most repressive measures to safeguard the interests of British capitalists in the African and West Indian colonies'.[103] 'People who can bomb Indians struggling for independence', the Labour Party was not very much more committed to the principle of self-determination than the Conservatives.[104] Within his old home, the Communist Party, Padmore identified a tragic contradiction between theory and practice, whereby a theoretical critique of capitalism and war did not prevent the pursuit of 'a policy identical with that of the Labour party … re-echoing all the shibboleths … about "bourgeois democracy" and "collective security through the League of Nations"'.[105] Worst of all, in Padmore's book, was the Comintern's division of the imperialist world into the 'good, peace-loving powers (Britain, France and America)' and those labelled 'bad, warlike' (Germany, Italy and Japan). The net result was that, once again, colonial subjects were expected to 'forego their struggle for self-determination and line up in defence of "democracy," something', Padmore pronounced damningly, 'they have never known'.[106] It also allowed for any 'kind of imperialistic or reactionary move' in the metropole 'so long as the politicians are shrewd enough to dress it up as part of the struggle against Hitlerism. Hitler is a godsend to our home-bred fascists'.[107]

While he deprecated the 'lamentable confusion' the party had shown in relation to the Ethiopia crisis, Padmore had qualified praise for the ILP's generally 'correct theoretical approach' to colonial questions.[108] Given that 'the heir to the October Revolution', the British Communist Party, had 'been swamped in a morass of opportunism' on colonial matters, Padmore declared his faith in the ILP instead, calling on it to uphold revolutionary Marxism and maintain 'an uncompromising and unswerving position, come what may'.[109] Above all, British workers should not 'help the capitalists to drown in blood the struggles of the colonial peoples'.[110] With characteristic incaution, but with a nose for the core truths, he pronounced that most colonial peoples 'were not concerned with the conflicting political conflicts going on in Europe. To them all whites are alike – a feeling which can hardly be otherwise when Labour and Popular Front Governments oppress and exploit them in the same way as Tory and other reactionary Capitalists.'[111] For this attitude to change, European workers' movements would have to 'show more solidarity in deeds and not words' with colonial aspirations to liberation. Padmore himself was drawing on resistance taking place in the colonies to make his observations, citing, for instance, the *Barbados Observer*, which had declared it 'sheer impudence on the part of the British ruling class to appeal to colonial workers to help them defend their ill-gotten gains' given the denial of 'elementary principles of democracy ... to the native masses'.[112] 'While the European scene is occupying our attention, the colonial "Fuehrers" are tightening their grip on the coloured workers in Africa and the West Indies', Padmore announced, as the Second World War finally broke out.[113] Quite simply, he noted, the British government 'cannot claim to be fighting for "freedom and democracy" in Europe without stimulating demands for "freedom and democracy" in its own Empire'.[114] He also repeatedly invoked the white European 'indifference to the suffering of the coloured people of Asia, Africa, and other backward lands', asking pointedly: 'How many whites who are now living under the Nazi jackboot ever concerned themselves with the life and struggles of the coloured races?'[115]

Padmore's imprint is immediately manifest in the *New Leader*'s first 'Empire Special', published ahead of May Day, 1938. Its front page lays out in pithily annotated bullet-points, 'What the Empire Is', from the countries and populations under its purview to the investments and profits it generates.[116] 'There is certainly much to commend from the point of view of the British Capitalist class', the article announces acerbically. 'Whether there is so much to commend from the point of view of the workers, the other pages of this "Empire Special" will serve to indicate.'[117] It is impossible not to see Padmore's analytical influence in every article which follows. Reginald Reynolds, laying out a litany of imperial crimes in India, familiar from his *White Sahibs in India*, now describes, as he had not in his book, the extent of resistance, as well as the brutal repression of it from the 'Mutiny' to the Amritsar massacre in 1919. Citing both Ernest Jones on the Indian revolt and Hutchinson's comment in the wake of the Meerut Conspiracy Case that British imperialism is 'in no respect different' from 'Fascist Terrorism' in Italy, Reynolds elaborates: 'Yet such is the system for which we are being invited to fight in the name of "Democracy"; and an attempt is actually being made to mix up the fight of the Spanish workers against Fascism with the defence of the British Empire against the rival bandits of Italy, Germany, and Japan!'[118] British workers 'will one day realise that they are used to keep their fellow-workers in slavery'. Reynolds rehearsed a point that was also made, we will recall, in the aftermath of the Indian rebellion in 1857 and Morant Bay uprising in 1865;

the end of empire 'means not only freedom for the other fellow but freedom for ourselves'. An unsigned piece lists 'humane' British campaigns of aerial bombing, observing: 'Imperialist aggression is not only infamous when it is committed by Japan and the Fascist powers. It is always infamous. It is infamous when committed by the British Government.'[119] The hitherto moderate Fenner Brockway posed a bold question in his article 'Has Hitler Anything to Teach Our Ruling Class?', before going to on to list the features of fascism practised by all empires, including the British, from racial persecution, forced labour and the suppression of worker organizations to censorship, detention without trial and even concentration camps. Noting that political democratic rights were only enjoyed by members of the conquering white race in the colonies, 'The British Empire is not a democracy,' Brockway declared passionately. 'It is the most extensive dictatorship in the world.'[120] Kenyatta and Padmore also contributed to the supplement, their pieces fleshing out Brockway's more general points, detailing respectively the violent expropriation of ancestral lands in East Africa and the brutal repression of labour organization in the West Indies, another form of 'colonial fascism'.[121] In an article telling the story of the Opium Wars, a young Jon Kimche, who would later become a noted historian of the Middle East, called for opposition to Japanese aggression in China, but ended thus: 'But don't think that the British ruling class is any better than the Japanese ruling class. They are both Imperialist robbers. And our first duty is to overthrow the robbers in our own midst.'[122]

A particularly trenchant voice on colonial affairs in the *New Leader* was that of Arthur Ballard. A carpenter by profession and a protégé of James, Ballard wrote frequently on colonial matters, and ran a series in the *New Leader* called 'In the Empire', which he aimed partly at 'the working-class student of Empire problems'.[123] One of Ballard's creations was a counter-exhibit to the much-hyped Empire Exhibition in Glasgow held that year, in which, as one contributor to the *New Leader* had it: 'Ideal conditions are being created for enticing young men to become murderous robots on behalf of the ruling caste.'[124] Ballard's 'Anti-Empire Exhibition' would instead 'show that the real owners of the Empire are not the people of Britain or of the colonies, but the big financial and commercial interests centred in London'.[125] The 'Anti-Empire Exhibition' would also involve 'remarkable lectures' to packed halls on colonial conditions by the likes of Kenyatta and Padmore, to counter the main exhibition in which, as Ballard trenchantly observed, 'All the resources of Capitalism have been used to glorify an Empire under whose flag conditions are equal to those within the Fascist countries.'[126] It is unlikely that Ballard's views were not indebted in some sense to James's writings and to Padmore's persistent repetition of this very point. Sarah Britton's useful historical account of the 'Workers' Exhibition', as it was also known, tells us that it sought to detail the 'harsh conditions in the colonies and the hardships endured by colonial workers' from their own perspective; from Australia and Ireland to India, Trinidad and China, it told the story of 'Empire from the bottom', as one socialist newspaper put it.[127] A report in the *New Leader* deemed the counter-exhibition a great success, its having 'received large-scale notice in all the Scottish papers' and 'a record sale of general anti-Imperialist literature'.[128] Given the high levels of support for the ILP in Glasgow, the exhibition was not an isolated call from the political fringe but 'an articulate, co-ordinated expression from a political party at the very centre of Glasgow life'.[129] An unsigned piece written around this time, most likely by Ballard, praised Comrade George Padmore as 'a great intellectual force and the voice of our negro brothers'.[130] On 9 December 1938, Ballard's review of James's *The Black Jacobins* described the Haitian Revolution as 'The Greatest Slave Revolt in History', and posed the question: 'What are the lessons we can learn from this story?'[131] One was that 'oppressed peoples should be ready to take advantage of the difficulties of the various Imperialist groups', and should be assisted in their quest for self-determination by white workers, even if only 'the revolutionary action of the masses can give freedom to the masses, whether white or coloured'.[132]

Unsurprisingly given these influences, reportage and opinion on the 'colonial question' in the *New Leader* was also distinctive in being shot through with the understanding that any concessions towards freedom and self-determination were wrested from colonial powers, in the first instance, by the actions of colonial peoples. In earlier pieces reporting on the unrest in the Caribbean, Ballard, noting that British warships had been dispatched to the West Indies, had demanded: 'Are we in Britain going to tolerate this? Are we going to allow the demands of the workers in the West Indies to be answered with armed force?'[133] Detailing the appalling conditions prevailing in the West Indian colonies, Ballard praised those workers who, not content to break stones for a pittance every day and demanding 'land to cultivate', had rioted only to meet with shootings and arrests.[134] The West Indies 'now occupy the centre of the stage of the anti-Imperialist struggle'.[135] Ballard would note in relation to India that it was only bitter struggle by the masses that had 'compelled the Government to grant certain political rights in the Provinces'.[136] Challenging Lord Halifax's claim that, contra Germany, British rule 'had left trail [sic] of freedom and self-government' behind, Ballard snapped: 'The West Indies alone give the answer to the lie.'[137] In another article he would note that methods 'in accord with the worst Fascist traditions' were used by the British Empire in the face of 'agitational movements' – that of the West African Youth League in Sierra Leone, for instance.[138] Indeed, to stop Hitler's appeal to the colonial masses, it was necessary to admit to imperial hypocrisies and to assist anticolonial struggles. Ballard's call for assistance based on solidarity rather than benevolence – 'We in Britain can help' – was based on the simple argument that to let such repression pass without protest was 'only bringing the open dictatorship of Imperialism one step nearer home'.[139]

Neither Ballard nor other *New Leader* contributors were unaware of Hitler's cynical and self-serving use of the British Empire's record to justify his depredations, and they were at pains to stress that Nazism had to be resisted unambiguously and strenuously; 'the whole liberty-crushing regime of Fascism is abhorrent to us', Brockway insisted.[140] No one doubted that 'it is the duty of the working-class movement to stop Hitler' and to 'give direct, large and constant assistance' to militant anti-Fascist working-class movements in Fascist-held countries.[141] The point was, rather, to hold the Empire to account as it imprisoned the likes of war veteran Uriah Butler in the West Indies 'for the crime of attempting to obtain a little of the democratic rights which were supposed to be Britain's aim'.[142] To this end, the false binary between freedom-loving democracies with colonies and tyrannical fascism had to be put under scrutiny. Brockway argued that fascism and British imperialism both 'trample upon liberty and embody the barbarity of racial suppression'.[143] Giving the example of Sierra Leone, Ballard observed that, as resistance in the colonies gathered steam, colonial rulers had been 'actively engaged in removing what small elements of "democracy" already existed'.[144] In September 1939, the *New Leader* published, through the India League, the Indian National Congress's famous declaration that it stood against both fascism and imperialism: 'Indian sympathy is entirely on the side of democracy and freedom but she is not able to associate herself with the present war when freedom is denied to her and even the present limited freedom is taken away'.[145] A few weeks later, with the war now underway, the paper carried extensive extracts from 'an outspoken manifesto' signed by multiple organizations from the West Indies and African colonies declaring that 'the African Peoples' in the British and French empires were following the Indian people in refusing to co-operate in the war: 'What did the Negroes get out of the last war which should make them enthusiastic about the present? Nothing. Today they enjoy less democracy in their own countries than they did in 1914.'[146] The manifesto itself, issued in Britain by the IASB executive and signed by Padmore, James, Kenyatta, Johnson and others, was a sharply worded response to the call for colonial subjects to contribute to the war effort:

> Let Mr Chamberlain get up at Westminster and M. Daladier in the French Chamber of Deputies and issue a declaration to the world granting their colonies full democratic rights and self-government – NOW! ... Already we have witnessed the shameful rejection of the legitimate demands of our Indian brothers. The struggles of the Indians, the Chinese and other oppressed peoples for freedom is also our struggle, and we pledge our support to them.[147]

It was endorsed by, among others, the West Africa Youth League, the Kikuyu (East African) Central Association, the TUC of Sierra Leone, the West Indian National Federation and the Abyssinian Freedom League.[148]

It is worth recording that such interventions were not restricted to the pages of the *New Leader* but given a wider airing as they percolated through to parliamentary debates via ILP MPs like John McGovern, who invoked the West Indian 'unrest' in the House:

I think everyone will agree that to hear these stories unfolded of the domination of race over race or class over class brings home to us the truth of the saying of the leader of what is termed the Oxford Group the other day that there is enough in the world for every man's human needs but there is not enough for some people's human greed. We see in this report, and in the statements of the right hon. Gentleman and of other Members of the House, that there is something radically wrong in what is termed by many speakers this great and glorious Empire of ours. The flag, and the tinsel, and the cheering of the Empire, are one thing, but when one gets down to hard economic facts, and sees the everyday life of the natives of our Colonial Empire, one finds something completely different from all these tales and stories that are told on platforms, in theatres and over the wireless.[149]

McGovern further noted that those in the West Indies who had sought to express suffering and demand changes

are not cheered, or applauded, or told that they deserve well of the Empire; they are clapped into prison for five, ten and twelve years because they express the human needs of men, women and children in those Colonies. Can anyone read the reports of human suffering and low standards in Jamaica, Trinidad and other parts of the Colonial Empire without a blush of shame that white men, who pretend to be the civilisers, keep their black brothers living, or existing, under such conditions?[150]

The conditions were shameful, but equally shaming was the fact that they had been brought to metropolitan attention not by the humanitarian British conscience that was constantly invoked in parliament, but by colonial subjects in unrest, actors who were now being punished for refusing to accept their lot. Even Arthur Creech-Jones, erstwhile colonial secretary and a Fabian socialist very much attached to the idea of Britain benignly 'bestowing self-government', would also note the significance of claims for humanity being *asserted*, rather than divined and addressed through imperial benevolence:

The truth is that until riots and disturbances occurred and we had unrest beginning to sweep from one end of our Colonial Empire to the other, very little was really being done. This burst of activity is largely due to the fact that at last the workers are demanding that something should be done. It is a sad commentary on our method of government when we have to wait for riots and disturbances to force us to do what is elementary [*sic*] right.[151]

Urging the extension of democratic reforms which had been stalled across the region, Creech-Jones suggested that it was a testament to the force of criticism emerging from the colonies 'that so wide an extension has now been given to the legal meaning of sedition that almost any searching criticism of a Colonial Government by a black man or even of the conditions of employment in a Colony has become a punishable offence'.

In parliament, James McGovern was also quite clearly drawing directly from Padmore's hymn-sheet when he went on to tell his colleagues: 'When we see what is happening in these parts of the Empire, we understand the seeds of war, because the struggle between Mussolini on the one hand and France and Britain on the other hand, is a struggle to see who is going to exploit these people.'[152] It was a point that Orwell would also make – undoubtedly, as Høgsbjerg notes,[153] influenced by James and Padmore – in a pointedly titled review essay in which he attacked the 'hypocrisy and self-righteousness' of pitting a 'Union' of 'democracies' against 'dictatorships':

The unspoken clause is always 'not counting niggers'. For how can we make a 'firm stand' against Hitler if we are simultaneously weakening ourselves at home? In other words, how can we 'fight Fascism' except by bolstering up a far vaster injustice?

For of course it *is* vaster. What we always forget is that the overwhelming bulk of the British proletariat does not live in Britain, but in Asia and Africa. It is not in Hitler's power, for instance, to make a penny an hour a normal industrial wage; it is perfectly normal in India, and we are at great pains to keep it so ... What meaning would there be, even if it were successful, in bringing down Hitler's system in order to stabilize something that is far bigger and in its different way just as bad?[154]

Fresh from fighting fascists in Spain, Orwell was hardly suggesting that the war against fascism did not matter. He was, rather, much as Padmore had been doing, querying the ways in which anti-Nazi and anti-fascist rhetoric was turned into an alibi, a talisman to obscure colonialism's own depredations.[155] Certainly, one point that Padmore and his associates repeatedly hammered home made it into many articles on the pages of the *New Leader*: 'How is it', asked the anti-colonial campaigner and erstwhile secretary of the short-lived British Centre against Imperialism, Dinah Stock, 'that people who will demonstrate in tens of thousands to "save Austria," who will send the Chinese all the money they can spare and more, who will even fight and die for the Spanish workers, remain so deaf and inattentive when Indians claim liberty or Africans demand democratic equality with whites?'[156] Deeming Britain 'the oldest and strongest Fascist Power in the world', Stock deprecated the ways in which Britons 'fix indignant eyes on Hitler and Mussolini, and persuade themselves that the Fascism of their own Empire is somehow less important'.[157] While calling for British socialists to do all they can to assist the struggles of colonized peoples, a few weeks later Stock, reviewing Kenyatta's *Facing Mount Kenya*, criticized what she called 'professional friends of the African' and their own deep-seated paternalism, which failed to recognize the existing resources for freedom and egalitarianism in other cultures:

> British people, even British Socialists, are sometimes too much inclined to think of their own anti-Imperialist activities in terms of 'doing something for' the Colonial peoples who are presumed to be backward and to need guidance. That is perhaps the permanent mark of a guilty Imperialist conscience, and it is difficult to get over. A book like this is a good cure for that mentality.[158]

Through the early 1940s, the *New Leader* maintained its insistence that the fight against fascism could not be won if colonialism persisted in its prevailing form of authoritarian rule. Colonial peoples could be relied on to fight for 'freedom' only if it had truly universal scope. Not just India, but Palestine, Kenya, West Africa, South Africa, the West Indies, Brockway wrote, all 'lie heavily on Britain as a continual denial of moral right to encourage the political and social freedom of other peoples'.[159] A week later, Padmore would reiterate the point: 'The support of the colonial peoples in the struggle for the overthrow of Fascism and Imperialism can only be won by renunciation of domination. Freedom is indivisible!'[160] Other anti-colonial figures, like the Sri Lankan organizer J. V. P. de Silva, echoed the point, declaring that 'when the workers of Britain realise that the effective way to fight Hitler and his hordes is to fight Fascism at home, then millions of exploited colonials will be ready to fight side by side'.[161] The *New Leader* also mocked the distinction made by imperial apologists between 'dominium', the reprehensible aim of Hitler and Mussolini, and Britain's 'imperium', which ostensibly functioned as 'a trusteeship for the bodies and souls of men'.[162] But it was Padmore who kept up the comparisons between fascism and imperialism, including colonial equivalents of *Lebensraum* and *Herrenvolk*, offering forensic examinations of policies and procedures as well as ideological origins, never giving ground on either:

> Nazism and all other manifestations of Fascism must be destroyed. There can be no compromise with this evil thing.
>
> This, however, is no justification for Socialists to apologise for, and even attempt to whitewash, so-called 'democratic' Imperialism which, in its colonial application, is indistinguishable from European Fascism. It is not a question of which is better: Fascism or Imperialism. Both are bad. Both have the same common origin – monopoly capitalism – and can only be eradicated by abolishing the social system which permits the exploitation of man by man, class by class, nation by nation, race by race.[163]

Indeed, he was able to write or publish this piece at all, he pointed out, because he was resident in the heart of the imperium; in the country of his birth, a British colony, he could not do so 'unless I wanted to spend the duration of the war in a concentration camp. British democracy is not for export. The whites are the *Herrenvolk*, the blacks the "lesser breed without the law"'.[164] When workers demanded their rights in the copper mines of Northern Rhodesia, they were met with immediate violence: 'The Negroes asked for bread, but their masters gave them hot lead!'[165]

Even labour movements in the settler colonies, Padmore noted with a provocative biblical allusion, were not immune to the virus of racism: 'It is as easy for a Negro to enter the South African and Southern Rhodesian Labour Parties as for a Jew to join the Nazi hierarchy.'[166] Hitler, he opined, was too late in the race to implement racial hierarchies and enslavement in the colonies: 'Cecil Rhodes did this long ago!'[167] The failure to pay attention to the parallels was not just of academic interest; in many ways, it accounted for the present-day sufferings of Europe: 'Now that imperialism has come home to roost, the victims are white. Europe has taken the place of Africa as "the Dark Continent".'[168] Fenner Brockway would also directly pose the question, 'How far is the empire a dictatorship?', undertaking a damning census of (the absence of) civil liberties in the colonies, making comparisons between colonial methods and Nazi techniques, and, as Padmore himself had done many times, dismissing trustee-ship as 'sheer hypocrisy' and a 'veil' to hide economic exploitation, given that most living under it were 'on a level nearer animal than human existence'.[169] Brockway echoed Padmore in pointing out that any 'democracy' under imperialism was restricted to whites, with the result that 'each white human being in the Empire governs six black, brown and yellow human beings'.[170] In bringing this situation to an end, British socialists, Brockway reiterated, had a role to play: 'We can express our solidarity by direct help and by agitation at the centre of Imperialism in this country ... We must accept the present opportunity of the war to demand the national liberation of the colonies'.[171]

The war and ensuing pressures for unity also did not stop Padmore from pushing the envelope on left-wing blind spots and paternalist failures in the pages of the *New Leader*. He had already noted that reportage of wartime unrest in the West Indies had been jettisoned in favour of 'feeding the British people and the American public with a lot of sunshine stories about the happy, smiling natives contributing their widow's mite to Spitfire funds'.[172] He observed that plans for colonial 'trusteeship' as a benign mode of rule were being fiercely challenged in the African and Caribbean press:

Conscious of the fact that the British imperialists cannot pretend to be fighting those 'evil things – brute force, bad faith, injustice, oppression and persecution' – to use the grandiloquent expression of our late lamented appeaser, Mr Neville Chamberlain – and at the same time practise Hitler methods in the colonies, the native Press is everywhere demanding their 'trustees' to state their war aims.[173]

In fact, the war had afforded colonial governments the chance to further repress resistance and suspend civil liberties in the name of security. Censorship prevailed widely and interning agitators was commonplace. This included two Irish women who had come to Trinidad to help organize the labour movement there. Padmore's tribute to Kathleen Donnellan, who died attempting to escape, and her comrade E. Cahill, was eloquent with anger: 'White men – even those calling themselves Socialists – do not usually associate with coloured people in the Colonies ... I am sure West Indian workers will remember them with affection and gratitude long after the little Hitlers who now sit on their backs have been relegated to the dustbin of history.'[174]

Padmore's other target for criticism in the pages of the *New Leader* was what he diagnosed as a frequent failure among liberals and socialists to understand that it was not possible to *alleviate* imperialism through humanitarianism, or to postpone liberation for an indefinite period. Assessing the works of two Fabians, Norman Leys's *The Colour Bar in East Africa* and Rita Hinden's *Plan for Africa*, Padmore observed that, while both liberals seemed to have a clear sense of the evils wrought by British imperialism in Africa, neither 'seems to wish to put an end to that Imperialism' itself.[175] 'It is peculiar', he wrote, 'that most British Left-Wing intellectuals who see the dire results which British colonial policy (supposedly the best in the world) has achieved, nevertheless refuse to see that the only possible and lasting solution is the complete liquidation of the system of Imperialism which has given rise to the conditions which they deplore.'[176] Padmore's stringent and uncompromising condemnation of the failure of British 'Internationalists' to 'see the claims of the coloured subject peoples of the Empire in the same light as the white ones under Nazi domination in Europe'[177] is reminiscent of Césaire's fierce later polemic against white Europeans' blindness to parallels, for forgetting of Nazism that

before they were its victims, they were its accomplices; that they tolerated that Nazism before it was inflicted on them, that they absolved it, shut their eyes to it, legitimized it, because, until then, it had only been applied to non-European peoples ... reserved exclusively for the Arabs of Algeria, the coolies of India, and the blacks of Africa.[178]

Even as he noted that the British press, which rightly condemned the Nazis, 'remains silent ... about the sufferings of the blacks in Southern Africa', Padmore would state the problem in political rather than racial terms:[179] 'Imperialism is incapable of offering freedom to its subject peoples, the only means by which it can secure their loyalty and support. To do so would be to commit hara kiri.'[180] He also deprecated the dishonest tendency to blame the Boers or the Dutch for fascist conditions in South Africa while overlooking British rule in Rhodesia: 'Are they responsible for the "native policy" in Kenya? And the colour bar practices in other parts of the Empire and even in Great Britain?'[181] In other articles, Padmore painstakingly detailed the appropriation of land in Rhodesia, in which natives had been corralled, 'concentrated' into reserves, amid declarations that whites and Africans could never be equal.[182]

As the Second World War continued its long course, Padmore began to write about an empire in crisis, unable to elicit the support of its colonies in its war aims. 'How', he asked pertinently, 'could a people whose existence had been entirely ignored, presumably because they were considered unfit to participate in the government of the country, suddenly resuscitate themselves as it were, and assume responsibility in defence of the system which had until then failed to recognise their existence?'[183] Where the *New Leader* had always had strong political and journalistic links to Indian nationalists like Nehru (with whom Brockway had a personal friendship), and covered the subcontinent regularly, it was only by the late 1930s, influenced by Padmore and James, that it began to pay sustained attention to Africa; this focus was kept up in the immediate post-war period. The veteran socialist Frank Ridley articulated the sense, correct as it turned out, that 'the storm centre of colonial revolt against Imperialism will inevitably shift to the Dark Continent'; the latter had now to be given pride of place in the annals of anticolonialism: 'After India, Africa!'[184] Clearly influenced by Padmore and James, Ridley invoked Toussaint as evidence that Africa was more than capable of parlaying with the

West on equal terms. Other writers in the *New Leader*, including Brockway, would point out that, while resistance movements against the Nazis were praised, those against British rule met with condemnation and worse: 'Whilst Germany fought to gain an Empire, Britain fought to retain one ... These territories are "occupied" by Britain. In these countries, also, Resistance Movements have arisen demanding independence.'[185] Padmore, characteristically, was more explicit in a series of articles on 'The New Imperialism', noting that, having supported the war against Hitler, colonized peoples were now laying claim to the equality, liberty and fraternity enshrined in the United Nations Charter. Imperialism could no longer hide behind anti-fascism: 'Truly, a spectre is haunting the Colonial Ministries of Britain, France and the Netherlands. The spectre of Colonial Revolution!'[186] Attention would have to be paid, as Padmore was doing in his running commentaries, to machinations in the corridors of Western power – and in the United Nations, where 'the statesmen are once again faced with the problem of finding some machinery for maintaining their imperialist system under a new disguise'.[187] With the South African, Jan Smuts, at the helm, the rhetoric and practice of 'trusteeship' – which was nothing new, having been 'the old formula of the Berlin Congress of 1885' – would replace the system of 'mandates' put in place after the previous war. Once again, the right to 'self-determination' was off the table.[188] Fenner Brockway argued similarly that where 'Germany had fought to gain an Empire, Britain fought to retain one'.[189] Both Ridley and Brockway wrote with a trenchant honesty that owed something to Padmore's dogged exposition of the false opposition between fascism and democratic imperialism. Both men also expressed sharp scepticism about proposals to reframe the Empire in terms of 'trusteeship' and the 'Commonwealth', Ridley pronouncing firmly: 'We do not advocate the retention of British Imperialism, nor believe that even by rebaptising it as a "Commonwealth" we change its essential nature.'[190] Brockway notes that areas under consideration for 'trusteeship' had originally been annexed 'for the same reason that Germany wanted to annex the rest of Europe – to gain markets and raw materials for its owning class'.[191]

When Labour took over the helm of government in post-war Britain, with India on the cusp of independence, efforts were made once again to give institutional form to the anticolonial dialogues and alliances of the last decade. After what appears to have been an abortive start in 1938, the British Centre against Imperialism was again launched, in late February 1946, at a London conference whose speakers included Padmore and Brockway. The gathering was acutely aware that it was taking place in London, 'centre of the greatest Imperialism the world has known'. Widespread militancy in the colonies – 'mutiny and riots in India, serious labour disturbances in the West Indies' – gave it 'a sense of a vast movement awake in the world, a gathering surge towards universal human liberty'.[192] The conference hoped to achieve 'a great unifying movement of anti-imperialist forces ... a consolidating instrument for a world-wide struggle'. The aim of the British Centre was to find a way of channelling information from the colonies into the British public sphere, linking with MPs who could raise colonial issues in the House of Commons, and finding 'agitational means' to raise working-class awareness of the need to end imperialism. Brockway's reported remarks at the conference offer a definitive warning against paternalism: 'The Centre must not begin in any attitude of patronage or philanthropy towards the coloured peoples. There must be a partnership of absolute equality. In fact, it would be a partnership in which the British would progressively become the junior partners.'[193] In that spirit – apart from British members including representatives of the ILP, the Labour Party and various trade unions – the Centre had formal representation from India, Ceylon, West Africa, Kenya and the Middle East. Its high-profile British 'sponsors' included Frank Horrabin, Harold Laski, the economist Michael Foot, Will Cove MP, F. A. Ridley and Fenner Brockway. In his speech, Brockway cites Padmore, who gave an extensive account of 'colonial Fascism' in the West Indies and Africa, urging British listeners to involve themselves in the struggle: 'You need our help as much as we need yours. Let us join hands together ... Let us make this anti-imperialist centre a worthy instrument in a worthy cause.'[194] He told them too about a conference that had taken place the previous year in Manchester, not picked up on by the wider British press, in which representatives of African peoples from various countries 'said, to their imperialist master, "We will be satisfied with nothing less than complete independence."'[195]

The End of Paternalism: The 1945 Pan-African Conference

We are here to tell the world that black peoples, supported by the semi-colonial people in America and millions of other people, are determined to emancipate themselves.

Amy Ashwood Garvey

The tempo of coloured people has changed. Either the British gov-ernment will extend self-government in West Africa and the West Indies or face open revolt.

W. E. B. Du Bois

The British are notoriously incapable of recognising democracy in any country unless it wears an English garb or expresses itself in terms intelligible to the English mind.

From a cable sent to delegates from the Gold Coast by the president of the Aboriginals Rights Protection Society of the Gold Coast

We were here with one understanding, that the Colonial Office will have to realise the time has come when we no longer beg for what we deserve, but that we are demanding that which is ours.

S. O. J. Andrews, labour organizer from Grenada

The Manchester Pan-African Congress, which was finally held in Chorlton Town Hall on 15 and 16 October 1945, was largely organ-ized by Padmore under the auspices of the Pan-African Federation (PAF), which brought together a number of black British organiza-tions.[196] The congress had about 200 delegates and several observers, and Padmore, who by now regarded himself as an elder statesman of sorts, wrote privately of his personal 'satisfaction of seeing concrete results for my years of labour'.[197] Although, as Immanuel Geiss notes, the mainstream British press largely ignored the event – only the *New Leader* was present – the congress remains of historical significance for the cast of characters it brought together, for the analyses and resolutions which emerged from it, and, not least, for apotheosiz-ing the currents of black self-assertion and radical anticolonialism that had emerged so powerfully in the previous decade.[198] The event was 'a landmark both in the history of Pan-Africanism and in that of decolonization ... [It] served as the pace-maker of decolonization in Africa and in the British West Indies', with strategies resolved on in the course of the conference often implemented 'with surprising ease'.[199] Christian Høgsbjerg has listed some of the posters and quotations visible at the conference, 'which give some sense of the politics and demands of the organisers':

'Labour with a white skin cannot emancipate itself while labour with a black skin is branded' (a quote from Karl Marx's *Capital*), 'Arabs and Jews unite against British Imperialism', 'Down with Trusteeship', 'Oppressed peoples of the earth unite!', 'Freedom for all subject peoples', 'Africa for the Africans' (a slogan popularised by the late Marcus Garvey), 'Down with Colour Bar', 'Ethiopia wants exit to the sea', 'Africa Arise', 'Freedom of the press in the colonies!', 'Down with lynching and Jim-Crowism', 'Down with anti-semitism', 'African peoples want the four freedoms'.[200]

The list of attendees itself reads like a Who's Who of anticolonialism and black nationalism: it includes, in addition to Padmore, Kenyatta and Nkrumah, who were part of the organizational team, Peter Abrahams and I. T. A. Wallace-Johnson. Delegates from an astonishing array of organizations were also present or sent felicitations, from the Kikuyu Central Association, the Nyasaland African Congress and the South African National Congress to numerous trade unions from the West Indies, the Federation of Indian Organisations in Britain, the Women's International League and the Ceylon Lanka Sama Samaj Party. For Padmore, the event marked the definitive end of paternalism: 'The days of dependence upon the thinking and direction of their so-called left-wing European friends who had so often betrayed them, were over. From henceforth Africans and peoples of African descent would take their destiny into their own hands and march forward under their own banner of Pan-Africanism in co-operation with their own selected allies.'[201]

This was a point repeatedly underscored by other prominent speakers. Amy Ashwood Garvey opened the proceedings, observing that the goals of 'freedom and peace' had been central to the war just concluded, and therefore ought to be applied to the British colonies. One delegate recalled that taking freedom by force, if necessary, was a recurrent theme: 'The notion was expressed that the British government would not, out of its free will, "donate" self-rule to a colony, and the application of some element of force might be necessary.'[202] Another delegate, Joe Appiah, was quoted in the *Manchester Guardian*: 'It is only force which will bring us out of this disgraceful condition in which we find ourselves.'[203] Nkrumah would insist unambiguously that mere 'internal self-government within the Empire' was unacceptable, and 'full and unconditional independence' would be the goal, even if that required 'revolutionary methods'.[204] Another delegate spoke of the need to 'help civilise the English people' through the black presence in England.[205] Self-assertion was a keynote in the congress's manifesto:

> The delegates to the Fifth Pan-African Congress believe in peace.
> How could it be otherwise when for centuries the African people
> have been victims of violence and slavery. Yet if the Western world
> is still determined to rule mankind by force, then Africans, as a
> last resort, may have to appeal to force in the effort to achieve
> Freedom, even if force destroys them and the world.[206]

In a further 'Declaration to the Colonial Workers, Farmers and Intellectuals', other demands were elaborated with greater specificity, but again drawing from insurgencies on colonial ground: strikes and boycotts, 'the right to form cooperatives, freedom of the press, assembly, demonstration and strike, freedom to print and read the literature which is necessary for the education of the masses', as well as 'the right to elect their own governments, without restrictions from foreign powers'.[207] During the first session of the congress, which Du Bois chaired after being felicitated, speaker after speaker also situated this self-assertion within a longer history of black resistance. The world and British people needed to be told by the congress 'that we want our freedom. We do not want freedom that is partially controlled – we want nothing but freedom.'[208] In his account of the East African picture, Kenyatta noted that the previous year a massive strike had gripped the Ugandan cotton industry, 'which the Government called a disturbance, but it was really a protest by the people against the political, as well as economic, oppression under which they suffer'.[209] The reports from the Caribbean unsurprisingly referenced the 'spontaneous outbreaks of strikes and riots' and the 'the perpetual agitation from the people' in the face of intolerable conditions: 'Since the wave of revolt which swept through the West Indies in 1937, the people have demonstrated in and out of season their resentment over Crown Colony rule.'[210] Ken Hill, the highly regarded Jamaican trade unionist, noted that the time had come for a reverse pedagogy: 'The first thing which people of the industrial powers want to be educated to recognise is that paternalism and benevolence are not adequate or just substitutes for national home rule or independence in Colonial territories.'[211] It was left to the Sierra Leonean trade unionist Wallace-Johnson to spell it out again, referencing an 1885 uprising against imperialism in his country: 'We are at this conference not to demand certain concessions for Africa and the West Indies, but to demand complete independence for the African peoples and peoples of African descent all over the world.'[212]

Once again, the wider background of actually occurring resistance and agitation is important. A few months before the Congress, on 15 July 1945, the PAF, along with the West African Students Union (WASU) and other organizations, hosted what was reportedly 'one of the largest rallies of coloured peoples ever witnessed in the British capital' in support of the Nigerian General Strike, which had begun a month previously and would last a total of fifty-two days.[213] Hakim Adi writes that the strike became a cause célèbre in Britain, galvanizing anticolonial militancy.[214] Driven by worker demands and famously joined by the market women of Nigeria, the strike is widely regarded as the first major anticolonial event in that country to garner international attention – 'the struggle that initiated the struggle for Nigeria by Nigerians'.[215] As in the West Indies, the scale and vigour of the strike took both trade union leaders and the government by surprise, an unprecedented mood of militancy having spread throughout the ranks of both labour and the wider populace. Meanwhile, in Britain, the election of a Labour government under Clement Attlee had 'temporarily increased optimism amongst Black people in Britain concerning the future of the colonies'.[216] In conjunction with the news coming in of widespread unrest in the colonies, this created an opportunity to demand that Clause Three of the Atlantic Charter, specifying the right of peoples to choose their own government – the subject of Padmore and Cunard's dialogue – be genuinely universalized. Testifying, once again, to the influence of Padmore's analysis, Harold Moody of the reformist organization the League of Coloured Peoples (LCP) recalled that English people were now beginning to see 'how incongruous it is to be fighting ostensibly against the Herrenvolk idea and then to be supporting it within their own communities'.[217] There had also been several other conferences during the 1930s, including a series organized by the reasonably militant WASU, which featured speeches by sympathetic Labour MPs and set up a parliamentary pressure group 'campaigning for the desired changes in West Africa'.[218] In 1944, the LCP held a conference in which a 'Charter for Coloured Peoples' had been drawn up and presented to an ever-truculent Churchill. Among other things, the charter had demanded 'that the colonial powers should assume the obligation to render account to an international body about their administration in Africa and about the steps they were taking to transfer sovereignty'.[219]

In 1945, the PAF had also sent an open letter to the Attlee government on behalf of various affiliated organizations. The letter spoke of the implications of both the Allied and the Labour victories, which it welcomed, though it noted again the kinship between the evil that had just been defeated and that under which colonial subjects laboured:

> The dark-skinned workers, no less than the pale-skinned, want freedom from war, want and fear. The victory of the common man here is the victory of the common man in Africa, Asia and other colonial lands.
>
> To consolidate this great victory, however, courage is needed. The courage to face squarely the fact that imperialism is one of the major causes of war. The courage to admit that any high-sounding blue-prints that beg the question of man's territorial and political domination by other men, whether their skins are white, yellow or black, is only staving off the day when the evils of war with their ghastly new scientific twists will again be unleashed on humanity. It is the challenge of our time that you, Comrade Attlee, and your Government, should give the Socialist answer to the Tory imperialism of Mr Churchill's 'What we have we hold.' What will your answer be?

To condemn the imperialism of Germany, Japan and Italy while condoning that of Britain would be more than dishonest, it would be a betrayal of the sacrifice and sufferings and the toil and sweat of the common people of this country. All imperialism is evil.[220]

There was no response from Attlee's government.

Writing of Padmore and the milieu of the IASB and the PAF, one scholar asks: 'Would the African liberation movement have succeeded in gaining political independence so rapidly in British colonies after the war if this little circle of writer-agitators had not laid the groundwork in London? Quite possibly not.'[221] It has also been suggested that the growth of African nationalism helped transform Labour left-wingers' colonial attitudes. The colonies, Nancy Cunard wrote in her prefatory comments to The White Man's Duty, were 'a national heartache to those who know them and who know also that the coloured peoples are as human as ourselves and deserve the kind of life we ourselves desire'.[222] Only such a recognition, and actions based upon it, could yield anything like a real commonwealth of peoples. Instead, Padmore observed, it was being made clear that 'the regime of exploitation and colonial fascism ... is to continue after the war; that the system of imperialism is to run on indefinitely'.[223] Padmore was also, one scholar argues, 'anticipating the Fanonian idea that once the colonized participates in his own liberation, a new culture emerges to sustain and energize the new collective identity which ultimately emerges'.[224] In Chapter 10, I will explore the unfolding of post-war resistance and rebellion in British Africa – Kenya in particular – and the impact it had on Britons, both individuals and groups, who would throw their weight decisively behind the process of decolonization that the Second World War had now set inexorably in motion, regardless of whether British leaders wished to 'preside over the liquidation of the British Empire'.[225] Fought for tenaciously, that liquidation was finally effected. The next chapter looks at a famous uprising that was a significant contributor to this ending.

10

A Terrible Assertion of Discontent: 'Mau Mau' and the End of Imperial Benevolence

[The Mau Mau crisis was] if not the bloodiest, then certainly among the most traumatic, of the conflicts attendant on British decolonisation – [it] loomed menacingly behind the later phases of constitutional talks and progress to self-government.

Stephen Howe

Mau Mau challenged not only the British sense of control – which was often challenged in these years – but officials' new-found sense of mission, the belief that they had a positive role in the future of their subjects.

Frederick Cooper

In 1953, George Padmore wrote of an impending revolution in Africa. The headache it posed for ruling British politicians was, he averred, a familiar one:

The distinguished Victorian Prime Minister, the Marquis of Salisbury, once asserted that 'Africa has been created to plague Ministers of Foreign Affairs'. This was never more true than today. For throughout the length and breadth of the once Dark Continent – from Egypt to South Africa, from Kenya to the Gold Coast, not to mention the vast Central African territories of the Rhodesias and Nyasaland – the indigenous races are struggling to throw off the yoke of colonialism and achieve their rightful place as free nations in a free world.[1]

Padmore was referring to increasingly fractious resistance across Africa, but his specific focus was on what became the most high-profile uprising of the post-war period: 'The agitation for self-government is nowhere more dramatically manifested than in Kenya, where the violence of the struggle of the African people against alien domination has captured the attention of the entire world.' For Padmore, Kenya, more than anywhere else other than perhaps South Africa, exemplified the workings of colonialism as a species of fascism. As we have seen, Kenyatta too had made that case in the pages of the *New Leader*. Detailing the expropriation of hundreds of thousands of acres of fertile Kikuyu land in that country, Padmore emphasized the ways in which punitive taxation, forced labour and widespread impoverishment were constitutive features of colonial rule in Kenya. Here 'democracy is interpreted as the right of a small white minority to rule an overwhelming black majority who have been denied all right of free political expression'.[2] Governance was based 'upon the *Herrenvolk* philosophy of "white supremacy"', such that the colour bar and discrimination operated in every aspect of public and social life.[3] Direct responsibility for the state of unrest in Kenya lay with the European settlers, 'aided and abetted' by the colonial administration. What the world was witnessing in Kenya was 'a spontaneous revolt of a déclassed section of the African rural population', which had been given the mysterious name of 'Mau Mau' by white settlers.[4] The name itself had been invented 'to discredit the Africans and justify the white man's legalized terror against a once peaceful and long-suffering people'.[5]

The uprising which unfolded in Kenya in the early 1950s had indeed begotten a mythology all its own. In the British cultural and political imagination, 'Mau Mau' had become a code word for demonic violence in excess of all justification. Novelists Robert Ruark and Elspeth Huxley, for instance, both wrote lurid popular fiction evoking what the latter famously called 'the yell from the swamp'.[6] Ruark's evocation of 'a symptomatic ulcer of the evil and unrest which currently afflicts the world', meaning anticolonial unrest, is not untypical of either colonial fiction or media representations of Mau Mau.[7] As Frederick Cooper observes,

Confronted with an opposition that was fundamental and violent, the dualism of British thinking about African society – imagining the modern while fearing the primitive – virtually became a schizophrenia, and like true madness, it had its own meticulous logic and its insistence that it was the Other who was mad. The savagery of British counterterrorism in Kenya was built against a belief that the terrorist was a savage.[8]

The representation of Mau Mau as a phenomenon that evaded all understanding and explanation, David Maughan-Brown suggests, had an expedient material basis to it: 'the settlers' justificatory ideology could not allow any admission of legitimate social and economic grievances, so a set of myths had to be elaborated to account for the revolt. If the causes of the revolt could not be social or economic they must be psychological' – a belief that resulted in the officially commissioned government report by J. C. Carothers, *The Psychology of Mau Mau*.[9] In another work, Maughan-Brown argues that even liberal discourse in Britain was fully in thrall to the language of poison, insanity and disease that prevailed in relation to Mau Mau. He is not wrong, and his examples are persuasive: the *Manchester Guardian* referred to 'the liberation of the Kikuyu people ... from the virus of Mau Mau', while Kingsley Martin, often thought of as an imperial dissident, wrote of the oath of unity as 'nasty mumbo-jumbo'.[10] With the exception of writings in the *Daily Worker*, the only consistently critical engagement with white settler discourse, many on the left 'also showed themselves convinced of the accuracy of the settlers' views of the movement, even while repudiating the justice of the settlers' cause'.[11]

And yet there was more to it. Despite the seeming hegemony of anti-insurgent discourse, Mau Mau and its attendant crises paradoxically also served to highlight wider resistance to colonial injustices in Kenya, and therefore the fragility of the paternalism that underlay increasingly desperate-sounding discourses of trusteeship. In a curious way, the violence and undoubted brutality of much Mau Mau activity, even if often exaggerated, enabled the emergence of an understanding that there was also wider resistance to settler colonialism in Kenya. This book has tracked the ways in which British dissent and criticism on imperial questions over a century were shaped by crises of conscience following bloodshed and repression in the colonies, by travels to areas of 'unrest' that unsettled and reshaped received ideas about 'reform', and by the pedagogical work of anticolonial campaigners and intellectuals in the metropole. This last chapter examines how all three of these strands are relevant to metropolitan criticism in relation to the Kenyan struggle against British colonialism, which is most prominently symbolized by 'Mau Mau', though not contained by it. The Mau Mau insurgency and concomitant metropolitan crisis of conscience helped British dissenters to make the case for Kenyan self-government and eventual independence – one that could not be delayed for much longer. Here I will explore three symptomatic responses to the situation: the first is that of the MP and campaigner Fenner Brockway, a founding member of the Movement for Colonial Freedom (MCF), whom we have already met as the editor of the *New Leader* and through his brief association with the League against Imperialism. Although Brockway was already a known critic of the Empire, his travels in Kenya and subsequent engagement with events there put pressure on his own tendencies to paternalism, and pushed him to qualify somewhat his hitherto unshakable faith in non-violence. He would never go so far as to endorse Mau Mau, but he came to an understanding of what had caused the insurgency in ways that deepened his own commitment to ending imperialism. Second, and closely related, are the crises of parliamentary and press conscience triggered by the ferocious repression of the insurgency that took place in the Emergency years, as manifested in the scandal caused by Eileen Fletcher's damning pamphlet *Truth about Kenya*, and British MP Barbara Castle's investigative findings revealing British atrocities in that colony. Lastly, in a perhaps eccentric choice, the chapter examines the impact of insurgency and anticolonialism on the work of the reformist advisor to the Colonial Office, the Oxford academic and commentator Margery Perham. For Brockway, Perham, and several others who were not distant from the corridors of British governance, the violence and persistence of the insurgency drove home the fact that imperial resistance to anticolonial resistance might well have been futile.

The Historical Background

> *Nearly everybody was a member of the Movement, but nobody
> could say with any accuracy when it was born: to most people,
> especially those in the younger generation, it had always been there,
> a rallying centre for action. It changed names, leaders came and
> went, but the Movement remained, opening new visions, gathering
> greater and greater strength, till on the eve of Uhuru, its influence
> stretched from one horizon touching the sea to the other resting on
> the great Lake.*
>
> Ngũgĩ wa Thiong'o, *A Grain of Wheat*

Prior to the uprising, undoubtedly the most notorious anticolonial
crisis of the post-war era, when there were many, Kenya had indeed
largely been figured as 'the land of sunshine, gin slings and smiling,
obedient servants' and 'of benign white paternalism and accepting
black subservience'.[12] For the bulk of Kenya's white settlers, apartheid
South Africa was the model polity; as they set about demanding more
self-governance in the immediate post-war years, they 'campaigned
against enhanced political representation for Africans, pushed themselves into key roles in the management of the colonial economy, and
tightened their grip over local and municipal governments'.[13] The
movement that came to be known as 'Mau Mau' was the culmination
of many years of resistance by those dispossessed of their lands and
put to work on European farms.[14] At the heart of the grievances –
which also included low wages, racist passbooks known as *kipande*,
and lack of electoral representation – was 'land hunger', large swathes
of arable land coming under settler occupation while poor Kenyans,
mainly Kikuyu, lived economically deprived lives in 'Reserves', or
tiny plots on settler land which they worked. The complex causes and
layered constitution of the network of insurgency that underlay the
uprising have been the subject of a substantial body of scholarship,
and I do not intend to revisit it here in any detail.[15] The roots of the
uprising lay in the post-war intensification of fear and anxiety among
'squatters' – the misleadingly named communities of farm labour
who worked settler plantations and faced intensification of repressive measures to contain them – and the resistance they frequently
put up to exploitative regimes of labour extraction. As 'vast estates

were expropriated and then largely underutilised', squatters became increasingly aware of the injustices they faced, 'especially since open intimidation, physical floggings and general ill-treatment were part and parcel of their day-to-day lives'.[16] Particular resentment was caused by increasingly aggressive *kifagio*, or settler attempts to dispossess squatters and severely limit how much stock they could keep and how much personal cultivation they could do.[17] Much as had happened in Morant Bay less than a hundred years before, squatter resistance, including strikes and refusals to sign contracts, was often shaped by rumours of working conditions which could be equated to enslavement or near-enslavement.[18] Low-waged labourers' refusal to be acquiescent was met with forced removals from the land into already overcrowded reserves; petitioning the government and the Colonial Office proved to be of little use. Much of this resistance was channelled through an organization known as the Kikuyu Central Association (KCA), which began as an informal network of contacts and 'acquired a relative degree of coherence in the 1940s' after it was declared illegal by the colonial government.[19]

In the late 1940s, to cement loyalty to the KCA and step up the drive to obtain land rights, a campaign of 'oathing' – a practice drawing on existing secret societies and their rituals in rural communities – was intensified; this is what became most famously associated with Mau Mau, the subject of much lurid speculation and demonic mythology in Britain. A younger, more militant wing of the banned KCA – now merged with the Kenya African Union (KAU), led by Jomo Kenyatta – sought to 'extend oathing on a mass scale to escalate resistance' and emphasize unity.[20] As a split between moderates and the more militant hardened, by late 1947, and repression intensified – culminating in the arrest of evicted Kikuyu squatters from the Olenguruone area – the oathing campaign sought to bind Kikuyu people 'behind an as yet undefined radical action'.[21] Kenyatta and others would caution against drastic measures such as burning the *kipande*, which several did at public meetings, but the idea of militant underground protest was steadily gaining traction. It was at Olenguruone that 'rural resistance – disobedience of orders, refusal to make agreements – reached a new level and where a new idiom was found'.[22] Here emerged a new oath to fight enemies, 'based on older Kikuyu traditions but modified in its contents and in its social significance', administered across ages and genders.[23] In the spring of 1952, in the face of increased state and settler repression – which included severely limiting the amount of land and stock squatters could own, as well as evictions of troublemakers – armed resistance emerged. Attacks and sabotage began on settler properties and cattle even as Kenyatta toured the Highlands speaking of political change. Assassinations and disappearances of police witnesses and headmen perceived to be collaborating with the government began to take place. While a small number of white settlers and colonial officials perished in the violence, by far the largest number of deaths was those of Africans deemed to be British 'loyalists'. Treating the resistance initially as just labour unrest with traditional practices attached to it, the colonial government worsened the situation by increased repression and indiscriminate preventive detentions. On 20 October 1952 the notorious State of Emergency was declared: if the possibility for legal and 'peaceful' protests had always been severely limited, now the turn to guerrilla warfare became inevitable.[24] The outcome would be disastrous for the Kikuyu – insurgents, their supporters and 'loyalists', as well as those caught in between. Shortly after the Emergency was declared, Kenyatta and many others were arrested under 'Operation Jock Scott', ahead of being charged and tried for instigating Mau Mau – something of an irony given Kenyatta's own firm commitment to moderate tactics.[25] Whatever their differences on strategy, however, Kenyatta was regarded even by the militants as the leader of the nationalist struggle. His trial in the deliberately remote location of Kapenguria in the Rift Valley would become a cause célèbre across and beyond Africa, the left-wing British barrister D. N. Pritt QC leading the defence, alongside distinguished Indian lawyers such as Chaman Lall. Kenyatta levied a counter-accusation with regard to the emergence of Mau Mau: that it was the colonial government which had 'made it what it is, not Kenyatta' – a point which would reverberate in metropolitan discussions of the crisis:[26]

> I blame the Government because knowing that Africans have grievances they did not go into these grievances ... instead of joining with us to fight Mau Mau they arrested all the leading members of KAU, accusing them of being Mau Mau ... They wanted to, I think, not to eliminate Mau Mau, sir, but what they wanted to eliminate

is the only political organisation – that is KAU – which fights constitutionally for the rights of the African people.[27]

Kenyatta's subsequent conviction on the charge of leading a proscribed organization – based on distinctly unsafe and uncorroborated
testimony which was infamously recanted later by the chief witness,
Rawson Macharia – would also cause a scandal. The presiding magistrate, brought hastily out of retirement for the trial, did not really
bother to conceal his partisan tendencies, himself noting that his
judgement 'means that I disbelieve ten witnesses for the defence and
believe one witness for the prosecution'.[28] As Pritt later wrote, the
trial was covered by half a dozen of the best foreign correspondents
in the British press, and 'aroused great interest in England, causing a
resurgence of genuine liberal sentiment, and even some public feeling
of responsibility for British colonial activities'.[29] To British observers
of a critical disposition, the patently unsound charge that Mau Mau
was directed by Kenyatta indicated a desire on the part of the colonial government to deprive Kenyan Africans of 'all lawful political
representation' by enabling the banning of the KAU, one of many
'reactionary follies that hastened the independence of Kenya'.[30]

In the post-war period, as David Goldsworthy has argued, 'the
over-all [sic] direction of colonial policy became an issue in metropolitan politics'.[31] As Britain became more powerless to control
events in the colonies, 'the search for solutions to colonial problems stimulated greater political activity at home than ever before.
Interactions among government, opposition, pressure groups, and
colonial leaders became continuous and lively'.[32] If insurgencies in
Malaya (where another brutal Emergency was imposed) and Cyprus
were also significant, events in Africa which provided a particular
stimulus to metropolitan political activity included the birth pangs
of the Central African Federation in early 1953, the British Guiana
crisis later that year, and the Seretse Khama controversy in 1956 over
the marriage of an African prince to a white Englishwoman.[33] But
it was Kenya that dominated the headlines in the 1950s. In 1954,
two years into the brutal counter-insurgency programme, Colonial
Secretary Lyttelton would suddenly announce 'constitutional changes
to accommodate the "legitimate" aspirations of all races' in Kenya,
including land reforms which could have been ceded much earlier.[34]

Even as the insurgents' brutal tactics were widely condemned back in Britain, there appeared to be a growing consensus that both the emergence and the suppression of Mau Mau demanded an urgent revisiting of British colonial policy in Kenya. An early day motion in the British parliament called for 'all practical measures to mitigate the most pressing hardships and frustrations of the African people' to be put in place.[35] As John Lonsdale has noted, the Emergency was, in reality, 'a pre-emptive attack carried out by the incumbent colonial authorities against a significant section of the African political leadership of Kenya and its supporters'; this fact was not lost on British dissidents.[36] Fenner Brockway was one of them.

'The member for Africa': Fenner Brockway and Unlearning Paternalism

> *They told with varying disagrees of exaggeration how [Mugo] organized the hunger-strike in Rira, an action which made Fenna Brokowi raise questions in the British House of Commons.*
>
> Ngũgĩ wa Thiong'o, *A Grain of Wheat*

> *The problems in Kenya are ... so symbolic of what is happening in Colonial Territories generally. In the minds of many of us there is the question whether the Colonies in Africa, and in East and Central Africa particularly, are to move towards racial equality and racial co-operation, or whether they will develop into the unhappy situation which exists in Kenya of violence, conflict and race war. I believe that our answer to the present problems in Kenya may determine not only the future of Kenya but the future of other territories in Africa as well.*
>
> Fenner Brockway in the House of Commons, March 1955

'I am instinctively a pacifist. It is literally true that I have never held a weapon in my hand (except a rubber bullet sent me from Northern Ireland)', Fenner Brockway would recall at the age of 98.[37] A founder member of the No-Conscription Fellowship – he was jailed for refusing to serve in the First World War – Brockway remained a lifelong anti-war campaigner, and also became devoted, first, to the cause of colonial reforms, and eventually to full freedom from colonial rule. His was a long twentieth-century life: he died in 1988, just short of his 100th birthday. A firm constitutionalist and pacifist, until the 1950s Brockway had only ever suspended his commitment to non-violence with respect to the war against Nazi Germany. Born in India to missionary parents, Brockway had been pro-Boer during the South African war and a Liberal for a short period before joining the ILP, from this point describing himself as a socialist, strongly influenced by Keir Hardie. He joined the Labour Party in 1946, serving first in the House of Commons and then, from 1964 onwards, in the House of Lords. Although he was formally disapproving of them, he regarded his own elevation to a peerage as providing a useful platform from which to raise questions and introduce bills. A prolific writer, Brockway produced several memoirs, biographies, pamphlets, journal articles and historical accounts. In addition to a long parliamentary career, which began in 1929, Brockway also took on leading roles in the British Committee of the Indian National Congress, the League against Imperialism, the British Centre for Colonial Freedom, the Congress of Peoples against Imperialism (COPAI), the No More War Movement (NMWN), and the Movement for Colonial Freedom (MCF). It is fair to say that no account of British anticolonialism in the twentieth century would be complete without some understanding of Brockway's role in it.

As a stalwart backer of the Indian National Congress, whose moderation of policy and non-violent methods appealed to his temperament, Brockway threw his weight behind full independence for India, but had always been something of a gradualist in relation to Africa, a region he knew less well in the interwar period than India, his 'first love'.[38] His close relationships with Gandhi, Nehru and others in the Indian National Congress from the 1920s on had made him a known advocate of the cause of Indian independence; in his pieces for the *New Leader* and elsewhere, Brockway tended to ventriloquize the INC leadership's line on India, rarely challenging it. The *New Leader* under Brockway's editorship, for instance, took an uncompromisingly hostile line towards the Muslim League and the demand for a Muslim homeland. Under Brockway, however, as we have already seen, the *New Leader* also provided a vital platform for radical black voices to be heard on the British left, challenging its

deep-rooted tendencies towards paternalism. Brockway's own paternalism, however, would not be disrupted thoroughly until after his
second 'African journey'. While well known as an advocate of self-
government throughout the 1930s and 1940s, Brockway really only
came into his own as one of the strongest voices in British anticolonialism in the 1950s, when he began to engage with Africa, and Kenya
in particular. In 1950, he took his seat in the Commons after having
left a highly weakened ILP, and re-joined the Labour Party – a parliamentary career he was able to parlay very effectively into becoming
a spokesman and campaigner for colonial liberation. It was then,
specifically because of his engagement with liberation movements,
he recalled, that he found himself 'beginning to specialise on the
colonies':[39]

> My contact with Third World movements through the Congress
> of Peoples against Imperialism meant that I had letters from all
> over Africa and Asia reporting injustices, and I continually raised
> them in the House. The Hansard index showed that in one week I
> put questions about Uganda, Nigeria, Trinidad, Sierra Leone and
> Gambia. I had been dubbed 'Member for Moscow'. With more
> justice I was now called 'Member for Africa'.[40]

When Seretse Khama of Bechuanaland was infamously deposed
from his chieftainship by a Labour government for the crime of marrying a white Englishwoman – for fear of offending South Africa,
where 'miscegenation' was illegal – Brockway stood against his own
party's ministers in his support for Khama.[41] As the *Dictionary of
Labour Biography* notes, Brockway, a vigorous early campaigner
against apartheid in South Africa and racial discrimination in Britain,
played 'a key part in attempts to secure – not always successfully
– a peaceful and fair transition to independence for numerous countries including Kenya, Tunisia, Madagascar, Ghana, Cyprus, Malta
and British Guiana'.[42] In the course of this campaigning, and going
very much against the grain of his cultural training, Brockway would
also attempt strenuously to slough off his paternalist tendencies in
order to become what he called a 'world citizen': 'Compassion is
not enough: that is concern by the better off for the worse off. There
should not be that sense of gulf. There should be identity'.[43] In many

ways, Brockway is an exemplary case study in how those of a reform-ist rather than oppositional bent were radicalized by insurgencies, and by learning from European and Asian anticolonialists.

How did this self-proclaimed 'Gandhian', pacifist, anti-war cam-paigner and insistent votary of non-violence come to resign from the Peace Pledge Union in the 1970s over his astonishing pronouncement that 'support for physical action could not always be withheld?'[44] 'Although no revolt had then begun', Brockway recalls, 'I told its annual meeting that I would support an insurgence by the Africans to win their right to self-government in Rhodesia … I would support a revolution in Southern Africa.'[45] Through a close reading of his memoir, *African Journeys*, and then examining some of his subse-quent interventions on the question of Africa and imperialism, I want to suggest that, although Brockway first came to Kenya convinced of the need for both moderation and gradualism, what he saw there of the operations of colonial violence and racialized dispossession shaped his transformation in the following decades into a full-time British anticolonalist who, without ever advocating violence, came to understand why it might be deployed under certain circumstances. Followed by his engagement, along with other Labour parliamentar-ians, with the crisis of the Emergency imposed on Kenya in 1952 and the related colonial atrocities visited upon Africans, Brockway's African journeys formed the seedbed for a more radical anticolonial politics. He subsequently became a founding member and first presi-dent of the Movement for Colonial Freedom in Britain.

Passages in Africa

Brockway made his first trip to East Africa on behalf of COPAI, vis-iting Uganda and Kenya in 1950. His notes from this period, which form the basis of his memoirs, as well as his parliamentary interven-tions, give us a flavour of his gradualist views on imperial rule and self-governance in Africa in the immediate post-war period. While he was clearly already critical of several aspects of colonial governance and policy, there is little to indicate that he was thinking in terms of bringing imperial rule to an immediate end. His object in travelling there was 'to get the point of view of the African population', but

Brockway was careful to note repeatedly that he had also consulted extensively with colonial officials.[46] 'I listened rather than spoke,' he would say of attending political meetings in Uganda. For all that he sought actively to be 'balanced', he did observe that 'positive' aspects of colonial governance were 'regarded with suspicion' by the Africans he met. His suggestions were nonetheless determinedly reformist:

It is clearly desirable that in the planning of Uganda the full co-operation of the people should be gained. The deepest conviction with which I return is that this co-operation cannot be obtained unless the people are given the democratic right of expressing their voice at every stage when plans for their country are under discussion.[47]

Brockway was not unaware that the gulf between rulers and ruled is 'deep', but hoped that violence might be averted by providing a 'constitutional opportunity for the expression of the feeling of the people'. On this first visit, Brockway spent only a week in Kenya, where he advised the colonial administration that the views of the Africans were 'of paramount importance when planning the future of Kenya because the Africans are, after all, the indigenous and major-ity population'.[48] Urging the introduction of a common electoral roll for Africans, Indians, Europeans and Arabs, Brockway repeatedly denounced racial segregation. Famously walking out of a Nairobi restaurant which would not serve his African companion, Brockway wrote: 'I could understand the bitterness of the Africans who accom-panied me when, pointing to the wooded hills where the Europeans lived, they asked why they should be condemned to the wilderness.' On the whole, however, he remained hopeful that 'the progressive elements would win through eventually'.[49] While Brockway was aware during this first trip of disturbances on the East Suk reserve, for instance, he had no time to visit it, and insisted that he 'had no knowledge of the Mau Mau Association'. Having given the last forty years to Asia, he did, however, intend now to 'devote the next 20 years to Africa'.[50] Would this entail going beyond identifying the mal-practices and inadequacies of colonial rule and suggesting reforms? We shall see.

If he was largely oblivious to Mau Mau during his first visit, Brockway certainly returned to Britain appalled by Kenya's brutal racial hierarchy and the resentment it had caused. He would introduce – for nine years running – a bill to make racial and religious discrimination illegal in public places in Britain. In due course he would also become a leading figure in British anti-apartheid activism. On his eightieth birthday, many years later, at a dinner in the House of Commons, Brockway would express his disappointment at the persistence of racism in Britain, America and elsewhere, making another startling statement: 'I am not opposed to the fundamentals of Black Power. When a people is oppressed the movement for freedom must come from within.'[51] This seed of support for a radical liberationist movement had clearly been sown during Brockway's Kenya visits, where he witnessed the material underpinnings of the racial oppression which resulted in violent resistance: 'African land hunger, European land space, African starvation wages, European comfort, African illiteracy, European expensive education'.[52] The colonial government compounded its problems by insisting on the repudiation not just of Mau Mau, but also of the grievances which had engendered it: no African was given credence 'unless he were prepared to put into cold storage his protest against the enforced social disintegration of the life of his people, the economic misery of Africans on the reserves, and the humiliations of the colour bar and racial segregation'.[53]

Bitterly resented by the majority of European settlers, Brockway's second visit to Kenya, along with his fellow MP Leslie Hale, was painted both by the settlers and by the British media as a propaganda exercise on the part of the Kenya African Union (KAU), which was both paying for the trip and hosting the two parliamentarians. The insurgency was now fully underway. Hale and Brockway were given an armed guard to protect them, not from insurgents, but from incensed settlers, 'fanatical Europeans'.[54] Brockway made a point, as he had previously, of staying with Chief Koinange's family, despite the fact that two of its members, the ex-chief included, were in prison accused of participating in political murders. Watchful this time around for signs of Mau Mau's influence on a visit to a Kikuyu independent school – among the institutions charged with fomenting insurgency – Brockway noted that all he could see was 'a passionate national patriotism', and that, contra settler propaganda, he had 'not found hatred of whites as whites nor any atmosphere of violence'.[55] Having also discussed matters with settlers and the government, including the governor, Brockway – still determinedly anti-Mau Mau – offered them an infuriating inversion of malady and symptom: 'The Europeans were complaining that the Kenya Government had shown no dynamic energy in crushing Mau Mau when first it lifted its ugly head. I think our criticism would be that it had shown no dynamic energy in removing the African frustration which had led to the emergence of Mau Mau.'[56] Many administrators and officials were well-meaning and sincere, Brockway acknowledged, but they 'did not realise that they were administering a volcano boiling to eruption'.[57] To complaints that Africans ought to be more loyal, Brockway responded merely that colonial administrators 'appeared to overlook the fact that no self-respecting African could be "loyal" to a Government in which at that time Africans, alone among the races, had no representative and which had been directly responsible for the frustrations, social, economic and psychological, from which they suffered so grievously'.[58] By refusing to acknowledge that injustices burned in African breasts, the colonial government had in fact allowed Kenyan Africans to 'come to the conclusion that there was no alternative to Mau Mau'.[59] All these were points he would raise in parliament upon his return.

African Journeys is not a radical text by any means. It prides itself on taking a 'balanced' view of colonial matters, and does not directly challenge any of the several demonizing stereotypes of Mau Mau in circulation. Indeed, Brockway himself frequently resorts to them himself, invoking bestiality, 'cold-blooded' oath ceremonies, and sanguinary atrocities. What seem to have unnerved him more, however, were the unabashedly supremacist white settler views he was exposed to. Invited by a group of settlers to 'hear their case', Brockway recalls listening to 'the most frightening words we heard in Kenya. They bruised themselves on my mind'.[60] ... He was told: "Every African is dishonest, a liar and lazy. Their language has no words for love, gratitude and loyalty."[61] (Upon inquiry Brockway found out that the corresponding Gikuyu words were, in fact, *wendu*, *ngatho* and *wathikai*).[62] As he struggled to work out whether his friend Jomo Kenyatta was its mastermind or not, Brockway's reflections on Mau

Mau's 'barbarism' also impelled him to turn the lens of criticism back upon 'the infamies which we, civilised and cultured, commit. The atom bomb on Hiroshima killed 1,000 infants for each one killed at Lari. More immediately relevant, the Government in Kenya has been executing fifty Africans a month.'[63] While he was not quite able to relinquish his attachment to the liberal notion (possibly 'pompous and hypocritical', he concedes) that the British Empire could take credit for disseminating an 'education and ethic' derived from Greece, Rome and Christianity, he leavened that claim with an important counterpoint: 'We have destroyed the old African society without replacing it by any satisfying substitute. We have spread frustration and given it no outlet.'[64] This was not a romantic position but an historical insight. 'I don't seek to idealise the old Kikuyu society', he insisted, noting that he had already criticized its treatment of women and inter-tribal wars.[65] Yet the historical reality – and Brockway was undoubtedly also drawing here on Kenyatta's insider ethnographical account, *Facing Mount Kenya* – was that the 'old Kikuyu community was a conscious society' with 'intimate loyalties which gave a social significance to living'.[66] In its place, colonialism had created fresh antagonisms and division without creating new social bonds or communal institutions. Despite his own deprecation of the practice, Brockway understood that the way in which the female circumcision issue had been handled – as a civilizational weapon rather than an issue of women's emancipation – had been counterproductive and divisive. Invoking Britain's own new post-war welfare state, Brockway also wrote eloquently of the Kenya land issue:

> To the African, land is what work is to us. Land is life ... Land-hunger in Kenya is equivalent to unemployment in Britain – unemployment without benefits, National Assistance, children's allowances or other social services. I can think of no parallel more exact to conditions in the Kikuyu and some other reserves than conditions in the valleys of South Wales in the Hungry 'Thirties, when 70 per cent unemployment drove thousands to seek a livelihood elsewhere.[67]

Those who had left their overcrowded reserves to work on European-owned farms had been transmogrified into 'squatters': 'When I first heard the name, I thought they must be trespassers. Not so. They were labourers on the European farms. The name should be "serfs" rather than "squatters".'[68] The final degradation came from racial discrimination and separation, 'fundamentally not different from South Africa's *apartheid*'.[69] Self-consciously established 'interra- cial clubs' were courageous and good ventures, but in themselves paternalist, 'a little too precious, too consciously good ... a Churchy atmosphere of doing good'.[70] It was 'a section of the whites' who would now have to be 'painfully ... educated to new human values', but there was no reason for Africans to wait for this new disposition to manifest itself.[71]

Back in Britain, Brockway would drive home these points in parliament:

> The greatest mistake which the Government have made in their Kenya policy has been to refuse to accept the co-operation of Africans who, while critical of the Government, abhor the methods of Mau Mau just as much as the methods of the Government. The attitude of the Government has been that unless any African was a 100 per cent supporter of their policy, he was outside the pale.[72]

Largely due to his efforts and those of other MPs like Hale, Arthur Creech-Jones, Barbara Castle and Aneurin Bevan, among others, the 'Kenya situation' became a frequent topic of discussion in Commons debates during the 1950s. Brockway was relentless in raising the land question – again, significant in the face of routine denials, that the land acquired by white settlers had been in use by Africans: 'The European population in Kenya should recognise that the African population has the first right to land in that territory.'[73] Modest as they may seem to us now, in the context of debates which included nakedly racist interventions, frequently unabashed in their insistence on white superiority and Christian values against a putative African primitivism, the contextual radicalism of Brockway's interventions must be recognized.[74] Brockway was clear that racism was a signifi- cant reason for the grievances of the colonized:

> I say without any doubt that it is the practice of the colour bar in Kenya which is largely responsible for the bitterness which has

now turned into the vicious movement of Mau Mau. One may suffer a social or an economic affront, but there is nothing which so pierces the personality as the humiliation of being treated as a lesser human being by another human being.[75]

This recognition impelled him to turn the critical lens back on Britain and its own 'colour bar' in a resonant biblical metaphor: 'Why should we behold the mote in the eye of South Africa and not consider the beam in our own? I would certainly say that, if we draw attention to the beam in the eye of South Africa, we should recognise, at least, that there is a mote in our own.'[76] Situating the present debate within the larger history of British radicalism, Brockway commented on the familiarity of the kinds of racial arguments now being put forward against a legislative end to racial discrimination:

I was reading last night the reports of the discussions in this House when the abolition of slavery was proposed. I was very interested to find that exactly the same arguments against legislation for the abolition of slavery were made by the reactionary circles in this country at that time as are now being made by the Conservative Party against the elimination of the colour bar. It was argued that slavery was inherent in human relations. There was one beautiful phrase which ran: 'The drive to obtain freedom from drudgery by the possession of and absolute control over one or more of one's fellow beings appears to be inherent in the nature of man.' That argument is now being urged against legislation for the elimination of the colour bar – that it is instinctive and inherent in man's mind, and, therefore, one must not move too rapidly or introduce legislation. Had that argument been listened to 120 years ago, we should never have had the Emancipation Act of 1833 which ended slavery.[77]

Echoing Brockway, Arthur Creech-Jones, erstwhile Labour colonial secretary, made the startling observation that 'this century may not be remembered for the two great German wars nor even for the cold war, but it may be remembered rather as the century of the coloured man and the inevitability of changes'.[78]

That both Hale and Brockway returned from their joint visit to Kenya prepared to push parliamentary discussion in more radical directions is clear. Six months after that trip, Brockway, now dubbed the 'Member for Africa', stood up to present a petition to parliament 'on behalf of 158,642 citizens of the Protectorate and Colony of Kenya'.[79] Many of the signatures took the form of thumb-prints, with some done in blood 'to indicate, in the phrase of the petitioners, that, in their view, "land is life"'. Among the petition's more radical demands: that 'Africans shall immediately be allowed to occupy and farm the large unused areas which are in the territories reserved to Europeans', and that further immigration of settlers 'be stopped in view of the land hunger from which the African community suffers'.[80] Hale too was unambiguous in his interventions: 'I think the time for being moderate in this matter has gone. It is time that people spoke up for what is right and what they sincerely believe.'[81] He noted that the atmosphere in the House itself was strikingly different:

> There is a real fear that the time is coming when every African will begin to hate every European. [An HON. MEMBER: 'That is not true.'] There is nobody who knows that it is not true. None of us who go out there can fail to be impressed by the gravity of the situation. We talked to Christian missionaries there, and I have been talking to them in London this morning. Let hon. Members talk to them and they will find a deep and abiding fear that Africa is marching with the majesty and inevitability of a Greek tragedy to what is for us a disastrous end ... Go into any large library and look at the books on Kenya from Macgregor Ross to Norman Leys and Negley Farson every one of which is a warning about Kenya. They are all of the type of 'Crisis Coming in Kenya', 'Clouds Over Kenya', warning all of us – and I have as much responsibility as anybody else – that this problem ought to be tackled.[82]

In a pamphlet issued not long after his second visit, and after the Emergency was declared, *Why Mau Mau? An Analysis and a Remedy*, written for the London Committee of COPAI, Brockway began by expressing the familiar deprecation of Mau Mau's putative atavism, and his 'shock' at finding 'some Africans reverting to methods of witchcraft and terrorism'. Yet, in bold italics at the centre of the page, he notes: '*But it is not enough to condemn, punish and protect. We must seek out the causes of Mau Mau and strive to remove them.*'[83] After discussing the causes of African 'land hunger' in Kenya, Brockway observes that the very idea of 'ownership' as adumbrated by the settler population was alien to the Kikuyu, for whom 'the ownership of the land could not have been transferred'.[84] What was deemed 'unoccupied' land by white settlers – in *terra nullius* mode – had in fact been used for nomadic grazing or left temporarily fallow. The conflict in Kenya bore witness not to a clash of civilizations, but to a clash of economies, moral and fiscal. Wounds of bitterness ran deep not only from this alienation of land, but also from the canny racial discrimination which debarred Africans from growing profitable crops like coffee on what little land they did have. 'Unless British policies are drastically changed', Brockway warned, speaking perhaps of his own change of heart from believing a multiracial cooperative society was possible to a position of greater pessimism, 'Kenya may descend, with the inevitability of a Greek tragedy, to the disaster of race conflict.'[85] This, it turned out, was absolutely correct.

'Oh, you don't want to feel sorry for *them*': Britain's Gulag

A sixteen-year-old African boy is taken into custody as a suspected insurgent. The next day his body is returned to his family; he had been shot 'while trying to escape'. When his father tries to find a lawyer, he and his friends are also taken into detention. A young boy shins up a tree in terror; though not an insurgent, he is shot by the security forces; wounded, he falls to the ground. A third young man is being made to 'confess' that he is Mau Mau. Tied up with his head between his knees, dirt forced down his throat, he is left out in the cold night air and refused food as he slowly slumps to death.[86] These were a few of the shocking stories *Daily Mirror* readers encountered in the run-up to Christmas 1955, in a syndicated set of articles focusing on the Emergency in Kenya. They were authored by the Labour MP Barbara Castle, who, commissioned by the tabloid, had undertaken a 'one-woman probe' into allegations of widespread abuse by British forces in Kenya during the Emergency. 'CAN the black men get white justice in Kenya today?' asked one article.[87] While in that country, Castle found herself in an unusual position; followed everywhere by the secret police just like the African trade unionists she met, she believed she now 'realised what it must be like to be black, and powerless'.[88] Were any African to complain, they would find themselves, like the father of the sixteen-year-old she reported on, disappearing into prison camps. Castle's articles, as the *Mirror* boasted a few days afterwards, caused a 'House of Commons storm'.[89] 'Labour to Fight Kenya Thugs' read the headline on the front page of the *Tribune*, referring not to Mau Mau, but to the hardliners of counterinsurgency operations, about whose conduct several Labour MPs would pose parliamentary questions.[90]

The 'excesses' on Colonial Secretary Lennox-Boyd's watch would generate widespread controversy, fuelled by 'leaks' from within Kenya's administrative service which included photographic evidence of torture and horrifying conditions in detention camps. 'Stories of colonial brutality and government evasiveness' were carried in several newspapers and magazines, including the *Manchester Guardian* and the *New Statesman and Nation*.[91] Hot on the heels of the Castle *Daily Mirror* probe came the bombshells dropped by Eileen Fletcher, in the pamphlet *Truth about Kenya*, published by the Movement for Colonial Freedom, in which the former rehabilitation officer, a Quaker reformer, detailed not only the brutal, overcrowded and lethally unsanitary conditions in the camps, but also the fact that female children as young as twelve were among the detainees.[92] Accompanied by several harrowing photographs, Fletcher's exposé spoke of the growing callousness of the British in Kenya, the wide 'sweeps' in which thousands were detained simply on suspicion and treated like cattle: 'I saw several men who were not moving quickly enough to please the Askaris being given great blows on naked shoulder blades with rifle butts, and when I protested the British Officers and even women officials standing by said, "Oh, you don't want to feel sorry for *them*."'[93] The process of 'screening' for Mau Mau entailed both torture – at the very least a 'light diet and a good thrashing' – and questionable psychological techniques. Undernourished and severely weakened prisoners were put to hard labour if they did not first die of disease. Fletcher's challenge to her British readers was emphatic: 'The defeat of Mau Mau is largely financed with money from this country. It is *our* money that is being spent on these brutal and repressive measures. What are we going to do about it?'

The unease about what was happening in Kenya was not restricted to the usual suspects. In the first two months of the Emergency, historian Joanna Lewis notes, 'the popular press across the board gave Kenya front- and back-page coverage, editorial comment and in-depth analysis'.[94] To the *Daily Mail*, Mau Mau was the gift that kept on giving sensational copy: secret primitive ceremonies, blood oaths, ritual cannibalism, diabolical murders of settlers and loyalists, and white settlers in 'terrorland' heroically braving 'terrorists' of the worst kind, from whom neither women nor children were safe.[95] But as the months went on, even the conservative *Times* noted that 'anxiety cannot fail to be felt at the high number of executions'.[96] The danger for the colonial government, the newspaper reflected, was that 'they would be building up in the name of Britain a terrible legacy of hatred and bitterness, for while deeds done in hot blood may be forgotten, the cold processes of law are apt not to be, in Africa any more than in Europe'.[97] This anxiety was borne out by a parliamentary delegation report noting that, towards the end of the long and brutal campaign, 'the influence of Mau Mau in the Kikuyu area ... has not declined; it has, on the contrary, increased'.[98] Indeed, even diehard apologists for empire such as F. D. Corfield, who strenuously denounced Mau Mau's 'atavism', would find themselves conceding that there was method in what they denounced as absolute madness. Commissioned to write a Command Paper for parliament published as *Historical Survey of the Origins and Growth of Mau Mau*, Corfield insisted that Mau Mau had to be seen in the wider context of the 'swift rise of African nationalism', if 'a violent and wholly evil manifestation of that nationalism'.[99] Noting that Mau Mau could not be reduced to a communist plot even if it had the sympathy of sections of the British left, Corfield's report also attested to the existence of much unrest before Mau Mau emerged fully onto the scene, in the form of strikes, upheavals and other 'subversive activities'.[100]

In *Histories of the Hanged*, his brilliant account of Mau Mau and the Kenyan Emergency, David Anderson notes that many Europeans objected to the idea of negotiations with the insurgents on the basis that they were 'sub-humans' who could not and should not be parlayed with.[101] Even the official government analysis of Mau Mau articulated an epidemiology of rebellion whereby the uprising was 'only an illness, a mental disease', afflicting the Kikuyu.[102] While

Anderson is correct to point to the salience of the 'mental-illness' analytic, it is necessary also to tease out the tensions in such pathologizing accounts which were rarely – even in the case of the most virulently hostile – solely about inhuman others. In inviting deprecation of its 'inhumanity', Mau Mau inevitably threw light upon the correspondingly inhumane aspects of colonial rule, putting uneasily into the frame the claims to humanity being made by the subjects of empire. It raised the question of whether Huxley's infamous 'yell from the swamp' could also be read as an insistence on recognition. The ferocity of the colonial state's response generated an uneasy sense that only the end of empire could end the savagery all around. Thus the *Daily Mirror* deprecated empire apologists: 'The gunboat. The bomb, the prison compound. That is what the monocle-flashing warriors of the Empah mean when they speak of determination. Will the sun never set on these bristling Blimps?'[103] In this opinion piece, the novelist and commentator Keith Waterhouse insisted that, while he sought no 'excuses' for the 'beastly' and 'revolting' Mau Mau whose defeat had raised jubilation in other quarters of the media, the British response to the insurgency also raised several questions about '*the thick catalogue of shameful things that have happened in Kenya in the name of the British Empire*'.[104] Waterhouse's disgust at what was being undertaken in the British name in Kenya – random floggings, the mutilation of corpses, and the torture and humiliations heaped on Mau Mau suspects and insurgents – inspired a stark warning, one resonant of Hale's caution in the House of Commons. Before long, Britain would see 'the eyes of the Empire staring back at it ... And those eyes will be full of hate'.[105]

Brockway and others raised similar concerns in parliament, the former asking the secretary of state for the colonies 'what provision is made to feed Africans when caged for screening in Kenya; what shelter is provided against rain; how far hooded interrogators are employed; and at what speed the individual screenings take place'.[106] Castle's findings had caused a political furore, and, along with Fletcher's charges, were the subject of much official denial and evasion. On 6 June 1956, a high-profile debate on Kenya was introduced by the former colonial secretary, Arthur Creech-Jones, himself no radical. He raised questions about the administration of justice in the colony and suggested that the events of the past few years

called for 'long overdue' political and economic changes of significance.[107] Brockway too spoke at length, defending Eileen Fletcher
from attack, mentioning the 'series of trials which have shocked hon.
Members and a large part of the British public', as well as the execution of over a thousand Kenyan Africans in the space of four years.
Barbara Castle revisited her findings, connecting the continuation of
Emergency measures in Kenya with 'the attitude of *baasskap*, white
domination', not unlike the attitudes that prevailed in South Africa,
'controls for control's sake' passing as the war against Mau Mau.
What was needed now was a decisive end to white domination and
'the recognition that Africans are human beings with fundamental
human rights as people'.[108]

Castle's comments here point to a remarkable feature of the debate
around Mau Mau and the Emergency: politicians and writers were
starting to make the connection between what was happening in
Kenya and imperial rule more broadly. Thus, Leslie Hale:

> This matter affects not only Kenya but the world as a whole. Our
> attitude in Kenya has a considerable effect on American opinion.
> But that was not the point that I wished to emphasise. Our attitude
> to the people of Kenya has its repercussion in Tanganyika, Uganda
> and the adjoining territories. At this moment a real struggle has
> started for the soul of Africa. The liberal conscience of Britain is
> becoming heard more than it has been for a long time; people are
> evolving a new conception of human rights and there is a new
> demand for human dignity. We cannot afford to allow a small body
> of settlers by a policy of repression to lose the fundamental moral
> integrity of Britain which is tied up in this struggle.[109]

Some of the most stentorian interventions in what is arguably one
of the most significant debates on colonial matters came from the
Labour icon Aneurin Bevan, best known today for his pivotal role in
instituting Britain's National Health Service. Observing that matters
pertaining to repression came to a head only when 'there is some
protest from someone in the Colonies about them', Bevan deprecated
the gradualism – 'the necessity of extending the franchise very slowly'
– which he heard articulated by some Members of the House who, he
averred, could have as easily been speaking a hundred years before:

'We do not like this weighted franchise. We do not like votes handed out as prizes for the establishment.' Bevan, like Hale, called on the House to 'read the situation at which we have arrived, especially in the supervision of colonial administration', in a world-historical frame:

> Very grave difficulties are arising in different parts of the world. We are faced with a very serious crisis in Cyprus. We may have very great difficulty in Singapore. Trouble is starting in Aden and may develop, and trouble has not been altogether removed in Kenya. It has been borne in upon me and upon my hon. Friends that the time has now arrived when the House of Commons should gravely consider an overhauling of our constitutional relationship to colonial administration.[110]

Charging government ministers with evading serious questions put to them by Brockway, Bevan reiterated the causal connections: 'We talk here as though the administration of Kenya, as though the seizure of land in Kenya and all those things were not responsible at all for Mau Mau.'[111]

Britons against the Empire: The Movement for Colonial Freedom

Within a decade of his return from Kenya, Brockway would write, much of what he had campaigned for had come to fruition: 'an elected African majority in the Legislature, African farms on the exclusive White Highlands, Africans allowed to grow coffee'.[112] He would also call for 'all progressive opinion in Britain' to 'support the African claims' in Kenya at a point in time when 'all over the Continent the African people are sweeping forward to democratic self-government'.[113] In April 1954, under Brockway's leadership, the COPAI merged with the Kenya Committee, the Central Africa Committee, the Seretse Khama Defence Committee and others to form the Movement for Colonial Freedom. Its archives, now housed at the School of Oriental and African Studies, University of London, indicate that the impetus came from events in Kenya and British Guiana; there was the sense that if the anticolonial struggle was about to hit a new stage of intensity, then Britain should have an organization that could offer solidarity and assistance, independent of direct political affiliation but calling on various wings of the Labour movement for support. In comparison to Brockway's more cautiously stated insights during his African journeys, the MCF's goals were explicitly radical and anticolonial, supporting 'the right of all peoples to full independence' and 'the substitution of internationalism for imperialism in all political and economic relations'.[114] Situating itself as a 'part of a world movement', the MCF sought to invert the direction of colonial tutelage, 'enlightening' Britain by rectifying Britons' ignorance about colonial affairs. With over a hundred affiliated MPs, the organization also sought to draft parliamentary questions and brief MPs on matters relating to Asia and Africa, and to highlight areas of shared interest – indeed, an identity of struggles between the Labour movement in Britain and liberation movements in colonial territories. It would provide assistance to representatives from various colonial liberation movements, arranging for them to speak at public meetings and meet with British trade union leaders and parliamentarians. Such speakers included Jomo Kenyatta, Julius Nyerere and Kenneth Kaunda; when Kenyatta was jailed, the MCF led a campaign in Britain to have him released. At one point, the organization could claim to have the support of nearly one hundred MPs and about twenty trade unions, in addition to various regional affiliates.

In its literature, much of it written with Brockway's imprimatur, the MCF explicitly espoused the right of all peoples to full independence, including freedom from external political, economic and military domination, as well as calling for the universal application of the Four Freedoms and the Declaration of Human Rights.[115] A pamphlet urging youth organizations to affiliate to it cautioned that the MCF was 'not a "charity" do-gooding organisation, which provides balm for uneasy consciences'.[116] Later, in his assessment of what he called 'the Colonial Revolution', Brockway would also describe the organization as carrying on continuous agitation in Britain – though, importantly, always taking its lead from crises of colonial insurgency:

Mau Mau in Kenya, the independence struggles in Nigeria, Ghana, Tanganyika and Uganda, the repression in Nyasaland, the tragic

Lumumba agitation for unity in the Congo, the military intervention in British Guiana, the opposition to the Central African
Federation and the violent resistance in Cyprus to British power (as
well as to national conflicts outside the British Empire in Algeria,
Tunisia, Morocco and Madagascar ...)[117]

The MCF produced leaflets, pamphlets and petitions (to demand the
release of Kenyatta, for instance), and organized meetings, lobbies,
special conferences, debates, marches, 'poster parades' and demonstrations across the country, facilitating speakers from Africa in
particular. There were film shows and half-day schools, and press
conferences for visiting anticolonial activists around whom the MCF
tried to generate publicity for its causes. In the mid 1950s, Brockway
recalled, 'there was great interest in the emerging anti-colonialist
struggle, but little knowledge'.[118] Providing information and a colonial
education became one of the campaigning organization's platforms.
With the assistance of others in the MCF, which noted that it was
supported by a range of trade unions, including the National Union
of Miners, the Amalgamated Engineering Union, and the National
Union of Tailors and Garment Workers, Brockway drafted Commons
questions and briefs for interested MPs.[119] MCF educational pamphlets covered a huge range of relevant issues from self-determination
for the colonies to nuclear disarmament, and from world hunger to
racism in Britain. These also spanned several contexts from Northern
Ireland, Cuba and Rhodesia (present-day Zimbabwe) to Vietnam,
Timor, Oman, Cyprus and Malaysia. The MCF was credibly seen as
'an articulate pressure group with much depth of support', giving
'a sense of centrality to colonial issues unknown in British history
since the First World War', Kenneth Morgan has argued – though he
somewhat predictably situates the organization in 'the grand tradition of British dissent'.[120] In an article he drafted for *Life* magazine in
1973, Brockway was clear that decolonization in colonies with white
settler populations had not taken place on metropolitan initiative,
but was the consequence of the defeat by African nationalism of the
white settler populations' attempts to dominate.[121] 'Moderates have
never achieved anything', he cited Hastings Banda of Nyasaland as
saying. 'It took extremists like Oliver Cromwell and Mrs Pankhurst
to get things done.'[122] The minutes of the MCF's Central Committee

would make a similar point: 'Whilst the attainment of colonial freedom depended mainly on the effort of the colonial movements, it also depended on the attitude of British governments.'[123] With this in mind, influencing British opinion was the real contribution which the MCF could make: 'Imperialism can only be ended by the British and Colonial people struggling jointly against the common enemy'.[124] Democratic pressure on parliament was key to the MCF's strategy, which included writing briefs and policy documents for Labour MPs to draw on. One such document noted the extent of repression that it had taken to keep the Empire in place:

> British colonialism, like all colonialisms, has a sad history in its denials of personal liberties and human rights. During the last twenty years of national struggles, it has been an almost continuous record of detentions without trial, imprisonments on political charges, deportations, enforced periods of exile, and of the repression of the freedoms of speech, writing, movement, association and trade unionism.[125]

Calling for overseas British bases to be shut down, the MCF tried repeatedly to show the connections between colonialism and Cold War militarism, pointing out the implications for British people including loss of social services to pay for a military budget and the constant threat of a world war. The organization also sought to explain 'neo-colonialism' in many of its pamphlets: 'This is not just a matter of winning political independence; Britain, America and other colonial powers are clever enough to concede this ... It is the struggle of half the world's population in the underdeveloped countries to rid themselves of poverty imposed on them by foreign or local rulers'.[126] This was, not, however, distant from the concerns of the British people who would also benefit from the fight against neo-colonial forms of domination: 'By helping the former colonial peoples to inherit their own resources we are weakening the very big monopolies and "take-over" tycoons who are the barriers to social advance in Britain'.[127] The MCF, in its capacity as 'Britain's anti-imperialist movement', combined its repudiation of the colonial project with an equally stringent attack on 'racialism' and anti-immigrant discourse, committing itself to fighting the Commonwealth Immigrants

Act (1962) and campaigning for amendments to the Race Relations Act.[128] It made clear, however, that its own role was secondary to that of colonial insurgents: 'We do not wish to claim over-much for the MCF. The growth of interest has been mainly due to the strength and vigour of the movements for freedom in Africa and Asia and to the liberation which they have brought about. We have been proud to be their voice in Britain.'[129]

Brockway himself would come to describe the MCF, with a touch of hyperbole, as a 'mass movement against imperialism ... in this country', which could be situated within a longer tradition of British radicalism going all the way back to Leveller solidarity with Irish peasants crushed by English landlords.[130] He had certainly come a long way himself. At his eightieth birthday dinner at the House of Commons in 1968, his speech had an element of irascible radicalism to it as he addressed himself partly to his fellow warrior, Barbara Castle:

> You said on TV, Barbara, that idealism must be wedded to reality. True; but idealism often creates reality. I think of racial equality and colonial freedom. I think of the fifties. When the Movement for Colonial Freedom was established I had to draft nearly every Question from the Labour Benches; the Fabian Colonial Bureau drafted a few. I had to brief Members of Parliament – I even briefed you, Barbara! But the whole climate of events (illustrated by Harold MacMillan's 'wind of change' speech) changed. Within two years I didn't have to draft any Question or brief any MP. I certainly didn't have to brief you. You were more effective on Hola than I could hope to be. What I want to say is this: the great change which took place regarding the colonies was due in part, at least, to the pioneer idealists – Hobson, Hilferding, Lenin, George Padmore, Jean Rous of Paris, Leon Szur and, later, to the MCF.[131]

Once again Brockway acknowledged the role played by African insurgencies in the gains of anticolonialism: 'The most liberal of Colonial Secretaries, Iain Macleod, told the truth. He said that if independence had not been granted to the African nations, the violence would have been far worse. Mau Mau and Algeria pointed to that.'[132] A decade later, he would flesh out a further genealogy for British anticolonial dissent, paying tribute to 'The Communist International [which] when it was formed in 1917, gave organised form to Lenin's theory and was active in colonialist spheres in opposing the opposition of colonialist powers. Less decisively the opposition to imperialism as a system arose within the Socialist International.'[133] Brockway noted that the League against Imperialism, which reflected a 'third period in the struggle against colonialism and imperialism', had itself been a response to 'the strong emergence of national movements within the Colonies and their active cooperation with the opponents of imperialism in the exploiting capitalist countries'.[134] Looking ahead to the coming decades through this lens, Brockway then took this acknowledgement of anticolonial agency and the struggle's centre of gravity to its logical conclusions:

> There is another possibility. It may be that the next stage in the advance to a new social order in the world may come, not from industrial countries, but from developing countries. It may be that from Vietnam a social revolution will expand across South East Asia, a new area of economic liberation, challenging America and the capitalist world. We live in exciting times and, if our horizons are broad, we see that the tempo is for radical change. Underneath, everywhere, is a great creative force for a new world, and we must recognise that our struggle against colonialism and imperialism is a part of it.[135]

Even more importantly, Brockway observed, 'efforts to end colonialism and imperialism' also led to one clear conclusion that had implications within Britain itself: 'we must identify with the movements for fundamental change in the basis of our society'.[136] The global and domestic orders were inextricably linked in this way.

Britain's Conscience on Africa and the Crisis of Paternalism

Over the course of this book, I have largely discussed figures who would have considered themselves to be, if not quite oppositional outliers, certainly dissidents. They were not, however, the only ones who found themselves responding to anticolonial insurgencies and contact with anticolonial figures. This book has not looked at twentieth-century reformist critics of imperial policies such as Leonard Woolf and his associates in the Labour Party Advisory Committee on Imperial Questions, or (except in passing, as with Arthur Creech-Jones) the liberal humanitarian members of the very moderate Fabian Colonial Bureau. More work also needs to be done on the impact of anticolonial thought and liberation movements on officials, politicians and administrators. In moving to a close, I want to touch on the question of how anticolonial struggles influenced those of a liberal imperialist but also reformist bent who would regard themselves as, if not quite the 'official mind' of British colonial thinking, certainly in some sympathy with it. One such figure is the Oxford don Margery Perham. Certainly no anticolonialist, over the course of a long and distinguished career as an Africa specialist and government advisor on colonial policy, Perham might have been regarded as much the opposite – a responsive liberal or 'constructive' imperialist with a penchant for urging reforms precisely in order to keep colonial rule stable and viable. That rare figure for her time, a female Oxford academic who came to be taken seriously as a specialist advisor on colonial African matters, Perham also wrote for newspapers and gave radio talks to inform a wider public about colonial questions. An early advocate of the rights of native people and of curbing the 'excesses' of white settler populations in Africa, Perham did not, however, start out as a dissenter from received colonial ideas; she 'shared a clear consciousness of race', for instance, with others who defended colonial rule.[137] What makes Perham worthy of closer attention is not only the extent to which her defences and critiques of the imperial project alike influenced both British public opinion and the vaunted 'official mind' in the Colonial Office. Her own trajectory – less susceptible to the vagaries of party lines – from an enthusiast of British rule in Africa to what one of her BBC colleagues described as 'a cautious, respectable radical' on colonial matters, who came to relinquish a dearly held gradualism on the matter of decolonization, had more than a little to do with witnessing – and learning from – the anticolonial insurgencies of the post-war period, the Mau Mau episode among them.[138] This is an aspect of Perham's intellectual and political biography that appears to have escaped scholarly attention: a professional teacher on matters to do with the Empire, she also came to be taught something by the colonized and their resistance. If she did indeed become 'the informed conscience of the English governing classes', African anticolonialists could take more than a little credit for it.[139]

One scholar and friend of Perham's who has written on her intellectual biography has described 'the two Miss Perhams' who emerged in the course of her career – one a liberally inclined imperialist wedded to good colonial government and not especially engaged with Christianity, and the second, who 'came into existence very suddenly, following the fall of Singapore to the Japanese in February 1942', returning to 'full Christian belief'.[140] While it is debatable whether this particular shift took place precisely in this manner and quite so suddenly, Roland Oliver is right to suggest that there was something of a split (albeit a messy one) in Perham's imperial worldview which became increasingly prominent from the war-torn 1940s into the decolonizing 1950s. Whether or not it began with Singapore – certainly Perham admitted that the 'disaster' had 'shocked us into sudden attention to the structure of our colonial empire' – by the 1950s, she had become far more explicitly engaged with the question of insurgency and its implications for the longevity of British rule.[141] Mau Mau and the attendant crisis of paternalism faced by the colonial state constituted a kind of watershed in Perham's thinking, compelling her to come to terms with the limitations of the gradualism she had championed for most of her career, which had underlain her own reformist critiques of imperial policy.[142] She came to see the demise of gradualism as inevitable, due partly to the Second World War and American opposition to Britain's empire, but also very substantially to 'the internal logic and irresistible dynamic of African nationalism itself ... propelling the move to independence at a rapidly increasing rate'.[143] Of course there were other movements, in West Africa for instance, which were pushing her towards this conclusion, but Mau Mau – and the wider context of Kenyan militancy – had a particular role in shaping her thinking about not just colonialism, but also anticolonialism.

Reading history at Oxford, Perham excelled in both academics and sport. Upon graduation she became a lecturer at Sheffield, and then returned to Oxford as one of a very small handful of women tutors. In between those appointments, she would make her first visit to Africa via British Somaliland, where her sister and brother-in-law were stationed, publishing *Major Dane's Garden* in 1925, a novel based on her experiences. Shortly after her appointment at Oxford, she would strike up a lifelong friendship with Lord Frederick Lugard, the famous architect of 'indirect rule' in West Africa, later becoming his biographer, and, until its viability became seriously questionable, an advocate of indirect rule. The establishment of Imperial and Commonwealth Studies at Oxford benefited her, as did that in 1904 of the Rhodes Trust, which would fund her first long stretch of travels to colonial outposts. These culminated in Africa, where she would spend nine months, in 1929–30, in 'the problem colony of Kenya', a place for which she would hold a special lifelong regard.[144] Writing frequently for outlets such as *The Times* and the *Manchester Guardian*, she also became what one scholar describes as 'a publicist in explaining African nationalism to the British people better than anyone else and therefore helping to ready them for the end of empire in Africa in the 1960s'.[145] One newspaper hyperbolically dubbed her 'Britain's African Queen'.[146] In all three positions, including her Oxford tutorship, Perham had clearly cracked hitherto male bastions, but in her relationship to imperial questions she exhibited – and sometimes held in tension – both an understanding of marginality in relation to power and an ability to voice a ferociously paternalist (and patriarchal) defence of British colonial aims and achievements. It is true, of course, as Joanna Lewis has argued, that something of Perham's ability to fashion 'a critique that gently coaxed colonial administrations into rethinking their ruling strategies' might have emerged from her own sense of critical distance as a single woman in a male world.[147] While the increase in 'the metropolitan focus on its own poor' may also have 'opened up her analysis of the African context', it is important to recognize that Perham also became a student of Africa and Africans, her own critique over time shaped by African criticism of and resistance to imperial policies.[148] The trajectory of her work is instructive in this regard.

Perham's first Kenya travelogues offer little that is out of the ordinary, comprising a series of vignettes combined with political observations, and those mainly about the behaviour and politics of the white settlers. At the time, Perham recalled in an introduction to a later memoir, a few African politicians 'had begun to organize and assert their grievances ... and there was now an increase of agitation and political expression by some Kikuyu over land and labour grievances'.[149] When told by a woman settler that the natives were like ungrateful animals, Perham retorted 'that if you choose to take land from a primitive, overcrowded people, you could not rely on getting civil and civilized labour'.[150] Although feisty and combative in tone, Perham did not articulate here a significant critique of colonial life, and African voices do not really figure in her account. She spoke of falling in love with the 'charm' of the Masai, and feeling that it was dangerous to use the female-circumcision issue to irritate the Kikuyu, 'already very politically self-conscious and tending to be anti-European'.[151] To the extent that she commented on the land issue at all, her views were carefully 'balanced', despite the pejorative language with which she evoked Kenyan farm labour: 'The squatter is a very significant figure in Africa. He clings to the white settler like a parasite and one which could eventually ruin its host. He would not be there if the native had enough land and the white man had not too much.'[152] Much of Perham's early commentary on colonial rule in Africa, written for outlets such as *The Times*, demonstrated a commitment to a kindly but stern paternalism. Of her 'uncritical, unforeseeing commendation' of indirect rule at that point, Perham would later assert, somewhat defensively: 'my first knowledge and experience of Africa was of the continent at its wildest and most dangerous, the Africa which dictated the character of much of Britain's earlier administration'.[153] It is not precisely that Perham's early writings ignored the voices of what she called 'native witnesses' – on the contrary, she reported their dissatisfaction and distrust as evidenced before government commissions – but that these voices and concerns were grist for a larger story in which the main actor was Britain. Even at the very moment Perham urged her British readers to remember that theirs was 'an alien government which has imposed itself upon subject peoples', Perham's initial aim was the intelligent consolidation of that government through local knowledge, 'stooping to discover the positive impulses that animate the smallest cells of their corporate life, and enlisting these in our work of civilization'.[154] The African is a 'partner' in this project, but without any doubt *in statu pupillari*, and a beneficiary. 'Trusteeship' had a necessarily temporary mandate, 'that of developing backward peoples until they can "stand by themselves"'.[155]

Even in those romantic early days, however, Perham was not unaware of brewing resentment, reminding her readers that the British could not 'shut our eyes to the beginning of native discontent in Kenya and of distrust between black and white'.[156] In an introduction to *Ten Africans*, a volume which sought specifically to voice African life experiences, Perham would note that African 'backwardness,' while an 'obvious and fundamental fact', was 'one upon which we are apt to lean a little too hard in order to make ourselves comfortable in a difficult situation'.[157] Moreover, she observes, there's a tendency to talk about Africans as an undifferentiated mass, whether as 'natives', 'hut and poll tax-payers', 'native labour' or even as the 'native problem', which serves to obscure, if not their humanity, their individuality.[158] This recognition does not prevent her, however, from prefacing *Ten Africans* with the unpromising assertion: 'The barriers between the civilized and the less civilized are there, and they are solid.'[159] Such distancing generalities surface frequently in Perham's own early critique of the colonial situation in Kenya – the only part of Africa she saw as *not* 'largely quiescent' during the interwar years. In a famous published exchange of bristling, often uncomfortable, letters with the British Kenyan settler-writer Elspeth Huxley, written in 1942–43, while referring sympathetically to the settler's fear of 'a great dark flood over the little island of privilege',[160] Perham does envision black resentment reaching the point of an active overthrow of white rule. While to some extent deserving of representation on matters that concerned them, Africans figured in Perham's letters not as acting subjects but as 'voiceless labourers',[161] passive recipients of injustice, negligence or benevolence.

Without a doubt, Perham's views at this point were shaped by a sense of 'British conscience' and the need to preserve the Empire by the exercise of that conscience: 'The partnership of conscience and criticism is the salt that saves the Empire from going bad and always has done since the days of Burke and the anti-slavery movement.'[162] At the point that she made the case for reformed leadership, figured as a negotiation mainly between settlers and imperial centre, Perham certainly did not conceptualize power shifting into African hands. Indeed, as Huxley was quick to note, Perham had herself suggested in the course of correspondence that 'Africans aren't ready for considerable political advances',[163] urging that any major changes be put off for a few decades while Africans were 'educated' into governance: 'I have not been pressing for the early transfer of power to those unready to make good use of it, but for the maintenance of imperial authority on their behalf, during the period of unreadiness.'[164] Yet, even as Perham avers that Africans cannot 'hold their own' right now, there is a glancing, uneasy reference to the now manifest fragility of colonial rule:

> We have been beaten out of some of our richest Eastern possessions by a 'coloured' people, and other coloured people, Chinese and Indians, have fought with and for us. The spell of our invincibility ... has been broken ... It is certainly the moment to modify our persistent delusion that other peoples *like* being ruled by us, or are going to accept our former political and social superiority any longer without question.[165]

In fact, the undoing of imperial paternalism in Africa would come earlier than Perham could have imagined. Over ten years after this initial published correspondence, in 1955, both Huxley and Perham would write retrospective reflections on it. In hers, Huxley would make a startling observation:

> Obviously – perhaps even too obviously to mention – one million people do not indulge in open revolt against the existing order unless the times are badly out of joint. The question then becomes: what sickness is it in society of which Mau Mau is the symptom? Many would answer in one word: inequality. The sort of things we have been discussing in these letters: the land hunger of the Kikuyu, the feeling that they have been cheated of their land, the low wages, resentment of the Europeans' wealth, the colour bar. All these things combined to accentuate in the minds of the Kikuyu a state of resentment which made just the right seedbed for the spores of Mau Mau to germinate in.[166]

While her account is replete with the familiar condemnatory tropes of savage rituals and bloody plots, Huxley notes that, even in their otherwise antagonistic correspondence, she and Perham had agreed ('for once'), with reference to the West Indies, 'that, in a British territory, you get nowhere unless you kick up a fuss, generally a violent fuss'.[167] Judging that her and Huxley's views had drawn closer, given the latter's attempts to understand Mau Mau in her novel *A Thing to Love*,[168] Perham pronounces that there is now an 'African Africa which must in no long time, given the new conditions of our world, emerge through the thin and recent layer of European control'.[169] The important departure for Perham here is the admission, contra prior assertions, that gradualism has had its day. 'Honesty demands', she acknowledges, 'the admission that the Mau Mau movement has to its credit that it has brought all races to the edge of the precipice of racial strife – many have indeed fallen over that edge – and forced them to draw back into the unattractive alternative of co-operation.'[170] The emergence of African assertion means that the settlers must now accept that there is no chance of consolidating their own supremacy; matters were no longer 'in the main a bilateral issue between the settlers and the British government'.[171] It is a concession from Perham that is laced with an unmistakable petulance, perhaps even animus, as she describes the 'new and bitter impatience' which appears to mark this assertive new phase:

> It is the desire for equality that seems to move individuals, classes and nations with an energy never shown before in history. There is also a wholly new impatience to get it *quickly* which is dictated by the speed of modern scientific discovery ... Now men use the powerful political forces they find at hand to get the desired results not in a lifetime, nor ten years hence, but in two years – next year! Not because they can prove they are ready for it but because they so passionately desire it and this principle of equality accords it.[172]

Definitions of 'freedom' had also been unmoored from their entrepreneurial-meritocratic connotations, for 'it is not freedom which these aspirants desire, freedom in which to work out their own salvation', or even just 'equality of opportunity', but something rather more threatening to the colonial order: 'equality in status and in material standards, a mass equality to be given or induced, almost irrespective of any qualifications'.[173] Perham was recognizing, albeit with anxiety, that 'freedom' had lineages and futures different from those put in place by imperialism as capitalism.

It is clear that, reflecting on her letters ten years later, Perham found herself having to shift her analysis away from an exclusive emphasis on imperial responsibility to thinking about the implications of black insurgency, the 'dearly bought opportunity *Mau Mau has made possible*'.[174] And so it was that, in 1954, well into the Kenyan Emergency and its brutal repression of Kenyan resistance, Perham would write an extraordinary opinion piece for *The Listener* in which, without quite relinquishing the idea of trusteeship, she conceded: 'we have shown ourselves capable of making great mistakes as rulers of other peoples. We should remember Ireland and Palestine, and the Mau Mau in Kenya, to go no further.'[175] She now posed far more fundamental questions to do with the limitations of both colonial knowledge and colonial practice: 'how far are we towards understanding the colonies in their present restless condition? In other words, are we dealing with the causes as well as the symptoms?'[176] The most remarkable aspect of this colonial specialist's responses to insurgency now was the admission that the demands for rights and freedoms could not be described as emerging from British initiative:

> In our dealings with colonial nationalism we are – let us admit it – finding ourselves obliged to make concessions we never meant to make so soon. We yield to pressures without fully understanding what they are and where they come from. We claim – but it is only a half-truth – that what is happening is merely the fulfilment of our own policy and promises.[177]

In a pronouncement that might well have issued from Frederick Douglass himself, Perham, theorist of British trusteeship, observes of the distrust that Britain faces: 'It lies surely in the truth that independence is something that cannot be given but must be taken. And first it has to be demanded by more than the first half-dozen lawyers and journalists who have learned to direct against us the civil liberties we wrested from the Stuarts.'[178]

It is easy to overlook the radical significance of Perham's concessions here, even when peevishly offered. It is not only that freedom from colonial rule has been wrested rather than conceded, but that the Caliban model of political education is inadequate to explaining anticolonial insurgency. The Mau Mau 'movement' too, she notes in another article, had 'the active or passive acceptance of it by – perhaps? – 90 percent of Kikuyu', a fact that had 'come as a profound shock to Kenya and to all connected with the colony'.[179] While she believed that radical leaders played upon discontent and thrust aside 'moderate' leaders as 'imperialist stooges', Perham did not advocate, unlike some, that a few 'agitators' be set aside in favour of 'the loyal masses who would then long remain content under our beneficent rule' – that moment, she appeared to suggest, has passed not least because of 'a powerful world force which at once inspires their demands and makes them almost irresistible'.[180] Without naming socialism as such, Perham invoked the 'desire for equality, for self-expression, for freedom from any kind of external mastery and its stigma of inferiority', a force which she noted was also moving through Britain at that point in the form of a 'peaceful revolution'.[181] To refuse to acknowledge its reach would be to leave a vacuum for that which is to be feared more than decolonization and the loss of empire: 'the pervasive indoctrination of communism'.[182] More worrying than the now inevitable end of colonial rule was the prospect of 'chronic opposition'.[183]

The Tutor Tutored

That it was, above all, Mau Mau which had finally impelled Perham to confront the question of oppression and resistance more directly is clear from her comments in articles written during the mid 1950s. This 'terrible assertion of discontent', she suggested, had changed perceptions for good: 'The Africans can never again be seen as they were before this event.'[184] Black self-assertion also meant, to put it mildly, that 'paternalism may be actively threatened'.[185] Perham's changing views on the Kenyan situation in the post-war period were also influenced by contact with Kenyan anticolonial campaigners such as the labour organizer Tom Mboya, a Luo who was then secretary of the Kenya Federation of Labour. Though not affiliated to Mau Mau, Mboya had a very clear and uncompromising vision of what freedom for Kenya would look like. His 1956 pamphlet written for the Fabian Colonial Bureau, which was not entirely happy with it, and introduced by Perham with enthusiasm though not without reservations, was pointedly titled *The Kenya Question: An African Answer*.[186] In his mid twenties, Mboya, who thought of himself as 'a socialist at heart and a believer in democracy', had spent the academic year (1955–56) leading up to the publication of the pamphlet studying political science and economics, specializing in industrial relations, at Ruskin College, Oxford, where he had interacted in some depth with Perham and other students.[187] During his time in Britain, he also met several political leaders, MPs and trade unionists. Introducing him as a 'mind of young Africa' who must be listened to, Perham flagged her own shift in position: 'We have to make terms with things as they are … there comes a moment when Britain can no longer effectively govern a subject people against the will of the educated minority.'[188] Aware that her own concessions to this tide would be deemed 'defeatist' in some quarters, she pronounced with a deliberate air of statesmanship: 'History teaches that the greater political courage lies more often in the fearless acceptance of change than in blind defiance of it.'[189]

Coming from a man Perham deemed a political 'moderate', if a 'magnificent brain', *The Kenya Question* is brutally unsparing in its analysis of the colonial situation in Kenya and the origins of Mau Mau.[190] Indeed, it suggests that Mau Mau had shifted Perham's own understanding of what constituted the 'moderate'. Opening his short essay with an uncompromising assertion of equality, Mboya notes that present conditions 'have forced the discussion into racial terms', which may mean that he will be charged with being 'anti-European' or 'pro-African'.[191] Significantly, Mboya does not distance himself or other Kenyans from Mau Mau as such: 'Most people agree that Mau Mau – apart from being a reflection of the failure of British colonial policy in Kenya – is the child of the political, economic and social frustrations experienced by the African people prior to 1952.'[192] The essay laid out a familiar charge-sheet against the British in Kenya: land alienation, discriminatory practices in licensing cash crops, and a thoroughly racial basis for establishing schools, hospitals and residential areas, in addition to the colour bar in public places. In the face of this tyranny, Mboya observes calmly, 'a violent reaction is understandable even if it is not justifiable'.[193] The Kenyan trade unionist also made short shrift of the standard explanations for the insurgency produced in Britain, including those offered by Perham herself as well as by the pathologizing studies she endorsed, such as that by Carothers: 'Psychologists may offer reasons why the Mau Mau ceremonies were primitive and barbaric, but these explain the form of the revolt and not the causes of it. It is absurd to represent Mau Mau as merely the result of too rapid a transition from primitive life to a modern complex society, or as a reversion from Christianity to barbarism.'[194] Those many Kenyans like himself who did not support Mau Mau's methods did not, however, 'sympathise with the government against which it is struggling'.[195] Nor could Mau Mau be dismissed as a 'struggle of differing factions among the Kikuyu people': 'All Africans, regardless of tribe, are agreed on the need to eliminate European dominance.'[196]

Mboya restates with simple clarity what Perham and others were coming grudgingly to concede: the time for reforms was over, and it was no longer possible to 'justify paternalistic government'.[197] Continued advocacy of gradualism and pandering to the wishes of settlers amounted to ignoring the 'rise of African political opinion', which 'leaves no room for the master/servant relations of the past'.[198] Africans would not 'be subject to the generosity of those who govern' but must be *recognized* – a word Mboya uses pointedly and repeatedly. Despite his distance from Mau Mau methods, Mboya's warning emphasis is on the violence of the colonial state and the effect of 'the methods used in the prosecution of the emergency, on future relationships in Kenya'.[199] Collective punishments often took illogical forms, Mboya notes, first evicting families onto the streets, then arresting them for being without shelter, but punishing those who did offer them shelter. Mboya recounted his own arrest and that of other trade unionists during the notorious Operation Anvil – the biggest sweep of the Emergency ostensibly undertaken to 'screen', 'blacklist' and detain actual and potential insurgents. However high the number of (largely Kenyan) lives taken by Mau Mau, the colonial government had more blood on its hands. Reflecting on the episode some years later, Mboya reiterated these views:

Of course it is true that Africans, more than anyone else, suffered from Mau Mau, and many more Africans died. But this is true of many revolutions and anti-colonial uprisings. It is normally the indigenous people who suffer most, and the Kenya situation does not appear to be unique historically. The trouble in the Kenya situation was that Mau Mau violence was met by even greater violence from the British Government and its security forces. If we must condemn the violence of the Mau Mau, we must equally condemn British violence against it.[200]

It was, he noted shrewdly, a point that had been made a long while ago by none other than the British reformer John Bright: 'I may say too that Force, to prevent freedom and to deny rights, is not more moral than Force to gain freedom and secure rights.'[201] Violence garnered attention in a way that 'working quietly and slowly' did not: 'Again, it is sad but true that until the eruption of violence in Algeria and Angola, the world had been content to remain silent about the suffering of those people under colonial rule.'[202]

The 'cult of anti-colonialism'

In 1961, Perham's stature as one of Britain's most recognized commentators on imperial rule was cemented when she was invited by the BBC to give that year's Reith Lectures, published subsequently as *The Colonial Reckoning*.[203] In part a spirited defence of the better motives and merits of the imperial project, now in terminal decline, the lectures were to some extent motivated by her belief that it had 'been misjudged and had misleading tests applied to it'.[204] In terms of her intellectual trajectory, these lectures came at the right moment, 'when I was ready to think over all I had been working upon, and generalize upon it'.[205] What is striking, however, is the prominence given in this synthetic overview of how empire was coming to an end not, as might have been expected, to an 'orderly' decolonization or 'the peaceful transfer of power', but to that novel phrase in circulation: 'anti-colonialism'. While attempting to explain the multiple 'overseas news items' in the daily broadsheets that concerned 'the relations of white peoples with coloured peoples', the lectures also became an account of a looming metropolitan existential crisis:[206]

People of my generation were taught from their schooldays that our empire was a splendid achievement, conducted as much for the good of its many peoples as for our own, peoples who, indeed, now owe to us the form of their existence as national states. The words 'trusteeship' and 'partnership' held serious meaning. To the generation before us the 'white man's burden' was not a rather bitter joke. Then how, we ask, has 'colonialism' suddenly become, as it seems, such a term of abuse? Have we been utterly blind? Was the idealism we so often professed merely a cloak in which we tried to hide our complete self-interest from the world, and indeed from ourselves?[207]

More startling than the actual loss of governing power in its global implications, for Perham, was 'this outburst of anti-colonialism which has accompanied it'.[208] This 'great movement of assertion among the non-European peoples ... suddenly changed the balance of forces in our world'.[209]

Perham flirted with the familiar self-consoling notion that the 'ideal of democratic freedom' had 'been learned very largely from Britain herself'.[210] And yet she found herself compelled to complicate the picture. Certainly, the 'Caliban' theory formed part of her account, in the form of African students who had come to London and, like Indian graduates before them, 'enjoy a sense – a conflicting sense – of freedom and equality' as they 'learn all about the civil liberties and observe a free political life'.[211] When they returned to their lands as 'pioneer nationalists', they 'quoted the Bible, Blackstone, Burke and Shakespeare. They were turning against Britain her own political and judicial weapons', enriching 'their great natural powers of oratory' with demands in sonorous English.[212] The first generation of nationalists were, however, imbued with the spirit of moderation and pragmatism that Perham herself saw as fundamental to British politics, wanting to 'grow into self-government rather than to seize independence'.[213] What, then, spurred the rebellions which hastened decolonization and the concomitant crisis of paternalism? Here Perham identified many factors, not least the outbreak of 'riots' in the West Indies, India's refusal to accept dependent self-government, the First World War's use of African soldiers, Wilsonian ideas of self-determination and, not least, the 'black racialism' articulated by the likes of Marcus Garvey.[214] Two international events had also acted as spurs: the invasion of Ethiopia, and Hitler's demand for the return of ex-German colonies, or what were known as the 'Mandated territories'. Meanwhile, both America and the Soviet Union positioned themselves differently as hostile to the continuance of the British Empire. Russia, of course, 'offered not only a condemnation of colonialism but also an alternative'.[215] And so it was that Perham found herself posing the question at the beginning of her second lecture: 'What is the nature of the force that in less than a decade has swept the rule of Europe out of almost the whole of tropical Africa and has bred more than twenty new nations in its place?'[216] Manifold circumstantial factors notwithstanding, what cannot be denied, Perham concedes, is the inevitability of human resistance to discrimination, to being treated as a lesser being. This returns her to the example of Kenya: 'We British, I think', Perham reflects, 'hate ever to admit that the blackmail of violence can pay.'[217] The fact remained that Mau Mau 'had disrupted the whole life of the colony', making clear that 'Kenya could never again face another tribal movement of this kind, still less a movement that was wider than a single tribe'.[218] Without quite relinquishing the stock figuration of Mau Mau, 'that most ghastly of rebellions', in terms of 'bestial oaths' and a 'cult of torture and murder', Perham offers what still, in 1961, ran counter to received ideas by acknowledging how necessary that violence must have been felt to be in order to so countermand the moral economy of an indigenous community: 'How deep must have been the frustrations of the Kikuyu to drive them to practices which quite deliberately violated the sanctities of their own sexual and tribal life!'[219]

If, on the one hand, Perham's figuring of African 'hatred' in familiar terms of emotion over reason pointed to her continuing participation in received colonial discourse, it is also the case that she took that 'intensity of feeling' seriously, suggesting that it be understood on its own terms.[220] Not only Africans, she notes, but even the 'so moderate' Indian writer Nirad C. Chaudhuri, had spoken of 'a ferocity of hate' he felt once when looking down upon a well-dressed English audience in a Calcutta theatre.[221] In what must surely count as an astonishing gesture from a supporter of the imperial project, Perham recited – on British public radio in the 1960s! – verses by the anticolonial poet of Négritude David Diop and Léopold Senghor's magnificent epic poem *Chaka*:

Je n'ai haï que l'oppression …

Ce n'est pas haïr d'aimer son peuple.

Je dis qu'il n'est pas de paix armée, de paix sous l'oppression

De fraternité sans égalité. J'ai voulu tous les hommes frères.[222]

Like Brockway, Perham identified colonial racism as the chief culprit: 'I remember the tone of voice and flash of eye with which a young leader from French Africa exclaimed to me, "*You* have never known what it is to live under colonialism. It's humiliating." '[223] Where Perham found it difficult to criticize colonialism directly, she was willing to condemn more fully the racism it legitimized. The resistance of the colonized, she finally admitted, was part of a very different historical trajectory from the Whig interpretation held by the metropole: 'We may try to equate Ghana with the Tudors or the Congo with the War of the Roses. But our immensely gradualist history cannot be exactly fitted to theirs.'[224] For Perham, the accelerated end of trusteeship was effected not by metropolitan will but by African leaders who, 'making full use of that changed balance of forces which I discussed in my second lecture, forced the pace'.[225] Congratulating them on this a few pages later, Perham finally admits the inadmissible. Decolonization was *not* the consequence of metropolitan initiative: 'Britain was answering a demand from her subjects which she was finding it difficult to refuse and nationalist leaders can congratulate themselves for forcing the pace.'[226]

If, in the final instance, Perham's Reith Lectures were not precisely a defence of anticolonialism, they were certainly a stringently honest account of how it had shaped the present, with Britain forced to accede to its claims. Why, Perham asked, had the official world of Britain been so myopic, made such serious miscalculations on the basis that anything resembling African independence was a long way off? 'Perhaps the reason for this degree of blindness is that British people do not understand nationalism, do not recognise it, or at least its strength, in others.'[227] This was not because Britain was immune to nationalism; on the contrary, 'the confidence arising from our former power, may have bred in us an unconscious kind of nationalism, one that seldom needed to assert or even to know itself'.[228] The fact also had to be acknowledged that the British Empire 'through most of its duration, like all other empires, had been created and conducted mainly in the interests of the ruling power'.[229] Perham never quite admits that it was wrong to deem colonial subjects unready to take on parliamentary democracy, but does concede with some admiration that 'Africans, following Asians, pressed on, as we saw, ignoring the doubts and negations of their rulers'.[230]

Ultimately, what is perhaps most remarkable is Perham's turn to something like dialectics, steering away from her own sense of 'pessimism' about Africa to the possibility that the newly independent nations of Africa would neither simply imitate the West nor turn to nativism, but rather attempt a 'synthesis' of the two sets of resources, a 'task of the greatest difficulty and value'.[231]

> When ... I saw the Union Jack flutter down the post I felt a wholly unexpected, almost physical shock. It may be that, having made some study of Nigeria's history, I realised just what it was that was being brought to an end, all the hopes and fears, the achievements and mistakes, all the work of hundreds of British lives, many of which ended up in this country. But immediately the Nigerian flag ran up, and the assembled Nigerians of all regions and tribes saluted it with unmeasured pride and hope. I realised then that, whatever our regrets or forebodings, the incalculable force of human energy and pride would be harnessed behind the new nation.[232]

Empire's Ends

Brockway too, if rather differently from Perham, arrived at the conclusion that what would emerge in Africa in the wake of decolonization would be dialectical, distinctive, and forged from its own historical struggles even as the 'trend is towards an Africanism independent of European influence'.[233] He also took seriously the claims made for African community structures as receptive to non-capitalist forms: 'Africans have no more need to be "converted" to socialism than they have to be "taught" democracy.'[234] Written shortly after Perham's Reith Lectures were delivered, and published as final negotiations for Kenya's transition to independence were underway, Fenner Brockway's *African Socialism* was also an attempt to think about the future of a decolonized Africa as breaking definitively from the regnant global economic order: 'What is not so fully realised is that African leaders and African national movements are to an extraordinary degree dedicated also to the task of repudiating the capitalism whose urges led to the occupation of their continent in the nineteenth century and of consciously directing their new independent states towards the creation of socialist societies.'[235] Both Brockway and Perham, for all their differences, believed that socialism would be a significant force in the era of decolonization. If empire was to be left behind, then the buccaneering capitalism that it had propagated would also need to be replaced with a more radically egalitarian system. The erosion of that possibility and the betrayals of the post-colonial moment belong to another book and another story.

Epilogue

That Wondrous Horse of Freedom

On 3 February 1960, British prime minister Harold Macmillan visited Cape Town and delivered a speech that did not go down too well with his hosts.[1] Macmillan began, benignly enough, by praising the Union of South Africa, its strong economy and the ports and skyscrapers of its great cities, Durban and Johannesburg. The economic union between Great Britain and South Africa had, he said, been one of beneficial interdependence, a marriage of capital and entrepreneurial skill. Then he uttered the now famous words:

> In the twentieth century, and especially since the end of the war, the processes which gave birth to the nation states of Europe have been repeated all over the world. We have seen the awakening of national consciousness in peoples who have for centuries lived in dependence upon some other power. Fifteen years ago this movement spread through Asia. Many countries there, of different races and civilisations, pressed their claim to an independent national life. Today the same thing is happening in Africa, and the most striking of all the impressions I have formed since I left London a month ago is of the strength of this African national consciousness. In different places it takes different forms, but it is happening everywhere. The wind of change is blowing through this continent, and whether we like it or not, this growth of national consciousness is a political fact. We must all accept it as a fact, and our national policies must take account of it.[2]

It is worth pausing on Macmillan's rhetorical moves here. He places African nationalism – as many would do – within a familiar teleology whereby the continent was deemed to be finally 'catching up' with a prior European historical stage, and a more recent one for Asia. Cannily, he exhorted his recalcitrant white South African audience to understand that what was blowing through black Africa was a version of their own legitimate national sentiments, they 'here in Africa' had 'created a new nation'.[3] Indeed, he was suggesting white South Africans – and the rest of the Western world – could take credit for African nationalism, totting it up as one of the many 'achievements of Western civilization' on this continent. Of course, to many in his audience the equivalence Macmillan was according to white and black nationalisms was in itself outrageous. Breaking through the fraternal pleading and civilizational credit-taking, however, was an unmistakable note of warning – the word 'fact' repeated twice with the 'frankness' of a friend. If the growth of African nationalism could not be accepted as a happy achievement, then grim reality would have to prevail: 'the growth of national consciousness in Africa is a political fact, and we must accept it as such. That means, I would judge, that we've got to come to terms with it.'[4] Not to do so would be to imperil 'the precarious balance' between East and West underlying the post-war settlement. The imperial era, Macmillan was saying more explicitly than any Western leader, and certainly more so than any British prime minister, was coming to an end. Only a few years before, Winston Churchill had sullenly pronounced that he had not become Britain's leader in order to preside over the liquidation of the British Empire. Macmillan was indicating not only that that liquidation was imminent, but that it had to be framed as the logical outcome of the project of empire.

Macmillan's speech in itself was only a sombrely realistic appraisal of the decade or so just gone. While nationalisms in Asia, and to a lesser extent in Africa, had clearly registered on the so-called 'official mind' of Britain, it would seem that 'virtually no one foresaw the scope of the decolonization process – much less its speed – in the immediate aftermath of the war'.[5] Neither France nor Britain, the two largest European colonial powers, had anticipated that the colonial world would become 'the major theatre of conflict' in the post-war era.[6] Macmillan hoped to exercise statesmanlike oversight of a process that was clearly going to be taken out of metropolitan hands; at the very least Britain needed a *narrative* of controlled and planned transfer of power to prevail. The long-cherished myth of the 'gifting' of freedom to those deemed ready for it would require some careful spin in the face of the manifest seizure of power from reluctant colonial hands. The uprising in Kenya was paralleled by one in Malaya (1948–60) where too a brutal counterinsurgency and Emergency were enacted by the British, who had been forced, in 1948, to give up their Mandate in Palestine. Counterinsurgency tactics developed in Palestine would be deployed in Malaya, which the British hoped to hold on to along with Singapore after the loss of India and Palestine; some of the same serving soldiers and high-ranking officials were redeployed from Palestine to Malaya. Though first targeting rubber planters and mine-owning interests, the Malayan Communist Party eventually broadened the resistance to encompass the 'Fascist colonial state' in its entirety; in colonial terms, they were, of course, 'terrorists' not nationalists. As Christopher Hale has noted, though Malaya has long been used as an example of a thoughtful and 'benign' counterinsurgency on Britain's record, unlike those in Cyprus (1955–59) and Kenya, 'The Emergency War in Malaya was a nasty and brutal business', involving, as it had in Kenya, subterfuge, illegality, collective punishment, forced resettlement and unjustifiable civilian bloodshed which, along with the lethal consequences of colonial divide-and-rule, manifests malign consequences even today; the paper trail itself may well only be partial.[7]

While it is traditional to pin the end of empire on the no doubt important moment of the Suez crisis in 1956, this was 'neither the first nor the last instance of imperial aggression to cause a public outcry'[8] – not even in relation to that country, as we have seen. A British ambassador to Egypt also made comparisons: 'In 1882, the bombardment of Alexandria and the British occupation of Egypt had divided British opinion on the same lines.'[9] As we have seen, the crises of empire did not begin at that fateful moment when President Gamal Abdel Nasser nationalized the canal. There were several other crises of insurgency and counterinsurgency in the period immediately following the Second World War: in Cyprus, Oman, the Gold Coast, British Guiana, Borneo, Aden and Nyasaland. The other great European empire of the time, the French one, had encountered an infamous defeat at Dien Bien Phu in 1954, and was facing its own crises of decolonization. France's infamous massacre at Setif in Algeria, just as the Nazis surrendered in 1945, had already cast severe doubts on the continuance of that empire in the face of anti-colonial resistance. By the time that Kenya achieved independence at long last in 1963, profound changes had also taken place in Britain. In the 1950s, the British Labour Party finally 'evolved a coherent, powerful critique of colonial affairs, one that helped to create a new cross-party consensus and effect the rapid demise of an empire that had lasted for 300 years'.[10] 'With Britain's Union Jack replaced by the black, red and green flag of the new states, political power in Britain's last East African colonial holding slipped from the grasp of its 55,759 whites and was taken up by its 8,365,942 Africans', wrote the *New York Times* in the wake of the handover ceremony in Nairobi.[11]

Half a century after Macmillan's speech, US president Barack Obama made a well-received speech of his own to both houses of parliament. On a high-profile state visit to Britain in 2011, he aimed to allay anxieties about the state of the so-called 'special relationship' and the possible decline of global Anglo-American influence. Reassuring his audience that the two countries were bonded through shared values, he began by invoking not Britain, but England, the nation at the heart of the Empire: 'Centuries ago, when kings, emperors, and warlords reigned over much of the world, it was the English who first spelled out the rights and liberties of man in the Magna Carta. It was here, in this very hall, where the rule of law first developed, courts were established, disputes were settled, and citizens came to petition their leaders.'[12] Having putatively identified the *fons et origo* of the very ideas of rights and liberties, America's first black president went on to graciously concede that mistakes had of course been made. For both his country and the one whose representatives he was addressing, there had been inevitable occasional failures to live up to ideals. So far, so predictable. But, then, a bolder move: 'But through the struggles of slaves and immigrants, women and ethnic minorities, former colonies and persecuted religions, we have learned better than most that the longing for freedom and human dignity is not English or American or Western – it is universal, and it beats in every heart'. This was encouraging. However, the acknowledgement of liberationist and human aspirations that just might exist beyond 'Western values' barely surfaced before it was quickly annexed to a familiar triumphalism:

> Perhaps that's why there are few nations that stand firmer, speak louder, and fight harder to defend democratic values around the world than the United States and the United Kingdom.
>
> We are the allies who landed at Omaha and Gold; who sacrificed side by side to free a continent from the march of tyranny, and help prosperity flourish from the ruins of war. And with the founding of Nato – a British idea – we joined a transatlantic alliance that has ensured our security for over half a century. Together with our allies, we forged a lasting peace from a Cold War.

Having skated surprisingly close to the suggestion that the struggles of the oppressed helped define Anglo-American understandings of freedom, tolerance, equality and democracy, Obama's speech now glossed freedom in rather more partisan and familiar terms, as an economic system 'we built' that takes hold and spreads across the world: 'There is no greater generator of wealth and innovation than a system of free enterprise that unleashes the full potential of individual men and women ... That's why countries like China, India and Brazil are growing so rapidly – because in fits and starts, they are moving toward market-based principles that the United States and the United Kingdom have always embraced.' As C.L.R. James noted at a different moment in relation to Africa, this was a familiar claim: 'Western civilisation was the norm and the African people spent their years in imitating, trying to reach or, worse still, if necessary going through the primitive early stages of the Western world.'[13]

The timing was important. Obama was giving this speech in the wake of the 'Arab Spring', a series of popular rebellions that had toppled authoritarian rulers, undermined existing political hierarchies in the Middle East and North Africa, and thus threatened to alter an international order geared to the strategic interests of his own nation. It was something of a geopolitical priority, then, to annex the diverse liberationist impulses and forces that had come together to constitute that widespread insurgency into an American project, to give it the imprimatur of the capitalist West. In an audacious reworking of the famous Douglass pronouncement with which this book began, Obama, himself of part-Kenyan descent, then declares: 'Power rarely gives up without a fight – particularly in places where there are divisions of tribe and divisions of sect ... What we are seeing in Tehran, in Tunis, in Tahrir Square, is a longing for the same freedoms that we take for granted here at home.' Young Arabs were rebelling in the streets, then, in order to become more like Americans, which indicated – and it is now that the real burden of the argument becomes clear – that Britain and the United States would need to start 'investing in the future of those nations that transition to democracy, starting with Tunisia and Egypt – by deepening ties of trade and commerce; by helping them demonstrate that freedom brings prosperity'. Aspirations to freedom made manifest in rebellion had now to be carefully channelled from above through the checkout lane.

It has been the argument of this book that British public life and political discourse have been mired in a tenacious colonial mythology in which Britain – followed by the remainder of the geopolitical West – is the wellspring of ideas of freedom, either 'bestowing' it on slaves and colonial subjects or 'teaching' them how to go about obtaining it. This assumption does not restrict itself to the undoubtedly copious body of writing on the idea of 'liberty' which is certainly a notable feature of British and American intellectual history; it extends, as we have just seen, to the very impulses that drive human beings to make their own history in circumstances not of their own choosing. It is this mythology which has enabled two successive twenty-first-century Labour prime ministers to make historically dubious pronouncements – in one case with lethal consequences:

> The days of Britain having to apologise for its colonial history are over ... We should talk, and rightly so, about British values that are enduring, because they stand for some of the greatest ideas in history: tolerance, liberty, civic duty, that grew in Britain and influenced the rest of the world.[14]

> If we can establish and spread the values of liberty, the rule of law, human rights and an open society then that is in our national interests too. The spread of our values makes us safer.[15]

To undo this mythology systematically, then, remains a project of the highest intellectual and political importance. In *Insurgent Empire*, I have tried to show not only that insurgencies were frequent during British colonial rule, but that resistance to empire and the crises it generated shaped dissent around the imperial project within Britain. Put another way, the resistance of the periphery helped radicalize sections of the metropole. In the process, ideas of freedom that were not reducible to Obama's ultimate 'triumph of a system of free enterprise that unleashes the full potential of individual men and women' did make their claims heard, even if they were not always heeded. Indeed, 'free enterprise' as such rarely formed the basis of claims to independence and self-determination, even though, from India and Jamaica to Egypt and Kenya, demands for land and control of labour power formed the basis of insurgencies. More often than not, capitalism was the target of insurgency, not its goal, and socialism in one form or the other, certainly in the twentieth century, was a strong influence. Tracking the lines of dissent and opposition within Britain and the ways in which these frequently emerged as part of a dialogical and transnational process is one way in which Britons today can both interrogate the seamless national mythologies they are routinely invited to consume. It enables Britons to lay claim to a different, more challenging history, and yet one that is more suited to a heterogeneous society which can draw on multiple historical and cultural resources.

An 'impudent fraud … upon the British people'

Reflecting on the independence struggle in Ghana which led to the formation of the first country on the African continent to be free of British rule, and on Nkrumah's central role in both the success of that revolution and its eventual tragic unravelling in a series of betrayals, C.L.R. James notes that what happened in the postcolonial period, 'the African degeneration', does not invalidate the promise and potential of the earlier moment.[16] This is, of course, in contrast to the many apologists for colonial rule, still wheeled out on radio and television programmes in Britain, for whom the blotted copy-book of many independent states is evidence of the inbuilt weaknesses

of anticolonialism itself – proof that African countries, and not a
few Asian ones, were not ready for independence. Without flinch-
ing from those failures – indeed, for him, Nkrumah's betrayals were
very deeply felt – James is clear about the significance of decolonization and the way in which it was fought for, contra 'the defensive
reiteration by the leaders of British public thought that the British
government "gave", "handed over" independence for which (God
save us) it had long been training [Africans]'.[17] James's ventriloquized
version of the mythologies of empire when it comes to liberation is
contemptuously precise:

> Africans are, and always have been, a backward and barbarous
> people who have never been able to establish any civilised society
> of their own. Some of the more liberal would qualify this by saying
> that this backwardness was due not to any natural inferiority but
> to the circumstances of their environment, the climate or the soil
> or the forests, or something of the kind. These barbarous people
> were brought in contact with civilisation by the brutalities of the
> slave trade. However, the unhappy slave trade is happily behind us,
> and as a result of their contact with Western European civilisation,
> primitive Africans became a part of our unified world. The British
> government has by and large aimed at bringing these peoples to the
> stage where they would be able to exercise self-government, despite
> certain lapses from principle to which all nations, all peoples and
> all individuals are of course subject, human nature being what it is.
> It was always a *principle* of the British colonial system, but within
> recent years with the rise of the colonial peoples, it has been clearly
> understood and is being carried out.[18]

In fact, this account could not 'stand concrete examination for a single
moment', being 'a tissue of falsehood, hypocrisy and empiricism, all
designed to present disorderly retreat as systematic advance.'[19] Invoking
the example of rebellions in the West Indies, James observes: 'Unless
the Colonial Office claims that it trains the masses of the people to
strike and revolt whenever a new stage of fiddling with the Legislature
is reached, its elaborate claims for training colonial peoples is an elaborate fiction.'[20] Each concession wrested from colonial governments
was the result of explosions causing loss of life and property, followed

by one step towards self-government being 'benevolently granted'.[21] Full self-government takes place when it becomes too costly to repress the determined resistance that will not be denied.

Myths matter because, unlike crude propaganda, they often drive action through sincerely held views, and possess a tenacity borne of limiting the horizon of possibilities: 'the vast majority of the British people having no other views placed before them ... have no other choice but to follow along the same lines of thought'.[22] Having argued that African polities also need to abjure such colonial mythologies, James goes on to make a point similar to that which has animated this study. In the post-war period, he judged, Britons themselves were 'now ready for new relations, human relations, with colonial peoples for the first time in four centuries' but remained 'choked and stifled by the emanations from the myth'.[23] Writing in 1962, with decolonization fully underway, James believed the same 'powerful current' of moral protests that animated popular anti-slavery in Britain in the past 'is now once more emergent under the blows imperialism has been receiving and the discredit which now colours all colonial adventures'.[24] 'Myth-making conceals another virulent poison for the myth-makers', James observes. 'It insists that they see themselves always as the givers, and Africans as the takers, themselves as teachers and Africans as the taught', and never 'the slightest hint' that anything which took place in the colonies could, conversely, 'instruct or inspire the peoples of the advanced countries in their own management of their own affairs'.[25] This was as true of those who are friendly towards Ghana, in this instance, as of those who are not. We might recall here Ernest Jones's exhortations to the British working-classes to learn from the acts of Hindustan's rebels. Several decades after James deprecated them, it remains the case that colonial mythologies have a tenacious hold on the British imagination – not least the idea that freedom was 'given to' or 'bestowed upon' former colonies. Generations of indoctrination, as James suggested, mean that such thinking remains 'an organic part of the thought processes of the nation, and to disgorge it requires a herculean effort'.[26]

My hope is that this study, along with others, will be able to contribute towards what will have to be a sustained unlearning, a monumental process but a necessary one in a heterogeneous twenty-first-century Britain. In the wake of Brexit, the imperial myth, 'whenever it is torn apart', shows itself to rest on deep foundations and is repeatedly mended, 'washed, dressed and tied with ribbons', to be presented to the British public.[27] James may well have the best formulation for why the myth of a unique, liberal, salvific and benign empire has been so profoundly damaging for Britain: 'A myth that has lost all contact with reality is the direct source of immeasurable confusion, catastrophes and disasters.'[28] As the sociologist and cultural historian Paul Gilroy puts it, despite the 'continued citation of the anti-Nazi war', it is in fact colonial history that provides a better explanatory context for contemporary British culture and its preoccupations – race, identity, multiculturalism, patriotism, religion, social cohesion, migration – providing 'a store of unlikely connections' and shaping political life.[29] Yet, he points out, that story remains 'marginal and largely unacknowledged, surfacing only in the interests of nostalgia and melancholia' in inflated imperial myths which then further entrench 'deluded patterns of historical reflection and self-understanding'.[30] For Gilroy, it is more than time for a 'frank exposure to the grim and brutal details of my country's colonial past'.[31] I would add to this the need for Britons, particularly young Britons, to be reminded of a long tradition of antislavery and anticolonialism that illuminates the ways in which those forms of dissent overlapped and intertwined with resistance outside Britain, specifically that asserted by black and Asian peoples. Scholars have begun to undertake the work of excavating similar dissidence and lines of influence in other European imperial metropoles: in France, Holland, Belgium, Italy, Germany, Portugal and Spain, among others.[32] Exciting work is also being done on the relationships between anticolonial movements across colonial and postcolonial contexts or the global South: Robbie Shilliam's pioneering account of the 'deep, global infrastructure of anti-colonial connectivity' in his study of the relationship between African and Māori anticolonial struggles is exemplary here.[33]

Some twenty years ago, the 'Parekh report' called for the writing of a new 'national story' in order to address difficult issues of national identity, culture, ethnicity and community relations.[34] It is a call that has been heeded largely through an emphasis on Britishness as constituted by a 'tolerance' and an 'inclusivity' which enable minority communities to be welcomed and 'integrated' into the larger fold of national life. The majority or 'host' community (implicitly figured as white, Christian and English-speaking) is enjoined to affirm its commitment to tolerance; 'tolerated' minority communities are called upon to 'integrate' with these values while retaining, to the extent that they are not incompatible with 'British values' (a concept affirmed by Parekh), their own distinctive identities and beliefs. The story of anticolonialism in Britain as I have attempted to tell it undoes this pernicious binary by offering something like a contrapuntal reading – a reading which, in Edward Said's words, is undertaken 'with a simultaneous awareness both of the metropolitan history that is narrated and of those other histories against which (and together with which) the dominating discourse acts'.[35] Such a reading rubs against not just the grain of imperial history but also the sort of unhelpful benign separatist liberalism which argues, 'It makes far more sense to teach British children of South Asian or Afro-Caribbean background about the parts of the world where their families originated – the history of the Mughal Empire, or of Benin or Oyo, for example – than to teach them about Alfred and the cakes or Drake and the Armada.'[36] Far from decentring Britain or enabling British ethnic minority communities to embrace 'their' history (why should *all* British children not know more about the Mughal Empire?), this form of liberal paternalism reinforces an unhelpful, to say the least, us-and-them model of social relations and a pernicious divide between imperial past and multicultural present. In fact, the two histories are profoundly connected, and it is precisely the British imperial project that provides a great deal of shared historical terrain in relation to both oppression and resistance. The pressure on non-white Britons – even those of the third or fourth generation – to 'constantly have to justify their presence on these islands' can only be lifted by a history that recognizes the processes of the past – imperialism – that account for their presence here.[37]

In her trenchant jeremiad *A Small Place*, the Antiguan writer Jamaica Kincaid pauses to ask what her fellow islanders might gain if they opted to undertake a more searching examination of their own history:

> And might not knowing why they are the way they are, why they
> do the things they do, why they live the way they live and in the

place they live, why the things that happened to them happened, lead these people to a different relationship with the world, a more demanding relationship, a relationship in which they are not victims all the time of every bad idea that flits across the mind of the world?[38]

In the British Isles, the project of developing a more demanding relationship to history than is offered by prevalent island stories must go beyond the performative largesse of 'including' ethnic and cultural minorities in the national. What Adorno calls 'seriously working upon the past' is a task that has also to be taken on by Britain's African, Caribbean and Asian communities.[39] What might be the resonances for these communities of reflecting on a history of agency and resistance, of the colonized-in-struggle, in terms of developing a different relationship to both Britain and the world? Could a consideration of the influence of that struggle on British radical traditions and domestic dissent in turn reshape the ways in which those communities are regarded more widely? It could certainly be one way out of the tedious and formulaic position-taking enjoined upon us when imperial apologetics are periodically instigated by professional controversialists who invoke 'an imagined history of Western endowments and free hand-outs: "Why don't they appreciate us, after what we did for them?"'[40] What if, rather than discourses of 'unappreciated magnanimity', Britons had access to more textured and dialogical but honest stories of ideological and personal encounters in the crucible of empire? Slavery and empire shape Britain's material and discursive inheritance; so, undoubtedly, do antislavery and anticolonialism.

Without an understanding of this backstory in which there is, firstly, British dissent on the question of empire, which is, secondly, shaped by anticolonial resistance, it becomes easy for present-day apologists to caricature all critiques of the British imperial project as undertaken by 'retrospective Jeremiahs denouncing the evils of a past colonialism'.[41] The patently false argument that criticism of empire involves judging the past by today's standards is given a free pass. Said himself suggests that there was 'very little domestic resistance' to European empire; but, as we have seen, there was certainly enough to constitute a distinct minority tradition available to those who sought a different form of engagement with non-European peoples.[42] It is evident, for instance, that E. M. Forster's great novel of India, which sought at once to think about the possibilities for friendship between Indian and Briton, and contemplated its impossibility in the face of imperialism, owes something of its dissident consciousness to the insurgent upheavals of its time.[43] We need to build an archive of dissidence, opposition and criticism in relation to the British Empire – one which might serve to caution us against levelling and self-serving assumptions about the past in order that we might engage in a more demanding way with the present. In the spring of 2016, controversy erupted over the demand by student campaigners at Oxford that a statue of the buccaneering colonial racist Cecil Rhodes be removed from the frontage of Oriel College, Oxford. The young activists were widely denounced by establishment historians and from other predictable quarters such as the *Daily Mail* and the *Telegraph*. They were accused by, among others, the eminent classical historian Mary Beard of wishing to 'whitewash' history while still benefiting from its legacies. One of Beard's charges was that the 'Rhodes Must Fall' campaigners were neglectful of history, and that Rhodes was simply of his time. The idea – not being propagated, as it happens – that he was a 'particularly dreadful lone racist wolf in the late 19th century is completely barking', she declared.[44] Rhodes was, of course, far from being a lone imperial ideologue. But was he so very completely endorsed in his time and by his peers? Here is another distinguished classicist writing in his memoirs about his return to Oxford where he had studied and taught for a number of years: 'I cannot say that I saw with pleasure my old University made a pedestal for the statue of such a man as Rhodes.'[45] Goldwin Smith, who wrote this, was not a revolutionary, but he had been a member of the Jamaica Committee, which had sought unsuccessfully to bring Governor Eyre to book. By the end of the nineteenth century, even a few literary works which had begun to ask troubling questions about the imperial project and white supremacy more broadly were well known: Joseph Conrad's very different novels *Almayer's Folly*, set in Dutch South East Asia, and *The Heart of Darkness*, set in the Belgian Congo, and Olive Schreiner's *Trooper Peter Halket of Mashonaland*, set in southern Africa. In the interwar period emerged Forster's *A Passage to India* and George Orwell's *Burmese Days*. Dissenters from the imperial status quo may not have carried the day, but they were no lone wolves either, as we have seen. These dissenters – and the insurgencies which inspired them – constitute a lineage that made its presence felt in the post-war period, and remain part of the genealogy towards which anti-war and anticolonial groups in Britain today can look back. Fenner Brockway and the Movement for Colonial Freedom, for instance, became deeply involved with the ultimately successful battle to end apartheid in South Africa, to which boycotts on the part of an international community were essential. Brockway was also the initiator, working together with ethnic-minority groups in Britain, of legislation to end racial discrimination in public places, successful only at the eighth attempt. In the face of disdainful dismissals and active silencing from various quarters of the establishment, it is these lines of resistance and genealogies of dissent that must continue to give heart and hope to those who look towards a more fully decolonized future for both Britain and the postcolonial world.

Notes

Introduction

1. Frederick Douglass, 'West India Emancipation, Speech Delivered at Canandaigua, New York, 3 August 1857'. Available at University of Rochester, Frederick Douglass Project, at rbscp.lib.rochester.edu. All other quotations from Douglass refer to this source, unless otherwise stated.
2. Ibid.
3. Ibid.
4. Edward Said, *Culture and Imperialism* (London: Chatto & Windus, 1994), pp. 240–1, emphasis in original.
5. Cited in John Oldfield, *Chords of Freedom: Commemoration, Ritual and British Transatlantic Slavery* (Manchester: Manchester University Press, 2007), p. 102.
6. David Cannadine, *In Churchill's Shadow: Confronting the Past in Modern Britain* (London: Penguin, 2002), p.26
7. John Darwin, *The End of the British Empire: The Historical Debate* (Oxford: Basil Blackwell, 1991), p. 5.
8. Joanna de Groot, *Empire and History Writing in Britain since 1750* (Manchester: Manchester University Press, 2013), p. 105.
9. The term is Niall Ferguson's, from his paper 'British Imperialism Revised: The Costs and Benefits of "Anglobalization"', Stern School of Business, New York University: Development Research Institute Working Paper Series 2 (April 2003).
10. Victor G. Kiernan, *The Lords of Human Kind: European Attitudes Towards the Outside World in the Imperial Age* (London: Serif, 1995), p. 2.
11. Many of these are detailed in Antoinette Burton, *The Trouble with Empire: Challenges to Modern British Imperialism* (New York: Oxford University Press, 2015) and John Newsinger, *The Blood*

Never Dried: A People's History of the British Empire, 2nd edn (London: Bookmarks, 2013).

12. Burton, *The Trouble with Empire*, p. 1.

13. Ibid. Burton also notes rightly that 'while imperial blockbusters fly off the shelves, wide-ranging accounts of those who struggled with and against imperial power ... have failed to materialize'. Ibid., p. 2.

14. See Roberto Fernández Retamar, 'Caliban: Notes towards a Discussion of Culture in Our America', in Robert Fernández Retamar, ed., *Caliban and Other Essays* (Minneapolis: University of Minnesota Press, 1989).

15. Darwin, *End of the British Empire*, p. 91. As Michael Goebel notes in the French context, this was not always a simple process: French republican slogans – *liberté, egalité, fraternité* – 'graced the entry gates of Indochinese prisons' in which anticolonialists often found themselves interned. They too, however, like many in the British Empire, would address the gap between rhetoric and reality, 'instead of outright dismissing these ideals altogether'. Michael Goebel, *Anti-imperial Metropolis: Interwar Paris and the Seeds of Third World Nationalism* (Cambridge: Cambridge University Press, 2015), p. 222.

16. Jan Nederveen Pieterse, *Empire and Emancipation: Power and Liberation on a World Scale* (London: Pluto, 1990), p. 361, emphasis in original.

17. 'What happens when, in the spirit of dialectics, we turn the tables, and consider Haiti not as the victim of Europe, but an agent in Europe's construction?' Susan Buck-Morss, *Hegel, Haiti, and Universal History* (Pittsburgh: University of Pittsburgh Press, 2009), p. 80.

18. There are presently five substantial historical studies that address British domestic critiques of empire at particular historical moments as their main subject: Stephen Howe, *Anticolonialism in British Politics: The Left and the End of Empire* (Oxford: Oxford University Press, 1993); Gregory Claeys, *Imperial Sceptics: British Critics of Empire, 1850–1920* (Cambridge: Cambridge University Press, 2010); Mira Matikkala, *Empire and Imperial Ambition: Liberty, Englishness and Anti-Imperialism in Late Victorian Britain* (London: I. B. Taurus, 2011); Bernard Porter, *Critics of Empire: British Radicals and the Imperial Challenge*, 2nd edn (London: I. B. Taurus, 2008 [1968]); and Nicholas Owen, *The British Left and India: Metropolitan Anti-imperialism 1885–1947* (Oxford: Oxford University Press, 2007).

19. Newsinger, *Blood Never Dried*, p. 17.

20. Timothy Brennan, *Borrowed Light: Vico, Hegel, and the Colonies* (Stanford: Stanford University Press, 2014), p. 3.

21. Said, *Culture and Imperialism*, p. xxii.

22. Ibid., p. 240.

23. Ibid., p. 241.

24. Ibid., p. 240.

25. Michel-Rolph Trouillot, *Silencing the Past: Power and the Production of History* (Boston, MA: Beacon, 1995), p. 96.

26. Ibid., p. 27.

27. Ibid., p. 98.

28. Ibid.

29. Ibid., p. 99.

30. Ibid., p. 95.

31. As Newsinger notes, 'the handful of books arguing an anti-imperialist case are completely swamped by the massive sales of the books of Niall Ferguson and company, some of which have been conveniently accompanied by successful television series'. 'Introduction to the Second Edition', in *Blood Never Dried*, pp. 7–8.

32. Despite important contestations, not least from historians of post-colonial polities, the 'imperial initiative school' of British imperial history has been influential, with debates about decolonization restricted to which British policy effected it.

33. Cited in Society for the Mitigation and Gradual Abolition of Slavery Throughout the British Dominions, *Report of the Committee of the Society for the Mitigation and Gradual Abolition of Slavery Throughout the British Dominions: Read at the General Meeting of the Society Held on the 25th Day of June 1824, together with an account of the proceedings which took place at that meeting* (London: Richard Taylor, 1824), p. 76.

34. Darwin, *End of the British Empire*, p. 87.

35. John Darwin, *Unfinished Empire: The Global Expansion of Britain* (London: Bloomsbury, 2012), p. 1.

36. Burton, *The Trouble with Empire*, p. 5.

37. Ibid., p. 2.

38. Stuart Ward, 'Introduction', in Ward, ed., *British Culture and the End of Empire* (Manchester: Manchester University Press, 2001), p. 4.

39. Ibid., p. 5.

40. Ibid., p. 6.

41. Ibid., p. 10.

42. Ibid., p. 12.

43. Martin Lynn, 'Introduction', in Lynn, ed., *The British Empire in the 1950s: Retreat or Revival?* (London: Palgrave Macmillan, 2005), p. 1.

44. John M. Mackenzie, 'The Persistence of Empire in Metropolitan Culture', in Ward, ed., *British Culture and the End of Empire*, p. 24.

45. De Groot, *Empire and History Writing in Britain*, p. 183.
46. Andrew S. Thompson, *Imperial Britain: The Empire in British Politics, c. 1880–1932* (Harlow: Longman, 2000), p. 10.
47. Ibid.
48. Neil Lazarus, *Nationalism and Cultural Practice in the Postcolonial World* (Cambridge: Cambridge University Press, 1999), p. 9.
49. Homi K. Bhabha, 'Sly Civility', *October* 34 (1985), p. 75. See also 'Signs Taken for Wonders: Questions of Ambivalence and Authority under a Tree outside Delhi, May 1817', *Critical Inquiry* 12: 1 (1985), p. 144. In the latter, Bhabha makes the influential case for 'mimicry' as marking 'those moments of civil disobedience within the discipline of civility: signs of spectacular resistance' (p. 162).
50. Lazarus, *Nationalism and Cultural Practice*, p. 133.
51. Lisa Lowe, *The Intimacies of Four Continents* (Durham, NC: Duke University Press, 2015), p. 3.
52. Ibid.
53. Ibid., p. 12.
54. Ibid., p. 26.
55. Buck-Morss, *Hegel, Haiti, and Universal History*, pp. 74–5, 74.
56. Satya P. Mohanty, 'Us and Them: On the Philosophical Bases of Political Criticism', *New Formations* 8 (Summer 1989), p. 73.
57. Said, *Culture and Imperialism*, p. 241.
58. Uday Singh Mehta, *Liberalism and Empire: A Study in Nineteenth-Century British Liberal Thought* (Chicago: University of Chicago Press, 1999), p. 191.
59. Gurminder K. Bhambra, *Rethinking Modernity: Postcolonialism and the Sociological Imagination* (New York: Palgrave MacMillan, 2007), p. 146.
60. Leela Gandhi, *Affective Communities: Anticolonial Thought, Fin-de-Siècle Radicalism, and the Politics of Friendship* (Durham, NC: Duke University Press, 2006), p. 7.
61. Ibid.
62. Ibid., p. 5.
63. Bill Ashcroft, Gareth Griffiths and Helen Tiffin, *The Empire Writes Back: Theory and Practice in Post-colonial Literatures* (London/New York: Routledge, 1989), p. 103.
64. Gandhi, *Affective Communities*, p. 5.
65. Ibid., p. 8.
66. Ibid., p. 2.
67. Ibid., p. 2–3.
68. Ibid., p. 6.
69. Ibid., p. 7.
70. See David Featherstone, *Solidarity: Hidden Histories and Geographies of Internationalism* (London: Zed, 2012), p. 5.

71. M. M. Bakhtin, *The Dialogic Imagination: Four Essays*, ed. Michael Holquist, transl. Caryl Emerson and Michael Holquist (Austin: University of Texas Press, 1981), p. 284.

72. M. M. Bakhtin, *Speech Genres and Other Late Essays*, ed. Caryl Emerson and Michael Holquist, transl. Vern W. McGee (Austin: University of Texas Press, 1986), p. 89.

73. Michael Holquist, *Dialogism: Bakhtin and His World*, 2nd edn (London/New York: Routledge, 1990), p. 29.

74. Ibid., p. 34.

75. Satya P. Mohanty, *Literary Theory and the Claims of History: Postmodernism, Objectivity, Multicultural Politics* (Ithaca, NY: Cornell University Press, 1997), p. 241.

76. Ibid., p. 240.

77. Ibid., p. 241.

78. Ibid., pp. 242, 243.

79. Ibid., p. 242

80. Elizabeth Heyrick, *Immediate not Gradual Abolition, or, An Inquiry into the Shortest, Safest, and Most Effectual Means of Getting Rid of West Indian Slavery* (London: J. Hatchard & Son, 1824). For a magnificent discussion of this image and Heyrick's reinterpretation of the Abolition Seal, see Marcus Wood's brilliant work, *The Horrible Gift of Freedom: Atlantic Slavery and the Repression of Emancipation* (Athens/London: University of Georgia Press, 2010), where he notes that the 'tremendous sentence ... in one daring move decimates the interrogative double negative of the original slogan' (pp. 75–7).

81. Pieterse, *Empire and Emancipation*, p. 368.

82. Ibid., p. 379.

83. Abdul R. JanMohamed and David Lloyd, 'Introduction: Minority Discourse: What Is to Be Done?', *Cultural Critique 7: The Nature and Context of Minority Discourse II* (Autumn 1987), p. 14.

84. Walter D. Mignolo, 'Delinking: The Rhetoric of Modernity, the Logic of Coloniality and the Grammar of De-coloniality', *Cultural Studies* 21: 2 (2007), p. 453.

85. Ibid.

86. Edward Said, *Humanism and Democratic Criticism* (New York: Palgrave Macmillan, 2004), p. 23.

87. Pieterse, *Empire and Emancipation*, p. 380.

88. Ibid., p. 381.

89. Paul Gilroy, *Darker than Blue: On the Moral Economies of Black Atlantic Culture* (Cambridge, MA and London: Belknap Press), 2010, p. 59.

90. Ibid., p. 66

91. Said, *Humanism and Democratic Criticism*, p. 28.

92. Ibid.

93. Pieterse, *Empire and Emancipation*, p. 380.

94. Ibid., p. 368.

95. Abdul Janmohamed and David Lloyd, 'Introduction: Towards a Theory of Minority Discourse', *Cultural Critique 6: The Nature and Context of Minority Discourse* (Spring 1987), p. 8.

96. Bakhtin, *Speech Genres and Other Late Essays*, p. 89, emphasis in original.

97. Said, *Culture and Imperialism*, p. 289.

98. Porter, *Critics of Empire*, p. 1.

99. Ibid., p. 32.

100. Ibid., p. 333.

101. Said, *Culture and Imperialism*, p. 290.

102. Ibid.

103. Ibid., p. 291.

104. Ibid., p. 292.

105. Darwin, *Unfinished Empire*, p. 293.

106. Ibid.

107. Said, *Culture and Imperialism*, p. 241.

108. Ranajit Guha, 'The Prose of Counter-insurgency', in Guha, ed., *Subaltern Studies: Writings on South Asian History and Society*, vol. 2 (Delhi: Oxford University Press, 1983), p. 46.

109. Ibid.

110. Frederic Harrison, 'Egypt', in *National and Social Problems* (London: Macmillan & Co., 1908), p.201.

111. D. Mackenzie Wallace, *Egypt and the Egyptian Question* (London: Macmillan & Co., 1883), p. 369.

112. Brennan, *Borrowed Light*, pp. 2–3.

113. Ibid., p. 13.

114. See Newsinger for a fairly comprehensive survey of nineteenth- and twentieth-century insurgencies.

115. Burton (*The Trouble with Empire*) has an extended discussion of the years leading up to Indian independence, and Newsinger (*Blood Never Dried*) discusses labour unrest in colonial India, including the famous naval-ratings mutiny.

116. See 'Professionals and Amateurs', in Edward Said, *Representations of the Intellectual* (New York: Vintage, 1996), pp. 73–83. Said defines 'amateurism' here as the desire to be moved not by profit or reward but by love for and unquenchable interest in the larger picture, in making connections across lines and barriers, in refusing to be tied down to a specialty, in caring for ideas and values despite the restrictions of a profession.

1. The Spirit of the Sepoy Host

1. Edward Thompson, *The Other Side of the Medal* (New York: Harcourt, Brace, 1926), p. 10.
2. Ibid., p. 25.
3. Ibid.
4. Ibid., pp. 27, 30.
5. Ibid., pp. 27–8.
6. Ibid., p. 32.
7. Ibid., p. 36.
8. John William Kaye, *A History of the Sepoy War in India, 1857–58*, vol. 3 (London: W. H. Allen, 1876), p. 654.
9. Jill C. Bender, *The 1857 Indian Uprising and the British Empire* (Cambridge: Cambridge University Press, 2016), p. 132.
10. Karuna Mantena, *Alibis of Empire: Henry Maine and the Ends of Liberal Imperialism* (Princeton: Princeton University Press, 2010), p. 1, emphasis in original
11. Rudrangshu Mukherjee, *Spectre of Violence: The 1857 Kanpur Massacre* (New Delhi: Penguin India, 2007), p. 37.
12. Thomas R. Metcalf, *The Aftermath of Revolt: India, 1857–1970* (Princeton: Princeton University Press, 1965), p. viii.
13. Ibid., p. ix.
14. Christine Bolt, *Victorian Attitudes to Race* (London: Routledge & Kegan Paul, 1971), p. 179.
15. Ibid., p. 180.
16. Mantena, *Alibis of Empire*, p. 2, emphasis in original.
17. Ibid., p. 9.
18. 'A vast literature has grown up around the Uprising, so vast that the bibliographies themselves have become a book,' writes Rosie Llewellyn-Jones. See *The Great Uprising in India, 1857–58: Untold Stories, Indian and British* (Woodbridge : Boydell, 2007), p. 21.
19. Sabyasachi Bhattacharya, 'Introduction', in Bhattacharya, ed., *Rethinking 1857* (Hyderabad: Orient Longman, 2007), p. ix. See also Crispin Bates, ed., *Mutiny at the Margins: New Perspectives on the Indian Uprising of 1857, Vol. 5: Muslim, Dalit and Subaltern Narratives* (New Delhi: SAGE Publications India, 2014).
20. Ibid., p. xv.
21. Bender, *1857 Indian Uprising*, p. 5.
22. William Cooke Stafford, cited in Donald Featherstone, *Victorian Colonial Warfare: From the Conquest of Sind to the Indian Mutiny* (London: Cassell, 1992), p. 105.
23. See 'Introduction: The Nature of 1857', in Biswamoy Pati, ed., *The 1857 Rebellion* (New Delhi: Oxford University Press India, 2007), p. xxii; Mukherjee, *Spectre of Violence*, 53.

24. Kim A. Wagner, *The Skull of Alum Bheg: The Life and Death of a Rebel of 1857* (London: Hurst, 2017), p. 80.

25. 'Appendix: The Azimgarh Proclamation: 25 August 1857', in Rudrangshu Mukherjee, *The Year of Blood: Essays on the Revolt of 1857* (New Delhi: Social Science Press, 2014), pp. 25–6.

26. Biswamoy Pati, 'Common People, Fuzzy Boundaries and 1857', in Pati, ed., *The Great Rebellion of 1857 in India* (Abingdon: Routledge, 2010). Pati also lists many tribal and peasant uprisings that took place in the decades leading up to 1857. He notes that 'the 1857 Rebellion neither started nor ended in 1857–8' (p. 58). The volume as a whole does an excellent job of mapping the multiple sites of insurgency.

27. See Rosie Llewellyn-Jones, *The Great Uprising in India*.

28. Mukherjee, *Spectre of Violence*, p. 58.

29. Ibid., p. 23.

30. Cited in Rebecca Merritt, 'Public Perceptions of 1857: An Overview of British Press Responses to the Indian Uprising', in Major and Bates, *Mutiny at the Margins, Vol. 2*, p. 13.

31. Cited in Mukherjee, *Spectre of Violence*, p. 24.

32. Cited in ibid., p. 43.

33. Quotation used by John Kaye, cited in ibid., p. 32.

34. Cited in Kim A. Wagner, *The Great Fear of 1857: Rumours, Conspiracies and the Making of the Indian Uprising* (Oxford: Peter Lang, 2010), p. 230.

35. Major and Bates, 'Introduction', in Major and Bates, *Mutiny at the Margins*, Vol 2, p. xv.

36. See Merritt, 'Public Perceptions of 1857'.

37. House of Commons Debate, 'India – State of Affairs', 27 July 1857, vol. 147 cc. 440–546 (c. 475).

38. Malik, 'Popular British Interpretations of "the Mutiny"', in *Mutiny at the Margins, Vol 2*, pp. 30, 32.

39. Gautam Chakravarty, *The Indian Mutiny and the British Imagination* (Cambridge: Cambridge University Press, 2005), p. 33.

40. Ibid., pp. 1, 16.

41. Christopher Herbert, *War of No Pity: The Indian Mutiny and Victorian Trauma* (Princeton/Oxford: Princeton University Press, 2008), pp. 2–3.

42. Ibid., pp. 28–9.

43. Ibid., pp. 16–17.

44. Ibid., p. 16.

45. Mantena, *Alibis of Empire*, p. 4.

46. John Bruce Norton, *The Rebellion in India: How to Prevent Another* (London: Richardson Brothers, 1857).

47. Michel-Rolph Touillot, *Silencing the Past: Power and the Production of History* (Boston, MA: Beacon, 1995), p. 88.

48. Norton, *Rebellion in India*, p. 2.

49. Ibid., pp. 95–6. 'Banchat' is an Anglicization of a Hindustani word translating to 'sister-fucker'.

50. Ibid., p. 96. The speech itself, of one rebel Puttawallah, is reported thus: 'Listen, all! *As the English people hurled the Rajah from his throne, in like manner do you drive them out of the country* ... Sons of Brahmins, Maharattas, and Musselmen, revolt! Sons of Christians, look to yourselves!'. Ibid. p. 97, emphasis in original.

51. 'Preface', in ibid., p. v.

52. Ibid., p. 3.

53. Ibid., p. 4, emphasis in original.

54. Ibid., p. 56.

55. Ibid., p. 7.

56. Ibid., p. 14.

57. Ibid., pp. 18–19.

58. Ibid., p. 7.

59. Ibid., p. 55.

60. Ibid., pp. 55–6.

61. Ibid., p. 56.

62. Ibid., p. 59.

63. Ibid., p. 60.

64. Ibid., pp. 62–3.

65. Ibid., p. 62.

66. Ibid., p. 59.

67. Metcalf, *Aftermath of Revolt*, p. 305.

68. Norton, *Rebellion in India*, p. 62.

69. Ibid.

70. Ibid., p. 326.

71. Ibid., p. 62.

72. Ibid.

73. Ibid., p. 137.

74. Ibid., p. 173.

75. Ibid., p. 175.

76. Ibid., p. 119.

77. Ibid., p. 146.

78. Ibid., p. 198.

79. Ibid., pp. 195–6.

80. Ibid., p. 197.

81. Ibid., p. 196.

82. John Bruce Norton, *Topics for Indian Statesmen* (London: Richardson Brothers, 1858), p. 35.

83. Ranajit Guha, 'The Prose of Counter-insurgency', in Ranajit Guha, ed., *Subaltern Studies: Writings on South Asian History and Society*, vol. 2 (Delhi: Oxford University Press, 1983), p. 6.

84. Ibid., p. 28.

85. Tim Pratt, 'Ernest Jones' Mutiny: The People's Paper, English Popular Politics and the Indian Rebellion 1857–58', in Chandrika Kaul, ed., *Media and the British Empire* (Basingstoke: Palgrave, 2006), p. 89.

86. Ibid., p. 89.

87. The People's Charter demanded 'manhood suffrage, annual parliaments, the secret ballot, equal electoral districts, no property qualifications for MPs, and payment for MPs'. See Hugh Cunningham, *The Challenge of Democracy: Britain 1832–1918* (London: Routledge, 2014), p. 47.

88. Miles Taylor, *Ernest Jones, Chartism, and the Romance of Politics, 1819–1869* (Oxford: Oxford University Press, 2003), p. 138.

89. John Belchem also notes 'constitutionalism offered the most successful formula in British politics: patriotism, retrenchment and reform'. John Belchem, *Popular Radicalism in Nineteenth-Century Britain* (London: Palgrave Macmillan, 1996), pp. 104–5.

90. Margot C. Finn, *After Chartism: Class and Nation in English Radical Politics, 1848–1874* (Cambridge: Cambridge University Press, 1993), p. 107.

91. Jones famously defended the Irish Fenians. See 'Introduction', in John Saville, *Ernest Jones: Chartist – Selections from the Writings and Speeches of Ernest Jones with Introduction and Notes by John Saville* (London: Lawrence & Wishart, 1952).

92. Ernest Jones, 'How Our Indian Empire Is Ruled', *People's Paper*, 14 May 1853. Included in Saville, *Ernest Jones: Chartist*, pp. 211, 212.

93. 'The Bengal Mutinies', *People's Paper*, 20 June 1857.

94. 'Whence Shall We Get Our Cotton?', *People's Paper*, 27 June 1857.

95. Ibid.

96. Ernest Jones, 'The British Empire', *People's Paper*, 18 July 1857.

97. Ernest Jones, 'Hindostan', *People's Paper*, 4 July 1857, and 'Hindostan', *People's Paper*, 11 July 1857.

98. The term is Trouillot's.

99. Ernest Jones, 'The Indian War', *People's Paper*, 8 August 1857.

100. Ibid.

101. Ibid.

102. Jones, 'British Empire'.

103. Ernest Jones, 'The Revolt of Hindostan', *People's Paper*, 29 August 1857.

104. Jones, 'Indian War'. It is worth noting that although Jones frequently uses 'Hindhus' to describe the 'nationality' of India, he is not leaving Muslims out of the equation. He notes in this piece, for instance, that although there had been 'Mahommedan invasions', the Muslim 'presence' had not 'dimmed' anything. On the contrary,

India's 'art and science, material prosperity and imperial grandeur were but enhanced by the admixture of the chivalric element that swayed more than half the then known habitable globe'.

105. Ibid.
106. Pratt, 'Ernest Jones' Mutiny', pp. 91, 92.
107. Ibid., p. 95.
108. Pratt, 'Ernest Jones' Mutiny', pp. 90–1.
109. Guha, 'Prose of Counter-insurgency', pp. 76–7.
110. Jones, 'Indian War'.
111. Ernest Jones, 'Palmerston and India', *People's Paper*, 15 August 1857.
112. Ibid.
113 Pratt, 'Ernest Jones' Mutiny', p. 96.
114. Guha, 'Prose of Counter-insurgency', p. 33.
115. Ibid. Taylor argues: 'But of most significance were not so much his views as the forums in which they were being expressed. Jones was now speaking alongside the very parliamentary radical and "middle-class" reformers whom he had dismissed as the enemy for most of the 1850s. Had he moved over to their way of thinking, or had they come round to his?' Taylor, *Ernest Jones, Chartism, and the Romance of Politics*, p. 182.
116. Pratt, 'Ernest Jones' Mutiny', p. 98.
117. Guha, 'Prose of Counter-insurgency', p. 2.
118. Jones, 'Palmerston and India'.
119. Ibid.
120. Ibid.
121. Ernest Jones, 'Progress of the Indian Insurrection', *People's Paper*, 19 September 1857.
122. Ibid.
123. Ibid.
124. Ernest Jones, 'Who Is the Torturer?', *People's Paper*, 12 September 1857, emphasis in original.
125. Ernest Jones, 'Indian Insurrection and British Democracy', *People's Paper*, 26 September 1857.
126. Ernest Jones, 'The Men of New York and the Working Classes' (signed), *People's Paper*, 10 October 1857.
127. Rico Vitz, 'Contagion, Community, and Virtue in Hume's Epistemology', in Jonathan Matheson and Rico Vitz, eds, *The Ethics of Belief: Individual and Social* (Oxford: Oxford University Press, 2014), p. 205, emphasis in original.
128. Cited in Bender, *1857 Indian Uprising*, p. 75. This book provides a useful overview of concerns that the Indian uprising might provoke similar rebellions across the colonies, including Jamaica, New Zealand and Ireland.

129. Jones, 'Men of New York and the Working Classes'.

130. Ibid.

131. Ibid.

132. Ernest Jones, 'The Indian Struggle', *People's Paper*, 5 September 1857.

133. Ibid.

134. Ibid.

135. Ibid.

136. Ibid.

137. Ibid.

138. Adam Smith, *The Theory of Moral Sentiments* (Cambridge: Cambridge University Press, 2002), pp. 15, 12.

139. Knud Haakonsen, 'Introduction', in ibid., p. xiv.

140. Ernest Jones, 'India', *People's Paper*, 24 October 1857.

141. Ernest Jones, 'How to Secure India', *People's Paper*, 2 January 1858.

142. Syed Abdoolah, 'Importance of the Study of the Indian Language', *People's Paper*, 23 January 1858.

143. Ibid.

144. Ernest Jones, 'The True Position in India', *People's Paper*, 17 October 1857.

145. Pratt, 'Ernest Jones' Mutiny', p. 99.

146. Jones, 'India'.

147. Jones, 'How to Secure India'.

148. Ibid.

149. Ibid.

150. Ernest Jones, 'The Siege of Lucknow', *People's Paper*, 10 April 1858.

151. Thierry Drapeau, '"Look at Our Colonial Struggles": Ernest Jones and the Anti-colonialist Challenge to Marx's Conception of History', *Critical Sociology*, 17 November 2017, p. 2.

152. Ibid., p. 3.

153. Ibid., p. 2.

154. Ibid.

155. 'Dispatches from India', in Karl Marx and Friedrich Engels, *The First Indian War of Independence 1857–1859* (Moscow/London: Foreign Languages Publishing House/Lawrence & Wishart, 1960), p. 56.

156. Pranav Jani, 'Karl Marx, Eurocentrism, and the 1857 Revolt in British India', in Crystal Bartolovich and Neil Lazarus, eds, *Marxism, Modernity, and Postcolonial Studies* (Cambridge: Cambridge University Press, 2002), pp. 88, 82.

157. 'The Indian Insurrection', in Marx and Engels, *The First Indian War of Independence*, p. 65.

158. 'British Incomes in India', in ibid., p. 90.

159. 'The Indian Revolt', in ibid., p. 91.

160. Ernest Jones, 'England's Rule in India, and the Cry for Vengeance', *People's Paper*, 31 October 1857.

161. Ibid.

162. Ibid.

163. Richard Congreve, *India [Denying England's Right to Retain Her Possessions], with an Introduction by Shyamaji Krishnavarma* (London: A. Bonner, 1907), pp. 5, 12.

164. Ibid., p. 12.

165. Ibid., p. 4.

166. Ibid., p. 8, my emphasis.

167. Ibid., p. 8.

168. I am referring here to Claeys's observation that Positivist anti-imperialism was generally based on these principles and on a respect for 'earlier forms of religious expression'. Gregory Claeys, *Imperial Sceptics: British Critics of Empire, 1850–1920* (Cambridge: Cambridge University Press, 2010), p. 57.

169. Congreve, *India*, p. 9.

170. Bernard Porter, *Critics of Empire: British Radicals and the Imperial Challenge*, 2nd edn (London: I. B. Tauris, 2008 [1968]), p. 27.

171. Ibid., pp. 28–9.

172. Christopher Kent, *Brains and Numbers: Elitism, Comtism, and Democracy in Mid-Victorian England* (Toronto: University of Toronto Press, 1978), p. 59. Positivism, with its commitment to 'The Religion of Humanity', came to England in the 1840s via the British disciples of Auguste Comte who sought to replace Christianity with a god-free religion rooted instead in morality and natural affections, which would, at the same time, acknowledge the virtues of other religions. Congreve emerged as the leader of a small band of fairly dedicated Comteans who included Frederic Harrison, Edward Beesly and John Henry Bridges.

173. Ibid.

174. Congreve, *India*, p. 37.

175. Ibid., p. 11.

176. Ibid., p. 15, my emphasis.

177. Ibid., p. 18.

178. Ibid., p. 9.

179. Ibid., p. 8.

180. Ibid., p. 20.

181. Ibid., p. 16.

182. Ibid., p. 22.

183. Ibid., p. 18.

184. Ibid., pp. 18, 23.

185. Ibid.
186. Ibid., p. 19.
187. Ibid.
188. Ibid., p. 24.
189. Ibid., p. 31.
190. Ibid.
191. Ibid., p. 32.
192. Ibid., p. 34.
193. Ibid., p. 35.
194. Ibid.
195. Ibid.
196. Ibid.
197. Ibid.
198. Smith, *Theory of Moral Sentiments*, p. 11.
199. Ibid.
200. Congreve, *India*, p. 37.
201. Ibid.
202. Smith, *Theory of Moral Sentiments*, p. 13..
203. Congreve, *India*, p. 37.
204. Ibid. Congreve's language is explicit with regard to this pressure: 'It is time that you should make clear to them the difference of your judgment from theirs. You should enforce on them a total change of policy, a concentration on home questions of the energies now wasted abroad'. Ibid., p. 38.
205. Ibid. p. 37. The ending of the pamphlet feels like a return to a more formulaic Positivism at odds with the tenor of the text as a whole: 'Listen then to no revolutionary appeals, accept no revolutionary doctrines, however time-honoured', suggesting instead a union of working class and philosopher as moderating influences towards social change. Ibid., 34.
206. Frederic Harrison, *Autobiographic Memoirs, Vol. 1, 1831–1870* (London: Macmillan, 1911), p. 181, emphasis in original.
207. Ibid., p. 173.
208. Ibid., p. 174.
209. Ibid.
210. Ibid., p. 175.
211. Ibid.
212. Ibid., p. 176.
213. Ibid., p. 177.
214. Ibid.
215. Ibid., p. 175.
216. Ibid., p. 181, emphasis in original.
217. Bolt, *Victorian Attitudes to Race*, p. 158.
218. Thompson, *Other Side of the Medal*, p. 86.

219. Ibid., p. 97: 'In January 1872, Deputy Commissioner J. L. Cowan responded to a minor *émeute* among the Kuka Sikhs by summarily executing sixty-eight prisoners by having them blown from cannon in the small principality of Malerkotla in Punjab'. See Kim A. Wagner, '"Calculated to Strike Terror": The Amritsar Massacre and the Spectacle of Colonial Violence', *Past and Present* 233: 1 (1 November 2016).

220. Ibid., p. 121.

2. A Barbaric Independence

1. This cautious bill, which sought to enfranchise some working-men – householders who were earning a minimum of twenty-six shillings a week – would be defeated in 1866. The Representation of the People Act 1867 was an even more limited measure; it doubled the number of enfranchised adult males to 2 million.

2. Catherine Hall, *Civilising Subjects: Metropole and Colony in the English Imagination, 1830–1867* (Cambridge: Polity Press, 2002), p. 48.

3. Marouf Hasian, Jr, 'Colonial Re-characterization and the Discourse Surrounding the Eyre Controversy', *Southern Communication Journal* 66: 1 (Fall 2000), p. 90.

4. Catherine Hall, 'Imperial Man: Edward Eyre in Australasia and the West Indies 1833–66', in Bill Schwarz, ed., *The Expansion of England: Race, Ethnicity and Cultural History* (London: Routledge, 1996), p. 132.

5. Tim Watson, *Caribbean Culture and British Fiction in the Atlantic World, 1780–1870* (Cambridge: Cambridge University Press, 2008), p. 156.

6. Ibid., p. 154.

7. R. W. Kostal, *A Jurisprudence of Power: Victorian Empire and the Rule of Law* (Oxford: Oxford University Press, 2005), p. 461.

8. Ibid., p. 25, emphasis in original.

9. Thomas Holt, *The Problem of Freedom: Race, Labor, and Politics in Jamaica and Britain, 1832–1938* (Baltimore, MD/London: Johns Hopkins University Press, 1992), p. 309.

10. Mimi Sheller, *Democracy after Slavery: Black Publics and Peasant Radicalism in Haiti and Jamaica* (Gainesville, FL: University Press of Florida, 2000), p. 199.

11. Watson, *Caribbean Culture*, p. 157.

12. Kostal, *Jurisprudence of Power*, p. 468.

13. Ibid., p. 20.

14. Edward Bean Underhill, *The Tragedy of Morant Bay: A Narrative of*

the Disturbances in the Island of Jamaica in 1865 (London: Alexander & Shepheard, 1895) – reprinted by Forgotten Books (2012), p. 136.

15. Holt, *Problem of Freedom*, p. 309.

16. Hall, 'Imperial Man', p. 132.

17. 'Indignation Meeting on the Jamaica Atrocities', *Bee-Hive*, 8 September 1866.

18. Charles Dickens, 'Letter to William de Cerjat, 30 November 1865', in *The Selected Letters of Charles Dickens*, ed. Jenny Hartley (Oxford: Oxford University Press, 2012), p. 397.

19. Douglas A. Lorimer, *Colour, Class and the Victorians* (Teaneck, NJ: Holmes & Maier, 1978), pp. 180–1.

20. Hall, 'Imperial Man', p. 132.

21. For a fuller account, see Gad Heuman, *The Killing Time: The Morant Bay Rebellion in Jamaica* (London: Macmillan, 1994).

22. Jamaica Committee, *Jamaica Papers No. 1: Facts and Documents Relating to the Alleged Rebellion in Jamaica and the Measures of Repression including Notes on the Trial of Mr Gordon* (henceforth *JC1*) (London: Jamaica Committee, 1866), p. 13.

23. As excerpted from the *Colonial Standard*, 21 October 1865, in *JC1*, p. 13.

24. Ibid.

25. Heuman, *Killing Time*, p. 13.

26. Ibid., p. 22, and Jamaica Royal Commission, *Report of the Jamaica Royal Commission 1866, Part 2: Minutes of Evidence and Appendix* (henceforth *JRC2*) (London: George Edward Eyre & William Spottiswoode, 1866), p. 34.

27. Jamaica Royal Commission, *Report of the Jamaica Royal Commission 1866: Part 1* (henceforth *JRC1*) (London: George Edward Eyre & William Spottiswoode, 1866), p. 41.

28. Ibid., p. 40.

29. 'Despatch from Maj. Gen O'Connor to Eyre', in *JRC2*, p. 621.

30. *The Times*, 13 November 1865, cited in Kostal, *Jurisprudence of Power*, pp. 25–6.

31. Kostal provides a detailed and clear account of the sequence of events. Ibid.

32. 'Governor Eyre's Despatch', in *JC1*, pp. 84, 91.

33. Ibid., p. 91.

34. Ibid., p. 86.

35. Ibid., p. 89.

36. Ibid., p. 92.

37. Ibid., p. 93.

38. Frederic Harrison, *Jamaica Papers No. V – Martial Law: Six Letters to 'The Daily News'* (London: Jamaica Committee, 1867), p. 37.

39. Kostal, *Jurisprudence of Power*, p. 37.
40. For a succinct account of various meetings held and representations undertaken, see ibid., pp. 40–8.
41. For a full account of the constitution of the Jamaica Committee, see Bernard Semmel's hugely important early study of the Eyre affair, *The Governor Eyre Controversy* (London: MacGibbon & Lee, 1962). Semmel notes that the membership of the committee included 'virtually all of the leading figures in the two principal pro-Northern societies' in relation to the American Civil War (p. 62).
42. Herbert Spencer, *An Autobiography*, vol. 2 (London: Watts & Co., 1926 [1904]), p. 143.
43. 'The Negro Controversy', *Saturday Review*, 13 October 1866. Cited in Lorimer, *Colour, Class and the Victorians*, p. 178.
44. Hall, *Civilising Subjects*, p. 48.
45. Holt argues that during this period 'British elite ideology and official policy moved from nonracist to racist premises, at the same time that the destruction of slavery cleared the way for that elite's more robust embrace of imperialist ambitions.' Revisiting the debate around Eric Williams, Holt notes that even Williams's critics now admit that 'the advent of slavery abolition was a function of the rise of capitalism'. Holt, *Problem of Freedom*, pp. xviii, 23.
46. *Spectator*, vol. 41 (London: John Campbell, 1868), p. 666. Cited in Semmel, *Governor Eyre Controversy*, p. 171.
47. Colley, *Britons: Forging the Nation 1707–1837* (New Haven/London: Yale University Press, 2005), p. 323.
48. Semmel, *Governor Eyre Controversy*, p. 140.
49. Cited in Sidney Haldane Olivier, *The Myth of Governor Eyre* (London: L. & Virginia Woolf, 1933), p. 305.
50. *The Times*, editorial, 13 November 1865. For a collation of such responses, see Anonymous, *Jamaica; Who Is to Blame, by a Thirty Years' Resident, with an Introduction and Notes by the Editor of the 'Eclectic Review'* (London: E. Wilson, 1866).
51. *JC1*, p. 59.
52. Ibid., p. 60.
53. Ibid.
54. Ibid., p. 59.
55. Carlyle, cited in Semmel, *Governor Eyre Controversy*, p. 106.
56. Abigail B. Bakan, *Ideology and Class Conflict in Jamaica: The Politics of Rebellion* (Montreal/London: McGill-Queen's University Press, 1990), p. 79.
57. Underhill, *Tragedy of Morant Bay*, p. 90.
58. Justin McCarthy, *A History of Our Own Times from the Ascension of Queen Victoria to the General Election of 1880*, vol. 3 (London: Chatto & Windus, 1882), p. 269.

59. Cited in Baptist Wriothesley Noel, *The Case of George William Gordon, Esq. of Jamaica* (London: James Nisbet, 1866), p. 6.

60. *Spectator*, vol. 41, p. 665, emphasis in original.

61. Cited in Noel, *Case of George William Gordon*, p. 7.

62. Gordon, cited in ibid., p. 13.

63. Ibid., p. 17.

64. McCarthy, *History of Our Own Times*, p. 270.

65. *JRC2*, p. 379.

66. Ibid., p. 444.

67. *JC1*, p. 91.

68. The Royal Commission's conclusion was as follows: 'Although, therefore, it appears exceedingly probable that Mr Gordon, by his words and writings, produced a material effect on the minds of Bogle and his followers, and did much to produce that state of excitement and discontent in different parts of the Island, which rendered the spread of the insurrection exceedingly probable, yet we cannot see, in the evidence which has been adduced, any sufficient proof either of his complicity in the outbreak at Morant Bay or of his having been a party to a general conspiracy against the Government.' *JRC1*, p. 38.

69. Geoffrey Dutton, *The Hero as Murderer: The Life of Edward John Eyre, Australian Explorer and Governor of Jamaica, 1815–1901* (Sydney/London: Collins, 1967), p. 293.

70. Cited in Sheller, *Democracy after Slavery*, p. 216.

71. David King, *A Sketch of the Late Mr G. W. Gordon, Jamaica* (Edinburgh: William Oliphant, 1866), p. 9.

72. This is English politician Justin McCarthy's reading of Gordon as a type of man who every 'really sensible politician' likes to have in a legislative assembly. McCarthy, *History of Our Own Times*, p. 269.

73. Thomas Harvey and William Brewin, *Jamaica in 1866: A Narrative of a Tour through the Island; With Remarks on Its Social, Educational and Industrial Condition* (London: A. W. Bennett, 1867), p. 21.

74. *JRC1*, p. 31.

75. Ibid.

76. 'Report of W. F. March', in *JRC2*, p. 888.

77. 'Paul Bogle and George William Gordon – Heroes or Idiots?', *Sunday Gleaner*, 17 October 2004. Cited in Howard Johnson, 'From Pariah to Patriot: the Posthumous Career of George William Gordon', *New West Indian Guide* 81: 3–4 (2008), p. 215.

78. Sheller, *Democracy after Slavery*, p. 146.

79. Cited in Johnson, 'From Pariah to Patriot', p. 205.

80. Cited in Sheller, *Democracy after Slavery*, p. 212.

81. Ibid., p. 213.

82. Ibid., p. 204.

83. Ibid., p. 211.
84. The Jamaica Royal Commission, cited in Underhill, *Tragedy of Morant Bay*, p. 136.
85. For a meticulously compiled and useful list of activists, many of whom had ties to Gordon, see Sheller, *Democracy after Slavery*, pp. 214–15. They include, in addition to Bogle and McLaren, Kelly Smith, E. J. Goldson, S. Clarke and W. F. March, as well as several others whose signatures also appear on various documents.
86. *Morning Herald*, 23 November 1865. Cited in Lorimer, *Colour, Class and the Victorians*, pp. 198–9.
87. *JRC2*, p. 993.
88. Ibid., p. 619.
89. Ibid.
90. Underhill, *Tragedy of Morant Bay*, p. 23.
91. Ibid., p. 24.
92. *JRC1*, p. 14.
93. Michel-Rolph Trouillot, *Silencing the Past: Power and the Production of History* (Boston, MA: Beacon, 1995), p. 24. Sheller points out that by the 1850s 'there seems to have been a new sense of agency among the less formally educated people that they too could make speeches and "put their hand to paper"'. She notes more petitions 'written in a local Creole idiom', and an increasing frequency of anonymous threat letters, all of which were also to be seen in the days leading up to and following the Morant Bay uprising. Sheller, *Democracy after Slavery*, p. 185.
94. Bakan, *Ideology and Class Conflict in Jamaica*, p. 79.
95. *JRC1*, p. 14.
96. Several white witnesses, including many planters, complained in their testimony to the Royal Commission about changed behaviour on the part of the Jamaican blacks they encountered in the months leading up to the rebellion. They speak of a marked difference in bearing, refusal to observe the rights of the road, and threatening comments. See, for instance, the testimony of Wellwood Maxwell Anderson in *JRC2*, p. 566.
97. *JRC2*, p. 619.
98. Edward Bean Underhill, *A Letter Addressed to the Rt Honourable E. Cardwell, with Illustrative Documents on the Condition of Jamaica and an Explanatory Statement* (London: Arthur Miall, 1865).
99. Heuman suggests that the 'Petition of the Poor people of St Ann's Parish' had, in fact, been in preparation before Underhill's own letter. Heuman, *Killing Time*, p. 48.
100. 'Petition of the Poor People of St Ann's Parish, and the Reply Thereto, Entitled "The Queen's Advice"', in Harvey and Brewin,

Jamaica in 1866, pp. 101–2. Another petition, written in September, came from St Thomas-in-the-East, signed by forty persons, speaking of 'heavy work' not even experienced when 'we were slaves' and of the 'advantage' taken of them by estate managers. Cited in Noel, *Case of George William Gordon*, p. 27.

101. Harvey and Brewin, *Jamaica in 1866*, p. 102.

102. *JC1*, p. 9.

103. Writing about the rebellion several decades later, Lord Olivier, himself a governor of Jamaica, would point out that the demand for land was based on 'the essentially sound fundamental axiom of African law, that land belongs to the King (or Chief) as trustee for his people ... to be held available for ... families for whose support unoccupied land is required'. Olivier, *Myth of Governor Eyre*, p. 176.

104. 'In 1857 a coloured man of the name of Ripley Edie told the people that the Queen had given them the lands when she gave them freedom'. *JRC2*, p. 566.

105. Ibid., my emphasis.

106. As with the 1857 uprising, rumour could have a galvanizing effect in the organization of resistance. As Scott also observes: 'As a rumour travels it is altered in a fashion that brings it more closely into line with the hopes, fears, and worldview of those who hear it and retell it'. James C. Scott, *Domination and the Arts of Resistance: Hidden Transcripts* (New Haven: Yale University Press, 1990), pp. 147, 145.

107. Jean Besson, cited in Sheller, *Democracy after Slavery*, p. 148.

108. *JRC1*, p. 40.

109. 'Testimony of W. Anderson', in *JRC2*, p. 165.

110. The rumour was not without historical foundation: certainly in the decades following Emancipation, planters talked of leaving British rule and joining the United States, which would have meant the re-enslavement of the black population.

111. 'Testimony of Venerable Archdeacon Rowe', in *JRC2*, p. 648.

112. *JRC1*, p. 16.

113. 'Testimony of W. Carr', in *JRC2*, p. 508.

114. Anonymous, *Jamaica; Who Is to Blame*, p. 24.

115. *The Times*, editorial, 13 November 1865.

116. Cited in Bedford Pim, *The Negro and Jamaica* (London: Trübner & Co., 1866), p. 55.

117. J. Radcliffe, 'To the Editor of *The Times*', *The Times*, 18 November 1865.

118. According to *The Times*, editorial, 20 November 1865.

119. Charles Savile Roundell, *England and her Subject-Races: With Special Reference to Jamaica* (London: Macmillan, 1866), pp. 25–6.

120. Editorial, *The Times*, 20 November 1865.

121. 'The telegraphic news from Jamaica', *The Times*, 4 November 1865.

122. Pim, *The Negro and Jamaica*, p. 34.

123. Ibid., pp. 64–5.

124. James Anthony Froude, *The English in the West Indies; Or, The Bow of Ulysses* (London: Longmans, Green, 1888), p. 248.

125. *The Eyre Defence and Aid Fund* (London: Pelican, 1866), p. 4, available at Rhodes House, Oxford (OC) 200.h.126 (1).

126. Ibid., pp. 26–31.

127. John Tyndall, 'Professor Tyndall's Reply to the Jamaica Committee', Appendix B in Hamilton Hume, *The Life of Edward John Eyre, Late Governor of Jamaica* (London: Richard Bentley, 1867), p. 273.

128. Ibid., p. 274.

129. Ibid., p. 275.

130. Ibid., p. 281.

131. John Ruskin, 'A Letter to the "Daily Telegraph"', 20 December 1865, in *The Works of John Ruskin*, vol. 18, ed. E. T. Cook and Alexander Wedderburn (London: George Allen, 1905), pp. 550–1.

132. John Ruskin, 'Liberty', in ibid., pp. 123–4.

133. From 'A Petition to the House of Commons', drawn up by Thomas Carlyle. Cited in Gillian Workman, 'Thomas Carlyle and the Governor Eyre Controversy: An Account with Some New Material', *Victorian Studies* 18: 1 (1 September 1974), p. 99.

134. Thomas Carlyle, 'Shooting Niagara, and After?', in *Works of Thomas Carlyle*, vol. 30 (London: Chapman & Hall, 1869), p. 12.

135. Harrison, *Jamaica Papers No. V*, p. 39.

136. McCarthy, *History of Our Own Times*, p. 274.

137. Semmel, *Governor Eyre Controversy*, p. 64.

138. Dickens, 'Letter to William de Cerjat, 30 November 1865', p. 397.

139. 'Gordon meant only to agitate, as men do here with us, and as men must ever be allowed to do in every free country; but he was unwise in his estimate of the materials with which he had to deal', wrote the barrister B. T. Williams. B. T. Williams, *The Case of George William Gordon, with Preliminary Observations on the Jamaica Riot of October 11th, 1865* (London: Butterworths, 1866), p. 58.

140. 'Statement of the Jamaica Committee', in *Jamaica Committee No. III: Statement of the Jamaica Committee and Other Documents* (London: Jamaica Committee, 1866), p. 3. Also included as Appendix E, 'Jamaica Committee: Public Documents', in John Stuart Mill, *Collected Works of John Stuart Mill*, vol. 21, ed. John M. Robson (Toronto: University of Toronto Press, 1984).

141. John Stuart Mill, *Autobiography and Literary Essays*, ed. John M. Robson and Jack Stillinger (London: Routledge, 1981), p. 281.

142. *JC1*, p. 17.

143. *JC1*, p. 10.

144. Ibid.

145. 'Statement of the Jamaica Committee', in Jamaica Committee No. III, *Statement of the Jamaica Committee and other Documents*, p. 7.

146. 'The Jamaica Committee', in *JC1*, p. 68.

147. Northumbrian, 'The Negro Revolt in Jamaica', *Reynolds Newspaper* (hereafter *RN*), 12 November 1865.

148. Northumbrian, 'The British Atrocities in Jamaica', *RN*, 26 November 1865.

149. Ibid.

150. 'The Blood-Thirsty Butcheries in Jamaica', *RN*, 3 December 1865.

151. Ibid.

152. Ibid., my emphasis.

153. Ibid.

154. 'Reported Negro Insurrection in Jamaica', *RN*, 12 November 1865.

155. Northumbrian, 'Jamaica and Its Tyrants', *RN*, 24 December 1865.

156. Ibid.

157. Ibid.

158. Ibid.

159. 'Indignation Meeting on the Eyre Southampton Banquet', *RN*, 2 September 1866.

160. Ibid.

161. 'Ex-governor Eyre at Southampton', *RN*, 26 August 1866.

162. Northumbrian, 'The Negro Revolt in Jamaica', *RN*, 12 November 1865.

163. 'Indignation Meeting'.

164. Ibid.

165. E. S. Beesly, 'Professor Beesly on the Trial of Mr Eyre', *RN*, 4 November 1866.

166. Ibid.

167. Ibid.

168. Ibid.

169. Ibid.

170. E. S. Beesly, 'Military Atrocities in Jamaica', *Bee-Hive*, 25 November 1865.

171. Ibid.

172. Ibid.

173. Ibid.

174. Ibid

175. E. S. Beesly, 'The Trial of Mr. Eyre', *Bee-Hive*, 16 August 1866.

176. Plain Dealer, 'The Working Men of Jamaica', *Bee-Hive*, 16 December 1865.

177. Plain Dealer, 'The Next House on Fire', *Bee-Hive*, 1 September 1866.

178. Ibid.

179. Ibid.

180. Ibid.

181. Plain Dealer, 'The Threefold Adversaries of the People', *Bee-Hive*, 15 September 1866.

182. Plain Dealer, 'Next House on Fire'.

183. Ibid.

184. Ibid.

185. Ibid.

186. Goldwin Smith, 'Public Liberty', *Bee-Hive*, 8 September 1866.

187. Ibid.

188. Harrison, *Jamaica Papers No. V*, pp. 37, 4.

189. Ibid., p. 38.

190. Ibid., p. 39.

191. Ibid., p. 23.

192. Ibid., p. 38.

193. Ibid., p. 41.

194. Ibid., p. 38.

195. Jennifer Pitts, *A Turn to Empire: The Rise of Imperial Liberalism in Britain and France* (Princeton: Princeton University Press, 2005), p. 154.

196. Ibid., p. 151.

197. HC Deb 31 July 1866, vol. 184, c. 1800.

198. Ibid.

199. Cited in Pitts, *Turn to Empire*, p. 158.

200. Ibid.

201. Ibid., p. 160.

202. Semmel, *Governor Eyre Controversy*, p. 61.

203. Goldwin Smith, *Reminiscences*, ed. Arnold Haultain (New York, Macmillan, 1910), p. 358.

204. Ibid.

205. J. M. Ludlow, *Jamaica Papers No. IV: A Quarter Century of Jamaica Legislation* (London: Jamaica Committee, 1866), p. 1.

206. Thomas Henry Huxley, *Life and Letters of Thomas Henry Huxley*, vol. 1 (London: Macmillan, 1903), p. 407.

207. Ibid.

3. The Accidental Anticolonialist

1. I have modernized the English spelling to 'Urabi', which is phonetically closer to the Arabic pronunciation; Victorian writers typically used 'Araby' or 'Arabi'.

2. Cited in John Marlowe, *Anglo-Egyptian Relations, 1800–1953* (London: Cresset, 1954), p. 118.

3. Wilfred [*sic*] S. Blunt, *The Secret History of the English Occupation of Egypt* (Dublin: Nonsuch Publishing, 2007), p. 196.

4. Ibid.

5. Ibid.

6. Ibid.

7. The term is Nicholas Owen's.

8. The term 'contact zone' refers to 'the space of colonial encounters, the space in which peoples geographically and historically separated come into contact with each other and establish ongoing relations, usually involving conditions of coercion, radical inequality and intractable conflict'. See Mary Louise Pratt, *Imperial Eyes: Travel Writing and Transculturation* (London: Routledge, 1992), p. 6.

9. Ibid., p. 7.

10. By Urabi's own account, he had given the canal engineer Ferdinand de Lesseps, who had pleaded with him, his personal assurance that he would respect the canal's neutrality. The British forces dispensed with these scruples, claiming that Urabi was planning to attack it. See A. M. Broadley, *How We Defended Arábi and His Friends: A Story of Egypt and the Egyptians*, illustrated by Frederick Villiers (London: Chapman & Hall, 1884), pp. 135–6.

11. The list of charges against Urabi is cited in ibid., p. 51.

12. Newsinger notes that 'Gladstone benefitted financially from the invasion of Egypt'. John Newsinger, *The Blood Never Dried: A People's History of the British Empire* (London: Bookmarks, 2013), p. 104.

13. *The Times* described Urabi thus: 'all kinds of projects are attributed to him, and public opinion invests him with an unnatural kind of importance. English members of Parliament interview him as a political notoriety, distinguished Orientalists make him an object of their study, Mahomedans go so far as to endow him with sacred descent'. 'Egypt: From Our Correspondent', 30 December 1881, p. 6. A few weeks later it would downgrade him to 'nothing more than a colonel of a regiment who has twice broken through all the rules of military discipline in the most flagrant manner'. 'Egypt', 14 January 1882, p. 8.

14. For a useful fuller discussion, see Marlowe, *Anglo-Egyptian Relations*.

15. Juan Cole, *Colonialism and Revolution in the Middle East: Social and Cultural Origins of Egypt's 'Urabi Movement'* (Princeton: Princeton University Press, 1993), p. 45.

16. Gregory Claeys, *Imperial Sceptics: British Critics of Empire 1850– 1920* (Cambridge: Cambridge University Press, 2010), p. 37.

17. Edward Walter Hamilton, cited in ibid. Malet himself would note that he had found it useful to deploy Blunt on missions of mediation.

18. Blunt, *Secret History*, pp. 183–4. Despite the obvious conflict of interest, British officials in Egypt like Auckland Colvin, the financial controller, doubled as correspondents to *The Times* and the *Pall Mall Gazette* – in a capacity we might today conceive of as that of an 'embedded' journalist, in similar contexts.

19. Claeys, *Imperial Sceptics*, p. 38.

20. See Michael D. Berdine, *The Accidental Tourist: Wilfrid Scawen Blunt, and the British Invasion of Egypt in 1882* (New York/ London: Routledge, 2005), p. xviii. Blunt gives this description of Gladstone in *Secret History*, p. 52. Blunt briefly joined the Liberal Party, running unsuccessfully as a parliamentary candidate.

21. For a lavishly illustrated account of the Blunts' journeys, drawing extensively on Lady Anne's journals, though with no interest in their political dimensions, see Richard Trench, *Arabian Travellers* (London: Macmillan, 1986), pp. 164–87.

22. Lady Anne Blunt, *Bedouin Tribes of the Euphrates* (London: J. Murray, 1879); and Lady Anne Blunt, *A Pilgrimage to Nejd, the Cradle of the Arab Race: A Visit to the Court of the Arab Emir and 'Our Persian Campaign'* (London: Cass, 1968 [1881]). For a useful scholarly engagement with this work, see Chapter 5 of Ali Behdad, *Belated Travelers: Orientalism in the Age of Colonial Dissolution* (Durham, NC/London: Duke University Press, 1994). Behdad notes that Wilfrid's authority over his wife also gave the 'discursive authority' of the male orientalist to her work. See also Lady Anne Blunt, *Journals and Correspondence 1878–1917*, ed. Rosemary Archer and James Fleming (Cheltenham: Alexander Heriot, 1986).

23. Dane Kennedy, *The Last Blank Spaces: Exploring Africa and Australia* (Cambridge, MA: Harvard University Press, 2013), p. 230.

24. Edward Said, *Humanism and Democratic Criticism* (New York: Palgrave Macmillan, 2004), p. 26.

25. Ibid., p. 28.

26. Wilfrid S. Blunt, 'The Thoroughbred Horse – English and Arabian', *Nineteenth Century: A Monthly Review*, September 1880.

27. Wilfrid S. Blunt, 'Recent Events in Arabia', *Fortnightly Review*, May 1880, p. 708.

28. Ibid., p. 719.

29. Blunt, *Secret History*, p. 71.

30. Ibid., p. 80.

31. Blunt, 'Recent Events in Arabia', p. 708.

32. Blunt, *Secret History*, p. 22.

33. Blunt, 'The Egyptian Revolution: A Personal Narrative', *Nineteenth Century: A Monthly Review*, September 1882, p. 325.

34. Edward Said, *Orientalism* (London: Routledge & Kegan Paul, 1978), p. 237.

35. Ibid.

36. Ibid., p. 197.

37. For an account of Burton's texts as 'operating different linguistic consciousnesses, enunciative set-ups and forms of authority' towards creating an 'unfixed, nomadic persona', see Fréderic Regard, 'Fieldwork as Self-Harrowing: Richard Burton's Cultural Evolution (1851–56)', in Regard, ed., *British Narratives of Exploration* (London: Pickering & Chatto, 2009), p. 181. Blunt was keenly attuned to difference without necessarily seeing himself as 'confronted with alterity'. Ibid.

38. Blunt, *Secret History*, p. 81.

39. Ibid., p. 96.

40. Ibid.

41. Wilfred S. Blunt, *The Future of Islam* (Dublin: Nonsuch, 2007 [1882]).

42. Ibid., p. 8.

43. Ibid., p. 22.

44. Ibid., p. 191.

45. Ibid., p. 25.

46. Ibid.

47. Ibid., p. 128.

48. Ibid., p. 129.

49. 'Medicine and Colonialism', in Fanon, *A Dying Colonialism*, transl. Haakon Chevalier (New York: Grove, 1959), pp. 126, 128.

50. Ibid., p. 126.

51. Blunt, *Future of Islam*, 135.

52. Ibid., pp. 135–6.

53. Ibid., p. 136.

54. Ibid., p. 175.

55. Blunt, 'Egyptian Revolution', p. 333.

56. Ibid., p. 324.

57. Ibid.; Blunt, *Secret History*, p. 217.

58. Blunt, *Secret History*, p. 115; Nikki R. Keddie, *Sayyid Jamal Ad-Din 'Al-Afghani': A Political Biography* (Berkeley, CA: University of California Press, 1972), p. 101. Newspapers established or edited by Afghani's followers included *Mirat ash-Sharq* and *Misr al-Fatat* (*Jeune Égypte*).

59. Blunt, *Secret History*, p. 166.
60. Ibid., p. 167.
61. *Annual Register: A Review of Public Events at Home and Abroad for the Year 1882* (London: Rivington's, 1883), p. 152.
62. Blunt, *Secret History*, p. 178.
63. Ibid., p. 154.
64. Ibid., pp. 177–8.
65. Ibid., p. 178.
66. Ibid., p. 179.
67. Lady Gregory, *Arabi and His Household* (London: Kegan Paul, Trench, 1882), p. 6.
68. Blunt, *Secret History*, pp. 148–9.
69. Ibid., p. 159.
70. Ibid.
71. Lady Anne Blunt, *Journals and Correspondence*, p. 145.
72. Ahmad Urabi, *Muthakirat Urabi: Kashf Al-sitar 'an sir al-Asrar fi al-nahda al-Masriya al-mashhura bi al-thawra al-Urabiya sanat 1298 Hijriya was sanat 1881–1882 Miliadiya* (The Urabi Memoirs: Uncovering Secrets of the Egyptian Awakening Commonly Known as the Urabian Revolution 1298 Hijri, 1881–1882 CE) (Cairo: Dar Al-Kutub Al-Misriya, 1925). I am grateful to Dr Heba Youssef for translations from this text.
73. The other term used to refer to Egyptians is *al-wataniyoon*, from *al-watan*, or homeland. So also *onsor* or 'national race'.
74. Urabi, *Muthakirat Urab*, p. 24.
75. Mounah A. Khouri, *Poetry and the Making of Modern Egypt (1882–1922)* (Leiden: E. J. Brill, 1971), p. 36.
76. Cole, *Colonialism and Revolution*, p. 20.
77. Ibid.
78. Blunt, 'Egyptian Revolution', p. 324.
79. Ibid., p. 328.
80. Ibid., p. 344.
81. Ibid.
82. Blunt, *Secret History*, p. 220.
83. Sir E. Malet to Earl Granville, no. 4 in House of Commons Command Papers, *Further Correspondence Respecting the Affairs of Egypt* (London: Harrison, 1882).
84. Blunt, *Secret History*, p. 213.
85. Blunt, 'Egyptian Revolution', p. 332.
86. Ibid., p. 345.
87. Mr W. S. Blunt to the Right Hon. W. E. Gladstone, MP, no. 7 in House of Commons Command Papers, *Further Correspondence*.
88. *Annual Register, 1882*, p. 147.
89. See William Gladstone, *Aggression on Egypt and Freedom in the*

East (London: National Press Agency, 1884 [first published in *The Nineteenth Century* in 1877]).

90. Blunt, *Secret History*, pp. 181–2, emphasis in original.

91. John Stuart Mill, 'A Few Words on Non-intervention', in Mill, *Dissertations and Discussions: Political, Philosophical, and Historical*, vol. 3 (London: Longmans, Green, Reader and Dyer, 1867 [first published in *Fraser's Magazine*, December 1859]), p. 168.

92. For an illuminating discussion of liberalism's demand for 'equivalence' in the context of empire, see Uday Singh Mehta, *Liberalism and Empire: A Study in Nineteenth-Century British Liberal Thought* (Chicago: University of Chicago Press, 1999).

93. Edward Dicey, 'England in Egypt', *Nineteenth Century: A Monthly Review* 12: 67 (November 1882), pp. 807–8.

94. Blunt, *Secret History*, p. 188.

95. 'Programme of the National Party of Egypt', *The Times*, 3 January 1882.

96. Ibid.

97. Ibid.

98. See Chapter 5 of Cole, *Colonialism and Revolution*.

99. Blunt, *Secret History*, p. 111.

100. Nikki R. Keddie, *An Islamic Response to Imperialism: Political and Religious Writings of Sayyid Jamal ad-Din 'al-Afghani', Including a Translation of the 'Refutation of the Materialists' from the Original Persian* (Berkeley, CA: University of California Press, 1968), p. 43.

101. Said, *Humanism and Democratic Criticism*, p. 73.

102. Blunt, *Secret History*, pp. 109–10.

103. Ibid., p. 112.

104. Keddie notes that 'Afghani used to spend long hours holding forth at cafés ... where he would drink tea, smoke cigarettes, and gather around him large groups of disciples and curious onlookers, as he expounded his ideas'. Keddie, *Sayyid Jamal ad-Din 'al-Afghani'*, p. 84.

105. Ibid., p. 110.

106. Dispatch to *The Times*, 20 August 1879, cited in ibid., p. 117. Elie Kedourie cites an account from M. E. Vauquelin's articles for the French left-wing newspaper *L' Intransigeant*, which claims that, on 3 August, 1879, Afghani preached at the Hasan Mosque before an audience of 4,000 people. The khedive, he told his audience, was 'compelled to serve – consciously or not – British ambitions, and ended his speech by a war-cry against the foreigner and by a call for a revolution to save the independence of Egypt and establish its liberty'. Ibid., pp. 29–30. Kedourie also points to claims that this speech directly caused a group of Syrian Christians to band together with some Muslims to form a society, publish a

newspaper and submit a plan of reforms to the prime minister. The official reason given for Afghani's expulsion a few days later was that he had organized a secret society aimed at 'the ruin of religion and rule'. Elie Kedourie, *Afghani and 'Abduh: an Essay on Religious Unbelief and Political Activism in Modern Islam* (Oxford: Routledge, 2008 [1966]), p. 31.

107. Pankaj Mishra, *From the Ruins of Empire: The Revolt against the West and the Remaking of Asia* (London: Allen Lane, 2012), p. 50.

108. 'Afghani's Egyptian followers continued to be active in politics after his expulsion, and several of them worked for the Urabi government after it took power, being subsequently exiled after the British victory and occupation of Egypt'. Keddie, *Islamic Response*, p. 21.

109. Keddie, drawing on Rida's *Tarikh*, in *Sayyid Jamal ad-Din 'al-Afghani'*, p. 101.

110. Ibid.

111. Ibid., pp. 101–2.

112. Ibid., p. 106. Keddie describes Afghani as one who 'in large part expressed a mood and viewpoint that was in any case beginning to come to the fore in the Muslim world ... a mood of many who did not wish simply to continue borrowing from the West or bowing to growing Western domination, but wished rather to find in indigenous traditions, both Islamic and national, precedents for the reforms and self-strengthening they wanted to undertake'. 'From Afghani to Khomeini: Introduction to the 1983 Edition', in Keddie, *Islamic Response*, p. xiii.

113. Afghani, 'Lecture on Teaching and Learning', in Keddie, *Islamic Response*, p. 101.

114. Mishra, *From the Ruins of Empire*, p. 84.

115. Afghani, 'Lecture on Teaching and Learning', p. 104.

116. Ibid., p. 107.

117. Afghani, 'The Benefits of Philosophy', in Keddie, *Islamic Response*, p. 110.

118. Ibid.

119. Ibid.

120. Ibid., p. 115.

121. Afghani, 'Answer of Jamal ad-Din to Renan, *Journal des débats*, May 18, 1883', in Keddie, *Islamic Response*, pp. 181–7.

122. Afghani, 'Benefits of Philosophy', p. 113.

123. Ibid., p. 114.

124. Ibid., p. 116.

125. Ibid., p. 114.

126. Ibid., p. 120.

127. Ibid., p. 122.

128. Keddie, 'Sayyid Jamal ad-Din's Ideas', in *Islamic Response*, p. 38.

129. Blunt, *Secret History*, p. 212.

130. Ibid., p. 211.

131. Ibid., p. 190.

132. Ibid., p. 212.

133. In his private papers, notebooks titled 'From Alms to Oblivion' (Part VI, Chapter 6), Blunt writes: 'I have been many times on the point of making my public declaration of faith, if only as a protest and proof of my standing on the side of Eastern right against Western wrong', but what has deterred him is lack of belief in a future life. He also says that, had he actually been in Egypt during the bombardment, he would have 'proclaimed myself a Moslem'. Blunt Papers, Fitzwilliam Museum, University of Cambridge.

134. Blunt, *Secret History*, p. 243.

135. *Annual Register, 1882*, p. 139.

136. Blunt, 'Egyptian Revolution', p. 346.

137. Ibid.

138. Blunt, *Secret History*, p. 225.

139. Ibid., p. 419; Blunt, 'Egyptian Revolution', p. 333.

140. *Annual Register, 1882*, p. 148.

141. Ibid., p. 152.

142. Ibid., pp. 151, 156.

143. Ibid., p. 147.

144. HC Deb 12 July 1882, vol. 272, c. 191.

145. Cole, *Colonialism and Revolution*, p. 3. Cole goes on to observe: 'The British invaded in order to ensure that a process of state formation did not succeed in creating a new sort of stable order that would end European privileges and threaten the security of European property and investments'. Ibid., p. 17.

146. Sir Wilfrid Lawson 'said the time had come when those who felt deeply the position of dishonour in which the country was placed should not hold their peace if they were not to be held responsible for a national crime. They had been drifting into war with their eyes open, and he took blame to himself for not having spoken out earlier. Now they were at war, and they had no distinct information for what they were fighting, and there had been no declaration of war ... It was said that the Government wished to maintain the rights of the people of Egypt, but the way they showed their regard was to go out and shoot them down'. Cited in the *Annual Register, 1882*, p. 147.

147. Blunt, *Secret History*, p. 417.

148. Ibid., p. 244.

149. 'Egypt', in Frederic Harrison, *National and Social Problems* (London: Macmillan, 1908), p. 209.

150. Ibid., p. 202.

151. Ibid., p. 200.

152. Ibid., p. 196.

153. Ibid., p. 198.

154. Ibid., p. 200. Harrison summarizes imperialism in Egypt as a series of manoeuvres involving bullying, coaxing and influencing as needed, and setting up the handy device of the Control. The latter allowed Egyptians to pay 'for the luxury of not being allowed to raise or to expend their own taxes as they please', even though half the total revenue was carried out of the country to foreign bond-holders. Ibid., 197–8.

155. Ibid., p. 201.

156. Ibid.

157. Ibid., p. 203.

158. Ibid.

159. Ibid.

160. 'An Appeal to Mr Gladstone', 1 July 1882, in Harrison, *National and Social Problems*, pp. 212–13.

161. Ibid., p. 218.

162. Ibid., p. 216.

163. Ibid., p. 222.

164. Ibid., p. 173.

165. John Seymour Keay, *Spoiling the Egyptians: A Tale of Shame, Told from the Blue Books*, 4th edn (London: Kegan Paul, Trench, 1882), p. 33, emphasis in original.

166. Ibid., p. 53.

167. Ibid., pp. 5, 49, 79.

168. Ibid., p. 54.

169. Ibid.

170. Ibid.

171. 'Empire and Humanity', in Harrison, *National and Social Problems*, p. 261.

172. Ibid., p. 260.

173. Ibid., p. 259.

174. Ibid., p. 193.

175. Harrison, *Autobiographic Memoirs, Vol. II (1870–1910)* (London: Macmillan and Co., 1911), p. 126.

176. Cited in Broadley, *How We Defended Arábi*, p. 349.

177. Ibid.

178. Ibid., pp. 350, 349.

179. Ibid., p. 350.

180. Wilfrid S. Blunt, *The New Situation in Egypt* (London: Burns & Oates, 1908), p. 15.

181. Wilfrid S. Blunt, *The Wind and the Whirlwind* (London: Kegan Paul, Trench, 1883), p. 5.

182. Ibid., p. 7.

183. Ibid., pp. 11–12, 14.

184. Mohammed Abdu, 'Interview with Sheyk Mohammed Abdu, as published in the "Pall Mall Gazette"', 17 August 1884, Appendix E in Wilfrid S. Blunt, *Gordon at Khartoum: Being a Personal Narrative of Events in Continuation of 'A Secret History of the English Occupation of Egypt'* (London: S. Swift, 1911), p. 623.

185. Ibid.

186. Ibid., p. 626.

187. Blunt, 'The Shame of the Nineteenth Century: (a Letter Addressed to the "Times")', (S.I., 1900).

188. Ibid., pp. 1–2.

189. Ibid., p. 4.

190. Ibid., p. 5.

191. Ibid.

192. Ibid., p. 1.

4. Passages to Internationalism

1. Wilfred S. Blunt, *India under Ripon: A Private Diary by Wilfrid Scawen Blunt, Continued from His 'Secret History of the English Occupation of Egypt'* (London: T. F. Unwin, 1909), pp. 7–8.

2. Wilfrid S. Blunt, *Ideas about India* (London: Kegan Paul, 1885), p. vii.

3. Ibid., p. xi.

4. Annie Besant, *India and the Empire: A Lecture and Various Papers on Indian Grievances* (London: Theosophical Publishing Society, 1914), pp. 3–4.

5. Blunt, *India under Ripon*, p. 1.

6. Ibid., p. 223.

7. Blunt, *Ideas about India*, p. 3.

8. Ibid., p. 7.

9. Ibid., pp. 5–6.

10. Ibid., p. 10.

11. Ibid., p. 74.

12. Ibid., pp. 74–5.

13. Ibid., pp. 26–7.

14. Ibid., p. 174.

15. Ibid., p. 71.

16. Allan Octavian Hume, *Old Man's Hope*, cited in Edward C. Moulton, 'The Early Congress and the British Radical Connection', in D. A. Low, ed., *The Indian National Congress: Centenary Hindsights* (Delhi: Oxford University Press, 1988), p. 48.

17. Besant, *India and the Empire*, p. 3.

18. Edward Thompson and G. T. Garratt, *Rise and Fulfilment of British Rule in India* (London: Macmillan, 1934), p. 540.

19. Edward C. Moulton, 'British Radicals and India in the Early Twentieth Century', in A. J. A. Morris, ed., *Edwardian Radicalism 1900–1914* (London/Boston, MA: Routledge & Kegan Paul, 1974), p. 26.

20. Gregory Claeys, *Imperial Sceptics: British Critics of Empire 1850–1920* (Cambridge: Cambridge University Press, 2012), pp. 125–6.

21. J. A. Hobson, *The Crisis of Liberalism: New Issues of Democracy* (London: P. S. King, 1909), p. 259.

22. Ibid., p. 259.

23. Ibid., p. 260.

24. Stephen Howe, *Anticolonialism in British Politics: The Left and the End of Empire, 1918–1964* (Oxford: Oxford University Press, 1993), p. 30.

25. Ibid., p. 32.

26. Marcus Morris, 'From Anti-colonialism to Anti-imperialism: The Evolution of H. M. Hyndman's Critique of Empire, c.1875–1905', *Historical Research* 87: 236 (May 2014), p. 293. For a full accounting of the ambiguities in how Hyndman was seen in relation to imperial matters, see Claeys, *Imperial Sceptics*.

27. H. M. Hyndman, *The Indian Famine and the Crisis in India* (London: Edward Stanford, 1877), p. 6.

28. H. M. Hyndman, *The Unrest in India* (London: Twentieth-Century Press, 1907), p. 1.

29. Ibid., p. 2.

30. Ibid., p. 7.

31. Ibid., p. 8.

32. Ibid.

33. Ibid., p. 9.

34. Ibid.

35. Ibid., p. 10.

36. Ibid., p. 11.

37. Stephen Howe, *Anticolonialism in British Politics*, p. 32.

38. Hyndman, *Unrest in India*, p. 15.

39. The term is Owen's.

40. Philip Snowden, 'Foreword to the Second Edition', in Keir Hardie, *India: Impressions and Suggestions* (London: Home Rule for India League [British Auxiliary], 1917), p. xi.

41. Sir Henry Cotton, *New India: Or, India in Transition* (London: Kegan Paul, Trench, Trübner, 1907), p. 37.

42. Nicholas Owen, *The British Left and India: Metropolitan Anti-imperialism 1885–1947* (Oxford: Oxford University Press, 2007), p. 17.

43. I take my descriptive cue in the subheading for this section from Nicholas Owen's 'Edwardian Progressive Visitors to India', Chapter 3 of *The British Left and India*. Owen writes: 'After 1907, four Labour figures – Keir Hardie, Ramsay MacDonald and Sidney and Beatrice Webb, as well as the Radical journalist H. W. Nevinson – visited India in quick succession, and their differing perceptions and recommendations provide a good cross-section of responses to the new Indian nationalism'. The phrase 'the line of most resistance' is used by H. W. Nevinson to describe the 'Extremists' in India. Ibid., pp. 84, 329.

44. Owen, *The British Left and India*, p. 50.

45. Ibid., pp. 61–2.

46. Ibid., p. 62.

47. Ibid., p. 81.

48. Ibid.

49. Ibid., p. 84.

50. Homi K. Bhabha, 'Sly Civility', *October* 34 (1985), pp. 324–46.

51. Cotton, *New India*, pp. 29, 16.

52. Ibid., p. vi.

53. Cited in D. V. Tahmankar, *Lokamanya Tilak: Father of Indian Unrest and Maker of Modern India* (London: John Murray, 1956), p. 136.

54. See Stanley A. Wolpert, *Tilak and Gokhale: Revolution and Reform in the Making of Modern India* (Berkeley/Los Angeles, CA: University of California Press, 1962), p. 191.

55. Thompson and Garratt, *Rise and Fulfilment of British Rule*, p. 541.

56. Viceroy Curzon, cited in Sumit Sarkar, *The Swadeshi Movement in Bengal, 1903–1908* (New Delhi: People's Publishing House, 1973), p. 20.

57. Ibid.

58. Ibid.

59. Ibid., p. 21.

60. Owen, *The British Left and India*, p. 83.

61. Sarkar, *Swadeshi Movement*, p. 23.

62. B. C. Pal, cited in ibid., p. 68.

63. Ibid., 28.

64. Sarkar notes that what is more surprising than the eventual alienation of Muslims is the level of their participation. Mosques offered prayers against partition, and declarations of fraternity and shared national unity were frequently made. A practice appears to have developed of sending out agitators in pairs consisting of a Hindu and a Muslim. The Muslim folk poet Mofiuddin Bayati composed Swadeshi songs. Ibid., pp. 425–6. See Chapter 8, below, for an extended account of the Muslim role in Swadeshi.

65. Rabindranath Tagore, *The Home and the World*, transl. Surendranath Tagore (London: Penguin, 1985).

66. Aurobindo Ghose, 'English Democracy Shown Up', in Haridas Mukherjee and Uma Mukherjee, *Sri Aurobindo and the New Thought in Indian Politics*, 2nd edn (Calcutta: Firma KLM, 1997), p. 178.

67. Ibid., p. 179.

68. Ibid.

69. Kenneth O. Morgan, *Keir Hardie: Radical and Socialist* (London: Weidenfield & Nicolson, 1975), p. 192.

70. Ibid.

71. Cited in ibid., p. 194.

72. Ghose, 'English Democracy Shown Up', p. 180, emphasis in original.

73. Morgan, *Keir Hardie*, p. 194.

74. Hardie, *India*, p. 42.

75. Ibid., p. 75.

76. Ibid., p. 46.

77. Ibid., p. 46. The plausible suggestion that Hardie may have been misled with regard to the question of loyalty is Jonathan Hyslop's. See his 'The World Voyage of James Keir Hardie: Indian Nationalism, Zulu Insurgency and the British Labour Diaspora 1907–1908', *Journal of Global History* 1: 3 (November 2006), pp. 343–62.

78. Hardie, *India*, p. 46.

79. Ibid., p. 72.

80. Ibid., p. 106.

81. Ibid., p. 88.

82. Hyslop, 'World Voyage', p. 348.

83. Hardie, *India*, pp. 125, 120.

84. Ibid., p. 139.

85. Morgan, *Keir Hardie*, p. 193.

86. Hardie, *India*, p. 131; William Stewart, *J. Keir Hardie: A Biography* (London: National Labour Press, 1921), p. 264.

87. Hyslop, 'World Voyage', pp. 352–3.

88. Theodore L. Shay, *The Legacy of the Lokamanya: The Political Philosophy of Bal Gangadhar Tilak* (New Delhi: Oxford University Press, 1956), p. 103.

89. Cited in D. V. Tahmankar, *Lokamanya Tilak* (London: John Murray, 1956), p. 136.

90. Bal Gangadhar, Tilak, 'Tenets of the New Party' in *Bal Gangadhar Tilak: His Writings and Speeches. Appreciation by Babu Aurobindo Ghose*, 3rd edn (Madras: Ganesh and Co., 1922), p. 56.

91. Ibid., p. 61.

92. Ibid., p. 65.

93. Ibid.

94. Ibid., p. 60.
95. Tilak, 'The Shivaji Festival', in *Tilak: His Writings and Speeches*, p. 77.
96. Tilak, 'Tenets of the New Party', p. 63.
97. Henry W. Nevinson, *More Changes, More Chances* (London: Nisbet, 1925), p. 226.
98. Cited in Angela V. John, *War, Journalism and the Shaping of the Twentieth Century: The Life and Times of Henry W. Nevinson* (London: I. B. Tauris, 2006), p. 105.
99. Henry W. Nevinson, *The New Spirit in India* (London: Harper, 1908).
100. John, *War, Journalism and the Shaping of the Twentieth Century*, p. 119.
101. Owen, *British Left and India*, p. 87.
102. Nevinson, *New Spirit of India*, p. 122.
103. Ibid., p. 43.
104. For a brief but heartfelt tribute to their friendship, see E. M. Forster, '"We Speak to India": "Some Books" – A Backward Glance over 1941', broadcast on 10 December 1941, in *The BBC Talks of E. M. Forster*, ed. Mary Lago, Linda K. Hughes and Elizabeth MacLeod Walls (Columbia, MO: University of Missouri Press, 2008), pp. 155–6.
105. E. M. Forster, *A Passage to India* (London: Penguin, 2015 [1924]), p. 190, my emphasis.
106. Benita Parry, 'Materiality and Mystification in "A Passage to India"', in *Novel: A Forum on Fiction* 31: 2 (Spring 1998), p. 185.
107. Ibid., p. 180.
108. Ibid., p. 177.
109. Ibid., p. 191.
110. Nevinson, *New Spirit of India*, p. 66.
111. Tilak, cited in ibid., p. 72.
112. Cited ibid., p. 74.
113. Ibid., p. 75.
114. Ibid., p. 76.
115. Ibid., p. 69.
116. Ibid., p. 74.
117. Ibid., p. 126.
118. Ibid., pp. 128–9.
119. Ibid., p. 131.
120. Ibid., p. 132.
121. Ibid., pp. 221–2.
122. Ibid., p. 223.
123. Cited in ibid., pp. 223, 221.
124. Ibid., p. 226.

125. Ibid.

126. Aurobindo Ghose, 'Look on This Picture, Then on That', in Mukherjee and Mukherjee, *Sri Aurobindo and the New Thought*, p. 51.

127. Aurobindo Ghose, 'The New Thought: Nationalism Not Extremism', in Mukherjee and Mukherjee, *Sri Aurobindo and the New Thought*, p. 19.

128. Ibid., pp. 20, 22.

129. Aurobindo Ghose, 'The New Thought: Shall India be Free? National Development and Foreign Rule', in Mukherjee and Mukherjee, *Sri Aurobindo and the New Thought*, p.25.

130. Aurobindo Ghose, 'The Man of the Past and the Man of the Future', in Mukherjee and Mukherjee, *Sri Aurobindo and the New Thought*, p. 6.

131. Aurobindo Ghose, 'English Obduracy and Its Reason', in Mukherjee and Mukherjee, *Sri Aurobindo and the New Thought*, p. 98.

132. Aurobindo Ghose, 'Morleyism Analysed', in Mukherjee and Mukherjee, *Sri Aurobindo and the New Thought*, p. 94.

133. Aurobindo Ghose, 'English Obduracy', in Mukherjee and Mukherjee, *Sri Aurobindo and the New Thought*, p. 100.

134. Ibid.

135. Aurobindo Ghose, 'The New Thought: Shall India be Free?', p. 33.

136. Ibid., p. 35.

137. Aurobindo Ghose, 'Look on This Picture', p. 52.

138. Ibid., 52.

139. Aurobindo, 'The Old Year', in Mukherjee and Mukherjee, *Sri Aurobindo and the New Thought*, pp. 38, 36.

140. Aurobindo, 'Graduated Boycott', in Mukherjee and Mukherjee, *Sri Aurobindo and the New Thought*, p. 46.

141. Aurobindo, 'Asiatic Democracy', in Mukherjee and Mukherjee, *Sri Aurobindo and the New Thought*, p. 252.

142. Aurobindo, 'Our Rulers and Boycott', in Mukherjee and Mukherjee, *Sri Aurobindo and the New Thought*, p. 123.

143. Ibid.

144. Forster, '"We Speak to India"', p. 155; Nevinson, *New Spirit of India*, p. 159.

145. Nevinson, *New Spirit of India*, p. 153.

146. Ibid.

147. Ibid., p. 155.

148. Ibid., p. 156.

149. Ibid.

150. Ibid.

151. Ibid., p. 159.

152. Ibid., p. 157.
153. Ibid., p. 159.
154. Ibid.
155. Nevinson, *More Changes, More Chances*, p. 272.
156. Nevinson, *New Spirit of India*, p. 188.
157. Owen, *British Left and India*, p. 89.
158. Ibid.
159. Nevinson, *New Spirit of India*, pp. 261–2.
160. Ibid., p. 320.
161. Ibid., p. 323.
162. Ibid.
163. Ibid., pp. 326–7.
164. Ibid., p. 327.
165. Ibid., p. 329.
166. Ibid., p. 34.
167. Owen, *British Left and India*, p. 89.
168. Edward Said, *Culture and Imperialism* (London: Vintage, 1994), p. 28.
169. Nevinson, *New Spirit of India*, p. 330.
170. Ibid., pp. 310, 328.
171. Ibid., p. 321.
172. Ibid., p. 329.
173. Ibid., p. 331.
174. Ibid., p. 335.
175. Ibid.
176. Henry W. Nevinson, 'India's Coral Strand', *Saturday Review of Literature*, New York, 1924, reprinted in Philip Gardner, ed., *E. M Forster: The Critical Heritage* (London: Routledge & Kegan Paul, 1973), pp. 256–7.
177. Ibid., p. 257.
178. John, *War, Journalism and the Shaping of the Twentieth Century*, p. 112.
179. Aurobindo Ghose, 'Mr Macdonald's Visit', *Karmayogin: A Weekly Review*, 27 November 1909, available at aurobindo.ru.
180. Peter Cain writes: 'Despite his close association with Hobson and Robertson through the Rainbow Circle, there is no trace of any attempt to link together a radical analysis of the domestic economy with imperialism; which meant, in effect, that his socialism was a good deal vaguer than their radical liberalism in pointing out the defects of capitalism'. Peter Cain, 'Introduction', in J. Ramsay MacDonald, *Labour and the Empire* (London: Routledge, 1998), p. vi.
181. J. Ramsay MacDonald, *The Awakening of India* (London: Hodder & Stoughton, 1910), pp. 211, 301.

182. Ibid., p. 119.

183. Ibid., p. 7.

184. Owen, *British Left and India*, p. 89.

185. MacDonald, *Awakening of India*, p. 297.

186. Ibid., pp. 65, 99.

187. Edward Said, *Culture and Imperialism* (London: Chatto & Windus, 1993), 214.

188. MacDonald, *Awakening of India*, p. 105.

189. Ibid., p. 215.

190. Ibid., p. 193.

191. Ibid., p. 121.

192. Owen, *British Left and India*, p. 90.

193. Macdonald, *Awakening of India*, p. 100.

194. Ibid., pp. 51, 103.

195. Ibid., p. 226.

196. Ibid., pp. 186, 189.

197. Ibid., p. 74.

198. Ibid., p. 122.

199. Ibid.

200. Ibid., p. 96.

201. Ibid., p. 138.

202. Ibid., p. 168.

203. Ibid., p. 213.

204. Ibid.

205. Ibid., pp. 211–12.

206. Ibid., p. 308.

207. Parry, 'Materiality and Mystification', p. 177; Forster, *A Passage to India*, p. 120.

208. MacDonald, *Awakening of India*, p. 5.

209. Ibid., p. 302.

210. Ibid., pp. 308–9.

211. Ibid.

212. Ibid., p. 310.

213. Ibid.

214. Ibid., p. 311.

215. Ibid., p. 214.

216. J. Ramsay MacDonald, *The Government of India* (London: Swarthmore, 1919), p. 16.

217. Owen, *British Left and India*, p. 92.

218. Edward C. Moulton, 'British Radicals and India in the Early Twentieth Century', in A. J. A. Morris, ed., *Edwardian Radicalism 1900–1914: Some Aspects of British Radicalism* (London/Boston: Routledge & Kegan Paul, 1975), p. 44.

219. Ibid.

220. Michael Adas, 'Contested Hegemony: The Great War and the Afro-Asian Assault on the Civilizing Mission Ideology', *Journal of World History* 15: 1 (March 2004), p. 50.

221. Hilda Howsin, *The Significance of Indian Nationalism* (London: A. C. Fifield, 1909), pp. 17–18.

222. V. H. Rutherford, 'Introductory Note by Dr Rutherford', in ibid., p. 7.

223. Ibid., 8.

224. Howsin, *Significance of Indian Nationalism*, p. 96.

225. Dilip M. Menon, 'The Many Spaces and Times of Swadeshi', *Economic and Political Weekly* 47: 42 (2012), available at epw.in.

5. The Interpreter of Insurgencies

1. Kris Manjapra, 'Communist Internationalism and Transcolonial Recognition', in Sugata Bose and Kris Manjapra, eds, *Cosmopolitan Thought Zones: South Asia and the Global Circulation of Ideas* (New York: Palgrave Macmillan, 2010), p. 162.

2. Dilip M. Menon, 'The Many Spaces and Times of Swadeshi', *Economic and Political Weekly* 47: 42 (2012), available at epw.in.

3. Shyamaji Krishnavarma, cited in Tilak Raj Sareen, *Indian Revolutionary Movement Abroad (1905–1921)* (New Delhi: Sterling, 1979), p. 4.

4. Ibid., p. 9.

5. For more on this, see Maia Ramnath, *Haj to Utopia* (Berkeley: University of California Press, 2011); Kate O'Malley, *Ireland, India and Empire* (Manchester: Manchester University Press, 2009); Ashwini Tambe and Harald Tiné, eds, *The Limits of British Colonial Control in South Asia* (Abingdon: Routledge, 2011).

6. Partha Chatterjee, 'Nationalism, Internationalism, and Cosmopolitanism: Some Observations from Modern Indian History', *Comparative Studies of South Asia, Africa and the Middle East* 36: 2 (August 2016), p. 323.

7. Erez Manela, *The Wilsonian Moment: Self-Determination and the International Origins of Anticolonial Nationalism* (Oxford: Oxford University Press, 2007), p. 5.

8. Ibid., p. 91. Manela notes that, in a pivotal speech given in Caxton Hall in January 1918, British prime minister David Lloyd George, 'in a promiscuous rhetorical flourish', elided 'the Bolshevik term "self-determination" together with Wilson's favourite phrase, "consent of the governed"'. Ibid., p. 39.

9. Heather Streets-Salter, 'International and Global Anti-colonial Movements', in Tony Ballantyne and Antoinette Burton, eds, *World*

Histories from Below: Disruption and Dissent from 1750 to the Present (London: Bloomsbury Academic, 2016), p. 48.

10. Ibid., p. 47.

11. For a brief overview of these terms and the relationships between them, see Ali Raza, Franzisca Roy and Benjamin Zachariah, 'Introduction', in Raza, Roy and Zachariah, eds, *The Internationalist Moment: South Asia, Worlds, and World Views, 1917–1939* (Los Angeles: Sage, 2015), p. xi.

12. Ibid., p. xii.

13. Ibid., p. xvii.

14. Ian Duffield, cited in Nicholas Owen, 'Critics of Empire in Britain', in J. M. Brown and W. M. R. Louis, eds, *The Oxford History of the British Empire, Vol. IV: The Twentieth Century* (Oxford: Oxford University Press, 1999), p. 202; Minkah Makalani, *In the Cause of Freedom: Radical Black Internationalism from Harlem to London, 1917–1939* (Chapel Hill: University of North Carolina Press, 2011), p. 194.

15. Marc Matera, *Black London: The Imperial Metropolis and Decolonization in the Twentieth Century* (Oakland, CA: University of California Press, 2015), p. 14.

16. As Maia Ramnath writes of this period, 'The center of activity then shifted to Paris, where prominent socialists and anticolonialists S. R. Rana and Madame Rustomji Cama presided over a well-established political circle.' Maia Ramnath, 'Two Revolutions: The Ghadar Movement and India's Radical Diaspora, 1913–1918', *Radical History Review* 92 (Spring 2005), p. 11.

17. As Timothy Mitchell notes, the principle of self-rule was not necessarily in contradiction with the idea of empire: 'On the contrary, the need for self-government could provide, paradoxically, a new justification for overseas settlement and control, because only the European presence in colonised territories made a form of self-rule possible.' Timothy Mitchell, *Carbon Democracy: Political Power in the Age of Oil* (London: Verso, 2011), p. 71. Later, this would be theorized via the doctrine of 'trusteeship', in which Europe would hold territories 'in trust for civilization'. *New Statesman*, 1916, cited in Mitchell, *Carbon Democracy*, p. 76.

18. Matera, *Black London*, p. 17.

19. Anthony Read and David Fisher, *The Proudest Day: India's Long Road to Independence* (London: Jonathan Cape, 1997), p. 207.

20. Shapurji Saklatvala, HC Deb 17 June 1927 vol. 207, c. 1388.

21. Ibid.

22. Ibid.

23. HC Deb 23 November 1927 vol. 210, c. 1826.

24. There are three biographical accounts of Saklatvala's personal

and political life: Mike Squires, *Saklatvala: A Political Biography* (London: Lawrence & Wishart, 1990); Marc Wadsworth, *Comrade Sak: Shapurji Saklatvala: A Political Biography* (Leeds: Peepal Tree, 1998); and Sehri Saklatvala, *The Fifth Commandment: Biography of Shapurji Saklatvala* (Salford: Miranda, 1991). The last of these is perhaps the fullest account of his personal and family life.

25. Secret Service files, cited in Wadsworth, *Comrade Sak*, p. 53.

26. Ibid., p. 30.

27. Ibid.

28. For brief accounts of all these figures and their relationships to each other, see Open University, *Making Britain: Discover How South Asians Shaped the Nation, 1870–1950*, at open.ac.uk.

29. Shapurji Saklatvala, 'The Second Indian Round Table Conference', *Labour Monthly* 13: 10 (October 1931), available at marxists.org. The Communist Party was deeply disapproving of Saklatvala's decision to hold a *navjote* or 'thread' ceremony in 1927 for his children. See Wadsworth, *Comrade Sak*, pp. 102–4.

30. Cited in ibid., p. 106.

31. Herbert Bryan to Arthur Field, 23 February 1937, typed copy in Saklatvala Papers, MSS.EUR D 1173/4; Saklatvala, *Fifth Commandment*, p. 97.

32. Herbert Bryan, 'Saklatvala: An Appreciation', *Daily Herald*, 24 November 1922 – typed copy in Saklatvala Papers, MSS.EUR D 1173/4.

33. Cited in Wadsworth, *Comrade Sak*, p. 51.

34. Susan D. Pennybacker, *From Scottsboro to Munich: Race and Political Culture in 1930s Britain* (Princeton: Princeton University Press, 2009), p. 149.

35. Arthur Field to Beram Saklatvala, 7 March 1937, in Saklatvala Papers, MSS.EUR D 1173/4.

36. Lord Snowden to Beram Saklatvala, 4 February 1937 – typed copy in Saklatvala Papers, MSS.EUR D 1173/4.

37. Nicholas Owen, *The British Left and India: Metropolitan Anti-imperialism 1885–1947* (Oxford: Oxford University Press, 2007), p. 108.

38. See ibid., pp. 198–9.

39. Though he made many significant interventions on matters pertaining to trade unions, unemployment, Emergency powers and housing conditions, Wadsworth notes that 'the bulk of his speeches related to India and other anti-imperialist issues' – which included Ireland. Wadsworth, *Comrade Sak*, p. 51.

40. Shapurji Saklatvala with Duncan Carmichael, 'Statement Submitted to the Joint Committee on Indian Reforms on Behalf of the Workers' Welfare League of India', in Saklatvala, *Fifth Commandment*, Chapter 7, Appendix A, p. 115.

41. Ibid., p. 94.

42. Ibid.

43. Wadsworth, *Comrade Sak*, p. 61. Tilak had visited Saklatvala at his home in 1910 while a guest at the ILP's annual conference. British intelligence files on Saklatvala noted in 1911 that he kept in touch with radical nationalists such as Bipin Chandra Pal, 'showing considerable interest in the extremist movement' (p. 53).

44. HC Deb 9 July 1925 vol. 186, c. 711.

45. Cited in Meerut Prisoners' Defence Committee, *The Meerut Trial: Facts of the Case* (London: Meerut Prisoners' Defence Committee, 1929), p. 10.

46. Gene D. Overstreet and Marshall Windmiller, *Communism in India* (Berkeley: University of California Press, 1959), p. 17.

47. Ibid., p. 29.

48. The main contours of the arguments on either side can be found in Marika Sherwood, 'The Comintern, the CPGB, Colonies and Black Britons, 1920–1938', *Science and Society* 60: 2 (Summer 1996); and John Callahan, 'Colonies, Racism, the CPGB and the Comintern in the Inter-war Years', *Science and Society* 61: 4 (Winter 1997–98). For a sober and fuller assessment, see Neil Redfern, *Class or Nation: Communists, Imperialism, and Two World Wars* (London/New York: Tauris Academic Studies, 2005).

49. James Klugman, cited in Sherwood, 'The Comintern, the CPGB, Colonies and Black Britons', p. 144.

50. Cited in ibid., p. 146.

51. Ibid., p. 160, emphasis in original.

52. Shapurji Saklatvala, 'India in the Labour World', *Labour Monthly* 1: 5 (November 1921), available at marxists.org.

53. HC Deb 9 July 1925 vol. 86, c. 706.

54. HC Deb 23 November 1922 vol. 159, c. 111.

55. Ibid., c. 114.

56. Ibid., cc. 113–14.

57. HD Deb 27 February 1923 vol. 160, c. 1835.

58. Ibid.

59. Ibid.

60. HC Deb 5 July 1923 vol. 166, c. 676.

61. HC Deb 9 July 1925, c. 708.

62. Ibid.

63. Ibid., c. 709.

64. Ibid.

65. Ibid.

66. Ibid., cc. 710–11.

67. Ibid., c. 709.

68. Ibid.

69. Ibid., c. 712.
70. Ibid., c. 712.
71. Ibid.
72. Ibid.
73. Ibid., c. 714.
74. Ibid., c. 718.
75. Maria Misra, *Vishnu's Crowded Temple: India since the Great Rebellion* (London: Allen Lane, 2007), p. 188.
76. HC Deb 17 June 1927, c. 1398.
77. HC Deb 27 November 1927, cc. 2280, 2282.
78. HC Deb 17 June 1927 vol 207, c. 1388.
79. Ibid.
80. Ibid.
81. Ibid., cc. 1388–9.
82. HC Deb 22 November 1927 vol. 210, c. 1642.
83. Ibid.
84. HC Deb 17 June 1927 vol. 207, cc. 1389–90.
85. HC Deb 23 Nov 1927 vol. 210, c. 1824.
86. Ibid., c. 1823.
87. HC Deb 25 November 1927 vol. 210, c. 2272.
88. Pennybacker, *From Scottsboro to Munich*, p. 159.
89. HC Deb 25 Nov 1927 vol 210, c. 2283.
90. HC Deb, *India Office*, 17 June 1927, c. 1392.
91. HC Deb 25 November 1927, c. 2282.
92. Shapurji Šaklatvala, 'India and Britain', *Labour Monthly* 9: 6 (June 1927), available at marxists.org.
93. Ibid.
94. Ibid.
95. Ibid.
96. Ibid.
97. HC Deb 23 November 1927, c. 1828.
98. Ibid. Saklatvala's rejoinder was: 'The Noble Lord knows all this, and he has reports in his possession showing that hundreds of thousands of the people of India approve of my plans and my policy, and they also approve of what I have been doing for India while residing in this country. If the Noble Lord would make a journey with me to India, I would be quite willing to organise open public meetings – not camouflaged and manœuvred meetings – and he would then find that 99 people out of every 100 at those meetings would declare in favour of my authority to speak on their behalf.' Ibid., cc. 1843–4.
99. Wadsworth, *Comrade Sak*, p. 59.
100. Cited in Saklatvala, *Fifth Commandment*, p. 332.
101. Wadsworth, *Comrade Sak*, p. 21.

102. Maria Misra notes: 'Amritsar was not in fact the wholly isolated event the British liked to believe. Elsewhere the Punjab disturbances had been met with lethal force ... unarmed market crowds and schoolhouses were strafed with hundreds of rounds of ammunition and then carpet-bombed.' Misra, *Vishnu's Crowded Temple*, p. 152.

103. Rabindranath Tagore, 'Letter to Lord Chelmsford', *Monthly Review* (Calcutta Monthly), July 1919.

104. Owen, *British Left and India*, p. 125.

105. Sumit Sarkar, *Modern India: 1885–1947* (London: Macmillan, 1983), p. 176; see p. 199 for a list of significant strike actions during the period 1919–20.

106. Sumit Sarkar notes correctly that the combination of pressures from below and Gandhian organization acting as a 'brake' to such pressures created a 'peculiar dialectic'. Sumit Sarkar, *'Popular' Movements and 'Middle Class' Leadership in Late Colonial India: Perspectives and Problems of a 'History from Below'* (Calcutta: Centre for Studies in Social Sciences, 1983), p. 44.

107. Cited in Overstreet and Windmiller, *Communism in India*, p. 56.

108. See Nirode K. Barooah, *Chatto: The Life and Times of an Anti-imperialist in Europe* (Delhi: Oxford University Press, 2004).

109. Sarkar, *Modern India*, p. 247.

110. Cited in Panchanan Saha, *Shapurji Saklatvala: A Short Biography* (Delhi: People's Publishing House, 1970), p. 40.

111. Shapurji Saklatvala, 'Mr Saklatwala's Message to His Countrymen' (message to Sarojini Naidu, president of Indian National Congress), reprinted in *Bombay Chronicle*, 15 January 1997, in Saklatvala Papers, British Library, MSS EUR D 1173/3.

112. Ibid. He continues: 'The old idea of ruling castes in each nation wanting to rule the masses within their nation, has been burnt and charred in the conflagration of the last great war and cannot be revived.'

113. Ibid.

114. Wadsworth notes that, on the eve of his departure from India, Saklatvala made a 'controversial speech' calling for peasants and workers to rally around the Congress. Roy complained to the CPGB, saying that 'Saklatvala was hobnobbing with all sorts of Indians who were not revolutionaries'. Ibid., p. 61. Another Indian leftist, Hasrat Mohani, claimed that the British Indian MP had become a 'Congress victim'. Ibid., p. 62.

115. Ibid., p. 51.

116. 'Saklatvala's Open Letter to Gandhi', *Amrita Bazar Patrika*, 12 March 1927. In Wadsworth, *Comrade Sak*, pp. 158–9.

117. Ibid., p. 159.

118. 'Saklatvala to Gandhi', 1 July 1927. In Wadsworth, *Comrade Sak*, p. 172.

119. Wadsworth, Saklatvala to Gandhi, *Amrita Bazar Patrika*, 12 March 1927, p. 156.

120. Ibid., p. 157.

121. Ibid.

122. Ibid., p. 159.

123. Ibid.

124. 'Mahatma Gandhi's Reply', *Amrita Bazar Patrika*, 18 March 1927. Cited in Wadsworth, *Comrade Sak*, p. 162.

125. Ibid., p. 165.

126. Ibid., p. 164.

127. Wadsworth, *Comrade Sak*, p. 65.

128. 'Saklatvala to Gandhi', 1 July 1927. In Wadsworth, *Comrade Sak*, p. 173.

129. HC Deb 25 November 1927, c. 2272.

130. Ibid.

131. Ibid., c. 2273.

132. Ibid., c. 2275.

133. Ibid.

134. Ibid., c. 2277.

135. Ibid., c. 2278.

136. Ibid., c. 2285.

137. Ibid.

138 HC Deb 21 March 1928 vol. 215, c. 426.

139. Shapurji Saklatvala in HC Deb 27 September 1926 vol. 199, cc. 338–9.

140. HC Deb 20 July 1926 vol. 198, c. 1117.

141. Sir Charles Wilson, in HC Deb 27 September 1926, cc. 343–4.

142. Shapurji Saklatvala, *Election Address, Parliamentary By-election, June 1930, Shuttleston Division*, Bridgeman Papers, U DBN/24.

143. Shapurji Saklatvala, 'The Indian Round Table Conference', *Labour Monthly* 12: 12 (December 1930), pp. 720–4, available at www.marxists.org.

144. Saklatvala, 'Second Indian Round Table Conference'.

145. Ibid.

146. Shapurji Saklatava, 'The Indian Round-Table Conference: A Danger to World Peace and Socialism', *Labour Monthly* 13: 2 (February 1931), pp. 86–92, available at www.marxists.org.

147. Shapurji Saklatvala, 'To My Countrymen', typescript of pamphlet, Bridgeman Papers, U DBN/24.

6. The Revolt of the Oppressed World

1. Lester Hutchinson, *Conspiracy at Meerut, with a preface by Harold J. Laski* (London: Allen & Unwin, 1935), p. 41.
2. A useful but brief account of the Meerut Conspiracy Case can be found in A. G. Noorani, *Indian Political Trials 1775–1947* (New Delhi: Oxford University Press, 2005).
3. See ibid., p. 238.
4. For an excellent account of revolutionary violence in this period, see Kama Maclean, *A Revolutionary History of Interwar India: Violence, Image, Voice and Text* (London: Hurst, 2015).
5. Political Dept, File 14, June 1927, Government of Bengal, cited in Panchanan Saha, *Shapurji Saklatvala: A Short Biography* (Delhi: People's Publishing House, 1970), p. 28. It continues: 'the peasants are grumbling that there is no reason why they should be forced to pay rent to the zamindar or land revenue to the sarkar; in the towns the labourers are complaining that while richmen [*sic*] live lives of comfort and ease, they are condemned to toil, early and late, to live in miserable hovels, to go clad in rags.' Ibid.
6. Hutchinson, *Conspiracy at Meerut*, p. 117.
7. Cited in Fredrik Petersson, 'The "Colonial Conference" and the Dilemma of the Comintern's Colonial Work, 1928–29', in Vijay Prashad, ed., *Communist Histories* (New Delhi: Leftword, 2016), p. 106.
8. Pramita Ghosh, *Meerut Conspiracy Case and the Left Wing in India* (Calcutta: Papyrus, 1998), p. 93.
9. 'The Speech of the Prosecutor in the Meerut Case' (Part 1), *Labour Monthly* 12: 1 (January 1930), available at marxists.org.
10. 'The Speech of the Prosecutor in the Meerut Case' (Part 2), *Labour Monthly* 12: 2 (February 1930), available at marxists.org.
11. 'Speech of the Prosecutor' (Part 1).
12. Ibid.
13. Ibid.
14. Cited in Noorani, *Indian Political Trials*, p. 254.
15. Cited in Ghosh, *Meerut Conspiracy Case*, p. 110. For a slightly longer account of Gandhi's relationship with communism as it pertained to this case, see Franziska Roy and Benjamin Zachariah, 'Meerut and a Hanging: "Young India," Popular Socialism, and the Dynamics of Imperialism', *Comparative Studies of South Asia, Africa and the Middle East* 33: 3 (2013). They describe Hutchinson as 'one of the more coherent and biting critics of Gandhi and of Gandhian politics within youth league circles' (p. 375).
16. Ghosh, *Meerut Conspiracy Case*, p. 111.
17. Hutchinson, *Conspiracy at Meerut*, p. 118.

18. Roy and Zachariah, 'Meerut and a Hanging', p. 360.

19. Ibid., p. 363.

20. HC Deb 25 March 1929 vol. 226, cc. 2041–3.

21. Hutchinson, *Conspiracy at Meerut*, p. 179.

22. Harold J. Laski, 'Preface', in Hutchinson, *Conspiracy at Meerut*, p. 7.

23. Cited in Ghosh, *Meerut Conspiracy Case*, p. 155.

24. 'The Meerut Case', *The Manchester Guardian*, 5 August 1933.

25. *Meerut: Release the Prisoners! A Statement upon the Meerut Trial and Sentences*, London: issued by the National Joint Council, representing the Trades Union Congress, the Labour Party and the Parliamentary Labour Party, 1933.

26. Hutchinson, *Conspiracy at Meerut*, p. 179.

27. Cited in Ghosh, *Meerut Conspiracy Case*, p. 159.

28. Pennybacker, *From Scottsboro to Munich*, p. 147.

29. 'Meerut Conspiracy Prosecution,' *Manchester Guardian*, 10 December 1929.

30. Pennybacker, *From Scottsboro to Munich*, p. 171.

31. *The Meerut Prisoners and the Charge against Them* (London: Modern Books, 1931).

32. Ibid., p. 6.

33. Ibid.

34. The provincial Workers and Peasants Parties (a plurality across India although run by the same organisation) were part of a tactic initiated by the Indian communist M. N. Roy. They were legal parties – 'established at a time when the British government of India was arresting anyone remotely connected to communism on charges of an international conspiracy'. They were looked upon askance by both the Comintern and, in particular, the CPGB, which called for them to be disbanded. For a fuller account, see Wendy Singer, 'Peasants and Peoples of the East: Indians and the Rhetoric of the Comintern', in Tim Rees and Andrew Thorpe, ed., *International Communism and the Communist International, 1919–1943* (Manchester: Manchester University Press, 1998), 276.

35. *The Meerut Prisoners*, p. 8.

36. Ibid., p. 18.

37. Ibid., p. 12.

38. Ibid., p. 42.

39. Ibid., p. 26.

40. Ibid., p. 29.

41. Ibid., p. 33.

42. Ibid., pp. 44–5.

43. Ibid., p. 5.

44. *Meerut: Workers Theatre Movement Play*, available at wcml.org.uk.

45. Charlie Mann, 'How to Produce Meerut (1933)', at ibid.
46. Ibid.
47. Ibid.
48. Jimmie Miller, 'Red Megaphones', available at wcml.org.uk.
49. Romain Rolland, 'For the Meerut Prisoners: Against Imperialist Terror', in *Meerut Conspiracy Case, Specially Written by a Barrister-at-Law* (London: Meerut Prisoners' Release Committee, 1933). Published in French as 'Pour les condamnés de Meerut', first published in *L'Humanité*, 18 March 1933.
50. Ibid., p. 1.
51. Ibid.
52. Ibid., p. 2.
53. Ibid., pp. 2–3.
54. Ibid., p. 3.
55. Ibid.
56. Ibid.
57. Ibid., p. 4.
58. Cited in Ghosh, *Meerut Conspiracy Case*, p. 167.
59. See Muzaffar Ahmad, 'Introduction', in Ahmad, ed., *Communists Challenge Imperialism from the Dock* (Calcutta: National Book Agency, 1967). Other documents pertaining to the case have been digitized and are available at 'Indian Communists and Trade Unions on Trial: The Meerut Conspiracy, 1929–1933', British Online Archives, at microform.digital.
60. Hutchinson, *Conspiracy at Meerut*, p. 81.
61. Ibid., p. 75. See also Ahmad, 'Introduction'.
62. Nicholas Owen, *The British Left and India: Metropolitan Anti-imperialism 1885–1947* (Oxford: Oxford University Press, 2008), p. 210.
63. Kevin McDermott and Jeremy Agnew, *The Comintern: A History of International Communism from Lenin to Stalin* (Basingstoke: Macmillan, 1996), p. xvii.
64. Nikolai Lenin, *'Left-Wing' Communism: An Infantile Disorder* (London: Communist Party of Great Britain, n.d. [1923?]), p. 7.
65. John Riddell, ed., *To See the Dawn: Baku, 1920 – First Congress of the Peoples of the East* (London/New York: Pathfinder, 1993), p. 27.
66. McDermott and Agnew, *Comintern*, p. 217.
67. For an engaging account of the discussion, see John P. Haithcox, 'The Roy–Lenin Debate on Colonial Policy: A New Interpretation', *Journal of Asian Studies* 23: 1 (November 1963), pp. 93–101.
68. 'Minutes of the Second Congress of the Communist International, Fourth Session, July 25', available at marxists.org. Also available in McDermott and Agnew, *Comintern*, pp. 223–4.

69. Pennybacker describes Arthur Creech-Jones, one of many 'cautious critics of empire' who would become the head of the liberal-imperialist Fabian Colonial Bureau, and later colonial secretary, as 'implacably hostile to any notion of Indian agency', insisting that 'unlike their comrades in the West the workers in India are mainly the illiterate, and are dependent almost entirely for their organization ... upon persons who are not themselves workers'. Pennybacker, *From Scottsboro to Munich*, p. 174.

70. Hutchinson, *Conspiracy at Meerut*, p. 188.

71. Lester Hutchinson, *Meerut 1929–1932: Statement Given in His Own Defence at Meerut Court, India, against a Charge of 'Conspiracy against the King'* (London: Meerut Defence Committee, 1932), p. 57.

72. Ibid., p. 57.

73. Ibid.

74. Ibid., pp. 58–9.

75. Robert Page Arnot, 'The Meerut Sentences', *Labour Monthly* 15: 2 (February 1933), available at marxists.org.

76. Ibid.

77. Ibid.

78. Ibid.

79. Ibid.

80. 'Meerut and the Colonial Struggle,' *Daily Worker*, 20 January 1933.

81. 'Meerut Sentences Arouse Anger', *Daily Worker*, 18 January 1933.

82. 'League against Imperialism Active to Release Meerut Prisoners', *Daily Worker*, 21 January 1933.

83. Petersson, 'The "Colonial Conference"', p. 106.

84. 'LAI British Section, Report of 2nd Annual Conference Held May 21st and 22nd, Friars Hall, London', p. 1, Bridgeman Papers, Hull University Archives, U DBN25/1.

85. The LAI's Meerut activities, reported by Bridgeman to the British Section's Second Annual Conference in 1932, included meetings, demonstrations, fundraising for the Prisoner Relief Fund, and publishing pamphlets, petitions and open letters.

86. Reginald Bridgeman, 'The Meerut Conspiracy Case: Open Letter to Delegates of the 31st Annual Conference of the Labour Party (5–9 October 1931)', dated 29 September 1931, Bridgeman Papers, Hull University Archives, U DBN19/1. The document dwells at some length on the resistance put up by Indian workers through strikes and agitation in the period 1920–29.

87. Ibid.

88. 'A Socialist Dandy', *Evening Standard*, 15 January 1929, Saklatvala Papers, D1173/3.

89. John Saville, 'Reginald Bridgeman', in Joyce M. Bellamy and John Saville, eds, *The Dictionary of Labour Biography* (London: Palgrave MacMillan, 1972).

90. *Daily Star*, 'An Aesthetic Socialist', 23 November 1927; no title, clipping from *Daily Record and Daily Mail*, 25 November 1927, Bridgeman Papers U DBN 6/1.

91. A recent two-volume history offers a compendious and painstaking account of the inner workings of the LAI over its short lifespan. See Fredrik Petersson, *Willi Münzenberg, the League against Imperialism and the Comintern, 1925–1933*, 2 vols (Lewiston: Queenston Press, 2013).

92. Stafford Cripps, *Empire* (London: India League, 1938), p. 11, Bridgeman personal copy, Bridgeman Papers U DBN 27/5.

93. Bridgeman to Noel Baker, 3 December 1938, Bridgeman Papers, U DBN 27/4.

94. See Bridgeman Papers U DBN/22, which contains papers pertaining to his speaking engagements.

95. Clemens Dutt, 'The Colonial Policy of the Labour and Socialist International', *Anti-imperialist Review* 1: 1 (July 1928), p. 14.

96. Ibid., p. 15.

97. The Covenant of the League of Nations, available at the Avalon Project at the Lillian Goldman Law Library at Yale Law School, at avalon.law.yale.edu.

98. For an informative account of the Mandates system, see Susan Pedersen, *The Guardians: The League of Nations and the Crisis of Empire* (New York: Oxford University Press, 2015).

99. Reginald Bridgeman, 'Britain and the System of Colonial Mandates', unpublished TS (n.d. [possibly 1934/1935]), Bridgeman Papers, 2. U DBN/26/1.

100. 'League against Imperialism and for National Independence (British Section), Fifth Annual Conference, Saturday and Sunday, January 25th and 26th 1936', Bridgeman Papers, Hull University Archives, U DBN 25/1.

101. Susan Pedersen, *Guardians*, p. 3.

102. Ibid., p. 5.

103. Petersson, *Willi Münzenberg*, vol. 1, p. 88. For another account of the organization's founding moment and subsequent history, see Vijay Prashad, *The Darker Nations: A People's History of the Third World* (New York, London: New Press, 2007).

104. Willi Münzenberg, 'From Demonstration to Organisation', *Anti-imperialist Review* 1: 1 (July 1928), p. 10.

105. 'Report of the First Annual Conference of the League against Imperialism (British Section), 1931', Bridgeman Papers, Hull History Centre, U DBN/25/1.

106. Saville, 'Reginald Bridgeman', in Bellamy and Saville, *Dictionary of Labour Biography*, p. 47.
107. Michele L. Louro, 'Where National Revolutionary Ends and Communist Begins: The League against Imperialism and the Meerut Conspiracy Case', *Comparative Studies of South Asia, Africa and the Middle East* 33: 3 (2013), p. 335.
108. Louro argues that, for the British Section of the LAI 'from 1929 to 1933, the Meerut Conspiracy Case consumed nearly all of its time and resources'. Ibid., p. 339.
109. J. Ayodele Langley, *Pan-Africanism and Nationalism in West Africa, 1900–1945: A Study in Ideology and Social Classes* (Oxford: Clarendon, 1973), pp. 301–2. For more on Senghor, see also David Murphy, 'Defending the "Negro Race": Lamine Senghor and Black Internationalism in Interwar France', *French Cultural Studies* 24: 2 (2013), pp. 161–73.
110. Ibid., p. 305.
111. Cited in Petersson, *Willi Münzenberg*, vol. 1, p. 272.
112. J. R. Campbell, 'J. R. Campbell, Introducing the Resolution on IMPERIALISM & WAR, Nov 1934', unpublished, Bridgeman Papers, U DBN/25/4, p. 5.
113. James Maxton, 'Foreword', *Anti-imperialist Review* 1: 1 (July 1928), p. 1.
114. Münzenberg, 'From Demonstration to Organisation', *Anti-Imperialist Review* 1:1 (July 1928), p. 8.
115. Petersson, *Willi Münzenberg*, vol. 2, p. 974.
116. Fenner Brockway, 'The Coloured People's International', *New Leader*, 26 August 1927.
117. Fenner Brockway, 'At the International', *New Leader*, 16 September 1927.
118. Ibid.
119. Brockway, 'Coloured People's International'.
120. Fenner Brockway, 'At Brussels', *New Leader*, 18 February 1927.
121. Brockway, 'Coloured People's International'.
122. Ibid.
123. George Lansbury, 'A Great Week-End at Brussels', *Lansbury's Labour Weekly*, 19 February 1927. Reprinted in the *Canton Gazette*, 25 March 1927.
124. Ibid.
125. Ibid.
126. Ibid.
127. Ibid.
128. Ibid.
129. Ibid.
130. Ibid.

131. Pedersen, *Guardians*, p. 112.

132. Ibid., p. 78; Dantés Bellegarde, cited in ibid., p. 84.

133. Ibid., p. 92.

134. Ibid., p. 93.

135. Christian Høgsbjerg rightly notes that assumptions about such durability and legitimacy were hegemonic among progressive British intellectuals of the period, and cites Lansbury's own later insistence (in 1934) that there could be no immediate decolonization even under a socialist government. This was, of course, a retreat from the insight Lansbury articulates here, representing his own retrenchment from the LAI into Labour conservatism. But the point still remains: the moment of the LAI represents a fracture in the hegemon. See Christian Høgsbjerg, *C. L. R. James in Imperial Britain* (Durham, NC: Duke University Press, 2014), p. 201.

136. 'Report of the National Conference of the League against Imperialism (British Section), February 1931', Bridgeman Papers, Hull University Archives, U DBN25/1.

137. Conrad Noel, *The Meaning of Imperialism* (London: League against Imperialism, 1928), p. 7.

138. Ibid., pp. 13, 2.

139. Ibid., p. 2.

140. Ibid., p. 3.

141. Ibid., p. 4.

142. Ibid., p. 5.

143. Ibid., p. 6.

144. Ibid., p. 12.

145. Ibid.

146. Ibid.

147. Cited in ibid., p. 15.

148. Ibid.

149. J. R. Campbell, 'J. R. Campbell, Introducing a Resolution on Imperialism and War, Nov 1934', unpublished, Bridgeman Papers, U DBN/25/4]

150. *The Colonies and Oppressed Nations in the Struggle for Freedom: Resolutions Adopted by the Executive Committee of the League against Imperialism and for National Independence* (Berlin: International Secretariat of the League against Imperialism, 1931), p. 3, in Bridgeman Papers, U DBN/25/1.

151. Ibid., p. 9.

152. Ibid.

153. Ibid., pp. 4–5.

154. Ibid., p. 5. The Special Restriction (Coloured Alien Seamen) Order, 18 March 1925, stated that "coloured" seamen who did not

possess documentary proof of their status as British must register as 'aliens' in Britain. National Archives, Kew, HO 45/12314.

155. See Petersson, *Willi Münzenberg*, especially vol. 2, for a very thorough if rather cluttered account of the various machinations and movements that brought the organization to its final end in 1937.

156. Ibid., p. 976.

157. Petersson, 'The "Colonial Conference"', p. 75.

7. Black Voices Matter

1. Pan-African Association, 'Address to the Nations of the World by the Pan-African Conference in London, 1900', in J. Ayodele Langley, ed., *Ideologies of Liberation in Black Africa 1856–1970: Documents on Modern African Political Thought from Colonial Times to the Present* (London: Rex Collins, 1979), pp. 738–9.

2. Owen Charles Mathurin, *Henry Sylvester Williams and the Origins of the Pan-African Movement, 1869–1911* (Westport, CT: Greenwood, 1976). Mathurin suggests that the first use of the term 'pan-African' is to be found in a letter written by Williams in 1899 with reference to the upcoming conference. Ibid., pp. 46, 52.

3. Ibid., p. 54.

4. Jonathan Derrick, *Africa's Agitators: Militant Anti-colonialism in Africa and the West, 1918–1939* (London: Hurst, 2008), p. 23.

5. 'Report of the Pan-African Conference', cited in Mathurin, *Henry Sylvester Williams*, p. 56.

6. W. E. B. Du Bois et al., 'Address to the Nations of the World by the Pan-African Conference in London, 1900', in Langley, ed., *Ideologies of Liberation*, p. 738.

7. Ibid.

8. Ibid., p. 739.

9. Ibid., p. 738.

10. Ibid, my emphasis.

11. Ibid.

12. Ibid., pp. 738–9.

13. Ibid., p. 739.

14. Ibid.

15. Laura A. Winkiel, *Modernism, Race and Manifestos* (Cambridge: Cambridge University Press, 2008), pp. 34, 27.

16. Pan-African Association, 'The London Manifesto (29 August 1921)', in Langley, *Ideologies of Liberation*, p. 748.

17. Ibid., p. 748.

18. Ibid., p. 750.

19. Ibid., p. 749.

20. Ibid.
21. Ibid., p. 750.
22. Ibid., p. 749.
23. Ibid., p. 750.
24. Ibid.
25. Ibid.
26. Ibid.
27. Ibid., p. 751.
28. Ibid.
29. Ibid.
30. Ibid.
31. Ibid., p. 752.
32. Ibid.
33. Ibid., p. 751.
34. Ibid.
35. The phrase 'rebel sojourner' that appears in the subheading is Wayne F. Cooper's. See his *Claude McKay, Rebel Sojourner in the Harlem Renaissance* (Baton Rouge: Louisiana State University Press, 1996).
36. Pan-African Association, 'London Manifesto', p. 751.
37. Satnam Virdee, *Racism, Class and the Racialized Outsider* (London: Palgrave, 2014), p. 74.
38. E. D. Morel, 'Black Scourge in Europe', *Daily Herald*, 10 April 1920. The subheadings on the front page included: 'Sexual Horror Let Loose by France on the Rhine', 'Disappearance of Young German Girls' and 'A Deliberate Policy'.
39. Ibid.
40. Ibid.
41. Ibid., emphasis in original.
42. R. C. Reinders, 'Racialism on the Left: E. D. Morel and the Black Horror on the Rhine', *International Review of Social History* 13: 1 (April 1968), p. 4. This is a full – and damning – account of Morel's pamphlet and its reception.
43. Morel, 'Black Scourge in Europe'.
44. Ibid.
45. E. D. Morel, 'Black Scourge in Europe', *Daily Herald*, 10 April 1920.
46. 'Black Peril on the Rhine: Wave of Indignation', *Daily Herald*, 12 April 1920.
47. Morel, 'Black Scourge in Europe'.
48. 'Brutes in French Uniform', *Daily Herald*, 13 April 1920.
49. Reinders, 'Racialism on the Left', p. 2.
50. Reinders offers a full list. Ibid., p. 7.
51. As just one example, the entry for Morel in the left-wing encyclopedia *Spartacus Educational* (spartacus-educational.com) also fails to refer to the 'Black Scourge' affair.

52. 'Democratic Control, Debate on Labour's Foreign Policy, the Black Troops', *Daily Herald*, 26 April 1920.

53. E. D. Morel, *The Horror on the Rhine, with a Preface by Arthur Ponsonby and New Foreword by the Author*, 8th edn (London: Union of Democratic Control, 1921), p. 23.

54. Barbara Foley, cited in Gene Andrew Jarrett, 'Introduction', in Claude McKay, *A Long Way from Home* (New Brunswick, NJ: Rutgers University Press, 2007), p. xxv.

55. Claude McKay, 'A Black Man Replies', in Wayne Cooper, ed., *The Passion of Claude McKay: Selected Prose and Poetry, 1912–1948* (New York: Schocken Books, 1973), pp. 55–6.

56. Ibid., p. 55.

57. Ibid.

58. Reinders notes that, many years later, McKay explained that he believed the Second International's fear that French militarism would destroy the German Social Democrats is what may have motivated the turn to race by Morel and others – the knowledge that an appeal to racial solidarity would be the only hope in the face of widespread anti-Germanism in Britain. Reinders, 'Racialism on the Left', p. 26.

59. McKay, 'A Black Man Replies', p. 56.

60. Ibid.

61. Ibid.

62. For a thorough account of these see Jacqueline Jenkinson, *Black 1919: Riots, Racism and Resistance in Imperial Britain* (Liverpool: Liverpool University Press, 2009). Jenkinson cites a letter from the African Races Association of Glasgow which condemns 'the unwarrantable attacks that have been made upon men of colour, without exception, as one common herd of inferior beings', also asking pertinently: 'Did not some of these men fight on the same battlefields with white men to defeat the same enemy and make secure the British Empire?' (p. 8).

63. Ibid., p. 4.

64. Virdee, *Racism, Class, and the Racialized Outsider*, p. 79.

65. McKay, *A Long Way from Home*, pp. 75.

66. Ibid.

67. Ibid.

68. Claude McKay, letter to Nancy Cunard, 18 September 1932, Harry Ransom Center Nancy Cunard Papers (hereafter HRC) 17.1.

69. Wayne F. Cooper and Robert C. Reinders, 'A Black Briton Comes "Home": Claude McKay in England, 1920', *Race and Class* 9: 1 (1967), pp. 80, 79.

70. Ibid., p. 80.

71. McKay, *A Long Way from Home*, p. 76.

72. Ibid.

73. Ibid., p. 68. He sought refuge in two clubs, one 'for colored soldiers' in a basement in Drury Lane which he felt obliged to withdraw from after describing in print the 'patronizing white maternal attitude toward her colored charges' of the Englishwoman who ran it. Ibid., p. 67–8.

74. McKay, letter to Nancy Cunard, 30 April 1932, HRC 17.1.

75. McKay, *A Long Way from Home*, p. 78.

76. Ibid., p. 77.

77. Ibid., p. 78.

78. Ibid., p. 61.

79. Claude McKay, 'Socialism and the Negro', in Cooper, ed., *Passion of Claude McKay*, p. 54.

80. Ibid.

81. Ibid., p. 51.

82. Ibid.

83. Ibid., p. 53–4.

84. Ibid., p. 54.

85. Leon Lopez, 'The Yellow Peril and the Dockers', *Workers Dreadnought* VII: 30 (16 October 1920).

86. Ibid.

87. Jarrett, 'Introduction', in McKay, *A Long Way from Home*, p. xxvii.

88. Cited in Winston James, 'A Race Outcast from an Outcast Class: Claude McKay's Experience and Analysis of Britain', in Bill Schwarz, ed., *West Indian Intellectuals in Britain* (Manchester: Manchester University Press, 2003), p. 85, emphasis in original.

89. Ibid., p. 72.

90. 'Stabbing Negroes in the London Dock Area', editorial, *Workers Dreadnought* VI: 11 (7 June 1919).

91. 'The Indian Reform Bill', editorial, *Workers Dreadnought* VI: 12 (14 June 1919).

92. 'India and Ireland: India Going Sinn Fein', *Workers Dreadnought* VIII: 43 (7 January 1922).

93. Cited in Mary Davis, *Sylvia Pankhurst: A Life in Radical Politics* (London: Pluto, 1999), p. 106.

94. Sylvia Pankhurst, *India and the Earthly Paradise* (Bombay: Sunshine, 1926), pp. 637–8.

95. McKay to Cunard, 1 December 1931, HRC 17.1, emphasis in original. Also cited in Lois Gordon, *Nancy Cunard: Heiress, Muse, Political Idealist* (New York: Columbia University Press, 2007), p. 164.

96. Jane Marcus, *Hearts of Darkness: White Women Write Race* (New Brunswick, NJ: Rutgers University Press, 2004). Marcus writes, correctly, that Cunard has too often been dismissed as an eccentric wealthy aristocrat whose sole claim to fame is her bohemianism:

'When the stories of African anticolonial struggles are finally written, perhaps it is here she will find her place in history' (p. 122). She also has a place in the histories of anti-racism in Britain and the United States.

97. For a fuller picture of the Scottsboro campaign in Britain and key figures associated with it, see Susan D. Pennybacker's excellent detailed study, *From Scottsboro to Munich: Race and Political Culture in 1930s Britain* (Princeton: Princeton University Press, 2009). Another LAI figure who was visible in the Scottsboro campaign was Willi Münzenberg, in addition to many other communists including Saklatvala.

98. For an account of how *Negro* sits within a wider modernist anthological culture, see Peter J. Kalliney, *Commonwealth of Letters: British Literary Culture and the Emergence of Postcolonial Aesthetics* (Oxford: Oxford University Press, 2013), especially Chapter 2, 'Race and Anthologies'.

99. Brent Hayes Edwards, *The Practice of Diaspora: Literature, Translation, and the Rise of Black Internationalism* (Cambridge, MA: Harvard University Press, 2003), p. 310.

100. Nancy Cunard to Dorothy Padmore, 'For Dorothy', HRC 17.10.

101. Edwards, *Practice of Diaspora*, p. 310.

102. Irina Rasmussen Goloubeva, 'Curating Art, Rewriting World History: Nancy Cunard's *Negro: An Anthology* (1934)', in Margrét Gunnarsdóttir Champion and Irina Rasmussen Goloubeva, eds, *Ethics and Poetics: Ethical Recognitions and Social Reconfigurations in Modern Narratives* (Newcastle: Cambridge Scholars, 2014), p. 283.

103. Cited in Hugh Ford, ed., *Nancy Cunard: Brave Poet, Indomitable Rebel, 1896–1965* (New York: Chilton Book Company, 1968), p. 114. Cited in Gordon, *Nancy Cunard*, p. 156.

104. Laura A. Winkiel, 'Nancy Cunard's Negro and the Transnational Politics of Race', *Modernism/Modernity* 13: 3 (September 2006), p. 513.

105. Alain Locke to Cunard, 14 April 1934, HRC 20.10.

106. Marcus, *Hearts of Darkness*, p. 123. Marcus is eloquent on Cunard's centrality to modernism as a 'living network, a one-woman permanent walking demonstration against racism and fascism, and a celebrant of black culture in all its forms. She had a voice in shaping many of the competing and conflicting discourses of modernism, but in their histories there is only the marginal trace of a husky whisper, a streak of kohl across those hooded piercing eyes, remembered in a malicious footnote, and a stunning visual history in photographs, portraits, and sculpture by major and minor modernist artists' (ibid.). Marcus argues that Cunard

changed art history by pioneering 'the revaluation of ethnic objects as art for museums and private collectors' (p. 126).

107. Ibid., p. 128.

108. HRC 10.8 contains several of these offensive letters that Cunard kept.

109. Alan Warren Friedman, 'Introduction', in Alan Warren Friedman, ed., *Beckett in Black and Red: The Translations for Nancy Cunard's Negro (1934)* (Lexington: University Press of Kentucky, 2014), p. xi.

110. Winkiel, 'Nancy Cunard's Negro', p. 515.

111. Winkiel, *Modernism, Race and Manifestos*, p. 162.

112. Robin D. G. Kelley, ' "But a Local Phase of a World Problem": Black History's Global Vision, 1883–1950', *Journal of American History* 86: 3 (December 1999), *The Nation and Beyond: Transnational Perspectives on United States History – A Special Issue*, p. 1,055.

113. Cunard, 'Review of *Africa Answers Back*', undated typescript, probably 1934 or 1935, HRC 8.6.

114. Cunard to the *Spectator* and Lothrop Stoddard, probably 6 June 1931, HRC 10.6.

115. James (Ford?) to Cunard, 2 April 1934, HRC 20.10.

116. Hughes to Cunard, HRC 15.11.

117. Cited in Anne Chisholm, *Nancy Cunard* (London: Sidgwick & Jackson, 1979), p. 191.

118. McKay to Cunard, 20 August 1932, HRC 17.1.

119. Hugh Ford, 'Introduction', in Cunard, *Negro*, p. xi.

120. A shortened version of the anthology was published in 1970 by Hugh Ford.

121. For more on Beckett's work with the anthology, see Friedman, *Beckett in Black and Red*.

122. Eugene Gordon to Cunard, 7 June 1934, HRC 20.10, emphasis in original.

123. Langston Hughes, 'Always the Same', in Cunard, *Negro*, p. 427.

124. Cunard, 'Black Man and White Ladyship: An Anniversary', in Maureen Moyhagh, ed., *Essays on Race and Empire* (Calgary: Broadview, 2002), p. 195.

125. Cited in Chisholm, *Nancy Cunard*, p. 192, and Hugh Ford, 'Introduction', in Cunard, *Negro*, p. xvii.

126. For a fuller account of the contents of the anthology, see 'Coda', in Edwards, *Practice of Diaspora*.

127. Cited in Robin D. G. Kelley, 'Introduction', in Aimé Césaire, *Discourse on Colonialism*, transl. Joan Pinkham, ed. Robin D. G. Kelley (New York: Monthly Review, 2000), pp. 25–6.

128. 'Curating Art, Rewriting World History', in Champion and Goloubeva, *Ethics and Poetics*, p. 275.

129. Ibid., p. 276.

130. Friedman, 'Introduction', in Friedman, ed., *Beckett in Black and Red*, p. xxxi.

131. Raymond Michelet, 'Nancy Cunard', in Hugh Ford, ed., *Nancy Cunard*, p. 128.

132. Kalliney, 'Cunard, Hughes, McKay, Pound', p. 73.

133. Nancy Cunard, foreword to Cunard, *Negro*, p. iv.

134. Ford, 'Introduction', p. xii.

135. Ibid., p. xiii–xiv.

136. Edwards, *Practice of Diaspora*.

137. Cunard, 'Foreword', p. iii.

138. Ibid., p. iii.

139. Ibid., p. iv.

140. Ibid., p. iii.

141. Ibid.

142. Winkiel, *Modernism, Race and Manifestos*, 175.

143. Ibid., p. iv.

144. Langston Hughes, introduction to Cunard, *Negro*, p. 4.

145. Taylor Gordon, 'Malicious Lies Magnifying the Truth', in Cunard, *Negro*, p. 79.

146. Ibid., p. 80.

147. John Frederick Matheus, 'Some Aspects of the Negro Interpreted in Contemporary American and European Literature', in Cunard, *Negro*, p. 108.

148. 'Nat Turner – Revolutionist', in Cunard, *Negro*, p. 14.

149. W. E. Burghardt Du Bois, 'Black America', in Cunard, *Negro*, p. 149.

150. Ibid., p. 150.

151. Ibid., p. 150.

152. Michel-Rolph Trouillot, *Silencing the Past: Power and the Production of History* (Boston: Beacon, 1995), p. 104.

153. Nancy Cunard, 'A Reactionary Negro Organisation', in Cunard, *Negro*, p. 146, emphasis in original.

154. James W. Ford, 'Communism and the Negro', in Cunard, *Negro*, p. 281.

155. Ibid., p. 284.

156. Ibid.

157. Ibid.

158. Nancy Cunard, 'Jamaica – the Negro Island', in Cunard, *Negro*, p. 449, emphasis in original.

159. Nancy Cunard, 'The Colour Bar', in Cunard, *Negro*, p. 552.

160. Ibid., p. 554.

161. George Padmore, 'Race Prejudice in England', in Cunard, *Negro*, p. 555.

162. Ibid.

163. George Padmore, 'Ethiopia Today: The Making of a Modern State', in Cunard, *Negro*, p. 612.

164. Ibid., p. 613.

165. Ben. N. Azikiwe, 'Liberia: Slave or Free?', in Cunard, *Negro*, p. 780.

166. Ibid., p. 781.

167. Ibid., p. 783.

168. George S. Schuyler, 'Black Civilisation and White', in Cunard, *Negro*, p. 785.

169. Ibid., p. 785.

170. Johnstone Kenyatta, 'Kenya', in Cunard, *Negro*, p. 805.

171. The Surrealist Group in Paris, 'Murderous Humanitarianism', transl. Samuel Beckett, in Cunard, *Negro*, p. 574. Signatories included André Breton, Roger Caillois and René Crevel.

172. T. K. Utchay, 'White-Manning in West Africa', in Cunard, *Negro*, p. 762.

173. Ibid.

174. Ibid., p. 765.

175. Ibid.

176. Ibid.

177. Raymond Michelet, 'African Empires and Civilisations', in Cunard, *Negro*, p. 598.

178. Michelet, '"Primitive" Life and Mentality', in Cunard, *Negro*, p. 739.

179. Ibid.

180. Ibid.

181. Ibid., p. 740.

182. Ibid.

183. Césaire, *Discourse on Colonialism*, p. 56.

184. Michelet, '"Primitive" Life and Mentality', in Cunard, *Negro*, p. 740.

185. Ibid.

186. Ibid., p. 742.

187. Césaire, *Discourse on Colonialism*, p. 69.

188. Michelet, '"Primitive" Life and Mentality', p. 745, emphasis in original.

189. Ibid., p. 746

190. Ibid., p. 747.

191. Ibid., 761.

192. Frantz Fanon, *A Dying Colonialism*, transl. Haakon Chevalier (New York: Grove, 1965), p. 125.

193. Raymond Michelet, 'The White Man Is Killing Africa', in Cunard, *Negro*, p. 839.

194. For a more extended discussion of the Cunard–McKay exchange on the question of payment, see Kalliney, *Commonwealth of Letters*. It is difficult not to sympathize with both parties in this case: the black writer in straitened circumstances who insisted on his right to remuneration; the disinherited white woman editor who was working with no budget to speak of for what she saw as a vital political project, though also no doubt operating within an aristocratic model of prestige and patronage, as McKay suggested.

195. McKay to Nancy Cunard, 25 January 1933, HRC 17.1.

196. Sylvia Pankhurst, 'The Fascist World War', in Kathryn Dodd, ed., *A Sylvia Pankhurst Reader* (Manchester: Manchester University Press, 1993), p. 215. First published in *New Times and Ethiopia News*, 1 August 1936.

197. Cited in Davis, *Sylvia Pankhurst*, 100.

198. Ibid., p. 111.

199. Nancy Cunard, untitled, HRC 8.6.

200. Ibid.

201. Ibid.

202. Cited in Gordon, *Nancy Cunard*, p. 374.

203. McKay to Cunard, 20 August 1932, HRC 17.1; Chisholm, *Nancy Cunard*, p. 222.

8. Internationalizing African Opinion

1. Kwame Nkrumah, *Ghana: Autobiography of Kwame Nkrumah* (Edinburgh: Thomas Nelson, 1957), p. 27.

2. Ibid.

3. Brent Hayes Edwards, *The Practice of Diaspora: Literature, Translation, and the Rise of Black Internationalism* (Cambridge, MA: Harvard University Press, 2003), p. 246.

4. Minkah Makalani, *In the Cause of Freedom: Radical Black Internationalism from Harlem to London, 1917–1939* (Chapel Hill, NC: University of North Carolina Press, 2011), p. 194.

5. Christian Høgsbjerg, *C. L. R. James in Imperial Britain* (London/ Durham NC: Duke University Press, 2014), p. 9.

6. Roderick J. Macdonald, '"The Wisers Who Are Far Away": The Role of London's Black Press in the 1930s and 1940s', in Jagdish S. Gundara and Ian Duffield, eds, *Essays on the History of Blacks in Britain* (Aldershot: Avebury, 1992), p. 151. Black-run journals included *The Keys*, issued by the moderate organization the

League of Coloured Peoples, while the *New Times and Ethiopia News*, edited by Pankhurst, had a significant number of black contributors.

7. James Walvin, *Black and White: The Negro and English Society, 1555–1945* (London: Allen Lane, 1973), p. 212.

8. 'Editorial: An Open Letter to West Indian Intellectuals', *International African Opinion* 1: 7 (May–June 1939).

9. Tony Martin, *Amy Ashwood Garvey: Pan-Africanist, Feminist, and Mrs Marcus Garvey No.1; or, a Tale of Two Amys* (Dover, MA: Majority Press, 2007), p. 143.

10. Ibid.

11. Gary Wilder, *Freedom Time: Negritude, Decolonization, and the Future of the World* (Durham, NC: Duke University Press, 2015), pp. 9–10.

12. Bill Schwarz, 'George Padmore', in Bill Schwarz, ed., *West Indian Intellectuals in Britain* (Manchester: Manchester University Press, 2003), p. 138. Schwarz's description here is specifically of Padmore's work.

13. Wilder is succinct and elegant on this point, noting of Césaire and Senghor among others: 'These black thinkers also produced important abstract and general propositions about life, humanity, history, and the world'. Wilder, *Freedom Time*, p. 100.

14. To read Haile Selassie's powerful 1936 speech at the League of Nations, see Haile Selassie, 'Appeal to the League of Nations', June 1936, available at mtholyoke.edu.

15. Ibid.

16. Robbie Shilliam notes that, in December 1935, 'details of a secret pact were made public wherein Britain and France had proposed to grant Italy significant territories in Ethiopia'. There was a public furore about this, forcing the resignation of Foreign Secretary Samuel Hoare. Robbie Shilliam, 'Ethiopianism, Englishness, Britishness: Struggles over Imperial Belonging', *Citizenship Studies* 20: 2 (2016), p. 246.

17. Frank Hardie, *The Abyssinian Crisis* (London: Batsford, 1974), p. 6. Hooker discusses the tendency even of sympathizers 'to talk of Africa as a European problem, as a piece of territory coveted by some white nations and controlled by others'. James R. Hooker, *Black Revolutionary: George Padmore's path from Communism to Pan-Africanism* (London: Pall Mall, 1967), p. 45. Padmore, representing the IAFE, apparently rebuked a conference called by the National Peace Council thus: 'you discuss the redivision of Africa to satisfy discontented nations like Germany and Italy, but the views and opinions of the Africans themselves are not solicited. It may have been nothing more than an oversight on your part, but it

certainly does not establish much confidence among the people of Africa'. Ibid.

18. Cited in C. L. R. James, 'Black Intellectuals in Britain', in Bhikhu Parekh, ed., *Colour, Culture and Consciousness: Immigrant Intellectuals in Britain* (London: Allen & Unwin, 1974), p. 159.

19. Ibid., p. 161.

20. Makonnen, *Pan-Africanism*, pp. 116–17.

21. C. L. R. James, 'Abyssinia and the Imperialists', in Anna Grimshaw, ed., *The C. L. R. James Reader* (London: Wiley-Blackwell, 1992), p. 63.

22. Ibid., p. 64.

23. Ibid., p. 66.

24. Ibid.

25. It is worth noting, however, that there was disagreement about how to deal with the situation. James opposed League of Nations sanctions against Italy, calling instead for 'workers sanctions'.

26. Robert G. Weisbord, 'British West Indian Reaction to the Italian–Ethiopian War: An Episode in Pan-Africanism', *Caribbean Studies* 10: 1 (April 1970), p. 34.

27. Marc Matera, *Black London: The Imperial Metropolis and Decolonization in the Twentieth Century* (Oakland, CA: University of California Press, 2015), p. 6.

28. Ibid., p. 3.

29. Ibid., p. 98.

30. Cedric J. Robinson, 'The African Diaspora and the Italo-Ethiopian Crisis', *Race and Class* 27: 2 (1985), p. 60.

31. Cited in S. K. B. Asante, *Pan-African Protest: West Africa and the Italo-Ethiopian Crisis, 1934–1941* (London: Longman, 1977), p. 202.

32. C. L. R. James, 'Is This Worth a War?', in *At the Rendezvous of Victory: Selected Writings* (London: Allison & Busby, 1984), pp. 15–16.

33. Ibid., p. 16.

34. A report of a speech given by James at the LCP's 1933 conference, cited Høgsbjerg, *C. L. R. James in Imperial Britain*, p. 66.

35. Cited in ibid., p. 87.

36. Ras Makonnen, *Pan-Africanism from Within* (Nairobi/London: Oxford University Press, 1973), pp. 114–15.

37. Davarian L. Baldwin, 'Introduction: New Negroes Forging a New World', in Davarian L. Baldwin and Minkah Makalani, eds, *Escape from New York: The New Negro Renaissance beyond Harlem* (Minneapolis: Minnesota University Press, 2013), pp. 4–5.

38. Anthony Bogues, *Caliban's Freedom: The Early Political Thought of C. L. R. James* (London: Pluto, 1997), p. 80.

39. *International African Opinion* 1: 2 (1938), quoted from back cover.
40. Stafford Cripps, 'Foreword', in George Padmore, *Africa and World Peace* (London: Secker & Warburg, 1937), p. ix.
41. Ibid., pp. 117–18.
42. 'Editorial', *International African Opinion* 1: 1 (July 1938). For a fuller account of the publishing activities mentioned here, see Carol Polsgrove, *Ending British Rule in Africa: Writers in a Common Cause* (Manchester: Manchester University Press, 2009).
43. Cited in Asante, *Pan-African Protest*, p. 205.
44. Eric Williams, *The Negro in the Caribbean*, foreword by George Padmore (Manchester: Panaf Service/International African Serice Bureau Publications, 1942). Quoted from back cover.
45. Edwards also lists Peter Milliard, William Harrison, Laminah Sankoh, Chris Jones and Babalola Wilkey as key members. See Edwards, *Practice of Diaspora*, p. 299.
46. Cedric J. Robinson, 'Black Intellectuals at the British Core: 1920s–1940s', in Gundara and Duffield, *Essays on the History of Blacks in Britain*, p. 180.
47. C. L. R. James, *Beyond a Boundary*, 50th anniversary edn, with an introduction by Robert Lipsyte (Durham NC: Duke University Press, 2013), p. 111.
48. Stephen Howe, 'C. L. R. James: Visions of History, Visions of Britain', in Schwarz ed., *West Indian Intellectuals in Britain*, pp. 168, 165.
49. Schwarz, 'George Padmore', pp. 145–6.
50. Cited in Makalani, *In the Cause of Freedom*, p. 205.
51. Cited in Høgsbjerg, *James in Imperial Britain*, p. 71.
52. For an interesting account of James's relationship to labour rebellions of the 1930s, see Christian Høgsbjerg, '"A Thorn in the Side of Great Britain": C. L. R. James and the Caribbean Labour Rebellions of the 1930s', *Small Axe* 15: 2 (July 2011).
53. *International African Opinion* 1: 1 (July 1938).
54. 'Why Such a Bureau?', *IASB Broadsheet*, cited in Asante, *Pan-African Protest*, p. 204.
55. Makalani, *In the Cause of Freedom*, p. 218. The pamphlets that came out formally under the aegis of the IASB include *The West Indies Today*, *Hands off the Protectorates*, *The Negro in the Caribbean* and *Kenya: Land of Conflict*.
56. James, 'Black Intellectuals in Britain', p. 161.
57. Macdonald, '"The Wisers Who Are Far Away"', p. 158.
58. Makalani, Matera and Edwards, among others, give enthusiastic praise to *International African Opinion*, but mention only a few highlights from its short run.
59. 'Editorial', *International African Opinion* 1: 1 (July 1938).

60. 'Editorial', *International African Opinion* 1: 1 (July 1938).
61. Ibid.
62. Ibid., emphasis in original.
63. Ibid.
64. Ibid.
65. Ibid., emphases in original.
66. Ibid.
67. Ibid.
68. George Padmore, 'Labour Unrest in Jamaica', *International African Opinion* 1: 1 (July 1938).
69. 'The Ethiopian Question', ibid.
70. 'The West Indian Royal Commission', *International African Opinion*, vol. 1, no. 2, August 1938.
71. Ibid.
72. 'Politics and the Negro', *International African Opinion* 1: 3 (September 1938).
73. Makalani, *In the Cause of Freedom*, p. 214.
74. H. Jeremy Curtis, 'Correspondence', *International African Opinion* 1: 2 (August 1938), p. 13.
75. The Executive Committee of the International African Service Bureau, 'Rejoinder to a Popular Retort', *International African Opinion* 1: 2 (August 1938), p. 14.
76. Ibid.
77. Ibid.
78. Macdonald, '"The Wisers Who Are Far Away"', p. 167.
79. George Padmore, 'Labour Unrest in Jamaica', *International African Opinion* 1: 1 (July 1938).
80. O. Nigel Bolland, *On the March: Labour Rebellions in the British Caribbean, 1934–39* (Kingston, Jamaica/London: I. Randle/J. Currey, 1995), p. 144.
81. Ibid., p. 145.
82. Ken Post, *Arise Ye Starvelings: The Jamaican Labour Rebellion of 1938 and Its Aftermath* (The Hague/Boston: Nijhoff, 1978), p. 296.
83. Bolland, *On the March*, p. 153.
84. Gordon K. Lewis, *The Growth of the Modern West Indies* (Kingston, Jamaica/Miami: Ian Randle Publishers, 2004), p. 82.
85. Butler's agitational methods, labelled 'extremist' and 'communistic' (despite his religious leanings), had unprecedented consequences when oilfield workers staged a stay-in strike for higher wages – actions then spreading across the island involving destruction of property and crowd violence. Black workers were joined by Indian ones demanding recognition of their unions, equal pay with whites, and forty-hour weeks (some suggest a share of the profits was also demanded).

86. C. L. R. James, *A History of Negro Revolt* (New York: Haskell House, 1969), p. 80.

87. Cedric J. Robinson, *Black Marxism: The Making of the Black Radical Tradition* (London/Chapel Hill, NC: University of North Carolina Press, 2000 [1983]), p. 273.

88. In addition to other works mentioned here, see Robert J. Alexander and Eldon M. Parker, *A History of Organized Labor in the English-Speaking West Indies* (Westport, CT: Praeger, 2004); O. Nigel Bolland, *The Politics of Labour in the British Caribbean: The Social Origins of Authoritarianism and Democracy in the Labour Movement* (Kingston, Jamaica/Oxford: Ian Randle Publishers/James Currey, 2001); and Richard Hart, *Caribbean Workers' Struggles* (London: Bogle L'Overture, 2012).

89. Richard Hart, *Labour Rebellions of the 1930s in the British Caribbean Region Colonies* (London: Socialist History Society, 2002), p. 24.

90. Post, *Arise Ye Starvelings*, p. 20.

91. Ibid., p. 148.

92. Cited in ibid., p. 193.

93. Cited in ibid., p. 372.

94. Bolland, *On the March*, p. 135.

95. Post, *Arise Ye Starvelings*, p. 206.

96. 'The African World: Barbados', *International African Opinion*, 1: 6 (February–March 1939).

97. Post, *Arise Ye Starvelings*, p. 297.

98. Ibid., p. 300.

99. 'The Ethiopian Question,' *International African Opinion* 1: 1 (July 1938).

100. 'Anti-imperialist Exhibition in Glasgow', *International African Opinion* 1: 1, July 1938.

101. 'The West Indian Royal Commission', *International African Opinion.*

102. 'Editorial: To the Delegates of the Trades Union Congress at Blackpool', *International African Opinion* 1: 3 (September 1938).

103. Ibid.

104. 'An Open Letter to West Indian Intellectuals', *International African Opinion*, 1:7 (May–June 1939).

105. Ibid.

106. Ibid.

107. Ibid.

108. Ibid.

109. 'Notes on the West Indies', *International African Opinion* 1: 1 (July 1938).

110. Ibid.

111. 'Editorial: Africa and World Peace', *International African Opinion* 1: 4 (October 1938).

112. 'Politics and the Negro', *International African Opinion* 1: 4 (October 1938).

113. International African Service Bureau, 'Manifesto against War', September 25, 1938; *International African Opinion* 1:4 (October 1938).

114. 'Politics and the Negro: Africa and the New Diaspora', *International African Opinion* 1: 3 (September 1938).

115. Ibid.

116. Ibid.

117. Makalani, *In the Cause of Freedom*, p. 204.

118. 'Editorial: Hitler and the Colonies', *International African Opinion* 1: 5 (November 1938).

119. Ibid.

120. Ibid.

121. Ibid.

122. Ibid.

123. Eric Williams, *The Negro in the Caribbean*, p. 52.

124. Ibid., p. 53.

125. Ibid., 57: 'At various periods before 1935 there had been labour unrest in the British West Indies and attempts at the formation of Workingmen's Associations. It is significant that one of the most important of these uprisings took place in Trinidad in 1919 during the international unrest which followed the World War.'

126. Ibid., p. 65.

127. George Padmore, 'Fascism in the Colonies', *Controversy* 2: 17 (February 1938).

128. International African Service Bureau, *The West Indies Today* (London: International African Service Bureau, 1956), p. 40.

129. Ibid., p. 41.

130. 'In carrying out this programme, the Bureau will be pleased to supply speakers to Labour Party Branches, Trade Unions, Co-operative Guilds, and other working-class and progressive organisations, in order to explain the present conditions under which the coloured populations in various parts of the Empire live'. Williams, *The Negro in the Caribbean*, quoted from 'What Is the International African Service Bureau', on inside back cover.

131. George Padmore, 'Manifesto against War', *International African Opinion* 1: 4 (October 1938).

132. C. L. R. James, *Nkrumah and the Ghana Revolution* (London: Allison & Busby, 1977), p. 69.

133. Edwards, *Practice of Diaspora*, p. 305.

134. Ibid.
135. Williams, *The Negro in the Caribbean*, p. 52.
136. James, *History of Negro Revolt*, pp. 5–6.
137. Ibid., p. 16.
138. Ibid., p. 18.
139. Ibid., p. 27.
140. Ibid., p. 45.
141. Ibid., p. 47
142. Walter Rodney, 'The African Revolution', in Paul Buhle, ed., *C. L. R. James: His Life and Work* (London: Allison & Busby, 1986), p. 32.
143. For a fuller account of such movements, see Michael Adas, *Prophets of Rebellion: Millenarian Protest Movements against European Colonial Order* (Cambridge: Cambridge University Press, 1979).
144. Rodney, 'African Revolution', pp. 34–5.
145. Ibid., p. 31.
146. James, *History of Negro Revolt*, p. 52.
147. Ibid., p. 62.
148. Ibid.
149. Ibid.
150. Ibid., p. 69.
151. Ibid., p. 71.
152. Ibid., p. 81.
153. Ibid.
154. Ibid.
155. Ibid., p. 83.
156. The Executive Committee of the International African Service Bureau, 'An open letter to the workers of the West Indies, British Guiana and the British Honduras', International African Opinion, vol. 1, no. 2, May–June 1939. Original emphasis. The letter was signed by Padmore, Makonnen, Kenyatta, James, Chris Jones, Peter Milliard, Laminah Sankoh, Babalola Wilkey and William Harrison.
157. Post, *Arise Ye Starvelings*, p. 238.
158. *The Times*, 4 May 1938, cited in ibid., p. 308.
159. Cited in Post, *Arise Ye Starvelings*, 330. 'By the end of August ... it was clear that the main response of the Colonial Office to the Jamaican labour rebellion was to accept it as final proof that some major action had to be taken to revise West Indian policy' (p. 336).
160. See ibid., p. 327.
161. Cited in Post, *Arise Ye Starvelings*, p. 367.
162. Arthur Calder-Marshall, *Glory Dead* (London: M. Joseph, 1939), p. 255. See also W. M. Macmillan, *Warning from the West Indies* (London: Faber & Faber, 1936).

163. W. Arthur Lewis, *Labour in the West Indies: The Birth of a Workers Movement* (London: New Beacon, 1977 [1939]), p. 41.

164. Ibid., pp. 18–19.

165. Ibid., p. 19.

166. Ibid., p. 40.

167. Ibid., my emphasis.

168. C. L. R. James, 'Notes on the Life of George Padmore', in Anna Grimshaw, ed., *The C. L. R. James Reader* (Oxford: Blackwell, 1992), pp. 294–5.

169. 'Between 1930 and 1945 all of us saw African emancipation as dependent upon the breakdown of imperialist power in Europe. Armed rebellion was sure to be crushed unless the imperialist powers were impotent; and this could only be the result of revolutions within the metropolitan powers themselves ... The need for a political reappraisal rose from the fact that, contrary to our pre-war speculations, nowhere had the proletariat of the metropolitan powers overthrown the imperialist state. The actual struggle of the Africans now had to depend on themselves alone.' Ibid., p. 294.

170. Makonnen, *Pan-Africanism*, p. 147.

9. Smash Our Own Imperialism

1. George Padmore to Nancy Cunard, n.d., Harry Ransom Centre, Nancy Cunard Papers (hereafter HRC) 17.10.

2. Nancy Cunard and George Padmore, 'The White Man's Duty: An Analysis of the Colonial Question in Light of the Atlantic Charter', in Maureen Moynagh, ed., *Essays on Race and Empire* (Peterborough, Ontario: Broadview, 2002), pp. 127–77.

3. Cunard and Padmore, 'White Man's Duty', p. 138.

4. Ibid., p. 139.

5. Ibid., p. 144.

6. Ibid., p. 160.

7. Ibid.

8. Ibid., p. 127.

9. Typescript of 'White Man's Duty', HRC 9.10.

10. Cunard and Padmore, 'White Man's Duty', p. 136.

11. Ibid.

12. Nancy Cunard and George Padmore, *The White Man's Duty* (London: W. H. Allen, 1942), front cover.

13. James R. Hooker, *Black Revolutionary: George Padmore's Path from Communism to Pan-Africanism* (London: Pall Mall, 1967), p. 12.

14. For more on this phase of Padmore's political career, see Imanuel

Geiss, *The Pan-African Movement*, transl. Ann Keep (London: Methuen, 1974).

15. Hooker, *Black Revolutionary*, pp. 17–18.

16. Leslie James, *George Padmore and Decolonization from Below: Pan-Africanism, the Cold War, and the End of Empire* (Basingstoke: Palgrave Macmillan, 2015), p. 5.

17. Robin D. G. Kelley, 'A Poetics of Anticolonialism', in Aimé Césaire, *Discourse on Colonialism*, transl. Joan Pinkham (New York: Monthly Review, 2000), p. 20.

18. Ibid.

19. 'George Padmore: Black Marxist Revolutionary', in C. L. R. James, *At the Rendezvous of Victory: Selected Writings* (London: Allison & Busby, 1984), p. 257.

20. James, *George Padmore and Decolonization from Below*, p. 11.

21. Susan D. Pennybacker, *From Scottsboro to Munich: Race and Political Culture in 1930s Britain* (Princeton: Princeton University Press, 2009); Minkah Makalani, *In the Cause of Freedom: Radical Black Internationalism from Harlem to London, 1917–1939* (Chapel Hill, NC: University of North Carolina Press, 2011); Carol Polsgrove, *Ending British Rule in Africa: Writers in a Common Cause* (Manchester: Manchester University Press, 2012); Brent Hayes Edwards, *The Practice of Diaspora: Literature, Translation, and the Rise of Black Internationalism* (Cambridge, MA: Harvard University Press, 2003); Fitzroy Baptiste and Rupert Lewis, ed., *George Padmore: Pan-African Revolutionary* (Kingston, Jamaica: Ian Randle, 2008).

22. C. L. R. James, 'Notes on the Life of George Padmore', in Anna Grimshaw, ed., *The C. L. R. James Reader* (Oxford: Blackwell, 1992), p. 290.

23. Cited in Anthony Bogues, 'C. L. R. James and George Padmore: The Ties That Bind – Black Radicalism and Political Friendship', in Baptiste and Lewis, *George Padmore*, p. 200.

24. Rupert Lewis, 'Introduction', in Baptiste and Lewis, *George Padmore*.

25. James, *George Padmore and Decolonization from Below*, p. 3.

26. Matera describes James's views as going 'beyond the cautious anti-imperialism of the ILP'. Marc Matera, *Black London: The Imperial Metropolis and Decolonization in the Twentieth Century* (Oakland, CA: University of California Press, 2015), p. 79. My suggestion here is that James, Padmore and others contributed to a degree of radicalization where the organization's engagement with the Empire was concerned.

27. As Cedric Robinson has noted, left politicians such as William Gallagher (of the Communist Party), Fenner Brockway and Reginald Sorensen were among those associated with the black intelligentsia

in Britain, who included, in addition to James and Padmore, Arnold Ward, Chris Jones, Ras Makonnen and Peter Blackman, among others. Cedric Robinson, *Black Marxism: The Making of the Black Radical Tradition* (London/Chapel Hill, NC: University of North Carolina Press, 1983), p. 261.

28. James, 'George Padmore: Black Marxist Revolutionary', in James, *At the Rendezvous of Victory*, p. 256.

29. Bert J. Thomas, 'George Padmore', in Thomas, ed., *The Struggle for Liberation: From Dubois to Nyerere* (New York: Theo Gaus, 1982), pp. 46–7.

30. George Padmore, 'Trusteeship – the New Imperialism', *New Leader*, 2 February 1946.

31. James, 'Notes on the Life of George Padmore', p. 293.

32. Peter Abrahams, *The Black Experience in the Twentieth Century: An Autobiography and Meditation* (Bloomington, IN: Indiana University Press, 2000), p. 38

33. Geiss, *Pan-African Movement*, p. 353.

34. Hooker, *Black Revolutionary*, p. 46.

35. Arnold Ward, cited in Makalani, *In the Cause of Freedom*, p. 185.

36. James, citing Padmore, in 'George Padmore: Black Marxist Revolutionary', p. 255.

37. Cited in Polsgrove, *Ending British Rule in Africa*, p. 4.

38. See James, 'George Padmore'.

39. Ibid., p. 254.

40. Cited in Hooker, *Black Revolutionary*, p. 31.

41. Ibid., p. 33.

42. James, 'George Padmore', p. 255.

43. Ibid.

44. James, 'Notes on the Life of George Padmore', p. 292.

45. George Padmore, *The Life and Struggles of Negro Toilers* (London: Red International Labour Unions Magazine for the International Trade Union Committee of Negro Workers, 1931), available at marxists.org.

46. James, *George Padmore and Decolonization from Below*, p. 22.

47. George Padmore to Cyril Olivierre, 11 December 1945, Padmore Papers, Schomburg Center for Research in Black Culture, MG.624.

48. Padmore, *Life and Struggles of Negro Toilers*.

49. George Padmore to Cyril Olivierre, 28 July 1934, Padmore Papers, MG.624.

50. James, *George Padmore and Decolonization from Below*, p. 28.

51. For an extensive discussion of Padmore's collaboration and friendship with Kouyaté, see Edwards, *Practice of Diaspora*, Chapter 5. Edwards writes that the two men developed an internationalist politics enabled by the Comintern in the first instance, but 'one

not wholly subsumed in a Comintern agenda, one that emphasizes race-based organizing and anti-colonial alliances among differently positioned revolutionaries of African descent' (p. 264).

52. James, 'Notes on the Life of George Padmore', p. 293.

53. See Hakim Adi, *West Africans in Britain: 1900–1960, Nationalism, Pan-Africanism and Communism* (London: Lawrence & Wishart, 1998), pp. 24–8.

54. James, 'Notes on the Life of George Padmore', p. 292.

55. Ibid., p. 293.

56. Nancy Cunard to Dorothy Padmore, 'For Dorothy', n.d., HRC 17.10.

57. Dorothy Padmore to Nancy Cunard, in ibid.

58. Cited in Nnamdi Azikiwe, *My Odyssey: An Autobiography* (London: C. Hurst, 1970), p. 198.

59. George Padmore, *How Britain Rules Africa* (London: Wishart, 1936), pp. 390–1.

60. Ibid., p. 391.

61. *Times Literary Supplement*, 27 June 1936, cited in Polsgrove, *Ending British Rule*, p. 17.

62. Padmore, *How Britain Rules Africa*, pp. 3–4.

63. Ibid., p. 4.

64. George Padmore to Otto Theis, cited in Polsgrove, *Ending British Rule in Africa*, p. 5.

65. Padmore, *How Britain Rules Africa*, p. 7.

66. Ibid.

67. Ibid.

68. Ibid., p. 9.

69. Ibid., p. 16.

70. Ibid., pp. 15–16.

71. Ibid.

72. Ibid., p. 17.

73. Ibid., p. 395.

74. C. L. R. James, '"Civilising" the "Blacks": Why Britain Needs to Maintain Her Colonial Possessions', *New Leader*, 29 May 1936.

75. Ibid.

76. Ibid.

77. Padmore, *How Britain Rules Africa*, p. 395. Polsgrove notes elegantly: 'Around the act of publication, a political community had formed.' This was, also, 'a collaborative work, an exercise in solidarity'. Polsgrove, *Ending British Rule in Africa*, p. 7.

78. Padmore, *How Britain Rules Africa*, pp. 395–6.

79. Ibid., p. 333.

80. Ibid.

81. Ibid., p. 335.

82. Ibid., p. 350.

83. Ibid., p. 360.

84. C. L. R. James, 'The Making of the Caribbean People', in C. L. R. James, *Spheres of Existence: Selected Writings* (London: Allison & Busby, 1980), p. 177.

85. Padmore, *How Britain Rules Africa*, p. 362.

86. Ibid., p. 363.

87. Ibid., pp. 394–5.

88. Gideon Cohen, *The Failure of a Dream: The Independent Labour Party from Disaffiliation to World War II* (London: Tauris Academic, 2007), p. 1.

89. Ibid.

90. Christian Høgsbjerg, 'C. L. R. James, George Orwell and "Literary Trotskyism"', *George Orwell Studies* 1: 2 (2017).

91. Sarah Britton, '"Come and See the Empire by the All Red Route!": Anti-imperialism and Exhibitions in Interwar Britain', *History Workshop Journal* 69: 1 (1 March 2010), p. 82.

92. Satnam Virdee, *Racism, Class, and the Racialised Outsider* (Basingstoke: Palgrave Macmillan, 2014), p. 83.

93. Ibid., p. 84.

94. 'National Liberation to Be Demanded in Empire', *New Leader*, 8 November 1941, p. 1.

95. James, *George Padmore and Decolonization from Below*, p. 29.

96. Ibid.

97. C. L. R James, 'Truth about "Peace Plan": Britain's Imperialist Game', *New Leader*, 20 December 1935.

98. Jomo Kenyatta, 'Hitler Could Not Improve on Kenya', *New Leader*, 21 May 1937.

99. Ibid.

100. George Padmore, 'Hands off the Colonies!', *New Leader*, 25 February 1938.

101. George Padmore, 'Whither the West Indies?', *New Leader*, 29 March 1941.

102. George Padmore, 'The Government's Betrayal of the Protectorates', *Controversy* 2: 21 (June 1938).

103. Padmore, 'Hands off the Colonies!'

104. Ibid.

105. Ibid.

106. Ibid.

107. 'West Indians Reply to Anglo–US Imperialism', *New Leader*, 4 January 1941.

108. Padmore, 'Hands off the Colonies!'.

109. Ibid.

110. Ibid.

111. George Padmore, 'Why Moors Help Franco', *New Leader*, 20 May 1938.
112. George Padmore, 'Police Sweep on Workers' Leaders in the Colonies', *New Leader*, 20 October 1939.
113. Ibid.
114. Ibid.
115. George Padmore, 'Not Nazism! Not Imperialism! But Socialism!', *New Leader*, 27 December 1941.
116. Trevor Williams, 'What the Empire Is', *New Leader*, Empire special supplement, 29 April 1938.
117. Ibid.
118. Reginald Reynolds, 'The Road to Empire: How Britain Won and Keeps India', *New Leader*, Empire special supplement, 29 April 1938.
119. 'British Govt Is Also "Imperialist Aggressor"', *New Leader*, Empire special supplement, 29 April 1938.
120. Fenner Brockway, 'Has Hitler Anything to Teach Our Ruling Class?', *New Leader*, Empire special supplement, 29 April 1938.
121. Jomo Kenyatta, 'Their Land Was Stolen: Slave Conditions in Kenya', *New Leader*, Empire special supplement, 29 April 1938; George Padmore, 'Colonial Fascism in the West Indies', *New Leader*, Empire special supplement, 29 April 1938.
122. Jon Kimche, 'How British Empire Got a Hold in China', *New Leader*, Empire special supplement, 29 April 1938.
123. 'In the Empire: West Indies to Burma in Revolt', *New Leader*, 13 January 1939.
124. Councillor W. R. Gault, 'Red Glasgow's Empire Exhibition,' *New Leader*, 6 May 1938.
125. Arthur Ballard, 'The "Other" Exhibition', *New Leader*, 12 August 1938.
126. Arthur Ballard, 'We Are Going to Run an Anti-Empire Exhibition!', *New Leader*, 3 June 1938.
127. Britton, 'Come and See the Empire', p. 78.
128. 'Success of Anti-imperialist Exhibition', *New Leader*, 19 August 1938.
129. Britton, 'Come and See the Empire', p. 82.
130. 'News from Somewhere: George Padmore', *New Leader*, 21 April 1939.
131. Arthur Ballard, 'The Greatest Slave Revolt in History', *New Leader*, 9 December 1938.
132. Ibid.
133. Arthur Ballard, 'Warships on the Way to Crush Jamaica Strikers', *New Leader*, 27 May 1938.
134. Arthur Ballard, 'Ten Years' Imprisonment for Stealing Two

Shillings', *New Leader*, 17 June 1938.

135. Arthur Ballard, 'Behind the Empire Exhibition: Police Fire on Jamaica Strikers', *New Leader*, 6 May 1938.

136. Arthur Ballard, 'Tyranny in the Empire,' *New Leader*, 24 March 1939.

137. Ibid.

138. Arthur Ballard, 'Empire "Sahibs" Bare Their Teeth', *New Leader*, 9 June 1939.

139. Ibid.

140. Fenner Brockway, 'How to Stop Hitler without War', *New Leader*, 24 March 1939.

141. Ibid.

142. Ballard, 'Tyranny in the Empire'.

143. Brockway, 'How to Stop Hitler without War'.

144. Ballard, 'Empire "Sahibs" Bare Their Teeth'.

145. 'India and the War', *New Leader*, 29 September 1939.

146. 'African Workers Ask, "What Can the Blacks Know of Democracy?"', *New Leader*, 24 November 1939.

147. Ibid., emphasis in original.

148. The IASB anti-war Manifesto drafted by Padmore and discussed in Chapter 8 was also carried by the *New Leader*. Executive Committee of the International African Service Bureau, 'A Manifesto from the Colonial Workers', *New Leader*, 23 September 1938.

149. HC Deb, *Colonial Office*, 14 June 1938, vol. 337, cc. 79–189 (c. 165).

150. Ibid.

151. Ibid., c. 157.

152. Ibid., c. 168.

153. Høgsbjerg, 'James, Orwell, and "Literary Trotskyism"', pp. 43–60.

154. George Orwell, 'Not Counting Niggers', in Sonia Orwell and Ian Angus, ed., *The Collected Essays, Journalism and Letters of George Orwell*, 4 vols, vol. 1 (Harmondworth: Penguin, 1968), p. 437. First published in the *Adelphi*, 1939, emphasis in original.

155. It is worth noting that, many decades later, James reflected on the unwitting underplaying of the dangers of Nazism that he and others might have been party to, in a comment on the failure to foresee the Holocaust: 'When it came, we were against it, but none of us really knew how mischievous fascism would be if it came to power. We thought it was merely some development of bourgeois hostility to proletarianism but it was more than that, it was an attempt to strike at everything that Europe had developed since the French Revolution in 1789. It wanted to take Europe back to class, and the subjugation of the people, it was a terrible thing altogether, but we saw it late.' 'Interview with C. L. R. James', in

Mackenzie Frank, *C. L. R. James: The Black Jacobin* (London: Hackney Council, 1985). I am grateful to Christian Høgsbjerg for drawing my attention to this.

156. Diana [*sic*] Stock (Dinah Stock), 'Anti-fascism Begins at Home', *New Leader*, 6 May 1938.

157. Ibid.

158. Dinah Stock, 'An African Describes His Own People', *New Leader*, 1 July 1938.

159. Fenner Brockway, 'Empire Must Be Freed if Britain Is to Lead European Revolution against Nazism', *New Leader*, 18 July 1940, p. 4.

160. George Padmore, 'To Defeat Nazism We Must Free Colonials', *New Leader*, 25 July 1940.

161. J. V. P. de Silva, 'Beaverbrook Thanks Ceylon', *New Leader*, 23 November 1940.

162. Arthur Sudbery, '"Imperialism" – from Z to A – and Even Further', *New Leader*, 9 May 1940, p. 4.

163. Padmore, 'Not Nazism! Not Imperialism! But Socialism!', *New Leader*, 27 April 1941.

164. Ibid.

165. George Padmore. 'We Gave Them Copper – They Gave Us Lead!' *New Leader*, 18 April 1940.

166. George Padmore, 'Lloyd Suppresses Another Report,' *New Leader*, 7 December 1940.

167. Ibid.

168. Padmore, 'Not Nazism! Not Imperialism! But Socialism!'

169. Fenner Brockway, 'How Far Is the Empire a Dictatorship?', *New Leader*, 30 August 1941.

170. Ibid.

171. Ibid.

172. George Padmore, 'Warning from the West Indies', *New Leader*, 3 May 1941.

173. George Padmore, 'Colonials Demand Britain's War Aims', *New Leader*, 15 February 1941.

174. George Padmore, 'Lifts the Veil of the Censorship over the Colonies', *New Leader*, 5 July 1941.

175. George Padmore, 'No Solution within Empires', *New Leader*, 9 May 1942.

176. Ibid.

177. George Padmore, 'Socialists Can't Bargain for India's Freedom', *New Leader*, 4 July 1942.

178. Césaire, *Discourse on Colonialism*, p. 14.

179. George Padmore, 'Imperialists Treat Blacks like Nazis Treat Jews', *New Leader*, 13 September 1941.

180. George Padmore, 'Imperialists Can't Solve African Question', *New Leader*, 11 July 1942, p. 3.

181. Padmore, 'Imperialists Treat Blacks like Nazis Treat Jews'.

182. 'How Natives Are Robbed of Their Lands', *New Leader*, 20 September 1941.

183. George Padmore, 'The Crisis in the British Empire', *New Leader*, 27 June 1942.

184. F. A. Ridley, 'Out of Africa', *New Leader*, 15 June 1946.

185. Fenner Brockway, 'Socialism Cannot Be Built on a Slave Empire', *New Leader*, 29 December 1945.

186. George Padmore, 'Trusteeship – the New Imperialism', *New Leader*, 2 February 1946.

187. George Padmore, 'The Old Firm under a New Name ...', *New Leader*, 23 February 1946.

188. George Padmore, 'There's No Real Difference', *New Leader*, March 1946.

189. Brockway, 'Socialism Cannot Be Built on a Slave Empire'.

190. F. A. Ridley, 'Where the ILP and the Labour Party Differ', *New Leader*, 29 December 1945, p. 3.

191. Brockway, 'Socialism Cannot Be Built on a Slave Empire'.

192. 'World-Wide Link-up against Imperialism', *New Leader*, 2 March 1946.

193. Fenner Brockway, cited in 'If Britain Had Statesmanship', *New Leader*, 9 March 1946.

194. 'World-Wide Link-up against Imperialism'.

195. Ibid.

196. For a pithy but full account of the congress and its context, see Christian Høgsbjerg, 'Remembering the Fifth Pan-African Congress', *Leeds African Studies Bulletin* 77 (Winter 2015/16), pp. 119–39, available at lucas.leeds.ac.uk.

197. George Padmore to Cyril Olivierre, 11 December 1945, Padmore Papers, Schomburg Center for Research in Black Culture, SMG.624.

198. Geiss, *Pan-African Movement*, 398.

199. Ibid., 408.

200. Høgsbjerg, 'Remembering the Fifth Pan-African Congress'.

201. George Padmore, *Pan-Africanism or Communism? The Coming Struggle for Africa* (London: D. Dobson, 1956), p. 152.

202. F. R. Kankam-Boadu, 'Reminiscences', in Adi and Sherwood, *The 1945 Manchester Pan-African Congress Revisited*, p. 36.

203. Cited in Sherwood, 'The Congress', in in Adi and Sherwood, *The 1945 Manchester Pan-African Congress Revisited*, p. 44.

204. Ibid., p. 45.

205. Cited in ibid.

206. 'The Challenge to the Colonial Powers', in Padmore, 'Colonial and

... Coloured Unity', in Adi and Sherwood, *The 1945 Manchester Pan-African Congress Revisited*, p. 55.

207. Ibid. p. 56.

208. G. Ashie Nikoi, chairman of the West African Cocoa Farmers' Delegation, cited in Padmore, 'Colonial ... and Coloured Unity', p. 81. He also notes that the congress should be the occasion when the 'British people and the world' are told.

209. Jomo Kenyatta, cited in ibid., p. 88.

210. Claude Lushington, cited in ibid., p. 95; J. F. F Rojas, cited ibid., p. 95.

211. Ibid., p. 93.

212. I. T. A. Wallace Johnson, cited in ibid., p. 100.

213. Cited in Hakim Adi, 'Pan-Africanism in Britain: Background to the 1945 Manchester Congress', in Adi and Sherwood, *The 1945 Manchester Pan-African Congress Revisited*, p. 21. See also George Padmore, 'The General Strike in Nigeria', in Padmore, ed., *The Voice of Coloured Labour: Speeches and Reports of Colonial Delegates to the World Trade Union Conference* (Manchester: Panaf Service, 1945).

214. Adi, 'Pan-Africanism in Britain', p. 21.

215. See Ahmed Aminu Yusuf, 'The 1945 General Strike and the Struggle for Nigeria', available at transforma-online.de.

216. Adi, 'Pan-Africanism in Britain', p. 23.

217. Cited in Geiss, *Pan-African Movement*, p. 386.

218. Adi, 'Pan-Africanism in Britain', p. 12.

219. Geiss, *Pan-African Movement*, p. 387.

220. Pan-African Federation, 'An Open Letter to the Prime Minister', in Padmore, *Pan-Africanism or Communism*, pp. 156–7. Cited also in Adi, 'Pan-Africanism in Britain', pp. 23–4.

221. Carol Polsgrove, 'George Padmore's Use of Periodicals to Build a Movement', in Baptiste and Lewis, *George Padmore*, p. 103.

222. Cunard and Padmore, *White Man's Duty*, p. 133.

223. Ibid., p. 139.

224. Thomas, 'George Padmore', p. 47.

225. Stephen Howe, *Anticolonialism in British Politics: The Left and the End of Empire, 1918–1964* (Oxford: Oxford University Press, 1993), p. 168.

10. A Terrible Assertion of Discontent

1. George Padmore, 'Behind the Mau Mau', *Phylon* 14: 4 (1953), p. 355.

2. Ibid., 360.

3. Ibid., 361.

4. Ibid., 365.

5. Ibid., 362.

6. Cited in David Anderson, *Histories of the Hanged: Britain's Dirty War in Kenya and the End of the Empire* (London: Weidenfeld & Nicolson, 2005), p. 1. Anderson notes that Huxley, who used it in her *No Easy Way* (1957), had borrowed the phrase from Gerald Hanley's *The Year of the Lion* (1956).

7. Robert Chester Ruark, *Something of Value* (London: Hamish Hamilton, 1955), p. 7.

8. Frederick Cooper, 'Mau Mau and the Discourses of Decolonization', *Journal of African History* 29: 2 (1988). p. 317.

9. D. A. Maughan-Brown, 'Myth and the "Mau Mau"', *Theoria: A Journal of Social and Political Theory* 55 (October 1980), p. 72.

10. Cited in D. A. Maughan Brown, *Land, Freedom and Fiction: History and Ideology in Kenya* (London: Zed, 1985), p. 158.

11. Ibid.

12. Anderson, *Histories of the Hanged*, p. 1.

13. Ibid., p. 3.

14. In his account of his becoming a 'Mau Mau' detainee, Josiah Kariuki suggests that the origins of the term lie in children's anagrams, where the warning 'Go, Go' or 'Uma, Uma' was turned into 'Mau, Mau', to warn those participating in oathing ceremonies to escape. Josiah Mwangi Kariuki, *'Mau Mau' Detainee* (London: Oxford University Press, 1963), p. 50.

15. See, for example, Daniel Branch, *Defeating Mau Mau, Creating Kenya: Counterinsurgency, Civil War, and Decolonization* (Cambridge: Cambridge University Press, 2009); Kinuthia Macharia and Muigai Kanyua, *The Social Context of the Mau Mau Movement in Kenya (1952–1960)* (Lanham, MD: University Press of America, 2006); David Throup, *Economic and Social Origins of Mau Mau, 1945–1953* (London: James Currey, 1987); Greet Kershaw, *Mau Mau from Below* (Oxford: James Currey, 1997); Bruce Berman and John Lonsdale, eds, *Unhappy Valley: Conflict in Kenya and Africa* (Oxford: James Currey, 1992); Atieno Odhiambo and John Lonsdale, eds, *Mau Mau and Nationhood: Arms, Authority and Narration* (Oxford: James Currey, 2003); Carl Gustav Rosberg and John Cato Nottingham, *The Myth of 'Mau Mau': Nationalism in Kenya* (New York: Praeger, 1966); Tabitha Kanogo, *Squatters and the Roots of Mau Mau, 1905–1963* (London: James Currey, 1987).

16. Kanogo, *Squatters and the Roots of Mau Mau*, p. 135–6.

17. Ibid., pp. 46, 136.

18. Frank Furedi, *The Mau Mau War in Perspective* (London: James

Currey, 1989), p. 78.

19. Ibid., 79.
20. Ibid., 103.
21. Ibid., 105.
22. Cooper, 'Mau Mau and the Discourses of Decolonization', p. 319.
23. Ibid.
24. Furedi, *Mau Mau War in Perspective*, p. 118.
25. Kenyatta's co-arrestees included Bildad Kaggia, Fred Kubai, Richard Achieng-Oneko, Paul Negei and Kungu Karamba, all of whom Pritt represented. For a fuller account, see Dennis Nowell Pritt, *The Autobiography of D. N. Pritt* (London: Lawrence & Wishart, 1965).
26. Montagu Slater, *The Trial of Jomo Kenyatta* (London: Secker & Warburg, 1957), p. 174.
27. Jomo Kenyatta, cited in ibid., pp. 174–5.
28. Ibid., p. 236.
29. Pritt, *Autobiography*, p. 71.
30. Ibid., p. 75.
31. David Goldsworthy, *Colonial Issues in British Politics 1945–1961: From 'Colonial Development' to 'Winds of Change'* (Oxford: Clarendon Press, 1971), p. 2.
32. Ibid., p. 2.
33. Ibid., p. 5.
34. Ibid., p. 27.
35. House of Commons, Early Day Motion (EDM) 21 (1952–1953), 4 December 1952, redrafted as EDM 29, 11 December 1952.
36. Bruce Berman, 'Bureaucracy and Incumbent Violence: Colonial Administration and the Origins of the "Mau Mau" Emergency', in Berman and Lonsdale, eds, *Unhappy Valley*, p. 253.
37. Fenner Brockway, *98 Not Out* (London: Quartet, 1986), p. 124.
38. Fenner Brockway, *Outside the Right: A Sequel to 'Inside the Left'* (London: Allen & Unwin, 1963), p. 169.
39. Fenner Brockway, *Towards Tomorrow: The Autobiography of Fenner Brockway* (London: Hart-Davis, MacGibbon, 1977), p. 161.
40. Ibid.
41. The Seretse Khama and Ruth Williams story is the subject of a 2016 film, *A United Kingdom* (dir. Amma Asante).
42. Greg Rosen, ed., *Dictionary of Labour Biography* (London: Politico's, 2001), p. 85.
43. Brockway, *98 Not Out*, p. 129.
44. Ibid., p. 124.
45. Ibid.
46. Fenner Brockway, 'Visit to Uganda, August/September 1950', Churchill Archives Centre (hereafter CAC), 518 FEBR, no. 48K.
47. Ibid.

48. Fenner Brockway, 'Visit to Kenya, September 1950. Report Presented to the Secretary of State for Colonial Affairs', CAC, 518 FEBR, no. 48K.

49. '"Big Chief" Brockway Flies Home after 30,000 Mile Tour of Africa', *Windsor, Slough and Eton Express*, 15 September 1950, CAC 22.99.

50. Ibid.

51. Fenner Brockway, 'Fenner Brockway's 80th Birthday Celebrations, 1968: Fenner's Speech', pamphlet, CAC, FEBR 16.62, 3.

52. Fenner Brockway, *African Journeys* (London: Gollancz, 1955), p. 117.

53. Ibid., p. 130.

54. Ibid., p. 120.

55. Ibid., p. 126.

56. Ibid., p. 131.

57. Ibid.

58. Ibid., p. 129.

59. Ibid., p. 130.

60. Ibid., p. 144.

61. Ibid.

62. Ibid.

63. Ibid., p. 169.

64. Ibid., p. 170.

65. Ibid.

66. Ibid., pp. 170–1.

67. Ibid., p. 173.

68. Ibid., p. 175.

69. Ibid., p. 179.

70. Ibid.

71. Ibid., 181.

72. HC Deb 4 November 1953 vol. 520 c. 276.

73. Ibid.

74. This is an example of the kind of *parliamentary* (not tabloid) discourse about Kenya that routinely surfaced in Commons Debates: 'Mr Craddock: I cannot give way. If my wife had had a family while we were in East Africa I would certainly not have allowed those children to be in charge of an African nurse because – and here I am going to be brutally frank, because I think these things should be appreciated – it is a common practice among Africans to put children to sleep by the excitation of their uro-genital organs. These are statements of fact and are the sort of things which bring about this situation ... The effect of alcohol upon an African is remarkable. I admit that sometimes alcohol has a remarkable effect on Europeans. But, speaking generally, alcohol seems to bring out all the evil instincts in the African in the most astonishing way. I mention

all these points to give the other side of the picture and to show that it is not just stupidity on the part of Europeans which has brought about a colour bar and racial discrimination.' HC Deb, 1 May 1953 vol. 514 c. 2534.

75. Ibid.
76. Ibid.
77. Ibid.
78. Ibid.
79. HC Deb 15 July 1953 vol. 517, c. 2029.
80. Ibid.
81. HC Deb 16 December 1952 vol. 509 c. 1291.
82. Ibid.
83. Fenner Brockway, *Why Mau Mau? An Analysis and Remedy* (London: Congress of Peoples against Imperialism, 1953), p. 1.
84. Ibid., p. 4.
85. Ibid., p. 14.
86. Barbara Castle, 'What Price Justice?', *Daily Mirror*, 7 December 1955.
87. Ibid.
88. Barbara Castle, 'The Truth about the Secret Police', *Daily Mirror*, 9 December 1955.
89. 'Barbara Castle's Articles in "The Mirror" Cause House of Commons Storm', *Daily Mirror*, 15 December 1955.
90. Cited in Caroline Elkins, *Britain's Gulag: The Brutal End of Empire in Kenya* (London: Jonathan Cape, 2005), p. 276.
91. Ibid., p. 286.
92. Eileen Fletcher, *Truth about Kenya – An Eye Witness Account*, foreword by Leslie Hale (London: Movement for Colonial Freedom, [n.d.]).
93. Ibid.
94. Joanna Lewis, '"Daddy Wouldn't Buy Me a Mau Mau": The British Popular Press and the Demoralization of Empire', in Odhiambo and Lonsdale, eds, *Mau Mau and Nationhood*, pp. 227–50.
95. See ibid., pp. 231–3.
96. *The Times*, cited in Slater, *Trial of Jomo Kenyatta*, pp. 245–6.
97. Ibid., p. 246.
98. Ibid., p. 248.
99. F. D. Corfield, *The Origins and Growth of Mau Mau: An Historical Survey* (Nairobi: Colony and Protectorate of Kenya, 1960), p. 5.
100. Ibid., p. 72.
101. Anderson, *Histories of the Hanged*, p. 281.
102. Ibid., p. 280.
103. Keith Waterhouse, 'The Newspaper with a Blind Eye', *Daily*

Mirror, 7 September 1955, p. 2, emphasis in original.

104. Ibid., emphasis in original.

105. Ibid.

106. HC Deb 9 March 1955 vol. 538, c.430.

107. HC Deb 6 June 1956 vol. 553, c. 1091.

108. Ibid.

109. Ibid.

110. Ibid.

111. Ibid.

112. Brockway, *Towards Tomorrow*, p. 208.

113. Brockway, 'Africa's Year of Destiny: A Political Guide to a Continent in Crisis', London, Movement for Colonial Freedom, n.d. School of Oriental and African Studies, London (hereafter SOAS), Movement for Colonial Freedom (hereafter MCF) Archives, Box 87.

114. Movement for Colonial Freedom, 'What Is the Movement for Colonial Freedom?', in Fletcher, *Truth about Kenya*, n.p.

115. Ibid.

116. MCF, *Young Socialists – Join the MCF*, n.d., SOAS, MCF Archives, Box 87.

117. Fenner Brockway, *The Colonial Revolution* (London: Hart-Davis, MacGibbon, 1973), p. 42.

118. Brockway, *Towards Tomorrow*, p. 216.

119. MCF, 'The Movement for Colonial Freedom', n.d. SOAS, MCF Archives, Box 87.

120. Kenneth O. Morgan, 'Imperialists at Bay: British Labour and Decolonization', in Robert D. King and Robin W. Kilson, eds, *The Statecraft of British Imperialism: Essays in Honour of Wm. Roger Lewis* (London: Frank Cass, 1999), p. 240.

121. Fenner Brockway, 'Winds of Change', draft article for *Time Life* magazine, CAC, FEBR 6.10.

122. Ibid.

123. Minutes of Special Central Council Meeting, 23 October 1958, MCF Archives, SOAS, Box 3.

124. MCF, 'Together against Imperialism', n.d. MCF Archives, SOAS, Box 87.

125. MCF, 'A Labour Government, the Colonial Peoples and the New Nations: A Policy Statement Offered for Consideration by the Movement for Colonial Freedom', MCF Archives, SOAS, Box 1.

126. MCF, *Young Socialists – Join the MCF*.

127. MCF, 'What Is Neocolonialism?', n.d. SOAS, MCF Archives, Box 87.

128. MCF, 'The Movement for Colonial Freedom Greets the All-African People's Conference', n.d. SOAS, MCF Archives, Box 87.

129. Brockway, 'What Is the MCF?'
130. MCF, 'Tasks for the Seventies: Based on the Speech of Lord Brockway, President of the MCF at Annual National Delegate Conference 1970', CAC, FEBR, 16.62.
131. Brockway, 'Fenner Brockway's 80th Birthday Celebrations, 1968', p. 3.
132. Ibid.
133. From MCF, 'Tasks for the Seventies'.
134. Ibid., p. 2.
135. Ibid., p. 7.
136. Ibid.
137. Lewis, *Empire State Building*, p. 91.
138. Prudence Smith, 'Margery Perham and Broadcasting: A Personal Reminiscence', in Alison Smith and Mary Bull, eds, *Margery Perham and British Rule in Africa* (New York/Abingdon: Routledge, 2013), p. 199.
139. Lewis, *Empire State-Building*, p. 89.
140. Roland Oliver, 'Prologue: The Two Miss Perhams', in Smith and Bull, *Margery Perham and British Rule in Africa*, p. 23.
141. Ibid. See also Margery Perham, *Colonial Sequence, 1949–1969: A Chronological Commentary upon British Colonial Policy in Africa* (London: Methuen, 1970).
142. Lewis writes that 'the late colonial state faced a crisis of paternalism and found a confusing array of prescriptions with which to read the problem and find a solution'. Lewis, *Empire State-Building*, p. 123.
143. Faught, *Into Africa*, p. 134.
144. Margery Perham, *East African Journey: Kenya and Tanganyika, 1929–30* (London: Faber & Faber, 1976), p. 15.
145. Faught, *Into Africa*, p. viii.
146. 'Newscheck on South Africa and Africa', 12 October 1962, cited in ibid., p. 127.
147. Lewis, *Empire State-Building*, p. 92.
148. Ibid., p. 100.
149. Perham, *East African Journey*, p. 16.
150. Ibid., p. 118.
151. Ibid., p. 32.
152. Ibid., p. 192.
153. Perham, *Colonial Sequence, 1930–1949*, pp. xv, xix.
154. Ibid., p. 42.
155. Ibid., p. 140.
156. Ibid., p. 45.
157. Margery Perham, 'Introduction', in Margery Perham, ed., *Ten Africans: A Collection of Life Stories* (London: Faber & Faber, 1963),

p. 9.

158. Ibid.

159. Ibid., p. 12.

160. Elspeth Huxley and Margery Perham, *Race and Politics in Kenya: A Correspondence between Elspeth Huxley and Margery Perham with an Introduction by Lord Lugard*, 2nd edn (London: Faber & Faber, 1956), p. 26.

161. Ibid., p. 120.

162. Ibid., p. 111.

163. Ibid., p. 192.

164. Ibid., p. 194.

165. Ibid., p. 212, emphasis in original.

166. Ibid., pp. 254–5.

167. Ibid., p. 258.

168. Elspeth Huxley, *A Thing to Love: A Novel* (London: Chatto & Windus, 1954).

169. Huxley and Perham, *Race and Politics in Kenya*, p. 265.

170. Ibid., p. 274.

171. Ibid., p. 268.

172. Ibid, emphasis in original.

173. Ibid.

174. Ibid., p. 276, my emphasis.

175. Perham, *Colonial Sequence 1949–1969*, p. 93.

176. Ibid.

177. Ibid., pp. 93–4.

178. Ibid., p. 94.

179. Ibid., p. 112.

180. Ibid., p. 95.

181. Ibid.

182. Ibid., p. 96.

183. Ibid., p. 97.

184. Ibid., p. 147.

185. Ibid., p. 148.

186. Tom Mboya, *The Kenya Question: An African Answer* (London: Fabian Colonial Bureau, 1956).

187. Cited in David Goldsworthy, *Tom Mboya: The Man Who Kenya Wanted to Forget* (Nairobi/London: Heinemann, 1982), p. 55.

188. Margery Perham, foreword in Mboya, *The Kenya Question*.

189. Ibid., p. 7.

190. Cited in Faught, *Into Africa*, p. 158.

191. Mboya, *The Kenya Question*, p. 13.

192. Ibid., p. 13.

193. Ibid., p. 17.

194. Ibid.

195. Ibid.
196. Ibid.
197. Ibid., p. 16.
198. Ibid., p. 31.
199. Ibid., p. 17.
200. Tom Mboya, *Freedom and After* (London: André Deutsch, 1963), p. 49.
201. Ibid., p. 52.
202. Ibid., p. 51.
203. Margery Perham, *The Colonial Reckoning* (London: Collins, 1961).
204. Ibid., p. 16.
205. Letter to Prudence Smith, cited in Faught, *Into Africa*, p. 140.
206. Perham, *The Colonial Reckoning*, p. 9.
207. Ibid., pp. 14–15.
208. Ibid., p. 13.
209. Ibid., p. 11.
210. Ibid., p. 22.
211. Ibid., p. 38.
212. Ibid., p. 40.
213. Ibid.
214. Ibid., p. 44
215. Ibid., p. 52.
216. Ibid., p. 26.
217. Ibid., p. 95.
218. Ibid., p. 96.
219. Ibid., pp. 94–5.
220. Ibid., p. 63.
221. Ibid.
222. Ibid.
223. Ibid., p. 62, emphasis in original.
224. Ibid., p. 70.
225. Ibid., p. 79.
226. Ibid., p. 130.
227. Ibid., p. 114.
228. Ibid.
229. Ibid., p. 102.
230. Ibid., p. 113.
231. Ibid., p. 154.
232. Ibid., p. 156.
233. Fenner Brockway, *African Socialism: A Background Book* (London: Bodley Head, 1963), p. 20.
234. Ibid., p. 31.
235. Ibid., p. 14.

Epilogue

1. The title of the Epilogue is taken from David Harvey, *The New Imperialism* (Oxford: Oxford University Press, 2003): 'If we were able to mount that wondrous horse of freedom, where would we seek to ride it?' (p. 198).

2. 'Address by Harold Macmillan to Members of both Houses of the Parliament of the Union of South Africa, Cape Town, 3 February 1960', Appendix One, in Harold Macmillan, *Pointing the Way, 1959–1961* (New York: Harper, 1972), p. 475.

3. Ibid., p. 476.

4. Ibid.

5. 'Introduction', in Tony Smith, ed., *The End of the European Empire: Decolonization after World War II* (Massachusetts: D.C. Heath & Co., 1975), p. xi.

6. Ibid., p. xii.

7. Christopher Hale, *Massacre in Malaya: Exposing Britain's My Lai* (Gloucestershire: History Press, 2013), p. 284. There was evidence that the Batang Kali massacre, the British High Court agreed in 2012, had involved 'a deliberate execution of 24 civilians' even as it refused to sanction a public inquiry. Arguably, Malaya caused less of a public outcry in its time than Kenya because of how much was successfully covered up.

8. A. J. Stockwell, 'Suez 1956 and the Moral Disarmament of the British Empire', in Simon C. Smith, ed., *Reassessing Suez 1956* (Aldershot: Ashgate, 2008), p. 232.

9. Humphrey Trevelyan, cited in ibid., p. 232.

10. Kenneth O. Morgan, 'Imperialists at Bay: British Labour and Decolonization', in Robin D. King and Robin W. Kilson, eds, *The Statecraft of British Imperialism: Essays in Honour of Wm. Roger Lewis* (London: Frank Cass, 1999), p. 238.

11. 'Dec. 12, 1963, Kenya Gains Independence', *New York Times* ('Learning Network'), 12 December 2011.

12. 'Obama's Speech to UK Parliament, in Full, with Analysis', *BBC*, 25 May 2011, available at bbc.co.uk.

13. C. L. R. James, *Nkrumah and the Ghana Revolution* (London: Allison & Busby, 1977), p. 214.

14. Gordon Brown, cited in Gary Younge, 'Cruel and Usual: The Outrages at Camp Breadbasket are Consistent with British Colonial Rule – Brutal, Oppressive, and Racist', *Guardian*, 1 March 2005.

15. Tony Blair, 'Doctrine of the International Community', 24 April 1999, available at webarchive.nationalarchives.gov.uk.

16. Ibid., p. 11.

17. Ibid., p. 14.

18. Ibid., pp. 29–30, emphasis in original.

19. Ibid., p. 31.

20. Ibid., p. 32.

21. Ibid.

22. Ibid., p. 29.

23. Ibid., p. 34.

24. Ibid., p. 35.

25. Ibid., p. 38.

26. Ibid., p. 36.

27. Ibid., p. 35.

28. Ibid., p. 36.

29. Paul Gilroy, *After Empire: Melancholia or Convivial Culture?* (Abingdon: Routledge, 2004), p. 2.

30. Ibid., pp. 2, 3.

31. Ibid., p. 3.

32. Some recent works that offer useful insights and accounts include: Michael Goebel, *Anti-imperial Metropolis: Interwar Paris and the Seeds of Third World Nationalism* (Cambridge: Cambridge University Press, 2015); Daniel Brückenhaus, *Policing Transnational Protest: Liberal Imperialism and the Surveillance of Anticolonialists in Europe, 1905–1945* (Oxford: Oxford University Press, 2017); Ian Birchall, ed., *European Revolutionaries and Algerian Independence, 1954–1062* (London: Merlin, 2012); Jennifer Anne Boittin, *Colonial Metropolis: The Urban Grounds of Anti-imperialism and Feminism in Interwar Paris* (Lincoln, NE: University of Nebraska Press, 2010). As is evident, there is much more on France than on other European imperial powers.

33. Robbie Shilliam, *The Black Pacific: Anti-colonial Struggles and Oceanic Connections* (London: Bloomsbury Academic, 2015), p.185

34. Runnymede Trust, *The Future of Multi-ethnic Britain: The Parekh Report* (London: Profile, 2000), p. 14.

35. Edward W. Said, *Culture and Imperialism* (London: Vintage, 1994 [1993]), p. 59.

36. Richard J. Evans, 'The Wonderfulness of Us (the Tory Interpretation of History', *London Review of Books* 33:6 (17 March 2011).

37. Jo Littler and Roshi Naidoo, 'White Past, Multicultural Present: Heritage and National Stories', in Robert Phillips and Helen Brocklehurst, eds, *History, Identity and the Question of Britain* (London: Palgrave, 2004), p. 338.

38. Jamaica Kincaid, *A Small Place* (New York: Farrar, Straus & Giroux, 2000 [1998]), p. 56.

39. 'The Meaning of Working through the Past', in Theodor W. Adorno,

Critical Models: Interventions and Catchwords, transl. Henry W. Pickford (New York: Columbia University Press, 2005), p. 89.

40. Said, *Culture and Imperialism*, p. 24.

41. Ibid., p. 19.

42. Ibid., p. 10.

43. E. M. Forster, *A Passage to India* (London: Penguin, 2005 [1924]).

44. Mary Beard, 'Cecil Rhodes and Oriel College, Oxford', *Times Literary Supplement* blog, 20 December 2015, the-tls.co.uk.

45. Goldwin Smith, *Reminiscences*, ed. Arnold Haultain (New York: Macmillan, 1910), p. 369.

Bibliography

I. Primary Texts and Archival Sources

NEWSPAPERS AND JOURNALS

Annual Register: A Review of Public Events at Home and Abroad for the Year
Anti-imperialist Review
Bee-Hive
Bombay Chronicle
Controversy
Daily Herald
Daily Mirror
Daily Worker
International African Opinion (IAO)
Labour Monthly
Manchester Guardian
New Leader
Nineteenth Century: A Monthly Review
People's Paper
Reynold's Newspaper
The Times
Workers Dreadnought
Spectator

ARCHIVE SOURCES

Wilfrid Scawen Blunt Papers, Fitzwilliam Museum, University of Cambridge

Papers of Reginald Orlando Francis Bridgeman (1921–53), Hull History Centre, U DBN.

Fenner Brockway Papers, Churchill Archives Centre, FEBR.

Nancy Cunard Collection (1895–1965), Harry Ransom Center, the University of Texas at Austin.

Maitland Sara Hallinan Collection, Modern Records Centre, University of Warwick, MSS.15X/1/121/1-6.

The Movement for Colonial Freedom and Liberation Archive, School of Oriental and African Studies, London, MCF.

Rhodes House Anti-slavery Collection, Rhodes House Library, Oxford University.

George Padmore Letters, Schomburg Center for Research in Black Culture, New York Public Library, Sc MG 624.

Papers of and relating to Shapurji Saklatvala (1874–1936), British Library, MSS Eur D1173.

E-SOURCES

Blair, Tony, 'Doctrine of the International Community', 24 April 1999. Available at <https://webarchive.nationalarchives.gov.uk/20080909041753tf_/http://www.number10.gov.uk/Page1297>

'Dec. 12, 1963, Kenya Gains Independence', *The Learning Network, New York Times*, 12 December 2011. Available at < https://learning.blogs.nytimes.com/2011/12/12/dec-12-1963-kenya-gains-independence>.

Douglass, Frederick, 'West India Emancipation, speech delivered at Canandaigua, New York, 3 August, 1857'. Available at University of Rochester, Frederick Douglass Project, <http://rbscp.lib.rochester.edu/4398>.

Ghose, Aurobindo, 'Mr Macondald's visit', *Karmayogin, a Weekly Review*, 27 November 1909. Available at <aurobindo.ru/workings/sa/37_08/0146_e.htm>.

'Indian Communists and Trade Unionists on Trial: The Meerut Conspiracy, 1929–1933', *British Online Archives*, <microform.digital/boa/collections/36/indian-communists-and-trade-unionists-on-trial-the-meerut-conspiracy-1929-1933>.

James, C. L. R, 'The Revolution and the Negro', *New International*, vol. V, December 1939, 339–43. Available at *Marxists*

Internet Archive, <https://www.marxists.org/archive/james-clr/works/1939/12/negro-revolution.htm>.

Mann, Charlie, 'How to Produce Meerut (1933)', in *Meerut: Workers Theatre Movement Play*. Available at <http://www.wcml.org.uk/our-collections/international/india/meerut-workers-theatre-movement-play/>.

Meerut: Workers Theatre Movement Play. Available at <http://www.wcml.org.uk/our-collections/international/india/meerut-workers-theatre-movement-play/>.

Miller, Jimmie, 'Red Megaphones'. Available at <https://www.wcml.org.uk/maccoll/maccoll/theatre/the-red-megaphones/>.

'Minutes of the Second Congress of the Communist International, Fourth Session, July 25'. Available at *Marxists Internet Archive*, <https://www.marxists.org/history/international/comintern/2nd-congress/ch04.htm>.

'Obama's speech to UK Parliament, in full, with analysis', *BBC*, 25 May 2011. Available at <http://www.bbc.co.uk/news/uk-politics-13549927>.

The Open University, *Making Britain: Discover How South Asians shaped the nation, 1870–1950*, <open.ac.uk/researchprojects/makingbritain>.

Selassie, Haile, 'Appeal to the League of Nations', June 1936. Available at <https://www.mtholyoke.edu/acad/intrel/selassie.htm>.

Yusuf, Ahmed Aminu, 'The 1945 General Strike and the Struggle for Nigeria'. Available at <www.transforma-online.de/deutsch/transforma2006/papers/yusuf.html>.

PUBLISHED MATERIALS

Peter Abrahams, *The Black Experience in the Twentieth Century: An Autobiography and Meditation*, Bloomington: Indian University Press, 2000.

——, *A Wreath for Udomo*, New York: MacMillan, 1971.

Ahmad, Muzaffar ed., *Communists Challenge Imperialism from the Dock*, Calcutta: National Book Agency, 1967.

Anonymous, *Jamaica; Who is to Blame, by a Thirty Years' Resident, with an introduction and notes by the editor of the 'Eclectic review'*, London: E. Wilson, 1866.

Azikiwe, Nnamdi, *My Odyssey: An Autobiography*, London: C. Hurst, 1970.

Besant, Annie, *India and the Empire: A Lecture and Various Papers on Indian Grievances*, London: Theosophical Publishing Society, 1914.

'"Big Chief" Brockway Flies Home after 30,000 Mile Tour of Africa', *The Windsor, Slough and Eton Express*, 15 September 1950, Churchill Archives Centre, 22.99.

Blunt, Lady Anne, *Bedouin Tribes of the Euphrates*, London: J. Murray, 1879.

——, *The Future of Islam*, Dublin: Nonsuch Publishing, 2007 [1882].

——, *Gordon at Khartoum: Being a Personal Narrative of Events in Continuation of 'A Secret History of the English Occupation of Egypt'*, London: S. Swift, 1911.

——, *Ideas about India*, London: Kegan Paul, 1885.

——, *India under Ripon: A Private Diary by Wilfrid Scawen Blunt, Continued from His 'Secret History of the English Occupation of Egypt'*, London: T. F. Unwin, 1909.

——, *Journals and Correspondence 1878–1917*, ed. Rosemary Archer and James Fleming, Cheltenham: Alexander Heriot & Co., 1986.

——, *The New Situation in Egypt*, London: Burns & Oates, 1908.

——, *A Pilgrimage to Nejd, the Cradle of the Arab Race: A Visit to the Court of the Arab Emir and 'Our Persian Campaign'*, London: Cass, 1968 [1881].

——, 'Recent Events in Arabia', *Fortnightly Review*, May 1880.

——, *Secret History of the English Occupation of Egypt*, Dublin: Nonsuch Publishing, 2007 [1907].

——, *The Shame of the Nineteenth Century, a Letter Addressed to the 'Times'*, London: [s.n.], 1900, Cambridge University Library Royal Commonwealth Society Collection.

——, 'The Thoroughbred Horse – English and Arabian', *The Nineteenth Century: A Monthly Review*, September 1880.

——, *The Wind and the Whirlwind*, London: Kegan Paul, Trench, and Co., 1883.

Broadley, A. M., *How We Defended Arábi and His Friends: A Story of Egypt and the Egyptians*, illustrated by Frederick Villiers, London: Chapman and Hall, 1884.

Brockway, Fenner, *African Journeys*, London: Gollancz, 1955.

——, *African Socialism: A Background Book*, London: Bodley Head, 1963.

——, *The Colonial Revolution*, London: Hart-Davis, MacGibbon, 1973.

——, *98 Not Out*, London: Quartet Books, 1986.

——, *Outside the Right: A Sequel to 'Inside the Left'*, London: Allen & Unwin, 1963.

——, *Towards Tomorrow: The Autobiography of Fenner Brockway*, London: Harl-Davis, MacGibbon Ltd, 1977.

——, *Why Mau Mau? An Analysis and Remedy*, London: Congress of Peoples against Imperialism, 1953.

Bryan, Herbert, 'Saklatvala: An Appreciation', *Daily Herald*, 24 November 1922, typed copy in Saklatvala Papers, MSS.EUR D 1173/4.

Calder-Marshall, Arthur, *Glory Dead*, London: M. Joseph, 1939.

Carlyle, Thomas, 'Occasional Discourse on the Negro Question', in *Fraser's Magazine for Town and Country*, vol. XL, February 1849.

——, 'Shooting Niagara, and After?', in *Works of Thomas Carlyle*, vol. 30, London: Chapman & Hall, 1869, 1–48.

Chirol, Valentine, *Indian Unrest*, London: Macmillan, 1910.

Congreve, Richard, *India [Denying England's Right to Retain Her Possessions], with an Introduction by Shyamaji Krishnavarma*, London: A. Bonner, 1907.

Cotton, Sir Henry, *New India: or, India in Transition*, London: Kegan Paul, Trench, Trübner & Co., 1907.

The Covenant of the League of Nations. Available at *The Avalon Project* at the Lillian Goldman Law Library at Yale Law School, <avalon.law.yale.edu/20th_century/leagcov.asp>.

Cripps, Stafford, 'Foreword', in George Padmore, *Africa and World Peace*, London: Secker and Warbury, 1937.

Cunard, Nancy ed., 'Black Man and White Ladyship: An Anniversary', in Maureen Moynagh, ed., *Essays on Race and Empire*, Calgary: Broadview Press, 2002.

——, *Negro*. London: Nancy Cunard at Wishart & Co., 1934.

——, and George Padmore, *The White Man's Duty*, London: W. H. Allen, 1942.

——, and George Padmore, 'The White Man's Duty: an Analysis of the Colonial Question in Light of the Atlantic Charter', in

Maureen Moynagh, ed., *Essays on Race and Empire*, Peterborough, Ontario: Broadview Press, 2002.

Dickens, Charles, 'Letter to William de Cerjat, 30 November 1865', in *The Selected Letters of Charles Dickens*, ed. Jenny Hartley, Oxford: Oxford University Press, 2012.

Dutt, Clemens, 'The Colonial Policy of the Labour and Socialist International', *The Anti-imperialist Review*, vol. 1, no. 1, July 1928.

The Eyre Defence and Aid Fund, London: Pelican Printing Company, 1866.

Fletcher, Eileen, *Truth about Kenya – An Eye Witness Account*, foreword by Leslie Hale, Movement for Colonial Freedom [n.d.].

Froude, James Anthony, *The English in the West Indies; Or, The Bow of Ulysses*, London: Longmans, Green, and Co., 1888.

Gladstone, William, *Aggression on Egypt and Freedom in the East*, London: The National Press Agency, 1884 [first published in *The Nineteenth Century* in 1877].

Gregory, Lady, *Arabi and His Household*, London: Kegan Paul, Trench & Co., 1882.

Hardie, J. Keir, *India: Impressions and Suggestions*, new edn, London: Home Rule for India League, 1917.

Harrison, Frederic, *Autobiographic Memoirs, Vol. 1, 1831–1870* and *Vol. 2, 1870–1910*, London: Macmillan and Co., 1911.

——, *National and Social Problems*, London: Macmillan and Co.,1908.

——, *Jamaica Papers No. V – Martial Law: Six Letters to 'The Daily News'*, London: The Jamaica Committee, 1867.

——, 'Letter to the Editor', *Pall Mall Gazette*, Friday 9 June 1882, iss. 5390.

Harvey, Thomas and William Brewin, *Jamaica in 1866: A Narrative of a Tour through the Island; With Remarks on Its Social, Educational and Industrial Condition*, London: A. W. Bennett, 1867.

House of Commons, Early Day Motion (EDM) 21 (1952–53), 4 December 1952, redrafted as EDM 29, 11 December 1952.

House of Commons Debate, *Abolition of Slavery, Fowell Buxton's Resolution*, 15 May 1823 vol. 9, cc. 257–360.

——, *Africans (Screening Conditions)*, 9 March 1955 vol. 538, cc. 430–1.

——, *Colonial Affairs*, 16 March 1955 vol. 358, cc. 1303–395.

——, *Colonial Office*, 14 June 1938 vol. 337, cc. 79–189.

——, *Colour Bar (Abolition)*, 1 May 1953 vol. 514, cc. 2505–95.

——, *Debate on the Address*, 4 November 1953 vol. 520, cc. 153–288.

——, *Debate on the Address*, 23 November 1922 vol. 159, cc. 44–166.

——, *Disturbances in Jamaica*, 31 July 1866 vol. 184, cc. 1763–1840.

——, *Egypt, Military Affairs*, 12 July 1882 vol. 272, cc. 162–98.

——, *Government of India Act*, 25 November 1927 vol. 210, cc. 2215–98.

——, *Government of India (Statutory Commission Bill)*, 22 November 1927 vol. 210, cc. 1633–51.

——, *Government of India (Statutory Commission) Bill, Clause 1*, 23 November 1927 vol. 210, cc. 1821–51.

——, *India*, 25 March 1929 vol. 226, cc. 2040–5.

——, *India Office*, 17 June 1927 vol. 207, cc. 1369–458.

——, *India Office*, 5 July 1923 vol. 166, cc. 655–779.

——, *India Office*, 9 July 1925 vol. 186, cc. 631–751.

——, *Indian States (Protection Against Disaffection) Act, 1922*, 27 February 1923 vol. 160, cc. 1799–1875.

——, *India – State of Affairs*, 27 July 1857 vol. 147, cc. 440–546.

——, *Kenya*, 16 December 1952 vol. 509, cc. 1212–52.

——, *Kenya (Situation)*, 6 June 1956 vol. 553, cc. 1087–1213.

——, *Perils of Socialism*, 21 March 1928 vol. 215, cc. 397–465.

——, *Petition (Kenya)*, 15 July 1953, cc. 2029–30.

——, *Present Situation*, 27 September 1926 vol. 199, cc. 269–384.

House of Commons Command Papers, *Further Correspondence Respecting the Affairs of Egypt*, London: Harrison and Sons, 1882.

Howsin, Hilda, *The Significance of Indian Nationalism*, London: A.C. Fifield, 1909.

Hume, Hamilton, *The Life of Edward John Eyre, Late Governor of Jamaica*, London: Richard Bentley, 1867.

Hutchinson, Lester, *Conspiracy at Meerut, with a Preface by Harold J. Laski*, London: Allen & Unwin, 1935.

——, *Meerut 1929–1932: Statement Given in His Own Defence at Meerut Court, India, against a Charge of 'Conspiracy against the King'*, London: Meerut Defence Committee, 1932.

Huxley, Elspeth, *A Thing to Love: A Novel*, London: Chatto & Windus, 1954.

——, and Margery Perham, *Race and Politics in Kenya: A Correspondence between Elspeth Huxley and Margery Perham*, 2nd edn, London: Faber and Faber, 1956.

Huxley, Thomas Henry, *Life and Letters of Thomas Henry Huxley*, vol. 1, London: Macmillan, 1903.

Hyndman, Henry Mayers, *The Unrest in India*, London: The Twentieth Century Press, 1907.

International African Service Bureau, *The West Indies Today*, London: The International African Service Bureau, 1956.

Jamaica Committee, *Jamaica Papers No. 1: Facts and Documents Relating to the Alleged Rebellion in Jamaica and the Measures of Repression Including Notes on the Trial of Mr. Gordon*, London: Jamaica Committee, 1866.

——, *Jamaica Papers No. III: Statement of the Jamaica Committee and Other Documents*, London: Jamaica Committee, 1866.

Jamaica Royal Commission, *Report of the Jamaica Royal Commission 1866: Part 1*, London: George Edward Eyre and William Spottiswoode, 1866.

——, *Report of the Jamaica Royal Commission, Part 2: Minutes of Evidence and Appendix*, London: HM Stationery Office, 1866.

James, C. L. R., 'Abyssinia and the Imperialists', in Anna Grimshaw, ed., *The C.L.R. James Reader*, London: Wiley-Blackwell, 1992.

——, *Beyond a Boundary*, 50th anniversary edn, with an introduction by Robert Lipsyte, Durham, NC: Duke University Press, 2013.

——, 'Black Intellectuals in Britain', in Bhikhu Parekh, ed., *Colour, Culture and Consciousness: Immigrant Intellectuals in Britain*, London: Allen and Unwin, 1974.

——, *The Black Jacobins: Toussaint L'Ouverture and the San Domingo Revolution*, London: Secker and Warburg, 1938.

——, 'George Padmore: Black Marxist Revolutionary', in C. L. R. James, *At the Rendezvous of Victory: Selected Writings*, London: Allison and Busby, 1984.

——, *A History of Negro Revolt*, New York: Haskell House, 1969.

——, 'Is This Worth a War?', in C. L. R. James, *At the Rendezvous of Victory: Selected Writings*, London: Allison and Busby, 1984.

——, 'The Making of the Caribbean People', in C. L. R. James, *Spheres of Existence: Selected Writings*, London: Allison and Busby, 1980.

——, *Nkrumah and the Ghana Revolution*, London: Allison and Busby, 1977.

——, 'Notes on the Life of George Padmore', in Anna Grimshaw, ed., *The C.L.R. James Reader*, Oxford: Blackwell, 1992.

Kankam-Boadu, F. R., 'Reminiscences', in Hakim Adi and Marika Sherwood, eds, *The 1945 Manchester Pan-African Congress Revisited*, 3rd edn, London: New Beacon Books, 1995.

Kaye, John William, *A History of the Sepoy War in India, 1857–58*, Vol. 3, London: W. H. Allen & Co., 1876.

Keay, J. Seymour, *Spoiling the Egyptians: A Tale of Shame, Told from the Blue Books*, 4th edn, London: Kegan Paul, Trench, 1882.

Keddie, Nikki R., *An Islamic Response to Imperialism: Political and Religious Writings of Sayyid Jamal ad-Din al-Afghani, Including a Translation of the 'Refutation of the Materialists' from the Original Persian*, Berkeley, CA: University of California Press, 1968.

King, David, *A Sketch of the Late Mr. G. W. Gordon, Jamaica*, Edinburgh: William Oliphant and Co., 1866.

Langley, J. Ayodele, ed., *Ideologies of Liberation in Black Africa 1856–1970: Documents on Modern African Political Thought from Colonial Times to the Present*, London: Rex Collins, 1979.

Lansbury, George, 'A Great Week-End at Brussels', *Lansbury's Labour Weekly*, 19 February 1927. Reprinted in the *Canton Gazette*, 25 March 1927.

Lewis, W. Arthur, *Labour in the West Indies: The Birth of a Workers Movement*, London: New Beacon Books, 1977 [1939].

Ludlow, J. M., *Jamaica Papers No. IV: A Quarter Century of Jamaica Legislation*, London: Jamaica Committee, 1866.

McCarthy, Justin, *A History of Our Own Times from the Ascension of Queen Victoria to the General Election of 1880*, vol. 3, London: Chatto & Windus, 1882.

——, *The History of Our Own Times*, vol. 4, London: Caxton Publishing, 1908.

MacDonald, J. Ramsay, *The Awakening of India*, London: Hodder and Stoughton, 1910.

——, *The Government of India*, London: The Swarthmore Press Ltd, 1919.

——, *Labour and the Empire*, London: Routledge, 1998.

McKay, Claude, 'A Black Man Replies', in Wayne Cooper, ed., *The Passion of Claude McKay: Selected Prose and Poetry, 1912–1948*, New York: Schocken Books, 1973, 55–6.

——, *A Long Way from Home*, New York: Arno Press and the New York Times, 1969.

——, 'Socialism and the Negro', in Wayne Cooper, ed., *The Passion of Claude McKay: Selected Prose and Poetry, 1912–1948*, New York: Schocken Books, 1973.

Macmillan, W. M., *Warning from the West Indies*, London: Faber & Faber, 1936.

Makonnen, Ras, *Pan-Africanism from Within; As Recorded and Edited by Kenneth King*, Nairobi and London: Oxford University Press, 1973.

Marx, Karl, and Friedrich Engels, *The First Indian War of Independence 1857–1859*, Moscow: Foreign Languages Publishing House and London: Lawrence and Wishart, 1960.

Maxton, James, 'Foreword', *The Anti-imperialist Review*, vol. 1, no. 1, July 1928.

Mboya, Tom, *Freedom and After*, London: André Deutsch, 1963.

——, *The Kenya Question: An African Answer*, London: Fabian Colonial Bureau, 1956.

The Meerut Prisoners and the Charge against Them, London: Modern Books, 1931.

Meerut Prisoners' Defence Committee, *The Meerut Trial: Facts of the Case*, London: issued by the Committee, 1929.

Meerut: Release the Prisoners! A Statement upon the Meerut Trial and Sentences, London: issued by the National Joint Council, representing the Trades Union Congress, the Labour Party and the Parliamentary Labour Party, 1933.

Mill, John Stuart, *Autobiography and Literary Essays*, ed. John M. Robson and Jack Stillinger, London: Routledge 1981.

——, *Collected Works of John Stuart Mill*, vol. 21, ed. John M. Robson, Toronto: University of Toronto Press, 1984.

——, 'A Few Words on Non-intervention', in *Dissertations and Discussions: Political, Philosophical, and Historical*, vol. 3, London: Longmans, Green, Reader, and Dyer, 1867 [first published in *Fraser's Magazine*, December 1859].

Morel, E. D., *The Horror on the Rhine, with a Preface by Arthur*

Ponsonby and New Foreword by the author, 8th edn, London: Union of Democratic Control, 1921.

Movement for Colonial Freedom, *Young Socialists – join the MCF*, [n.d.].

Mukherjee, Haridas and Uma Mukherjee, *Sri Aurobindo and the New Thought in Indian Politics*, Delhi: Oscar Publications, 1997 [1964].

Münzenberg, Willi, 'From Demonstration to Organisation', *Anti-imperialist Review*, vol. 1, no. 1, July 1928.

Nevinson, Henry W., *More Changes, More Chances*, London: Nisbet and Co., 1925.

——,*The New Spirit in India*, London: Harper & Brothers, 1908.

Ngũgĩ wa Thiong'O, *A Grain of Wheat*, London, Heinemann Books, 1967.

Nkrumah, Kwame, *Ghana: Autobiography of Kwame Nkrumah*, Edinburgh: Thomas Nelson and Sons, 1957.

Noel, Baptist Wriothesley, *The Case of George William Gordon, Esq. of Jamaica*, London: James Nisbet and Co., 1866.

Noel, Conrad, *The Meaning of Imperialism*, League against Imperialism British Section, 1928.

Norton, John Bruce, *The Rebellion in India: How to Prevent Another*, London: Richardson Brothers, 1857.

——, *Topics for Indian Statesmen*, London: Richardson Brothers, 1858.

Orwell, George, 'Not Counting Niggers', in Sonia Orwell and Ian Angus, eds, *The Collected Essays, Journalism and Letters of George Orwell*, 4 vols, vol. 1, Harmondsworth: Penguin Books, 1968.

Padmore, George, 'Behind the Mau Mau', *Phylon*, vol. 14, no. 4, 1953.

——, 'Colonial and ... Coloured Unity: A Programme of Action: History of the Pan-African Congress' (1963), in Hakim Adi and Marika Sherwood, eds, *The 1945 Manchester Pan-African Congress Revisited*, 3rd edn, London: New Beacon Books, 1995.

——, 'The General Strike in Nigeria', in George Padmore, ed., *The Voice of Coloured Labour: Speeches and Reports of Colonial Delegates to the World Trade Union Conference – 1945*, Manchester: Panaf Service Ltd, 1945.

——, *How Britain Rules Africa*, London: Wishart Books Ltd., 1936.

——, *The Life and Struggles of Negro Toilers*, London: The Red International of Labour of Unions Magazine for the International

Trade Union Committee of Negro Workers, 1931. Available at *Marxists Internet Archive*, <https://www.marxistsfr.org/archive/padmore/1931/negro-toilers/ch06.htm>.941.

——, *Pan-Africanism or Communism? The Coming Struggle for Africa*, London: D. Dobson, 1956.

Pan-African Association, 'Address to the Nations of the World by the Pan-African Conference in London, 1900', in J. Ayodele Langley, ed., *Ideologies of Liberation in Black Africa 1856–1970: Documents on Modern African Political Thought from Colonial Times to the Present*, London: Rex Collins, 1979.

——, 'The London Manifesto (29 August 1921)', in J. Ayodele Langley, ed., *Ideologies of Liberation in Black Africa 1856–1970: Documents on Modern African Political Thought from Colonial Times to the Present*, London: Rex Collins, 1979.

Pankhurst, Sylvia, 'The Fascist World War', in Kathryn Dodd, ed., *A Sylvia Pankhurst Reader*, Manchester: Manchester University Press, 1993.

——, *India and the Earthly Paradise*, Bombay: Sunshine Publishing Company, 1926.

Perham, Margery, *The Colonial Reckoning*, London: Collins, 1961.

——, *Colonial Sequence, 1930–1949*, London: Methuen, 1967.

——, *Colonial Sequence, 1949–1969: A Chronological Commentary upon British Colonial Policy in Africa*, London: Methuen, 1970.

——, *East African Journey: Kenya and Tanganyika, 1929–30*, London: Faber and Faber, 1976.

——, ed., *Ten Africans: A Collection of Life Stories*, London: Faber and Faber, 1963.

Pim, Bedford, *The Negro and Jamaica*, London: Trübner and Co., 1866.

Rolland, Romain, 'For the Meerut Prisoners: Against Imperialist Terror', in *Meerut Conspiracy Case, Specially Written by a Barrister-at-Law*, London: Meerut Prisoners' Release Committee, 1933.

Roundell, Charles Savile, *England and Her Subject-Races: With Special Reference to Jamaica*, London: Macmillan and Co., 1866.

Ruskin, John, 'A Letter to the "Daily Telegraph"', 20 December 1865, in *The Works of John Ruskin*, vol. 18, ed. E. T. Cook & Alexander Wedderburn, London: George Allen, 1905.

——, 'Liberty', in *The Works of John Ruskin*, vol. 19, ed. E. T. Cook & Alexander Wedderburn, London: George Allen, 1905.

Rutherford, V. H., 'Introduction', in Hilda Howsin, *The Significance of Indian Nationalism*, London: A. C. Fifield, 1909.

Saklatvala, Shapurji, 'India and Britain', *Labour Monthly*, vol. 9, no. 6, June 1927, 361–4. Available at *Marxists Internet Archive*, <marxists.org/archive.saklatvala/1927/06/x01.htm>.

——, 'India in the Labour World', *Labour Monthly*, vol. 1, no. 5, November 1921, 440–51. Available at *Marxists Internet Archive*, <marxists.org/archive/saklatvala/1921/11/x01.htm>.

——, 'The Indian Round Table Conference', *Labour Monthly*, vol. 12, no. 12, December 1930, 720–4. Available at *Marxists Internet Archive*, https://www.marxists.org/archive/saklatvala/1930/12/x01.htm.

——, 'The Indian Round-Table Conference: A Danger to World Peace and Socialism', *Labour Monthly*, vol. 12, no. 2, February 1931, 86–92. Available at *Marxists Internet Archive*, https://www.marxists.org/archive/saklatvala/1931/02/x01.htm.

——, 'Letter to Sarojini Naidu, President of Indian National Congress', reprinted in *Bombay Chronicle*, 15 January 1997, Saklatvala Papers, British Library, MSS EUR D 1173.

——, Parliamentary By-election Flyer, Shettleston Division, June 1930, Bridgeman Papers, Hull University Archives, U DBN/24/5.

——, 'The Second Indian Round Table Conference', *Labour Monthly*, vol. 13, no. 10, October 1931. Available at *Marxists Internet Archive*, <marxists.org/archive/saklatvala/1931/10/x01.htm>.

Smith, Goldwin, *Reminiscences*, ed. Arnold Haultain, New York: Macmillan, 1910.

Snowden, Philip, 'Foreword to the Second Edition', in Keir Hardie, *India: Impressions and Suggestions*, London: Home Rule for India League (British Auxiliary), 1917.

'The Speech of the Prosecutor in the Meerut Case' (Part 1), *Labour Monthly*, vol. 12, no. 1, January 1930, 24–9. Available at *Marxists Internet Archive*, <https://www.marxists.org/history/international/comintern/sections/britain/periodicals/labour_monthly/1930/01/x01.htm>.

'The Speech of the Prosecutor in the Meerut Case' (Part 2), *Labour Monthly*, vol. 12, no. 2, February 1930, 97–105. Available at *Marxists Internet Archive*, <https://www.marxists.org/history/international/comintern/sections/britain/periodicals/labour_monthly/1930/02/x01.htm>.

Spencer, Herbert, *An Autobiography*, vol. 2, London: Watts & Co. 1926 [1904].

Tagore, Rabindranath, 'Letter to Lord Chelmsford', *Modern Review* (Calcutta Monthly), July 1919.

Thompson, Edward, *The Other Side of the Medal*, New York: Harcourt, Brace and Co., 1926.

——, and G. T. Garratt, *Rise and Fulfilment of British Rule in India*, London: Macmillan and Company Ltd, 1934.

Tilak, Bal Gangadhar, *Bal Gangadhar Tilak: His Writings and Speeches. Appreciation by Babu Aurobindo Ghose,* 3rd edn, Madras: Ganesh and Co., 1922.

Underhill, Edward Bean, *A Letter Addressed to the Rt. Honourable E. Cardwell, with Illustrative Documents on the Condition of Jamaica and an Explanatory Statement*, London: Arthur Miall, 1865.

——, *The Tragedy of Morant Bay: A Narrative of the Disturbances in the Island of Jamaica in 1865*, London: Alexander and Shepheard, 1895, reprinted by Forgotten Books, 2012.

Urabi, Ahmad, *Muthakirat Urabi: Kashf Al-sitar 'an sir al-Asrar fi al-nahda al-Masriya al-mashhura bi al-thawra al-Urabiya sanat 1298 Hijriya was sanat 1881–1882 Miliadiya* (The Urabi Memoirs: Uncovering the Secrets of the Egyptian Awakening Commonly Known as the Urabian Revolution 1298 Hijri, 1881–1882), Cairo: Dar Al-Kutub Al-Misriya, 1925.

Visram, Rozina, *Ayahs, Lascars, and Princes: Indians in Britain 1700–1947*, London: Pluto, 1986

White, T. Baker, 'The Anti-British League: Plotting against the Empire', Letters to the Editor, *Morning Post*, 2 June 1927.

Williams, B. T., *The Case of George William Gordon, with Preliminary Observations on the Jamaica Riot of October 11th, 1865,* London: Butterworths, 1866.

Williams, Eric, *The Negro in the Caribbean*, foreword by George Padmore, Manchester: Panaf Service, 1942.

II. Secondary Works

Peter Abrahams, *The Black Experience in the Twentieth Century: An Autobiography and Meditation*, Bloomington: Indian University Press, 2000.

——, *A Wreath for Udomo*, New York: MacMillan, 1971.

Adas, Michael, 'Contested Hegemony: The Great War and the Afro-Asian Assault on the Civilizing Mission Ideology', *Journal of World History*, vol. 15, no. 1, March 2004, 31–63.

——, *Prophets of Rebellion: Millenarian Protest Movements against European Colonial Order*, Cambridge: Cambridge University Press, 1979.

Adi, Hakim, 'Pan-Africanism in Britain: Background to the 1945 Manchester Congress', in Hakim Adi and Marika Sherwood, eds, *The 1945 Manchester Pan-African Congress Revisited*, 3rd edn, London: New Beacon Books, 1995.

——, *West Africans in Britain: 1900–1960, Nationalism, Pan-Africanism and Communism*, London: Lawrence and Wishart, 1998.

Adi, Hakim and Marika Sherwood, eds, *The 1945 Manchester Pan-African Congress Revisited*, 3rd edn, London: New Beacon Books, 1995.

Adorno, Theodor W., *Critical Models: Interventions and Catchwords*, transl. Henry W. Pickford, New York: Columbia University Press, 2005.

Alexander, Robert J. and Eldon M. Parker, *A History of Organized Labor in the English-Speaking West Indies*, Westport, Connecticut: Praeger, 2004.

Anderson, David, *Histories of the Hanged: Britain's Dirty War in Kenya and the End of the Empire*, London: Weidenfeld & Nicolson, 2005.

Aptheker, H., *American Negro Slave Revolts*, New York: International Publishers, 1969.

Asante, S. K. B., *Pan-African Protest: West Africa and the Italo-Ethiopian Crisis, 1934–1941*, London: Longman, 1977.

Ashcroft, Bill, Gareth Griffiths and Helen Tiffin, *The Empire Writes Back: Theory and Practice in Post-colonial Literatures*, London and New York: Routledge, 1989.

Azikiwe, Nnamdi, *My Odyssey: An Autobiography*, London: C. Hurst, 1970.

Bakan, Abigail B., *Ideology and Class Conflict in Jamaica: The Politics of Rebellion*, Montreal and London: McGill-Queen's University Press, 1990.

Bakhtin, M. M., *The Dialogic Imagination: Four Essays*, ed. Michael Holquist, transl. Caryl Emerson and Michael Holquist, Austin: University of Texas Press, 1981.

——, *Speech Genres and Other Late Essays*, ed. Caryl Emerson and Michael Holquist, transl. Vern W. McGee, Austin: University of Texas Press, 1986.

Baldwin, Davarian L., 'Introduction: New Negroes Forging a New World', in Davarian L. Baldwin and Minkah Makalani, eds, *Escape from New York: The New Negro Renaissance beyond Harlem*, Minneapolis: Minnesota University Press, 2013.

Baptiste, Fitzroy and Rupert Lewis, eds, *George Padmore, Pan-African Revolutionary*, Kingston: Ian Randle Publishers, 2008.

Barooah, Nirode K., *Chatto: The Life and Times of an Anti-imperialist in Europe*, Delhi: Oxford University Press, 2004.

Bates, Crispin, ed., *Mutiny at the Margins: New Perspectives on the Indian Uprising of 1857, Vol. 5: Muslim, Dalit and Subaltern Narratives*, New Delhi, India: SAGE Publications India, 2014.

Bayly, Christopher, 'European Political Thought and the Wider World', in Gareth Stedman Jones and Gregory Claeys, eds, *The Cambridge History of Nineteenth-Century Political Thought*, Cambridge: Cambridge University Press, 2011.

Beard, Mary, 'Cecil Rhodes and Oriel College, Oxford', *Times Literary Supplement* blog, December 20, 2015. Available at https://www.the-tls.co.uk/cecil-rhodes-and-oriel-college-oxford.

Behdad, Ali, *Belated Travelers: Orientalism in the Age of Colonial Dissolution*, Durham, NC and London: Duke University Press, 1994.

Belchem, John, *Popular Radicalism in Nineteenth-Century Britain*, London: Palgrave MacMillan, 1996.

Bender, Jill C., *The 1857 Indian Uprising and the British Empire*, Cambridge: Cambridge University Press, 2016.

Berdine, Michael D., *The Accidental Tourist: Wilfrid Scawen Blunt, and the British Invasion of Egypt in 1882*, New York and London: Routledge, 2005.

Berman, Bruce and John Lonsdale, *Unhappy Valley: Conflict in Kenya and Africa*, London: James Currey, 1992.

Bhabha, Homi K., 'Signs Taken for Wonders: Questions of Ambivalence and Authority under a Tree outside Delhi, May 1817', *Critical Inquiry*, vol. 12, no. 1, 1985, 144–65.

——, 'Sly Civility', *October*, vol. 34, 1985, 324–46.

Bhambra, Gurminder K., *Rethinking Modernity: Postcolonialism and the Sociological Imagination*, New York: Palgrave MacMillan, 2007.

Bhattacharya, Sabyasachi, ed., *Rethinking 1857*, Hyderabad: Orient Longman, 2007.

Birchall, Ian, ed., *European Revolutionaries and Algerian Independence, 1954–1962*, London: Merlin Press, 2012.

Blackburn, Robin, *The Overthrow of Colonial Slavery 1776–1848*, London: Verso, 1988.

Blair, Tony, 'Doctrine of the International Community', 24 April 1999. Available at <http://webarchive.nationalarchives.gov.uk/+/www.number10.gov.uk/Page1297>.

Bogues, Anthony, *Caliban's Freedom: The Early Political Thought of C. L. R. James*, London: Pluto Press, 1997.

——, 'C. L. R. James and George Padmore: The Ties That Bind – Black Radicalism and Political Friendship', in Fitzroy Baptiste and Rupert Lewis, eds, *George Padmore, Pan-African Revolutionary*, Kingston: Ian Randle Publishers, 2008.

Boittin, Jennifer Anne, *Colonial Metropolis: The Urban Grounds of Anti-imperialism and Feminism in Interwar Paris*, Lincoln: University of Nebraska Press, 2010.

Bolland, O. Nigel, *On the March: Labour Rebellions in the British Caribbean, 1934–39*, Kingston, Jamaica: I. Randle and London: J. Currey, 1995.

——, *The Politics of Labour in the British Caribbean: The Social Origins of Authoritarianism and Democracy in the Labour Movement*, Kingston: Ian Randle Publishers and Oxford: James Currey, 2001.

Bolt, Christine, *Victorian Attitudes to Race*, London: Routledge & Kegan Paul, 1971.

Branch, Daniel, *Defeating Mau Mau, Creating Kenya: Counter-insurgency, Civil War, and Decolonization*, Cambridge: Cambridge University Press, 2009.

Brennan, Timothy, *Borrowed Light: Vico, Hegel, and the Colonies*, vol. 1, Stanford: Stanford University Press, 2014.

Britton, Sarah, '"Come and See the Empire by the All Red Route": Anti-imperialism and Exhibitions in Interwar Britain', *History Workshop Journal*, vol. 69, no. 1, 1 March 2010, 68–89.

Brückenhaus, Daniel, *Policing Transnational Protest: Liberal Imperialism and the Surveillance of Anticolonialists in Europe, 1905–1945*, Oxford: Oxford University Press, 2017.

Buck-Morss, Susan, *Hegel, Haiti, and Universal History*, Pittsburgh: University of Pittsburgh Press, 2009.

Burton, Antoinette, *The Trouble with Empire: Challenges to Modern British Imperialism*, New York: Oxford University Press, 2015.

Cain, Peter, 'Introduction', in J. Ramsay MacDonald, *Labour and the Empire*, London: Routledge, 1998.

Calder-Marshall, Arthur, *Glory Dead*, London: M. Joseph, 1939.

Callahan, John, 'Colonies, Racism, the CPGB and the Comintern in the Inter-war Years', *Science and Society*, vol. 61, no. 4, Winter 1997/1998, 513–25.

Cannadine, David, *In Churchill's Shadow: Confronting the Past in Modern Britain*, London: Penguin, 2002.

Césaire, Aimé, *Discourse on Colonialism*, New York: Monthly Review Press, 1972.

Chakrabarty, Dipesh, *Provincialising Europe: Postcolonial Thought and Historical Difference*, Princeton: Princeton University Press, 2000.

Chakravarty, Gautam, *The Indian Mutiny and the British Imagination*, Cambridge: Cambridge University Press, 2005.

Chatterjee, Partha, 'Nationalism, Internationalism, and Cosmopolitanism: Some Observations from Modern Indian History', *Comparative Studies of South Asia, Africa and the Middle East*, vol. 36, no. 2, August 2016, 320–34.

Chisholm, Anne, *Nancy Cunard*, London: Sidgwick and Jackson, 1979.

Claeys, Gregory, *Imperial Sceptics: British Critics of Empire, 1850–1920*, Cambridge: Cambridge University Press, 2010.

Cohen, Gideon, *The Failure of a Dream: The Independent Labour Party from Disaffiliation to World War II*, London: Tauris Academic Studies, 2007.

Cole, Juan, *Colonialism and Revolution in the Middle East: Social and Cultural Origins of Egypt's 'Urabi Movement*, Princeton: Princeton University Press, 1993.

Colley, Linda, *Britons: Forging the Nation 1707–1837*, New Haven and London: Yale University Press, 2005.

Cooper, Frederick, 'Mau Mau and the Discourses of Decolonization', *Journal of African History*, vol. 29, no. 2, 1988, 313–20.

Cooper, Wayne F., *Claude McKay, Rebel Sojourner in the Harlem Renaissance*, Baton Rouge: Louisiana State University Press, 1996.

——, and Robert C. Reinders, 'A Black Briton Comes "Home": Claude McKay in England, 1920', *Race and Class*, vol. 9, no. 1, 1967, 67–83.

Corfield, F. D., *The Origins and Growth of Mau Mau: An Historical Survey*, Nairobi: Colony and Protectorate of Kenya, 1960.

Cotton, Sir Henry, *New India: Or, India in Transition*, London: Kegan Paul, Trench, Trübner & Co., 1907.

The Covenant of the League of Nations. Available at *The Avalon Project* at the Lillian Goldman Law Library at Yale Law School, <avalon.law.yale.edu/20th_century/leagcov.asp>.

Cunningham, Hugh, *The Challenge of Democracy: Britain 1832–1918*, London: Routledge, 2014.

Darwin, John, *The End of the British Empire: The Historical Debate*, Oxford: Basil Blackwell, 1991.

——, *Unfinished Empire: The Global Expansion of Britain*, London: Bloomsbury, 2012.

Davis, Mary, *Sylvia Pankhurst: A Life in Radical Politics*, London: Pluto Press, 1999.

'Dec. 12, 1963, Kenya Gains Independence', *The Learning Network, New York Times*, 12 December 2011. Available at < https://learning.blogs.nytimes.com/2011/12/12/dec-12-1963-kenya-gains-independence/>.

de Groot, Joanna, *Empire and History Writing in Britain since 1750*, Manchester: Manchester University Press, 2013.

Derrick, Jonathan, *Africa's Agitators: Militant Anti-colonialism in Africa and the West, 1918–1939*, London: Hurst, 2008.

Drapeau, Thierry, '"Look at Our Colonial Struggles": Ernest Jones and the Anti-colonialist Challenge to Marx's Conception of History', *Critical Sociology*, 17 November 2017, 1–14.

Dutton, Geoffrey, *The Hero as Murderer: The Life of Edward John*

Eyre, Australian Explorer and Governor of Jamaica, 1815–1901, Sydney and London: Collins, 1967.

Edwards, Brent Hayes, *The Practice of Diaspora: Literature, Translation, and the Rise of Black Internationalism*, Cambridge, MA: Harvard University Press, 2003.

Elkins, Caroline, *Britain's Gulag: The Brutal End of Empire in Kenya*, London: Jonathan Cape, 2005.

Evans, Richard J., 'The Wonderfulness of Us (the Tory Interpretation of History)', *London Review of Books*, vol. 33, no. 6, 17 March 2011.

Fanon, Frantz, *A Dying Colonialism*, transl. Haakon Chevalier, New York: Grove Press, 1965.

Faught, C. Brad, *Into Africa: The Imperial Life of Margery Perham*, London: I. B. Tauris, 2012.

Featherstone, David, *Solidarity: Hidden Histories and Geographies of Internationalism*, London: Zed Books, 2012.

Featherstone, Donald, *Victorian Colonial Warfare: From the Conquest of Sind to the Indian Mutiny*, London: Cassell, 1992.

Ferguson, Niall, 'British Imperialism Revised: The Costs and Benefits of "Anglobalization"', Stern School of Business, New York University: Development Research Institute Working Paper Series no.2, April 2003.

Finn, Margot C., *After Chartism: Class and Nation in English Radical Politics, 1848–1874*, Cambridge: Cambridge University Press, 1993.

Ford, Hugh, 'Introduction', in Nancy Cunard and Hugh Ford eds, *Negro: An Anthology,* edited and abridged by Hugh Ford, New York: Frederick Ungar Publishing Co., 1970.

——, ed., *Nancy Cunard: Brave Poet, Indomitable Rebel, 1896–1965*, New York: Chilton Book Company, 1968.

Forster, E. M., *The BBC Talks of E. M. Forster*, ed. Mary Lago, Linda K. Hughes and Elizabeth MacLeod Walls, Columbia, MO: University of Missouri Press, 2008.

Frank, Mackenzie, *C. L. R. James: The Black Jacobin*, Hackney Council, 1985.

Friedman, Alan Warren, ed., *Beckett in Black and Red: The Translations for Nancy Cunard's Negro (1934)*, Lexington: University Press of Kentucky, 2014.

Fryer, Peter, *Black People in the Empire: An Introduction*, London: Pluto Press, 1993.

Furedi, Frank, *The Mau Mau War in Perspective*, London: James Currey, 1989.

Gandhi, Leela, *Affective Communities: Anticolonial Thought, Fin-de-Siècle Radicalism, and the Politics of Friendship*, Durham, NC: Duke University Press, 2006.

Gardner, Phillip, ed., *E. M. Forster, The Critical Heritage*, London: Routledge and Kegan Paul, 1973.

Geiss, Imanuel, *The Pan-African Movement*, transl. Ann Keep, London: Methuen, 1974.

Genet, Jean, 'The Palestinians', *Journal of Palestine Studies*, vol. 3, no. 1, Autumn 1973, 3–34.

Ghosh, Pramita, *Meerut Conspiracy Case and the Left Wing in India*, Calcutta: Papyrus Publishing House, 1998.

Gilroy, Paul, *After Empire: Melancholia or Convivial Culture?*, Abingdon: Routledge, 2004.

——, *Darker than Blue: On the Moral Economies of Black Atlantic Culture*, Cambridge, MA and London: Belknap Press of Harvard University Press, 2010.

Goebel, Michael, *Anti-imperial Metropolis: Interwar Paris and the Seeds of Third World Nationalism*, Cambridge: Cambridge University Press, 2015.

Goldsworthy, David, *Colonial Issues in British Politics 1945–1961: From 'Colonial Development' to 'Winds Of Change'*, Oxford: Clarendon Press, 1971.

——, *Tom Mboya: The Man Who Kenya Wanted to Forget*, Nairobi and London, Heinemann, 1982.

Gordon, Lois, *Nancy Cunard: Heiress, Muse, Political Idealist*, New York: Columbia University Press, 2007.

Gott, Richard, *Britain's Empire: Resistance, Repression and Revolt*, London: Verso, 2011.

Goloubeva, Irina Rasmussen, 'Curating Art, Rewriting World History: Nancy Cunard's *Negro: An Anthology* (1934)', in Margrét Gunnarsdóttir Champion and Irina Rasmussen Goloubeva, eds, *Ethics and Poetics: Ethical Recognitions and Social Reconfigurations in Modern Narratives*, Newcastle: Cambridge Scholars Publishing, 2014.

Guha, Ranajit (ed.), *Subaltern Studies: Writings on South Asian History and Society*, vol. 2, Delhi: Oxford University Press, 1983.

Haakonsen, Knud, 'Introduction', in Adam Smith, *The Theory of Moral Sentiments*, Cambridge: Cambridge University Press, 2002.

Haithcox, John P., 'The Roy–Lenin Debate on Colonial Policy: A New Interpretation', *Journal of Asian Studies*, vol. 23, no. 1, November 1963, 93–101.

Hale, Christopher, *Massacre in Malaya: Exposing Britain's My Lai*, Gloucestershire: The History Press, 2013.

Hall, Catherine, *Civilising Subjects: Metropole and Colony in the English Imagination, 1830–1867*, Cambridge: Polity Press, 2002.

Hallas, Duncan, 'Revolutionaries and the Labour Party', *International Socialism*, vol. 2, no. 16, Spring 1982, 1–35. Available at <https://www.marxists.org/archive/hallas/works/1982/revlp/index.htm>.

Hannah, Simon, *A Party with Socialists in It: A History of the Labour Left*, London: Pluto Press, 2018.

Hardie, Frank, *The Abyssinian Crisis*, London: Batsford, 1974.

Hart, Richard, *Caribbean Workers' Struggles*, London: Bogle L'Overture Press, 2012.

——, *Labour Rebellions of the 1930s in the British Caribbean Region Colonies*, London: Socialist History Society, 2002.

Harvey, David, *The New Imperialism*, Oxford: Oxford University Press, 2003.

Hasian, Marouf, Jr, 'Colonial Re-characterization and the Discourse Surrounding the Eyre Controversy', *Southern Communication Journal*, vol. 66, no. 1, Fall 2000, 79–95.

Hatch, John, 'The Decline of British Power in Africa', in Tony Smith, ed., *The End of the European Empire: Decolonization after WWII*, Massachusetts: D. C. Heath & Co., 1975.

Henderson, Mae G., ed., *Borders, Boundaries, and Frames: Essays in Cultural Criticism and Cultural Studies*, New York: Routledge, 1995.

Herbert, Christopher, *War of No Pity: the Indian Mutiny and Victorian Trauma*, Princeton and Oxford: Princeton University Press, 2008.

Heuman, Gad, *The Killing Time: The Morant Bay Rebellion in Jamaica*, London: Macmillan, 1994.

Hobson, J. A., *The Crisis of Liberalism: New Issues of Democracy*, London: P. S. King & Son, 1909.

Høgsbjerg, Christian, 'C. L. R. James, George Orwell and "Literary Trotskyism"', *George Orwell Studies*, vol. 1, no. 2, 2017, 43–60.

——, *C. L. R. James in Imperial Britain*, Durham, NC: Duke University Press, 2014.

——, 'Remembering the Fifth Pan-African Congress'. Available at *Centre for African Studies (LUCAS)*, <http://lucas.leeds.ac.uk/article/remembering-the-fifth-pan-african-congress-christian-hogsbjerg/>.

——, '"A Thorn in the Side of Great Britain": C. L. R. James and the Caribbean Labour Rebellions of the 1930s', *Small Axe*, vol. 15, no. 2, July 2011, 24–42.

Holquist, Michael, *Dialogism: Bakhtin and His World*, 2nd edn, London and New York: Routledge, 1990.

Holt, Thomas, *The Problem of Freedom: Race, Labor, and Politics in Jamaica and Britain, 1832–1938*, Baltimore, MD and London: Johns Hopkins University Press, 1992.

Hooker, James R., *Black Revolutionary: George Padmore's Path from Communism to Pan-Africanism*, London: Pall Mall Press, 1967.

Howe, Stephen, *Anticolonialism in British Politics: The Left and the End of Empire*, Oxford: Oxford University Press, 1993.

Howsin, Hilda, *The Significance of Indian Nationalism*, London: A. C. Fifield, 1909.

Hume, Hamilton, *The Life of Edward John Eyre, Late Governor of Jamaica*, London: Richard Bentley, 1867.

Huxley, Elspeth, *A Thing to Love: A Novel*, London: Chatto & Windus, 1954.

Hyslop, Jonathan, 'The World Voyage of James Keir Hardie: Indian Nationalism, Zulu Insurgency and the British Labour Diaspora 1907–1908', *Journal of Global History*, vol. 1, iss. 3, November 2006, 343–62.

James, Leslie, *George Padmore and Decolonization from Below: Pan-Africanism, the Cold War, and the End of Empire*, Basingstoke: Palgrave Macmillan, 2015.

Jani, Pranav, 'Karl Marx, Eurocentrism, and the 1857 Revolt in British India', in Crystal Bartolovich and Neil Lazarus, eds, *Marxism, Modernity, and Postcolonial Studies*, Cambridge: Cambridge University Press, 2002.

JanMohamed, Abdul R., and David Lloyd, 'Introduction: Minority Discourse: What Is to Be Done?', *Cultural Critique*, no. 7, The Nature and Context of Minority Discourse II, Autumn 1987, 5–17.

Jarrett, Gene Andrew, 'Introduction', in Claude McKay, *A Long Way from Home*, New York: Arno Press and the New York Times, 1969.

Jenkinson, Jacqueline, *Black 1919: Riots, Racism and Resistance in Imperial Britain*, Liverpool: Liverpool University Press, 2009.

John, Angela V. *War, Journalism and the Shaping of the Twentieth Century: The Life and Times of Henry W. Nevinson*, London: I. B. Tauris, 2006.

Johnson, Howard, 'From Pariah to Patriot: the Posthumous Career of George William Gordon', *New West Indian Guide*, vol. 81, no. 3/4, 2008, 197–218.

Kalliney, Peter J., *Commonwealth of Letters: British Literary Culture and the Emergence of Postcolonial Aesthetics*, Oxford: Oxford University Press, 2013.

Kanogo, Tabitha, *Squatters and the Roots of Mau Mau, 1905–1963*, London: James Currey, 1987.

Kennedy, Dane, *The Last Blank Spaces: Exploring Africa and Australia*, Cambridge, MA: Harvard University Press, 2013.

Kent, Christopher, *Brains and Numbers: Elitism, Comtism, and Democracy in Mid-Victorian England*, Toronto: University of Toronto Press, 1978.

Kershaw, Greet, *Mau Mau from Below*, Oxford: James Currey, 1997.

Khouri, Mounah A., *Poetry and the Making of Modern Egypt (1882–1922)*, Leiden: E. J. Brill, 1971.

Kiernan, Victor G., *The Lords of Human Kind: European Attitudes Towards the Outside World in the Imperial Age*, London: Serif, 1995.

Kincaid, Jamaica, *A Small Place*, New York: Farrar, Straus and Giroux, 2000 [1998].

Kostal, R. W., *A Jurisprudence of Power: Victorian Empire and the Rule of Law*, Oxford: Oxford University Press, 2005.

Langley, J. Ayodele, ed., *Ideologies of Liberation in Black Africa 1856–1970: Documents on Modern African Political Thought from Colonial Times to the Present*, London: Rex Collins, 1979.

——, *Pan-Africanism and Nationalism in West Africa, 1900–1945: A Study in Ideology and Social Classes*, Oxford: Clarendon Press, 1973.

Lazarus, Neil, *Nationalism and Cultural Practice in the Postcolonial World*, Cambridge: Cambridge University Press, 1999.

Le Gassick, Trevor J., *Major Themes in Modern Arabic Thought: An Anthology*, Ann Arbor: University of Michigan Press, 1979.

Lenin, Nikolai, *'Left-Wing' Communism: An Infantile Disorder*, London: The Communist Party of Great Britain, [n.d. (1923?)].

Lewis, Gordon K., *The Growth of the Modern West Indies*, Kingston: Jamaica and Miami: Ian Randle Publishers, 2004.

Lewis, Joanna, '"Daddy Wouldn't Buy Me a Mau Mau": The British Popular Press and the Demoralization of Empire', in Atieno Odhiambo and John Lonsdale, eds, *Mau Mau and Nationhood: Arms, Authority and Narration*, Oxford: James Currey, 2003.

——, *Empire State-Building: War and Welfare in Kenya 1925–1952*, Oxford: James Currey, 2000.

Lewis, Rupert, 'Introduction', in Fitzroy Baptiste and Rupert Lewis, eds, *George Padmore: Pan-African Revolutionary*, Kingston: Ian Randle Publishers, 2008.

Littler, Jo and Roshi Naidoo, 'White Past, Multicultural Present: Heritage and National Stories', in Robert Phillips and Helen Brocklehurst, eds, *History, Identity and the Question of Britain*, London: Palgrave, 2004.

Llewellyn-Jones, Rosie, *The Great Uprising in India, 1857–58: Untold Stories, Indian and British*, Woodbridge: Boydell Press, 2007.

——, 'Marginalised Victims of 1857', in Andrea Major and Crispin Bates, eds, *Mutiny at the Margins: New Perspectives on the Indian Uprising of 1857, Vol. 2: Britain and the Indian Uprising*, New Delhi, India: SAGE Publications India, 2013.

Lorimer, Douglas A., *Colour, Class and the Victorians: English Attitudes to the Negro in the Mid-nineteenth Century*, Leicester: Leicester University Press and New York: Holmes and Meier Publishers, 1978.

Louro, Michele L., 'Where National Revolutionary Ends and Communist Begins: The League against Imperialism and the Meerut Conspiracy Case', *Comparative Studies of South Asia, Africa and the Middle East*, vol. 33, no. 3, 2013, 331–44.

Lowe, Lisa, *The Intimacies of Four Continents*, Durham, NC: Duke University Press, 2015.

Lynn, Martin, 'Introduction', in Martin Lynn, ed., *The British Empire in the 1950s: Retreat or Revival?*, London: Palgrave MacMillan, 2005.

McCarthy, Justin, *A History of Our Own Times from the Ascension of Queen Victoria to the General Election of 1880*, vol. 3, London: Chatto and Windus, 1882.

——, *The History of Our Own Times*, vol. 4, London: Caxton Publishing, 1908.

McDermott, Kevin, and Jeremy Agnew, *The Comintern: A History of International Communism from Lenin to Stalin*, Basingstoke: Macmillan. 1996.

Macdonald, Roderick J., ' "The Wisers Who Are Far Away": The Role of London's Black Press in the 1930s and 1940s', in Jagdish S. Gundara and Ian Duffield, eds, *Essays on the History of Blacks in Britain*, Aldershot: Avebury, 1992.

Macharia, Kinuthia and Muigai Kanyua, *The Social and Economic Origins of the Mau Mau Movement in Kenya (1952–1960)*, Oxford: University Press of America, 2006.

——, *The Social Context of the Mau Mau Movement in Kenya (1952–1960)*, Lanham, MD: University Press of America, 2006.

Mackenzie, John M., 'The Persistence of Empire in Metropolitan Culture', in Stuart Ward, ed., *British Culture and the End of Empire*, Manchester: Manchester University Press, 2001.

Maclean, Kama, *A Revolutionary History of Interwar India: Violence, Image, Voice and Text*, London: Hurst, 2015.

Macmillan, Harold, *Pointing the Way, 1959–1961*, New York: Harper, 1972.

Macmillan, W. M., *Warning from the West Indies*, London: Faber & Faber, 1936.

Major, Andrea and Crispin Bates, eds, *Mutiny at the Margins: New Perspectives on the Indian Uprising of 1857, Vol. 2: Britain and the Indian Uprising*, New Delhi, India: SAGE Publications India, 2013.

Makalani, Minkah, *In the Cause of Freedom: Radical Black Internationalism from Harlem to London, 1917–1939*, Chapel Hill: University of North Carolina Press, 2011.

Makonnen, Ras, *Pan-Africanism from Within; As Recorded and Edited by Kenneth King*, Nairobi and London: Oxford University Press, 1973.

Malik, Salahuddin, 'Popular British Interpretations of "the Mutiny": Politics and Polemics', in Andrea Major and Crispin Bates, eds, *Mutiny at the Margins: New Perspectives on the Indian Uprising of 1857, Vol. 2: Britain and the Indian Uprising*, New Delhi, India: SAGE Publications India, 2013, 25–49.

Manela, Erez, *The Wilsonian Moment: Self Determination and the International Origins of Anticolonial Nationalism*, Oxford: Oxford University Press, 2007.

Manjapra, Kris, 'Communist Internationalism and Transcolonial Recognition', in Sugata Bose and Kris Manjapra, eds, *Cosmopolitan Thought Zones: South Asia and the Global Circulation of Ideas*, New York: Palgrave Macmillan, 2010.

Mansfield, Peter, *The British in Egypt*, London: Weidenfeld and Nicolson, 1971.

Mantena, Karuna, *Alibis of Empire: Henry Maine and the Ends of Liberal Imperialism*, Princeton: Princeton University Press, 2010.

Marcus, Jane, *Hearts of Darkness: White Women Write Race*, New Brunswick, NJ: Rutgers University Press, 2004.

Marlowe, John, *Anglo-Egyptian Relations, 1800–1953*, London: Cresset Press, 1954.

Martin, Tony, *Amy Ashwood Garvey: Pan-Africanist, Feminist and Mrs. Marcus Garvey No. 1, or, A Tale of Two Amies*, Dover, MA: The Majority Press, 2007.

Marx, Karl, and Friedrich Engels, *The First Indian War of Independence 1857–1859*, Moscow: Foreign Languages Publishing House and London: Lawrence and Wishart, 1960.

Matera, Marc, *Black London: The Imperial Metropolis and Decolonization in the Twentieth Century*, Oakland: University of California Press, 2015.

Mathurin, Owen Charles, *Henry Sylvester Williams and the Origins of the Pan-African Movement, 1869–1911*, Westport, CT: Greenwood Press, 1976.

Matikkala, Mira, *Empire and Imperial Ambition: Liberty, Englishness and Anti-imperialism in Late-Victorian Britain*, London: I. B. Taurus, 2011.

Matthews, Gelien, *Caribbean Slave Revolts and the British Abolitionist Movement*, Baton Rouge, LA: Louisiana State University Press, 2006.

Maughan Brown, D. A., *Land, Freedom and Fiction: History and Ideology in Kenya*, London: Zed Books, 1985.

——, 'Myth and the "Mau Mau"', *Theoria: A Journal of Social and Political Theory*, no. 5, October 1980, 59–85.

Mehta, Uday Singh, *Liberalism and Empire: A Study in Nineteenth-Century British Liberal Thought*, Chicago: Chicago University Press, 1999.

Menon, Dilip M., "The Many Spaces and Times of Swadeshi", *Economic and Political Weekly*, vol. 47, no. 42, 20 October 2012. Available at <http://www.epw.in/journal/2012/42/swadeshi-time-nations-special-issues/many-spaces-and-times-swadeshi.html>.

Merritt, Rebecca, 'Public Perceptions of 1857: An Overview of British Press Responses to the Indian Uprising', in Andrea Major and Crispin Bates, eds, *Mutiny at the Margins: New Perspectives on the Indian Uprising of 1857, Vol. 2: Britain and the Indian Uprising*, New Delhi, India: SAGE Publications India, 2013.

Metcalf, Thomas R., *The Aftermath of Revolt: India, 1857–1970*, Princeton: Princeton University Press, 1965.

Mignolo, Walter D., 'Delinking: The Rhetoric of Modernity, the Logic of Coloniality and the Grammar of De-coloniality', *Cultural Studies*, vol. 21, no. 2, 2007, 449–514.

Mishra, Pankaj, *From the Ruins of Empire: The Revolt against the West and the Remaking of Asia*, London: Allen Lane, 2012.

Misra, Maria, *Vishnu's Crowded Temple: India since the Great Rebellion*, London: Allen Lane, 2007.

Mitchell, Timothy, *Carbon Democracy: Political Power in the Age of Oil*, London: Verso, 2011.

Mohanty, Satya P., *Literary Theory and the Claims of History: Post-modernism, Objectivity, Multicultural Politics*, Ithaca: Cornell University Press, 1997.

——, 'Us and Them: On the Philosophical Bases of Political Criticism', *New Formations*, no. 8, Summer 1989, 55–80.

Morgan, Kenneth O., 'Imperialists at Bay: British Labour and Decolonization', in Robert D. King and Robin W. Kilson, eds, *The*

Statecraft of British Imperialism: Essays in Honour of Wm. Roger Lewis, London: Frank Cass, 1999.

——, *Keir Hardie: Radical and Socialist*, London: Weidenfield and Nicolson, 1975.

Morris, Marcus, 'From Anti-colonialism to Anti-imperialism: The Evolution of H. M. Hyndman's Critique of Empire, c.1875–1905', *Historical Research*, vol. 87, no. 236, May 2014.

Moulton, Edward C., 'British Radicals and India in the Early Twentieth Century', in A. J. A. Morris, ed., *Edwardian Radicalism 1900–1914*, London and Boston: Routledge and Kegan Paul, 1974.

——, 'The Early Congress and the British Radical Connection', in D. A. Low, ed., *The Indian National Congress: Centenary Hindsights*, Delhi: Oxford University Press, 1988.

Mukherjee, Rudrangshu, *Spectre of Violence: The 1857 Kanpur Massacre*, New Delhi: Penguin India, 2007.

——, *The Year of Blood: Essays on the Revolt of 1857*, New Delhi: Social Science Press, 2014.

Murphy, David, 'Defending the "Negro Race": Lamine Senghor and Black Internationalism in Interwar France', *French Cultural Studies*, vol. 24, no. 2, 2013, 161–73.

Newsinger, John, *The Blood Never Dried: A People's History of the British Empire*, 2nd edn, London: Bookmarks Publications, 2013.

Nkrumah, Kwame, *Ghana: Autobiography of Kwame Nkrumah*, Edinburgh: Thomas Nelson and Sons, 1957.

Noorani, A. J., *Indian Political Trials 1775–1947*, New Delhi: Oxford University Press, 2005.

Odhiambo, Atieno and John Lonsdale, eds, *Mau Mau and Nationhood: Arms, Authority and Narration*, Oxford: James Currey, 2003.

Oldfield, John, *Chords of Freedom: Commemoration, Ritual and British Transatlantic Slavery*, Manchester: Manchester University Press, 2007.

Olivier, Sidney Haldane, *The Myth of Governor Eyre*, London: L. & Virginia Woolf, 1933.

O'Malley, Kate, *Ireland, India and Empire*, Manchester: Manchester University Press, 2009.

Orwell, George, 'Not Counting Niggers', in Sonia Orwell and Ian Angus, eds, *The Collected Essays, Journalism and Letters of*

George Orwell, 4 vols, vol. 1, Harmondsworth: Penguin Books, 1968.

Overstreet, Gene D. and Marshall Windmiller, *Communism in India*, Berkeley: University of California Press, 1959.

Owen, Nicholas, *The British Left and India: Metropolitan Anti-imperialism 1885–1947*, Oxford: Oxford University Press, 2007.

——, 'Critics of Empire in Britain', in J. M. Brown and W. M. R. Louis, eds, *The Oxford History of the British Empire, Vol. 4: The Twentieth Century*, Oxford, Oxford University Press, 1999.

Parry, Benita, 'Materiality and Mystification in "A Passage to India"', in *Novel: A Forum on Fiction*, vol. 31, no. 2, Spring 1998, 174–94.

Pati, Biswamoy, ed., *The 1857 Rebellion*, New Delhi: Oxford University Press India, 2007.

Pederson, Susan, *The Guardians: The League of Nations and the Crisis of Empire*, Oxford: Oxford University Press, 2015.

Pennybacker, Susan D., *From Scottsboro to Munich: Race and Political Culture in 1930s Britain*, Princeton: Princeton University Press, 2009.

Petersson, Fredrik, 'The "Colonial Conference" and the Dilemma of the Comintern's Colonial Work, 1928–29', in Vijay Prashad, ed., *Communist Histories*, New Delhi: Leftword Books, 2016.

——, *Willi Münzenberg, the League against Imperialism and the Comintern, 1925–1933*, 2 vols, Lewiston: Queenston Press, 2013.

Pieterse, Jan Nederveen, *Empire and Emancipation: Power and Liberation on a World Scale*, London: Pluto, 1990.

Pitts, Jennifer, *A Turn to Empire: The Rise of Imperial Liberalism in Britain and France*, Princeton: Princeton University Press, 2005.

Polsgrove, Carol, *Ending British Rule in Africa: Writers in a Common Cause*, Manchester: Manchester University Press, 2012.

——, 'George Padmore's Use of Periodicals to Build a Movement', in Fitzroy Baptiste and Rupert Lewis, eds, *George Padmore, Pan-African Revolutionary*, Kingston: Ian Randle Publishers, 2008.

Porter, Bernard, *Critics of Empire: British Radicals and the Imperial Challenge*, 2nd edn, London: I. B. Taurus, 2008 [1968].

Post, Ken, *Arise Ye Starvelings: The Jamaican Labour Rebellion of 1938 and Its Aftermath*, The Hague: Martinus Nijhoff, 1978.

Prashad, Vijay, *The Darker Nations: A People's History of the Third World*, New York and London: The New Press, 2007.

Pratt, Mary Louise, *Imperial Eyes: Travel Writing and Transculturation*, London: Routledge, 1992.

Pratt, Tim, 'Ernest Jones' Mutiny: The People's Paper, English Popular Politics and the Indian Rebellion 1857–58', in Chandrika Kaul, ed., *Media and the British Empire*, Basingstoke: Palgrave, 2006.

Pritt, Dennis Nowell, *The Autobiography of D. N. Pritt*, London: Lawrence & Wishart, 1965.

Ramnath, Maia, *Haj to Utopia*, Berkeley: University of California Press, 2011.

——, 'Two Revolutions: The Ghadar Movement and India's Radical Diaspora, 1913–1918', *Radical History Review*, no. 92, Spring 2005, 7–30.

Raza, Ali, Franzisca Roy and Benjamin Zachariah, 'Introduction', in Ali Raza, Franzisca Roy and Benjamin Zachariah, eds, *The Internationalist Moment: South Asia, Worlds, and World Views, 1917–1939*, Los Angeles: SAGE Publications, 2015.

Read, Anthony, and David Fisher, *The Proudest Day: India's Long Road to Independence*, London: Jonathan Cape, 1997.

Redfern, Neil, *Class or Nation: Communists, Imperialism, and Two World Wars*, London and New York: Tauris Academic Studies, 2005.

Regard, Fréderic, 'Fieldwork as Self-Harrowing: Richard Burton's Cultural Evolution (1851–56)', in Fréderic Regard, ed., *British Narratives of Exploration*, London: Pickering and Chatto, 2009.

Reinders, R. C., 'Racialism on the Left: E. D. Morel and the Black Horror on the Rhine', *International Review of Social History*, vol. 13, no. 1, April 1968, 1–28.

Retamar, Roberto Fernández, 'Caliban: Notes towards a Discussion of Culture in Our America', in Roberto Fernández Retamar, *Calibán and Other Essays*, Minneapolis: University of Minnesota Press, 1989.

Riddell, John, ed., *To See the Dawn: Baku, 1920 – First Congress of the Peoples of the East*, London and New York: Pathfinder Press, 1993.

Robinson, Cedric J., 'The African Diaspora and the Italo-Ethiopian Crisis', *Race and Class*, vol. 27, no. 2, 1985, 51–65.

——, 'Black Intellectuals at the British Core: 1920s–1940s', in Jagdish

S. Gundara and Ian Duffield, eds, *Essays on the History of Blacks in Britain*, Aldershot: Avebury, 1992.

———, *Black Marxism: The Making of the Black Radical Tradition*, London and Chapel Hill: University of North Carolina Press, 2000 [1983].

Rodney, Walter, 'The African Revolution', in Paul Buhle, ed., *C. L. R. James: His Life and Work*, London: Alison & Busby, 1986.

Rolland, Romain, 'For the Meerut Prisoners: Against Imperialist Terror', in *Meerut Conspiracy Case, Specially Written by a Barrister-at-Law*, London: Meerut Prisoners' Release Committee, 1933.

Rosberg, Carl Gustav and John Cato Nottingham, *The Myth of 'Mau Mau': Nationalism in Kenya*, Stanford, CA: Published for the Hoover Institution on War, Revolution, and Peace by Praeger, New York, 1966.

Rosen, Greg, ed., *Dictionary of Labour Biography*, London: Politico's, 2001.

Roy, Franziska and Benjamin Zachariah, 'Meerut and a Hanging: "Young India," Popular Socialism, and the Dynamics of Imperialism', *Comparative Studies of South Asia, Africa and the Middle East*, vol. 33, no. 3, 2013, 360–77.

Ruark, Robert Chester, *Something of Value*, London: Hamish Hamilton, 1955.

The Runnymede Trust, *The Future of Multi-ethnic Britain: The Parekh Report*, London: Profile Books, 2000.

Saha, Panchanan, *Shapurji Saklatvala: A Short Biography*, Delhi: People's Publishing House, 1970.

Said, Edward, *Culture and Imperialism*, London: Chatto & Windus, 1993.

———, *Humanism and Democratic Criticism*, New York: Palgrave Macmillan, 2004.

———, *Orientalism*, London: Routledge and Kegan Paul, 1978.

———, *Representations of the Intellectual*, New York: Vintage Books, 1996.

Saklatvala, Sehri, *The Fifth Commandment: Biography of Shapurji Saklatvala*, Salford: Miranda Press, 1991.

Samuel, Raphael, *Island Stories: Unravelling Britain; Theatres of Memory, Volume II*, London: Verso, 1998.

Sareen, Tilak Raj, *Indian Revolutionary Movement Abroad*

(1905–1921), New Delhi: Sterling Publishers, 1979.

Sarkar, Sumit, *Modern India: 1885–1947*, London: Macmillan, 1983.

——, *'Popular' Movements and 'Middle Class' Leadership in Late Colonial India: Perspectives and Problems of a 'History from Below'*, Calcutta: Centre for Studies in Social Sciences, 1983.

——, *The Swadeshi Movement in Bengal, 1903–1908*, New Delhi: People's Publishing House, 1973.

Sartori, Andrew, *Liberalism in Empire: An Alternative History*, Berkeley: University of California Press, 2014.

Saville, John, *Ernest Jones: Chartist – Selections from the Writings and Speeches of Ernest Jones with Introduction and Notes by John Saville*, London: Lawrence and Wishart, 1952.

——, 'Reginald Bridgeman', in Joyce M. Bellamy and John Saville, eds, *The Dictionary of Labour Biography*, London: Palgrave MacMillan, 1972.

Scheckner, Peter, ed., *The Anthology of Chartist Poetry: Poetry of the British Working Class, 1830s–1850s*, London and Toronto: Associated University Press, 1989.

Schwarz, Bill, ed., *The Expansion of England: Race, Ethnicity and Cultural History*, London: Routledge, 1996.

——, ed., *West Indian Intellectuals in Britain*, Manchester: Manchester University Press, 2003.

Scott, James C., *Domination and the Arts of Resistance: Hidden Transcripts*, New Haven: Yale University Press, 1990.

Semmel, Bernard, *The Governor Eyre Controversy*, London: MacGibbon and Lee, 1962.

Shay, Theodore L., *The Legacy of the Lokamanya: The Political Philosophy of Bal Gangadhar Tilak*, Mumbai: Indian Branch, Oxford University Press, 1956.

Sheller, Mimi, *Democracy after Slavery: Black Publics and Peasant Radicalism in Haiti and Jamaica*, Gainesville, FL: University Press of Florida, 2000.

Sherwood, Marika, 'The Comintern, the CPGB, Colonies and Black Britons, 1920–1938', *Science and Society*, vol. 60, no. 2, Summer 1996, 137–63.

——, 'The Congress', in Hakim Adi and Marika Sherwood, eds, *The 1945 Manchester Pan-African Congress Revisited*, 3rd edn, London: New Beacon Books, 1995.

——, 'Introduction', in Hakim Adi and Marika Sherwood, eds, *The 1945 Manchester Pan-African Congress Revisited*, 3rd edn, London: New Beacon Books, 1995.

Shilliam, Robbie, *The Black Pacific: Anti-colonial Struggles and Oceanic Connections*, London: Bloomsbury Academic, 2015.

——, 'Ethiopianism, Englishness, Britishness: Struggles over Imperial Belonging', *Citizenship Studies*, vol. 20, no. 2, 2016, 243–59.

Singer, Wendy, 'Peasants and the Peoples of the East: Indians and the Rhetoric of the Comintern', in Tim Rees and Andrew Thorpe, eds, *International Communism and the Communist International, 1919–1943*, Manchester: Manchester University Press, 1998

Slater, Montagu, *The Trial of Jomo Kenyatta*, London: Secker and Warburg, 1957.

Smith, Adam, *The Theory of the Moral Sentiments*, Cambridge: Cambridge University Press, 2002.

Smith, Alison and Mary Bull, eds, *Margery Perham and British Rule in Africa*, New York and Abingdon: Routledge, 2013.

Smith, Tony, ed., *The End of the European Empire: Decolonization after World War II*, Massachusetts: D.C. Heath & Co., 1975.

Squires, Mike, *Saklatvala: A Political Biography*, London: Lawrence & Wishart, 1990.

Stewart, William, *J. Keir Hardie: A Biography*, London: The National Labour Press, Ltd, 1921.

Stockwell, A. J., 'Suez 1956 and the Moral Disarmament of the British Empire', in Simon C. Smith, ed., *Reassessing Suez 1956*, Aldershot: Ashgate, 2008, 227–38.

Streets-Salter, Heather, 'International and Global Anti-colonial Movements', in Tony Ballantyne and Antoinette Burton, eds, *World Histories from Below: Disruption and Dissent from 1750 to the Present*, London: Bloomsbury Academic, 2016.

Tagore, Rabindranath, *The Home and the World*, transl. Surendranath Tagore, London: Penguin, 1985.

——, 'Letter to Lord Chelmsford', *Modern Review* (Calcutta Monthly), July 1919.

Tahmankar, D. V., *Lokamanya Tilak: Father of Indian Unrest and Maker of Modern India*, London: John Murray, 1956.

Tambe, Ashwini and Harald F. Tiné, eds, *The Limits of British Colonial Control in South Asia*, Abingdon: Routledge, 2011.

Taylor, Miles, *The Decline of British Radicalism, 1847–1860*, Oxford: Clarendon Press, 1995.

——, *Ernest Jones, Chartism, and the Romance of Politics, 1819–1869*, Oxford: Oxford University Press, 2003.

Thomas, Bert J., 'George Padmore', in Bert J. Thomas, ed., *The Struggle for Liberation: From Dubois to Nyerere*, New York: Theo Gaus, 1982, 42–55.

Thompson, Andrew S., *Imperial Britain: The Empire in British Politics, c.1880–1932*, Harlow, Essex: Longman, 2000.

Thompson, Dorothy, *The Chartists: Popular Politics in the Industrial Revolution*, London: Temple Smith, 1984.

Thornton, A. P., *The Imperial Idea and Its Enemies: A Study in British Power*, New York: St Martin's, 1985 [1959].

Throup, David, *Economic and Social Origins of Mau Mau, 1945–1953*, London: James Currey, 1987.

Trench, Richard, *Arabian Travellers*, London: Macmillan, 1986.

Trouillot, Michel-Rolph, *Silencing the Past: Power and the Production of History*, Boston, MA: Beacon Press, 1995.

Vardo, Gregory, '"Outworks of the Citadel of Corruption": The Chartist Press Reports the Empire', *Victorian Studies*, vol. 54, no. 2, Winter 2012, 227–253.

Virdee, Satnan, *Racism, Class and the Racialized Outsider*, Basingstoke: Palgrave Macmillan, 2014.

Vitz, Rico, 'Contagion, Community, and Virtue in Hume's Epistemology', in Jonathan Matheson and Rico Vitz, eds, *The Ethics of Belief: Individual and Social*, Oxford: Oxford University Press, 2014.

Wadsworth, Marc, *Comrade Sak: Shapurji Saklatvala, a Political Biography*, Leeds: Peepal Tree Press, 1998.

Wagner, Kim A., '"Calculated to Strike Terror": The Amritsar Massacre and the Spectacle of Colonial Violence', *Past and Present*, vol. 233, no. 1, 1 November 2016, 185–225.

——, *The Great Fear of 1857: Rumours, Conspiracies and the Making of the Indian Uprising*, Oxford: Peter Lang, 2010.

——, *The Skull of Alum Bheg: The Life and Death of a Rebel of 1857*, London: Hurst, 2017.

Walvin, James, *Black and White: The Negro and English Society, 1555–1945*, London: Allen Lane, 1973.

——, *Slaves and Slavery: The British Colonial Experience*, Manchester: Manchester University Press, 1992.

Ward, Stuart, 'Introduction', in Stuart Ward, ed., *British Culture and the End of Empire*, Manchester: Manchester University Press, 2001.

Watson, Tim, *Caribbean Culture and British Fiction in the Atlantic World, 1780–1870*, Cambridge: Cambridge University Press, 2008.

Weisbord, Robert G., 'British West Indian Reaction to the Italian–Ethiopian War: An Episode in Pan-Africanism', *Caribbean Studies*, vol. 10, no. 1, April 1970, 34–41.

Wilder, Gary, *Freedom Time: Negritude, Decolonization, and the Future of the World*, Durham, NC: Duke University Press, 2015.

Winkiel, Laura A., *Modernism, Race and Manifestos*, Cambridge: Cambridge University Press, 2008.

——, 'Nancy Cunard's Negro and the Transnational Politics of Race', *Modernism/Modernity*, vol. 13, no. 3, September 2006, 507–30.

Wolpert, Stanley A. *Tilak and Gokhale: Revolution and Reform in the Making of Modern India*, Berkeley and Los Angeles, CA: University of California Press, 1962.

Wood, Marcus, *The Horrible Gift of Freedom: Atlantic Slavery and the Repression of Emancipation*, Athens and London: University of Georgia Press, 2010.

Workman, Gillian, 'Thomas Carlyle and the Governor Eyre Controversy: An Account with Some New Material', *Victorian Studies*, vol. 18, no. 1, 1 September 1974, 77–102.

Young, Robert J. C., *Postcolonialism: An Historical Introduction*, Oxford: Blackwell, 2001.

Younge, Gary, 'Cruel and usual: The Outrages at Camp Breadbasket Are Consistent with British Colonial Rule – Brutal, Oppressive, and Racist', *Guardian*, 1 March 2005. Available at <https://www.theguardian.com/uk/2005/mar/01/military.iraq>.

Index